THE INDIGENOUS WORLD 2015

Copenhagen 2015

THE INDIGENOUS WORLD 2015

Compilation and editing: Cæcilie Mikkelsen
Regional editors:
    Arctic & North America: Kathrin Wessendorf
    Mexico, Central and South America: Alejandro Parellada
    Australia and the Pacific: Cæcilie Mikkelsen
    Asia: Christian Erni and Christina Nilsson
    The Middle East: Cæcilie Mikkelsen
    Africa: Marianne Wiben Jensen and Geneviève Rose
    International Processes: Lola García-Alix and Kathrin Wessendorf

Cover and typesetting: Jorge Monrás
Maps: Jorge Monrás
English translation: Elaine Bolton
Proof reading: Elaine Bolton
Prepress and Print: Eks-Skolens Trykkeri, Copenhagen, Denmark
© The authors and The International Work Group for Indigenous Affairs (IWGIA), 2015
    All Rights Reserved

HURRIDOCS CIP DATA

Title: The Indigenous World 2015
Edited by: Cæcilie Mikkelsen
Pages: 571
ISSN: 1024-0217
ISBN: 978-87-92786-52-4
Language: English
Index: 1. Indigenous Peoples – 2. Yearbook – 3. International Processes
BISAC codes: LAW110000 Indigenous Peoples
REF027000 Yearbooks & Annuals
POL035010 Political Freedom & Security / Human Rights
Geografical area: World
Publication date: April 2015

Executive Director: Orla Bakdal
Head of Finance: Morten Bjørn Nielsen

Distribution in North America:
Transaction Publishers
300 McGaw Drive
Raritan Center - Edison, NJ 08857
www.transactionpub.com

This book has been produced with financial support from the Danish Ministry of Foreign Affairs (DANIDA) and the Norwegian Agency for Development Cooperation (NORAD)

INTERNATIONAL WORK GROUP FOR INDIGENOUS AFFAIRS

Classensgade 11 E, DK 2100 - Copenhagen, Denmark
Tel: (45) 35 27 05 00 - Fax: (45) 35 27 05 07
E-mail: iwgia@iwgia.org - Web: www.iwgia.org

CONTENTS

PART II – INTERNATIONAL PROCESSES

PART III – GENERAL INFORMATION

EDITORIAL

EDITORIAL

The World Conference on Indigenous Peoples

"Indigenous people will always have a home at the United Nations," said Secretary-General Ban Ki-moon when opening the UN High Plenary meeting on indigenous peoples.

The opening of the World Conference on Indigenous Peoples (WCIP) took place in the great assembly hall of the UN headquarters in New York on 22 September 2014. But while many representatives of the world's indigenous peoples could not get a pass for one of the limited observers´ seats on the balcony, on the plenary floor, quite a few of the official blue name tags of States and UN agencies shone on empty chairs.

Despite the near universal endorsement of the UN Declaration on the Rights of Indigenous Peoples (UNDRIP) and the adoption by consensus of the World Conference Outcome Document, many States still don't recognise the existence of indigenous peoples in their own countries and their rights are not high on the political agenda. The human rights of indigenous peoples are also far from reflected in the daily lives of most of the world's 370 million indigenous people.

Indigenous peoples remain among the poorest and most marginalized; they have far greater risk of not having access to education, clean water and safe housing, of ending up in prison, and of dying during pregnancy and childbirth than other people, said the UN High Commissioner for Human Rights Zeid Ra'ad Al Hussein, in his opening speech at the World Conference. "This clear statistic translates to thousands of human tragedies. Thousands of violations of human rights," Al Hussain said, and urged all parties to use the outcome document to ensure that the UNDRIP is turned into reality.

The world conference was not an initiative of indigenous peoples, but for three years they have joined forces in a global preparatory process to ensure direct and full participation in the whole process, including the negotiations of the programme and outcome of the meeting, and to make sure that the high plenary would not be used as a pretext for watering down the rights they have fought for and got recognised in the UNDRIP.

The World Conference Outcome Document

Not least as a result of indigenous peoples' thorough preparation, persistent advocacy and alliance building, the WCIP outcome document confirms and reaffirms the language of the UNDRIP and includes many of the priorities identified by indigenous peoples at the Global Indigenous Preparatory Conference in Alta, Norway (See *The Indigenous World 2014*), particularly on issues related to rights to land and natural resources, and free, prior and informed consent.

The outcome document contains requirements to take action both at the national and international level. For example, States are requested to develop national action plans, strategies or other measures to achieve the ends of the UNDRIP. Furthermore, States are encouraged to include information on the situation of the rights of indigenous peoples, including measures taken, to pursue the objectives of UNDRIP in reports to Treaty Bodies and during the universal periodic review process. At the international level the Secretary-General is requested to begin the development of an UN system-wide action plan to ensure a coherent approach to achieving the ends of the UNDRIP.

It is also positive that the outcome document acknowledges the need to pay special attention to the rights of indigenous women, including furthering their empowerment and equal participation in decision-making processes at all levels. There is also a special mentioning of the need to examine the causes and consequences of violence against indigenous women, and to disaggregate data and conduct surveys to address the situation and need of indigenous peoples and individuals based on holistic indicators of well-being.

On the other hand, States did not accept the inclusion of articles suggested by indigenous peoples on issues related to treaty rights and demilitarization of indigenous peoples' lands. It is also important to note that some issues of major concern to indigenous peoples such as the reference to the impact of extractive industries, and the need of State action in this regard, is much weaker than the text suggested by indigenous peoples.

Land Grabbing

Investments in extractive industries and large-scale agriculture are at the core of the everyday struggle of indigenous peoples to maintain their land, livelihood and culture.

According to the International Land Coalition, between 2000 and 2011, large-scale plots of land acquired or negotiated through deals brokered on behalf of foreign governments or transnational corporations covered, in total, 203 million hectares of land worldwide. This is equivalent to over eight times the size of the United Kingdom.[1] But only very few of these large-scale land deals for commercial or industrial purposes take place in Western Europe. Most involve the land of indigenous peoples in developing countries and are closed without any consultation of the local communities, no compensation, and with a lack of regard for environmental sustainability and equitable access to, or control over, natural resources. In other words, most of these land deals involve what has been termed "land grabbing." Land grabbing poses the greatest threat to the survival of indigenous peoples today and is thus a recurrent concern in the articles included in *The Indigenous World*. This year's edition is no exception.

Under the pretext of enhancing food security by making so-called "under-utilised land" productive, Ethiopia continues to lease out millions of hectares of land to private foreign and domestic agricultural investors while forcing pastoralist families to settle in villages. Presented as a national development strategy, the local indigenous population is facing acute poverty, losing its customary land and traditional pastoralist livelihood to export agriculture, non-food production and an influx of migrant workers.

In Cambodia, this year´s article criticises the World Bank's large investment in rubber production, which has been carried out without the free, prior and informed consent and without satisfactory compensation of the affected communities. In contrast to the World Bank's stated mission of "reducing poverty," the investments have dispossessed indigenous peoples of their land and lead to "deforestation, a loss of biodiversity and the pollution of water sources, (which have) severely impacted upon peoples' livelihoods, disrupted children's education, limited religious expression, (and) triggered food insecurity."

Similar examples can be found from all the seven geo-regions of the world and new projects are in the making, such as the Lamu Port (Kenya), South Sudan and Ethiopia Transport Corridor Project (LAPSSET), the Southern Agricultural Growth Corridor of Tanzania (SAGCOT) and the Nicaragua Interoceanic Grand Canal – three large scale projects, among many, that promise development but could wreak havoc on indigenous peoples' right to food, to water, to adequate housing, to land, to free, prior and informed consent, to self-determination and to a safe, clean, healthy and sustainable environment, land and livelihood.

Diversified local strategies

The WCIP outcome document reiterates the commitments of states to acknowledge and advance indigenous peoples' rights to land. Some countries are already taking steps in this direction. Indonesia, which is home to up to 70 million indigenous peoples, has seen positive development in regards to clarification of land rights and the solving of land disputes. On the backdrop of continued land grabbing and human rights violations related to land disputes, many of which involve indigenous peoples, the Indonesian government has launched a 'one-map' initiative to make one standardised national map and include cross-sectorial data into a single, open portal. Indigenous peoples have since 2013 been collecting geospatial data and mapping their traditional territories, and in 2014, maps covering 4,8 million hectares of indigenous land were accepted into the One-Map initiative, thus making way for greater recognition of indigenous peoples' land rights and greater inclusion of indigenous peoples in land related decision-making processes.

In Paraguay, while the economic policy favours a continuation of displacements of indigenous communities, indigenous peoples are seeking legal assistance to reclaim land. In 2014, the Sawhoyamaxa community won back its traditional territory. 30 years since their land was unlawfully appropriated by cattle ranchers and eight years after a favourable ruling on their case by the Inter-American Court, the Paraguayan Supreme Court finally confirmed the expropriation and return of the 14.000 ha land to the community. This is an example on how indigenous peoples in the Americas are increasingly seeking redress of violations committed against their right to land and territories through the Inter-American Human Rights, but the case also points to the pitfalls in a system that ultimately relies on the good will of the national government for implementation.

In Cambodia, disillusioned as to the state´s willingness to protect their rights, the indigenous movement now directly targets the finance institution behind the land grabs. So far this seems like a promising strategy, yet it requires the particular company or finance institution to actually care for its public image. It is therefore key to uphold the pressure on states to guarantee the rights of indigenous peoples in relation to business interventions. As indigenous peoples are one of the groups most at risk of business-related human rights violations, it is imperative, that National Action Plans on Business and Human Rights include specific targets and measures introducing robust safeguards for indigenous peoples' rights, including improved access to justice in home states of transnational corporation, and recognition of their customary laws and land rights. [2]

Repression of civil society

The ever more brutal race for land and natural resources, spurred by greed but explained as necessity, marketed as development but resulting in inequality, is opening a broad range of local battle fields where indigenous peoples keep fighting back to save their territory, their environment, their culture and their survival as peoples.

With such great economic interests at stake, many States take unsavoury measures to silence criticism and alternative visions for development from indigenous peoples.

As reported in several of this year's articles, private investments and national development strategies are often backed by the military, the police or paramilitary groups. Harassment of indigenous peoples, violent evictions, and even murder of indigenous human rights defenders occur with impunity while their forest is cleared away at unprecedented rates.

Several articles also highlight the special vulnerabilities of indigenous girls and women in relation to loss of land, militarization and violent conflicts. In for example Bangladesh, where transmigration programmes illegally settling Bengalis in the Chittagong Hill Tracts have been backed up by military forces since the mid-1970s, the mixture of land grabbing and militarization has deeply affected the safety and security of indigenous women and girls.[3] In 2014 alone, 122 indigenous women and girls were victims of violence while their perpetrators have enjoyed near complete impunity.

Less brutal, but just as effective, are administrative measures to restrict the working of indigenous organisations and the freedom of expression of indigenous human rights defenders. In 2014, the hindering of several indigenous representatives from the Russian federation to participate in the World Conference on Indigenous Peoples in New York, drew international attention as it was denounced from the podium of the UN by the Presidents of Finland and Estonia, the UN High Commissioner for Human Rights, and the Chair of the UN Permanent Forum at the Opening Plenary of the General Assembly on 22 September. Back home in Russia, however, the repression of indigenous civil society organisations continued.

After having co-opted the national indigenous umbrella organisations RAIPON in 2013 and required NGO's engaged in political activity and receiving foreign funding to register as "foreign agents," in 2014, the Federal Government took additional measures to limit the right to free association of indigenous peoples, when, in December, it decreed that the authorities could unilaterally register political NGOs. Apart from heavily stigmatising the legitimate political agenda of these organisations (which include professional associations of e.g. hunters and reindeer herders), the label as "foreign agent" entails being put under extremely close scrutiny by the authorities and being subjected to a range of additional restrictions and administrative obligations.

Also in Algeria, the law on associations, adopted in December 2011, is beginning to have an effect in terms of restricting Amazigh freedoms. Particularly the requirement to communicate solely in Arabic and the ban on any relationship with Amazigh associations abroad or foreign NGOs, is repressing the legitimate Amazigh protest against lack of benefits from resource extraction and the increasing militarization of their traditional territories.

Ethiopia is another country where land grabbing by foreign investors goes hand in hand with state repression of civil society. Here, legal restrictions on freedom of association and speech are impeding the indigenous peoples from formally organising to lobby the Ethiopian government to live up to regional human rights standards on indigenous peoples.

Implementation

The WCIP outcome document is an important step forward in the affirmation of indigenous peoples' rights as enshrined in the UNDRIP. However, the real value of the document is still to be seen, as its implementation will require political will from States and a coordinated lobby action from indigenous peoples to ensure that the commitments are followed up at the international and national level.

There is no doubt that the commitment expressed by States to develop national action plans should be prioritized and pushed forward by indigenous peoples at the country level and this will show whether or not States are ready to translate the good intentions expressed in the outcome document about the protection of indigenous peoples rights into concrete results.

An urgent task for States is to ensure that the Post 2015 development agenda and the new Sustainable Development Goals respect the contribution of indigenous peoples to ecosystem management and sustainable development and give due consideration to all the rights of indigenous peoples, including their right to determine and develop priorities and strategies for exercising their right to development.

The UN also has a great task ahead to implement and normalise its commitments throughout the organisation. One example is the World Bank, whose draft *environmental and social standards (EAS) 7*, presented in July 2014, outline the future policy of the Bank in relation to indigenous peoples. On the positive side, the draft reinforces the right of indigenous peoples to grant or withhold their free, prior and informed consent and increases protection against forced evictions. On the negative side, diluted safeguards are established in several key areas. Paragraph 9 of EAS7 contains a clause that allows governments to opt not to apply and adopt an "alternative approach" in case the application of the EAS could create a serious risk of increased ethnic tensions and civil strife, or when the identification of various cultural groups as outlined in the EAS is not consistent with the provisions of the national constitution. This clause is a trap of incredible magnitude and has been widely criticized because it will effectively allow the Bank and its borrowers to ignore its own policy on indigenous peoples and the provisions of the UNDRIP in countries where indigenous peoples are not officially recognised.[4]

Another case of great concern remains the need for the World Heritage Convention to be aligned with the UNDRIP and for the Convention's Operational Guidelines to be amended accordingly. Despite increased focus on indigenous peoples rights on the part of UNESCO in recent years, nomination, establishments and management of World Heritage Sites on indigenous peoples' lands and territories are, as reflected in several of this year's articles, still taking place without the full and effective participation or the free, prior and informed consent of indigenous peoples.[5]

About this book

First and foremost, IWGIA would like to thank all the contributors to this volume for their commitment and their collaboration. Without them, IWGIA would never have been able to publish such a comprehensive overview of the past year's developments and events in the indigenous world. The authors of this volume are indigenous and non-indigenous activists and scholars who have worked with the indigenous movement for many years and are part of IWGIA's network. They are identified by IWGIA's regional coordinators on the basis of their knowledge and network in the regions. This year, the volume includes 54 country reports and 15 reports on international processes. We are especially happy to include an article on indigenous women, reflecting on the crucial work being done by indigenous women to raise the issues of women in indigenous contexts and of indigenous peoples in international arenas specifically dedicated to women. 2015 will stage several opportunities for promoting the rights of indigenous women, such as the Beijing+20 and Cairo+20 conferences and the setting of the Post 2015 Sustainable Development Goals, and we hope to receive regular updates on these struggles in the future.

All the contributions to this volume are offered on a voluntary basis – this we consider a strength, but it also means that we cannot guarantee to include all countries or all aspects of importance to indigenous peoples every year. We would like to stress that omissions of specific country reports should not be interpreted as "no news is good news." In fact, sometimes, it is the precarious human rights situation that makes it difficult to obtain articles from specific countries. In other cases, we have simply not been able to get an author to cover a specific country. In case you would like to contribute to this book, please contact the IWGIA team.

The articles in this book express the views and visions of the authors, and IWGIA cannot be held responsible for the opinions stated herein. We therefore encourage those who are interested in obtaining more information about a specific country to contact the authors directly. It is, nonetheless, our policy to allow those authors who wish to remain anonymous to do so, due to the political sensitivity of some of the issues raised in their articles.

The Indigenous World should be seen as a reference book and we hope that you will be able to use it as a basis for obtaining further information on the situation of indigenous peoples worldwide.   ○

Cæcilie Mikkelsen, editor, and Orla Bakdal, director
Copenhagen, April 2015

Notes and references

1   W. **Anseeuw, L. Alden Wily, L. Cotula, and M. Taylor, 2012:** *Land Rights and the Rush for Land.* International Land Coalition: Rome

2   See also: **Johannes Rohr & José Aylwin, 2014:** *Business and Human Rights: Interpreting the UN Guiding Principles for Indigenous Peoples.* IWGIA Report 16. IWGIA and the European Network for Indigenous Peoples (ENIP): Copenhagen.

3   See also: **Dr Bina D' Costa, 2014:** *Marginalisation and Impunity - Violence Against Women and Girls in the Chittagong Hill Tracts.* Chittagong Hill Tracts Commission (CHTC), IWGIA, and Bangladesh Indigenous Women's Network: Dhaka. Available for download on www.iwgia.org/publications

4   Read more at: http://www.iwgia.org/human-rights/policiesstrategies-on-indigenous-peoples/world-bank-environmental-and-social-safeguard-policies

5   See also: **Stefan Disko and Helen Tugendhat, 2014:** *World Heritage Sites and Indigenous Peoples' Rights.* IWGIA, Forest Peoples Programme and the Gundjeihmi Aboriginal Corporation: Copenhagen.

PART I

REGION AND COUNTRY REPORTS

THE ARCTIC

GREENLAND

Kalaallit Nunaat (Greenland) has, since 1979, been a self-governing country within the Danish Realm. In 2009, Greenland entered a new era with the inauguration of the new Act on Self-Government, which gave the country further self-determination within the State of Denmark. Greenland has a public government, and aims to establish a sustainable economy in order to achieve greater independence. The population numbers 56,000, of whom 50,000 are Inuit. Greenland's diverse culture includes subsistence hunting, commercial fisheries, tourism and emerging efforts to develop the oil and mining industries. Approximately 50 per cent of the national budget is financed by Denmark through a block grant. The Inuit Circumpolar Council (ICC), an indigenous peoples' organisation (IPO) and an ECOSOC-accredited NGO, represents Inuit from Greenland, Canada, Alaska and Chukotka (Russia) and is also a permanent participant in the Arctic Council. The majority of the people of Greenland speak the Inuit language, Kalaallisut, which is the official language, while the second language of the country is Danish. In 1996, at the request of Greenland, Denmark ratified ILO Convention No. 169.

A turbulent year

The Government of Greenland, under the leadership of Premier Aleqa Hammond, has been very active on the international scene over the past year. Elected into office in 2013, Aleqa Hammond has strongly promoted Greenland as a nation on its way to independence from Denmark. At the same time, Hammond has displayed solidarity with indigenous peoples around the world through various statements at international conferences – a prominent one of these being the World Conference of Indigenous Peoples (WCIP) at the United Nations Headquarters in New York in September 2014.

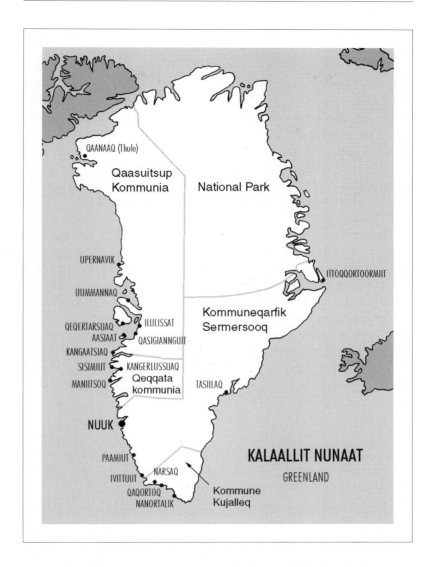

When UN Secretary-General Ban Ki-moon paid an official visit to Greenland in the spring of 2014 to personally experience the impacts of climate change on the country, he invited Aleqa Hammond to speak at the United Nations Climate

Summit, which coincided with the WCIP and resulted in a wealth of media coverage.

However, at home, Premier Hammond and her coalition government have taken many beatings on controversial political statements and actions, and this has failed to convince people of any progress in national politics. Calls for an election sounded louder and louder last year given that the government remained reluctant to listen to any constructive criticism and failed to introduce overdue financial and other reforms. In the end, the Premier had to step down as leader of the social democratic party, Siumut, when evidence of her private spending of public finances surfaced. The exit was cemented by a loud public demonstration during the traditional opening ceremony of parliament.

Parliamentary elections were called for 28 November and, for a long time, it looked as if the socialist party, Inuit Ataqatigiit (IA), would be back in power headed by its new leader, Sara Olsvig. Olsvig replaced former Premier Kuupik Kleist, who stepped down earlier in the year to allow for generational change in the party leadership. Sara Olsvig, who was both a member of the Danish and Greenland parliaments, before taking on the leadership of IA, won the election with the most personal votes. However, the newly-elected leader of Siumut, Kim Kielsen and his team, managed to maintain their lead, albeit by a very small margin, giving Siumut the opportunity to form a new government.

One of the most controversial issues during the election campaign was the call for a nation-wide referendum on uranium mining by Inuit Ataqatigiit and the newly-formed Partii Naleraq, a breakaway party established by a former Premier of Siumut, Hans Enoksen. The uranium issue came to a head in 2013 when the Siumut party, in coalition with Atassut, took the controversial step to abolish the zero-tolerance policy which had been in place since 1988. The policy was seen as standing in the way of attracting mining companies into the country (see also *The Indigenous World 2014*).

A new coalition

Many expressed hopes for a broad coalition between the two largest parties, Siumut and Inuit Ataqatigiit, despite their differences with regard to uranium mining. Instead, Siumut opted to form a narrow coalition with the small liberal party, the Democrats, and the even smaller conservative party, Atassut, citing the uranium policy as the defining issue. The new government has only a marginal lead, placing it in a vulnerable position.

Time and again, during the election campaign, the new Premier Kim Kielsen promised to lead a responsible government. However, the coalition agreement contains a long list of unfinanced projects as well as huge new expenditure. It is difficult to see how the government is going to implement many of its electoral promises and, at the same time, close the huge deficit in the fiscal budget.

The growing deficit in public finances, for instance, is dramatic and reinforced by fundamental structural problems in Greenland due to an aging population and a steady decline in GNP. These problems have sparked urgent demands for political reforms, which experts argue are needed to increase the level and quality of education, to reduce unemployment and to establish new and broader export-oriented business and industrial development. Experts and advisors argue that the focus should be on sustaining the fisheries economy, establishing new mineral resource activities and increasing tourism.

Loss of Thule Air Base contract

The shocking news that a US company had unexpectedly won the tender for a multi-million Danish Kroner contract to supply and maintain the Thule Air Base (TAB) in North Greenland hit hard. The contract had been held for many years by Danish and Greenlandic companies under the Greenland Contractors company umbrella, and the Greenland treasury is now in danger of losing both tax revenues and jobs. According to the 1951 defence agreement, US citizens and US companies are exempt from paying taxes while working on TAB. This wake-up call coincides with the recent high profile opening of the Greenland Representation in Washington D.C., affiliated to the Royal Danish Embassy, precisely with the purpose of promoting closer cooperation between the US and Greenland.

The companies around the present contract holder have appealed the result and the Danish Prime Minister and the Minister of Foreign Affairs are facing pressure from both Danish and Greenlandic MPs to overturn the result of the tender.

Extractive industries

Greenland has for many years invested heavily in attracting extractive industries in the hope that it will create Greenlandic jobs and better tax revenues, thus improving the economy. Despite an increased interest on the part of foreign companies, this strategy has not met expectations. However, in October 2013, London Mining and the Greenland government signed an agreement for an exploitation license for the open-pit iron mine located 150 km from the capital, Nuuk. Although the construction costs were going to be astronomical, high hopes were placed on Chinese investments. The mine was expected to create hundreds of direct and indirect jobs but was, however, put on hold in 2014 when London Mining went into administration. The company had difficulty in finding a buyer for the business as it struggled with debts following a slump in iron ore prices and production problems in the company's Sierra Leone mine in the wake of the Ebola outbreak. London Mining Greenland has now been taken over by the large Chinese company, General Nice Development Ltd.

Transparency and inclusion

Attracting extractive industries to Greenland remains high on the agenda, as it is believed to be one way of relieving the dire financial situation. The former government, however, had come under increasing civil society pressure to disseminate more information and to engage the public more effectively in decision-making concerning the extraction of oil and minerals. In particular, there had been a call for improved procedures with regard to public consultation – even to the extent of calls for free, prior and informed consent.

The ICC and World Wildlife Fund (WWF) published a survey on participation in decision-making related to uranium mining, showing that only one in three were satisfied with civil society's involvement in consultation and decision-making procedures concerning the abandonment of the zero-tolerance policy on uranium.

A number of Greenlandic civil society organisations had been on the alert during the Hammond government due to a lack of transparency and involvement of the public in decision-making with regard to oil and mineral exploration and exploitation activities more generally. In 2013, organisations such as ICC, WWF, the Hunter's and Fishermen's Association - KNAPK, Earth Charter, Avataq (Greenland's environmental organisation) and Transparency International Greenland formed the NGO Coalition of 2013. The NGO Coalition is promoting improved procedures for involving civil society in relation to mineral resources extraction. It is also recommending that the government ratify and implement relevant international conventions, such as the Aarhus Convention (the UNECE Convention on Access to Information, Public Participation in Decision-making and Access to Justice in Environmental Matters) and the UN Convention on Corruption.

The NGO Coalition and others often refer to the UN Declaration on the Rights of Indigenous Peoples or ILO Convention No. 169 as important sources of inspiration in terms of improved inclusion and information dissemination, in particular with regard to resource extraction projects.

Claim to the North Pole

On 15 December, together with Greenland, Denmark presented its claim to the United Nations for an area covering 895,000 sq. km stretching all the way from Greenland to the Russian 200 nautical mile zone. This claim is based on data collected since 2002 and on evidence that the Lomonosov Ridge is a natural extension of the Greenland continental shelf. Canada and Russia are expected to make similar claims. Denmark ratified the UN Convention on the Law of the Sea (UNCLOS) in 2004, meaning that 2014 was the deadline for submitting claims to extend the continental shelf, as these must be made within 10 years of ratification. It is expected that the processing of claims will take another 12-14 years. Denmark and Greenland, along with Russia, Norway, Canada and the US, have agreed that the territorial dispute should be settled under UNCLOS.

Greenland Human Rights Council

In 2013, the Government of Greenland took the first steps towards establishing a human rights institution, something that had been unanimously decided upon by parliament in 2008. The Greenland Human Rights Council (GHRC) is composed of representatives from civil society organisations and from social and political institutions in Greenland that are engaged in human rights in their daily work. It is based on the UN Paris Principles for national human rights institutions (NHRI) and has a seat on the board of the Danish NHRI (DNIHR).

One of the main objectives of the GHRC is to raise awareness of human rights in Greenland and to build capacity in this area. In 2014, GHRC and DNIHR published the first joint status report providing a snapshot of the overall human rights situation in Greenland in seven selected areas, including key recommendations on how to strengthen human rights in these areas. This report has now been followed up by a GHRC report on the status and implementation of international instruments in Greenland aimed at securing the rights of persons with disabilities.

World Conference on Indigenous Peoples

One of the important issues of the WCIP was indigenous peoples' participation in the UN. The joint participation of the Premier of Greenland, Aleqa Hammond, and the Danish Minister of Foreign Affairs, Martin Lidegaard, who shared their speaking time, was an illustration of good cooperation between indigenous peoples and states. In her presentation, Aleqa Hammond expressed the view that: "Just as the Declaration on the Rights of Indigenous Peoples continues to inspire us in Greenland, Greenland hopes that this model for cooperation within the Kingdom of Denmark may inspire other indigenous peoples."

While Greenland participated actively in the preparations for the WCIP and the conference itself, the WCIP outcome document is not explicitly mentioned in the coalition agreement. However, the fact that Greenland enjoys an extensive self-government and works in close cooperation with Denmark on indigenous rights issues implies that the principles and recommendations of the WCIP outcome document remain on the table for future implementation.

One Arctic – One Future

The Inuit Circumpolar Council (ICC) (representing Inuit from Canada, Greenland, Russia and the US) holds its general assembly every four years in a different Arctic country and on a different theme. This year's theme was One Arctic – One Future. The general assemblies are important venues for Inuit from the four Arctic nations to meet and exchange views on Arctic issues and developments affecting the Inuit world and to celebrate their cultural heritage.

The 12th General Assembly of the ICC, held in Inuvik, Canada, was attended by a large delegation from Greenland, including the former government and parliament, and representatives of various civil society organisations, of which 18 are official delegates. During the meeting, a new executive council was elected and Aqqaluk Lynge, Greenland's International Chair, handed over the chairmanship to Canada and the incoming International Chair, Okalik Eegeesiak from Nunavut.

For Aqqaluk Lynge, this event marked the end of an era of more than 30 years at the helm of Arctic indigenous politics. The incoming President of ICC Greenland, Hjalmar Dahl, also has a long history of working on Arctic indigenous peoples' rights. Hjalmar Dahl is one of the Arctic members of the Global Coordination Group of the World Conference on Indigenous Peoples.   O

Frank Sejersen is a Danish anthropologist employed as an associate professor in the Department of Cross-Cultural and Regional Studies (University of Copenhagen), where he has been pursuing research into the Arctic in general, and Greenland in particular, since 1994. Frank Sejersen was appointed a member of IWGIA's Board in June 2011 and has been its chair since January 2012.

Marianne Lykke Thomsen has a background in Inuit studies and anthropology and has been living and working in Greenland in various capacities for close to 30 years. In her earlier capacity as senior policy advisor to the Government of Greenland, she played an active part in UN's work concerning human and indigenous peoples' rights, and in the Arctic Council process. Prior to this, she worked with the Inuit Circumpolar Council on environmental issues and Traditional Knowledge. Marianne Lykke Thomsen was elected a member of IWGIA's Board in January 2015.

THE RUSSIAN FEDERATION

Of the more than 180 peoples inhabiting the territory of contemporary Russia, 40 are officially recognized as "indigenous small-numbered peoples of the North, Siberia and the Far East". These are groups of less than 50,000 members, perpetuating some aspects of their traditional ways of life and inhabiting the Northern and Asian parts of the country. One more group is actively pursuing recognition, which continues to be denied. Together, they number about 260,000 individuals, less than 0.2 per cent of Russia's population. Ethnic Russians account for 78 per cent. Other peoples, such as the five million Tatars, are not officially considered indigenous peoples, while their self-identification varies.

The latest official population figures from the 2010 national census do not provide disaggregated data on the socio-economic status of indigenous peoples. Indigenous peoples are predominantly rural dwellers, while Russia on the whole is a highly urbanized country.

Indigenous peoples as such are not recognized by Russian legislation; however, the constitution and national legislation set out the rights of "indigenous small-numbered peoples of the North", including rights to consultation and participation in specific cases. However, there is no such concept as "Free, Prior and Informed Consent" enshrined in legislation. Russia has not ratified ILO Convention 169 and has not endorsed the UNDRIP. The country has inherited its membership of the major UN Covenants and Conventions from the Soviet Union: the ICCPR, ICESCR, ICERD, ICEDAW and ICRC.

There is a multitude of regional, local and interregional indigenous organizations. RAIPON, the national umbrella organization, operates under tight state control.

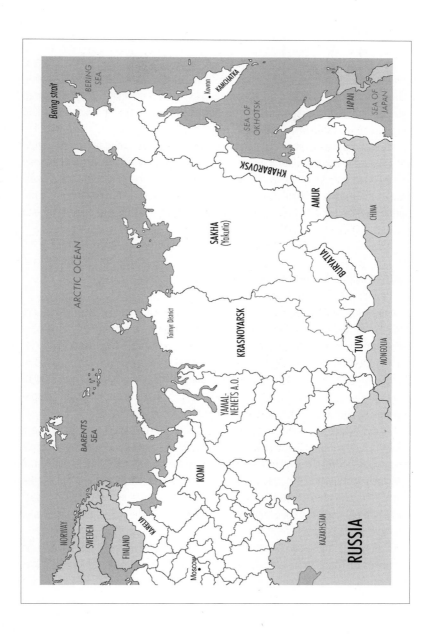

I n 2014, the conflict between Russia and Ukraine had repercussions for the indigenous peoples of the North. For one, in the wake of the annexation of
Crimea, the Kremlin stepped up policies to stifle dissent and further control and
constrain civil society, including indigenous peoples' organizations. Furthermore,
indigenous peoples' status as collective subjects of international law endowed
with the right to self-determination has become even more of a toxic item within
Russian politics than it was before.

With the annexation of Crimea, several peoples of the peninsula, self-identifying as indigenous, are now living under Russian control. The largest of these
are the Crimean Tatars, who are Sunni Muslims and speak a language closely
related to modern Turkish. Two other groups, the Krymchaks and Karaim, numbering several thousand each, are also Turkic-speaking; however, they adhere to
the Karaite branch of Judaism.

Land and natural resource rights

A number of legislative changes have affected indigenous peoples' rights and
control over their lands and natural resources and have increasingly restricted
their participation in decision-making processes with regard to these lands, including the Federal law "On specially protected natural territories" amended in
December 2013, which excluded the Territories of Traditional Nature Use (TTNU)[1]
of indigenous peoples of the North, Siberia and the Far East from the list of specially protected conservation areas (see *The Indigenous World 2014*).

On 21 July 2014, changes to the Land Code of the Russian Federation were
adopted by the State Duma, the Russian Parliament, which narrow the ability of
indigenous peoples to participate in decision-making regarding the allocation of
land for construction of industrial facilities on their traditional settlements. At the
same time, changes to the Land and Urban Planning Codes have eased industrial expansion into the places of traditional residence and economic activities of
the indigenous peoples of the North.

Proposed draft laws concerning the regulation of traditional fishery and on
Territories of Traditional Nature Use submitted to parliament by the Federal Government in late 2013 and in 2014 also severely limit the rights of indigenous
peoples. The draft law on traditional fishery thus stipulates that indigenous peoples are granted fishing quotas for personal consumption only. The law excludes

indigenous cooperatives (*obshchinas*) from the realm of traditional fisheries and the possibility of obtaining fishing plots. Moreover, "personal consumption" is defined in a very narrow manner, as it considers only a person's food intake while also ignoring actual findings on personal consumption amounts. The annual allowed volume of fish catch per person is set at 30 to 100 kg, depending on the region. This is not even enough to meet the traditional dietary requirements. Scientific studies have shown that indigenous peoples annually consume between 100 kg (reindeer herders) and 300 kg of fish (in regions where fish is the principal staple food and also used to feed dogs) but these findings have not been taken into account.

Major revisions to one of the three framework bills on the rights of indigenous peoples have also been suggested. The draft revised bill on Territories of Traditional Nature Use (TTNU) provides for the unilateral establishment of TTNU by the federal and regional governments without the participation of indigenous peoples in the choice of location of the TTNU, without the establishment of self-government structures within the TTNU and without an environmental expert review of the project.

Arctic development

The weakening of environmental and human rights safeguards is reflected in two relevant draft laws under discussion in the State Duma, "On the Arctic zone of the Russian Federation" and "On territories of accelerated development in Siberia and the Far East of the Russian Federation". These aim to create favourable conditions for attracting industrial investments into these areas at the cost of reduced compliance with environmental regulations.

The general weakening of environmental legislation, especially in the so-called "areas of accelerated development in the Arctic and the Far East", has resulted in industrial development without the mandatory consultation of residents and without considering their concerns. Examples are the "Power of Siberia" pipeline,[2] hydrocarbon exploration in the Chukchi sea, the development of military facilities on Wrangel island, the seizure of lands in Nenets and Khanty-Mansi Autonomous districts for oil production, the construction of the Vostochny space centre in Amurskaja oblast and others (see also *IWGIA Report 18*).[3]

In September 2014, the Ministry of Regional Affairs (which oversaw indigenous affairs) was dissolved. As a consequence, indigenous affairs and the management of Arctic and Far Eastern territories has been split up. The Arctic has been reassigned to the Ministry of Economic Development while indigenous peoples are now under the Ministry of Culture. This sparked angry reactions from indigenous activists, who saw themselves relegated to the realm of "singing and dancing" and far removed from land and resource rights.[4]

Socio-economic conditions

The socio-economic conditions of the indigenous peoples of Russia are heavily affected by the seizure of lands for industrial development, and the transfer of reindeer pastures, fishing and hunting areas into the control of commercial structures in the regions. This is complemented by cuts in the federal budget for social services (free education, health care, housing, etc.), which particularly affect indigenous peoples who, being from rural areas, live in a non-cash environment.

Aggravated persecution of NGOs

In July 2012 the State Duma adopted a law obliging NGOs that are engaged in "political activity" and receiving foreign funding to register as "NGOs performing the functions of foreign agents" (see also *The Indigenous World 2013*).

The law was amended in February 2014, introducing unannounced inspections of NGOs suspected of "political activity" or "extremism" and, in December 2014, the Federal Government issued a decree stipulating that the authorities should register any NGOs that did not register themselves as foreign agents. With this decree, any "unwanted" organization can unilaterally be registered as a "foreign agent" by the authorities.

The first indigenous peoples' organization to be affected by the new rules was the Chukotka Association of Traditional Sea Mammal Hunters (ChAZTO). In early December 2014, the head of ChAZTO was summoned to the regional Department of Justice and asked to voluntarily request the inclusion of ChAZTO on the list of organizations performing the functions of foreign agents. When he refused and stated that ChAZTO was not engaged in any political activity and that all foreign funding was earmarked for scientific research and the protection of marine mammals, the department's representatives informed him that, should he refuse, ChAZTO would be subjected to checks by all supervisory authorities and would end up being declared a foreign agent anyway.[5]

They did not explain precisely what it was about the activities of ChAZTO that the supervisory bodies considered "political activity". However, during the 2013-2014 period, representatives of ChAZTO had taken the floor during public hearings on proposed oil exploration and extraction in the continental shelf of Wrangel island in the Chukchi sea to express their concern at the potential negative impacts on populations of marine mammals and polar bears and the traditional lifestyle of the indigenous peoples of Chukotka. This might just have been enough to trigger the above action by the authorities. When even the participation of an indigenous peoples' organization from Chukotka in international environmental projects is now considered "political activity", this signals a sharp increase in state pressure.

"Association of Indigenous Peoples of the Russian Federation"

In 2014, representatives of several larger non-Russian peoples living in the Russian Federation formed an "Association of Indigenous Peoples of the Russian Federation". The peoples which this new organization purports to represent, such as the Tatars, Udmurt, Bashkir and Chuvash, vastly outnumber the 260,000 indigenous Northerners, with the Tatars alone numbering over five million. The classification of the Tatars and other peoples as indigenous is controversial. While they are linguistically and culturally distinct from the majority Russians and their languages and cultures are being marginalized by the Russian majority, their way of life does not differ significantly from the rest of the population. At the time of writing, the new association does not yet appear to have a website and has made a limited number of public pronouncements and actions.

The UN World Conference on Indigenous Peoples

The UN World Conference on Indigenous Peoples, held in September in New York, had unexpected repercussions for the indigenous peoples' movement in the

Russian Federation. The preparations for the conference were marked by a division between the original national organizing committee, which had been formed in 2012, and a new organizing committee, set up by the RAIPON leadership, which was elected in 2013. Rodion Sulyandziga, long-time indigenous activist and former first vice-president of RAIPON, had been representing the East European region within the Global Coordinating Group (GCG), and played a key role in negotiating the outcome document to be adopted by the World Conference.

One of the points of contention in the preparations for the conference was the demand for the high-level participation of indigenous representatives in the conference proceedings. Russia was among the states most fiercely opposed to any high-level role of non-state actors in the WCIP.

As Rodion Sulyandziga prepared to fly from Moscow to New York on 18 September to attend the WCIP, he was not allowed to leave the country on allegations of an invalid passport, and was therefore unable to attend the conference he had spent literally years helping to prepare.[6] At the same time, news came in that other indigenous activists had been held up in various ways, including one assault during which masked men snatched the passport and cell phone of Crimean Tatar activist Nadir Bekirov; slashed car tyres and extensive traffic police checks preventing Sami Parliament chair Valentina Sovkina from catching her flight; and yet another passport, that of former member of the UN Permanent Forum on Indigenous Issues, Anna Naikanchina, presumably invalidated by border guards.[7] During the WCIP, the harassment of Russian participants was denounced strongly, i.a. by two heads of state, and UN officials and mandate holders expressed their concern, including the UN High Commissioner for Human Rights and the Chair of the UN Permanent Forum.

The activists whose passports were suspected of having been invalidated by border police were furthermore charged with administrative offences, alleging that they themselves had cut the missing pages from their travel documents. The story was widely reported, including by the BBC and Al Jazeera. Eventually, all charges were dropped in the wake of the protests and outrage that the events had sparked.

In September 2014, a group of indigenous activists from various regions gathered in Moscow to consider their response to the changed political environment and the dysfunctional state of RAIPON. They resolved to form a new coalition named "Aborigen Forum", designed as an informal, non-hierarchical network of independent activists and experts jointly monitoring the situation of indigenous peoples in Russia.

Oil in the Komi Republic

The north of Komi republic, a region west of the Ural mountains, is a centre of the Russian oil industry, operated by the regional branch of Russia's LUKOil and its subsidiaries. The local indigenous people are the Izvatas, a subgroup of the Komi people, who despite their distinct language, culture and way of life are not recognized as indigenous by the Russian government. The Izvatas' main traditional activities and sources of income are hunting, fishing, gathering and reindeer herding. Since recognition is withheld from them, they do not enjoy the limited legal protections that apply to other peoples, in particular with regard to consultation, consent and compensation for damage to their lands and resources. While corporate misconduct on the side of LUKOil-Komi is nothing new, a culmination of incidents in 2014 sparked an unprecedented wave of protests. Incidents included unannounced pipeline construction, cover-ups and disastrous mismanagement of oil spills, the erection of oil rigs in the immediate vicinity of villages, unlicensed exploration works and the use of particularly harmful drilling techniques where tailings are disposed of in open mud pits that often leak into the environment. In February 2014, inhabitants of Krasnobor village in Izhma district discovered several oil rigs had been deployed right on the edge of the village. The construction had commenced without agreement and without notice to the local inhabitants or the administration. On 3 April, more than 150 attendees gathered in the culture house of Krasnobor village, representing 12 settlements. The gathering was also attended by the prosecutor's office, the environmental group the "Committee to Save Pechora", the indigenous peoples' organization "Izvatas", the head of administration of the Izhma district and members of the district and village councils. Representatives of "LUKOil" had been invited but declined the invitation. In a move very rare in contemporary Russia, the participants unanimously passed a resolution to terminate the operations of the "LUKOil-Komi" oil company within their territory. On 11 April, the Izhma district council voted unanimously to support this move. Unsurprisingly, the company failed to respect either resolution. The protests continued throughout 2014 and also spread north to neighbouring Usinsk district, which in 1994 was the site of the world's largest on-land oil spill ever.

Greenpeace and 350.org ran supporting on-line campaigns and the issue was reported by Al Jazeera. Yet still no substantial improvement in LUKOil's conduct was observed. LUKOil is a member of the Russian Global Compact Network but its conduct in Komi shows no sign of attempting to comply with the UN Guiding Principles on Business and Human Rights.

Open cast mining in Kemerovo Oblast

Another conflict hotspot in 2014 was the South Siberian coal mining region in Kemerovo oblast. Here, several villages, predominantly inhabited by Shors, a Siberian Turkic indigenous group, are under intense pressure from open cast coal mining, which has been consuming their ancestral territory for many years. In 2014, the long-standing conflict around the village of Kazas culminated in the all-out destruction of the village, which is entirely surrounded by mining concessions. Those inhabitants who refused to sell their houses have seen them burnt down in nightly arsons. The former villagers are now scattered across the city and other settlements. They have received neither adequate financial compensation nor suitable resettlement land. Some are reported homeless. The mining company is operating an armed checkpoint which prevents the inhabitants from reaching their village and their cemetery. The nearby sacred mountain of Karagai-Nash has been destroyed by mining operations. Inhabitants of neighbouring Chuvashka village fear that their community may be next in line for removal.[8]

Interference with indigenous peoples' internal affairs

The authorities continued to massively interfere in indigenous peoples' internal affairs throughout 2014 by putting pressure on their decision-making bodies, failing to recognize elected representatives and imposing their own proposals on them. Such interventions were particularly visible on Sakhalin, where the authorities refused to accept the outcomes of the indigenous peoples' congress held in December 2013, and in Murmansk region, during the Kola Saami Congress, where they intervened to break up the Kola Saami Parliament.[9]

Contentious national parks

A major issue of contention were plans announced by the Federal Government to create a national park along the Bikin river in Primorsky Krai in the Far East. The Bikin valley is the ancestral territory of the Udege people and, at the same time, the home of the Siberian tiger, whose protection is an issue of national prestige for Russia. The indigenous peoples of Russia have abundant negative experiences with the creation of national parks, as these are usually run by state authorities with very little or no regard to indigenous rights and customs. The Udege have for many years been demanding the establishment of a Territory of Traditional Nature Use (TTNU) within their territory, which would ensure that their right to participation in decision-making is respected. Their response to the plans for a national park were therefore overwhelmingly negative. Protest rallies were held in the main village of Krasny Yar.[10] At a roundtable meeting held in Vladivostok in April, the regional authorities indicated that they might be prepared to make some concessions and delay the park's establishment until pending rights issues were resolved.

UN mechanisms and mandate holder review of the Russian Federation

In January 2014, Russia was reviewed by the UN Committee on the Rights of the Child (CRC) during its 65th Session. The CRC had received information from civil society organizations during the pre-session held in 2013, where among others, one submission on the situation of indigenous children had been presented. The concluding observations were adopted on 25 February 2014.[11] In the observations, the CRC expressed its concern at the fact "that oil- and gas-extracting businesses continue to have a negative impact on the traditional lifestyle of persons belonging to small-numbered indigenous groups, including children, through deforestation and pollution and by endangering the species that are crucial to their livelihoods."

The mechanism made a number of recommendations with regard to the regulatory framework for the oil and gas industries, coal, environmental and health standards and monitoring thereof, and assessments of the human rights impacts of business activities, as well as reparations with regard to potential damage to the health and development of children.

The committee specifically recommended that these measures be guided by the UN Guiding Principles on Business and Human Rights (UNGP), which Russia officially supports, making this the first decision by a UN human rights mechanism to reference the UNGP in their jurisprudence in relation to indigenous peoples in Russia.

In late 2013, the then UN Special Rapporteur on the rights of indigenous peoples, together with the UN Working Group on Business and Human Rights, had jointly submitted an allegation letter to the Russian government regarding economic discrimination against indigenous peoples in the case of Dylacha, an indigenous *obschina* (cooperative). The cooperative had been one of the oldest and most successful of its kind in Russia until it was raided and forcibly closed by the authorities (see *The Indigenous World 2013*), virtually ripping out the economic backbone of the indigenous Evenk community of Buryatia.

In May 2014, Russia responded to the allegations. The response letter confirmed that the cooperative was terminated because one of its activities, namely mining of nephrite jade, was not officially recognized as an indigenous peoples' traditional economic activity. Russia therefore implicitly confirmed the gist of the allegation of economic discrimination against indigenous peoples, namely that indigenous peoples in Russia are not free to determine their own path of economic development. In his report on communications, the Special Rapporteur noted the substance of Russia's response and recalled his own earlier recommendations to the Russian government to support indigenous entrepreneurship in both traditional and non-traditional areas.[12]   ◯

Notes and references

1   The term "Territories of Traditional Nature Use" is defined in a Federal law "Territories of Traditional Nature Use of indigenous peoples of the North, Siberia and the Far East" 7 May 2001; they are a type of protected territory created with the purpose of protecting indigenous peoples' traditional ways of life. Indigenous peoples' customary ownership of these lands is not acknowledged; however, they do have certain decision-making rights when it comes to use of these territories by third parties, including extractive industries. For details, see I.a. *IWGIA Human Rights Report 18: Indigenous Peoples in the Russian Federation*,
      http://www.iwgia.org/publications/search-pubs?publication_id=695

2 See: *Russia: Major new gas pipeline to China to be built without impact assessment*, 17 July 2014 http://www.iwgia.org/news/search-news?news_id=1043

3 See note 1 for full reference for IWGIA Report 18.

4 See *Russia: Ministry in charge of indigenous affairs to be dissolved* 10 September 2014 http://www.iwgia.org/news/search-news?news_id=1073

5 Cf. "*Russia: Indigenous hunters association pressured to register as 'foreign agents'*". 11 December 2014, http://www.iwgia.org/news/search-news?news_id=1139

6 See *Russian delegates denied exit from country to participate in World Conference*, 22 September 2014 http://www.iwgia.org/news/search-news?news_id=1082

7 See *Russia: President of Kola Saami Parliament harassed while travelling to UN World Conference on Indigenous Peoples* 21 September 2014 http://www.iwgia.org/news/search-news?news_id=1078

8 See 2012 IWGIA briefing note "Coal Mining in Kemerovo Oblast, Russia", http://www.iwgia.org/iwgia_files_publications_files/0595_Coal_Mining_in_Kemerovo_Oblast_Briefing_note_Sept_2012.pdf and IWGIA Human Rights Report 18, Indigenous Peoples in the Russian Federation, p. 42-43, http://www.iwgia.org/iwgia_files_publications_files/0695_HumanRights_report_18_Russia.pdf

9 See Russia: Sakhalin authorities and Exxon playing Divide and Conquer. 22 May 2014 http://www.iwgia.org/news/search-news?news_id=995, Russia: Kola Saami Congress held amidst massive state pressure, authorities push back against Saami Parliament. 28 November 2014, http://www.iwgia.org/news/search-news?news_id=1122

10 *Russia: Bikin Udege community vows to rally to defend land rights* 11 June 2014 http://www.iwgia.org/news/search-news?news_id=1013

11 *Concluding observations on the report submitted by the Russian Federation under article 8, paragraph 1, of the Optional Protocol to the Convention on the Rights of the Child on the involvement of children in armed conflict*, UN Doc CRC/C/RUS/CO/4-5, Download from http://undocs.org/CRC/C/RUS/CO/4-5

12 See Report on observations to communications sent and replies received by the Special Rapporteur on the rights of indigenous peoples, James Anaya, 3 September 2014. http://undocs.org/A/HRC/27/52/Add.4

Olga Murashko is a Russian anthropologist and one of the co-founders of the former IWGIA Moscow. She works as a consultant for the Centre for the Support of Indigenous Peoples of the North (CSIPN).

Johannes Rohr is a German historian who has been working with indigenous peoples' organisations in Russia since 1995, focusing on their economic, social and cultural rights. He is currently working as a consultant for IWGIA and INFOE.

INUIT REGIONS OF CANADA

In Canada, the Inuit number 60,000 people, or 4.3% of the Aboriginal population. Inuit live in 53 Arctic communities in four regions collectively known as "Inuit Nunangat" (Inuit homeland): Nunatsiavut (Labrador); Nunavik (Quebec); Nunavut; and the Inuvialuit Settlement Region of the Northwest Territories. The *Nunatsiavut* government, created in 2006, is the only ethnic-style government to be formed among the four Inuit regions to date. It was formed following the settling of the Labrador Inuit Land Claims Agreement in 2005. The Agreement covers 72,520 square kilometres of land, including 15,800 square kilometres of Inuit owned land.

The *Nunavut* Land Claims Agreement (NLCA), which covers two million square kilometres, was settled in 1993. The Nunavut government was created by the NLCA in April 1999. It represents all Nunavut citizens. Nunavut Tunngavik Incorporated (NTI) represents Inuit who are beneficiaries of the Nunavut Land Claims Agreement.

The first *Nunavik* land claim (James Bay and Northern Quebec Agreement) was settled in 1975. The second land claim Agreement, which applies to the offshore region around Quebec, northern Labrador and offshore northern Labrador, came into effect on 10 July 2007. The Nunavik area covers 550,000 square kilometres, which is one-third of the province of Quebec. Makivik Corporation was created to administer the James Bay Agreement and represent Inuit beneficiaries. Nunavik is working to develop a regional government for the region.

The *Inuvialuit* land claim celebrated its 30th anniversary on 5 June 2014. The Inuvialuit Final Agreement (IFA) is a Constitutionally-protected Agreement covering 91,000 square kilometres in the Northwest Territories, including 13,000 square kilometres with subsurface rights to oil, gas and minerals. The Inuvialuit Regional Corporation (IRC)[1] represents collective Inuvialuit interests in dealings with governments and industry, with the goal of improving the economic, social and cultural well-being of its beneficiaries, and protecting and preserving Arctic wildlife, environment and biological productivity. The Inuvialuit are negotiating for self-government.

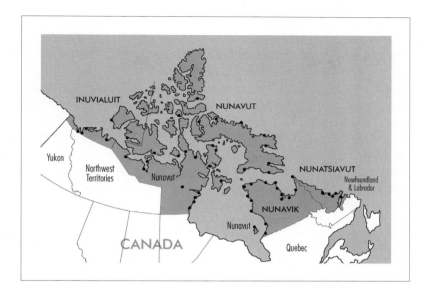

U ndoubtedly the highlight for Inuit in Canada in 2014 was the international gathering of the Inuit Circumpolar Council (ICC) held in Inuvik, Northwest Territories, in July. Inuit from Greenland, Canada, Alaska and Russia gathered for a week, as outlined in greater detail in the report from the Inuvialuit Settlement Region below.

On 22 May 2014, following Canada and Norway's appeal of a decision of the World Trade Organization's (WTO) Dispute Resolution Panel in January 2014, the WTO Appellate Body issued its much anticipated Report on *European Communities Measures Prohibiting the Importation and Marketing of Seal Products.* The report presents the Appellate Body's conclusions that certain aspects of the European Union regulations prohibiting the importing of seal products do not comply with the *General Agreement on Tariffs and Trade* (GATT). In particular, the report concluded that the Indigenous Community Exception has not been designed and applied in a manner that meets the requirements of Article XX of the GATT, namely, that such measures must not be applied in a manner which would constitute a means of arbitrary or unjustifiable discrimination between countries where the same conditions prevail. The report further recommended that the European Union bring these regulations into compliance with the rules of international trade. In a parallel political process, On 8 August 2014, Canada and the EU issued a Joint Statement on "Access to the European Union of Seal Products from Indigenous Communities of Canada". The Joint Statement envisions that an expert group representing both sides will work expeditiously towards establishing the administrative arrangements required to enable access to the European Union on the part of seal products from Canadian indigenous communities. Much work remains to make this document a living reality.

At the national level, Inuit Tapiriit Kanatami (ITK), the national Inuit organization, participated in the annual Council of the Federations meeting with premiers of the 13 Canadian provinces and territories. Held in Charlottetown in late August 2014, a consensus emerged to hold a National Roundtable on the issue of Missing and Murdered Aboriginal Women in early 2015.

The Report of the Special Rapporteur on the rights of indigenous peoples, Mr. James Anaya's visit to Canada was made public in May 2014. Inuit met with Mr. Anaya when he visited Canada in 2013 and discussed the critical issue of social housing. In his report, Mr. Anaya addressed this issue head on. The report states:

The housing crisis has been identified by Inuit representatives as a high priority issue. It is worth noting that the chronic housing shortage has a severe negative effect on a wide variety of economic and social conditions. Overcrowding contributes to higher rates of respiratory illness, depression, sleep deprivation, family violence, poor educational achievement and an inability to retain skilled and professional members in the community.

Canada's Auditor General issued a report in late November 2014 that was heavily critical of the "Nutrition North Canada" (NNC) program aimed at ensuring nutritious food reaches Inuit in Canada's northern communities at affordable prices. National Inuit Leader Mr. Terry Audla commented, "The reality is that it still costs twice as much to feed a family in the North than what it costs to feed a family in many places in Southern Canada. As an example, the rate of food insecurity in Nunavut is six times the national average – the highest rate in any Aboriginal population in a developed country." The Canadian Department of Aboriginal Affairs and Northern Development agreed with all of the Auditor General's Recommendations. The issue, however, touched a nerve among Canadians living in the South, who responded by using social media to organize nationwide food drives to send food directly to Inuit in the Arctic.

Inuvialuit Settlement Region

2014 was a significant year in the Inuvialuit Settlement Region (ISR), most nota-bly for the celebrations of the 30th anniversary of the signing of the Inuvialuit Final Agreement (IFA) on 5 June. Inuvialuit across the region held Inuvialuit Day events to commemorate the milestone. The IFA provides Inuvialuit with a voice in the future development of the ISR, as well as land, financial compensation and con-trol of wildlife harvesting.

In July, Inuvik played host to the 2014 Inuit Circumpolar Council (ICC) General Assembly with a theme of *Ukiuqtaqtumi Hivuniptingnun - One Arctic One Fu-ture*. The honorary patron of the General Assembly, Prime Minister Stephen Harper, opened the conference with a video presentation. At the conclusion of the formal meeting, the Kitigaaryuit Declaration was signed, which is intended to promote bet-ter knowledge sharing between Inuit organizations and the rest of the world.

The ICC General Assembly drew more than 600 delegates: youth, elders, cultural performers, non-governmental organizations, media and observers from Chukotka (Russia), Greenland, Alaska and Canada. Highlights included the nightly gala evenings of entertainment featuring international, national and re-gional participants. More than 200 participants came from the surrounding com-munities for the Traditional Inuit Northern Games and Circumpolar Drum Dance Workshop.

Nunavut

Progress continued on the Nunavut Tunngavik Incorporated (NTI) historic CDN $1 billion lawsuit against the Government of Canada, launched in 2006 because of the government's failure to implement the Nunavut Land Claim Agreement (NLCA). In 2014, NTI won two legal decisions related to the case. In April, it won an appeal launched by the Crown to the Nunavut Court of Appeal. In November, NTI won in the federal court with the result that the Crown must produce its final statement of documents and make them available to all parties by January 2015. The trial of the case has been set to begin on 9 March 2015.

Meanwhile, NTI continued to work towards making progress on the Nunavut Land Claims Agreement Implementation Contract Renewal Negotiations for the period 2013-2023. The ten-year implementation contract was up for renewal in 2003; however, the federal government walked away from the negotiations at the time, only to come back in 2013 with a proposal that was rejected by NTI and the Government of Nunavut. In early 2014, NTI submitted a new proposal, comprehensive in scope for the vast territory, and in the spirit of the NCLA. As of December 2014, the federal government had not accepted or rejected NTI's proposals.

Nunavik

The Makivik Corporation, along with the other Nunavik organizations, completed the Parnasimautik Consultation Report after extensive consultations with Nunavik Inuit in 2013 and 2014. This report gives Nunavik Inuit one voice and calls for governments to commit to a comprehensive, integrated, sustainable and equitable approach to improving Nunavik Inuit lives and communities.

For the last few years, as Nunavik has witnessed a significant increase in mineral resource exploration and mining projects, Makivik decided to develop a mining policy to better monitor and guide mining projects in the region. The Nunavik Inuit Mining Policy clearly sets out the conditions for mineral resource development in Nunavik as follows: 1) Maximize the short- and long-term social and economic benefits for Nunavik Inuit. 2) Minimize the negative environmental and social impacts of mining activities. 3) Ensure open dialogue and good communication between project developers and Nunavik Inuit.

Nunavik continues to be in the midst of a serious housing crisis, which is affecting the majority of its families. In September 2014, Canadian Government Minister Bernard Valcourt responded to Makivik's numerous requests for a catch-up housing program, indicating that he was committed to working with his colleagues to find additional avenues beyond the Five-Year Housing Agreement to address the housing concerns in Nunavik.

Nunatsiavut

The Nunatsiavut government tabled a balanced budget in March 2014 for CDN \$66.9 million. Finance Minister Daniel Pottle listed housing, and the revitalization of Inuit culture and language, as major priorities for the region. CDN $7.5 million was budgeted for housing issues and initiatives.

An extensive Housing Needs Assessment Report was made public later in March 2014. The Assessment, conducted in 2012 in all Nunatsiavut communities, had over a 90% participation rate.

A population survey of the George River Caribou Herd, made public in August, indicated a shocking decline in the herd's numbers, down to 14,200 animals. The herd numbered between 700,000 – 800,000 in the 1980s. The Nunatsiavut government called on the provincial governments of Newfoundland and Labrador, and Quebec, to commit the necessary resources and work with all stakeholders to establish a comprehensive management strategy.

The Government of Nunatsiavut expressed strong disappointment in the delay of a trial which could have seen the settlement for Inuit survivors of the residential schools in Newfoundland and Labrador. Five class-action suits were filed. The government wrote to the Prime Minister of Canada early in 2014 appealing for justice in the matter, and asking Canada to agree to mediate, and work towards an out-of-court settlement. The trial has been postponed to September 2015.

Nain resident Joey Angnatok won the inaugural "Inuit Recognition Award" at the annual ArcticNet Scientific Conference in December 2014. Mr. Angnatok helped champion a number of Arctic research projects throughout Nunatsiavut using his blend of traditional knowledge, skills and values in achieving positive results.   O

Notes and references

1   NTI, the Makivik Corporation and the IRC were incorporated under provincial or federal laws for the purpose of representing the rights and interests of Inuit in their respective regions through the land claims agreement negotiation process. Since the ratification of those agreements, NTI, Makivik Corporation and IRC have carried the general mandate of ensuring the improvement of the economic, social and cultural well-being of their land claims agreement beneficiaries through the implementation of the promises and proper flow of financial compensation due to the beneficiaries under those agreements. These corporations operate democratically through elected boards of directors which represent the communities within the regions. These corporations also fulfil their mandates through the operation of subsidiary companies dedicated to specific development goals.

Stephen Hendrie *is Executive Director of Inuit Tapiriit Kanatami (ITK) - Canada's national Inuit organization based in Ottawa. He came to ITK in 2002 following 10 years of work in the field of communications at Makivik Corporation in Nunavik, northern Quebec. He has a BA from Concordia University in Montreal (1984) and an MA in Political Science from McGill University in Montreal (1991), along with many years of journalistic experience.*

*With contributions from **Kate Darling**, Senior Political and Legal Advisor (ITK), staff at the Inuvialuit Regional Corporation (IRC), **Kerry McCluskey** (NTI), **Teevi Mackay** (Makivik) and **Bert Pomeroy** (Nunatsiavut).*

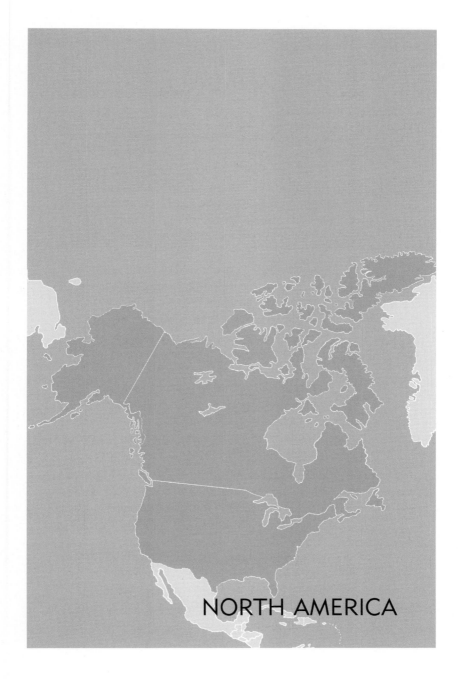

NORTH AMERICA

CANADA

The Indigenous peoples of Canada are collectively referred to as "Aboriginal peoples". The Constitution Act, 1982 of Canada recognizes three groups of Aboriginal peoples: Indians, Inuit and Métis. According to the 2011 National Household Survey, 1,400,685 people in Canada had an Aboriginal identity, representing 4.3% of the total Canadian population. 851,560 people identified as a First Nations person, representing 60.8% of the total Aboriginal population and 2.6% of the total Canadian population.

First Nations (referred to as "Indians" in the Constitution and generally registered under Canada's Indian Act) are a diverse group, representing more than 600 First Nations and more than 60 languages. Around 55% live on-reserve and 45% reside off-reserve in urban, rural, special access and remote areas. The Métis constitute a distinct Aboriginal nation, numbering 451,795 in 2011, many of whom live in urban centres, mostly in western Canada.

Canada's Constitution Act, 1982 recognizes and affirms the existing Aboriginal and Treaty rights of Aboriginal peoples. The Supreme Court has called the protection of these rights "an important underlying constitutional value" and "a national commitment". Canada's highest Court has called for reconciliation of "pre-existing aboriginal sovereignty with assumed Crown sovereignty".[1] Canada has never proved it has legal or *de jure* sovereignty over Indigenous peoples' territories, which suggests that Canada is relying on the racist doctrine of discovery.[2]

In 2010, the Canadian government announced its endorsement of the United Nations Declaration on the Rights of Indigenous Peoples (UNDRIP), which was adopted by the UN General Assembly in September 2007. This decision comes as a reversal of Canada's earlier opposition to the Declaration, which it had pursued together with Australia, the USA and New Zealand, and who have all since revised their attitude towards the UNDRIP. Canada has not ratified ILO Convention No. 169.

2014 is most noted for the historic Supreme Court decision, *Tsilhqot'in Nation v British Columbia*,[3] affirming Aboriginal title to traditional lands – including rights to own, benefit from and determine future use of these lands. This decision marked the first time a Canadian court has provided legal recognition to Indigenous land title based on the Indigenous Nation's traditional use and control of the lands. In opposition to the Supreme Court decision and the efforts of Indigenous peoples and their allies, the federal government of Canada has intensified its efforts to undermine Indigenous peoples' human rights both domestically and internationally. The government remains hostile to the UN Declaration on the Rights of Indigenous Peoples, despite its 2010 endorsement (see also *The Indigenous World 2011*).

Tsilhqot'in Nation victory

On 26 June, the Supreme Court of Canada unanimously recognized the right of the Tsilhqot'in people to own, control and enjoy the benefits of approximately 2,000 km^2 of land at the heart of their traditional territory in central British Columbia (see *The Indigenous World 2014* for an introduction to the SCC hearing). This

decision marks the first time that a Canadian court has affirmed the land ownership of a particular Indigenous Nation, rather than relying on negotiations to address land rights.

Responding to the landmark decision, the Tsilhqot'in Nation said, "The Supreme Court of Canada's ruling ends a long history of denial and sets the stage
for recognition of Aboriginal title in its full form."

The legal principles articulated in the Court's decision are widely applicable
and should be adopted as part of a principled framework for the recognition of
Indigenous land rights in Canada. Indeed, this jurisprudence could be used by
Indigenous peoples in other countries. Highlights of the decision include:

- Aboriginal title confers ownership rights including "the right to decide how
  the land will be used; the right of enjoyment and occupancy of the land;
  the right to possess the land; the right to the economic benefits of the
  land; and the right to pro-actively use and manage the land," [4] as well as
  the "right to control" the land.[5]
- The doctrine of *terra nullius* "never applied in Canada." [6] The Court affirmed that Indigenous peoples exercised rights to control, use and benefit from their lands prior to the arrival of Europeans and that the assertion
  of European sovereignty in British Columbia did not extinguish this "independent legal interest".[7]
- The Court repeatedly emphasized the constitutional requirement of obtaining Indigenous peoples' "consent".[8] The right to "control" title land
  "means that governments and others seeking to use the land must obtain
  the consent of the Aboriginal title holders".[9] If the Aboriginal group does
  not consent to the use, "the government's only recourse is to establish
  that the proposed incursion on the land is justified under s. 35 of the
  Constitution Act, 1982".[10]
- In regard to federal and provincial governments, "incursions on Aboriginal
  title cannot be justified if they would substantially deprive future generations of the benefit of the land".[11]
- The Court rejected assertions by the province that Indigenous title lands
  are necessarily limited to small tracts of continuous intensive use. Instead, the Court found that Indigenous societies that historically exercised control over large territories could establish ongoing title to these
  lands.[12]

- The "Crown had... a legal duty to negotiate in good faith to resolve land claims".[13] "The governing ethos," the Court said, "is not one of competing interests but of reconciliation."[14] Further, "What is at stake is nothing less than justice for the Aboriginal group and its descendants, and the reconciliation between the group and broader society."[15]
- Finally, the Court cautioned, "if the Crown begins a project without consent prior to Aboriginal title being established, it may be required to cancel the project upon establishment of the title if continuation of the project would be unjustifiably infringing. Similarly, if legislation was validly enacted before title was established, such legislation may be rendered inapplicable going forward to the extent that it unjustifiably infringes Aboriginal title." [16]

Indigenous Peoples and their allies have celebrated this ruling as a "game-changer".[17] Government and industry have been slower to respond. The federal government had not yet engaged with the Tsilhqot'in Nation in any constructive manner by the end of the year. The province of BC was urged to meaningfully work with Indigenous peoples on the eve of a significant gathering of provincial government and First Nations leaders.[18]

Report of the Special Rapporteur on the rights of indigenous peoples

Former UN Special Rapporteur James Anaya visited Canada in the fall of 2013 (*see The Indigenous World 2014*) and his report was presented to the Human Rights Council in 2014.[19] Key conclusions of Anaya's report echo concerns raised repeatedly by Indigenous peoples. In his conclusions, Anaya states:

Canada faces a continuing crisis when it comes to the situation of indigenous peoples of the country. The well-being gap between aboriginal and non-aboriginal people in Canada has not narrowed over the last several years, treaty and aboriginal claims remain persistently unresolved, indigenous women and girls remain vulnerable to abuse, and overall there appear to be high levels of distrust among indigenous peoples towards government at both the federal and provincial levels.[20]

Anaya's report details ongoing challenges with regard to rights violations and lack of implementation of the court decisions that support Indigenous peoples. He touches on many topics that have been covered in previous issues of *The Indigenous World:* child welfare, murdered and missing Indigenous women, the Truth and Reconciliation Commission, resource development and the right of free, prior and informed consent and the need for implementation of the *UN Declaration on the Rights of Indigenous Peoples.*

There has been no substantive response from the Government of Canada. Canada is increasingly a state participating in "rights ritualism",[21] agreeing to and participating in the visit of the Special Rapporteur in the appearance of good faith while having no plan to seriously engage in implementing the recommendations of the report. As described by Hilary Charlesworth: "Rights ritualism can be understood as a way of embracing the language of human rights precisely to deflect real human rights scrutiny and to avoid accountability for human rights abuses." [22]

Indigenous peoples and their allies have welcomed the report and are using the Special Rapporteur's work in their own.

World Conference on Indigenous Peoples

Indigenous peoples' and human rights organizations were outraged that the federal government used the World Conference on Indigenous Peoples as an opportunity to continue its unprincipled attack on the UN Declaration on the Rights of Indigenous Peoples.[23] After the consensus adoption of the Outcome Document, Canada was the lone state that insisted on an Explanation of Vote. Canada then filed a two-page statement of objections, including that it could not commit to upholding provisions in the UN Declaration that deal with free, prior and informed consent (FPIC) since these provisions "could be interpreted as providing a veto to Aboriginal groups".

The notion that the Declaration could be interpreted as conferring an absolute and unilateral veto power has been repeatedly raised by Canada as justification for its continued opposition. This claim, however, has no basis either in the UN Declaration or in the wider body of international law.

Much as there has been no visible engagement with the report of the Special Rapporteur, Canada has not engaged domestically with Indigenous peoples with any dialogue with regards to an action plan for implementation of the Outcome

Document of the WCIP. The Coalition on the UN Declaration on the Rights of Indigenous Peoples, which is made up of Indigenous peoples' and human rights
organizations, is engaging with the Outcome Document and exploring strategies
for advancing the recommendations, with or without the engagement of the State.

Murdered and missing Indigenous women

Indigenous peoples' and human rights organizations have been raising awareness on the issue of murdered and missing Indigenous women and girls for many
years, with calls for a national inquiry and national plan of action.[24] In May 2014,
Canada's national police, the RCMP, published the first national statistics on the
numbers of missing and murdered Indigenous women known to police. The RC-
MP reported that 1,017 Indigenous women and girls were murdered between
1980 and 2012 (a rate 4.5 times higher than homicides of non-Indigenous wom-
en). As of November 2013, at least 105 Indigenous women and girls remained
missing under suspicious circumstances or for undetermined reasons.[25]

In August, the body of 15-year-old Tina Fontaine was pulled from Winnipeg,
Manitoba's Red River – having been murdered and dumped into the river in a
plastic bag. The horror of the story hit the national consciousness. Media coverage, rallies and vigils took place across the country. In November, another Indigenous teen, Rinelle Harper, was found almost dead after crawling out of the
Assiniboine River (also in Winnipeg, Manitoba). Shockingly, the federal government refused to engage – the Prime Minister repeatedly denying the issue was a
"sociological phenomenon".[26] In an end-of-year interview, the Prime Minister re-
plied to a question about whether the federal government would respond to the
call for an inquiry by saying: "It isn't really high on our radar, to be honest." [27]

Education Act

The long-standing need to ensure equity in funding for Indigenous education was
intended to be addressed in federal legislation introduced in 2014.[28] On 7 February, the federal government announced legislation, and 1.9 billion dollars of funding, with the support of the National Chief of the Assembly of First Nations. Quickly, the draft legislation, ironically titled "First Nations Control of First Nations Edu-

cation", was heavily criticized for, among other things, placing too much control in the hands of the Minister of Aboriginal Affairs. On 2 May, the National Chief resigned.[29] The following week, the Minister of Aboriginal Affairs put the legislation "on hold". The budgeted funds did not flow and Indigenous education remains starkly underfunded. The Prime Minister insists that funds will not be released until the Indigenous leadership agrees to the terms set by the government. As of year-end, no progress had been made.

Review of the Comprehensive Land Claim Policy

One of Canada's processes for addressing land rights violations is the comprehensive land claim policy (CCP). For Indigenous peoples who do not have a Treaty or other arrangement, this is intended to be a method of redress for land dispossession. In August 2014, the federal government unilaterally appointed a ministerial special representative, Mr. Douglas Eyford, to develop recommendations for the reform of the CCP. The government also released an interim policy on resolution of comprehensive claims.[30] The interim policy is described by government "as a starting point for discussions with partners and outlines the Government of Canada's current approach to the negotiation of treaties, including the developments that have occurred since the publication of the last policy in 1986". However, the interim policy does not depart in any significant way from existing policies and fails to incorporate either the standards established in the *Tsilhqot'in* decision or international human rights law, including the UN Declaration on the Rights of Indigenous Peoples. Many substantive submissions were made to Eyford by Indigenous organizations and others.[31]

Specific Claims Tribunal

Another form of intended redress for past violations is the specific claims process. This process differs from the CCP as it deals with compensation not exceeding 150 million dollars for specific violations of agreements, including treaties, or the mismanagement by the government of an Indigenous Nation's assets.

In 2008, a Specific Claims Tribunal was established to make the process more efficient and improve access to justice.[32] In November 2014, the Tribunal issued its report, including grave concerns about its ability to function. Tribunal Chair Justice Harry Slade warned:

> *The Tribunal has neither a sufficient number of members to address its present and future case load in a timely manner, if at all. Nor is it...assured of its ability to continue to function with adequate protection of its independence... Without the appointment of at least one additional full time member and several part time members...The Tribunal will fail.*[33]

This pronouncement is another example whereby Canada appears to be engaging in rights ritualism, as described above. Canada has created a body to address past violations yet does not give the body the resources or the independence to function properly.

In *Aundeck Omni Kaning* v. *Canada*, the Tribunal ruled that the federal government's negotiating position was

> *paternalistic, self-serving, arbitrary and disrespectful of First Nations. It falls short of upholding the honour of the Crown, and its implied principle of 'good faith' required in all negotiations Canada undertakes with First Nations. Such a position affords no room for the principles of reconciliation, accommodation and consultation that the Supreme Court ... has described as being the foundation of Canada's relationship with First Nations.*[34]   ○

Notes and references

1   Canada is part of the British Commonwealth. The British Crown is the symbolic head of state and the term refers to government. The federal government is the Crown in right of Canada and each of the provincial governments is the Crown in right of the province.

2   See Permanent Forum on Indigenous Issues, *Study on the impacts of the Doctrine of Discovery on indigenous peoples, including mechanisms, processes and instruments of redress.* UN Doc. E/C.19/2014/3 (20 February 2014) Study by Forum member Edward John, available at http://daccess-dds-ny.un.org/doc/UNDOC/GEN/N14/241/84/PDF/N1424184.pdf?OpenElement.

3   *Tsilhqot'in Nation* v. *British Columbia*, 2014 SCC 44.

4   *Tsilhqot'in Nation*, *supra* note 1, para. 73. See also paras. 94 and 121.

5   *Ibid.*, paras. 2, 18, 75 and 76.

6   *Tsilhqot'in Nation*, *supra* note 1, para. 69.

7   *Ibid.*, para 69.

8   In regard to "consent", see *Tsilhqot'in Nation*, paras. 2, 5, 76, 88, 90-92, 97 and 124; and *UN Declaration*, article 32(2).

9   *Ibid.*, para. 76. In regard to "control", see also paras. 2, 15, 18, 31, 36, 38, 47, 48, 50, 75 and 119; and *UN Declaration*, article 26(2).

10   *Ibid.*, para. 76.

11   *Tsilhqot'in Nation*, *supra* note 1, para. 86.

12   *Tsilhqot'in Nation*, *supra* note 1, para. 50.

13   *Tsilhqot'in Nation*, *supra* note 1, para. 17.

14   *Tsilhqot'in Nation*, *supra* note 1, para. 17.

15   *Tsilhqot'in Nation*, *supra* note 1, para. 23

16   *Tsilhqot'in Nation*, *supra* note 1, para. 92.

17   For example, Tears and cheers greet historic Supreme Court ruling handing Tsilhqot'in major victory, *APTN National News*, 26 June 2014. Online at: http://aptn.ca/news/2014/06/26/supreme-court-hands-tsilhqotin-major-victory-historic-ruling/.

18   Amnesty International and Canadian Friends Service Committee, *Open Letter to the Premier of British Columbia*, 10 September 2014. Online at: http://quakerservice.ca/wp-content/up-loads/2014/09/Open-Letter-to-the-Government-of-British-Columbia-10-Sept-14.pdf

19   UN Human Rights Council, 2014: *Report of the Special Rapporteur on the rights of indigenous peoples, James Anaya: Addendum: The situation of indigenous peoples in Canada*, UN Doc. A/HRC/27/52/Add.2 (4 July 2014), Annex.

20   *Ibid.*, para. 80.

21   For more on this concept, see Fleur Adcock, 2012: The UN Special Rapporteur on the Rights of Indigenous Peoples and New Zealand: A study in compliance ritualism. *New Zealand Yearbook of International Law*, Vol. 10 at 97 (2012).

22   Hilary Charlesworth 2010: Kirby Lecture in International Law: Swimming to Cambodia. Justice and Ritual in Human Rights After Conflict. *29 Australian Yearbook of International Law* 1 at 12-13, quoted in *The Limitations of the Current International Human Rights Law System in Regard to Monitoring of Rights? Does it Encourage 'Rights Ritualism'?*, Presentation by Ms Fleur Adcock, The Australian National University, at the International Expert Group Meeting, Dialogue on an optional protocol to the United Nations Declaration on the Rights of Indigenous Peoples, hosted by the Secretariat of the Permanent Forum on Indigenous Issues in New York, January 2015. UN Doc. PFII/2014/EGM, New York, 27 - 29 January 2015, para. 10.

23   Ad hoc coalition on the UN Declaration on the Rights of Indigenous Peoples, 24 September 2014: *Canada uses World Conference to continue indefensible attack on UN Declaration on the Rights of Indigenous Peoples*. Available online: http://quakerservice.ca/wp-content/uploads/2014/09/Joint-Public-statement-following-WCIP-24-Sept-2014.pdf

24   See generally Native Women's Association of Canada and Amnesty International Canada

25   Canada, RCMP 2014: *Murdered or Missing Aboriginal Women: National Operational Overview.* Available online : http://www.rcmp-grc.gc.ca/pubs/mmaw-faapd-eng.pdf

26   Alex Boutilier, 2014: Native teen's slaying a 'crime', not a 'sociological phenomenon', Stephen Harper says. *Toronto Star*, 21 August 2014. http://www.thestar.com/news/canada/2014/08/21/native_teens_slaying_a_crime_not_a_sociological_phenomenon_stephen_harper_says.html.

27   The full text of the interview is available online: http://www.cbc.ca/news/politics/full-text-of-peter-mansbridge-s-interview-with-stephen-harper-1.2876934

28   Minister of Aboriginal Affairs and Northern Development. Bill C-33, An Act to establish a frame-work to enable First Nations control of elementary and secondary education and to provide for-

related funding and to make related amendments to the Indian Act and consequential amendments to other Acts (*First Nations Control of First Nations Education Act*) , 2nd Session, Forty-first
Parliament. http://www.parl.gc.ca/content/hoc/Bills/412/Government/C-33/C-33_1/C-33_1.PDF

29   See: How the First Nations education act fell apart in matter of months, *Canadian Press*. 11 May
     2014. Online at http://www.cbc.ca/news/politics/how-the-first-nations-education-act-fell-apart-in-
     matter-of-months-1.2639378

30   Aboriginal Affairs and Northern Development Canada, 2014: *Renewing the Comprehensive
     Land Claims Policy: Towards a Framework for Addressing Section 35 Aboriginal Rights*, Septem-
     ber 2014 ["Interim Policy"], Online at
     http://www.aadnc-aandc.gc.ca/eng/1408631807053/1408631881247

31   Coalition on the UN Declaration on the Rights of Indigenous Peoples: Amnesty International
     Canada; Assembly of First Nations; Canadian Friends Service Committee (Quakers); Chiefs of
     Ontario; First Nations Summit; Grand Council of the Crees (Eeyou Istchee); Indigenous World
     Association; Inuit Tapiriit Kanatami; KAIROS: Canadian Ecumenical Justice Initiatives; Native
     Women's Association of Canada; Québec Native Women/Femmes Autochtones du Québec;
     Union of British Columbia Indian Chiefs. 27 November 2014: *Renewing the Federal Comprehen-
     sive Claims Policy: Submission to Douglas Eyford, Ministerial Special Representative*. Available
     online at http://quakerservice.ca/wp-content/uploads/2014/11/Joint-submission-Renewing-the-
     Comprehensive-Claims-Policy.pdf

32   *Specific Claims Tribunal Act*, Statutes of Canada 2008, c. 22.

33   Specific Claims Tribunal, ANNUAL REPORT, For Presentation to the Honourable Bernard Val-
     court, Minister of Aboriginal Affairs and Northern Development Canada, 30 September 2014,
     http://www.sct-trp.ca/pdf/Annual%20Report%202014.pdf, at 2.

34   *Aundeck Omni Kaning* v. *Canada*, 2014 SCTC 1, para. 89.

Jennifer Preston *is the Program Coordinator for Indigenous Rights for Canadian
Friends Service Committee (Quakers). Her work focuses on international and
domestic strategies relating to indigenous peoples' human rights and implementing the United Nations Declaration on the Rights of Indigenous Peoples. She
works in close partnership with indigenous peoples' and human rights representatives. She is the co-editor of: Jackie Hartley, Paul Joffe & Jennifer Preston (eds.),
Realizing the UN Declaration on the Rights of Indigenous Peoples: Triumph,
Hope and Action. (Saskatoon: Purich Publishing, 2010). Special thanks to Paul
Joffe and Craig Benjamin for edits to this article.*

UNITED STATES

Approximately 5.1 million people in the U.S., or 1.7% of the total population, identify as Native American or Alaska Native alone or in combination with another ethnic identity. Around 2.5 million, or 0.8% of the population, identify as American Indian or Alaska Native only.[1] Five hundred and sixty-six tribal entities are federally recognized,[2] and most of these have recognized national home-lands. Twenty-three per cent of the Native population live in American Indian areas or Alaska Native villages. The state with the largest Native population is California; the place with the largest Native population is New York City.[3]

While socioeconomic indicators vary widely across different regions, per capita income in Indian areas is about half that of the U.S. average, and the poverty rate is around three times higher.[4] The United States announced in 2010 that it would support the UNDRIP after voting against it in 2007. The United States has not ratified ILO Convention 169.

Recognized Native nations are sovereign but wards of the state. The federal government mandates tribal consultation but has plenary power over indigenous nations. All American Indians are American citizens.

Federal recognition

In May 2014, The Bureau of Indian Affairs (BIA) announced a proposal to change the rules for tribal recognition. Only indigenous nations that are federally recognized or acknowledged exist as Native nations for the federal government, fall under the provisions of federal Indian law, and are therefore eligible to receive services from the BIA. The federal government can add new tribes to the list of federally acknowledged tribes and can take acknowledged tribes off that list. There are basically two potential paths to acknowledgment: a congressional decision or a petition through the Office of Federal Acknowledgment. These new

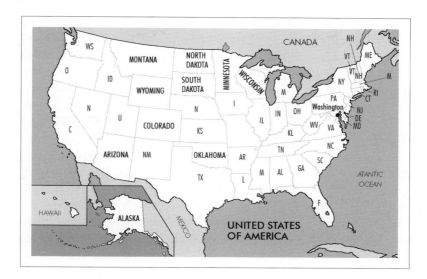

proposed guidelines would simplify the process and eliminate some of the burden of proof on applicant indigenous nations.[5] Because federal recognition or non-recognition creates or denies the official existence of an indigenous nation, it is fundamental to all other issues.

The reactions to the proposed guidelines have been mixed. While tribes currently in the process and tribes that were denied recognition but could apply anew under the new guidelines see this as a very positive development, some local, state, and federal legislators are opposed. For example, the whole congressional delegation from Connecticut opposed the proposed changes, purportedly because recognized tribes would become sovereign nations, no longer bound by local and state laws, and because people hold fears that recognized tribes would build casinos.[6] The same fears surface in comments by county and state officials in California.[7] No deadline is currently available for a finalized proposal or for when new guidelines might come into effect.

Federal policy

In June, President Obama visited the Cannon Ball community on the Standing Rock Sioux Reservation in North Dakota. This was the first visit to a Native nation by a sitting U.S. president since Bill Clinton's 1999 visit. In an opinion piece before the visit, Obama highlighted the engagement of the federal government under his administration with indigenous nations and wrote, "The history of the United States and tribal nations is filled with broken promises. But I believe that during my Administration, we've turned a corner together." [8] He echoed this sentiment in his remarks at Cannon Ball, where he said that "my administration is determined to partner with tribes, and it's not something that just happens once in a while. It takes place every day, on just about every issue that touches your lives. And that's what real nation-to-nation partnerships look like."[9] The National Congress of American Indians applauded the visit and wrote that it "builds on ongoing efforts of his Administration to work closely with tribal nations on policy that affects their citizens."[10] At the White House Tribal Nations Conference in December, the president announced several policy initiatives to help indigenous youth. These initiatives, he remarked, came as a consequence of his meeting with young people at Standing Rock, which had left a deep impression on him: "We're all one family. Your nations have made extraordinary contributions to this country. Your children represent the best of this country and its future. Together, we can make sure that every Native young person is treated like a valuable member not only of your nation, but of the American family." [11]

In August, the Secretary of the Interior, Sally Jewell, published an order to reaffirm the federal trust responsibility to recognized tribes and individual American Indians. This document is a response to the Cobell litigation over mismanagement of American Indian funds (see *The Indigenous World 2012*). It establishes seven guiding principles for all bureaus and offices within the Department of the Interior, the first one of which reads, "Respect tribal sovereignty and self-determination, which includes the right of Indian tribes to make important decisions about their own best interests." [12]

While, in principle, the federal government wants to support the self-determination and perhaps even sovereignty of indigenous nations, in practice, indigenous interests are often overlooked when national interests are at stake. In December, for example, it became apparent that supporters of a copper mine project in Arizona had written supportive legislation into the national defense budget bill in order to hide it. This legislation will give National Forest lands that include Apache sacred sites to a subsidiary of Rio Tinto in a land swap that has failed to gain congressional authorization so far (see *The Indigenous World 2014*). Secretary Jewell called the move "profoundly disappointing" [13] but the bill passed and was signed into law by President Obama without any attempts to strip it of this amendment, such that the land swap is now a reality and the way for the mine cleared.

Elections

Alaskans elected a new governor in November and, with the help of the votes from Native villages, chose Independent candidate Bill Walker. Walker had been running with an Athabaskan candidate for lieutenant governor, Craig Fleener, but in mutual understanding replaced him with Byron Mallott, the Democratic nominee and former president of the Alaska Federation of Natives (AFN). Former governor Parnell tried to gain the Native vote by signing a language bill into law at the AFN convention in October. This law made 20 Native languages official state languages. However, official business can still be conducted in English only, and official documents do not have to reflect these Native languages. There are 229 federally recognized Native entities in Alaska but they are recognized as corporations and not as nations. Issues of Native sovereignty, jurisdiction, fishing rights and law enforcement face the new governor.

The Mandan, Hidatsa and Arikara, or Three Affiliated Tribes on the Fort Berthold reservation in North Dakota, elected Mark Fox as their new chairman. The tribe is situated in the middle of the Bakken oil boom and has become one of the wealthiest tribes in the U.S., although many tribal members do not profit from the boom. Growing inequalities as well as concerns over environmental regulations and tribal government transparency were contributing factors to the ousting of former chairman, Tex Hall, in the primaries.

The Navajo nation had to postpone the election of a new president. Two candidates who did not make it past the primary elections in August filed a complaint against run-off candidate, Chris Deschene, arguing that he was not fluent in Navajo. After Deschene refused to submit to a fluency exam, the tribe disqualified him shortly before the November elections were scheduled. Navajo nation law states that the president must be fluent in the language, although there is no official definition of what that means. The election dispute has set off an important debate about language, culture, and revitalization and preservation efforts.

UN World Conference on Indigenous Peoples

The so-called "World Conference on Indigenous Peoples" (WCIP), a meeting organized by the UN General Assembly, took place in September and produced an
outcome document that sets out the direction of the UN and its member states in
their relations with indigenous nations.[14] The meeting had been debated among
indigenous peoples in the United States beforehand, with some groups opposing
its legitimacy. Others, including the National Congress of American Indians, the
oldest and largest organization representing Native interests in the United States,
saw it as an opportunity "to dialogue with States, present their concerns and advance the full and effective implementation of the UN Declaration on the Rights of
Indigenous Peoples".[15] The outcome document raises several important issues
but, seen in the context of indigenous nations in the United States, the lack of any
meaningful mentioning of sovereignty is a shortcoming. The United States did
propose an additional paragraph to commit "to recognize, observe, and enforce
our nation to nation treaties" but that did not make it into the document.[16]

Keith Harper, Cherokee and U.S. Ambassador to the UN Human Rights
Council, said that the document "underscores the commitments of member states
to advance and uphold the principles and goals of the UN Declaration on the
Rights of Indigenous Peoples" and expressed his gratitude "that the document
supports the empowerment of indigenous women and eliminating violence and
discrimination against them." [17] He saw three main issues on which the United
States wanted to focus: measuring the progress of states in achieving UNDRIP
objectives, enlarging indigenous participation in UN meetings, and coordinating
the work towards achieving the objectives of the UNDRIP throughout the UN
system.

In the phase leading up to the WCIP, the United States made recommendations on almost all the proposed statements for the eventual outcome document.
These recommendations included replacing language of commitment with language of encouragement, intention and affirmation, in line with the government's
view that the UNDRIP is a moral and not a legal document. The United States
also recommended an individual approach wherever possible (for example, in
health care), and tried to exclude lands, territories and resources in the context of
free, prior and informed consent.[18] These recommendations are not necessarily a
sign that the current administration does not want to work with indigenous na-

tions; that commitment is evident. However, indigenous interests and indigenous sovereignty, over land and resources especially, are consistently ignored when they run counter to national interests. Sovereignty thus becomes a vague moral concept rather than a legal reality enforceable by law.

Resource extraction

Conflicts over resource extraction and energy-related issues continue to be at the center of sovereignty issues, and this might explain the reluctance to grant the right to free, prior and informed consent in this area. Native American tribes lay claim to lands that are outside established reservation boundaries, especially if those lands were taken illegally. In South Dakota, for example, resistance against the Keystone XL pipeline, which would increase the flow of oil from the Canadian tar sands, continues from Lakota people and their Native and non-Native allies. When, in November, the House of Representatives approved a bill to build the pipeline (although President Obama has not given his final approval), Cyrill Scott, the President of the Sicangu Oyate on the Rosebud Sioux Reservation declared this an "act of war" and vowed to protect the land.

In Oregon, the state denied a permit for a coal terminal in August, in part responding to Columbia River tribes, who feared for their fisheries. The terminal would have loaded coal from Montana and Wyoming for export to Asia. Two other coal terminals are planned in the area.

The planned expansion of the Kayenta coal mine on the Navajo reservation in Arizona is encountering resistance from Navajo and Hopi people concerned with archaeological artefacts and human remains. The current lease with the Navajo nation expires in 2019. So far, 400 million tons of coal have been extracted to fire the Navajo Generating Station (NGS), which produces electricity for the Southwest. Accompanying archaeological investigations found over a million artefacts and around 200 human remains, housed in partially unsecured university collections. The NGS is also one of the worst carbon dioxide emitters in the United States. The federal government announced new lower emission standards for power plants in May but excluded power plants on reservations.

Tribes with high unemployment rates and few economic opportunities do support resource extraction and energy generation as an opportunity to create revenues. In Montana, the Crow tribe is continuing the development of its coal reserves. Cloud Peak Energy started the exploration of a 1.4 billion ton coal reserve on the reservation in June which has paid the tribe 5 million dollars so far, with a possible 10 million more over the next five years. Crow Tribal Chairman Darrin Old Coyote has pointed to coal as the only development possibility for his nation. Referring to organizations opposed to further coal development on tribal lands, Old Coyote said, "Unless these NGOs can tell me how else to feed my people, we're going to pursue development." [19] The Crow nation has an unemployment rate of close to 50%.

In Alaska, Native tribes continue to fight against the planned Bristol Bay copper and gold mine by Pebble Partnership (see *The Indigenous World 2014*). President Obama blocked the bay from oil and gas drilling in December but the mine is still a possibility. The bay has the world's largest sockeye salmon run, and tribes fear that toxic chemicals from a megamine in its watershed would endanger the fishery. Forty percent of the wild seafood consumed in the United States comes from Bristol Bay. The Environmental Protection Agency (EPA) took initial steps to reject the mine in February but the company and the state of Alaska have filed a lawsuit against the agency.

Sovereignty

In December, the Bureau of Indian Affairs (BIA) announced a change in rules that will allow the Secretary of the Interior to acquire land in trust for Native individuals and tribes in Alaska. Previously, this was only allowed for one Alaska community, the Metlakatla Indian Community. Taking land into trust means that the federal government holds the title to lands in trust for indigenous people. While this imposes federal decision-making over the land, it also removes the land from state jurisdiction and sovereignty. In Alaska, the 1971 Alaska Native Claims Settlement Act (ANCSA) constituted Native tribes as corporations, without protected territories. This new rule will allow for a considerable extension of Native sovereignty, taxation and jurisdiction if lands are approved for taking into trust. The historic decision was in part a response to litigation but also followed a 2013 recommendation by the Indian Law and Order Commission, which "brought to light the shocking and dire state of public safety in Alaska Native communities" (see *The Indigenous World 2014*).[20]

In Wyoming, the Wind River Reservation has been involved in two separate sovereignty-related disputes. The reservation is home to the Eastern Shoshone and the Northern Arapaho and, in September, the Northern Arapaho Tribe announced that it would dissolve the Joint Business Council, which had representation from both tribes. Instead, they would pursue their interests through a separate governing body. Although the Eastern Shoshone have resisted the move and want to keep the joint council intact, in October the BIA acknowledged the dissolution. It is unclear how this will affect the reservation, as it will have two separate tribal governments. The Wind River Reservation is also involved in a border dispute with the state of Wyoming. The EPA ruled that the establishment of the city of Riverton, which lies on reservation land that was opened for non-Native settlement and removed from trust land status in 1905, did not diminish the reservation as has been argued by the state of Wyoming. The city would still therefore lie within the reservation boundaries, although the tribe does not have any direct sovereignty over or jurisdiction on its territory. In response, the state drafted legislation that would declare Riverton to be outside the reservation, and filed a brief against the EPA decision with the 10th U.S. Circuit Court of Appeals in October.

Violence against women and children

In December, Congress repealed the "Alaska exemption" in the 2013 Violence against Women Act (VAWA). The law allows tribes to prosecute non-Native offenders in limited circumstances but had excluded Alaska Native villages (see *The Indigenous World 2014*). Representative Don Young (R) who led the effort in the House to overturn the exemption, said the repeal would "empower Alaska's tribes and uplift Alaska Native women" Senator Lisa Murkowski (R), who had put the exemption in the bill, co-sponsored the repeal with her Alaskan colleague Mark Begich (D) and said, "Alaska tribes asked me to repeal [the exemption], and I heard them loud and clear." [21] Together with the new potential for trust lands in Alaska, the hope is that Native villages will be able to establish local tribal law enforcement and court systems that will help curb the epidemic of violence against women. Currently, 100 Alaskan villages have tribal courts and 129 do not.

While the VAWA enlarged tribal jurisdictional powers, in September, an opinion by the 9th U.S. Circuit Court of Appeals dealt tribal courts a severe blow. The Sixth Amendment of the U.S. Constitution guarantees defendants the right to an attorney but this does not apply to tribal courts. In *U.S. v Bryant*, a panel of the court found that tribal convictions for which the defendant did not have legal representation do not stand up in federal law. In this case, a man was indicted as a habitual domestic assault offender based on two previous convictions by the Northern Cheyenne tribal court in Montana. The court decided that these two convictions could not be counted. As one of the judges who called for a review by the Supreme Court wrote, "The implication is that, if the defendant lacks counsel, tribal court convictions are inherently suspect and unworthy of the federal courts' respect.... [R]espect for the integrity of an independent sovereign's courts should preclude such quick judgment." [22]

In November, the Attorney General's Advisory Committee on American Indian/Alaska Native Children Exposed to Violence published a report that called for the inclusion of violence against children in legislation similar to the VAWA, in order to fund a meaningful tribal juvenile justice system and to coordinate efforts against suicide, gang violence, and sex and drug trafficking. While there are very little quantitative data on Native children, anecdotal data indicate that Native children face much higher rates of exposure to violence than other children in the United States. Violence accounts for 75% of deaths of Native youths, and Native youths are over-represented in federal and state juvenile justice systems. [23]

In December, the Executive Office of the President released the 2014 Native Youth Report. It was inspired in part by the presidential visit to Standing Rock, and identifies the barriers for Native youth as "nothing short of a national crisis". The administration proposes doing more for Native youth through efforts in education, economic development and health. One in three Native children live in poverty, suicide is the second highest cause of death for Native youths aged between 15 and 24, and graduation rates for schools are well below the national average. [24] Native students saw a four-year high school graduation rate of 67% in 2011-12, while White students were at 86%. [25] A report by the Government Accountability Office in November focused on the lack of oversight over Bureau of Indian Education (BIE) school budgets, but gave some insight in the system: the BIE "administers 185 elementary and secondary schools that serve approximately 41,000 students on or near Indian reservations in 23 states. Of the 185 schools, 58 are directly operated by BIE, and 127 are operated by tribes mostly through federal grants. These schools serve about 7 percent of the Indian student population, mostly low-income students in rural communities." [26] Numbers from previous reports reveal that students in BIE schools lag behind American Indian students in public schools, who are below the national average in reading and mathematics. Sixty-one percent of BIE high school students graduated. This is a higher graduation rate for Native students than public schools in eight states - Minnesota shows the lowest rate at 42% - but is lower than the national average, and this level of achievement puts the academic preparation into question. A GAO report from 2013 came to conclusion that "the extent to which [the Department of the] Interior is effectively meeting its responsibilities is questionable." [27]

Billy Frank, Jr.

In May, Billy Frank, Jr., treaty rights activist and long-term chairman of the Northwest Indian Fisheries Commission, passed away. He was a national leader of the ongoing treaty rights movement. Tribes in Wisconsin, Minnesota and elsewhere are still following his legacy and trying to enforce the rights to fish and hunt off-reservation promised to them in treaties. In October, the 7th U.S. Circuit Court of Appeals ordered that a decades-old ruling against Chippewa hunting deer at night in northern Wisconsin should be reconsidered, for example. Around 6,000 people attended the service for Billy Frank, Jr., whose leadership during the fish-ins in the 1960s turned Frank's Landing on the Nisqually reservation in Washington into a symbol of the fight for American Indian sovereignty.   ○

Notes and references

1   U.S. Census Bureau. *American Fact Finder*.
    http://factfinder2.census.gov/faces/tableservices/jsf/pages/productview.xhtml?src=CF
2   Bureau of Indian Affairs. 2014. Indian Entities Recognized and Eligible To Receive Services From the United States Bureau of Indian Affairs. *Federal Register* 79 (19): 4748-4753
3   U.S. Census Bureau. 2012. *The American Indian and Alaska Native Population: 2010.*
4   Randall K.Q. Akee & Jonathan B. Taylor. *Social and Economic Change on American Indian Reservations. A Databook of the US Censuses and the American Community Survey, 1990–2010.*
5   See http://www.bia.gov/WhoWeAre/AS-IA/ORM/83revise/index.htm6 Christopher Keating. 2014. Lawmakers Oppose Easing Rules On Tribal Recognition, Adding More Casinos. *Hartford Courant*, 10/1/2014
7   Evan Halper. 2014. Effort to reform rules on tribal recognition has communities concerned. *Los Angeles Times*, 11/1/2014
8   Barack Obama. 2014. On my Upcoming Trip to Indian Country. *Indian Country Today*, 6/5/14

9   Barack Obama. 2014. *Remarks by the President at the Cannon Ball Flag Day Celebration.* Office of the Press Secretary, The White House.

10   http://www.ncai.org/news/articles/2014/06/12/ncai-applauds-president-obama-s-historic-visit-to-indian-country

11   Barack Obama. 2014. *Remarks of the President at the Tribal Nations Conference.* Office of the Press Secretary, The White House.

12   Secretary of the Interior. 2014. Order No. 3335.

13   Reid Wilson. 2014. Jewell "profoundly" disappointed by land exchange at sacred Native American sites. *Washington Post*, 12/6/14.

14   United Nations General Assembly. 2014. *Outcome document of the high-level plenary meeting of the General Assembly known as the World Conference on Indigenous Peoples.*

15   The National Congress of American Indians. 2014. Resolution #SAC-12-078.

16   United Nations General Assembly. 2014. *Draft outcome document to be adopted by the General Assembly on 22 September 2014*, 5 Sept 2014.

17   Keith Harper. 2014. *The World Conference on Indigenous People a Call for Further Action.* https://geneva.usmission.gov/2014/09/23/the-world-conference-on-indigenous-people-a-call-for-further-action/

18   United Nations General Assembly. 2014. *Draft outcome document to be adopted by the General Assembly on 22 September 2014*, 5 Sept 2014.

19   Alex Sakariassen. 2014. Coal's long shadow. *Missoula Independent*, 5/29/2014.

20   Department of the Interior. 2014. Land Acquisitions in the State of Alaska. *Federal Register* 79 (246): 76888-76897.

21   Sari Horwitz. 2014. Repeal of "Alaska exemption" gives tribes more power to protect Alaska Native women. *Washington Post*, 12/18/2014.

22   United States Court of Appeals for the Ninth Circuit. *U.S. v Bryant*. No. 12-30177. 9/30/2014.

23   Attorney General's Advisory Committee on American Indian/Alaska Native Children Exposed to Violence. 2014. *Ending Violence so Children Can Thrive.* http://www.justice.gov/sites/default/files/defendingchildhood/pages/attachments/2014/11/18/finalaianreport.pdf

24   Executive Office of the President. *2014 Native Youth Report.* www.whitehouse.gov/sites/default/files/docs/20141129nativeyouthreport_final.pdf

25   U.S. Department of Education. 2014. *Public High School Four-Year On-Time Graduation Rates and Event Dropout Rates: School Years 2010–11 and 2011–12.* NCES 2014-391.

26   Government Accountability Office. 2014. *Bureau of Indian Education Needs to Improve Oversight of School Spending.* GAO-15-121.

27   Government Accountability Office. 2013. *Better Management and Accountability Needed to Improve Indian Education.* GAO-13-774.

Sebastian Felix Braun, *an anthropologist, is associate professor and chair of the department of American Indian Studies at the University of North Dakota. He works on issues of sustainability in the broadest sense.*
sebastian.braun@und.edu

MEXICO AND
CENTRAL AMERICA

MEXICO

Mexico has the largest indigenous population of all Latin American countries and the greatest number of native languages spoken within its territory, with a total of 68 languages and 364 dialects recorded. The National Institute for Statistics and Geography (*Instituto Nacional de Estadística y Geografía* / INEGI), the National Population Council (*Consejo Nacional de Población* / CONAPO) and the Economic Commission for Latin America (ECLAC) record a total of 16,933,283 indigenous people in Mexico, representing 15.1% of the total population (112,236,538).[1] This figure demonstrates sustained growth due to high birth rates among indigenous groups, tempered slightly by the generally higher mortality rate (with significant, persistent and worrying differentials in mother-and-child mortality which, in some states, is triple the national average).

Mexico ratified ILO Convention 169 in 1990 and, in 1992, Mexico was recognised as a pluricultural nation when Article 6 of the Constitution was amended. In 2001, as a result of the mobilization of indigenous peoples claiming the legalization of the "San Andres Accords" negotiated between the government and the Zapatista National Liberation Army (Ejército Zapatista de Liberación Nacional - EZLN) in 1996, the articles 1,2,4,18 and 115 of the Mexican Constitution were amended. From 2003 onwards, the EZLN and the Indigenous National Congress (Congreso Nacional Indígena - CNI) began to implement the Accords in practice throughout their territories, creating autonomous indigenous governments in Chiapas, Michoacán and Oaxaca. Although the states of Chihuahua, Nayarit, Oaxaca, Quintana Roo and San Luís Potosí have state constitutions with regard to indigenous peoples, indigenous legal systems are still not fully recognised. Mexico voted in favour of the UN Declaration on the Rights of Indigenous Peoples in 2007.

I ndigenous peoples' health continues to be a factor of significant influence 'for their vulnerable status. This is recognised by the state but addressed only poorly due to insufficient programmes and projects. The "universal coverage" proclaimed by the Mexican state "requires expenditure of 6% of GDP", according to the World Health Organization, whereas "in Mexico it stands at between 3.05% and 3.2%", clearly disproportionately affecting the poorest sectors of society (rural indigenous and urban poor).[2]

The Ministry of Health's *National Health Programme,* published after nearly a year's delay on the part of the current administration, highlights the importance of two strategies: *Popular Health Insurance* and the *National Crusade against Hunger*, this latter coordinated by the Ministry of Social Development (SEDESOL). In addition, the government has promoted *Prospera* as the programme to overcome poverty. However, after more than a year of implementation, the results have proved disappointing: the proportion of people below the poverty line remains the same as in 1992, and 600,000 people who left the *Oportunidades* programme because they had "overcome their poverty" have had to be reincorporated into *Prospera.* It is significant that the municipalities chosen by the National Council for the Evaluation of Social Policy (CONEVAL) to evaluate the strategy are, almost without exception, largely indigenous municipalities in the north, centre, south and south-east of the country.[3]

Popular Insurance, which has proved attractive to a large proportion of the indigenous population, in reality offers a "medical package" of restricted cover, with rights and services below those recognised constitutionally. "Lack of access to social security" (evaluated by CONEVAL) shows that 81% of indigenous people were suffering from this, as opposed to the national average of 59.1%, while "Lack of access to health services" was 24.3% for indigenous peoples as opposed to 21.2% for non-indigenous. In addition, according to CONEVAL itself and the National Council for the Prevention of Discrimination (CONAPRED), "the percentage of indigenous population in poverty has shown no statistically significant change (71% in 2008, 74.4% in 2010 and 72% in 2012). In 2012, seven out of every ten indigenous individuals was living in poverty while around five out of every ten of the non-indigenous population were in such a situation." Moreover, "Lack of access to basic housing services" (clean or piped water, sanitation and drainage, overcrowding, etc.) was 37% for indigenous peoples and 12.6% for non-indigenous Mexicans.

Over the last year, there have been growing complaints of indigenous peoples' health being affected by exposure to contamination from mining and agroindustrial companies, deteriorating ecosystems, acute and chronic malnutrition, alcoholism and severe gynaecological/obstetric problems, with a significant increase in chronic/degenerative diseases (different kinds of cancer, cardiovascular problems, diabetes and cirrhosis of the liver, primarily), while high rates of infectious/contagious diseases persist. The most objective evaluations (including those of CONEVAL) highlight the problem of low-quality services and "a lack of adequate conditions at the primary care level, where 30% of state-run primary care units only have one trainee doctor with no supervision whatsoever".[4]

The scourge of violence, on the one hand, and the criminalisation of indigenous and popular protest, on the other, have, however, meant that the impact of these problems on morbidity and mortality rates has been somewhat obscured.

Indigenous migration and remittances to Mexico

Given the changes caused by growing globalisation, increasing numbers of indigenous people are migrating, either internally within Mexico or internationally, and this is becoming one of the main phenomena influencing their economic, political, social and cultural situation, even their spatial distribution. These migrations explain the presence of indigenous peoples on international borders (north and south), at crossing points to other countries, in small, medium and large towns, areas of agricultural development, places of importance to tourism, even the United States and more recently Canada, where they are joining the different labour markets.

The prevailing social and economic inequality in Mexico goes a long way to explaining this migratory process and is reflected, for example, in high levels of marginalisation. Among the municipalities with the greatest indigenous presence from across the country's different states, the highest levels of marginalisation can be seen in 48 municipalities in Chiapas, 43 in Guerrero, 220 in Oaxaca, 39 in Puebla and 41 in Veracruz. The employment situation of the working population that speak an indigenous language is also illuminating. In 2010, male employees or workers represented 25.9% and female 38%; male agricultural day labourers 19.8% and female 9% (INEGI, 2010).

Some researchers have estimated that indigenous remittances could amount to as much as a third of all known transfers sent home, and there is also probably a significant amount of informal money that also passes between hands. If this is true, and purely as a hypothetical example deriving from this estimate, indigenous remittances would equate to far more than the financial resources devoted by the National Commission for Indigenous Peoples' Development (CDI), a specialist government body, to native peoples. It would also represent more than all federal sectoral investment for indigenous peoples put together.

Dispossession of indigenous peoples continues

The dispossession of indigenous peoples that the government has been encouraging for decades in favour of transnational companies continued throughout 2014. As has already been documented in previous years, the government has amended the law and transformed the government institutions responsible for implementing it so that companies wishing to exploit the natural resources located on indigenous territories can do so, even riding roughshod over internationally-recognised rights as well as the established case law of the Inter-American Court of Human Rights when ruling on cases submitted for their consideration.

The indigenous peoples are, however, resisting such policies. Some, such as the Nahua of Jalisco, Guerrero, Colima and the Sierra Norte de Puebla, along with the Wixaritari from Jalisco, the Na savi from Guerrero, the Zapotecos from Oaxaca and the Tononacos from the Sierra Norte de Puebla (to name only those with the highest profiles) are waging war on the exploitation of their mineral resources.

In terms of water resources, most notable is the resistance of the Yaqui to the Independencia aqueduct; the Guarijios, who have been displaced by the construction of the Pilares dam; the peoples of Cacahuatepec, Guerrero, grouped together in the Council of Cooperatives and Communities in Opposition to the Parota Dam; the Council of Peoples United in Defence of the Río Verde (COPU-DEVER), who are opposed to the Paso de la Reina dam, on the Oaxaca coast; the Wixaritari and Coras peoples who are fighting the construction of Las Cruces dam in Nayarit; and the Cucapá who are unable to fish, an activity essential to their subsistence, because the government is making the issuing of permits conditional upon their acceptance of a consultation process.

Other important struggles are being fought against wind farms, for example by the Ikoots (Huaves) and Zapotec from the Oaxaca isthmus and by the Maya from the Yucatán peninsula; and against the invasion of GM maize (the Kiliwa of Baja California), which is being grown in various communities of Jalisco, Oaxaca, Tlaxcala, Chiapas and Guerrero, along with the commercialisation of biodiversity through environmental services.

Claims brought before the courts with regard to the right to consultation have had varying results. The district courts (which operate as courts of first instance in such cases) generally rule in favour of the claimants; however, when the authorities appeal the ruling before a higher court (the collegial courts or Supreme Court of Justice), while this also recognises the right and grants protection, it almost never stops the offending action, as it should do, but allows it to continue. This effectively rules out any protection that might have been provided. Such was the case of the Yaqui and the Independencia Aqueduct, the Huetosachi in Chihuahua and the Na savi in Guerrero.

Moreover, observing that the courts were ruling in favour of peoples when demanding their right to consultation as a way of defending their territories, the federal government has hijacked this right, turning it into state privilege: it has not revoked the right but has claimed the power to decide where, when and how it is exercised. As part of this strategy, it pieces together protocols which it then proposes to the indigenous peoples; in the stages prior to the proposed consultation it offers funding for much-needed facilities in the villages and, if that does not work then it resorts to threats and violence to control the claimants.

Repression is another mechanism used by the government and companies to prevent indigenous peoples' struggles when legal and economic means have failed. Such is the case of Enedina Fuentes Vélez, Chair of the Cooperative Committee of San Felipe Xonacayucan, Puebla, currently in prison for defending her lands from a gas pipeline that is planned to cross the states of Morelos, Puebla and Tlaxcala; it is also the case of Marco Antonio Suástegui, spokesperson of CECOP, Bettina Cruz Velázquez, member of the General Coordinating Body of the Assembly of Indigenous Peoples of the Isthmus in Defence of Land and Territory (*Coordinación General de la Asamblea de Pueblos Indígenas del Istmo en Defensa de la Tierra y el Territorio*), and Néstora Salgado García, commander of the Community Police in Olinalá municipality, Guerrero.

Numerous social and environmental conflicts have broken out in the northwest of Mexico over the use of territory and natural resources. These conflicts largely affect indigenous peoples as they occupy a large part of the cooperative and communal lands, forests and woods of that area. Notable conflicts involve the Yaqui people and the Independencia aqueduct in Sonora, which is intended to carry 75 million cubic metres of water each year from the Plutarco Elías Calles (El Novillo) dam on the Yaqui River to the town of Hermosillo, where a number of large transnational companies are located, including Ford Motors, the Holcim Apasco cement company, and the Coca-Cola, Pepsico and Big Cola drinks companies. The aqueduct, 172 kilometres of steel piping costing 3,860 million pesos, was tendered, built and is now being operated (at 25% capacity) without any of the five precautionary suspensions issued by the judicial federal power having been respected. These suspensions required the state to halt the work. After three years of legal action, the Supreme Court of Justice ruled in favour of the Yaqui tribe (2013) and ordered that a consultation process be commenced, in line with their traditions and customs. In September 2014, Mario Luna and Fernando Jiménez, spokespersons for the Yaqui tribe, were arrested on the basis of a formal order for their imprisonment.

The Guarijíos of Sonora are also putting up active resistance to the project known as *Sonora Sistema Integral*: the construction of the Los Pilares-Bicentenario dam on their territory, which commenced in April 2014. The state government developers simulated a process of consultation and approval of the dam on the part of the Guarijíos, obtaining the signature of the traditional authorities through threats and manipulation, without the leaders reporting back to their assemblies. This was in violation of agreements reached in what initially looked as though it was going to be the first exemplary indigenous consultation process involving different government agencies. An appeal for unconstitutionality lodged before the 7th District Court of Sonora in 2013 is still awaiting a decision. In addition to the threat of the dam, the indigenous people are faced with increasing corporate interest in their territory, 33% of which has already been awarded in concessions. Their habitat is one of the least contaminated, despite a biodiversity in decline particularly since the construction of the Mocúzarit dam on the Mayo River in 1954.

Another conflict over the use of water in the north-west is taking place on the San Pedro River in Nayarit, the only large river in the country not to have a dam built on it. The indigenous and *mestizo* peoples living in this basin have been actively resisting the construction of Las Cruces hydroelectric plant by CFE since 2010, as this will affect numerous sacred sites of the Náyeris, Wixárikas, Tepehuanos and Mexicaneros, and cause irreparable damage to the ecological balance of the Marismas Nacionales, one of the most important reserves for biodiversity on the planet. It will also cause considerable financial harm to the peoples in neighbouring valleys.

The above cases are just a handful of examples of the ongoing dispossession of indigenous peoples in Mexico, illustrating a policy that is in open violation of their rights. And they are resisting this policy, because they know that therein lies not only their future but that of all humanity.

The EZLN and Ayotzinapa

On 1 January 2014, the Zapatista National Liberation Army (EZLN) celebrated the 20th anniversary of its armed uprising in Chiapas. Twenty years of demanding autonomy for its communities and reaffirming its desire for greater resistance in the face of harassment from the authorities and the Mexican army. Although the government has never implemented the San Andrés Accords, signed 18 years ago, the EZLN has continued to grow as an organisation, as can be seen in the opening up to civil society of its educational project known as the *Zapatista little schools*, the *caracoles* (autonomous Zapatista regions) and the Good Governance Councils.

On 2 May 2014, members of the Independent Centre for Agricultural Workers and Peasants (*Central Independiente de Obreras Agrícolas y Campesinos* / CIO-AC), paramilitary forces and the state counter-insurgency general command planned and carried out the murder of the head of the local Good Governance Council and teacher in the "La Realidad" autonomous Zapatista school, José Luis Solís López, better known as "Galeano". The Zapatista grassroots members and EZLN therefore held a meeting on 24 May in "La Realidad" to commemorate the life of Lieutenant Galeano. At that meeting, Sub Comandante Marcos announced that he would be standing down as a "persona" and as the spokesperson of the EZLN, leaving Sub Comandante Insurgente Moisés in charge and instead taking the name of Sub Comandante Galeano, as a member of the Zapatista community.

Following the unfortunate events that took place on 26 September, during which 43 students from Ayotzinapa were disappeared and murdered, the EZLN met with their parents and relatives on 15 November 2014 to listen to them and express their total support in the difficult task of seeking justice for their disappeared children.

On 26 September, students from the "Raúl Isidro Burgos" Rural School in Ayotzinapa, Guerrero, were attacked by municipal police from Iguala and Cocula; three died, 25 were injured and a further 43 detained, their whereabouts still unknown. Since then there has been no official news of the students. Eleven days later, President Enrique Peña Nieto spoke for the first time about this case and, that same day, the Inter-American Commission on Human Rights (IACHR) called on the Mexican state to grant precautionary measures for students of the rural school. The Organization of American States described the crime as inhuman and absurd, and called on Mexico to conduct a full and transparent investigation. The local UN office urged Mexico to conduct a comprehensive search for the youths, and called for measures to protect the survivors and relatives of those disappeared. Representatives of the Mexican government and those affected by the Iguala case signed an agreement for the IACHR to provide technical assistance to the investigations.[5] As of the time of writing this article, the UN Committee on Enforced Disappearances, based in Geneva, had just reviewed Mexico's situation with regard to enforced disappearances for the first time (2 and 3 February 2015). The mothers and fathers of the disappeared students from Iguala attended the session.[6]

This is undoubtedly a case that has shaken both Mexico and the international community and yet virtually no media coverage mentioned the fact that a large number of the students from Ayotzinapa were of indigenous extraction. Most of them were Nahuas, Mixtecs or Amuzgos attending one of the few higher education options open to the children of indigenous peasant farmers in the region, for Guerrero is one of the poorest states in the country. This is despite a mineral wealth that ranks it first for gold production in the country. It is, however, also number one for poppy growing. Ayotzinapa is a memorial to the Mexican state's failure to protect the individual guarantees of its indigenous citizens; it exemplifies the authorities' collusion with organised crime in actions that violate human rights. It lifts the lid on the involvement of the municipal and federal police, and of the army itself, in the forced disappearance of young indigenous students and clearly illustrates a situation in which thousands of people are unable to access justice in Mexico.   ○

References

Conapo, 2010: Estimaciones del CONAPO con base en INEGI, *Censo de Población y Vivienda 2010*.
INEGI, 2011: *Censo de Población y Vivienda 2010*, INEGI.
Rojas Rangel, Teresa, 2010: "Las niñas y los niños jornaleros migrantes en México; condiciones de vida y trabajo", *Revista Sociedad Latinoamericana*, Mexico, Vol. 1, No. 7, FES-Aragón, UNAM.
Sanchez García, Carolina, 2003: Territorio, cultura e identidad: la reconfiguración de la identidad colectiva y la territorialización de los mixtecos en la colonia Obrera 3ª. Sección de Tijuana, Baja California, IIA, FFyL, UNAM, Master's thesis.
Conapo, 2001: Población indígena internacional en la migración temporal a Estados Unidos, Newsletter published by Consejo Nacional de Población, Year 5, No. 14, 2001.
Fundación BBVA y Servicio de Estudios Económicos México de BBVA Bancomer: Migración México, available at: https://www.bbvaresearch.com/wp-content/uploads/2015/02/2015-02-03-FlashMigracionMexico_01.pdf, consulted on 16 February 2015.

Notes

1   Ecomonic Commission for Latin America (ECLAC), Los Pueblos Indiígenas de América Latina:: *Avances en el último decenio y retos pendientes para la garantía de sus derechos*, ECLAC, Santiago, Chile, 2015, p. 27.
2   Asa Cristina Laurell, "Cobertura sin atención", www.jornada.unam.mx/2014/07/08.

3   Consejo Nacional de Evaluación de la Política de Desarrollo Social (CONEVAL), *Informe de evaluación de la Política de Desarrollo Social 2014, México, CONEVAL, 2014*, pp. 32-35.
4   Gustavo Leal, "Salud: el mito de la universalidad", www.jornada.unam.mx/2014/04/26. Asa Cristina Laurell, Art. Cit.
5   http://www.animalpolitico.com/2014/11/cronologia-el-dia-dia-del-caso-ayotzinapa/
6   Ayotzinapa en Ginebra: no aplauden al Estado mexicano: http://www.jornada.unam.mx/2015/02/10/opinion/016a1pol

José del Val, *Director of the University Programme of Cultural Diversity and Intercultural Studies (PUIC-UNAM).*

Jesús Armando Haro, *Researcher at the Colegio de Sonora*

Francisco López Bárcenas, *Mixteco lawyer and adviser to indigenous communities.*

Juan Mario Pérez Martínez, *Technical Secretary of PUIC-UNAM.*

Carolina Sánchez, *Academic Secretary of PUIC-UNAM.*

Carlos Zolla, *Research Coordinator at PUIC-UNAM.*

GUATEMALA

The more than 6 million indigenous inhabitants (60% of the country's total population), are made up of the indigenous peoples: Achi', Akateco, Awakateco, Chalchiteco, Ch'orti', Chuj, Itza', Ixil, Jacalteco, Kaqchikel, K'iche', Mam, Mopan, Poqomam, Poqomchi', Q'anjob'al, Q'eqchi', Sakapulteco, Sipakapense, Tektiteko, Tz'utujil, Uspanteko, Xinka and Garífuna. The indigenous population continue to lag behind the non-indigenous population in social statistics: they are 2.8 times poorer and have 13 years' less life expectancy; meanwhile, only 5% of university students are indigenous. The human development report from 2008 indicates that 73% of the indigenous population are poor (as opposed to 35% of the non-indigenous population), and 26% are extremely poor. Even so, indigenous participation in the country's economy as a whole accounts for 61.7% of output, as opposed to 57.1% for the non-indigenous population.

Guatemala voted in favour of the UN Declaration on Rights of Indigenous Peoples in 2007 and ratified ILO Convention 169 in 1996.

2014 showed no progress with regard to the inclusion and recognition of indigenous peoples' rights into government decision-making on laws, public policies and specific support programmes. Any progress made has come about through the struggle of the social movements, who have had to mobilise international mechanisms and spaces to enforce their rights.

Little progress in legislation or public policies

No new laws were approved on indigenous peoples by Congress in 2014, although at least 10 proposals have been submitted to this body in recent years. The intended Law on Rural Development remains shelved despite constant protests by the social, peasant and indigenous sectors. There was also no progress on public policies specifically for indigenous peoples.

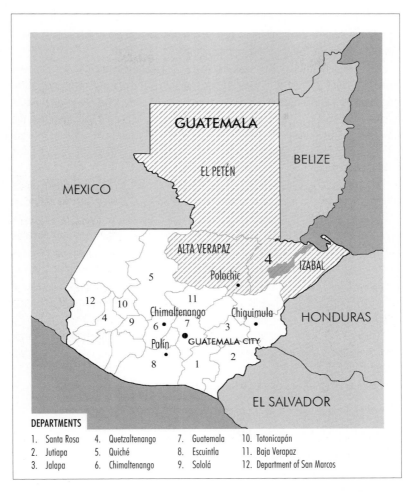

DEPARTMENTS

1. Santa Rosa	4. Quetzaltenango	7. Guatemala	10. Totonicapán
2. Jutiapa	5. Quiché	8. Escuintla	11. Baja Verapaz
3. Jalapa	6. Chimaltenango	9. Sololá	12. Department of San Marcos

The only step taken by this government was the creation of an Indigenous Peoples and Interculturality Office on 31 March 2014. This has been defined as a consultative and deliberating body reporting to the President of the Republic with the aim of coordinating the actions and policies of all public bodies, through the President, to ensure their cultural relevance. In addition it is intended to discuss and formulate proposals for political, legal, administrative and budgetary reforms as well as proposals for the country's politico-administrative division, within the concept of national unity and territorial integrity, with the aim of bringing the structure of the state institutions into line with the cultural, ethnic and linguistic diversity of the peoples living on the national territory.[1]

The creation of this office was, however, questioned by indigenous peoples' representatives as they consider it unrepresentative and of insufficient capacity to negotiate with and influence the government system. There has been no news of its achievements or actions since it was established. It should be noted that the only indigenous minister in this body was removed from post after an intense media campaign against him, which various analysts considered to be racist and discriminatory.

The government also launched its Agrarian Policy at the end of the year, which is intended to establish objectives, strategies and instruments aimed at facilitating and extending access to land, resolving conflicts, providing legal assurances and security and access to other productive assets, in order to address the country's land problems. This may offer an opportunity to indigenous peoples because part of this instrument is based on the Voluntary Guidelines on the Responsible Governance of Tenure of Land, Fisheries and Forests in the Context of National Food Security, issued by the UN Food and Agriculture Organization (FAO) in 2012.

These FAO guidelines advocate recognising traditional or customary landholding systems as practised by indigenous peoples. In this regard, the Agrarian Policy may offer an opportunity for resolving the historical land conflicts caused by the constant dispossessions suffered by the country's indigenous peoples.

Revocation of the "Monsanto Law"

In a rushed process, Congress approved the Law on Protection of Plant Varieties, popularly known as the Monsanto Law, referring to one of the world's leading producers of seed and agricultural inputs. This law protects the rights of those who modify plant species for the purpose of improving their genetic potential. No other law has engendered so much popular rejection in recent years, nor managed to achieve the coordination of such wide sectors of Guatemalan society. Social protest right across the country led Congress to revoke the law, as it was in clear violation of legitimate rights to food and, above all, to traditional knowledge of local seeds, particularly maize, for which Guatemala is one of the centres of origin. The indigenous peoples have been legitimately involved in building the genetic diversity of this plant and the ancestral knowledge that exists in its regard.

Legal claims for violations of rights

Case of genocide

The historic 80-year sentence passed on former President General Ríos Montt on 10 May 2013 following the court's ruling of genocide was rapidly overturned by the Constitutional Court on 20 May, claiming procedural errors (see *The Indigenous World 2014*). The trial itself was merely postponed, however, with a retrial due to commence on 5 January 2015. The social organisations have thus remained active in this regard, particularly in terms of opposing the media campaign launched by pro-military actors aimed at throwing the case out completely. By the end of the year, everything pointed to the retrial going ahead as planned.

Case of the burning of the Spanish Embassy

The trial of Pedro García Arredond opened on 2 October. This was the main defendant accused of storming and setting fire to the Spanish Embassy on 31 January 1980, when he was Head of Sixth Command of the former National Police. There was a huge media sensation around this case, as it was the first to bring to trial officers from the state security services who had perpetrated acts of repression against the civilian population during the internal armed conflict. Thirty-seven people died during the embassy fire, most of them indigenous individuals from Quiché department, including Sr. Vicente Menchú, father of Nobel Peace Prize winner, Rigoberta Menchú, who was there to report on the repression being suffered by that department's indigenous population at the hands of the armed forces. The defence team unsuccessfully tried to prevent the opening of the trial, citing the right to amnesty established in the Peace Agreements signed in 1996, which effectively provides an amnesty to members of groups involved in the internal war but not those involved in crimes against humanity. After an intense hearing in which testimonies were heard from eye witnesses and related actors, including embassy officials from that time, the court finally sentenced the accused to 90 years in prison, in addition to the previous 70 years imposed on him for the murder of a university student.

Chixoy case

The 33 indigenous communities of the Maya Achi' people, 440 of whom were massacred and the rest involuntarily displaced during the construction of the Chixoy hydroelectric plant, the largest in the country and built at the start of the 1980s, finally obtained assurance that they would receive compensation from the state. It has been a long struggle and they encountered many difficulties in the beginning due to the surviving population's fear and because the national courts had ruled against their claim. The families therefore decided to approach the Inter-American Commission on Human Rights where they obtained a favourable ruling requiring the Guatemalan state to pay compensation. The government and Coordinating Body of Communities Affected by the Construction of the Hydroelectric Plant (*Coordinadora de Comunidades Afectadas por la Construcción de la Hidroeléctrica*) established a Reparations Plan in 2010 which includes: a cash payment of US$154.5 million to be paid within a 15-year period, the construction of 445 houses, an official apology from the President of Guatemala, community access to documents in the Historic Archives of the National Police, an integrated management plan for the Chixoy Basin and projects for infrastructure, basic education, health and development, all things these communities have lacked for many years, ever since losing their lands.[2]

Despite this agreement, the government has shown little desire to implement its provisions. In 2014, President Otto Pérez publicly stated that Guatemala was a sovereign country and thus not obliged to comply with the rulings of international bodies. However, the Consolidated Appropriations Act 2014, passed by the US Congress, requires the US directors of the World Bank and Inter-American Development Bank to report to the Appropriations Committees on fulfilment of the Plan for the Reparation of Damages Suffered by Communities Affected by the Construction of the Chixoy Hydroelectric Plant in Guatemala, and this was sufficient to get the President to sign a Plan to provide compensation to the Maya Achi' people from Baja Verapaz department, given that the support received from both the United States government and the international organisations was at risk.

This demonstrates yet again that the Guatemalan state only addresses indigenous demands when it feels that its economic benefits are being threatened and not because it has taken any public commitment to recognise indigenous peoples' rights. It also highlights the fact that local courts have no political desire to respond favourably to these demands, for which reason the international bodies have to be approached.

Chuarrancho case

The Constitutional Court finally ruled in favour of the indigenous community of Chuarrancho in the municipality of the same name, Guatemala department, some 40 kms north of the capital. In 1897, this community recorded its name on the title for its communal lands in the General Property Register but, in 2001, the local mayor asked for the title to be transferred to the name of Chuarrancho municipality. This was without the consent of the community and a licence was subsequently granted to a private company for the construction of a hydroelectric plant. The indigenous peoples took a case against the officials of the General Property Register to court and finally managed to obtain the return of the title to their communal lands.[3] This case sets an interesting precedent on which to base demands for recognition of the right to indigenous lands and territories which, throughout history, has been violated. Many of the indigenous peoples' ancestral lands have been unlawfully recorded in the names of private owners and municipalities.

Extractive industries: moratorium and repression

The moratorium on mining licences proposed by President Otto Pérez as a strategy for avoiding serious social conflict has proved to be mere lip service as no current licence has been suspended and the proposal has never been discussed in Congress, which is the only body with the power to establish a moratorium on current laws. In contrast, the government has continued to support the implementation of current extractive projects, above all making the security forces available to companies when required to suppress popular protests.

On 19 September, violence between the staff of a cement factory and members of the Maya Kaqchikel community of San Juan Sacatepéquez in Guatemala department, 25 km north of the capital, resulted in 11 deaths. The local people have been categorically rejecting the installation of the cement factory on their ancestral territory, undertaken without any consultation, for several years now but the government has merely supported the company and repressed the population. One of the government's favourite options has been to declare a so-called

"State of Emergency" in areas of conflict, thereby limiting constitutional guarantees of the local population's right to freedom of movement, assembly and organisation with the aim of ensuring the security of the extractive industries' investments and criminalising the resistance movements.[4] Back in 2011, in the report on his visit to Guatemala, the UN Special Rapporteur on the rights of indigenous peoples warned that the presence of extractive industries on indigenous territories was becoming a source of serious conflict and division between the communities.

For its part, the Indigenous Ch'orti' Council, in Chiquimula department, denounced the arrest of two of its leaders, accused of crimes they had not committed, due to their active opposition to the construction of the El Orégano hydroelectric project on the Jupilingo River, in the indigenous territory of the Maya Ch'ortí people. This project was able to go ahead due to the illegal and deceitful sale of communal lands, supported by Jocotán municipality without any consultation. In this same regard, the government authorities have continued to close community radio stations around the country, at the request of the large communications companies and as a strategy for eliminating alternative forms of broadcasting, particularly those fighting for indigenous rights.

Indigenous peoples and the forthcoming elections

With an eye to the general elections due to take place in September 2015, various entities are promoting the greater inclusion and participation of indigenous peoples, not only as voters but also as candidates. In the past, indigenous representation in parliament has barely reached 10%, with indigenous women not even making up 2% of the deputies. Even these deputies follow traditional party lines and do not necessarily propound the proposals of the indigenous peoples. It is important to note that, despite forming a majority of the population, Guatemala has never had an indigenous president nor a political proposal that might unify the indigenous sector. In contrast, it is more common to find councils with indigenous representatives in municipalities that have an indigenous majority.

In order to overcome this poor representation in political spaces, a number of social organisations have therefore formed a largely indigenous electoral proposal known as Democratic Revolutionary Convergence (*Convergencia Revolu-*

cionaria Democrática), which seeks to unify popular aspirations that have long been excluded or manipulated by the traditional political parties.

On 5 April, indigenous leaders from across the country elected the new members of the National High Council of Ancestral Authorities, which works for the social, political and cultural coordination and rebuilding of the peoples and supports the territorial defence movements.

Firm steps towards restitution of rights to lands and territories

After decades of legal struggles, and at great cost and sacrifice, including the murder of many of their leaders, a number of communities from the Maya Q'eqchi' people have now taken firm steps to recover the lands and territories taken from them unlawfully. Through the National Council for Protected Areas, the Land Fund and the Ministry of Agrarian Affairs, the Guatemalan state has finally recognised the rights of six indigenous communities living in the vicinity of protected areas. Other cases are progressing through the Constitutional Court, for example the claim of a Q'eqchi' community that lost its land to a palm oil-producing company. This was with the connivance of the General Property Register as this company's rights were registered in violation of the indigenous community's legitimate title. Similar demands are being made in other parts of the country, and it is hoped that, gradually, a body of case law will be established that can support the return of lands to their legitimate indigenous owners.

The return of the land title to the Chuarrancho indigenous community, mentioned above, sets a precedent on which other demands for ancestral rights to lands and territories can be based. This community recently managed to re-establish its system of traditional authorities with the aim of consolidating forms of government that will be able to guarantee the enjoyment of its territorial rights in the future. ○

Notes and references

1   http://mcd.gob.gt/el-presidente-instala-el-gabinete-de-pueblos-indigenas-e-interculturalidad/

2   http://www.internationalrivers.org/resources/pr-%E2%80%93-reparations-due-for-chixoy-dam-
     atrocities-8208
3   https://www.cronica.com.gt/cronica-del-dia/corte-de-constitucionalidad-restituye-tierra-a-comu-
     nidad_857901/
4   http://www.elperiodico.com.gt/es/20140922/pais/2229/Observatorio-ind%C3%ADgena-rechaza-
     despliegue-represivo.htm

Silvel Elías *is a lecturer in the Faculty of Agronomy of the San Carlos de Guate-*
mala University. He runs the Rural and Territorial Studies Programme, PERT
FAUSAC, and supports initiatives aimed at recognising the collective rights of in-
digenous peoples

HONDURAS

Given the lack of an official census, it is estimated that the nine indigenous and Afro-descendant peoples living in Honduras number 1.27 million inhabitants, divided between the following groups: Lenca, 720,000; Garífuna, 380.000; Miskito, 87,000; Tolupan, 47,500; Nahua, 20,000; Chortí, 10,500; Pech, 3,800 and Tawahka, 1,500. The territory claimed by the indigenous peoples accounts for approximately two million hectares out of a total national land mass of 11.2 million. Only ten % have a guaranteed property title. Each of the indigenous peoples retains a degree of individuality, in line with their customs, and this is reflected in their day-to-day practices in terms of, for example, their community councils.

Honduras ratified ILO Convention 169 in September 1994. In 2007 it voted in favour of the Declaration on the Rights of Indigenous Peoples. Apart from Convention 169, there is no case law to protect the rights of indigenous peoples.

The path towards militarisation, authoritarianism and a lack of human rights protection[1]

President Juan Orlando Hernández Alvarado (2014-2018) took office in January 2014, succeeding Porfirio Lobo Sosa in the post, both of them nationalist and self-proclaimed "governments of national reconciliation and transition" following the 2009 *coup d'état*. Hernández' government has been essentially characterised by its focus on "privatising everything and militarising everything".[2]

According to the economist Martin Barahona "Hernández' government is likely to draw together the main directions of the previous governments of the new right[3] under the banner of the National Party (NP); apart from continuity and strategic vision this will also mean a clearly class-based political, economic and social project in which the financial and agroindustrial sectors, the *maquila* manufacturing industry, the mining industry and foreign and national investors are all beneficiaries of the new division of the national territory into Special Development Zones (ZEDES) or 'model towns', the new panacea of neoliberalism in Honduras".[4]

This "new right" in Honduras is characterised primarily by is consolidation of neoliberalism through a rolling back of the state's social commitments, and a strengthening of the private sector. In this regard, the ZEDES are the epitome of its planned vision for the country, presenting a new kind of state that is completely controlled by private investment and which – they argue – will form a "development hub"[5] that "will benefit" the Honduran population. The trauma following the *coup d'état* of June 2009 continues to weigh heavy on the country's social reality. It is rapidly moving to consolidate the economic power of transnationals, particularly in areas where concessions for communal lands and resources granted by the last two post-coup governments are giving free rein to the destruction of the territories and, consequently, to the dispossession and repression of the communities. Proof of this can be seen in the dispossessions that are taking place along the Honduran Caribbean coast, affecting Garífuna communities particularly. The post-coup governments have finished laying the legal foundations in terms of laws and concessions and now the government of Juan Orlando Hernández intends to consolidate transnational capital.

Hydroelectric dams on Lenca territory

2014 began with a series of events that bore witness to a greater liberalisation of natural resources. One example was the privatisation of 47[6] rivers as part of the process of granting rights over the country's heritage (protected areas and archaeological zones) to private companies, a process that is being driven by businessmen who themselves own the country's thermal energy companies. This particular privatisation process has its roots in the Law on the Promotion of Public/Private Alliances, approved in 2010.

The Independent Legal Lenca Movement of La Paz Honduras (*El Movimiento Independiente Indígena Lenca de La Paz Honduras* / MILPAH),[7] has been active in defending its territories from the construction of a hydroelectric dam, approved without the consultation or participation of the main communities affected. The communities had managed to avoid the construction until 6

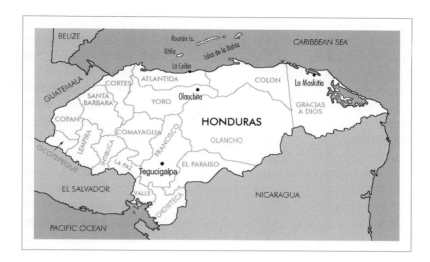

October, when they held open councils (form of community consultation in line with the Honduran law on municipalities) and the mayor, accompanied by a strong police and military presence, not only managed to approve the permit for the company but also to intimidate the leaders of MILPAH, for example Martín Gómez Vázquez.

Moreover, between September and November 2014, MILPAH reported continuing intimidation from police and military units reminiscent of the political repression and persecution of the 1980s: profiling the indigenous community leaders and issuing constant threats and accusations of sedition and treason.

It should be noted that almost two years have now passed[8] since the Lenca people of Río Blanco (in Intibucá department) blockaded the dam on the Gualcarque and Canje rivers as part of a process of struggle and territorial defence. COPINH (Civic Council of Popular and Indigenous Organisations of Honduras) played an important role in this, mobilising the people in defence of water and territory. It should therefore be noted that, in recent months (to January 2015), Berta Cáceres (general coordinator of COPINH) has been systematically persecuted and threatened. Implicated in this persecution[9] are the Chinese company Desarrollos Energéticos S.A. (DESA) and Blue Energy, now part of the Honduran company Grupo Terra, which holds strategic energy and infrastructure concessions in the country.

In addition, it has been one year since the takeover of San Francisco de Opalaca Town Hall in opposition to the corruption of the local authorities, calling for their replacement with Lenca structures and ancestral authorities. "The struggle of the Lenca communities, organised via COPINH, has not stopped despite the constant criminalisation – including the murder of members – and will not stop because our lives are tied to Mother Earth, to the rivers, the mountains, the biodiversity we have cherished for centuries," [10] argues COPINH in a press release denouncing the aggression against the Lenca people and summarising their position in defence of their territories.

On 29 October 2014, Maycol Ariel Rodríguez García was found murdered. He was a 15-year-old Lenca boy from Río Blanco community, also a member of COPINH and an active defender of the Gualcarque River and its territory. In addition, the Indigenous Community Council of Río Blanco reported that the National Police was harassing and intimidating communities involved in the recovery of land around the Gualcarque River. Incidents such as the abuse of power by the authorities and the murder of Maycol have thus far gone totally unpunished, indicating the complete defencelessness of the indigenous communities involved in resistance processes.

Measures to protect intangible cultural heritage while neglecting human rights of the Tolupán

While in 2014, the Honduran state inscribed the oral traditions of the Tolupanes from la Montaña de la Flor community on the UNESCO list of intangible cultural heritage in need of urgent safeguarding,[11] it did nothing to amend its historic abandonment of this people in terms of their health, education and housing or improve their security and access to justice. The indigenous Tolupán people from the San Francisco de Locomapa tribe, in Yoro department, have denounced the impunity and insecurity that is being suffered on their territory. Their complaint states that they are being systematically threatened and persecuted by armed groups linked to organised crime and mining companies. The most alarming incident was the murder –on 23 August 2013– of three indigenous Tolupán: María Enriqueta Matute (71), Armando Fúnez Medina (46) and Ricardo Soto Fúnez (40). All were involved in defending their territory from the extraction of antimony. Paradoxically, despite the Inter-American Commission on Human Rights' call, on 19 December 2013, for protection to be provided to 38 members of the San Francisco tribe, the authorities have not yet taken any action to comply with these precautionary measures.[12]

The Garifuna´s struggle for recognition

On the Caribbean coast of Honduras, the Garífuna people and their organisations, such as OFRANEH (*Organización Fraternal Negra Hondureña*) are involved in an important and vital debate on the indigenous status of the Garífuna people.[13] The importance of being recognised as indigenous lies in the fact that ILO Convention 169 would then be applicable, and this would enable the Garífuna people to defend themselves legally in the face of the evictions and dispossessions they are suffering, primarily those living on territories with concessions superimposed on them. The Honduran state has maintained the same position before the Inter-American Court of Human Rights (IA Court) for decades, not recognising the indigenous status of the Garífuna and instead calling them ethnic or Afrodescendant minorities.

Possible off shore oil exploration to affect the Miskito and Garífuna

The US oil company Chevron has asked the government for more than 38,000 km for exploratory purposes in waters offshore of Honduras,[14] alongside the oil explorations already being conducted by British Gas International Limited (BG). Part of BG's oil exploration area overlaps with the Mesoamerican Barrier Reef System (Caribbean coast between Honduras, Guatemala, Belize and Mexico) and covers the Honduran Mosquitia region. BG's offices are in Reading, United Kingdom, and it was awarded this concession under Lobo Sosa's government. In April 2014, Chevron opened offices in San Pedro Sula, Cortés and, although public information on its negotiations with the Honduran government has been limited, there are signs of a possible impending oil operation concession.

There is no doubt that Chevron's involvement in oil exploration and possible exploitation would place the Miskito and Garífuna peoples under even greater threat. As those directly affected, they should be key players in the decisions that the state and successive governments are taking in relation to concessions over communal lands and natural resources.

Threats against indigenous community radio

Since 1995, the network of indigenous Garífuna radio stations has been undertaking a monumental work of publicising and defending their culture and territories in the different communities. They now have a network of six transmitters all working independently, managed by each community where they are established. However, the National Telecommunications Commission (CONATEL), the state telecoms institution, has threatened to close some of the community radio stations: Radio Garífuna Sugua de Sambo Creek in September 2014, and Radio Garífuna Waruguma de Trujillo in May 2013. It should also be noted that CONATEL has made OFRANEH responsible for the network of transmitters. The government of Porfirio (Pepe) Lobo Sosa (2010-2014) commenced a reform of the Framework Law on the Telecommunication Sector, arguing that there was a need to democratise the communications sector. Despite the reaction from the main media companies and the lack of clarity in relation to the community stations, it has not enabled a better positioning of the community stations, which are constantly threatened and, in some cases, ransacked.

Murders of indigenous peoples continue to rise

The Broad Movement for Dignity and Justice (*Movimiento Amplio por la Dignidad y la Justicia* / MADJ) reports that at least nine members of the Tolupán de San Francisco tribe have been murdered since 2002. In addition, Honduran indigenous and human rights organisations report that, between 2009 and 2014, at least 43 indigenous individuals from different peoples were murdered: Lenca, Maya-Chortí, Tolupán and Garífuna. These murders were committed with total impunity by armed groups paid by landowners, and there are also a number of cases in which evidence of the involvement of police and soldiers has been found. As far back as 2005, the UN Commission on Human Right reported that 58 Tolupán had been murdered by landowners.[15]   ○

Notes and references

1   This section is based on **Marvin Barahona, 2014:** "El ascenso de la 'nueva' derecha en el Partido Nacional (4) El gobierno de Juan Orlando Hernández: ¿Hacia la militarización y la radicalización del neoliberalismo?", in Envío, Year 12, No. 44, December 2014, pp. 21-30.

2   **Marvin Barahona:** *art. cit., p. 24.*

3   See the series of four articles describing the rise of a new right through the National Party, from 1990 to 2014, in **Marvin Barahona:** El ascenso de la "nueva" derecha en el Partido Nacional (1, 2, 3 and 4) in Envío, Year 12, in No. 41 (March 2014), No. 42 (June 2014), No. 43 (September 2014) and No. 44 (December 2014), respectively.

4   Ibíd., p. 24.

5   *La Prensa, "Honduras: aprueban Ciudades Modelos en el Congreso Nacional", in http://www. laprensa.hn/honduras/tegucigalpa/331319-98/honduras-aprueban-ciudades-modelo-en-el-congreso-nacional*

6   See "El Estado transfiere fondos a la empresa privada y le otorga bienes patrimoniales, áreas protegidas y 47 ríos", at *http://www.defensoresenlinea.com/cms/index.php?Itemid=181&catid =58:amb&id=1033:emilio-d-cuire-el-estado-transfiere-fondos-a-la-empresa-privada-y-le-otor-ga-bienes-patrimoniales-aereas-protegidas-y-47-rios&option=com_content&view=article*

7   For more information see "Honduras: Preocupación por la situación de indefensión del Movimiento Independiente Indígena Lenca de La Paz-Honduras (MILPAH)" at *http://www.defensoresenlinea.com/cms/index.php?option=com_content&view=article&id=3362:impactos-del-cc-en-la-caficultura-peruana&catid=58:amb&Itemid=181*

8   22 months, to January 2015.

9   See press release of the National Network of Human Rights Defenders in Honduras, Tegucigalpa, 28 January 2015 at *http://redefensorashn.blogspot.com/2015/01/comunicado_43.html*

10   See "COPINH: Denuncia Nuevas Agresiones contra el Pueblo Lenca: Fuera Blue Energy, Los Ríos se Defienden", 30 January 2015, at *http://www.copinh.org/article/copinh-denuncia-nue-vas-agresiones-contra-el-pueblo/*

11   La Prensa, "Los Tolupanes, candidatos a patrimonio de la humanidad", 29 October 2014, *http://www.laprensa.hn/honduras/762631-410/los-tolupanes-candidatos-a-patrimonio-de-la-humanidad*

12   See "Indígenas Tolupanes denuncian casos de impunidad e inseguridad en Yoro", published on 18 November 2014 at Adital: *http://site.adital.com.br/site/noticia.php?lang=ES&cod=82541*

13   See "Estado de Honduras deniega condición de indígena al pueblo Garífuna" at *https://ofraneh.wordpress.com/2014/08/20/estado-de-honduras-deniega-condicion-de-indigena-al-pueblo-garifuna/*

14   See (also with a map of where the oil exploration is located) "Más de 38.000 k² pide Chevron a Honduras" in El Heraldo, 24 October 2013, http://www.elheraldo.hn/csp/mediapool/sites/El-Heraldo/Economia/story.csp?cid=610859&sid=294&fid=216

15   See **Greg McCain:** "Honduras: Indigenous Tolupanes Return to Their Territory with IACHR Orders of Protection", 6 March 2014, Upside Down World, at http://upsidedownworld.org/main/

honduras-archives-46/4734-honduras-indigenous-tolupanes-return-to-their-territory-with-ia-chr-orders-of-protection

Regner Asís Castellanos Álvarez *is a sociologist from the National Autono-mous University of Honduras (UNAH).*

NICARAGUA

The cultural and historic roots of the seven indigenous peoples of Nicaragua lie both in the Pacific region, which is home to the Chorotega (221,000), the Cacaopera or Matagalpa (97,500), the Ocanxiu or Sutiaba (49,000) and the Nahoa or Náhuatl (20,000), and also on the Caribbean (or Atlantic) Coast, which is inhabited by the Miskitu (150,000), the Sumu-Mayangna (27,000) and the Rama (2,000). Other peoples who enjoy collective rights in accordance with the Political Constitution of Nicaragua (1987) are the black populations of African descent, known as "ethnic communities" in national legislation. These include the Creole or Afro-descendants (43,000) and the Garífuna (2,500). Among the most important regulations are Law 445 on the Communal Property System of Indigenous Peoples and Ethnic Communities of Nicaragua's Atlantic Coast and of the Bocay, Coco, Indio and Maíz Rivers which, from 2003 on, also stipulates the right to self-government in the titled communities and territories. The 2006 General Education Law also recognises a Regional Autonomous Education System (SEAR). In 2007, Nicaragua voted in favour of the UN Declaration on the Rights of Indigenous Peoples and, in 2010, ratified ILO Convention 169.

The Sandinista National Liberation Front (FSLN) came to power in Nicaragua in 1979, subsequently having to face an armed insurgency supported by the United States. Indigenous peoples from the Caribbean Coast, primarily the Miskitu, took part in this insurgency. In order to put an end to indigenous resistance, the FSLN created the Autonomous Regions of the North and South Atlantic (RAAN/RAAS[1]), on the basis of a New Political Constitution and the Autonomy Law (Law 28). Having lost democratically held elections in 1990, Daniel Ortega, of the FSLN, returned to power in 2007. Ortega is in the middle of his third presidential term in office (2011-2016) and has now managed to amend the Constitution to enable perpetual re-election.

The Nicaragua Interoceanic Grand Canal

The process that has attracted the most attention in 2014, both on the part of the Nicaraguan public in general and particularly the Náhuatl and Rama indigenous peoples and Afro-descendant communities, has been the planned "Nicaragua Interoceanic Grand Canal". This initiative will involve land expropriations that will most likely affect the country's indigenous territories, among other ways by removing the guarantee of inalienability of collective lands in the Autonomous Regions of Nicaragua, as contained in Laws 28 and 445.

To begin the process, Law 840 was approved and published on 14 June 2013 as the "Special Law for the Development of Nicaraguan Infrastructure and Transport Relating to the Canal, Free Trade Zones and Associated Infrastructure". Thirty-two different appeals were lodged by different groups and citizens denouncing the law as unconstitutional because it violated at least 44 of the Constitution's articles. However, without giving any reason to the plaintiffs, the Supreme Court declared Law 840 constitutional (see *The Indigenous World 2014*).

The indigenous and Afro-descendant peoples' main concern is that law 840 will expropriate any tangible assets that may be reasonably necessary for the project, whether private (property), communal, belonging to the Autonomous Regions or in the hands of any government body...". Furthermore, the Commission for Developing the Grand Interoceanic Canal will be the body that consents to the project's use of the natural resources found on the collective lands of the South Caribbean Autonomous Region (RACCS), usurping indigenous and Afro-descendant rights.

The concession holder, a Chinese company under the name of the Hong Kong Nicaragua Development Group (HKND), and the Government of Nicaragua publicly announced on 7 July 2014 that the route chosen for the interoceanic canal would pass through the mouth of the Brito River, to the south of Rivas on the Pacific side, with its entry near the mouth of the Punta Gorda River in the Caribbean.

The official aim of the canal is to link the Pacific and Atlantic oceans, enabling the passage of larger ships than can currently navigate the Panama Canal and bringing development to the country. The contract also includes sub-projects: a railway line, a highway, an oil pipeline, an artificial lake, two deep-water ports,

1. Mayangna territories   2. Rama y Kriol territory

airports and a free zone, at an estimated cost of 50 billion dollars, according to official information from the Nicaraguan government.

As soon as the route was announced, HKND began to conduct surveys along the whole length of the proposed canal, trying to generate a map of the landholdings affected in order to define the route in detail, and identify the settlements to be expropriated.

The canal zone indirectly includes the lands of the Náhuatl people living in Rivas department and on the island of Ometepe, and directly affects the Rama y Kriol territory that was titled in December 2009. The canal will cut their territory in two and forcibly displace the indigenous Rama community of Bangkukuk. This community is the only one in which all the inhabitants still speak Rama, a language that has been declared of world cultural heritage by UNESCO.

On 5 December 2014, representatives of the indigenous Miskito community of Tasbapounie, the indigenous Rama people, the Communal Government of the Kriol Community of Monkey Point and the Communal Creole Government of Bluefields asked the Inter-American Commission on Human Rights (IACHR) "to grant protective measures as soon as possible to ensure that the State of Nicaragua commences no project associated with the canal until those affected have been adequately consulted, in line with case law and the safeguards of the Inter-American Court, in order to obtain their due consent".[2] Carlos Wilson Willis, traditional leader of the indigenous Rama community of Bangkukuk, where the state and HKND intend to build a deep-water port, said: "We do not know what is going to happen to our community... where we will go... how we will live...and no-one has even asked us if we want this canal".

No process of consulting the peoples and communities affected in order to obtain their free, prior and informed consent had been commenced by year end. The Creole community of Bluefields finds itself in a very specific situation as its collective claim to title is the only one that was not resolved by means of Law 445, in addition to which it is located in the path of the canal. In an apparent attempt to weaken the community's claim, officials from the RACCS Regional Council attempted to remove their authority via an unlawful assembly that consequently left two parallel authorities in operation.

Wang Jing from HKND (which was awarded the mega-project concession without any bidding process) and Daniel Ortega announced the official launch of the canal project on 22 December 2014, without any social or environmental impact assessment (EIA) having been conducted and without any study published on its financial, economic and commercial viability.

The consultancy firm handed responsibility for the studies, Environment Resource Management (ERM), had however already raised a number of serious environmental issues, in addition to the problem of the forced evictions:

- The disappearance of species habitat, including some in danger of extinction (jaguar, tapir, macaw, manatee, anteater, etc.).
- Negative impact on internationally-protected wetlands / migratory birds (Ramsar sites).
- Conflict with national protected areas legislation.

- Conflict with the Biosphere Reserve, which is internationally-protected by UNESCO.
- Fragmentation of the Meso-American Biological Corridor.
- Destruction of freshwater habitat and deterioration of drinking water (contamination of Lake Nicaragua and the Punta Gorda river basin).

The fear, however, is that the forest territories of the indigenous peoples will suffer not only due to the forced evictions of their inhabitants but also due to the threat of a massive influx of settlers from the 277 villages that are all facing expropriation. According to Law 840 and the Framework Concession Agreement, neither the state nor HKND have any obligation to resettle these displaced people. The state's lack of will to find a legal solution to the ongoing conflicts between *mestizo* peasant farmers who are already living unlawfully on indigenous territories titled under Law 445 shows that it sees these territories as the answer to the problem of impoverished peasants. In some cases, farmers are even being given incentives to settle there (access roads, schools and donations of inputs). In other more politically complicated cases, such as the invasion of the heartland of protected areas, the authorities are intervening in a purely symbolic manner.

The government's position is clear because the state institutions have made no progress with regard to completing the indigenous land titling process, i.e. via their regularisation.[3] Political work to reform Law 445 is, however, continuing, encouraging the indigenous and Afro-descendant peoples to accept "cohabitation" with the *mestizos* unlawfully settled on their territories. In contrast with last year, however, where the government was keen to forge ahead with the legislative process, its strategy for achieving this now appears to be more political, first seeking greater indigenous support for the governing party so that they can then seek the indigenous movement's acceptance from within.

In the search for territorial alliances aimed at achieving social peace and promoting the application of environmental standards, using its powers in line with its territorial statutes and Law 445, the Rama y Kriol territorial government (GTR-K) in particular celebrated the first certifications of co-existence with *mestizos* unlawfully settled on their titled territory in April 2014.

The people who are going to be directly affected because they live in the path of the canal have also been organising and protesting vigorously against a project about which they have not been consulted. They are now facing compulsory purchase orders with compensation equal to or possibly less than the official land registry valuation (if the valuation is considered to be more than a fair market price). They will receive no compensation at all if they do not hold legal title to their land. In accordance with Law 840 but in contrast with the stipulations of the Political Constitution, the police and the army are now acting to protect a private company, HKND, rather than to defend the people, and they are facilitating surveys, preventing access to protest points, breaking up legal protests and arresting people who are demonstrating or protesting against the canal.

Given the multi-ethnic and multidisciplinary nature of those likely to be affected, an alliance has been established between civil society organisations and the indigenous and Afro-descendant authorities. This is known as the Cocibolca Group and it has taken a leading role in trying to encourage the planning process to respect political, civil and human rights. It is conducting independent scientific studies, analysing standards and publicly pronouncing on every significant step of the canal process.[4]

The interoceanic canal project has proved to be the number one national issue during the FSLN's third term in government, capable of stirring public opinion regardless of religion, ethnic group or party political persuasion. In fact, the Catholic Church, traditionally an ally of the government, is also calling for transparency and for real participation in decision-making on the part of those affected by the project, alongside a movement of pastors from different churches and denominations from the South Autonomous Region. This social movement against the project is, however, faced with the challenge of maintaining this struggle as a pro-human and environmental rights agenda rather than a political campaign taken up by the opposition parties, because this is not its purpose.

Internationally, there are actors apparently committed to individual, collective and environmental rights that are allowing themselves to be used for the sake of expedience. The clearest example of this is the maritime company, Maersk, which has its headquarters in Denmark. This company will probably be the canal's biggest global client, given that it is currently the Panama Canal's number one customer. Maersk staff has stated their support for the project, and this is being used by HKND to influence the political debate both in Nicaragua and abroad. Maersk is, in turn, a UN Global Compact lead company, supposedly committed to and proactive in human and environmental rights work in its sector. The company is no longer commenting publicly on the project, stating that it has no opinion on or interest in the project either way (for or against).

Denmark as a country has devoted 10 years to ensuring the collective titling of the indigenous Rama y Kriol territory through its human and environmental rights programmes, establishing regulations for the joint management (indigenous authorities and the Ministry of the Environment and Natural Resources/ MARENA) of protected areas in this territory with the aim of biodiversity conservation.

The Danish NGO, Forests of the World, has consequently approached the Danish Minister for Development and Trade, Mogens Jensen, with regard to Maersk, requesting that it comply with the UN Guiding Principles on Business and Human Rights:

States should set out clearly the expectation that all business enterprises domiciled in their territory and/or jurisdiction respect human rights throughout their operations.

The consultancy firm ERM, for its part, is currently lending its name, as a world-renowned environmental consultancy, to an unlawful process in all senses of the word, at a high business risk to itself. Not only was the start of project construction announced on 22 December without any real knowledge of the environmental and social impacts of the project but clear violations of the rights of indigenous peoples are continuing to take place, given that the principle of free, prior and informed consent is not being implemented, indigenous lands are being expropriated and the communities are being relocated without their consent.

If there were relevant studies available, and a law that had been submitted to a national consultation process with due respect for the specific consultation needs of indigenous peoples, Nicaraguans could have assessed the pros and cons and might have decided to give the green light to a transparent bidding process. Law 840 and the immediate and direct award of the concession instead seem more of a strategy by which to expropriate individual and collective lands throughout the national territory for an international consortium registered in the Cayman Islands, with a shareholder structure and links to the governments of China and Nicaragua that are far from transparent. The company is exempt from all requirements to pay tax without a guaranteed return – and the Nicaraguan state has used its supposed financial reserves to guarantee the contract. In other words, whether the canal is built or not, a part of Nicaragua has been sold off without public consent. And it is the indigenous peoples who are destined to pay the highest price because they depend not only economically but also culturally on their lands and territories.

Continued invasion into Biosphere reserves

The issue of the deforestation and invasion of the indigenous territories in the BOSAWAS Biosphere Reserve and the Río San Juan-Nicaragua Biosphere Reserve has been addressed in previous editions of *The Indigenous World* and was, yet again, not effectively addressed in 2014.[5] The deputies sitting on the Commission for Indigenous, Afro-descendant and Autonomous Regime Affairs consequently stated that they were going to link the complaints of settler invasions and timber extraction from the nature reserves on the Caribbean Coast in order to lodge a complaint regarding the Nicaraguan state's lack of protection, first before the Supreme Court of Justice (CSJ) and then, if necessary, internationally.

The parent organisation of the Mayangna nation, the Government of the Sumu-Mayangna Nation (GNSM) suffered a series of internal disputes at the beginning of the year related to external party political manipulation. The Mayangna leaders therefore publicly issued a resolution suspending their governing board's duties until an assembly or *"Asanglawana"* could be held to appoint a new leadership team. The year ended with some of its leaders concluding that:

> the national government has this year provided even less access to relevant information on the state's priorities in its territories and has not been consistent with its rhetoric, which is supposedly favourable to the interests of indigenous peoples. There is a perception that it would like to see the indigenous peoples no longer existing as institutions and a feeling that the public institutions are misinterpreting the indigenous movement's concerns as if they were their enemies. It is, however, of great concern that the agents of economic interests and politicians continue to interfere in and hinder the internal affairs of the indigenous peoples.[6]

The authorities of the new Mayangna territorial governments, GNSM's base, and sector studies all agree that the failure to protect the BOSAWAS Biosphere Reserve and the corresponding indigenous forest territories is due to the following national government priorities: 1) an agricultural policy that seeks to increase exports of beef and basic grains, primarily to member countries of the Bolivarian Alliance for Peoples of Our America (ALBA); 2) an interest in maintaining confusion in the forest sector, which encourages illegal logging by private companies, including the Alba-Forestal company, linked to the President of the Republic; and 3) a national and local electoral strategy that encourages the settlement of indigenous territories.

IACHR hearing on the situation of indigenous peoples in Nicaragua

Restating most of the issues raised, on 25 March 2014 the IACHR granted a hearing to the Centre for Indigenous Peoples' Legal Assistance (CALPI), the Centre for Justice and Human Rights of Nicaragua's Atlantic Coast (CEJUDHCAN), the Nicaraguan Human Rights Centre (CENIDH), the Centre for Justice and International Law (CEJIL) and the Rama y Kriol Territorial Government (GTR-K) with regard to five issues: 1) violation of the indigenous and Afro-descendant peoples' right to territory due to lack of regularisation; 2) violation of the right to free, prior and informed consent, taking the case of the Interoceanic Grand Canal and the oil concessions in the Nicaraguan Caribbean as examples; 3) the systematic and repeated violation of the right to life being suffered by the Buzos Miskitos of the Caribbean Coast; 4) the party political interference from the state in the autonomous and internal regional elections of the indigenous and Afro-descendant communities and peoples, in violation of their right to self-determination; and 5) the fact that the UN Committee on the Elimination of Racial Discrimination has repeatedly informed the Nicaraguan state of the need to include and consider the indigenous communities and peoples of the Pacific, Centre and North in the state's policies and to adopt a specific law that recognises, promotes and protects their rights. The organisations asked the IACHR to reiterate its request to the Nicaraguan state, made for a number of years now, to authorise an IACHR visit to the country in order to verify the situation and the allegations made in the hearing.　　　　○

Notes and references

1　Recently renamed "South and North Caribbean Coast Autonomous Regions" (RACCS/RACCN)
2　Previously, on 17 June 2014, the subjects themselves, in their own name and on behalf of their communities and territories, presented a petition to the Inter-American Commission on Human

Rights (IACHR) requesting that the state provide them with relevant information on the Interoceanic Canal megaproject so that they could find out about and consider the possible ways in which their lands and territories would be affected. They also called for adequate consultation, arguing that their collective and constitutional rights had been violated.

In July 2013, these peoples and communities submitted an Appeal for Unconstitutionality to the Supreme Court of Justice, in relation to the anomalous approval of Law 840 but, in December of that year, the Supreme Court declared it inadmissible, along with 31 other appeals that different bodies and sectors of Nicaraguan society had also lodged.

3   "Regularisation" refers to resolving conflicts with third parties, which may be private or corporate bodies claiming property rights within a titled communal land.

4   Self-presentation by the Cocibolca Group (name of the lake that will be dredged and through which 105 km of canal will pass): We are a self-convened national platform of non-governmental organisations, academics, technicians, professionals, indigenous and Afro-descendant peoples with experience of environmental, social, research and educational work that has been monitoring and studying Law 840 and the Concession's Framework Agreement for the so-called Interoceanic Canal being promoted by the Government of the Republic of Nicaragua.

5   With the exception of an initial and positive inter-institutional action in the Indio-Maíz Biological Reserve between the Fundación del Río, MARENA, GTR-K and the Nicaraguan Army, in compliance with the Joint Management Agreement signed between the state and the traditional Rama y Kriol authorities of the GTR-K.

6   Information from Noé Coleman Damacio, representative of the Mayangna nation / substitute deputy in the National Assembly.

Claus Kjaerby *is Danish, a civil engineer with a Master's degree in International Development Studies. He has worked for 18 years in the Amazon, the Andes and Central America on indigenous affairs, territorial governance, forest conservation, protected areas management and ecotourism. He has coordinated conservation, titling and infrastructure projects in the Nicaraguan Caribbean Coast with funds from DANIDA and the World Bank/DFID. He is the regional Central American representative of the organisation Forests of the World.*

COSTA RICA

Eight indigenous peoples occupy 3,344 km^2 of the Costa Rican landmass, divided into 24 distinct territories. There are 104,143 people in the country who self-identify as indigenous. Of these, 78,073 state that they belong to one of the country's eight indigenous peoples while the rest do not specify their belonging. With a total Costa Rican population of around four and a half million, indigenous peoples therefore represent little more than 2.5%. Nonetheless, this percentage belies the fact that they represent a significant sector of society with specific rights, both collective and individual, laid down in national and international legislation. Costa Rica ratified ILO Convention 169 more than two decades ago although this does not mean that indigenous rights are recognised in the country. The indigenous peoples continue to be discriminated against and suffer higher levels of social exclusion, in addition to less public investment than other sectors. The indigenous territories continue to be invaded by non-indigenous persons and the organisations designated to administer them lack legitimacy as they do not correspond to the traditional power structures. Quite the contrary, the forms and structures of these associations are alien to indigenous culture and were imposed on them more than three decades ago. The right to consultation continues to be denied them.

Seven of the eight peoples who inhabit the country's 24 indigenous territories are of Chibchense origin and the other is Meso-American (Chorotega in Matambú). Some 48,500 people live on these territories, 35,943 of them indigenous.

A legislative agenda that continues to exclude indigenous rights

Indigenous peoples' political demands have, for more than two decades, been focused on getting the "Law on the Autonomous Development of Indigenous Peoples" enacted, as this establishes the mechanisms for true self-determination and forms of political and territorial management that are in accord with the rights established in Convention 169. In the lead-up to the 2014 elections, enactment of this law featured in the manifesto of the victorious party. Now in government, however, discussion of this law has not been placed on the legislative agenda and, just as before, its approval is not considered a priority. Whenever a deputy attempts to place the text on the agenda of Congress, there is a clear and negative reaction with arguments to the effect that the matter is a secondary one, that further consultation of the indigenous peoples and constitutional experts is required, that it would stymie private investment on indigenous territories or that it represents a danger to national unity, all demonstrating an inherent and underlying tendency to racism.

Consultation processes still not commenced

The right to consultation is constantly being denied indigenous peoples in their relationship with the Costa Rican state. When state institutions are of the opinion that they have put an issue out to consultation this has often been limited to holding informative workshops with territorial leaders or with the Governing Boards of the Indigenous Integral Development Associations (*Juntas Directivas de Asociaciones de Desarrollo Integral Indígena*), the legitimacy of which is seriously questioned. In 2014, the environmental authorities held informational meetings on REDD+ with some territories, calling these a pre-consultation. The indigenous organisations maintain that these did not fulfil the minimum requirements for a process of this nature, being limited to meetings at which technical information was disseminated.

Two hydroelectric projects (Diquís in the South Pacific and Ayil in the Caribbean region) being developed by the Costa Rican Electricity Institute (ICE) are at a halt due to a lack of consultation with indigenous peoples. In both cases, the Institute has stated its willingness to conduct a consultation process, as established in Convention 169, and has the studies and basic elements with which to commence a pre-consultation on the methodology to be used. The decision, however, lies with the highest political authorities, who are failing to show the same commitment, instead dragging their heels and looking for legal loopholes that would allow them to circumnavigate this right.

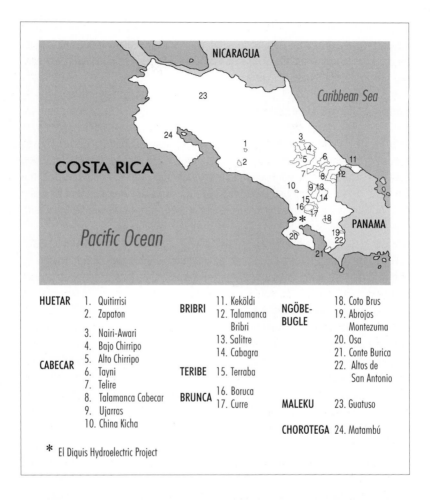

HUETAR	1. Quitirrisi	BRIBRI	11. Keköldi	NGÖBE-BUGLE	18. Coto Brus
	2. Zapaton		12. Talamanca Bribri		19. Abrojos Montezuma
	3. Nairi-Awari		13. Salitre		20. Osa
	4. Bajo Chirripo		14. Cabagra		21. Conte Burica
CABECAR	5. Alto Chirripo	TERIBE	15. Terraba		22. Altos de San Antonio
	6. Tayni				
	7. Telire		16. Boruca		
	8. Talamanca Cabecar	BRUNCA	17. Curre	MALEKU	23. Guatuso
	9. Ujarras				
	10. China Kicha			CHOROTEGA	24. Matambú

* El Diquis Hydroelectric Project

Although each of Costa Rica's indigenous peoples has different decision-making structures, and each issue requiring consultation will have a different impact on the people, their social structure and territory, although it is clear that consultations will differ depending on whether a society is clan-based or not and that issues of interest to women will require different participation systems to issues of interest to fisherpeople, for example, some national and international organisations and bodies in the country insist on promoting a "single protocol for indigenous consultation". This position does not enjoy the support of the main indigenous organisations and leaders, who consider that each consultation must be considered individually and its method be the object of a specific agreement.

Land conflicts in the Salitre indigenous territory

In 2011, the authorities of the Bribri indigenous territory of Salitre began a process to recover their land. By 2014, they had been able to recover more than 2,000 hectares of land that was previously in non-indigenous hands. According to Timoteo Ortiz, Vice President of the Salitre Indigenous Integral Development Association (ADII), this represents around 85% of the lands illegally occupied by non-indigenous people.

The state's commitments made during the Round Table Discussions in 2013 included the accurate delimitation of the indigenous territories of the South Pacific in order to clearly establish the areas occupied by non-indigenous people and ascertain which rights could or could not be compensated. In the case of Salitre, the National Registry was responsible for delimiting the territorial boundary during 2014, and this work was completed in November. There is, nevertheless, still some disagreement with the indigenous authorities, who consider that their ancestral territory has been reduced in size to the benefit of multinational-owned plantations and other non-Bribri owners. It is important to note that, in Costa Rica, the legal power to establish the boundaries of indigenous territories lies with the Rural Development Institute (Inder), an institution which, for the moment, has not had institutional responsibility for this process. The National Indigenous Council of Costa Rica (*Mesa Nacional Indígena de Costa Rica*), believes this institution must be involved in the work of territorial delimitation, otherwise the established boundaries could be challenged by illegal settlers in the future.

During 2014, primarily in July and December, groups of non-indigenous peoples attacked indigenous families living on the recovered lands, destroying and setting fire to homes and crops. They have put relentless pressure on them, threatening and intimidating the families involved in the land claim. Acts of racist violence aimed at indigenous peoples have been reported to the Ombudsman's Office, which has called on the government to ensure that such crimes are not repeated. In response, the police placed a control post at the entry to the territory but the aggression has continued as these people are able to gain entrance elsewhere. There is currently no case lodged with the Public Prosecutor's Office.

In December 2014, a court decision declared that a lawyer and former judge were illegally occupying lands in Salitre, claiming to be indigenous even though the traditional authorities had denied this. These lands have now been recovered in what the indigenous organisations feel was a positive court ruling.

Progress in recovering lands in Salitre has also had other consequences, however, the most visible of which has been the imprisonment of Sergio Rojas, president of the Salitre ADII and leader of the National Indigenous Peoples Front (Frenapi), accused of misusing funds from the Ecosytem Services Programme. A whole range of discriminatory consequences have also been unleashed in terms of local public services: in Buenos Aires, indigenous peoples are reporting discrimination at the public health clinic where one of the doctors was himself the illegal occupier of a farm in Salitre that was subsequently reclaimed; the situation is the same at the local council offices where some of the staff also illegally held land that was later recovered from them.

Payment for ecosystem services and REDD+ on indigenous territories

Payment for ecosystem services (PES) in Costa Rica is a public policy tool based on a selective tax on fuels. One argument to suggesting that it has a positive impact on indigenous territories is that such payments for conservation have prevented indigenous peoples in financial difficulties from selling their lands to settlers, who would then clear the trees and use the land for pasture. The ADII receives the payments from the National Forest Finance Fund (Fonafifo) and then distributes them to the individual beneficiaries, retaining a percentage for public works and management costs. Although these funds have contributed to preserving the forest and mitigating basic needs, they also give the state a reason for not investing in the indigenous territories, instead demanding that the ADII invest the PES funds in public works which, in non-indigenous communities, would be entirely covered out of the state budget.

PES is serving as a basis for the implementation of the REDD+ Programme in the country. This requires consulting with all indigenous territories, in accordance with ILO Convention 169. During 2014, Fonafifo commenced a pre-consultation process which the leaders considered insufficient and inadequate given the realities of the decision-making structures in the territories. Civil servants and consultants met with selected informants and then presented these meetings as part of a consultation process the workings of which had not been previously agreed with the indigenous authorities. This was in violation of the principle of consultation established in legislation and detrimental to the right to self-determination. In that same year, indigenous leaders in the South Pacific region proposed that the ADIIs' use of funds be audited by the state given that there was no transparency and the communities and beneficiaries were being given no clear information, thus making an indigenous audit of the handling of these funds necessary. Fonafifo responded by saying that, once the payments had been made to the associations, the state was no longer responsible. During the second half of the year, the president of the Salitre ADII was thus remanded in custody charged with improper use of PES funds. He was refused bail despite no evidence to support these accusations. It would not appear to be a coincidence that this is the same leader that is heading up the processes for the recovery of indigenous lands in the region.

The indigenous organisations believe that if the impact of PES funds is to be scaled up then there needs to be greater formulation, implementation and strengthening of local development strategies, with PES funds being channelled both individually and collectively. The prevalent view within the country's environmental institutions, namely that forest and biodiversity conservation can only be achieved by preventing the indigenous "from touching the forest" also has to be overcome, as it ignores their systems of traditional use and their tropical forest production systems which, far from simply not destroying the forest have actually preserved them for centuries. The organisations believe that ecosystem services must go beyond this vision to become more in line with indigenous productive traditions and cultures.

The regularisation and titling of indigenous territories is another crucial aspect of this process. Both from the perspective of ecosystem services and REDD+ itself, regularisation can prevent such payments from going to non-indigenous actors within the indigenous territories (as has already happened). Convention 169 would allow for a process of this kind and would undoubtedly be a step in the right direction towards re-establishing the rights of indigenous peoples.

One important aspect to highlight in the context of this whole discussion is that one of the UN's commitments in these processes is for a consultation to be conducted as stipulated in ILO Convention 169. This means obtaining the full participation and free, prior and informed consent (FPIC) of the indigenous peoples, as established in the UN Declaration on the Rights of Indigenous Peoples. It is on this basis that indigenous peoples must define their position with regard to REDD+ but, for this to happen, information must be provided in a timely and appropriate manner.

No progress in dialogue

In January 2013, a Round Table Dialogue commenced with the involvement of representatives from the country's seven indigenous territories, four ministries and with observers from the Ombudsman's Office and UNDP. One of the outcomes of this space has been progress in the delimitation of the indigenous territories. However, since the start of the current government's term in office, on 8 May 2014, these discussions have been at a standstill.

One issue that has not yet been discussed is that of defining a procedure for indigenous consultation. Indigenous peoples have made discussion of this issue conditional upon concrete progress being made in resolving structural problems such as territorial regularisation. ○

Carlos Camacho Nassar is an anthropologist specialising in international development. He has conducted a number of studies into indigenous peoples, conflicts, refugees, displaced and returning indigenous populations and intercultural public policies in Guinea, Mexico, Belize, Guatemala, Honduras, El Salvador, Nicaragua, Costa Rica, Panama, Ecuador, Chile, Paraguay and Bolivia.

PANAMA

The seven indigenous peoples of Panama (Ngäbe, Buglé, Guna, Emberá, Wounaan, Bribri, Naso-Tjërdi) numbered 417,559 inhabitants in 2010, or 12% of the total Panamanian population.[1] The following five regions (*comarcas*) are recognised by independent laws and are based on their constitutional rights: Guna Yala (1938), Emberá-Wounaan (Cémaco and Sambú) (1983), Guna Madungandi (1996), Ngäbe-Buglé (1997) and Guna Wargandi (2000).[2] These *comarcas* cover a total area of 1.7 million hectares. The Afro-descendant population, which is significant in Panama, does not claim its rights as collective subjects.

There has, since 2008, been another way of obtaining the titling of collective lands. Law 72, which sets out the *special procedure for awarding collective title to the lands of indigenous peoples not within comarcas*.[3] To date, only three territories have been titled under this law, and these were smaller in size than the actual area of traditional territory claimed. It is estimated that, once the process of collective land titling has been completed, either by means of *comarcas* or Law 72, a total area of 2.5 million hectares will have been returned to the indigenous peoples, incorporating an estimated 75% of the country's forests.[4] A number of protected areas have been superimposed on these territories, without consulting with or having gained the consent of the indigenous peoples. Territorial titling is a right that has not been fully implemented and it is an urgent need given that it has been shown to be an effective way of preserving Panama's forests, which have been cleared at a rate of around 16,000 hectares a year over the last 10 years.

The indigenous peoples are organised into 12 representative organisations (10 congresses and two councils) affiliated to the Coordinating Body of Indigenous Peoples of Panama (*Coordinadora de los Pueblos Indígenas de Panamá* / COONAPIP).[5]

The government announced at the 2010 ILO Congress that it would ratify Convention 169, although no progress has yet been made in this regard.

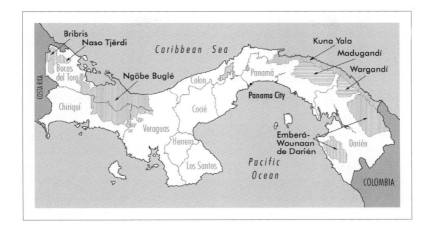

Agreements between the indigenous movement and the national government

President Juan Carlos Varela of the Panameñista party took office in May 2014. Shortly afterwards, bilateral meetings commenced between COONA-PIP, supported by advisors from the Organisation of Emberá and Wounaan Youth of Panama (OJEWP), and the Ministry of the Interior, the Ministry of Foreign Affairs (Vice President) and the National Assembly's Indigenous Affairs Commission. The outcomes of these meetings included a reaffirmed commitment to implement a Development Plan for Indigenous Peoples with a special infrastructure fund in the Ngäbe Bugle *comarca*, along with an agreement to ratify ILO Convention 169, to proceed with the titling of the indigenous territories, to grant territorial security to the Naso and Bribri territories bordering Costa Rica and to respect their right to free, prior and informed consent. In addition, there was a commitment to respect their internal electoral processes and provide financial support to the *caciques* (traditional leaders) as well as to address the political processes linked to climate change as such and not merely as a problem to be resolved via the REDD mechanism. A commitment was also made to establish a vocational programme for indigenous youth and raise the status of the state institution responsible for indigenous affairs to the level of Ministry.

Without further explanation, however, a process of "municipal decentralisation" was mentioned, which is seen as a possible threat to the indigenous peoples' right to self-determination.

UN-REDD process revived following indigenous immobilisation

The UN-REDD programme was revived in 2014 on the basis of an "Indigenous Environmental Agenda", having been at a standstill for more than a year due to COONAPIP's complaints of the programme officials' failure to implement consultation, inclusion and management mechanisms. Gerardo González, director of integrated watershed management and, focal point of the REDD+ process of the National Environmental Authority (ANAM), said of this new situation: "Their (indigenous peoples' (ed.)) participation is now guaranteed and we know they are the main protectors of the forests." [6]

Titling process stalled but movement's unity offers hope for its revival

In November, the 12 representative indigenous organisations met with the aim of creating unity, pursuing territorial defence and seriously commencing the titling of all 30 territories still pending.

With six years passed since the enactment of Law 72, only three territories have been titled under this law (Caña Blanca and Puerto Lara of the Wounaan people and Piriatí of the Emberá people) and, even then, at a reduced size that is insufficient to sustain the peoples' development needs. In some cases, the people are continuing to invade the territories and areas claimed, sometimes negotiated by the national government and accepted by the authorities. There is a misconception that, by showing their cooperation in resolving a national socio-demographic problem, their territory will be titled more rapidly. In 2010, the organisation responsible for this, the National Lands Administration Authority (ANATI) passed a resolution banning rights of possession from being issued to claimed lands. Since then, the cases have been at a virtual standstill, given the great opposition from third parties to the requests for collective land titles to be awarded. Studies conducted by indigenous jurists have discovered, however, that ANATI tends to send these contested claims to court, despite the fact that Law 72 specifies that the National Agrarian Reform Department (now ANATI) is responsible for resolving these cases through a process of amicable agreement rather than improperly placing them at the mercy of judges who have an inadequate understanding of collective rights and a traditional inclination to oppose indigenous peoples' interests.

During the six and a half years that Law 72 has been in force, ANATI has managed to lose a number of files, and be completely unaware of other procedures. At the end of the year, and after six months in power, there appeared to have been no progress made in the 30 claims pending titling.

All the congresses have agreed to work together until the titling of their territories has been achieved and, to this end, they intend to: demand a state budget to finance ANATI's operating costs and a public titling plan; prevent counter-claims from being referred to the courts; and refuse to accept reduced areas or areas that do not respect their territorial rights in the spirit of ILO Convention 169.

Three international cooperation agencies have offered to support the indigenous movement in the titling process: Forests of the World,[7] Rainforest Foundation US and the Rights and Resources Initiative (RRI), although the challenge for 2015 will be for these agencies to coordinate their support while respecting a titling strategy agreed between COONAPIP and the 12 indigenous organisations.

Significant rulings of the Supreme Court of Justice and the OAS

It is hoped that the titling process will speed up in 2015, particularly given the unity and strength the indigenous movement has found around two significant rulings:

On 12-13 December 2014, the Inter-American Court of Human Rights convicted the Panamanian state of violating the right to collective property and legal protection of the indigenous Guna people of Madungandi and the Emberá Piriatí and Ipetí communities of Alto Bayano. Since 1990, when Panama recognised the Court's competence, "it has had a duty to delimit, demarcate and title the lands... which in many cases it has not thus far done," states the ruling. It amounts to a failure on the part of the Panamanian state to fulfil its obligation to provide an adequate and effective procedure for ensuring access to their territory and for obtaining a response in the face of the multiple complaints of interference from third parties in relation to their territories and natural resources.

The origins of the case date back to 1972, when the Panamanian state removed a number of communities from their ancestral lands in order to build a hydroelectric dam on their territories. The case was sent to the Court in 2013 because the Inter-American Commission considered that the state had failed to comply with the recommendations contained in its Merits Report on the case. In this report, the Inter-American Commission recommended that the state, among other things, rapidly conclude the process of formalising, delimiting and physically demarcating the territories of the two peoples and their members.

In 2012, the indigenous Arimae and Emberá Puru communities presented 11 appeals for unconstitutionality against 11 rulings issued by the joint municipal court in favour of 11 peasant farmers who had invaded their traditional territory, requesting its titling in accordance with Law 72.

On 12 November 2014, the judgment of the Supreme Court of Justice indicated that the occupation had not been unconstitutional. This ruling is of major consequence as it could set a precedent for the continuing invasion of any territories involved in a titling process. As a consequence, indigenous women charged the door to the Supreme Court with a traditional baton, as used by the head of the *zarras* (traditional police), in an unsuccessful attempt to get their voices heard. The Ministry of the Presidency subsequently met with an indigenous commission and ANATI then undertook to investigate the important fact that the constitutional chamber's analysis maintained that, in previous administrative cases, ANATI had awarded ownership to the indigenous communities and clarifying that, in the final analysis, it had to be ANATI that gave the final response to the community's request. Come end of the year, ANATI consulted with the Public Prosecutor's Office in order to determine whether ANATI's administrative misconduct, in favour of the communities, should prevail over the ruling in favour of the *mestizos*.   ○

Notes and references

1   According to the 2010 national census.
2   The Naso have, since 1973, been struggling to establish a *comarca* and have developed and submitted a draft bill of law in this regard.
3   Regulated via Executive Decree No. 223 of 29 June 2010.
4   Each and every indigenous *comarca* is established under its own law with reference to Article 5 of the Political Constitution (PC): "The territory of the Panamanian state is divided politically into provinces, these into districts and districts into villages. The law may create other political divi-

sions, whether to subject them to **special regimes** or for reasons of administrative convenience or public service,*"* referring to *comarcas*.

Law 72 has been interpreted as an implementation of Art. 127 of the PC: "The State will guarantee the indigenous communities the reservation of the necessary lands and their collective ownership in order to achieve their social and economic well-being. The Law will regulate the procedures that must be followed to achieve this aim and the corresponding demarcations within which the private appropriation of lands will be prohibited".

For its part, a *comarca* establishes, in addition to the size of the territory, the nature of self-government and autonomy recognised as a consequence of negotiations during the legislative process. In the case of titling under Law 72, this aspect does not form part of the titling process. Article 3 of Law 72 states simply that "a collective title to lands guarantees the cultural, social and economic well-being of people living in the indigenous community. **To this end, the traditional authorities will maintain close cooperation with the national, provincial and municipal authorities."**

5   The number of councils and congresses affiliated to COONAPIP varies according to the themes is decides to focus on and the level of representativeness the authorities of each territory/people feel they have at that particular political juncture. Come the end of 2014, the following had not been involved in COONAPIP's dynamic: the Congress of Guna Yala Comarca, the Guna Congress of Madungandi Comarca and the Wounaan Congress.

6   http://www.un-redd.org/UNREDD_Launches_Panama_NP_Evaluation_EN/tabid/106063/Default.aspx

7   This is a Danish NGO that has been supporting COONAPIP for a number of years in the process of enacting Law 72 and supporting the Guna people obtain recognition of the Wargandi Comarca.

Claus Kjaerby *is Danish, a civil engineer with a Master's degree in International Development Studies. He has worked for 18 years in the Amazon, the Andes and Central America on indigenous affairs, territorial governance, forest conservation, protected areas management and ecotourism. He has coordinated conservation, titling and infrastructure projects in the Nicaraguan Caribbean Coast with funds from DANIDA and the World Bank/DFID. He is the regional Central American representative of the organisation Bosques del Mundo (Forests of the World).*

SOUTH AMERICA

COLOMBIA

Projections from the National Statistics Department for 2012 established an indigenous population of around 1,450,000 inhabitants (3.5% of the national population). The departments of Cauca, Nariño and Guajira are home to only a few peoples but account for 80% of the country's indigenous population. Most of the peoples (70), some of them on the verge of extinction, live in regions such as Amazonía and Orinoquía, where the demographic density is very low. Sixty-five different Amerindian languages are spoken in the country, with five of them classified as "dying" (with no possibility of revival) and another 19 "in serious danger" of disappearing. Almost a third of the national territory is formed of Indigenous Reserves, a large proportion of them invaded by oil and mining companies, banana and palm oil plantations, livestock rearing and illicit crops. The armed conflict has become the driving force behind the expropriation of the ethno-territorial peoples' land and is resulting in their marginalisation and exclusion. Over the 1990-2000 period, funds from drug trafficking were used to grab more than five million hectares of the country's agricultural land.

At national level, the indigenous peoples are represented by two organisations: the National Indigenous Organisation of Colombia (*Organización Nacional Indígena de Colombia* / ONIC) and the Indigenous Authorities of Colombia (*Autoridades Indígenas de Colombia* / AICO). There are also a number of different macro-regional organisations: the Organisation of Indigenous Peoples of the Colombian Amazon (*Organización de los Pueblos Indígenas de la Amazonia Colombiana* / OPIAC) and the Tairona Indigenous Confederation (*Confederación Indígena Tairona* / CIT).

The 1991 Political Constitution recognised the fundamental rights of indigenous peoples and ratified ILO Convention 169 (now Law 21 of 1991). Colombia decided to support the UN Declaration on the Rights of Indigenous Peoples in 2009. By means of Order 004 of 2009, the Consti-

tutional Court required the state to protect the fundamental rights of 34 indigenous peoples at risk of disappearance because of the armed conflict, a situation it described as "an unconstitutional state of affairs". President Santos signed Decree 1953 of 7 October 2014 creating a special system to operationalise the administration of indigenous peoples' own systems on their territories, until Congress can issue the Organic Law on

Territorial Regulation. This will set out the relationships and coordination between the Indigenous Territorial Bodies and the administrative areas of which they form a part (municipalities, departments). This radical step in relations with the state has been well-received by the national indigenous leadership as they feel it is a step in the right direction towards full autonomy.

The peace process

November 2014 marked two years of dialogue and negotiations between the government of President Juan Manuel Santos and the Revolutionary Armed Forces of Colombia (FARC)[1] aimed at bringing more than 50 years of armed conflict to an end. This conflict has been characterised by the violent plundering of the lands and property of peasant farmers, indigenous peoples and Afro-Colombian peoples.

Although the timeframe stipulated by President Santos for the signing of the peace accords was six months, the truth is that after two years of negotiations they have only reached agreement on three of the six points established in the agenda:[2] comprehensive agricultural development policy (May 2013), political participation (November 2013) and illicit drugs and drug trafficking (May 2014). The issue of victim reparation is currently being discussed and technical work groups are preparing the path for the termination of hostilities and the implementation and counter-signing of the agreements. Although there is still some way to go, it is acknowledged that these three issues were the most complex and difficult on the agenda and that things have never before gone this far in the efforts to achieve peace. Many analysts therefore believe that the process has now reached a point of no return.

Peace process scenarios

The peace process is moving forward on four political fronts: the first, most visible, is the one taking place in Havana between representatives of the government and the FARC in the dialogue and negotiations talks (*"Havana scenario"*). The second is the one taking place within the state and its institutions (*"state scenario"*). The third is taking place within the guerrilla organisation, its activists and social base (*"FARC* scenario"). The fourth and final one is taking place within society, the social organisations, political parties and academia (*"social scenario"*). There are different dilemmas facing each of these four scenarios, and they all have an impact on the peace process. The discussions that have taken place on the scope and validity of the results obtained thus far have been so intense and the obstacles so difficult to overcome that, two years after the start of the negotiations, with important issues yet to be discussed and agreed, the Colombian people are beginning to wonder if these negotiations can actually be concluded successfully. The only things that have kept this process going are the persistence of the government, the audacity of the negotiators in Havana, the backing of the international community, the direct support of Cuba, Norway, Chile and Venezuela, the support of UNDP and the National University of Colombia in the holding of civil society consultations and, last but by no means least, the desire of the Colombian peoples themselves to turn their backs on the internal war they have been suffering.

Surveys have shown that Colombians want peace, and this is the image the country is projecting to the outside world. When consulted on the possibility of making it real, however, Colombians reveal a caution that verges on pessimism. And there are good reasons for this because, in the *social scenario*, far removed from that of Havana, the ideological and political contradictions surrounding the process are severely affecting the state. The many years of so-called narco-paramilitaristic presence and its impact on local and regional politics (although also reaching into national politics) have penetrated the country's institutions, making them malleable to the ebbs and flows of money and giving a "Sicilian" flavour to the country. Moreover, it is noticeable that the economic interests that benefited from the armed conflict are able to move easily within this scenario.. These interests do not approve of and will certainly oppose any agreements to return the lands, assets and resources of the peasant farmers, Afro-Colombians and indigenous peoples, acquired illegally or at very little cost.

The biggest difficulty in the peace process lies in negotiating in the midst of hostilities. In the *state scenario,* but also in the *social scenario*, there is increasing dissatisfaction at continuing actions of war (kidnappings, attacks, ambushes of the army and police and other criminal acts on the part of the FARC) that affect the civilian population, such as the murders of two indigenous guards in Cauca department.

The problem becomes yet more complex when we realise that those in favour of the peace process, in both the *state* and *social scenarios*, have different and sometimes contradictory ideas of what peace is and how to achieve it, contradictions that are not insignificant and which promote the idea of a military solution to the armed conflict and encourage Colombians such as former Colombian president and now senator Álvaro Uribe Vélez and his political movement, *Centro Democrático*, to oppose the process.[3] For its part, the far right is attempting to sabotage the peace process and, dangerously, incite those sectors of the Armed Forces opposed to the process.

The kidnapping of General Rubén Darío Alzate in November 2014 carries a great deal of weight in the *state scenario*. President Santos was forced to suspend the talks in order to support the Armed Forces, the upper echelons of which were not prepared to accept that a high-ranking army officer was in the hands of the enemy. This action, which cast doubt over the continuity of the peace process, was resolved when, faced with pressure from wide sectors of the *social scenario*, the FARC decided to release the general after only 14 days in captivity.

This shows that the main challenge facing the state is that of avoiding a scaling-up of the clashes in the country and of shielding the process from conspiracies, attacks and obstacles placed in its path by those who – from within the *state scenario* – are seeking to sabotage it, a little like swimming in a pool of sharks. Nonetheless, the great challenge for the state is to create an environment favourable to the counter-signing of the agreements within the *social scenario*, once the negotiations have been completed. For no-one knows what might happen if the agreements reached in Havana are not counter-signed by the Colombian people.

In this regard, the victims of the conflict are key players in the negotiation process within the *social scenario* in terms of mobilisation, reporting and lobbying. It is first and foremost in this scenario that the Havana agreements will be counter-signed. This is one of the most difficult points to resolve because, for the two negotiating parties, it means acknowledging that they have committed criminal acts against society and that it will not be possible to bring about closure in the armed conflict unless there is a willingness to recognise and assume responsibilities, and build a truth that creates trust within society. Demands for justice, truth, recognition of responsibilities, compensation of rights and guarantees of non-repetition for the victims are thus basic to the counter-signing of the agreement by the Colombian people. And the Attorney-General's proposal to suspend investigations into members of the FARC and the public forces involved in crimes (including crimes against humanity) committed against the population if peace is achieved in Colombia may be seen as an act hostile to society and offensive to the victims. It is a proposal that has generated much controversy within the state (Attorney-General's Office and Congress) and has been rejected by the *social scenario*. And yet, from the *Havana scenario,* the FARC have made it known that they are not prepared to spend a single day in prison, even knowing full well that they have committed crimes against humanity. This position is threatening the process as President Santos has sensed that it is the negotiations that will guarantee good governance during his mandate. This demonstrates yet again the paradox that both war and nationalism are factors of unity while peace, and particularly its achievement, merely disunites and polarises.

It is causing some concern in the *social scenario* that the process is being delayed in Havana to the point that it could affect the local and regional elections (mayors, governors, councillors and deputies) on 25 October 2015, the results of which will have an effect on the negotiations. The FARC have realised that the *Havana scenario* is very important for them because, militarily weakened, largely delegitimised and with public opinion against them, it is the only scenario from which they are able to continue sending messages and generating information with which to influence the peace process. Hoping to turn around their negative image in the *social scenario*, they are delaying the process, clinging onto rhetoric and legend concerning their leaders (dead or not) as a way of reaffirming beliefs which, in reality, they no longer hold. It is nonetheless noteworthy and satisfying that they in December, declared (for the first time in the history of the negotiations) an indefinite ceasefire and apologising to the victims of the massacre that took place in Bojayá (Chocó) in 2002, in which 76 Afro-Colombians died, including 45 children.

There is uncertainty in the *social scenario* about the conversations taking place between the government and the country's second guerrilla force, the National Liberation Army (ELN), with a view to commencing a peace process. No-one knows what these guerrillas are proposing to the government, and expectations are therefore growing with regard to the content of the negotiations, all the more so given that almost everything is being negotiated with the FARC. The ELN commander, Nicolás Rodríguez Bautista, recently stated that progress was being made on a negotiation agenda with the government and that conversations had begun with the FARC with a view to the two sets of talks taking place in parallel but then coming together at the end of the peace process. Apart from some speculation in this regard, however, no-one knows for sure what this means.

It is absolutely clear in the *state scenario* that to maintain the good governance of the country, the *Havana scenario* needs to come up with more than just an agreement and an agenda for implementing it. This governance requires deep reforms of both Colombian state and society. It requires, above all, the conditions for a return to the rule of law so that society can once more have faith in its institutions and justice system, something that will not be possible without reparation for the wounds of the internal war, returning land to the displaced and helping the victims. This also involves responding to the urgent social needs of the peasant farmers, Afro-Colombians and indigenous peoples, and to the neglect and abandonment that resulted in the recent agricultural strike and protests on the part of these sectors, united around two political proposals: *Marcha Patriótica* and the *Congreso de los Pueblos*. These sectors are seeking more than mere reform for they know that if the conflict is to be stamped out and the peace sealed then the country's unequal land ownership structure needs to completely overhauled. It is this unequal land structure that has been at the root of all of Colombia's wars. In other words, the fundamental issue is to change a rural model that has been damaging the country for years.

These are the challenges of the post-conflict agenda, the point of which is to bring the conflict and violence to an end in order to usher in a period of transition as they move towards the transformation and reconstruction of the state. And it is at this stage that the *social scenario* will play an important role for the reconstruction of the state cannot be the exclusive affair of the *Havana* and *state scenarios*.

Indigenous peoples and the peace negotiations

The indigenous peoples have repeatedly stated that they support the peace process because they know that there can be no peace for them while there is no peace in Colombia. Nonetheless, they are not prepared to accept just any kind of peace. Some organisations (if not all of them) are clear that, in the interests of peace, they will have some difficult decisions to take. In the interests of rebuilding the Colombian nation and forging a future within it, they will have to decide which things to renounce, which to accept from other sectors but also which they cannot give up. For at stake in this process is the ability to retain what is fundamental to their lives as peoples, such as their territory, while at the same time contributing to achieving peaceful coexistence.

The future of the indigenous peoples will depend on the capacity of their organisations to forge a place for themselves in the process of transforming and reconstructing the state and society. The greatest challenge facing the indigenous organisations is that of ensuring their participation in a democratised political system and, from there, beginning to negotiate with the state, autonomously and without intermediaries, an agenda and a methodology for the restitution of rights violated by the armed conflict.

While the current *Havana scenario* is an exclusive state/FARC space that does not admit third parties, the post-conflict space in which a new country will be built is a democratic one open to all sectors of Colombian society. In this context, the FARC will withdraw from the political scene in order to make way for the political, social and community action of different sectors of civil society. This would be of huge importance for indigenous peoples because, for the first time since the 1991 Constitution was enacted, they would be making use of what, constitutionally, it means to be an organic part of the Colombian nation (defined as multi-ethnic and pluricultural) in order to participate in the collective and democratic construction of Colombian state and society.

Indigenous issues affected by the armed conflict

According to information from the National Indigenous Organisation of Colombia (ONIC), there are 73,200 indigenous people displaced from their lands, or 6.1% of their population. Most of these displacements were caused by paramilitary groups or drug traffickers but there are areas (mainly in Córdoba and Vichada) where the guerrillas were the cause of the displacements. In this regard, indigenous peoples share the status of victim with the peasant farmers and Afro-Colombians, as these are all peoples who have been affected not only by the occupation of their territories by different armed actors but also by the penetration of economic interests onto their lands: mining, hydrocarbon exploitation, logging and plantation monocropping, including coca, have all destroyed their economies and undermined their livelihoods. Indigenous peoples' separation from their territories has forced on them an *extreme economic exclusion* that has resulted in their "uprooting", a precursor to ethnocide.

Removal from their land destroys the livelihoods of indigenous peoples and puts their very existence as peoples at risk. And yet the right to life is a fundamental right in the Political Constitution of Colombia, ahead of any other public or private right or interest. Article III of Decree Law 4633 of 2011 regarding the definition of victims also states that, "… for indigenous people the territory is the victim, taking into account their world vision and the special and collective bond that links them to Mother Earth."

In the *Havana scenario,* a consensus has been reached between the parties that the transition process from armed conflict to peace will be considered territorially. For the FARC it is fundamental that there are guarantees ensuring that their demobilised combatants can be reintegrated into civilian life without any danger. Past experience weighs heavily in this regard, as around 3,000 activists from the Patriotic Union, a party that emerged from the previous failed peace process, were murdered following similar negotiations.

In the *Havana scenario* they are therefore considering the possibility of forming territories for the demobilised combatants, under state protection. They are discussing, in this regard, whether the status of "Peasant Reserve" would be most appropriate for this. Theoretically, this proposal is of great significance and enormous innovative value because, if given this status, it would not be a question of the rural sectors demanding "land redistributions" in the context of an agrarian reform but rather a change of a more reformist nature that would not question the logic of capital. It would, instead, be a matter of seeking the "recognition of peasant territories" which, being collectively owned (similar to the Indigenous Reserves and the Collective Territories of Black Communities,) would remain outside the market, forming a barrier to any possible concentration of land.

We do not know if this would work in practice, however. It would not be a problem in terms of regulations, as these already exist, but rather in terms of the practical way in which these reserves would operate, even the extent to which they would be accepted in areas of indigenous, Afro-Colombian or even peasant influence. To give one example, albeit perhaps not the most appropriate: it would be hard to imagine a Peasant Reserve in the north-eastern Cauca or on one of the Pacific rivers, where indigenous and Afro-Colombian population, respectively, predominate. Highly creative ways will clearly need to be found if these peasant reserves are to function properly.

When conceiving of peace along these lines, a territorial scenario takes on more importance for the indigenous peoples (*'territorial scenario'*), not only because it is through territory that they will come into contact (and collision!) with other social actors (peasants, settlers, Afro-Colombians, miners, coca growers, estate owners and now demobilised combatants) but also because it is on their territory that many of the indigenous peoples' rights to self-government, participation and autonomy will be concretely implemented. In this regard, the vexatious *territorial scenario* of the indigenous peoples is affected by the double standards of the *state scenario:* while their negotiators in Havana are signing agreements on land and victims' right, the government is submitting a draft bill of law (PL 133 of 2014c) over-ruling the social meaning of the current land law and giving priority to the provision of vacant plots to megaprojects in Areas of Rural Development and Economic Interest (ZIDRES) which, in the Altillanura region, affect the territoriality of the indigenous peoples.

In this same *territorial scenario*, the indigenous peoples are becoming increasingly desperate because, despite the Law on Victims and Decree Law 4633 of 2011 establishing measures of assistance, care, comprehensive reparation and the return of territorial rights to indigenous victims, the only land returned in the last three years has been the territory of one indigenous reserve (*Resguardo Unificado del Alto Andágueda*) in the Chocó. Moreover, to the detriment of indigenous peoples' interests, the National Mining Agency (ANM) and Ministry of Defence have not complied with the protective measures ordered to protect the indigenous territory from damage caused by the mining activities of AGA. And the Land Restitution Unit has only asked the courts to adopt protective measures for the indigenous territory of Alto Andágueda.

Given the above, in the *social scenario* and particularly in the *territorial scenario,* the peasants, Afro-Colombians and indigenous peoples have doubts over the land agreements because, if these are not accompanied by a commitment and willingness on the part of the state to ensure that territorial rights are respected, then the land that the rural sectors gain as a result of the agreements may be lost in just a few years, as has happened in the past.[4]

These are clearly the challenges facing Colombia, challenges that must be confronted if we are to build a more democratic society, more in line with the principles of a multicultural nation, for a *territorial peace* needs to become an ideal enjoyed by all and not merely the demobilised.   ○

Notes and References

1   In August 2012, the government and the FARC guerrilla group signed a "*General Agreement for the Termination of the Conflict and the Construction of a Stable and Lasting Peace*".

2   According to the "General Agreement" for the talks, the themes are: 1) Comprehensive agricultural development policy, 2) Political participation, 3) End of the conflict, 4) Solution to the problem of illicit drugs, 5) Victims, and 6) Implementation, verification and countersignature.

3   In the text: *"Las 25 capitulaciones del gobierno ante las FARC en La Habana"* (The government's 25 capitulations to the FARC in Havana), the large landowners are called on to oppose any change in land ownership or any kind of land reform.

4   The most flagrant case of this affirmation is what happened to the Afro-Colombians: with the ink scarcely dry following the signing of collective land titles granted to the Afro-Colombian communities in the Colombian Pacific by means of Law 70 of 1993, they were violently evicted.

Efraín Jaramillo Jaramillo *is an anthropologist and member of the Jenzera Work Collective (Grupo de trabajo Jenzera).*

VENEZUELA

Venezuela is a multicultural country. According to the XIV National Census of Population and Housing conducted in 2011, Venezuela's indigenous population totals 725,128 people out of a total population of around 27 million. This represents an increase of 41.8% between 2001 and 2011. The census recorded declarations of individuals belonging to 51 indigenous peoples in the country. Among these the Wayuu counted for the majority of the population with 58% of the total, followed by the Warao with 7%; Kariña 5%; Pemón 4%; Jivi, Cumanagoto, Anu, and Piaroa 3% each; Chaima and Yukpa 2%; Yanomami 1% and others 9%. The 1999 Constitution recognised the country's multi-ethnic and pluricultural nature and includes a chapter specifically dedicated to indigenous peoples' rights, opening up indigenous spaces for political participation at national, state and local level. The Organic Law on Demarcation and Guarantees for the Habitat and Lands of the Indigenous Peoples came into force in 2001; ILO Convention 169 was ratified in 2002; and the Organic Law on Indigenous Peoples and Communities (LOPCI) was developed in 2005, broadly consolidating this framework of rights. Venezuela voted in favour of the UN Declaration on the Rights of Indigenous Peoples in 2007.

2014 was marked by serious political conflict and a resulting growing economic crisis. President Nicolás Maduro had been calling for talks with the opposition *Mesa de la Unidad Democrática* (Coalition for Democratic Unity) since the end of 2013 but these efforts came to a halt when a breakaway faction of the opposition began demanding that his government step down. The resulting street protests that took place in some middle and upper class areas (known as "*La Salida*" or "The Ousting") ended in more than 40 deaths, and the destruction of public goods and highways. The economic crisis intensified as the year went on, reflected in a lack of some basic products, inflation running at more than 60% due to destabilising factors, currency devaluation caused by a lack of foreign exchange and a strong system of exchange controls, all exacerbated by the collapse of oil prices, the main source of income for the Venezuelan economy.

Price controls on subsidised goods, currency devaluation and the immoral actions of sectors devoted to providing contraband products have all resulted in a lack of basic goods such as foodstuffs and medicines. The national government has accused the opposition of conducting an "economic war", and led a fight against smugglers and hoarders.

Given the collapse in the oil price and the crisis of an oil-dependent rentier economy, the Venezuelan government is facing a need to diversify its sources of income, drawing on the potential of the agricultural, tourism, mining and industrial sectors. Significant progress was made during 2014 in legal and institutional terms to establish the foundations for the large-scale exploitation of mineral and hydrocarbon resources in the so-called "Orinoco Mining Arc" and the Perijá Mountains, which will have largely unpredictable socio-environmental effects on the indigenous peoples living in these areas.

There were few improvements in the situation of constitutionally-recognised rights for indigenous peoples in 2014. The indigenous peoples' main demand – the demarcation and titling of their lands – is still pending but also represents an obstacle to the state's plans to continue with a development model focused on natural resource extraction, particularly hydrocarbons and minerals. In addition, the unregulated growth of illegal gold, diamond and coltan mining in the south of the country, along with the increasing presence of non-state armed actors, are issues of concern for indigenous peoples given the negative impacts they are having on the environment and on the communities themselves in their ancestral territories.

Creation of the Presidential Council for Indigenous Peoples and the National Institute for Indigenous Languages

On 12 October, Vice-President Jorge Arreaza announced the creation of the Presidential Council of Popular Power for Indigenous Peoples (*Consejo Presidencial del Poder Popular para los Pueblos Indígenas*). The members of this Presidential Council were present on the occasion, with one representative for each of the country's indigenous peoples. According to the Vice-President, this

institution will have the same rank as the Council of Ministers and the objective of "creating a direct channel of communication between these communities and the Executive".[1] At the inauguration of the Council, President Nicolás Maduro, made a number of announcements:

1. That indigenous peoples over 50 years of age would now be eligible for a retirement pension.
2. That 2,963 million Bolivars were to be approved for the construction of 5,000 new homes in 2015, benefiting 23,698 indigenous people.

3. That 575,792 Bolivars were to be approved for the provision of comprehensive assistance to 396 indigenous communities living in extreme poverty.
4. That a further 265 million Bolivars were to be set aside for financing socio-productive projects in the 396 indigenous communities.
5. That branches of the state bank were to be established in indigenous communities.
6. That the members of the Presidential Council for Indigenous Peoples were to be provided with tablet computers.
7. That resources were to be provided to improve communication with indigenous communities, through the support of the Armed Forces for air or river access and through the provision of satellite communication systems for the indigenous communities.

In addition, the creation of the National Institute for Indigenous Languages (*Instituto Nacional de Idiomas Indígenas*) was announced. The Minister for Indigenous Peoples specified that this institute would be established within the context of the Law on Indigenous Languages, decreed in 2008, emphasising that "of the 44 native peoples in the country, 34 speak the language of their ethnic group and 10 have lost their language. We have been working on the proposal for this institute and its research process in order to strengthen or rescue the indigenous languages that have been lost."

Demarcation and recognition of Indigenous Lands

The Minister for Indigenous Peoples announced a 2014 target of providing 21 indigenous land titles in eight of the country's states.[2] On 13 October, President Maduro delivered six indigenous land titles to communities of the Cumanagoto and Kariña peoples in Anzoátegui state:

1. Guatacarito community (Cumanagoto indigenous people), for 1,891.24 ha.
2. Jabillote community (Cumanagoto indigenous people), for 438.68 ha.
3. Capachal community (Kari´ña indigenous people), for 983.52 ha.
4. Pedregal community (Kari´ña indigenous people), for 3,294.53 ha.
5. Guayabal community (Cumanagoto indigenous people), for 657.07 ha.
6. Mapiricurito community (Kari´ña indigenous people), for 1,119.33 ha.

To celebrate the 15th anniversary of the approval of the Constitution (15 December 2014), the Coordinating Body of Indigenous Organisations of Amazonas (*Coordinadora de Organizaciones Indígenas de Amazonas* / COIAM), issued a press release giving an assessment of the national demarcation process for indigenous lands. Based on an analysis of official information on indigenous communities that have already been demarcated and on all communities nationally (around 3,000), they conclude that "87.6% of the indigenous habitat and lands still remains to be demarcated" in the country, demonstrating a "lack of political will to implement the demarcation process". Finally, "in order to move forward with the national demarcation process", they propose that the national government should: a) urgently review all outstanding requests for demarcation, in order to reach favourable decisions covering a sufficient area, in agreement with the peoples, communities and organisations involved; and b) produce and implement, with the active involvement of the indigenous organisations, a Plan of Action to Advance the Demarcation Progress, with clear criteria and giving priority to collective demarcations for indigenous and multi-ethnic peoples, based on the requests submitted via self-demarcation.[3]

The Yukpa people's struggle for their territories

Nine members of the families of community leaders Sabino Romero and Carmen Fernández have been murdered since 2008 in the struggle to recover their ancestral lands, invaded by large estate owners and smallholders in the Perijá Mountains, Zulia state.[4] Although the lands have already been demarcated by the national government and officially handed over to the indigenous peoples, the former owners have not yet been compensated for their land and property and so some of them have sworn to do away with Sabino Romero and his whole family. The Yukpa are nonetheless continuing to recover their territories, occupying estates that have not yet been compensated by the government. "On 11 February, they occupied the Mi Deleite estate and, on 19 March, the Las Delicias estate, leaving Araguaney, Carmen and another two small farms to be occupied in this area, along with the Estrella lands." [5]

The response of the cattle ranchers, with hired assassins at their service and with the alleged support of members of the National Bolivarian Armed Forces (FANB), has been to continue the aggression against these people. On 3 January

2014, they attempted to murder Silverio Romero, 18 years of age, one of the younger sons of Sabino Romero. The aggressors, armed with shotguns, turned out to be hired assassins linked to the landowners. On 16 February, Rodolfo Fernández, 16-year-old son of Carmen Fernández (Kuse community leader and Sabino's niece), was beaten up by members of the army in Kuse community and, on 20 February, Leandro Romero Izarra, Sabino's brother, was detained and brutally beaten by a group of soldiers.

On 24 June, five members of the Bolivian National Guard from the El Tokuko border post attacked Carmen Fernández's children near the former Las Delicias estate, killing Cristóbal Fernández and injuring his brother, Leonardo. Cristóbal was an important witness in the case underway against six individuals charged with the murder of Sabino Romero. With this new crime, the number of Carmen Fernández's children who have been killed now comes to three, with another five family members injured. All these cases have gone unpunished.

On 30 June, after the burial and wake of Cristóbal Fernández, a group of more than 100 Yukpa from Tukuko and *criollos* from Machiques laid siege to Carmen Fernández's house for eight hours.* She was seriously injured by a shot to the neck, and her son, Luis Adolfo Fernández, and a nephew were also injured. The whole family was evicted from Las Delicias and later arrested when they went to make a complaint.[6] On 15 August, five municipal police officers from Machiques were sentenced to seven years in prison after admitting their involvement in the murder of Sabino Romero Izarra on 3 March 2013, an attack during which his wife, Lucía Martínez, was also injured. Activists linked to the Yukpa cause condemned the sentence for being too lenient. Ángel Romero, alias El Manguera (former member of the Anti-Extortion and Kidnapping Group of the Bolivarian National Guard and bodyguard to the Machiques municipal mayor) is still on trial for the same case, alleged to have been the one who fired at the leader and his wife.[7] Lucía Martínez, Sabino's widow, Carmen Fernández and *Sociedad Homo et Natura* have denounced the delays in the case, given that the hearings have now been postponed seven times, and are demanding that the intellectual authors of the crime, linked to the Machiques cattle farmers' association, be brought to justice and punished.[8]

---

*   The Yukpa are not unified on the issue of demarcation of their territory and about the relationship they have with the government. Some Yukpa do not support the struggle spearheaded by Sabino Romero, Carmen Fernández and others to recover their lands and are, conversely, allies of the ranchers and large landowners.

Illegal mining and the presence of non-state armed groups on indigenous territories

In the Venezuelan Amazon, the boom in illegal mining of gold, diamonds and coltan, the presence of irregular armed groups and the national government's plans to develop the so-called "Orinoco Mining Arc" have led to reactions from different sectors – particularly the indigenous organisations – concerned at the social and environmental impacts of mining on their territories.

COIAM published a statement in 2014 expressing its concern at the increase in illegal mining in the Atabapo river basin, in the Yapacana National Park and in the lower reaches of the Ventuari River, largely being undertaken by foreigners coming from Colombia and Brazil, and causing the destruction of large areas of forestland, altering the course of rivers and contaminating them with mercury. They also highlighted the fact that the illegal mining was being accompanied by other unlawful activities such as the smuggling of goods, fuel trafficking, prostitution and human trafficking, the illegal entry onto the national territory of foreigners, the presence of armed groups causing violence and the trafficking of banned substances. Finally, they called on the state's civilian and military authorities to take urgent action to control the mining and other unlawful activities.[9]

The Organisations of Indigenous Women of Amazonas (*Organizaciones de Mujeres Indígenas de Amazonas*) also published a press release on "the presence of non-state armed groups and illegal miners on our ancestral territory". The document noted the presence of non-state armed groups, who self-identify as members of the FARC, and who are "attacking, harassing and threatening our elders – leaders and active members of the indigenous organisations -, protecting the illegal miners, using coercion, threats and intimidation to create fear and to contribute to the displacement of indigenous communities, capturing and recruiting children, and invading the sacred places of the indigenous territories, affecting the spiritual well-being". They also noted that "illegal mining is plundering our ancestral territories and affecting indigenous women disproportionately, as they are an easy target for networks wishing to traffic them for sexual and labour exploitation, along with women, children and adolescents who choose or are forced into prostitution, a situation that results in high levels of unwanted pregnancies, sexually-transmitted infections and sexual violence".[10]

Illegal mining in the Caura River basin, Bolívar state

The "Kuyujani" Indigenous Organisation of the Caura River Basin (*Organización Indígena de la Cuenca del Caura "Kuyujani"*), which groups together 53 communities of the Yek'wana and Sánema peoples, has denounced the exponential increase in mining activity in the upper reaches of the Caura River, in Bolívar state. According to Mayraleno Cortés, leader of the organisation, there are currently more than 3,000 miners working with machines on the Yuruaní River and where it meets the Caura. There has also been a proliferation of bars with under-age prostitutes and the sale of drugs and alcohol. All this is taking place despite the existence of four FANB control posts along the Caura River. Instead of ensuring the security of the indigenous communities, these guards are attacking and mistreating them.

On 14 May 2014, the Supreme Court of Justice passed a decision urging the National Executive to reclassify the Caura Forest Reserve under a more restrictive status as provided by the Organic Law for Land Planning. In addition, it ordered "an immediate halt to all exploitation, use, extraction of or trade in metal or non-metal minerals (…) in the region of the current Caura Forest Reserve and its hydrographic basin". It also instructed the Ministry for the Environment to commence a programme to rehabilitate the areas degraded by mining.[11]

The "Kuyujani" Indigenous Organisation issued a statement following the ruling of the Supreme Court of Justice in which it called for the collective titling of the lands of the Ye'kwana and Sánema peoples of the Caura basin, a process which has been pending since 2006. It also rejected the fact that "under the pretext of 'environmental conservation' attempts are being made to impose protected areas and any other concept of Areas Under the Special Administration Scheme (ABRAE) on our ancestral territories, without previously granting collective title to our traditional habitats and territories in the Caura basin".[12]

State mining policy and development of the "Orinoco Mining Arc"

On 20 March 2014, President Nicolás Maduro approved Decree No. 841[13] establishing the creation of the Presidential Commission for the Protection, Development and Integral Promotion of Legal Mining Activity in Guayana Region,[14] with the aim of producing and implementing an Action Plan to comprehensively address the problem of illegal mining in the area, in line with the objectives of the Nation's Second Socialist Plan, 2013-2019.

In June, COIAM published a press release on the enactment of Decree No. 841. According to the indigenous organisations, this regulation seeks to implement the so-called "Orinoco Mining Arc", developing and promoting mining activity in the Guayana region (part of the Amazon) and natural resource extraction as established in the Nation's Second Socialist Plan.

In the press release, they expressed their concern that the decree was approved without the prior and informed consultation of the indigenous peoples affected, and without the Venezuelan state having conducted the effective demarcation of the indigenous lands. They also repeated their rejection of mining in all its different forms, as it is having serious environmental and sociocultural impacts on indigenous peoples' living conditions. They concluded by requesting that the national government review its development policies for the Venezuelan Amazon, that it studies and explores alternative and environmentally-sustainable development models and decrees a moratorium on mining activity in the south of Orinoco in order to ensure the protection of the great water and forest resources of the Amazon as well as the important biological and social diversity of these territories.[15]

On 11 June, Nicia Maldonado, Minister for the Comprehensive Development of the Guayana Region and former Minister for Indigenous Peoples, officially inaugurated the Presidential Commission for the Protection, Development and Integral Promotion of Legal Mining Activity in Guayana Region. This is the government's fifth attempt to put a stop to illegal mining.

On 9 August, a meeting was held with representatives of indigenous organisations from Bolívar state, convened by the Presidential Commission for the Protection, Development and Integral Promotion of Legal Mining Activity in Guayana Region. The meeting was in response to indigenous complaints at their exclusion and the absence of prior and informed consent with regard to the creation of this Commission and the approval of Decree No. 841. The indigenous representatives made a series of complaints referring to the problems they are suffering due to mining: mafias allied to FANB officials; drug, fuel and food trafficking; hired assassins; invasions by armed groups; the devastation of protected areas; and contamination of the rivers with mercury.

Juan Blanco, a leader of the Pemón people, stated that "our communities have gradually been devastated by foreigners who have virtually fenced us in, and by of the poorly named "unions"[16] who come from who knows where with so many weapons. Soldiers on active duty are offering to support the mining mafia." He also mentioned the involvement of indigenous communities in mining: "We are local people who depend on mining; we indigenous communities have immense needs and, because of these needs, we have been abandoning our customs and our culture." [17]

The "Kuyunu" organisation of the Ye´kwana and Sánema peoples of the Upper Ventuari River, in Amazonas state, rejected the agreement reached between the governments of Venezuela and the People's Republic of China in 2012 for mineral exploration and exploitation in various regions of the south of the country. In their press release, they stated that they were against mineral exploration and exploitation on their territory and had not been consulted over the signing of the agreement with the CITIC Chinese mining company in this regard. They called for the titling of the lands of the Upper Ventuari basin, the request for which has been lodged with the Regional Demarcation Commission since December 2009.[18]

Decree No. 1,396, approved on 18 November 2014, announced the Organic Law Reserving Activities of Gold Exploration and Exploitation for the State, along with everything connected with and auxiliary to this[19] "with the aim of reversing the serious effects of the capitalist mining model, characterised by environmental degradation, lack of respect for land planning, and attacks on the dignity and health of miners and of the people living in communities around the mining areas". Article 40 of this law states that gold mining and gold mining areas are strategic for the Nation, and should be declared as National Security Zones. This means it will be the FANB's responsibility, among other things, "to participate actively in assisting and developing the indigenous communities and peoples that make a living in the mining zones".

Developmentalist and extractivist projects in Zulia state

In Zulia state, social and environmental movements are continuing to confront regional and national government plans to open new coal mines in the Perijá Mountains and construct a coal-powered thermoelectric plant and a deep-water port at the exit to the Maracaibo Lake. These large-scale projects form part of the

Zulia State Economic / Productive Development Plan for 2013-2016, which aims to increase coal production from 7 to 22 million tonnes.[20]

Coal extraction from the Paso Diablo and Mina Norte mines has resulted in a decrease in the volume of the Guasare River and its tributaries and a number of indigenous Wayúu communities have been displaced and are suffering environmental and health impacts. The plans to open new coal mines would affect the Socuy, Cachirí and Maché rivers, displacing Wayúu communities that traditionally live in these basins and affecting the rivers and the provision of water to Maracaibo and other nearby towns, which are already suffering from poor supplies.[21]

The construction of highways and the América or Bolívar port for the transportation and export of the coal and oil produced could have large-scale environmental impacts on the ecosystems of the Maracaibo Lake and the Gulf of Venezuela. This would also affect the islands of San Bernardo, San Carlos, Pájaro and Zapara, which form part of the ancestral territory of the indigenous Añú people, not yet demarcated.[22]

Mapoyo oral tradition recognised by UNESCO as intangible heritage

The Mapoyo are an indigenous people living on the grasslands that extend from the Los Pijiguaos mountain range to the Orinoco River, in the far west of Guayana region. They comprise a population of around 400 people, living primarily in the community of El Palomo. The Mapoyo language is related to the Carib language and is in danger of extinction, with only three speakers left.

In November 2014, through the Centre for Diversity and Cultural Identity (*Centro de la Diversidad e Identidad Cultural*), the Venezuelan government proposed that UNESCO recognise "the oral Mapoyo tradition and its symbolic references in the ancestral territory" and include it on the list of Intangible Cultural Heritage requiring urgent safeguarding measures.

The oldest people in the community maintain this oral tradition but its transmission to new generations is being threatened by factors such as: the emigration of young people for educational and economic opportunities; the expansion of the mining industry; and the influence of the formal state education system, which does not encourage the use of a person's mother tongue.[23]   ◯

Notes and references

1   "Arreaza instala Consejo Presidencial de los Pueblos Indígenas", in *El Universal*, 12.10.14.
2   AVN. "Este año está prevista la entrega de 21 títulos de tierra y hábitat indígenas". 08.01.14.
3   COIAM. "Comunicado de la COIAM sobre el proceso nacional de demarcación de hábitat y tierras indígenas a los 15 años de aprobación de la Constitución de la República Bolivariana de Venezuela". 28.11.14.
4   Barrios, D. "Van 9 yukpas asesinados en la lucha por sus tierras", in Últimas Noticias, 07.08.14.
5   Sociedad Homo et Natura. "El Estado Gobierno sigue en deuda con los Yukpa". 20.05.14.
6   Sociedad Homo et Natura. "S O S por las familias de Carmen Fernández y Sabino Romero Izarra". 25.07.14
7   "Condenan a cinco hombres por muerte de Sabino Romero", in *Diario La Verdad*, 18.08.14.
8   Lucía Martínez y Carmen Fernández. "Lucía Martínez Romero y Carmen Fernández Romero hace un llamado". 10.11.14.
9   COIAM. "Comunicado de la COIAM sobre la minería ilegal en el municipio Atabapo". 05.05.14.
10   OMIDA – Wanaaleru. "Comunicado de las Organizaciones de Mujeres Indígenas de Amazonas sobre la situación de las mujeres indígenas en el municipio Autana". 11.12.14.
11   Supreme Court of Justice. Constitutional Chamber. Case No. 12-1166. 14.05.14.
12   Kiyujani Indigenous Organisation of the Caura Basin. "Pronunciamiento de los pueblos y comunidades Ye´kwana y Sánema del Caura ante la Sentencia del Tribunal Supremo de Justicia Sala Constitucional. EXP. 12-1166". 15.05.14.
13   *Gaceta Oficial*, No. 40.376, 20.03.14
14   The Guayana region covers three states in the south of the country: Amazonas, Bolívar and Delta Amacuro.
15   COIAM. "Segundo Comunicado de la COIAM sobre la nueva política minera del Estado venezolano". 02.06.14.
16   In the mining zones of Bolívar state, the so-called "unions" are non-state armed groups that extort miners in exchange for their security.
17   Rangel, C. "En las minas los militares están prestándose para apoyar a la mafia", in *Correo del Caroní*, 09.08.14.
18   "Los pueblos Ye´kwana y Sánema rechazan la presencia de la empresa minera china (CITIC) y de grupo generador de violencia en el Alto Ventuari, in *La Iglesia en Amazonas*, No. 144, June 2014.
19   *Gaceta Oficial* No. 6.150 Extraordinario, 18.11.14
20   Gil B., M. "La Sociedad Homo et Natura: No al Puerto América", in *Tal Cual*, 26.05.14.
21   Sociedad Homo et Natura. "No a la carboeléctrica en el Zulia ni a la explotación de carbón en el río Socuy, si al agua y a la energía limpia del Parque Eólico de la Guajira". 01.09.14; "Desde PDVSA/ Carbozulia, Ministerio de Energía y la Gobernación del Zulia se conjura la muerte de los ríos Guasare, Socuy y Maché y el desplazamiento de los pueblos wayuu aledaños". 28.12.13.
22   Sociedad Homo et Natura. "La salvación del Lago de Maracaibo no es cerrarlo para construir Puerto Bolívar". 13.05.14.
23   UNESCO. "La tradición oral mapoyo y sus referentes simbólicos en el territorio ancestral", in http://www.unesco.org/culture/ich/index.php?lg=es&pg=00011&USL=00983

Aimé Tillett. *Grupo de Trabajo Socioambiental de la Amazonía - Wataniba*

SURINAME

The Indigenous peoples of Suriname number approximately 20,344 people, or 3.8% of the total population of 541,638[1] (census 2012). The four most numerous Indigenous peoples are the Kali'ña (Caribs), Lokono (Arawaks), Trio (Tirio, Tareno) and Wayana. In addition, there are small settlements of other Amazonian Indigenous peoples in the south of Suriname, including the Akurio, Apalai, Wai-Wai, Katuena/Tunayana, Mawayana, Pireuyana, Sikiiyana, Okomoyana, Alamayana, Maraso, Sirewu and Sakëta. The Kali'ña and Lokono live mainly in the northern part of the country and are sometimes referred to as "lowland" Indigenous peoples, whereas the Trio, Wayana and other Amazonian peoples live in the south and are referred to as "highland" peoples.

Suriname is one of the few countries in South America that has not ratified ILO Convention 169. It did vote in favour of adopting the UN Declaration on the Rights of Indigenous Peoples in 2007 but the legislative system of Suriname, based on colonial legislation, does not recognize Indigenous or tribal peoples, and Suriname has no legislation governing Indigenous peoples' land or other rights. This forms a major threat to the survival and well-being of Indigenous and tribal peoples, along with respect for their rights, particularly given the strong focus that is now being placed on Suriname's many natural resources (including bauxite, gold, water, forests and biodiversity).

Land rights issues

Suriname again made little concrete progress in recognizing Indigenous and tribal peoples' rights in 2014, and remains the only country with Indigenous peoples in the Western hemisphere without specific national legislation on these rights, including land rights. This, predictably, once again resulted in various tense situations. Notable among these were renewed clashes with small-scale miners from the local Maroon communities of Nieuw Koffiekamp, where the Canadian company Rosebel Gold Mines/Iamgold has a gold mining concession, and Merian, where the American company Surgold/Newmont is operating. In both cases, the local miners, who are treated as illegal within these concessions, are claiming their traditional land and resource rights which, however, are neither recognized nor enforceable under Surinamese legislation. The community organization of Nieuw Koffiekamp has threatened to take their situation through the Inter-American human rights' system, particularly in light of the 2007 Saramaka judgment[2] of the Inter-American Court of Human Rights, which obliged Suriname to legally recognize the land and resource rights of the Saramakaner Maroons, of which Nieuw Koffiekamp is a part. This judgment has not yet been implemented.

Work on legislation aimed at recognizing land and other Indigenous and tribal peoples' rights, coordinated by the Presidential Commissioner on Land Rights, a position established in 2013 for this particular objective, has also moved little. A government consultant drew up a draft law on the traditional authorities' (the traditional community leaders, including chiefs and paramount chiefs) position with regard to central government but this was without any meaningful participation of Indigenous and Maroon representatives, who have categorically rejected the draft itself as well as the process by which it was produced.

There was also little respect for Indigenous and tribal peoples' rights to full and effective participation and free, prior and informed consent (FPIC) in decisions affecting their lives in 2014. Only through the media did communities hear about plans for large-scale projects such as a railroad from the capital Paramaribo to the international airport and a highway to neighbouring country Brazil, to be built through the Amazon region. An announcement from the Presidential Commissioner on Land Rights that a FPIC protocol would be developed in close consultation with Indigenous and Maroon representatives remained mere words.

The Trio and Wayana communities of south Suriname held a conference in December 2014 to discuss common issues in the south and ways of protecting their area in relation to sustainable development. This conference was funded by international environmental organizations who are attempting to create a corridor of protected areas throughout the Guianas. While the communities certainly agree on the need to protect their territories, there are serious concerns that current Surinamese legislation on protected areas lacks the standards necessary to implement the "new paradigm" in terms of respecting Indigenous peoples' rights in relation to nature conservation.

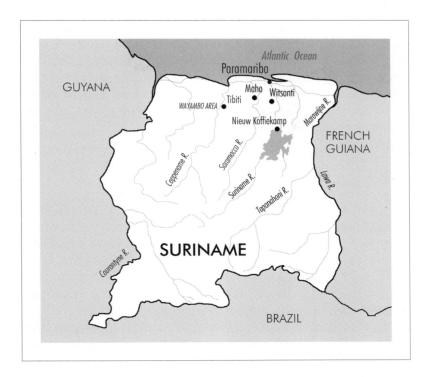

Cases considered by the Inter-American Human Rights System

In January 2014, the Inter-American Commission on Human Rights (IACHR) formally submitted the case of "the Kaliña and Lokono Peoples versus Suriname"[3] to the Inter-American Court of Human Rights. Having gone through the usual court procedures, hearings were held of the victims (the eight Indigenous villages of the Lower-Marowijne region), international experts and the Suriname state in February 2015. A judgment in this case may come as early as the end of 2015.

Another case related to Indigenous peoples concerns the community of Maho, whose 2009 petition to the IACHR was declared admissible in 2010.[4] Precautionary measures were not, however, acted on by Suriname. A working session on this petition was held with the IACHR in 2014, and a proposal to work towards a friendly settlement was agreed by the community under certain conditions. Dialogue regarding this possibility has started and is currently ongoing. Threats to Maho have not stopped, however; on the contrary, the village has been pestered by people who claim to have, or to be obtaining, land or sand mining concessions on the community's territory. In one instance, the perpetrators beat up a villager, whose subsequent complaint was not taken seriously by the local police station.

REDD+

After previous submissions failed to gain approval, in particular due to the limited meaningful participation of Indigenous and tribal peoples in their elaboration, the Government of Suriname finally obtained approval for its renewed REDD Readiness Preparation Proposal (R-PP) to the Forest Carbon Partnership Facility (FCPF) of the World Bank in 2013[5] with UNDP as delivery partner. The FCPF Participants Committee, however, also adopted an accompanying resolution outlining some specific conditions related to the more effective participation of stakeholders and consideration of the rights of Indigenous and tribal peoples in implementing the R-PP. The UNDP project to implement the R-PP was designed and approved in 2014, and will be implemented by the National Institute for Environment and Development in Suriname (NIMOS), the government environment agency.

One of the components of the R-PP, namely capacity strengthening of the Government of Suriname on Indigenous and tribal peoples' rights and FPIC, has been taken up by Conservation International who obtained funding from the US State Department for its project "Widening Informed Stakeholders Engagement in REDD+" (WISE-REDD+). Implementation of this project started in late 2014, with discussions on establishing a project steering committee and defining an implementation and communication strategy.

The Association of Indigenous Village Leaders in Suriname, VIDS, has been working to develop a "toolkit" for rights-based, culturally-sensitive information on REDD+, which will be finalized and rolled out in 2015. This "toolkit" will contain written and audio-visual materials, and training for community facilitators will also be provided.

Other activities and developments

Representatives of Suriname's Indigenous peoples actively participated in two major international events in 2014, namely the World Conference on Indigenous Peoples (WCIP) and the 20th Conference of the Parties (COP20) to the UN Framework Convention on Climate Change (UNFCCC). Follow-up on relevant issues under these processes in Suriname is coordinated by VIDS, which is organizing discussions on community-based "planning for the future".

Various Indigenous villages, including Witsanti and Tibiti, changed their leadership in 2014, accompanied as is usual by VIDS, as the umbrella Indigenous traditional authority. The latter village has recently learned that a private company is requesting large parts of its territory as a concession for a biofuel plantation and processing industry.

VIDS has completed a series of workshops in various regions and villages both in order to promote the discussion of written village regulations and to promote awareness of the UN Declaration on the Rights of Indigenous Peoples (UN-DRIP), as part of its efforts to enhance Indigenous peoples' right to self-determination in Suriname. This process received funding from the Indigenous Peoples Assistance Facility (IPAF) of the International Fund for Agriculture Development (IFAD).

Four Indigenous villages in the Para East region of Suriname have begun their land and resource mapping, under the coordination of VIDS and with financial support from the Worldwide Fund for Nature (WWF). VIDS has already coordinated Indigenous land mapping in East Suriname, West Suriname and the Wayambo area.

The World Bank, as well as the Caribbean Development Bank, held informative meetings with VIDS in 2014 as part of the formulation of their Country Strategy. VIDS expressed, among other things, its hope that these development banks would ensure that their cooperation does not result in human rights violations or further marginalization of Indigenous peoples, that there is effective participation in project formulation and implementation and that there are also opportunities for Indigenous peoples to have (direct) access to development funds.   ◯

Notes and references

1   The population is highly ethnically and religiously diverse, consisting of Hindustani (27.4%), Ma-
    roons ("Bushnegroes", 21.7%), Creoles (16%), Javanese (14%), mixed (13%), Indigenous peo-
    ples ("Amerindians", 3.8%) and Chinese (1.5%) (*census 2012*). At least 15 different languages
    are spoken on a daily basis in Suriname but the only official language is Dutch, while the *lingua
    franca* used in less formal conversations is *Sranan Tongo* (Surinamese).
2   http://www.corteidh.or.cr/docs/casos/articulos/seriec_172_ing.pdf
3   http://www.oas.org/en/iachr/media_center/PReleases/2014/009.asp
4   http://www.oas.org/es/cidh/decisiones/2013/SUAD1621-09ES.doc
5   http://www.forestcarbonpartnership.org/Node/175

Max Ooft *is Policy Officer at the Bureau of the Association of Indigenous Village
Leaders in Suriname (Vereniging van Inheemse Dorpshoofden in Suriname,
VIDS). He holds a doctorandus (drs) in medical sciences and a Master's in Busi-
ness Administration (MBA).*

ECUADOR

Ecuador has a total population of 16,189,044 inhabitants, including 14 nationalities that together comprise around 1,100,000 people. These peoples are organised into a number of local, regional and national organisations. 60.3% of the Andean Kichwa live in six provinces of the Central-North Mountains; 24.1% live in the Amazon and belong to 10 different nationalities; 7.3% of the Andean Kichwa live in the Southern Mountains; and the remaining 8.3% live along the coast and in the Galapagos Islands. 78.5% still live in rural areas and 21.5% in the towns and cities. A number of nationalities have very low population numbers and are in a highly vulnerable situation: in the Amazon, the A'i Cofán (1,485 inhabitants); Shiwiar (1,198 inhabs); Siekopai (689 inhabs); Siona (611 inhabs.); and Sapara (559 inhabs); in the coastal areas, the Epera (546 inhabs) and the Manta (311 inhabs.).

Article 1 of the 2008 Constitution of the Republic recognises the country as a "...constitutional state of law and social justice, democratic, sovereign, independent, unitary, intercultural, plurinational and secular". Despite clear progress in the law and in recognising collective rights, the trend over the last few years has continued to be towards disagreements and conflict between the state and the indigenous peoples.

Ecuador ratified ILO Convention 169 in 1998 and voted in favour of the adoption of the UN Declaration in the Rights of Indigenous Peoples in 2007.

Aftermath of the massacre of Taromenane families

Following the massacre on a Taromenane family living in voluntary isolation, by a group of indigenous Waorani in March 2013 (see *The indigenous World 2014*), in the beginning of 2014, the Orellana Second Court of Criminal Guarantees ordered five indigenous Waorani, arrested on 26 November 2013 and charged with alleged "genocide of peoples in voluntary isolation" to be remanded in custody.[1] The men detained were taken to the Sucumbíos Centre for Social Rehabilitation.

For José Miguel Goldáraz, Capuchin missionary, the case was never probably investigated and the prison sentence was culturally inappropriate, "...the whole group (Waorani (ed.)) is terrified. Prison, torture, isolation, means they have lost all will to express themselves as Waos. Prison has destroyed them, taken away everything that made them men: dignity, respect." [2]

In this regard, the well-known chronicler of Waorani affairs, Miguel Ángel Cabodevilla, a former Capuchin missionary, wrote a letter to the president of the Constitutional Court, proposing 13 points that would ensure that the Waorani understood the sentence handed down to them, and questioning whether prison was appropriate given their cultural and civic position: "...justice cannot consist of an incomprehensible, and thus oppressive, punishment for the Waorani; instead their knowledge, agreement and observance of Ecuadorian law must be sought. If we do it right, it could be the start of a new era between two societies (Waorani and national society) that have ignored each other and battled each other for too long".[3]

The case against those accused of murdering the Taromenane was suspended until the Constitutional Court could be consulted and, on 6 August, it was decided that the Waorani should be tried under principles of "interculturality" rather than ordinary law.[4] In the resolution, the Constitutional Court recommended that the Orellana Court Judge "take into account international agreements and judgements relating to the crime of genocide". In June, the Public Defence Service proposed three alternatives for trying the murder cases: the ordinary justice system could declare itself incompetent and the case be dealt with as an internal conflict by the indigenous justice system; the sentence could be reduced on the basis of an intercultural interpretation of the case; or negotiations could take place between the Constitutional Court and the Waorani people.

In August, the judge of the Orellana Second Court of Criminal Guarantees, Álvaro Guerrero, considered the request for a review of the precautionary measures and decided to pass replacement measures in favour of the accused. The five Waorani had spent a total of 10 months in custody and, according to the new legal provisions, must present themselves to the judge every fortnight, and are banned from leaving the country.

Conflict related to oil exploitation in Block 66

In Block 66 on Waorani territory, the Brazilian Petrobell Inc.- Grantmining S.A, oil company are producing around three million barrels of oil a day from the Tigüino and Cachiyacu wells. In this area there has been a succession of incidents dating back to December 2011 when the inhabitants of Bataburo closed the access roads to the operations zone, accusing the company of reducing the number of jobs and the state of failing to build 67 houses and appoint bilingual teachers as agreed. On that occasion, there were struggles between the Waorani and the forces of law and order. According to Roberto Ima, a young leader from Bataburo, "the discontent has arisen due to reforms of the Law on Hydrocarbons. Previously, we used to sign agreements directly with the oil companies but now these royalties go to the state and the resources are then channelled back down. The different ministries ask us for projects but, when we provide them, they take absolutely no notice." [5]

In April 2014 when, in circumstances that are still unclear, the 10-year-old son of David Enkeri died and, in revenge, he murdered two workers from the state "Ecuador Estratégico" company who were working to install a drinking water system in the community.[6] A commission made up of the government authorities and leaders of the Waorani (Naw) people are still looking into the situation but have come to no final agreement in this regard.

Oil operations in Yasuní Biosphere National Park

Months after the Ecuadorian government opposed the initiative to leave the oil inside Yasunì in the ground (see *The Indigenous World 2014*), the controversy over oil exploration in this protected area grew more intense. In May, environmental group known as "Yasunidos" called on the Inter-American Commission on Human Rights to declare that the Ecuadorian state had violated the political rights of both the group and more than 750,000 people who had signed a petition calling for a referendum with regard to leaving the crude oil from Block 43, in a protected area, in the ground.[7] In the document, the group alleged that the state had committed an illegal and unconstitutional act by refusing to hold a consultation on oil exploitation in Yasuní. The National Electoral Council (CNE) ruled that the group had gathered insufficient signatures to call a referendum[8] and the Electoral Disputes Court, which has the final say in electoral matters, ratified the CNE's position, thus allowing the government's promotion of oil exploitation in the area to continue unabated.

Meanwhile, the state company Petroamazonas has begun constructing access facilities for oil operations, including a loading area, access roads and drilling platforms. All this has given rise to questions from environmental groups and subsequent replies from the government authorities and Biodiversity Committee of the National Assembly, which issued a second report in January 2015. Initial production of around 10,000 barrels is planned for March 2016. Peak ITT production of around 180,000 barrels a day should be reached by 2019.

CONAIE, congress and clashes with the government

In an environment fuelled by the ever more radical positions of groups opposed to Rafael Correa's government, the 5th Congress of the Confederation of Indigenous Nationalities of Ecuador (CONAIE) was held from 15 to 17 May in the town of Ambato in the central mountains. A new leadership team was elected at this meeting, headed by a Kichwa from Cotopaxi, Jorge Herrera. This time, there was no agreement for a united front between the candidates, as on other occasions.

The congress ended with the approval of a resolution that included 13 main points including, in particular, a series of proposals such as[9]: "...Work towards a National Demonstration for Life, in defence of our territories; demand that the results of the pre-legislative consultation on the Water Law should be binding; reject the high cost of domestic gas, the criminalisation of the social struggle, political persecution, the Free Trade Treaty with the European Union and the expansion of extractivism".[10]

CONAIE also called for "...political independence from successive governments to be maintained, alliances to be built with likeminded social organisations and movements working for national and international social transformation" and "policies aimed at changing the productive matrix to be rejected, as they exacerbate the plundering of the ancestral knowledge of the peoples and nationalities and benefit transnational corporations and national and international power groups".[11]

On the basis of these broad outlines, the indigenous groups opposed to the government, headed by Herrera and the current mestizo president of the Kichwa Confederation, Ecuarunari, Carlos Pérez Guartambel, continued their actions.

In July, they headed the so-called "March for Water" in opposition to the so-called Law on Water Resources. Pérez Guartambel stated: "We have 10 mandates from the Resistance Front not only to defend water but also the right to education, and to reject the removal of the gas subsidy, among other things".[12]

With regard to water, Pérez Guartambel stated: "Prior consultations must comply with the international principles or standards set out in international law. In this case, the pre-legislative consultation process on the Water Law has not been completed and, what is worse, a number of defects have occurred in the process (...) We have proposals to make in this regard: firstly, we call for the plateaux and water sources to remain free from mining concessions; secondly, we want access to water to be deprivatised. Just 1% of private properties hold 64% of the total volume of water. Thirdly, we ask that the indigenous peoples are able to participate with both voice and vote in the proposed Plurinational Water Council and, finally, we demand that the community water systems should not be transferred into the hands of the autonomous decentralised governments." [13]

In October, Pérez Guartambel travelled to Washington to attend a hearing called by the IACHR to denounce "the concrete violation of collective rights and of nature; the restrictions on the administration of indigenous justice; the possible annihilation of the social organisations through Decree 16, and the lack of prior consultation for oil exploitation in Blocks 31 and 43 of the Yasuní National Park". [14]

In November, CONAIE's leadership decided to join the protests of the opposition unions, headed by the Unitarian Workers Front (*Frente Unitario de Trabajadores*), who are opposed to the government's proposed reforms of the Labour Code and are also rejecting a "Water Law that has neither deprivatised nor decentralised water, and removes power from the community systems with regard to irrigation and drinking. Moreover, according to Herrera, "The Land Law being debated in the Assembly protects companies and large-scale property." [15]

However, other organisations and factions close to the government, such as the National Confederation of Peasant, Indigenous and Black Organisations (*Confederación Nacional de Organizaciones Campesinas, Indígenas y Negras / Fenocin*) decided to reject the destabilising attempts of the "conservative opposition", as Santos Villamar, president of the organisation, explains: "...some organisations are only looking after their own interests and not those of the community. There is a serious need to raise awareness of the laws on territories and the indigenous sector. There is now a serious and responsible government that has improved issues such as education, health and road construction in the Amazon. Nonetheless, it is indebted to the agricultural sector and had made no investment in rural areas." [16]

Mining and violence in the Shuar territory of the Condor Mountain range

Finally, on 3 December, in an obscure incident in the south-east of the Amazon, where a number of mining projects are operating, some motorcyclists found the body of José Isidro Tendetza, a 47-year-old Shuar and representative of the

Yanua community, in Zamora Chinchipe. He had been missing since 28 November, when he left his home for a meeting with another leader and friend, Domingo Ankuash, one of the historic leaders of the Shuar nation. The intention was to make a complaint against the Ecuacorriente mining company to the Court for Rights to Nature at the Peoples' Summit in Lima on 5 December.[17]

The death of the leader took place in a context of growing violence due to the presence of mining in the area, which has already resulted in the deaths of three Shuar leaders in defence of their territories.   ◯

Notes and references

1   The five Waorani men were arrested in Yarentaro commune, Coca, after taking a young girl from the people into custody. In relation to this precise point, in the middle of January, the Inter-American Commission on Human Rights (IACHR) called on the Ecuadorian state to protect the integrity of two Taromenane girls who were separated during the incidents. One was apparently being held by a state body, the other under the control of the community. "The State must take immediate precautionary measures to protect the right to life, physical, moral, cultural integrity, family and identity of the two Taromenane sisters, separated from their community following an apparent confrontation," indicated the IACHR's press release (see: "CIDH exige a Ecuador proteger Niñas Taromenane separadas de su Comunidad" 28.01.2014. Available at http://servindi.org/actualidad/100056).

2   "Si Labaka hubiese ingresado ahora a territorio taromenane sería acusado de etnocidio", *El Comercio* 31.03.2014.

3   Letter to Dr. Patricio Pazmiño Freire, president of the Constitutional Court of Ecuador, Quito 10.01.2014 Available at: http://i.hoy.ec/wp-content/img/Carta%20a%20Patricio%20Pazmi%-C3%B1o,%20Presidente%20de%20la%20Corte%20Constitucional.pdf

4   Constitutional Court of Ecuador. Judgment No. 004-14-SCN-CC. Case No.0072 of 6 August 2014. Available at: http://www.corteconstitucional.gob.ec/images/stories/pdfs/Sentencias/0072-14-CN.pdf

5   Cf. Vicariato Apostólico de Aguarico: "Huaoranis amenazan por labor petrolera y juicio por terrorismo", por José Olmos, Tigüino, Pastaza, 20.01.13. Available at: http://www.vicariatoaguarico.org/index.php/noticias/ecuador/68-huaoranis-amenazan-por-labor-petrolera-y-juicio-por-terrorismo

6   Cf. *El Telégrafo*, "Asesinato de dos obreros motiva reunión de Waoranis". 08.04.2014. Available at: http://www.telegrafo.com.ec/noticias/informacion-general/item/asesinato-de-dos-obreros-motiva-reunion-de-waoranis.html

7   Yasunidos website: http://sitio.yasunidos.org/es/prensa/blog/80-carta-de-yasunidos-para-la-cidh-30-de-mayo-2014.html

8   *El Comercio*, "CNE descartó pedido de Yasunidos para Consulta Popular", 08.05.2014. Available at: http://www.elcomercio.com.ec/actualidad/politica/cne-descarto-pedido-de-yasunidos.html Also in: *El Telégrafo*, "Yasunidos no alcanza firmas para consulta popular sobre Yasuní". 07.05.2014.   At: http://www.telegrafo.com.ec/politica/item/yasunidos-no-alcanza-firmas-para-consulta-popular-sobre-yasuni.html

9   "Ecuador. El Supremo Congreso de la CONAIE aprueba las 13 resoluciones las cuales serán cumplidas por el nuevo consejo de gobierno", *Kaos en la Red*. At: http://2014.kaosenlared.net/america-latina-sp-1870577476/al2/ecuador/88063-ecuador-el-supremo-congreso-de-la-conaie-aprueba-las-13-resoluciones-las-cuales-ser%C3%A1n-cumplidas-por-el-nuevo-consejo-de-gobierno
10   Resolutions V Congress CONAIE 18.05.2014 http://ecuador.indymedia.org/es/2014/05/41780.shtml
11   Resolutions V Congress CONAIE 18.05.2014 http://ecuador.indymedia.org/es/2014/05/41780.shtml
12   *El Universo*, "Marcha Indígena contra la Ley del Agua llegó a Quito", 1.07.2014. At: http://www.eluniverso.com/noticias/2014/07/01/nota/3176921/marcha-indigena-contra-ley-agua-llego-quito
13   Ley de Recursos Hídricos: Ecuarunari advierte con movilizaciones. In *Ecuadorinmediato.com* 05.06.2014. At http://www.ecuadorinmediato.com/index.php?module=Noticias&func=news_user_view&id=2818763888&umt=ley_de_recursos_heddricos3a_ecuarunari_advierte_con_movilizaciones
14   Pérez Guartambel, "Justicia Ecuatoriana Vergüenza causa", in *Ecuarunari*, 28.10.2014, http://www.ecuarunari.org.ec/index.php/ecuachaski/206-justicia-ecuatoriana-vergueenza-causa .
15   *Ecuador en Vivo*. 11.11.2014. In http://www.ecuadorenvivo.com/politica/24-politica/23147-organizaciones-sociales-llaman-a-la-unidad-y-movilizacion-del-pueblo-movilizacion-el-19-de-noviembre-a-nivel-nacional.html#.VOZHXvmG9ps
16   Santos Villamar, president of FENOCIN in *Notimundo*. http://www.notimundo.com.ec/articulo/11791/la_relacion_entre_el_gobierno_y_los_indigenas%2C_ocho_anos_despues
17   Plan V, ¿Quién mató a José Tendetza? 04.12.2014 Available at: http://www.planv.com.ec/historias/sociedad/quien-mato-jose-tendetza

Pablo Ortiz-T. *Doctor of Latin American Cultural Studies,. MSc in Political Science. Lecturer at the UPS Salesian Polytechnic University –Girón Campus, Quito. Post-graduate Unit. Contact: mushukster@gmail.com*

PERU

The Census of Indigenous Communities, carried out in 1,786 Amazonian communities during 2007, gathered information on 51 of the 60 ethnic groups existing in the forests. Nine of them were not recorded "because some ethnic groups no longer form communities, having been absorbed into other peoples; in addition, there are ethnic groups which, given their situation of isolation, are very difficult to reach".[1] An Amazonian indigenous population of 332,975 inhabitants was recorded, mostly belonging to the Asháninka (26.6%) and Awajún (16.6%) peoples. 47.5 % of the indigenous population is under 15 years of age, and 46.5% has no health insurance. 19.4% stated that they were unable to read or write but, in the case of women, this rose to 28.1%, out of a population in which only 47.3% of those over 15 have received any kind of primary education. In addition, the Census noted that 3,360,331 people spoke the Quechua language and 443,248 the Aymara,[2] indigenous languages predominant in the coastal-Andes region of Peru. Peru has ratified ILO Convention 169 on Indigenous and Tribal Peoples and voted in favour of the UN Declaration on the Rights of Indigenous Peoples.

The regional and local elections

The regional and local elections of 5 October set the annual agenda and the electoral campaigns were riddled with social and environmental conflict. Most noteworthy was the case of Cajamarca where Gregorio Santos, leader of the Movement for Social Affirmation (*Movimiento de Afirmación Social* / MAS) was re-elected at the first round with 44.27% of the vote, despite being on remand in prison for the duration of the campaign. The population of Cajamarca has been bitterly divided over the Conga mining megaproject and analysts put his triumph down to the rural vote, which supported his opposition to this project.

In contrast to Cajamarca, where opposition to mining won the day, Luis Ot-suja Salazar, President of the Madre de Dios Mining Federation (*Federación Min-era de Madre de Dios*) triumphed in the Amazonian region of Madre de Dios. According to reports, this professional association not only includes miners wish-ing to be involved in the formalisation process commenced by the government but also illegal miners working with banned machinery and in areas of high environ-mental impact. Both informal and illegal forms of mining will undoubtedly continue to wreak havoc as they expand across the country. In Madre de Dios alone, 40,000 hectares of forest have been destroyed by illegal mining.

The controversial Tía María mining project is located in Arequipa region. This is a project which the Southern Cooper company has, since 2010, been attempt-ing to implement with an investment of USD 1,400 million. The young newly-elected regional president, Yamila Osorio, has expressed an interest in establish-ing a dialogue between the Ministry of Energy and Mines and the local population with regard to this project, which has been rejected by sectors of the population.

In Puno, Juan Luque Mamani, regional president elect, has stated his support for the Santa Ana mining project, situated on the border with Bolivia, despite the fact that opposition to this project resulted in the so-called "Aymarazo", a serious social conflict that paralysed the initiative in 2011 at the end of Alan García's term in office. Luque has also given his backing to the formalisation of artisanal mining, an activity that has resulted in the deaths of more than 50,000 head of cattle in Puno over the last two years.

The southern region of Tacna also appears, like other regions, to be greatly affected by large-scale mining due to Southern Cooper's licence to use 1,950 li-tres of water per second in the Tacna region, despite the region's water capacity being only 400 litres per second, thus seriously exacerbating the water shortage. The new regional president, Omar Jiménez, is not standing firm in defending the interests of the local population and says it is the central government's responsi-bility for having drafted the contract signed with the company.

Pollution without compensation

One of the most serious ways in which this affects the lives and environment of indigenous communities is through the pollution of four Amazonian basins: the Tigre, Corrientes, Pastaza and Marañón. The year came and went without the

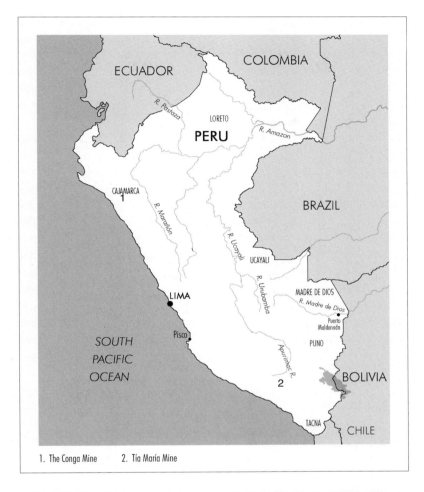

1. The Conga Mine   2. Tía María Mine

state making any progress in cleaning up and compensating the affected populations. The *apus* or traditional chiefs of the four basins' representative indigenous
federations[3] actively denounced the state's failure to address their most pressing
demands, such as the formation of an emergency fund and the appointment of a
public body responsible for resolving urgent issues and preventing, for example,
the population from continuing to ingest water contaminated with heavy metals
and petroleum by-products.

A report by the Environmental Oversight and Evaluation Body (*Organismo de Evaluación y Fiscalización Ambiental* / OEFA) dated 20 October 2014 confirmed the lamentable environmental performance of the company Pluspetrol, which is responsible for the cumulative impact of more than 40 years of oil activity in the four basins. Pluspetrol is accused of failing to clean up the environmental damage left by its predecessor and for spills that have occurred since it commenced its activities more than a decade ago.

The basins are affected by oil concessions 1AB and 8X, this latter situated within the Pacaya Samiria National Park. The concession contract for Plot 1AB, the largest in the country, expires in 2015 and the government intends to expand or resize it to become Plot 192, without having first addressed the request for remediation, titling, indemnity and compensation made as prior conditions by the affected populations.[4] James Anaya, former UN Special Rapporteur on the rights of indigenous peoples, considered these conditions to be "fair and conducive to a productive consultation process" following his visit to the zone. During the global Climate Change Summit (COP 20), held in Lima in December, two UN rapporteurs - Victoria Tauli-Corpuz, Special Rapporteur on the rights of indigenous peoples and Baskut Tuncak, Special Rapporteur on hazardous substances, jointly signed a communiqué urging Peru to meet its obligation to clean up the contamination and force companies to assume their responsibilities with regard to human rights before granting further concessions and making a dreadful situation worse.[5]

Oil spill in Cuninico

Environmental irresponsibility is not the sole preserve of the private sector. In June the state company, Petroperú, suffered a spillage from its oil pipeline in Cuninico, Urarinas district, Loreto region, directly affecting five communities of the Kukama people. The situation was exacerbated by the use of local inhabitants – some of them children – to clear up the oil, without providing either appropriate clothing or equipment, and without informing them of the risks to their health. By the end of the year, only Cuninico community itself had received water and food.[6] The Cocama Association for Development and Conservation San Pablo de Tipishca (*Asociación Cocama de Desarrollo y Conservación San Pablo de Tipishca* / Acodescopat) announced in January 2015 that it would be filing a lawsuit against Petroperú to obtain reparations for those affected. Juan Carlos Ruiz Molleda, a lawyer from the Legal Defence Institute (*Instituto de Defensa Legal* / IDL), states that fishing, the main subsistence activity of the Kukama people, has been affected by the spill and that the government has to compensate and indemnify those affected. The damaged pipeline is more than 40 years old and the state has not yet made it safe.

Murder in Alto Tamaya-Saweto and illegal felling

On 1 September, four Ashéninka leaders from Alto Tamaya-Saweto community in Ucayali region, were murdered by alleged illegal loggers in an area bordering Brazil. They were: Edwin Chota, head of the community, and leaders Jorge Ríos, Leoncio Quinticima and Francisco Pinedo. According to David Salisbury, a geographer and lecturer at the University of Richmond, Virginia, USA, who has advised the community for more than 10 years, Chota had sent more than 100 letters to Peruvian and Brazilian institutions requesting protection and that their demands be addressed. The murders gained significant national and international coverage. The New York Times reminded the Peruvian government – shortly before the start of the UN Climate Summit in Lima in December (COP 20) – that the problem of illegal felling and the serious threats to defenders of the forest would not be resolved by mere statements alone.

The Environmental Investigation Agency (EIA) published an important piece of research in 2012 describing the impunity enjoyed by the illegal felling mafia in Peru.[7] Alongside this, a World Bank report maintained that trees felled in the Peruvian Amazon were being trafficked and laundered using methods similar to those used by arms and drugs traffickers, resulting in high-level corruption. It concluded that illegal felling is a form of international organised crime that is undermining the rule of law and that it represents a significant threat since it encourages the development of criminal groups.[8] It stated that up to 80% of the timber exported from Peru, primarily to China and other Asian markets, is illegal and, according to the Loreto regional government, Peru loses USD 250 million every year through illegal felling. Fabiola Muñoz, director of the National Forestry Service (*Servicio Nacional Forestal* - SERFOR), under the Ministry of Agriculture and Irrigation, has stated that drug trafficking corridors are also operating in zones where illegal felling is known to be taking place, and that areas there are also being sown with coca. The Alto Tamaya-Saweto community itself has complained that drugs traffickers are using illegally felled timber to conceal the drugs trade.[9]

Ollanta Humala's government responded to the situation by creating a High Commissioner for illegal felling, reporting to the Presidency of the Council of Ministers. A retired police general, César Fourment Paredes, was appointed to the post despite having no experience in the extraction and marketing of timber, and despite the fact that he used to work closely with senior police chiefs linked to the sinister Vladimiro Montesinos, former security advisor to ex-president - and now prison inmate - Alberto Fujimori (1990-2000).

At the end of the year, the bombastic promises of the government with regard to the Saweto case remained empty words. The search for the body of Jorge Ríos was halted for lack of funds with which to conduct a specialised search, the communal titling of Saweto is still pending, the investigations into the perpetrators of the crime are at a standstill and the widows and children of the murdered leaders are unable to return to their community for fear of reprisals and a lack of security.

Cajamarca: the unenforced precautionary measure

Following a petition filed by the Unity Pact (*Pacto de Unidad*) on 5 May, the Inter-American Commission on Human Rights (IACHR) granted a precautionary measure in favour of 46 male and female leaders from the communities and peasant patrols of Cajamarca, the Chauper family, the patrolman Luis Mayta and the indigenous communicator César Estrada Chuquilín. The IACHR confirmed the three essential conditions: threat to the life and personal integrity of the beneficiaries in a serious, urgent and irreparable manner. This situation came about as a consequence of their opposition to the Conga mining project. The Peruvian state has failed to enforce the three provisions specified by the IACHR: adopt the measures necessary to guarantee the life and integrity of the beneficiaries; reach agreement with these latter regarding measures to be taken; and provide information on actions aimed at investigating the events that gave rise to the precautionary measure in order to "avoid its repetition". The Supranational Public Prosecutor of the Ministry of Justice and Human Rights[10] argued that it lacked the regulations, staff and funds to deal with the requests for protection made by the beneficiaries, and that a law was needed to regulate compliance with the IACHR's precautionary measures. This was despite the fact that the Vienna Convention on the Law of Treaties provides that the state cannot use deficiencies in its domestic legislation as a pretext for failing to comply with its international obligations, as pointed out by the International Law and Society Institute (*Instituto Internacional Derecho y Sociedad* / IIDS), an association that is advising the beneficiaries.

The indigenous peoples and the Peoples' Summit

The Conference of the Parties to the UN Framework Convention on Climate Change (COP 20), held from 1 to12 December in Lima, resulted in civil society's organisation of the Peoples' Summit on Climate Change as a parallel event. This summit was organised by a Political Committee made up of 13 national organisations, six of them members of the Unity Pact of Indigenous Organisations of Peru (*Pacto de Unidad de Organizaciones Indígenas del Perú*). The Peoples' Summit promoted the Global March of Peoples in Defence of Mother Earth on 10 December, together with social, union, youth and environmental organisations, and civil society in general.

The Unity Pact held its III National Meeting: "Territory, Climate Change and the Self-Determination of Indigenous Peoples" on 8 and 9 December against the backdrop of the Peoples' Summit and, in the presence of nearly 500 delegates, reaffirmed their identity as native peoples with a right to self-determination. They also reaffirmed their aim of achieving the decolonisation of relations between indigenous peoples, the state and society, moving towards their reconstitution and strengthening as native peoples and fighting for a Plurinational Constitution in which all native peoples can participate as constituent members of a plurinational state that recognises the pre-existence of indigenous peoples and their integral ancestral territory.

The Unity Pact has proposed a National Community Climate Change Adaptation Programme (PRONACC) as an appropriate and realistic alternative for the whole country and, in particular, vulnerable populations. This seeks to make the native communities and peoples the true protagonists of and main state allies in the struggle against climate change. The proposal is the result of proven ecosystemic and social inter-relationships between the high Andean and Amazonian zones, making it necessary to prioritise adaptation measures that address vulnerable populations in an integral manner. PRONACC has two main components:

territorial security and food sovereignty. Territorial security includes the titling and ownership of ancestral lands. Food sovereignty is subdivided into three areas: agricultural and livestock production, fishing and water. It also proposes four basic focal points: law, gender, interculturality and governance.[11]

For its part, the Inter-ethnic Association for the Development of the Peruvian Forest (*Asociación Interétnica de Desarrollo de la Selva Peruana* - AIDESEP) – outside of the Unity Pact – signed an agreement with the Ministry of Environment (MINAM) to participate in COP 20 through the Indigenous Pavilion and the *maloca* or traditional hut established by the government. AIDESEP and COICA distributed an Amazonian proposal focused on defending the collective rights of indigenous communities and titling indigenous territories. One area of its lobbying involves challenging "extractivist developmentalism" as a strategic driver of deforestation and degradation, highlighting the "Indigenous Full Life Plans" (*Planes de Vida Plena Indígena*) as effective alternatives for mitigation, adaptation and resilience in the face of the climate crisis, and Indigenous REDD+, a variant of the Reducing Emissions from Deforestation and Forest Degradation (REDD+) mechanism that is endeavouring to go beyond carbon and the market to take into account indigenous world visions, rights and proposals.[12]

The pending climate agenda

COP 20 led to and fostered the production of a national climate agenda and one of the outstanding issues in this regard is the discussion and approval of a mutually-agreed and transparent Framework Law on Climate Change. The year came to an end with the publication of a preliminary report by the Commission for Andean, Amazonian and Afro-Peruvian Peoples, Environment and Ecology of the Congress of the Republic (CPAAAEA), which was commented on by some Congressmen/women while awaiting the drafting of a "consensual" version. In addition, although the government presented an updated version of the National Strategy on Climate Change, this was challenged due to its lack of indicators, deadlines, procedures and sources of funding. The government tried to submit a new version during 2014 but the year ended without a strategy having been validated by civil society and formally approved.

Restricting prior consultation

In February, by means of Vice-ministerial Resolution 004-2014-VMI-MC, the Ministry of Culture approved "Guidelines establishing instruments for gathering social information and setting criteria for their application in the context of identifying indigenous and native peoples".[13] These guidelines take lifestyle and spiritual and historic links to the territory they traditionally occupy as an objective criterion for identifying indigenous peoples, and add to this other previously established objective criteria of a "concurrent and complementary" nature, such as indigenous and native language and "communal lands recognised by state bodies".[14] As noted in the report of the Working Group on Indigenous Peoples of the National Coordinating Body of Human Rights (*Coordinadora Nacional de Derechos Humanos*), the state continues to apply a narrow interpretation in its recognition of indigenous peoples, and this diminishes the right to consultation, particularly in the case of the native communities and peoples of the Peruvian coast and Andes. This can be seen in the fact that no consultation process has been conducted on the mining activity being developed primarily in the Andean area. The stated guidelines were approved without any consultation of the indigenous peoples. This is a serious matter if one considers that, in 2014, no progress was made in terms of creating public institutions for indigenous peoples that might provide channels and procedures to ensure their participation in the decision-making processes that affect them.

Threat to the legal security of indigenous territories

One of the state's great historic debts lies in the lack of progress that has been made in the titling of peasant and native communities in order to strengthen their rights to own and possess the lands they traditionally occupy. In June, the Ombudsman published a report: "*Análisis de la política pública sobre reconocimiento y titulación de las comunidades campesinas y nativas*"[15] (Analysis of Public Policy on Recognition and Titling of Peasant and Native Community Lands) in which it warns of a lack of budget with which to implement titling processes and the absence of guidelines with which to resolve controversies arising from the superimposition of rights. Adding fuel to the fire, the following month the government expedited Law 30230, known as the Law on Environmental Policies because it comprises different measures (fiscal, environmental, etc.) The regulation was initially rejected because it weakened OEFA's powers of environmental evaluation and supervision. However, as people began to analyse its different articles, its real threat became clear. The Safe Territories Collective for Peru's Communities (*Colectivo Territorios Seguros para las Comunidades del Perú*), the Platform for Territorial Planning (*Plataforma de Ordenamiento Territorial*), the Muqui Network (*Red Muqui*) and the Responsible Land Governance Platform (*Plataforma Gobernanza Responsable de la Tierra*) all denounced the fact that it was an attack on the peasant and native communities' right to private property and on the country's territorial organisation and because it "places more than 8,000 peasant and indigenous communities in a vulnerable situation".

Section III of this law allows the state, by means of "special procedures", to hand land over to investment projects, wherever and in whatever quantity they require, regardless of the owners' property rights. The organisations also warned that all lands, whether private or state, and whether or not supported by regularised titles or certificates of ownership, would be subject to special procedures, with no exception whatsoever. The Unity Pact denounced the fact that Law 30240 distorts the aim of regularisation by granting priority ownership to business interests over and above the ancestral rights of the native peoples. The regulation extends the area affected to the benefit of investment interests and leaves it at the discretion of the state and private companies to identify and decide what areas or plots are needed for the implementation of their projects and which therefore need to be "regularised".

In addition, the indigenous organisations of the Unity Pact and AIDESEP have stated their concern that the Inter-American Development Bank's Titling and Registration of Lands Project (PTRT- Phase 3), to be implemented from 2015 on, will focus on individual ownership rather than communal titling, disappointing the communities yet again. According to information gathered from the project, which is the responsibility of the Department for Regularisation of Agricultural Property and Rural Cadastre of the Ministry of Agriculture and Irrigation (MINAGRI), the aim is to formalise 441,000 individual plots and only 190 Amazonian indigenous communities when, according to AIDESEP, the regularisation of some 20 million hectares of land for 1,124 Amazonian communities is pending. Of these, 294 are demanding their recognition, 613 their titling and 262 their expansion. According to the Institute of the Common Good (*Instituto del Bien Común* - IBC) data from the Ministry of Housing suggests that there are some 934 native communities on the coast and in the Andes awaiting titling.

Indigenous peoples in isolation and initial contact

There was a continued failure to protect the indigenous peoples in voluntary isolation and initial contact throughout 2014, despite sightings reported primarily in Madre de Dios. As of September, at least four sightings had been recorded, according to the Vice-Minister for Interculturality, Patricia Balbuena. The most critical event occurred in December when a group of around 200 indigenous Mascho Piro entered the community of Monte Salvado, Tambopata province, in Madre de Dios. The state agency, Perupetro, interested in submitting a tender for Plot 187 in this region, had denied the existence of peoples in isolation in this area. Hydrocarbon activity is not the only danger for these peoples, however. In addition to reports of package holidays offered by some tourist agencies that include contact with peoples in isolation in areas such as Yanayacu, in the Upper Madre de Dios, Manu province, the anthropologist Beatriz Huertas has warned of the presence of drug trafficking, something very few people are willing to talk about.

This lack of protection is a continuing state of affairs given that, at the start of 2014, the Vice-Ministry of Interculturality considered that the observations regarding the extension of Plot 88 in Camisea within the Kugapakori, Nahua, Nanti and Others Territorial Reserve (RTKNN) had been addressed, despite a lack of up-to-date and relevant information on the health situation of vulnerable populations in the area of impact. Such is the case of the important Analysis of Intercultural Health (ASIS) of the Nanti People of Alto Camisea, produced in 2013 but which was only published in November 2014 due to difficulties in its production. According to the association Law, Environment and Natural Resources (*Derecho, Ambiente y Recursos Naturales* / DAR), inputs of this kind should be provided with all necessary support to ensure their publication and presentation before any activity is approved within the RTKNN.

Juan Carlos Ruiz Molleda has suggested that the four-stage strategy posited is really an intention to wind up the RTKNN in order to expand extractive activities in Plot 88. The four-stage strategy consists of: providing identity documents and promoting their self-recognition as Matsigenka; recruiting linked indigenous organisations; registering and titling the communities in the area of the reserve;

and, finally, incorporating the peoples in isolation into focused poverty reduction programmes. Ruiz Molleda believes this is the intention lying "behind a set of apparently isolated measures", as set out in *"La batalla por los Nanti. Intereses y discursos superpuestos a favor de la extinción de la Reserva Territorial Kugapakori Nahua Nanti y otros"* (The battle for the Nanti. Superimposed interests and rhetoric in favour of extinguishing the Kugapakori Nahua Nanti and Others Territorial Reserve), published by Perú Equidad and IWGIA.[16]

In conclusion, a concern to prioritise extractive activities over and above defending the lives of peoples in isolation explains the state's lack of interest in implementing the framework of protection contained in Law No 28736. The five existing territorial reserves do not have Protection Plans but President Ollanta and some of his ministers have been happy to project a social welfare image by personally delivering plastic cradles and nappies to the Nanti of Camisea, where chronic malnutrition affects 67.3% of children under five, five times the national average; acute malnutrition is double the national average.   ○

Notes and references

1   National Institute of Statistics and information (INEI), 2009: Definitive results on indigenous communities. National Census 2007: XI on Population and VI on Housing, Lima, January 2009, p. 7
2   Ibid, Book 1, p. 563.
3   The indigenous federations are: the *Asociación Cocama de Desarrollo y Conservación San Pablo de Tipishca* (ACODECOSPAT) of the Marañón River basin, the *Federación de Comunidades Nativas del Corrientes* (FECONACO), the *Federación de Comunidades Nativas del Alto Tigre* (FECONAT) and the *Federación Indígena Quechua del Pastaza* (FEDIQUEP). These four federations form the *Pueblos Indígenas Amazónicos Unidos en defensa de sus Territorios* (PUINAMUDT) platform and are conducting active monitoring and reporting of oil impacts: http://observatoriopetrolero.org/
4   One of Perupetro's first decisions in 2015 was to extend, without calls for tenders, the seven oil concessions, including Plot 192 (ex-1AB). See: La República: http://www.larepublica.pe/04-01-2015/perupetro-prorroga-contratos-petroleros-sin-licitacion
5   See: http://www.un.org/spanish/News/story.asp?NewsID=31240#.VK0x-XsYl7Y y http://unsr.vtaulicorpuz.org/site/index.php/es/declaraciones-comunicados/55-peru-oil-project
6   See: El drama de los menores del petróleo, at: http://servindi.org/actualidad/119613
7   EIA: "The Laundering Machine. How Fraud and Corruption in Peru's Concession System are destroying the future of its forests", in:
    http://launderingmachine.files.wordpress.com/2012/04/english_report_eia_final2.pdf
8   See note on Servindi: http://servindi.org/actualidad/96116
9   See Noticias Aliadas: http://www.noticiasaliadas.org/articles.asp?art=7075
10 *"La Procuraduría Supranacional del Ministerio de Justicia y Derechos Humanos"*

11 See: http://pactodeunidadperu.org/?p=7766
12 See Redd+ más allá del carbono y del mercado: Integralidad del Redd+ Indígena Amazónico: http://www.aidesep.org.pe/redd-mas-alla-del-carbono-y-del-mercado-integralidad-del-redd-indi-gena-amazonico/ and http://servindi.org/actualidad/104916
13 The regulation can be found at: http://transparencia.cultura.gob.pe/sites/default/files/transparen-cia/2014/02/resoluciones-del-viceministerio-de-interculturalidad/rvmi004-aprobarladirecti-va001-2014.pdf
14 See http://bdpi.cultura.gob.pe/identificacion-de-pueblos-indigenas 7 January 2015.
15 The report can be found at: http://www.defensoria.gob.pe/Downloads/descarga/Informe-002-2014-DP-AMASPPI-PPI.pdf
16 The publication can be found at: http://www.iwgia.org/publications/search-pubs?publication_id=685

Jorge Agurto is a journalist and social communicator. He is president of the Intercultural Communication Services association, Servindi.
Website: www.servindi.org - E-mail: jorgeagurto@gmail.com

BOLIVIA

According to the most recent data from the 2012 National Census, 2.8 million people over the age of 15 - 41% of the total population – are of indigenous origin. Of the 36 recognised peoples, the Quechua and the Aymara are most prevalent in the western Andes while the Chiquitano, Guaraní and Moxeño are the most numerous of the 34 peoples living in the lowlands, in the east of the country. To date, almost 20 million hectares of land have been consolidated as communal property under the concept of Community Lands of Origin (*Tierras Comunitarias de Origen* / TCO). With the approval of Decree No. 727/10, the TCOs changed their name constitutionally to Peasant Native Indigenous Territory (*Territorio Indígena Originario Campesino* / TIOC). Bolivia has been a signatory to ILO Convention 169 since 1991. The UN Declaration on the Rights of Indigenous Peoples was approved, with Law 3760, on 7 November 2007. With the entry into force of the new Constitution, Bolivia became a Plurinational State.

Evo Morales president for third consecutive term

Elections were held on 5 October for the presidency and vice-presidency along with a complete renewal of both chambers of the Plurinational Legislative Assembly. President Evo Morales and his vice-president, Álvaro García Linera, were re-elected with an overwhelming majority of the vote, 61.36%,[1] for their Movement to Socialism (MAS) party. In second place came the cement tycoon, Samuel Doria Medina, with 24.23%, representing the forces of the centre-right grouped within Democratic Unity. Former president Jorge Quiroga Ramírez[2] (Christian Democrat Party) received 9.04%. The former mayor of La Paz, Juan del Granado, at one time thought the likely successor to Evo Morales in the context of a deepening of the process of change and democratic renewal, gained

only 2.71%, resulting in a loss of the legal identity of his party (Movement without Fear).[3]

The indigenous organisations, divided since 2012, chose to include their representatives on the list of the different political parties as they could not agree on a coordinated indigenous response, as had been the case for the general elections of 2009 and the regional elections of 2010. This time, the "organic" Confederation of Indigenous Peoples of Bolivia (*Confederación de Pueblos Indígenas de Bolivia* / CIDOB)[4] supported the alliance between the Green Party of Bolivia (PVB) and the Indigenous Freedom Movement-TIPNIC (MIL-TIPNIS). Candidates were elected onto these lists by regional and local organisations that had separated from the "pro-government" CIDOB, linked to the MAS. The Green Party's presidential candidate was Fernando Vargas Mosúa, a leader from the TIPNIS regional office and driving force behind the previous marches in defence of territory and against construction of the Villa Tunari-San Ignacio de Mojos highway.[5]

Although the PVB won only 2.65% of the vote, this was an impressive performance given that it had virtually no resources with which to promote its innovative environmentalist and rights-based agenda. The Green Party secured one deputy by virtue of the percentage of the vote it won in Oruro department but, due to the controversial application of the Electoral System Law, this was subsequently allocated to the majority party (the MAS) as the Greens did not gain the minimum 3% nationally to retain their legal identity.

Indigenous peoples hold seven seats in the Plurinational Legislative Assembly (bicameral congress) elected by individual and secret ballot via the political parties in special departmental constituencies.[6] The MAS won six of these seven special seats, with one going to Democratic Unity in Oruro department. There are a number of reasons why the other constituencies do not have indigenous representatives in the chambers: on the one hand, the indigenous movement's clashes with the government and the MAS have led to ebbs and flows that have left it in a marginal place on its lists of candidates. There was a clear absence from the MAS lists not only of indigenous candidates but also of the social sectors in general, particularly peasants, as the party has decided to make space for "guests" from the middle classes, and even former activists from right-leaning parties, due to the good relationship the national government is fomenting with the business world and the traditional landowning sector.

The case of indigenous judge, Gualberto Cusi

One of the most serious political incidents to occur in the country was the case of Gualberto Cusi Mamani, an indigenous judge in the Plurinational Constitutional Court, elected in 2011 with 15.7% of the vote. He was the candidate that received the most popular support for this position. Cusi began to annoy the national government with public statements revealing the pressure and government interference being suffered by the Court with the aim of influencing certain politically-sensitive cases. One of the most serious cases in this regard was the appeal for unconstitutionality lodged by two deputies from Movement without Fear and by indigenous leaders against Law 222/12 on Prior Consultation in TIPNIS. It was through this law that the government was attempting to impose the construction of a highway through the indigenous territory, despite opposition from the communities living there. Judgment No. 300/12, adopted by three judges, proposed a form of prior consultation that was at odds with current international standards and from which Judge Cusi therefore dissented. In the days that followed, he denounced government interference in the wording of the judgment, drawing criticism and calls for his resignation from a large number of pro-government legislators and ministers.

Cusi and two other Court judges (out of a total of seven) were subsequently prosecuted after admitting an appeal for unconstitutionality lodged by two opposition deputies against the Law of Public Office, and then suspending the application of this law. It had been drafted by the executive and challenged by the opposition and so its suspension created great controversy within the government ranks. The judges involved in hearing the appeal were subsequently suspended and impeachment proceedings heard in the Senate. This was made possible by controversial Law 044/10, one of the elements of which allows the Senate to hear and rule on cases, including the passing of prison sentences.

Judge Cusi was suffering from ill health and this temporarily prevented him from attending the trial, which led to great speculation that the lawyer was faking some illness to avoid the case being made against him and his two colleagues. The judge claimed that his temporary suspension from post was preventing him from continuing his treatment because he was no longer covered by social security.

When a representative of the Office of the UN High Commissioner for Human Rights in La Paz stated that the case was inadmissible because a legislative body could not lawfully send senior state officials to prison, the section of Law 044/10 that gave the Senate this power was revoked in record time, with a new provision being incorporated through Law 365/14 to include the possibility of bringing the trial to a conclusion with the resignation of the defendants. The judges did not resign, however, as had been hoped by the pro-government bloc.

Faced with the impossibility of physically keeping Judge Gualberto Cusi in the dock and, apparently, in an attempt to discredit him, he was publicly ordered to state what kind of illness he was suffering from. Then, on 22 December, the Minister of Health, Dr. Juan Carlos Calvimontes, publicly announced that the lawyer was suffering from HIV/AIDS and had known this for two years. This led to a public outcry because Article 2d of Law 3729/07[7] expressly sets out a *principle of confidentiality* for anyone living with the illness[8] in order to protect their dignity and prevent them from suffering any social discrimination.[9] Moreover, Article 9 of the same Law establishes a *right to secrecy,* which means preserving the identity and status of people living with HIV/AIDS, who "shall not be subjected to publicity in the written or televisual media without their express consent". The publication of this information caused the judge to slide into a serious depression because, according to him, his family were not aware of his status. Amid general surprise, the Minister next day clarified that the announcement of Cusi's illness was done to "preserve the health of those around him, for fear of contagion",[10] only further deepening the vulnerable status of the Court, quite apart from demonstrating a clear lack of knowledge of the most fundamental elements of medical ethics. President Evo Morales publicly apologised for his colleague's outburst but refused to remove him from office. In the face of the scandal caused by this violation of his rights as an indigenous judge and an HIV/AIDS sufferer, the government (through its representatives in the Legislative Assembly) instructed the temporary suspension of the case but did not reinstate Judge Cusi to his post.

Mining law

On 28 May, President Evo Morales enacted new Law 535/14 on Mining and Metallurgy to replace the Mining Code (Law 1,777/97 of 17 March) adopted by then President Gonzalo Sánchez de Lozada.[11] This latter law was suspected of favouring this president's interests as he was heavily involved in mining operations in the country. Law 535/14 was rejected by the indigenous organisations, including Conamaq[12] and CIDOB, along with a number of environmental and human rights organisations, for being in violation of their rights. The new law does not anticipate mechanisms to guarantee consultation or free, prior and informed consent, as established in ILO Convention 169 and the UN Declaration on the Rights of Indigenous Peoples, when mining operations are conducted in indigenous communities or territories. Moreover, the law itself was not put out to consultation and nor was consent for its approval obtained, as it was negotiated only with the cooperativist mining sector (small and medium-sized private operators) and with some organisations of corporate water users in Cochabamba department.[13] In this law, the whole of the national territory has been declared state lands open to the granting of mining concessions regardless of whether it is an ecologically fragile area or protected by law. It violates the right to access and use water, as it grants preferential and exclusive use of this and other natural resources to mining operations being implemented on indigenous territories, permitting mining in glaciers, protected areas and mountain basins, and putting the ecosystems and tropical forests, as well as the snow-capped mountains that feed the territories inhabited by indigenous peoples, at serious risk. In addition, it strengthens private and transnational mining, consolidating the primary export model with minimal state intervention that has dominated this activity since colonial times. Finally, the organisations challenged the fact that, in breach of the current Environment Law, this new law granted the Ministry of Mining cumulative powers to prevent control of and participation in environmental management, along with a decentralisation of tasks to the regional and local levels for this purpose.

Indigenous autonomies

Nearly five years ago, Framework Law 31/10 on Autonomies and Decentralisation was passed. Under pressure from the 7th Indigenous March, this included a policy for developing the right to form own governments with legislative, executive, patrimonial and jurisdictional powers in the territories titled and/or occupied by indigenous peoples. In 2009, through a referendum, the peoples in 11 municipalities[14] decided to convert the local authority in their area into an Indigenous Autonomy, in line with their norms and procedures. To date, of these 11 peoples, not one has managed to fulfil the requirements demanded by Law 31/10. The Constitutional Court has declared only two autonomies compliant with the Constitution of Autonomous Statutes.[5] Five have completed the drafting but have not yet presented their text to the Court and four are encountering various difficulties in complying with one or other of the 11 stages established by the Law.[6]

Another way of accessing indigenous self-government is via territorial titling, and 12 indigenous settlements are moving along this path towards autonomy. The Constitutional Court has issued opinions with regard to rectifications to be made to the statutes of two of these peoples. This is, however, the furthest that "regionally-based" autonomy has ever gone. The other 10 are at the stage of organising and completing the preliminary stages.

Alongside the slow progress noted in implementing one of the most important and significant demands of the 2006/2007 Constituent Assembly to be included in the Constitution, consideration must also be given to the fact that the state has still not brought in tax legislation aimed at providing resources for the functioning of the new indigenous bodies. In fact, the Framework Law on Autonomies establishes that the allocation of resources and funding to the bodies created by this legislation will be the result of a "fiscal pact" linked to the results of the 2012 Census. However, the information from this was officially published in 2013 and the state has yet to commence the discussion. Given the stated difficulties, the organisations have a perception that the issue of autonomy, and possibly of indigenous peoples themselves, has dropped off the agenda (of a government that proclaims itself to be indigenous), as has the issue of land, where there has been no significant progress for years in terms of titling pending indigenous territories. All of this, added to other contradictory policies with respect to indigenous rights, shows very clearly that official policy has changed course, and that this is due to the new alliances being forged with the business and traditional landowning sectors, whose demands are now a priority for the national government.   ◯

Notes and references

1   According to data from the Supreme Electoral Court, 5,139,554 million people voted, including Bolivians living in 33 countries around the world. Turnout was 94.21%. CEJIS, Bolivia Plurinacional Nº 7.

2   He was vice president to Gen. Hugo Banzer Suárez (1997-2001) and took from him to complete his term in office when he died (2001-2002).

3   All data obtained from www.oep.org.bo/computo/index.html

4   This refers to the governing body of the Confederation, which was forcibly removed from its office and its representation taken over by a board accused of being supported and financed by the national government.

5   See *The Indigenous World 2014*

6   In other words, one representative is elected per department. The Constitution stipulates that the special seats favour minority peoples. Bolivia has nine departments; indigenous peoples are a minority in eight of them, excluding Potosí. However, only seven are elected because, in Chuquisaca, the indigenous organisations and the MAS agreed that this provision would not apply in exchange for a place for them on the list of party deputies.

7   Law for the Prevention of HIV/AIDS, protection of human rights and integral multidisciplinary assistance to people living with HIV/AIDS.

8   *Article 2 (Principles). This law sets out the following principles: d) Confidentiality: the clinical condition of people living with HIV/AIDS must be subject to the rules of confidentiality estab-*

lished in codes of ethics, medical and epidemiological protocols and this Law. Law No. 3729/07 Bolivia Official Journal.

9   *Article 5 (Rights and Guarantees). All people living with HIV/AIDS and with the guarantee of the state, have the following rights: d) To respect to privacy, maintaining confidentiality of their serostatus and banning obligatory testing, providing this is not affecting third parties. Except in cases specified in this law.*

10 As has been known for several years, HIV/AIDS is not "contagious" but instead "transmissible" in three ways: sexual relations, blood and from mother to baby in the uterus. One of the main reasons for the discrimination against this illness is precisely this mistaken belief that it is "contagious" and not "transmissible".

11 He resigned during his second term of office (2002-2003) forced out by a popular revolt known as the "Gas War", in opposition to the decision to export this gas to neighbouring Chile.

12 National Council of Markas and Ayllus of Qollasuyu, national representative organisation of the indigenous nations of the Andes of Bolivia.

13 In the context of a dialogue convened *in extremis,* some of the observations of these organisations were included, but this did not overcome the stated violations.

14 Thirteen referenda were held: in two of them the people rejected the possibility of converting the municipalities into Peasant Native Indigenous Autonomies (AIOC).

15 This refers to the municipality of Totora, in the Andean department of Oruro, inhabited by the Jach'a Karangas nation and Charagua municipality, in the subtropical department of Santa Cruz, inhabited by the Guaraní people.

16 There are six more peoples who have begun the path to autonomy, from different departments in the country.

Leonardo Tamburini *is a lawyer trained in natural resources, the environment and indigenous territorial rights with a human rights focus; he is currently the executive director of the Centre for Legal Studies and Social Research (Centro de Estudios Jurídicos e Investigación Social/CEJIS).*

BRAZIL

According to information from the 2010 census of the Brazilian Institute for Geography and Statistics, there are 305 indigenous peoples in Brazil speaking 274 different languages. Of these people, 37.4% of those over the age of five speak an indigenous language. The indigenous peoples number 896,917 persons in total, corresponding to 0.47% of the country's population. Of these, 324,834 live in urban and 572,083 in rural areas. Most of these people (57.7%) live spread across 698 so-called Indigenous Lands (*terras indígenas*) (106.7 million ha). Eighty-three of these Indigenous Lands are inhabited by fewer than 100 individuals. There are 28 indigenous peoples living in voluntary isolation.[1] The Indigenous Land with the greatest indigenous population is that of the Yanomami, in Amazonas and Roraima states, with 25,700 individuals.

Brazil has signed the UN Declaration of Human Rights, the International Covenant on Civil and Political Rights, the International Covenant on Economic, Social and Cultural Rights, ILO Convention 169 and the UN Declaration on the Rights of Indigenous Peoples.

President Dima Rousseff was re-elected in 2014 and her new term in office seems to be showing the same lack of respect in its policies towards indigenous peoples as the previous. The President's first term resulted in the smallest area of indigenous lands demarcated since the country's return to democracy, reflecting the lack of priority given to FUNAI (National Indian Foundation), which has been under the temporary management of the Attorney General, Flavio de Azevedo,[2] for the past 20 months, with a growing reduction in its budget.[3] Dilma Rousseff's government is clearly developmentalist in its outlook, and is failing to comply with either the Brazilian Constitution or the international agreements to which Brazil is a signatory.

1. Belo Monte Hydro-Electric Project   2. Teles Pires Hydro-electric Dam

Constitutional amendment can threaten demarcation of indigenous lands

A number of measures are taking shape that would be in clear violation of the few indigenous rights currently enforced. These include a Proposed Amendment to the Constitution (PEC-215) which would transfer the power for approving Indigenous Lands from the Executive to the National Congress.

With the election of the new Minister for Agriculture, Kátia Abreu in 2014, who is aligned with the rural caucus in National Congress, PEC 215 now has a good chance of being approved. If this happens, it will become more difficult for the lands intended for the use of the indigenous populations to actually be transferred to them.

"There is a clear process of attacking indigenous rights in Brazil. In addition, a series of exemptions seems to have been established with regard to possessing the usufruct of the lands already demarcated, in addition to the opening up of a possibility of reviewing already established demarcation procedures", announced the indigenous leadership.[4]

The rural caucus is one of the most active in Congress: of the 191 deputies that form part of the "Agricultural and Livestock Parliamentary Group" in the Federal Chamber, 126 were re-elected in 2014.

Kátia Abreu states that "there are no more large estates in Brazil", adding that "the whole of Brazil was theirs (the indigenous peoples), but this is quite different from providing them with certain areas, because the Indians will probably leave the forests and probably move into move productive sectors." [5]

According to Wagner, a member of the Kraho Kanela people: "The economy that the minister wants to create for our country is destroying the environment".[6] "If it were approved, it would result in the extermination of the indigenous and *quilombos* (Afro-descendant) peoples," adds Dinama Tuxá from the Tuxá people.[7]

If this proposal were to go ahead, FUNAI would lose one of its few remaining powers, that of requesting the demarcation of indigenous lands from the Executive, as this would henceforward be decided by National Congress, even though FUNAI is the only body with direct responsibility for promoting the rights of indigenous peoples. The institution is being slowly run down, however, with cuts to its budget. While it received 174 million reais or 58 million dollar in 2013, this had fallen to 154 million by 2014. As noted above, FUNAI has been under temporary management for the last 20 months, demonstrating a clear lack of interest in indigenous affairs. FUNAI has also had to cut back its workforce, particularly those working on the demarcation of indigenous territories. According to FUNAI, the demarcations team has fallen from 21 to 16 permanent staff and the number of anthropologists on the team based in Brasilia from six to two.[8] Dilma Rousseff's government has approved the least indigenous lands out of all governments over the last 20 years: only 11 lands in a period of four years, covering an area of two million hectares.[9]

In May 2014, Brazil was denounced for violations of indigenous rights before the UN Permanent Forum on Indigenous Issues by the indigenous leader, Lindomar Tenera, from Mato Grosso do Sul, a representative of APIB. He denounced the rural caucus in National Congress for approving changes to indigenous constitutional rights. He stated that, "Brazil is in the midst of a series of actions and initiatives that are seeking to reduce and remove the rights of indigenous peoples as recognised by Brazil's Federal Constitution and reaffirmed by international treaties (...) The Brazilian developmentalist model is using the territories of the indigenous communities and other segments of traditional communities as areas for the uncontrolled exploitation of natural resources, the expansion of agribusiness and the implementation of large-scale projects (...) This is why the Brazilian government has brought the constitutional process of demarcating our territories to a halt, seriously increasing the territorial conflicts in various regions of Brazil".[10]

No consultations regarding hydroelectric dams in the Amazon

In March 2014, the indigenous organisations and civil society denounced the Brazilian government at the 25th session of the UN Human Rights Council for violating indigenous rights during the process of building large hydroelectric plants in the Amazon. These complaints were made by the coordinator of the Coordinating Body of Brazil's Indigenous Peoples (*Articulação dos Povos Indigenas*/APIB), Alexandre Sampaio. He considers that violations of indigenous peoples' right to consultation and to free, prior and informed consent with regard to the ventures and administrative measures affecting their territories, as stipulated in ILO Convention 169 but not applied by Brazil, have created a dangerous precedent of illegality in terms of adhering to international treaties and that this is putting the survival of the indigenous peoples at risk. "An alliance of political and economic interests is exacerbating an unprecedented crisis in the application of legislation protecting our rights. It is inadmissible that the government should violate indigenous rights guaranteed by the Brazilian Constitution and international treaties," stated Guajajara. The government has conducted no consultations in order to obtain the free, prior and informed consent for either the Belo Monte hydroelectric power station (Pará state) or for the large dams on the Tapajós.

The power plants at Teles Pires and São Manoel have even already received the corresponding environmental licences. This situation is causing growing conflict with local communities, such as the Munduruku, Kayabi and Apiaka indigenous peoples, who have protested at the violation of their rights.[11]

The Belo Monte hydroelectric plant, under construction in the heart of the Brazilian Amazon since 2011, is probably the most notorious case of a megadam being built in flagrant violation of national legislation and international agreements on human rights and environmental protection. Belo Monte has already formed the object of 20 civil cases through the Federal Prosecution Service (*Ministerio Público Federal*) since 2001.

One of the key actions relates to approval of Legislative Decree No. 788/2005 by the National Congress, which authorised the construction of Belo Monte without any prior consultation of the indigenous peoples affected, as stipulated by Article 231 of the Federal Constitution and ILO Convention 169. The Federal Prosecution Service brought an action in 2006 calling for the suspension of Decree 788/2005 and fulfilment of the constitutional requirement to conduct prior consultation with the indigenous peoples of Xingú, whose territories and lives are threatened by the construction of Belo Monte. Finally, on 13 August 2012, the Regional Federal Court ruled on the merits of the case, suspending Decree 788/2005 and the construction of Belo Monte. A few days later, the then President of the Supreme Federal Court, Carlos Ayres Britto, at the request of the Office of the Attorney General (Advocacia Geral da União/AGU), unilaterally suspended the court decision, without hearing the Federal Prosecution Service, indigenous leaders or other representatives of civil society, ignoring the arguments on the merits of the case and postponing the final judgment.

In the case of Belo Monte, the National Public Security Force (established in 2004) is now acting as if it were a private security service for the Belo Monte Construction Consortium and the Norte Energía SA company (holder of the government concession to build the dam) while the leaders of the Xingú Vivo Movement are being criminalised. Dilma Rousseff's administration has, since 2008, embarked on a military operation known as "Operation Tapajós", sending the National Public Security Force and Federal Police into the area to protect the teams that are conducting the technical studies on the Munduruku people's territory, along with the preparatory work for the construction of megadams for which no-one was consulted. At the same time, the federal government has, on various occasions, questioned the legitimacy of the Munduruku leaders' involvement in the movement of resistance to the Tapajós dams.[12]

Indigenous peoples face increasing violence

The result of the measures described above can be seen in the increased violence against indigenous peoples. The Indigenous Missionary Council (CIMI) presented a report in July 2014 entitled "Violence against Brazil's Indigenous Peoples" [13] in which the issue of "Violence against Property" showed a 26% increase in terms of violations of indigenous lands. In the case of "Violations due to Omission of the Public Authorities", the figures were alarming, with a 72% increase, while "Violence against the Person" had increased a full 237%. This latter included death threats, murders, attempted murders, physical injuries and sexual violence. The report noted that the conflict over land was likely to continue since a large part of the indigenous lands remain unregulated.   ○

Notes and references

1   http://censo2010.ibge.gov.br/noticias-censo?busca=1&id=3&idnoticia=2194&t=censo-2010-poblacao-indigena-896-9-mil-tem-305-etnias-fala-274&view=noticia
2   Flavio de Azevedo is Attorney General in the AGU.
3   *Estadão* 15 February 2015.
4   http://agenciabrasil.ebec.com.br
5   OESP, Espaço Aberto, p.A2.
6   Idem.
7   http://brasil.elpais.com
8   *Estadão* 15 February 2015.
9   http://pib.socioambiental.org/pt/c/0/1/2/demarcacoes-nos-ultimos-governos
10 http://www.brasildefato.com.br/node/28582
11 http://pib.socioambiental.org/pt/noticias?id=137198
12 http://www.socioambiental.org/sites/blog.socioambiental.org/files/nsa/arquivos/brasil-pt-marco-2014_final-1.pdf
13 http://www.cnbb.org.br/imprensa-1/14581-cimi-lanca-relatorio-com-dados-de-violencia-contra-os-povos-indigenas-em-2013

Maria de Lourdes Beldi de Alcantara is an anthropologist and works as an invited professor in medical anthropology at the Faculty of Medicine, São Paolo. She is coordinator of the Support Group for Guaraní Youth of Mato Grosso do Sul (GAPK/AJI).

PARAGUAY

There are approximately 112,848 indigenous people living in Paraguay, belonging to 19 peoples from five different linguistic families: Guaraní (Aché, Avá Guaraní, Mbya, Pai Tavytera, Guaraní Ñandeva, Guaraní Occidental), Maskoy (Toba Maskoy, Enlhet Norte, Enxet Sur, Sanapaná, Angaité, Guaná), Mataco Mataguayo (Nivaclé, Maká, Manjui), Zamuco (Ayoreo, Yvytoso, Tomáraho) and Guaicurú (Qom).[1] According to preliminary data from the 2012 National Census of Indigenous Population and Housing, published in 2013, the Oriental region is home to the highest proportion of indigenous peoples (52.3%) while the Chaco region has the greatest diversity of peoples. They form, in all, 531 communities and 241 villages.

Although the indigenous peoples of Paraguay represent a great diversity and cultural wealth for the country, they are the victims of systematic and structural discrimination on the part of both state and non-indigenous society. In this regard, they are the poorest, most excluded and most marginalised sector of the country's population.[2]

In this context, all indigenous rights – civil, cultural, economic, social and political – are constantly violated and neglected. This situation is due, primarily, to the invasion, destruction and dispossession of indigenous peoples´ traditional and ancestral territories, where they live and which are deeply connected to their worldview, survival and cultural practices.

Paraguay has ratified the main international human rights instruments such as ILO Convention 169 (Law 234/93). However, the state is mainstreaming, interpreting and applying these instruments inadequately, if at all, meaning that the fundamental rights of indigenous peoples are constantly being violated.

The ideologically conservative and heavily business-oriented budget of Horacio Cartes' government is having a negative impact on indigenous rights. This can be seen in the rhetoric of a number of the state's current representatives, for example, Jorge Servín, President of the Paraguayan Indigenous Institute (INDI),

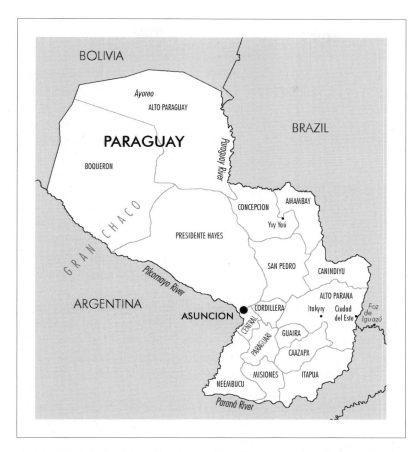

whose actions in the international arena have been revealing. During a hearing organised by the Inter-American Commission on Human Rights (IACHR) in Washington on the rights of indigenous Totobiegosode living in voluntary isolation, Servín requested, on behalf of Paraguay, and with absolutely no shame whatsoever: "the rejection of precautionary measures over the whole 550,000 hectares claimed, as this would result in local ungovernability",[3] thus echoing the position of the large landowners and cattle farmers of the northern Chaco, whose extractivist activities are putting the survival of the last uncontacted indigenous communities of the region at risk and who carry great weight in a region that enjoys little, if any, government presence.

Rather than focus on providing appropriate attention to indigenous rights, the dominant rhetoric and ideological framework is thus excluding and limiting them, to the benefit of investment and business deals which are now increasingly acquiring the facilities and privileges of political projects focused around imaginary "progress" to be achieved on the basis of large-scale investments, without compensating the rights of the indigenous peoples, whose lands are seen not as spaces in which to live their life and enjoy their culture but as areas of expansion for agribusiness, cattle farming and, ultimately, the exploitation of hydrocarbons.

Rural guards (or paramilitaries?) exercising state functions

A most serious incident of forced displacement took place on 15 June. This affected the Y'apó community of the Avá Guaraní people in the area of Corpus Christi, Canindeyú department, and was all the more concerning because it involved armed civilians, acting with total impunity and without any control whatsoever from the state.

The statements given following the attack refer to the perpetrators as being civilians in the pay of the Laguna S.A. company. This allegation was subsequently expressly acknowledged by the government in a statement[4] published via the state-run Human Rights Network.[5] The use of such private guards is incompatible with the principle of the state's constitutional monopoly of the forces of law and order

In another similar event, also in Canindeyú, in a settlement located within the boundaries of the districts of Corpus Christi and Puente Kyha, around 30 families from the indigenous Takuara'í Marilú community were attacked on 7 May by an unidentified armed group of people of Brazilian and Paraguayan origin, who fired weapons at around 01.30 in the morning, waking up and dispersing the people and then subsequently setting fire to their homes, vehicles and all their belongings.[6] According to a community member, Mr. Portillo, a few hours later, at around 05.00 am, members of the National Police arrived but, to the surprise of the distressed families, merely completed the eviction by throwing everyone off the land.

Neither of these cases has resulted in any legal proceedings being taken to investigate, bring to justice and convict those responsible for these serious acts, and this impunity merely gives the perpetrators *carte blanche* to continue their crimes. In the last case noted, not even an official statement was issued with regard to what had happened.

Also noteworthy is the publication of a report,[7] possibly the first of its kind in Paraguay, that bears witness to a significant number of extrajudicial executions and murders attributed to armed groups in the pay of drug traffickers in Amamba department and part of Concepción.

Worlds' fastest deforestation rate

The increasing rate of deforestation in the Western region of Paraguay throughout 2014 attracted a great deal of public attention. It is considered to be the fastest in the world, compromising not only the environmental balance and ecosystem of the area but also the rights of, among others, the Ayoreo people who are still living in voluntary isolation in the north and west of the Chaco.[8]

Maryland University's study on the situation of the world's forests, published in January 2014, provides some truly alarming data that sheds light on the events taking place in this region.[9]

A study published by the NGO Amotocodie Initiative notes that:

In February 2014, the area cleared was around 2,593,000 hectares. This represents a loss of Ayoreo ancestral territory to the order of 54% over nine years. However, the most worrying aspect is that, between December 2012 and February 2014, 442,450 hectares were turned over to pastureland. In other words, almost the same amount of forest that disappeared between 1927 (with the arrival of the first Mennonite settlers) and 2004 (77 years) has ceased to exist in just 14 months. This rapid transformation is marked not only by its extent but also by the degree of fragmentation of the forests. A large proportion of the forest that remains, and which does not appear on the lists of forests that have been lost, now exists in small islands of just a few hectares (reserves required by environmental legislation) or "wind breaks" of no more than 100 metres across in the best of cases. This means that they are transformed forests. This increases the amount of territory lost to isolated groups in the north of Chaco by at least 25%.[10]

One of the most worrying cases is the situation of the Totobiegosode, an Ayoreo group living in isolation and whose traditional territory is being invaded by numerous companies with the aim of clearing the forest. One of these, Yaguareté Porã S.A., a Brazilian company, has purchased land in the very heart of the Totobiegosode Cultural and Natural Heritage Area.

In March 2014, this company obtained an environmental licence authorising it to clear up to 78,549 hectares,[11] after which there would be no more deforestation for a number of years, due to evidence placed before the environmental authority with regard to the presence of Ayoreo Totobiegosode individuals living in the area.

One example that demonstrates the incompatibility of the state's attitude with its obligations to guarantee environmental and territorial rights is Executive Decree No. 453/2013,[12] which removes the requirement to conduct environmental impact assessments on properties measuring less than 2,000 hectares in the Chaco and less than 500 hectares in the Eastern region. In practice, this provision renders Law No. 294/93 on Environmental Impact Assessments completely null and void.[13]

The Inter-American Court of Human Rights (IA Court)

The most remarkable event of 2014 was undoubtedly the expropriation[14] of 14,404 hectares of land for the indigenous Sawhoyamaxa community, albeit five years after the deadline set by the IA Court. Moreover, the ruling of the Constitutional Chamber of the Supreme Court of Justice set an important precedent because, by throwing out the appeal for unconstitutionality lodged by the expropriated companies, it ratified the full constitutionality of the expropriating law,[15] thus concluding an important stage in the already long path of this community to recover its lands.

The indigenous Yakye Axa community, who are still living along the side of the road between Pozo Colorado and Concepción in Presidente Hayes department, has an agreement with the state by which these people are to be resettled on their lands, which have been legally guaranteed since the start of 2012. Before they can live there, however, road infrastructure is required to link their future settlement to the departmental road and a complete lack of progress has been seen in this regard. This is preventing the Enxet from accessing their lands, and perpetuating a state of affairs by which the community's rights continue to be violated.

The Xákmok Kásek, a community of the Sanapaná people, obtained a favourable ruling from the IA Court in 2010 but, on 24 September 2014, the additional time period granted by the Court within which the state was to implement the decision with regard to returning their lands came to an end without any significant progress having been made. It is thought that the state is negotiating the purchase of one of the farms, which is in private hands, in order to return it to the community. According to information from INDI, it covers an area of 7,701 hectares.

Visit of the UN Special Rapporteur

Victoria Tauli-Corpuz conducted the first visit of her term in office as UN Special Rapporteur on the rights of indigenous peoples to Paraguay. From 21 to 28 November 2014, she visited Paraguay to discuss territorial rights and natural resources, as well as the issue of prior consultation. The situation of the Ayoreo people, particularly those living in isolation and who are suffering the deforestation of their territories, the violence by private guards towards the Avá Guaraní of Y'apó community who are fighting to defend their lands in Canindejú, and the extent to which the ruling of the IA Court has been fulfilled with regard to the communities of the Enxet people were all issues that were keenly raised withe the rapporteur.

The final statement of Rapporteur Tauli's mission[16] bears witness to a number of concerns, including: a lack of access to land, a lack of social protection policies, extreme poverty, problems accessing clean drinking water in the Western region of the country, etc. The final version of the report has not yet been published.

Effective remedy for land claims and indigenous participation

The IA Court ruled against Paraguay for a third time in 2010 demanding that, among other things, the state adopt legislative, administrative and any other measures necessary to create an effective system for claiming the ancestral or traditional lands of the indigenous peoples, in order to give concrete expression to their right to property. The period stipulated for fulfilment of this ruling was two years, which has now passed.

As central elements of this reform, the Court also ruled that the state had to guarantee: a) that the importance of traditional land to indigenous peoples should be taken into account; and b) that it would not be sufficient for the lands claimed to be privately owned and under rational exploitation for a claim to be rejected. In addition, it noted that the reforms would need to ensure that a legal authority had the power to resolve any conflicts that might occur between the property rights of individuals and those of indigenous communities.

No progress has been made on this particularly important issue, not even in terms of discussing an institutional mechanism that would guarantee an adequate consultation procedure and enable free exercise of the right to participation, something which is part and parcel of the principle of self-determination.

One example of this negligence on the part of the state can be seen in INDI's management report, which includes a reference to "spaces for the participation of indigenous peoples"[17] but limits these to promotional and training events rather than spaces for real institutional debate in which the indigenous communities would be able to express their points of view and defend their rights and interests with regard to the state's management of relevant policies. This report demonstrates that the state's actions, through INDI, are limited to the creation of temporary spaces for the sale of handicrafts, participation in workshops on housing and communication and the establishment of a joint state/indigenous delegation to attend international events. None of these activities could in any way be considered equivalent to a policy of guaranteeing indigenous peoples' right to participation. There is therefore a clear political vacuum in this regard, and Paraguay is continuing to ignore its obligation to pass relevant domestic legislation.   ○

Notes and references

1   There is no mention of the Toba ethnic group of the Maskoy linguistic family in the 2012 National Census of Indigenous Population and Housing.

2   This can be seen in the data provided by the 2008 Survey of Indigenous Households from the DGEEC.

3   Cf. Management Report of the Paraguayan Indigenous Institute, August 2013/August 2014, p. 17. Available at: http://www.indi.gov.py/archivos/documentos/INDI%20INFO%20Gestion2013-2014_jx751qbd.pdf

4   INDI, 25 June 2014, Available at: http://www.indi.gov.py/noticia/54-comunicado-sobre-los-hechos-ocurridos-en-la-comunidad-indgena-yapo-del-pueblo-av-guaran-del-distrito-de-corpus-christi-departamento-de-canindey-el-domingo-15-de-junio-de-2014.html#.VF_aOvmG_RY

5   For more information on this issue please see the piece on the Y´apó case elsewhere in this article.

6   Proyecto Democratización de la Información, 7 May 2014, Available at: http://demoinfo.com.py/en-canindeju-desalojan-indigenas-queman-sus-pertenencias/

7   Tierraviva, Available at: http://www.tierraviva.org.py/wp-content/uploads/2014/08/Violencia-e-impundad.pdf

8   For more information please refer to "IWGIA Report 4. Paraguay: The Case of the Ayoreo". Unión de Nativos Ayoreo de Paraguay (UNAP), Iniciativa Amotocodie (IA), International Work Group for Indigenous Affairs (IWGIA). May 2010. Available at: http://www.iwgia.org/publications/search-pubs?publication_id=4

9   GAT, 21 January 2014. Available at:
    http://www.gat.org.py/v5/index.php?detalle=712&titu=7&sec=39

10 "La situación de los pueblos aislados en el Paraguay", Iniciativa Amotocodie, October 2014. Available at: http://www.iniciativa-amotocodie.org/

11 Abc Color, 31 March 2014. Available at: http://www.abc.com.py/edicion-impresa/locales/seam-autorizo-desmonte-en-tierra-donde-habitan-indigenas-silvicolas-1230088.html

12 SEAM, 28 January 2014. Available at: http://www.seam.gov.py/component/content/article/1713.html

13 Abc Color, 17 January 2014, Available at: http://www.abc.com.py/edicion-impresa/locales/decreto-de-horacio-cartes-facilita-la-deforestacion-1206276.html

14 Official Journal, 12 June 2014, Available at:
    http://www.gacetaoficial.gov.py/uploads/pdf/2014/2014-06-12/gaceta_2348_IJGEFHBFHCK-DIKCGHEGGEHGGBHHKFBFCKAHEIIKE.pdf

15 Agreement and Ruling of the Supreme Court of Justice No. 981 of 30 September 2014

16 Cf. http://unsr.vtaulicorpuz.org/site/index.php/es/declaraciones-comunicados/44-end-mission-to-paraguay

17 INDI, Management Report, August 2013/August 2014, p 32. Available at: http://www.indi.gov.py/archivos/documentos/INDI%20INFO%20Gestion2013-2014_jx751qbd.pdf

Oscar Ayala Amarilla is a lawyer with the Paraguayan NGO Tierraviva that works with the indigenous peoples of the Chaco region,

ARGENTINA

Argentina is a federal state comprising 23 provinces with a total population of over 40 million. The results of the Additional Survey on Indigenous Populations (2004-5), published by the National Institute for Statistics and Census, gives a total of 600,329 people who recognise themselves as descending from or belonging to an indigenous people,[1] while the latest national census from 2010 include a total of 955,032 persons self-identifying as descending from or belonging to an indigenous people.[2] There are today 35 distinct indigenous peoples officially recognized.

Legally, the indigenous peoples have specific constitutional rights at federal level and also in a number of provincial states. ILO Convention 169 and other universal human rights instruments such as the International Covenant on Civil and Political Rights and the International Covenant on Economic, Social and Cultural Rights are also in force, with constitutional status. Argentina voted in favour of the adoption of the UN Declaration of the Rights of Indigenous Peoples in 2007.

A t the end of 2014, the serious health situation being suffered by indigenous peoples in the north of the country has come to the fore once more. Tuberculosis and Chagas disease are the main endemic diseases affecting these people. Because of these illnesses, deaths due to malnutrition have risen among children and adults alike. A seven-year-old boy recently died in Chaco province after being admitted to hospital for TB treatment but then discharged with no-one to provide follow-up or ensure continuity of his treatment. The head of the Nelson Mandela Studies Centre (*Centro de Estudios Nelson Mandela*), a local NGO, considers that the health system in Chaco province "operates very poorly due to political patronage, abuse, and even open and clear discrimination of indigenous communities", and is revealing how "completely dehumanised and disorganised" it is. One additional problem is that the Ministry of Health's Vital Statistics System conceals the cause of death: in general, death certificates state the cause of death as "illness" and do not specify the patient's clinical history. In the case of the

above child, there was no mention of the underlying illnesses of TB and associated malnutrition.[3]

The situation is the same in other provinces of northern Argentina. On hearing of nine deaths due to malnutrition, the Governor of Salta admitted to the press that there were 135,000 extremely vulnerable children in his province[4] but emphasised indigenous peoples' misinformation and nomadic ways as the reasons why it was difficult to address their health situation. The indigenous organisations, in contrast, maintained that this situation was due to forced displacements caused by increasing deforestation and the advancing agricultural and livestock frontier.

People have been warning about this health crisis for many years. Two years ago, the National Council for Indigenous Policy (*Consejo Nacional de Políticas Indígenas*), comprising representatives from various provinces of the country's north and south, asked the President of the Chamber of Deputies to hold urgent discussions with representatives from different communities on the state's lack of attention to health issues. This request met with no response. In an election year such as this, it is hardly surprising that candidates are now showing a concern to produce proposals and plans and are making promises of environmental conservation, water provision and attention to primary health care.

All this is taking place while there are ongoing delays in the effective implementation of Law 26160 on the "Emergency situation of indigenous community property". This law, passed in November 2006, stipulated the suspension of legal evictions for four years, and established that land and territory surveys would be conducted in the first three years. This deadline has twice been passed and had to be extended, in 2009 and 2014, without the work yet being completed.

In order to coordinate joint efforts, the National General Auditor's Office held a meeting with indigenous and civil society organisations in June 2014 to agree on the points to be implemented in a future audit of the National Institute for Indigenous Affairs (*Instituto Nacional de Asuntos Indígenas*). The issues considered included: access to land, legal status, and the effective participation of indigenous communities in policies that involves them.[5]

Forest clearing in the north of Argentina

According to the Argentine Chaco Agro-forestry Network (*Red Agroforestal Chaco Argentina* / REDAF), the Chaco National Park incorporates around 70% of all of Argentina's native forest. It is also the most heavily deforested area. It is estimated that some 34% of the native forest of the Chaco National Park, Misionero Forest and Tucuman-Bolivian forest has now been cleared. In 2008, an alliance of non-governmental organisations and indigenous and Creole communities requested that the Supreme Court of Justice put in place precautionary measures prohibiting the "deforestation and felling of native forest in the Chaco Salteño region". Since the enactment of the Forests Law five years ago, more than 330,000 hectares have been cleared in the province, 98,894 hectares of these in areas prohibited by the Land Management Plan (Law 7543/2009). In addition, between 2008 and 2011, 53,202 hectares have been cleared in violation of the resolution passed by the Supreme Court of Justice.[6] Despite this, felling continues in prohibited areas, and has resulted in numerous complaints from local inhabitants and organisations. Furthermore, the ambiguity of the law has enabled the Provincial Ministry of the Environment to authorise a change in forest category in order to permit the clearing. One emblematic case is that of the Wichí community of San José de Cuchuy. In clear defiance of Provincial Decree 2789 prohibiting the clearing of areas inhabited by communities in which the survey established by Law 26160 had not yet been conducted, authorisation was given to clear 10,000 hectares around Cuchuy. Deceived and pressurised, the community members signed an agreement accepting 300 hectares and 10 houses, thereby losing 9,700 hectares of their land.[7]

Lack of guarantees protecting territorial rights

On 28 July 2014, various members of the Wichí community of El Colorado in Formosa province were beaten up by local police who entered their settlement with numerous officials to implement a court order. The community members were accused of removing a fence that a non-indigenous family had erected on community lands. They were prosecuted and imprisoned in the local municipality for defending their territory.[8]

Also in Formosa province, violence is continuing against the Qom leader, Félix Díaz, from Potae Napocna Navogoh-La Primavera community. A physical attack has been reported against his son, along with shots heard during the night in the area. Also, on 3 January 2015 a 17-year-old Qom, Esteban Medina, was found dead at the side of Route 86. Medina was found near where his aunt, Norma Artaza, was found dead on 12 December. The woman had received blows to the head and Díaz believes the police were responsible, "Qom deaths are always due to a heart attack or road traffic accident, they never allow informed community members give evidence during the autopsies". According to the journalist, Darío Aranda, "all these events are taking place in an unfavourable context because the provincial government has just suffered a serious setback in relation to the Inter-American Commission on Human Rights (IACHR), the main human rights body for the Americas; [...] this Commission has just ratified precautionary measures requiring the state to protect members of the Qom community. The provincial government requested this measure be removed but this was refused on 29 December [...]".[9]

Violence erupted in the area when the territorial demands led to clashes between the community, its leader and the provincial government. On 22 December, a community assembly declared a state of alert and mobilisation due to the lack of response received from the authorities with regard to the illegal occupation of their lands by a non-indigenous settler.

In order to face up to these violent attacks, denounce the violations of their rights and keep up their struggle for lands, the Nivaclé, Pilagá, Qom and Wichí communities of Formosa province have formed an association of 33 members, chosen by self-convened community assemblies. In December, they signed a petition asking UN Special Rapporteur Victoria Tauli-Corpuz to visit the area to see for herself what was going on. They will hold their 5th meeting in early 2015, where they will consider, among other issues, two new orders for the evictions of the communities of Campo del Veinte and Santo Domingo.[10]

Territorial struggles in Tucumán

In Tucumán province, Diaguita communities grouped together in the Union of Peoples of the Diaguita Nation of Tucumán (*Unión de los Pueblos de la Nación Diaguita de Tucumán* / UPNDT) have completed the surveys of the indigenous communities and submitted technical files for 14 communities covering an area of 450,000 hectares, 5% of which are state lands. Provincial-level prospects for getting land legalised on behalf of indigenous communities, however, are not good. Although a draft bill of law (proposed by different actors involved in the surveying) is making progress, this would not directly transfer ownership to the indigenous peoples but would instead create a State Land Commission involving indigenous peoples, state bodies and civil society representatives to conduct tasks aimed primarily at achieving the transfer of these state lands to the indigenous communities. This lack of any formal demarcation and titling procedure that would truly take the community's rights and interests into account is threatening to paralyse the slow process commenced with the approval of Law 26160 in 2006. This legal vacuum, which amounts to a failure on the part of the state to fulfil its obligations, leaves the titling process in an uncertain situation, all the more so given that 2015 will be an election year.

This clear lack of policy and failure to implement the rules is directly linked to indigenous peoples' lack of consultation and participation in government decisions. One illustration of this is UNESCO's granting of World Heritage status to the Inca road system (Qhapaq Ñan) in June 2014. This declaration affected the archaeological site of "La Ciudacita",[11] located within the territory of the indigenous community of Solco Yampa (Diaguita people) and yet their rights to consultation and participation were not respected in this regard. The provincial government merely limited itself to quoting the indigenous community's representative at the working meetings, without instigating a process of genuine participation, as stipulated in international legislation. This was despite the community, supported by UPNDT, having demanded it be involved in any decisions involving the territorial management of their community.[12]

The return and management of the Sacred City of the Quilmes,[13] which has been under discussion since 2002, is the first case of its kind in the province, and is coming up against legal, technical and political problems both between the community and the government and within the community itself.[14] The Quilmes are faced with the challenge of setting a precedent in terms of administering and managing their heritage in alliance with the state, and this latter cannot ignore its responsibility as guarantor of the conservation of the site and of the rights of its owners and heirs.

In addition, a violent conflict involving attempted land grabbing by *criollos* in El Nogalito community of the Lule people continues unresolved. Given the serious human rights violations suffered by this community, the Inter-American Commission on Human Rights issued a court order protecting the community in 2012, calling on the state to adopt effective measures to safeguard the life and integrity of the community and its members.[15] In March 2014, the IACHR convened a working meeting of the community, its legal advisors[16] and the Argentine state to assess the progress made in this regard. The assessment made at the meeting was not a positive one as it highlighted the state's failure to effectively protect the rights of community members. This failure has resulted in a situation of violent conflict on the community's territory along with regular threats and harassment of community members. The persistence of this situation not only represents a constant violation of their human rights but also deters members from participating in their community. The precautionary measure granted by the IACHR offers, at least in theory, a permanent platform for dialogue and negotiation with the state, albeit not without complications, delays and negotiations on the part of the authorities. Despite the Argentine state's commitment to organise a round table in order to discuss the conditions (safety, territorial and social) that gave rise to this precautionary measure, this did not take place during 2014 and the community remains in the same dangerous situation as before.

On 28 and 29 March, the 4th Indigenous summit (*Parlamento*) of the Calchaquí Valley was held in the indigenous community of Amaicha del Valle, Tucumán province, to commemorate the 40th anniversary of the first indigenous summit"Juan Calchaquí"[17]", with the participation of peoples from the northern provinces of Argentina. The issues discussed at this event included the delays in the territorial surveying (established by Law 26160), particularly for Catamarca, Salta and Jujuy provinces, and one of the greatest problems affecting their territories: mineral exploitation and soya plantations. In addition, a proposal was made to exercise territorial control by occupying the land and managing its natural resources, supportive actions were agreed between settlements and it was decided to seek solidarity with other social organisations in order to face up to the conflicts on their territories.

Resistance and struggle: some legal outcomes

Campo Maripe community (Mapuche people) – Neuquén province

"[The oil company] YPF does not wish to admit that it is responsible for applying a law that we indigenous peoples have, namely the right to be consulted on any project the company may want to commence on indigenous territory...", stated one of the community leaders of Campo Maripe as they continued to erect a perimeter fence around the community. Subsequently, on 2 September an oil well was drilled in Campo Campana, (operated by YPF-Chevron using fracking technology). As a result, a toxic cloud enveloped the community, affecting both people and animals. The protest organisation established by the community in the face of this constant conflict forced the provincial government to give Campo Maripe legal status in October. From now on, any action that affects its territory will need to be preceded by a proper consultation process. This outcome is extremely important because the government and oil companies have been denying the community its indigenous identity and its legal status has not been recognised for the last 14 years.

Recognition of the right to own justice

The Pulmarí Declaration, signed by the Office of the Attorney General (*el Ministerio Público Fiscal*) and the board of the Corporación Interestadual Pulmarí, established in 1987,[18] along with the indigenous communities and national and provincial (Neuquén) authorities that form part of this corporation, was published in August 2014. This establishes "recognition of and respect for the identity of the Neuquén indigenous peoples in the way that their conflicts are resolved within the context of human rights and current legislation". In September, the Attorney General instructed prosecutors to respect this declaration in all its facets.

Ruling of the Office of the Attorney General
(*la Procuración General de la Nación*)

On 8 September, the Attorney General issued a ruling in favour of the community of Catalán in Neuquén. This community had lodged an extraordinary appeal before the court following the Neuquén High Court's rejection of an appeal for unconstitutionality submitted by the community due to the enactment of Provincial Law 2439, which created the municipality of Villa Pehuenia, and Provincial Executive Decree 2/04, calling elections for the respective municipal committee. Two primary arguments were cited by the Attorney General in his ruling: 1) the state's failure to consult duly with the communities on a legislative decision that affects their lives; and 2) mechanisms for electing authorities that were alien to the ancestral traditions of the Mapuche people. Both arguments enabled him to conclude that, in this case, there had been a violation of indigenous rights as established and protected by domestic constitutional and international law. For this reason, the Attorney General ruled that the extraordinary appeal made by the community was admissible and that the decision should be annulled.

Vitality of the Mapuche people's language

On 18 June 2014, in the town of Zapala and in the context of the Apache-Pelayes case, the Court of Appeal convened a hearing to consider the defendants' request for interpreters or cultural facilitators from the Mapuche people. This request had been dismissed because, according to the prosecution, the members of Winkul Newen community did not speak *mapuzugun*, and were able to understand and communicate in Spanish. With the help of anthropologist, Diana Lenton, as expert witness, the validity and centrality of the Mapuche language was confirmed. Despite the prosecutor's and the complainant's refusal, the court decided to agree to the request for an interpreter in the subsequent stages of the case and, for this, it proposed initially approaching the Mapuche Confederation of Neuquén (*Confederación Mapuche Neuquina*) for a list of possible interpreters.   ◯

Notes and references

1   Instituto Nacional de Estadística y Censos (INDEC), 2004: *Resultados de la Encuesta Complementaria de Pueblos Indígenas—ECPI— surveyed in 2004.
     http://www.indec.mecon.ar/webcenso/ECPI/index_ecpi.asp
2   See the results of the 2010 National population survey (in Spanish), INDEC: *Censo Nacional de población, hogares y viviendas 2010.* Available from:
     http://www.indec.mecon.ar/nivel4_default.asp?id_tema_1=2&id_tema_2=21&id_tema_3=99
3   http://www.centromandela.com/?p=11147
4   http://argentina.indymedia.org/news/2015/02/872005.php
5   https://agnparticipacionciudadana.wordpress.com/
6   REDAF 2012, Informe Bosque nativo en Salta: les de bosques, análisis de la deforestación y situación del bosque chaqueño en la provincia. http://redaf.org.ar/
7   Aranda, D. 2014 "Arrasando vida".
     http://ctanacional.org/dev/2014/09/periodico-cta-105-septiembre-de-2014/
8   More information can be requested from: vicariapueblosoriginarios@gmail.com
9   Aranda, D. "Debate con dos versiones por una muerte." *Página 12*: http://www.pagina12.com.ar/diario/sociedad/3-263611-2015-01-10.html
10   http://qoomih-qom.blogspot.com.ar/
11   This is an archaeological site that was located within the native territory of the Diaguita people before they were conquered by the Incas, who then incorporated it into the Qhapaq Ñan Inca road system.
12   More information on "La Ciudacita": http://www.elsigloweb.com/nota.php?id=140982; http://www.primerafuente.com.ar/noticia/551250-una-comunidad-diaguita-denuncia-que-nunca-fue-consultada-sobre-el-destino-de-la-ciudacita;
     https://www.facebook.com/UPNDT/posts/677252469011584.
13   The Sacred City of the Quilmes is situated in the Calchaquí Valley. It is the site of the remains of the greatest pre-Colombian settlement in our country. It occupies around 30 hectares and is located at the foot of the Alto del Rey mountain. The site was first owned by the indigenous community, then the provincial state, then later a private concession, before finally returning into the hands of the descendants of the India Quilmes community. The ruins have been rebuilt.

14 Seizure of the Sacred City of the Quilmes on 07 March 2014 by a group of people from outside the community. The case that was commenced on this basis demonstrated yet again the ineffectiveness of our courts in this regard. See UPNDT press release: http://uniondiaguita.org.ar/comunicacion-de-la-comunidad-de-quilmes-ante-la-nueva-usurpacion-de-la-ciudad-sagrada/

15 http://www.lagaceta.com.ar/nota/532965/politica/exigen-al-estado-proteja-comunidad-indigena-nogalito.html

16 Fundación ANDHES (lawyers from the north-west of Argentina working on human rights and social studies). http://andhes.org.ar/

17 Considered to be one of the main Diaguita chiefs who opposed the Spaniards.
    In 1987, the national and provincial governments approved Law 23,612 (national) and Law 1,758 (provincial) in order to contribute 67,900 and 45,000 hectares respectively to the territorial space of (primarily) the communities of Aluminé and Villa Pehuenia.

*Prepared by the **Neuquén Indigenous Peoples' Human Rights Observatory** and **Morita Carrasco**. Morita is an anthropologist working at the University of Buenos Aires, where she teaches and researches issues relating to the rights of indigenous peoples and their relationship with the state. Since 1998, she has been working as an advisor to the Lhaka Honhat organisation in Salta and the Centre for Legal and Social Studies, CELS in relation to the Lhaka Honhat case before the Inter-American Commission on Human Rights (IACHR). Currently the claim is in the phase of implementation of the recommendations issued in 2012 by the IACHR.*

CHILE

The population that self-identifies as belonging to or descending from Chile's legally-recognised indigenous peoples[1] numbers 1,369,563 individuals, or 8% of the country's total population,[2] and comprises Aymara (0.59%), Lickanantay (0.14%), Quechua (0.07%), Colla (0.06%) and Diaguita (0.06%) living in the Andean valleys and *altiplanos* of the north; Rapa Nui in Polynesian *Te Pito o Te Henua* (Easter Island) (0.03%); Mapuche (6.97%) in *Wallmapu* in the centre-south of the country; and Kawashkar (0.01%) and Yamana (0.01%) in the southern canals.[3]

Chile's 1980 Political Constitution is still in force, approved under the dictatorship, and this recognises neither indigenous peoples nor their rights. The draft constitutional reform referring to these peoples and submitted to Congress in 2007/08 made no progress in 2014.

The rights of indigenous peoples are governed by Law No. 19,253 of 1992 on "encouragement, protection and development of indigenous peoples", a law that is not in line with international legislation on indigenous peoples' rights to land, territory, natural resources or participation and political autonomy. They are also governed by Law No. 20,249 of 2008 which "creates the marine coastal spaces of native[4] peoples" although its implementation has been minimal.[5] ILO Convention 169 was ratified by the Chilean state in 2008. Its implementation to date has also been insufficient, particularly in terms of the right to prior consultation.

Political rights

The indigenous peoples remain unrepresented in the bodies responsible for taking decisions that affect them. Although President Bachelet announced a specific legislative proposal in June 2014 that would make indigenous representation in the National Congress possible, this has not yet commenced its legislative path and was excluded from the draft bill of law replacing the binominal elec-

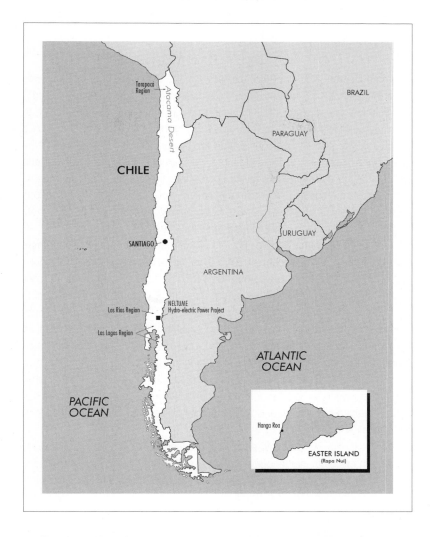

toral system with an inclusive proportional system and strengthening the representativeness of the National Congress, which is currently under consideration by
the chamber.

Right to consultation

Supreme Decree (SD) No. 66 of the Ministry of Social Development came into effect in March 2014. This "regulates the procedure for indigenous consultation".[6] It falls below the standard of ILO Convention 169 since it limits consultation to legislative projects likely to have a direct and significant impact on indigenous peoples. It also states that a consultation can be considered complete even if the agreement or consent of the indigenous peoples has not been obtained, and without having established culturally-appropriate procedures. For this reason, and because the decree itself was not put out to consultation with the indigenous peoples' representative organisations using appropriate procedures prior to its approval, this regulation was seriously questioned by those concerned.[7]

Moreover, Supreme Decree (SD) No. 40 of the Ministry of the Environment came into effect on 25 December 2013. This "approves regulations for the System of Environmental Impact Assessments (SEIA)" [8] and contains rules on "consulting" indigenous peoples with regard to investment projects that are subject to the SEIA. In addition to consultation procedures, the SD establishes ways of publicising and disseminating information on projects. This is so that, should an agreement not be reached with the indigenous peoples with regard to investment projects, they can still be approved. According to this SD, only high-impact projects that directly affect the peoples are subject to consultation, and this is to be determined by the authority in advance. The validity and scope of this decree has been challenged by a number of indigenous organisations, who have called for it to be repealed.[9]

Since SD No. 66 came into effect, two pre-legislative consultation processes have been held with indigenous peoples regarding draft bills of law that directly affect them: one creating the Ministry of Indigenous Affairs and the Council of Indigenous Peoples, the other the Ministry of Culture and Heritage.[10] The first of these two processes was convened by the Ministry of Social Development on 29 May 2014.[11] According to the notification issued for this process, the consultation was to be governed exclusively by the procedure established in SD No. 66. It was thus rejected by the indigenous peoples, who called for its repeal as a condition for commencing a dialogue with regard to any consultation process.[12] Despite the opposition and low turn-out of the indigenous organisations, the consultation went ahead and the first stage was completed in December, although the results have not yet been published.[13]

For its part, the consultation relating to the draft bill of law creating the Ministry of Culture and Heritage was convened by the National Council for Culture on 6 June 2014 by means of Exempt Resolution 2131[14] which, although it refers to SD No. 66 in its recitals, states that it will be implemented on the basis of ILO Convention 169 and must be undertaken in good faith, in a manner appropriate to the circumstances and with the aim of reaching an agreement or consent on the proposed actions. It should be noted that, in both its written and verbal communications in this regard, the National Council for Culture has shown its willingness to be flexible in order to ensure an intercultural dialogue that will enable the indigenous peoples' representative organisations to have an impact on the process and an agreement or consent to be reached on the draft submitted for consultation. This process is still under consideration.

Situation of the Mapuche people

No significant progress was made with regard to the situation of Mapuche rights during 2014. One landmark event was President Bachelet's appointment of a lawyer of Mapuche origin, Francisco Huenchumilla, to the post of Governor of Araucanía Region,[15] the region which is home to the largest number of indigenous people. This is the first time that a Mapuche has held this post. On taking office, Huenchumilla asked for "forgiveness from the Mapuche people for the land they have been dispossessed of by the Chilean state".[16] This was the first time a government authority had ever made such a declaration.

In terms of their right to lands and territories, although President Bachelet's administration, which commenced in March 2014, has stated its willingness to reinforce the policy on indigenous lands, the mechanism used to return these lands remains the Indigenous Lands and Waters Fund (FTAI) of the National Indigenous Development Corporation (CONADI), created under Law No. 19,253. The FTAI operates by purchasing lands for indigenous peoples on the open market, at speculative values. These purchases usually relate to lands already recognised to indigenous peoples but subsequently grabbed. The purchase of traditionally occupied lands is not generally considered, despite international standards.

Between 1994 and 2014, land purchases made by the FTAI through subsidies to indigenous communities lacking land (Article 20 of Law 19,253) came to 17,527.27 ha, most of which (17,266.77 ha) was for the Mapuche.[17] In terms of lands purchased by the FTAI that had already been recognised by the state but subsequently lost (Article 20 b Law 19,253), these totalled 120,321.73 ha, of which 119,885.82 ha were for the Mapuche.[18]

However, the legally-owned and/or ancestral lands and territories of the Mapuche continue to be threatened by a large number of extractive, productive or infrastructure projects which have been or are being assessed by the state through the SEIA (SD No. 40) without adequate consultation processes and without considering the right to free, prior and informed consent, as enshrined in international law, and without these people sharing in the benefits of this economic activity. These investment projects include: fish farming production and hatching projects for salmon breeding in the foothills; forestry, in constant expansion with monocropping of exotic species of pine and eucalyptus for cellulose production; hydroelectric companies, with dam projects or "run-of-river plants", supposedly environmentally friendly, in the foothills and mountainous regions. Mineral prospecting and geothermal exploration projects have also been identified. These investment projects affect the Mapuche communities by causing changes in their ecosystems and sacred sites, contaminating their water courses, affecting their production systems, and violating their right to define their own development priorities (Article 7.1 of ILO Convention 169). This is why such projects are widely rejected by the communities, and have led to great conflict in the regions in which they live (Araucanía, Los Ríos and Los Lagos).

One of the most notable cases is that of the Neltume Hydroelectric Power Project, which is being developed by the transnational company ENDESA-ENEL, a project involving USD 781 million of investment,[19] located on the Neltume Lake in Panguipulli commune (Los Ríos region). This is the ancestral territory of the Juan Quintuman, Inalafken and Valeriano Cayicul communities. The water discharged from the plant into the Neltume Lake will result in an increase in its level, threatening to flood the *nguillatue* where a most important Mapuche ceremony takes place. The project is also seriously threatening the tourist activities of the communities and, therefore, their development priorities. The state has commenced a consultation process for the project but this has been seriously questioned by the local communities because it fails to meet international standards. The affected communities therefore went to court in an effort to halt the ongoing consultation process and agree a new one in line with international standards. This appeal was rejected by the Courts of Justice,[20] arguing that there could be no violation of any right if the initial consultation process was not yet complete.

Another case is the construction of the hydraulic works for the Osorno Hydro-electric Power Plant, being developed by Eléctrica Pilmaiquén S.A.. This project involves USD 75 million of investment[21] and is located in the Valdivia and Osorno provinces, Los Ríos and Los Lagos regions. It will affect the Mapuche-Williche communities and traditional authorities of the territory as the dam will flood the religious and ceremonial site where the *Ngen Mapu Kintuante* lives. This is a site of great cultural significance to the Mapuche-Williche. The project's environmental authorisation, granted in 2009, and the 2014 authorisation of the General Waters Directorate (DGA) to conduct work on the water system were granted without prior consultation and without the consent of the Mapuche-Williche communities in question. As a result, they lodged an appeal for protection[22] against the DGA for issuing a resolution authorising commencement of these works. This case was considered inadmissible by the Courts of Justice on the basis that the people were not directly affected as the *Ngen Mapu Kintuante* site was not on indigenous lands.

Criminalisation of social protest

Mapuche social protest has continued to be repressed and persecuted by the Chilean state. Crimes committed against community members by police officers have gone unpunished, not least because they are heard through the military courts. In this regard, during 2014, eight cases in which Mapuche individuals were being prosecuted by means of the Anti-terrorist Law came to their conclusion.[23] All have now been ruled on by the courts, with six resulting in a dismissal of the charges; one in a common-law conviction of 4 of the 19 defendants who had originally been charged with terrorist offences in 2011; and one in the Machi (spiritual authority of the Mapuche people), Celestino Córdova, being sentenced to 18 years in prison. None of the convictions were therefore for terrorist activity as set out in Law 18,314 and yet the evidence used to convict them was the result of a legal process in accordance with the Anti-terrorist Law, with testimony being accepted from witnesses with concealed identities, in breach of the right to due process. The high rate of dismissals of cases in which Mapuche were prosecuted under the Anti-terrorist Law demonstrates the discretional and political use being made of this law by the state.

It should be noted that, in its judgment of 29 May 2014 in the case of *Norin Catriman et al v Chile,* the Inter-American Court of Human Rights convicted the Chilean state of violating the fundamental rights of eight members of the Mapuche people, as guaranteed in the American Convention, by using the Anti-terrorist Law. In this judgment, the Court concluded that "Chile violated the principle of the rule of law and the right to be presumed innocent, to the detriment of the eight victims of this case, by maintaining and applying Article 1 of Law No. 18,314, which contained a legal assumption of the subjective nature of a terrorist crime, this being a fundamental element of Chilean law with which to distinguish actions of a terrorist nature from those that are not."[24] The Court also established that, when substantiating the convictions, arguments has been used that were based on stereotypes and prejudice, and which represented a violation of the principle of equality and non-discrimination and the right to equal protection before the law.[25] The judgment drew attention to the existence of legislation that does not guarantee the right to due process, focusing particularly on and making recommendations with regard to the use of witnesses with concealed identities, thus preventing the right to cross-examination, and ordering that this legislation be amended.[26]

Situation of the Rapa Nui people (Easter Island)

The Rapa Nui people's struggle for territory continued in 2014. In January, a consultation took place with the aim of approving a new plot for the Vaitea fund, which controls around a quarter of the island's land.[27] There was very poor participation in this consultation on the part of the people, and it was moreover rejected by the Rapa Nui, who argued that the land included communally-owned heritage sites and would result in a break-up of the communal territory. However, there is an underlying pressure to transfer lands into individual properties in order to cover housing needs. This is why there has been no progress in recognising the territorial rights of this people since 2002.

In terms of political rights, a migration policy was discussed during 2014 aimed at limiting the population of the island in order to ensure its environmental, social, cultural and economic sustainability. A commitment was also made to produce a special statute for Easter Island in order to recognise Rapa Nui autonomy. The government drafted the migration policy and established its content jointly with the Easter Island Development Commission. This bill of law is now pending consideration by parliament. There has been no progress with regard to the autonomy statute, however.

Andean peoples' rights to natural resources

Violations of the collective rights of the Andean peoples of the north of Chile (Aymara, Quechua, Lickanantay, Colla and Diaguita) continued apace in 2014 due to natural resource extraction projects linked to large-scale mining. The current legislative framework[28] enables mining project holders to define the productive function of the territory and remove the natural resources necessary for their economic and cultural survival from the communities' control. One particularly problematic situation is that of water, given its scarcity in the region.

In terms of consultation, the inadequacies already noted in environmental regulations[29] and in the SEIA Regulation (SD No. 40) also apply to mining projects affecting the Andean peoples. To this must be added the fact that this legislation does not require independent environmental or social impact assessments. In addition, although there are mechanisms for the regularisation of land in Law No. 19,253 of 1993, many of the territories claimed are still under the control of the Chilean state and have not been formally demarcated or titled, as in the case of the Lickanantay territory of Alto Loa[30] and the Aymara-Quechua territory of the Tarapacá Basin.[31] This makes it difficult to protect them from mining projects. The studies commissioned by the authorities with the aim of identifying lands ancestrally occupied by indigenous communities in the north are now out of date, and so the demand is not clear and the land claim has not been satisfied. To this must be added the lack of an institutional mechanism that would make the return of property rights to the land under traditional occupation possible,[32] as possession has to be accredited by means of the rules of Decree Law 1939 on the administration of state lands.

Below is a summary of the most notable extractive projects on the territories of the Andean peoples during the year that gave rise to court cases for violation of the right to consultation:

The Manganeso Los Pumas project of the Hemisferio Sur S.C.M mining company, a Chilean subsidiary of the Australian Southern Hemisphere Mining, relating to the exploitation of a manganese deposit at a rate of 220,000 tonnes a month in order to produce concentrate from this mineral for the international markets. The deposit will have a useful life of 10 years and is located in the Lluta river basin, in the Arica y Parinacota region, where it is threatening the availability of water, discharging toxic waste and causing adverse effects on the valley's agriculture and on tourism. Although the Arica Court of Appeals overturned the Environmental Qualification Resolution that approved the project,[33] for lack of consultation and for violating freedom of religion (because of the possible effects on the river's waters, which are a source of the communities' world vision), the Supreme Court revoked the ruling, stating that it was for the new Environmental Courts to hear issues relating to environmental assessment processes, including consultation and indigenous rights. This sets a worrying precedent as it involves an abdication on the part of the Supreme Court of its role in protecting fundamental rights, which could be detrimental to the indigenous communities' right of access to justice, as noted by human rights organisations.[34]

Paguanta Prospecting Project, which involves 30% Chilean capital and is 70% owned by the Australian Herencia Resources. This project envisages drilling 14,000 m of holes, of which 3,000 m using reverse air method and 11,000 m. by diamond drilling. Thirteen drilling platforms will be constructed along with 1 kilometres of access roads to them. In addition, 53 watertight pools will be constructed in which to decant the sludge produced. The project is located in the headwaters of the Tarapacá River, in Tarapacá region. The communities' main issue has been that the environmental authority has only allowed for the consultation of one community close to the project, and this community has entered into negotiations with the project holder. The environmental authority has ignored the claims of other communities located in the same basin and whose access to water will be compromised. It should be noted that the authority has denied these communities the right to consultation, in violation of a legal ruling that explicitly recognised the right and called for an environmental impact assessment.[35] This situation has forced the communities in question to take further legal action. Appeals are currently pending with the Environmental Courts.[36]

The El Morro Project, of the Canadian company Goldcorp Inc., which holds 70% of the capital of this project and New Gold the rest. It consists of the construction and operation (for 14 years) of an open pit mine for the extraction of gold and copper. The aim is to produce 90,000 tonnes of mineral a day. The established reserves amount to 6.7 million ounces of gold and 4.9 billion pounds of copper. The project covers 2,463 h., of which 362 correspond to the open pit mine. The project is located on the legal and ancestral territory of the Diaguita Agricultural Community of the Huascoaltinos (CADHA), Atacama region, whose members are complaining that it will be impossible to continue the agricultural activities they have conducted since time immemorial and, moreover, that it will compromise indigenous territorial rights, creating the displacement of Huascoaltino cattle farmers. The project has had environmental approval since October 2013. The CADHA and, in parallel, other indigenous organisations, have made appeals for protection, which were admitted for a second time by the Supreme Court,[37] declaring the environmental authorisation null and void and arguing that the National Indigenous Development Corporation (CONADI) had not adequately substantiated the unilateral suspension of consultation in respect of CADHA, considering the authority's reasoning arbitrary when it described the organisation as acting in bad faith by undertaking delaying tactics such as lodging legal appeals. In addition, it considered that there was no basis for suggesting that other indigenous communities would not be affected. In this context, it considered the authority's actions illegal in suspending the indigenous consultation and subsequently granting the environmental licence to the project without safeguarding indigenous rights.

The Pascua Lama project, run and owned by Canadian Barrick Gold, the largest gold mining company in the world. Pascua Lama is a binational mining project involving both Chile and Argentina, which consists of exploiting seams of gold, silver and copper in order to obtain doré (unrefined gold and silver bullion bars) and copper concentrate. It is located at an altitude of more than 4,000 m. Gold production is likely to reach between 675,000 and 700,000 ounces/year (750,000 to 775,000 ounces/year for the first 10 years); silver between 24 and 25 million ounces/year (30 million in the first 10 years) and copper a projected 4,800 tonnes/year. The Huascolatino community has complained that, among other things, the project is being conducted without its consent, despite its magnitude and the violation of their territorial rights, in particular with regard to their ancestrally-owned territory and waters, including the glaciers that supply the whole hydrological system of the upper valley of the Huasco River. In addition, they claim that parallel indigenous structures have been set up alongside their own traditional authorities precisely for the purpose of entering into conversations with the company. CADHA currently has a complaint pending with the Inter-American Commission on Human Rights (IACHR),[38] which it has declared admissible.[39] In Chile, the project has been at a standstill since July 2013 by virtue of a court decision, given its failure to implement its Environmental Qualification Resolution (which required the production of a glacier management plan and a residual waters and drainage plan) and due to the serious environmental damage it has caused by dumping acid waste in the Chollay River.

Lastly, it should be noted that the Inter-American Commission on Human Rights (IACHR) is currently considering cases against the state of Chile for discriminatory acts in relation to Andean communities and persons, namely the Chusmiza-Usmagama[40] and G.B.B cases,[41] and that, during 2014, consistent efforts were made to reach a friendly agreement in both cases.   ○

Notes and references

1   Indigenous Law No. 19,253 of 1993. This law, however, only recognises the existence of ethnic groups and not peoples.
2   CASEN 2011 survey database. Statistical projection made by the team of *Observatorio Ciudadano*.
3   The results of the 2012 Population Census, published in 2013, showed a substantial increase in the country's indigenous population, which was estimated at 1.7 million, or 11.11% of the country's total population. National Institute of Statistics, Summary of 2012 Census Results at www.censo.cl. This census, however, was ruled as inadmissible due to its lack of accuracy, as recognised by the government.
4   In Spanish:"*pueblos originarios*" (ed.)
5   Only an area of approximately 100 hectares has been recognised in the case of the Altue Mapuche- Williche community, Los Lagos region.
6   Available at: http://www.leychile.cl/Navegar?idNorma=1059961
7   Including the Alianza Territorial Mapuche, Asociación Indígena de Mujeres del Valle de Lluta "Warmi Chamampi", Asociación Indígena Wila Pampa (Aymara), Asociación de Estudiantes de Pueblos Originarios AESPO, Consejo de Pueblos Atacameños, Consejo Territorial de Chapiquiña (Aymara), Comunidad Indígena de Chapiquiña, Coordinadora Aymara de Defensa de los Recursos Naturales, Identidad Territorial Lafkenche, el Pacto por la Autodeterminación Mapuche which groups together the organisations, leaders and traditional authorities of Araucanía (includ-

ing Ad-Mapu, Consejo de Todas las Tierras, Lonkos de Temucuicui, Parlamento de Coz Coz, Temulemu, etc.), Parlamento Aymara del Pueblo Qullana, Pueblos Indígenas Autoconvocados, Pueblos Indígenas Aymara de Arica-Parinocata y Tarapacá, Pueblos Indígenas Quechua de Tarapacá, Pueblos Lickanantay de Antofagasta, Consejo Nacional Aymara de Mallku y Talla de la comuna de Arica Urbano. In addition, the leaders and representatives of the Rapa Nui people (elected by the Easter Island Development Commission and the elected representative to CON-ADI's National Council) stated they would not participate and decided to independently organise the consultation for *Te pito o te henua*/Easter Island (INDH. 2013. *Informe Misión de Observación Mesa de Consenso Indígena*. Available online: <http://bibliotecadigital.indh.cl/bitstream/handle/123456789/588/Informe?sequence=1>

8   Available at: http://www.leychile.cl/Navegar?idNorma=1053563

9   Some statements from indigenous organisations in this regard can be found at:
      http://www.mapuexpress.org/2014/09/04/organizaciones-mapuche-de-concepcion-exigimos-la-anulacion-del-decreto-ndeg66-y-el%20
      http://www.mapuexpress.org/2014/09/05/atacamenos-y-quechuas-en-alto-loa-exigen-derogacion-decretos-66-y-40-y-se-reservan%20#sthash.Nz0I8Aq8.dpbs

10   Organisation of consultation process, Ministry and Council or Councils of Indigenous Peoples available at:
      http://www.consultaindigenamds.gob.cl/Convocatoria.html
      Organisation of consultation process, Ministry of Culture available at: http://consultaindigena.cultura.gob.cl/mapuche/portada

11   Exempt Resolution 275 of D.O. Ministry, 24 June 2014

12   Some statements from indigenous organisations in this regard can be found at:
      http://www.mapuexpress.org/2014/09/04/organizaciones-mapuche-de-concepcion-exigimos-la-anulacion-del-decreto-ndeg66-y-el%20
      http://www.mapuexpress.org/2014/09/05/atacamenos-y-quechuas-en-alto-loa-exigen-derogacion-decretos-66-y-40-y-se-reservan%20#sthash.Nz0I8Aq8.dpbs
      http://www.mapuexpress.org/2014/09/09/declaracion-comunidad-autonoma-de-temucuicui-sobre-la-consulta-indigena-del-gobierno

13   http://www.consultaindigenamds.gob.cl/articulo.php?id=13686

14   Available at: http://consultaindigena.cultura.gob.cl/wp-content/uploads/2014/08/Rex-16-de-junio-2014.pdf

15   The Governor is the most senior representative of the Executive at regional level.

16   http://www.soychile.cl/Temuco/Politica/2014/03/12/235984/En-su-primer-dia-como-intendente-Huenchumilla-pidio-perdion-a-mapuches-y-colonos-de-La-Araucania.aspx

17   National Indigenous Development Corporation (Ministry of Social Development), information provided to the *Observatorio Ciudadano* in October 2014.

18   Ibid.

19   http://seia.sea.gob.cl/expediente/ficha/fichaPrincipal.php?modo=ficha&id_expediente=5124693

20   Valdivia Court of Appeals Roll147-2014, Supreme Court Roll: 12450-2014.

21   http://seia.sea.gob.cl/expediente/ficha/fichaPrincipal.php?modo=ficha&id_expediente=2369587

22   Santiago Court of Appeals Roll No. 12.625-2014, Supreme Court Roll No. 23.046-2014.

23   The cases that resulted in a judgment during 2014 were that of the attack and murder of the Luchsinger Mackay family, with a conviction, the Fundo Brasil terrorist firebomb attack, with the case dismissed for all defendants, and the Fundos San Leandro terrorist attack, with the case dismissed against all defendants.

24 Inter-American Court of Human Rights, case of "Norín Catrimán et al v Chile", 29 May 2014, paras 168 to 177.

25 Ibid. paras 223 to 228 and 230

26 Ibid. para 20 operative part of the ruling.

27 More information on the Rapa Nui people from: IWGIA & Observatorio Ciudadano, 2012. *IWGIA Informe 15: Los derechos del pueblo Rapa Nui en Isla de Pascua: Informe de Misión Internacional*. IWGIA & Observatorio Ciudadano: Copenhagen.

28 The Mining Code and the Organic Constitutional Law No. 18,097 of 1982 on mining concessions.

29 Law No. 19,300 of 1994 on the General Bases of the Environment and its modifications.

30 See National Human Rights Institute. *Informe Misión Observación Alto Loa. 9 a 12 agosto de 2013*. Available from http://bibliotecadigital.indh.cl/bitstream/handle/123456789/643/Informe%20 Mision?sequence=1

31 See Neira. *Informe antropológico Oposición al proyecto Sondajes de Prospección Paguanta 04 de marzo de 2013*.

32 See National Human Rights Institute. *Situación de los derechos humanos en Chile. Informe Anual 2014*. National Human Rights Institute, 2014.

33 Arica Court of Appeals Roll 182-2013, judgment of 25 November 2013.

34 See National Human Rights Institute, *ibid*, pp. 249.

35 Supreme Court Roll No. 11,040-2011, judgment of 30 March 2012.

36 Santiago Environmental Court, Roll R-54-2014.

37 Supreme Court Roll 11,299, dated 7 October 2014.

38 Case 12,741.

39 Inter-American Commission on Human Rights. Report on Admissibility No. 1411/09, dated 30 September 2009.

40 Inter-American Commission on Human Rights, Report on Admissibility No. 29/13, dated 10 March 2013. Case 12,904.

41 Petition 687/2011.

José Aylwin, Hernando Silva and Nancy Yáñez, members of Observatorio Ciudadano.

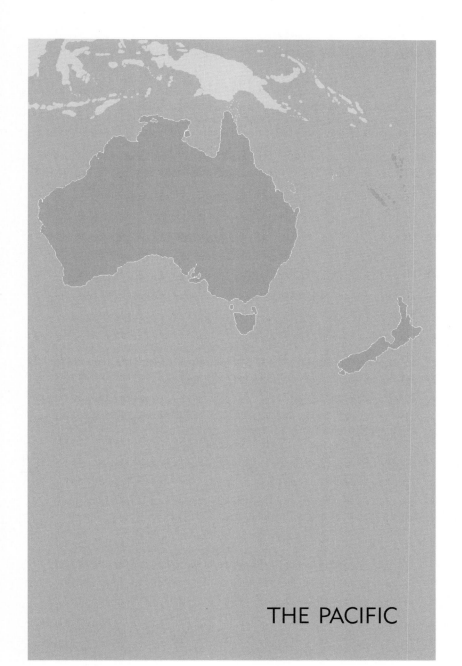

THE PACIFIC

AUSTRALIA

Indigenous peoples hold a long and complex connection with the Australian landscape, including marine and coastal areas. Some estimates maintain that this relationship has endured for at least 40,000 years.[1] At colonisation in 1788, there may have been up to 1.5 million people in Australia.[2] In June 2011, Indigenous peoples were estimated to make up 3.0% of the Australian population, or 670,000 individuals.[3] Throughout their history, Aboriginal people have lived in all parts of Australia. Today the majority live in regional centres (43%) or cities (32%), although some still live on traditional lands.

Despite recent minor improvements, the health status of Indigenous Australians remains significantly below that of other Australians. Rates of infant mortality among Indigenous Australians remain unacceptably high at 10-15%, and life expectancy for Indigenous Australians (59 for males and 65 for females) is 17 years less than that of others. Recent suicide figures report 105 deaths per 100,000, for Indigenous males between the ages of 25 to 34 years, as compared to 22 deaths per 100,000 for their non-Aboriginal counterparts.[4] According to the Australian Bureau of Statistics (ABS), there were 996 suicides reported across Australia between 2001 and 2010 among Indigenous peoples.[5] 1.6% of all Australians die by suicide but, for Aboriginal peoples, this rate is more than 4.2%, or one in every 24 Aboriginals or Torres Strait Islanders.[6] The ABS Corrective Services report recently noted that the number of Aboriginal men in prison had risen by 8% and women by 12% in the past year, compared to a national prison population increase of 6%.[7] Aboriginal and Torres Strait Islander peoples now comprise 30% of the prison population.[8]

The 1975 Racial Discrimination Act has proved a key law for Aborigines but was overridden without demur by the Howard government in 2007 when introducing the Northern Territory Emergency Intervention (see *The Indigenous World, 2008).* States and Territories also have legislative power on rights issues, including Indigenous rights, where they choose to use them and where these do not conflict with national laws.

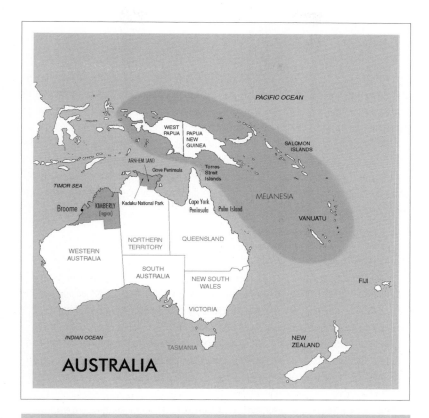

AUSTRALIA

Australia has not ratified ILO Convention 169 but, although it voted against the UN Declaration on the Rights of Indigenous Peoples (UN-DRIP) in 2007, it went on to endorse it in 2009.

At the end of 2014, Indigenous Australia faces what political commentators might call "existential" threats. The national government has been cutting essential services such as water and power to remote communities, why the Western Australian government wishes to displace Indigenous people and communities from its vast territory to save money.[9] Other state governments are also talking about closing communities. For Indigenous nations and cultures so attached to local landscapes, ceremony sites, and eco-systems, this could threaten their cultural and social survival.

Respected national Aboriginal elder Patrick Dodson says that "Aborigines will become refugees" and has elaborated the many ills which will result for people displaced and communities in which the displaced seek refuge, such as increased substance abuse and   social tensions.[10] Unfortunately, Australia has many of these problems in the North and Centre of the continent, but few solutions.

As if that were not enough, a provocative public policy commentator and former national Labor minister ended the year calling for Indigenous people to be denied the right to child-bearing unless free of any form of governmental aid![11] These population removal and social hygiene proposals should provide loud national and international comment and debate in 2015.

"Closing the Gap"

The latest official report on the 2009 national indigenous policy "Closing the Gap",[12] which aimed at addressing indigenous disadvantage, was met in national media with headlines such as "Australia's shame".[13]

Nevertheless, Prime Minister Tony Abbott remains the most reliable and consistent public advocate of Indigenous peoples and their interests, as well as advancing their hopes for constitutional recognition. His goodwill and ease with Indigenous people is dramatically different from the previous Coalition government, 1996-2007. However, the problems of passing the national Budget and fragmenting of power in the Senate (the upper House of Parliament ed.) have left national spending and policy in much confusion in 2014, meaning that, so far, promised improvements in e.g. education and health for indigenous groups have been stalled.

Torres Strait sea walls

The construction of sea walls to protect people, homes, and community facilities from rising seas is underway on six islands of Torres Strait, at the northern end of the Great Barriers Reef.[14] This is partly funded by the national government despite its official scepticism about rising sea levels and climate change. Indeed, great anger was shown by national political elites and their media supporters when American President Barack Obama referred to climate threats to Australia's Great Barrier Reef during a visit to Brisbane in November 2014.[15] His audience of young Australians was pleased by his speech, leaving the government elite looking silly and muttering about bad manners and respect for his Australian hosts.

Bloody deeds

Just before Christmas, national attention focused on the killing of eight Torres Strait children in Cairns, Far North Queensland, apparently by their troubled mother in a mixed Aboriginal-Islander neighbourhood. 2015 will see much official attention to the causes of such calamity and dysfunction after national and state government leaders attend the funerals.

Debate on constitutional recognition

The debate on constitutional recognition of aboriginal Australians gained momentum in 2014. Both the prime minister and opposition leaders support constitutional recognition for Indigenous peoples, and it seems likely that the constitutional referendum will be held in 2017, or later. Aboriginal lawyer, academic and land rights activist Noel Pearson delivered important input to the debate with his 2014 essay, *A Rightful Place: Race, Recognition and a More Complete Commonwealth*.[16] The essay discusses how to unite Australia's immigrant and Indigenous political cultures in terms acceptable to conservative, liberal, and other progressive voters who must approve any constitutional change.

Pearson won national acclaim speaking at the memorial service for former prime minister Whitlam (in office 1972-75), who died late in the year, attracting virtually all the political, social, cultural, and media elite of Australia to one televised event.[17] Australians rarely hear or listen to Indigenous voices, although eloquence is an important part of Indigenous leadership. Pearson's studied and solemn style impressed many and ensured his role in the constitutional debate.

The National Congress of Australia's First Peoples has reminded the Prime Minister in a public letter of the government's longstanding constitutional role vis-à-vis Indigenous peoples and has demanded that it ensure that service reductions and displacement of people not occur.[18] Congress co-chairs Kirstie Parker and Les Malezer wrote that, e.g.,

> *The WA (Western Australia (ed.) government apparently intends to target Aboriginal Peoples on the one hand, whilst continuing to provide high standards of municipal services to non-Indigenous citizens on the other. We cannot accept the WA and SA (Southern Australia ed.) governments have legitimate authority under Australian or international law to racially discriminate to disrupt or destroy the livelihoods, accommodations or habitat of the First Peoples of Australia.*
>
> *... Constitutionally, the Australian Government has the highest authority in the nation in order to promote and protect the rights of the First Peoples of Australia.*
>
> *It is part of the international responsibilities and it is a responsibility that should not and cannot be discarded or devolved to other levels of government.*
>
> *... These standards to which we refer are enshrined in the human rights treaties that Australia has signed and ratified, along with the UN Declaration on the Rights of Indigenous Peoples.*

One of the issues vexing national political and legal debate is the role of international covenants in determining Australian policy and law. The constitutional debates ahead will better inform Australians of these issues. Information and precedents from abroad will play an important role, and not only among Indigenous rights lawyers as at present.

The outcome of the World Conference on Indigenous Peoples

In September, the UN convened a World Conference of Indigenous Peoples (WCIP) at its Headquarters in New York, which came out with an action oriented Outcome Document (OD) intended at furthering the implementation of the UNDRIP. The National Congress of Australia's First Peoples participated in the preparation of the OD, and considers the OD to be highly useful to pursue the acknowledgement of rights for the Aboriginal and Torres Strait Islander Peoples through closer engagement with the national government along with renewed efforts for improving awareness amongst the Indigenous population. Congress has assumed the role to oversight its usage and implementation in Australia at the domestic level.

Following the WCIP, Congress convened a meeting with community organisations in Australia which focus upon rights at the domestic and international level and met with ministers and senior officials of government to seek cooperation in dealing with the resolutions in the OD. Congress is also campaigning with the government for take-up of a national action plan for implementation of the rights of the Aboriginal and Torres Strait Islander Peoples, and considers submissions and shadow reports on Australia to address the implementation of the OD during preparation for the Universal Periodic Review of Australia at the UN Human Rights Council in 2015.   ◯

Notes and references

1   Many Aboriginal people maintain that they were created when distinct Creator Beings formed the land at the beginning of time (often termed "the Dreaming"). It is now widely accepted among archaeologists that the earliest undisputed age for the occupation of Australia by human beings is 40,000 to 50,000 years ago. **O'Connell J.F. and Allen F.J., 1998**: When did humans first arrive in greater Australia and why is it important to know? *Evolutionary Anthropology*, 6:132–146.

2   The actual numbers are highly disputed because of the difficulty in estimating a population so very much changed by colonisation. Numbers range from 300,000 to 1.5 million, the latter being widely accepted nowadays. **Butlin, N., 1993:** *Economics and the Dreamtime*. Cambridge, Cambridge University Press; **Reynolds, H. 2001:** *An indelible stain? The question of genocide in Australia's history.* Ringwood Victoria, Penguin; **Gray, A., 2001:** Indigenous Australian: Demographic and Social History in J. Jupp (ed.) *The Australian People: an Encyclopaedia of the nation, its people and their origins.* Cambridge: Cambridge University Press, pp.88-93.

3   http://www.abs.gov.au/AUSSTATS/abs@.nsf/featurearticlesbyCatalogue/DB52AB9278B0C818CA257AD7000D1067?OpenDocument

4   http://www.abs.gov.au/AUSSTATS/abs@.nsf/39433889d406eeb9ca2570610019e9a5/8F08EF0297F11CC6CA2574390014C588?opendocument

5   http://www.abs.gov.au/ausstats/abs@.nsf/Products/3309.0~2010~Chapter~Aboriginal+and+Torres+Strait+Islander+suicide+deaths?OpenDocument

6   http://www.abs.gov.au/ausstats/abs@.nsf/Products/3309.0~2010~Chapter~Aboriginal+and+Torres+Strait+Islander+suicide+deaths?OpenDocument

7   http://www.abs.gov.au/ausstats/abs@.nsf/mf/4512.0/

8   http://www.abs.gov.au/ausstats/abs@.nsf/mf/4512.0/

9   E.g, **Nicolas Rothwell:** "Remote prospects of rejuvenation". *The Australian*, 15-11-2014; **Don Tout:** "Settler Colonial Closures", *Arena Magazine* No 133, 12-2014.

10 **Dan Harrison:** "Patrick Dodson warns…". *Sydney Morning Herald*, 22-11-2014

11 **Gary Johns:** "No contraception, no dole". *The Australian*, 30-12-2014

12   http://www.pc.gov.au/research/recurring/overcoming-indigenous-disadvantage
13   **Michael Gordon:** "Australia's shame". *Sydney Morning Herald*, 19-11-2014.
14   http://www.tsirc.qld.gov.au/sites/tsirc.qld.gov.au/files/seawalls_factsheet.pdf
15   E.g. **Mungo MacCallum:** "G20: The climate elephant just couldn't be ignored", *The Drum, ABC Online*, 20-11-2014.
16   *Quarterly Essay*, Black Inc. Melbourne.
17   http://www.smh.com.au/comment/noel-pearsons-eulogy-for-gough-whitlam-in-full-20141105-11haeu.html
18   http://nationalcongress.com.au/open-letter-to-prime-minister-remote-communities/ 28-11-2014

Peter Jull is a member of IWGIA's international advisory board.

The paragraph on the World Conference Outcome Document has been provided by **Les Malezer**, *Co-Chair of the National Congress of Australia's First Peoples. As a well known indigenous rights advocate, he was appointed co-advisor to the President of the General Assembly in the preparation for the UN World Conference on Indigenous Peoples during 2014.*

AOTEAROA (NEW ZEALAND)

Māori, the indigenous people of Aotearoa, represent 15% of the 4.5 million population. The gap between Māori and non-Māori is pervasive: Māori life expectancy is 7.3 years less than non-Māori; household income is 78% of the national average; 45% of Māori leave upper secondary school with no qualifications and over 50% of the prison population is Māori.[1]

The Treaty of Waitangi (the Treaty) was signed between the British and Māori in 1840. There are two versions of the Treaty, an English-language version and a Māori-language version. The Māori version granted a right of governance to the British, promised that Māori would retain sovereignty over their lands, resources and other treasures and conferred the rights of British citizens on Māori. The Treaty has, however, limited legal status; accordingly, protection of Māori rights is largely dependent upon political will and ad hoc recognition of the Treaty.

New Zealand endorsed the UN Declaration on the Rights of Indigenous Peoples in 2010. New Zealand has not ratified ILO Convention 169.

National elections a blow

General elections were held in New Zealand on 20 September 2014. The centre-right National Party obtained 60 of the 121 seats and secured a third three-year term by entering into coalition agreements with the rightist ACT and United Future parties, each of whom obtained one seat. The Labour Party won 32 seats, the Green Party 14 and New Zealand First 11. The two parties with an explicit Māori *kaupapa* (vision) – the Māori Party and Mana – did not fare well. The Māori Party saw a reduction in the number of its seats to two: Te Ururoa Flavell retained his seat and new party co-leader Marama Fox secured one. In a surprise loss, the leftist Mana Party, led by Hone Harawira, lost its only seat.[2]

Once again, the Māori Party entered into a relationship accord and confidence and supply agreement with the National Party (Confidence Agreement), under which the Māori Party will support the National-led government on confidence and supply in return for a number of commitments from National. National's commitments include consulting the Māori Party on relevant policy issues and legislative measures and working with them on a collection of policy priorities, including ongoing investment in Whānau Ora (a cross-agency culturally-anchored social programme) and Māori economic and regional development. The Māori Party will also again hold ministerial posts outside of Cabinet: Te Ururoa Flavell is appointed Minister for Māori Development, Minister for Whānau Ora and Associate Minister for Economic Development.[3] Notably, the Confidence Agreement does not contain the same firm social welfare and development commitments as in previous years, reflecting the weakened position of the Māori Party.

For Māori, the election results were a blow. The weakened position of the Māori Party and the Mana Party's failure to secure any seats means that Māori do not have strong party representation in the House. Despite occupying ministerial posts (in addition to those negotiated under the Confidence Agreement, National's cabinet includes Hekia Parata as Minister of Education),[4] Māori remain a numerical minority in Parliament and those with seats are constrained by their respective party's policy positions.

International concerns regarding Māori rights

A host of international bodies expressed concern at the human rights situation of Māori in 2014. **The United Nations (UN) Committee on the Rights of Persons with Disabilities** considered New Zealand's initial report on implementation of the Convention on the Rights of Persons with Disabilities in September. In its concluding observations, the Committee expressed concerns at the ability of Māori children with disabilities to access some government services, including health and education; the ability of Māori people with disabilities to access information in their own language; the higher prevalence of disability among the Māori population as a result of poverty and disadvantage; and the fact that employment levels in New Zealand for Māori and Pacific persons with disabilities remain especially low.[5] Government action on the Committee's recommendations[6] has yet to be forthcoming.

Pacific Ocean

North
Island

NORTHLAND

Tasman sea

Bay of
Plenty

TUHOE COUNTRY

WELLINGTON

Cook Strait

NGĀTI TOA RANGATIRA
COUNTRY

South
Island

Christchurch

Pacific Ocean

Stewart Island

NEW ZEALAND

In addition, the **UN Working Group on Arbitrary Detention** undertook its first official country mission to New Zealand in early 2014. At the conclusion of the visit, the Working Group identified signs of systemic bias against Māori "at all levels of the criminal justice process". In a strongly phrased statement it recommended:

that a review is undertaken of the degree of inconsistencies and systemic bias against Maori at all the different levels of the criminal justice system, including the possible impact of recent legislative reforms. Incarceration that is the outcome of such bias constitutes arbitrary detention in violation of international law.[7]

The Working Group encouraged the state to search "for creative and integrated solutions to the root causes which lead to disproportionate incarceration rates of the Maori population".[8] It will publish a report on its mission in 2015. The New Zealand government rejected the suggestion of institutional bias against Māori within its justice system, despite evidence to the contrary.[9]

Further, in 2014, the **UN Subcommittee on the Prevention of Torture and other Cruel, Inhuman or Degrading Treatment or Punishment** undertook its first periodic country visit to New Zealand. Its delegation visited places where persons may be deprived of their liberty. The Subcommittee expressed concerns at the "disproportionately high number of Māori at every stage of the criminal justice system"; at proposed amendments to the Bail Act 2000 given that these could further increase Māori prison numbers; at the absence of reintegration programmes for Māori in most prisons, particularly women's prisons; at the high rates of Māori recidivism; and at the absence of specific Māori literacy programmes at the residencies it visited. The Subcommittee's recommendations included placing greater focus on social reintegration programmes, "as well as more active involvement with the Māori community"; further developing and replicating programmes aimed at reducing Māori recidivism, including Māori literacy programmes; and considering Māori literacy programmes for Youth Justice Residences.[10] New Zealand's written response to the Subcommittee whitewashed these concerns. New Zealand stated that it was, *inter alia*, enhancing and expanding its Māori Focus Units to foster reintegration; that its own analyses indicated "that Māori prisoners perform equally well in mainstream prison-based programmes, including literacy"; and that the Māori language was already a feature of the New Zealand Curriculum taught in Youth Justice residencies.[11]

In April, New Zealand also updated the **Committee on the Elimination of Racial Discrimination** on its follow-up to concluding observations made regarding M ori in 2013. The update confirmed New Zealand's failure to announce a timetable for implementing the Waitangi Tribunal's decision on the Wai 262 claim (see *The Indigenous World 2012*) and detailed insufficient measures to preserve the Māori language, despite the Committee's recommendations on these matters.[12]

Outcome Document potential lobbying tool

The Outcome Document of the September 2014 UN World Conference on Indigenous Peoples is a potentially useful lobbying tool for Māori and indigenous rights advocates in Aotearoa as it reflects some of the priorities for action singled out by Māori.[13] These priorities include the establishment of effective mechanisms to implement indigenous peoples' rights. This is reflected, to some degree, in the Outcome Document's commitments whereby states will take, in consultation and cooperation with indigenous peoples, measures to achieve the ends of the UN-DRIP, including developing and implementing national action plans; the UN will support, the implementation, upon request, of national action plans, strategies or other measures to achieve the ends of the Declaration; and the Secretary-General is requested to develop an action plan to achieve the ends of the UNDRIP and submit recommendations at the General Assembly's 70th session on using, modifying and improving existing UN mechanisms to do so.[14]

The Outcome Document could also form an important focal point for lobbying on a host of other rights issues for which it makes commitments. Its commitments regarding education, health, the position of indigenous peoples with disabilities, justice, indigenous women, indigenous children and youth, traditional knowledge, free, prior and informed consent and lands, territories and resources may all prove especially useful in Aotearoa given that these are matters repeatedly highlighted by human rights bodies as requiring the state's attention (see, for example, *The Indigenous World 2014* and *2013*).

Tribunal affirms sovereignty not ceded

A particularly important development for Māori in 2014 was the Waitangi Tribunal's affirmation that the Treaty of Waitangi did not cede Māori sovereignty. This finding was made in the Waitangi Tribunal's report on stage one of the Wai 1040: Te Paparahi o te Raki inquiry, relating to the Northland region.[15] The report, entitled *He Whakaputanga me te Tiriti – The Declaration and the Treaty*, focused on the meaning and impact of the Treaty and the Declaration of Independence. The Declaration of Independence, which was signed by 34 *rangatira* (Māori leaders) from the North in 1835, proclaimed New Zealand's sovereign independence. The Tribunal found:

> *Our essential conclusion, therefore, is that the rangatira did not cede their sovereignty in February 1840; that is, they did not cede their authority to make and enforce law over their own people and within their territories. Rather, they agreed to share power and authority with the Governor. They and Hobson were to be equal, although of course they had different roles and different spheres of influence. The detail of how this relationship would work in practice, especially where the Māori and European populations intermingled, remained to be negotiated over time on a case-by-case basis.*[16]

In the report, the Tribunal made it clear that, at this initial stage of the inquiry, it was not making findings regarding the claims or about the contemporary exercise of Crown sovereignty in Aotearoa.[17]

Haka Act offers recognition

In 2014, legislation aimed at acknowledging and protecting the significance of the *haka* (dance) *Ka Mate* was passed. The Haka Ka Mate Attribution Act 2014 acknowledges the significance of *Ka Mate* to the *iwi* (nation) Ngāti Toa Rangatira (it was composed by Ngāti Toa Rangatira leader Te Rauparaha) as part of their Treaty settlement.[18] It seeks to address some of the concerns surrounding the disrespectful use of this important cultural *taonga* (treasure). However, the Act does not prevent the *haka* from being performed (whether respectfully or disrespectfully). Nor does it require that the *iwi* be compensated for commercial exploitation of the *haka*. Rather, it provides that where *Ka Mate* is published for commercial purposes, communicated to the public, or featured in a film shown in, or issued to, the public it must include a statement that Te Rauparaha was the composer of *Ka Mate* and a leader of Ngāti Toa Rangatira. This legislation is the first of its kind in Aotearoa and seeks to give some intellectual property-like protection to an *iwi taonga* as a result of Treaty settlement negotiations. The Act will be reviewed after five years to assess whether it offers sufficient protection.[19]

Police apologise to Tuhoe

In August, the Police Commissioner offered a landmark belated apology to the *iwi* Ngāi Tuhoe for police actions during the 2007 "terror" raids on Tuhoe country (see *The Indigenous World 2014* and *2010*). The apology included an acknowledgement of "the distress experienced by innocent community members, caught up in the execution of the search warrants, and the impact of subsequent media stigmatisation of Tuhoe as terrorists". Those Tuhoe who were present reportedly accepted the apology, although some *iwi* members declined to participate.[20]

Significant Treaty settlement progress

The year saw a significant number of completed settlements regarding Māori claims for historical Treaty breaches, spurred on by the National Party's (unmet) target of securing deeds of settlement with all groups by 2014. According to the Office of Treaty Settlements, at least one group signed an Agreement in Principle;[21] two groups agreed that their deeds of settlement were ready for presentation to their members for ratification;[22] three groups signed deeds of settlement with the Crown;[23] and a staggering 15 had the legislation giving effect to their settlements enacted.[24]   O

Notes and references

1   Statistics New Zealand http://www.stats.govt.nz.
2   New Zealand Electoral Commission "Official Count Results – Overall Status" 10 October 2014 http://www.electionresults.govt.nz/electionresults_2014/partystatus.html (last accessed 3 January 2015); New Zealand Parliament "Parliamentary Parties: National Party" www.parliament.nz/ en-nz/mpp/parties/national/00PlibMPPNational1/national-party (last accessed 3 January 2015).
3   National Party and Maori Party *2014 Relationship Accord and Confidence and Supply Agreement with the Maori Party* 5 October 2014 www.parliament.nz (last accessed 3 January 2015) at pp. 1-2.
4   Department of Prime Minister and Cabinet *Ministerial List* ,13 October 2014. www.dpmc.govt.nz/cabinet/ministers/ministerial-list (last accessed 3 January 2015).
5   Committee on the Rights of Persons with Disabilities, *Concluding observations on the initial report of New Zealand* 31 October 2014 UN Doc CRPD/C/NZL/CO/1 at [17], [43], [53], [55].
6   Ibid at [18] [44] [54] [56].
7   Working Group on Arbitrary Detention *United Nations Working Group on Arbitrary Detention statement at the conclusion of its visit to New Zealand (24 March -7 April 2014)* http://www.hrc. co.nz/wp-content/uploads/2014/04/WG-on-Arbitrary-Detention-statement-at-conclusion-of-visit. pdf (last accessed 5 January 2015) at 3.
8   Ibid.
9   Radio New Zealand News "Maori offenders not targetted [sic] – minister" 8 April 2014 http://www. radionz.co.nz/news/national/241079/maori-offenders-not-targetted-minister (last accessed 5 January 2015).
10 Subcommittee on Prevention of Torture and Other Cruel, Inhuman or Degrading Treatment or Punishment ['Subcommittee'], *Report on the visit of the Subcommittee on Prevention of Torture and Other Cruel, Inhuman or Degrading Treatment or Punishment to New Zealand* 25 August 2014 UN Doc CAT/OP/NZL/1 at [21], [33], [34], [50], [51], [52], [94].

11   Subcommittee, *Replies of New Zealand to the recommendations and questions put forward by the Subcommittee on Prevention of Torture in its report on its first periodic visit to New Zealand (CAT/OP/NZL/1)* 25 August 2014 UN Doc CAT/OP/NZL/Add.1 at [59], [60], [116].
12   Committee on the Elimination of Racial Discrimination, *Information received from New Zealand on follow-up to the concluding observations* 24 April 2014 UN Doc CERD/C/NZL/CO/18-20/ Add.1 at [14]-[15].
13   *Maori Priorities*, email to World Conference on Indigenous Peoples' Pacific Caucus, 12 June 2014 (on file with author).
14   UN General Assembly, *Outcome document of the high-level plenary meeting of the General Assembly known as the World Conference on Indigenous Peoples* 25 September 2014 UN Doc A/ RES/69/2 at [7], [8], [31], [32], [40].
15   Waitangi Tribunal *He Whakaputanga me te Tiriti The Declaration and the Treaty: The Report on Stage 1 of the Te Paparahi o Te Raki Inquiry* 2014 http://www.justice.govt.nz/tribunals/waitangi-tribunal/Reports/he-whakaputanga-me-te-tiriti-the-declaration-and-the-treaty-the-report-on-stage-1-of-the-te-paparahi-o-te-raki-inquiry (last accessed 5 January 2015).
16   Ibid at 10.4.4.
17   Carwyn Jones *He Whakaputanga me te Tiriti – The Declaration and the Treaty* 23 November 2014 https://ahikaroa.wordpress.com/2014/11/ (last accessed 5 January 2015).
18   The Act can be accessed through the New Zealand Legislation website: www.legislation.govt.nz.
19   Carwyn Jones *Ka Mate, Ka Mate; Ka Ora, Ka Ora* 12 May 2014 https://ahikaroa.wordpress.com (last accessed 5 January 2015); AJ Park *The Haka Ka Mate Attribution Act: The right of attribution* 7 May 2014 http://www.ajpark.com/ip-central/news-articles/2014/05/the-haka-ka-mate-attribution-act-the-right-of-attribution/ (last accessed 5 January 2015).
20   James Ihaka "Police Commissioner makes landmark apology to Tuhoe" 13 August 2014 http:// www.nzherald.co.nz/nz/news/article.cfm?c_id=1&objectid=11308261 (last accessed 5 January 2015).
21   Rangitāne o Wairarapa and Rangitāne o Tamaki Nui-ā-Rua.
22   Whanganui Iwi and Te Atiawa.
23   Ngā Ruahine, Ngāti Kuri and Te Kawerau â Maki.
24   Ngāi Tuhoe, Tāmaki Makaurau Collective Settlement, Ngāti Apa ki te Rā Tō, Ngāti Kuia, Rangit ne o Wairau, Ngāti Kōata, Ngāti Rārua, Ngāti Tama ki Te Tau Ihu, Te Ātiawa a Māui, Ngāti Toa Rangitira, Ngāti Rangiteaorere, Ngāti Rangiwewehi, Tapuika, Maungaharuru Tangitu Hapū and Raukawa. Office of Treaty Settlements http://www.ots.govt.nz/ (last accessed 5 January 2015).

Dr Fleur Adcock *(Ngāti Mutunga and English) is a Research Associate with the National Centre for Indigenous Studies at the Australian National University. Email: fleur.adcock@anu.edu.au*

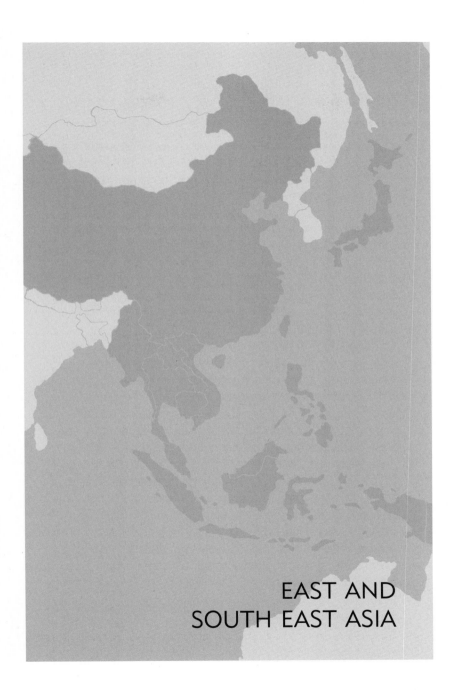

EAST AND
SOUTH EAST ASIA

JAPAN

The two indigenous peoples of Japan, the Ainu and the Okinawans, live on the northernmost and southernmost islands of the country's archipelago. The Ainu territory stretches from Sakhalin and the Kurile Islands (now both Russian territories) to the northern part of present-day Japan, including the entire island of Hokkaido. Hokkaido was unilaterally incorporated into the Japanese state in 1869. Although most Ainu still live in Hokkaido, over the second half of the 20th century, tens of thousands migrated to Japan's urban centers for work and to escape the more prevalent discrimination on Hokkaido. Since June 2008, the Ainu have been officially recognized as an indigenous people of Japan. Most recent government surveys put the Ainu population in Hokkaido at 16,786 (2013) and the rest of Japan at 210 (2011).[1]

Okinawans, or Ryūkyūans, live in the Ryūkyū Islands, which make up Japan's present-day Okinawa prefecture. They comprise several indigenous language groups with distinct cultural traits. Although there has been some migration of ethnic Japanese to the islands, the population is largely indigenous Ryūkyūans. Japan colonized the Ryūkyūs in 1879 but later relinquished the islands to the US in exchange for its own independence after World War Two. In 1972, the islands were reincorporated into the Japanese state and Okinawans became Japanese citizens although the US military remained. Today, 50,000 US military personnel, their dependents and civilian contractors occupy 34 military installations on Okinawa Island. The island is home to 1.1 million of the 1.4 million people living throughout the Ryūkyūs.

The Japanese government has adopted the UNDRIP (although it does not recognize the unconditional right to self-determination). It has not ratified ILO Convention 169.

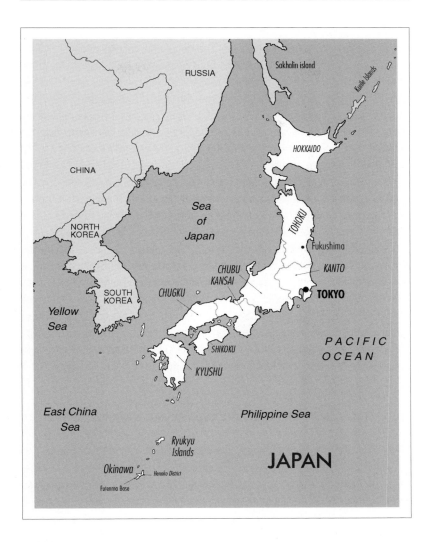

The Ainu

The Ainu and Japan's hate speech problem

2014 saw the Ainu thrust into the spotlight of Japan's growing hate speech problem. Not only have policies seeking to improve the socioeconomic situation of the

Ainu and promote Ainu culture been attacked but the attacks have often been directed at the Ainu people themselves. The issue drew national attention in September when a member of the Sapporo City Assembly in Hokkaido, the traditional homeland of the Ainu, posted on Twitter that "Ainu no longer exist". Despite calls for his resignation and his ousting from the Liberal Democratic Party (LDP), he continues to serve in the city assembly, using his social media platform to galvanize anti-Ainu sentiment among his supporters. He later went on to "favorite" a tweet by a supporter demanding that Koreans and Ainu leave the country. In the Hokkaido Prefectural Assembly, too, a member of the LDP stated in November that the indigeneity of the Ainu was "highly questionable" and proceeded to deny that the Japanese had inflicted any hardship on the Ainu in the past. The Prefectural Assembly member, also known for his active social media presence in promoting the anti-Ainu cause, faced no sanction for his comments.

Such statements have been criticized as "hate speech", an issue that drew a significant amount of attention from the UN Committee on the Elimination of Racial Discrimination in its consideration of the periodic report from Japan in August. In terms of its policies towards the Ainu, however, the emphasis of the Japanese government's report was on its efforts to promote Ainu language and culture. These developments demonstrate that the Ainu face challenges that require not only support for their language and culture but their rights to land and resources as indigenous people as well as their fundamental human right to non-discrimination.

World Conference on Indigenous Peoples and ancestral remains

Meanwhile, the Ainu saw some positive developments with their participation in the World Conference on Indigenous Peoples (WCIP). Kazushi "Yupo" Abe, vice-president of the Ainu Association of Hokkaido, participated in the conference as an official member of the Japanese government delegation, the first time an Ainu person had joined an international conference in that capacity. At the conference, the Japanese government emphasized its intention to create the "Symbolic Space for Ethnic Harmony" in time for the Tokyo Olympics in 2020, which will be used to restore traditional Ainu living space as well as to consolidate and memorialize Ainu ancestral remains.[2] The outcome document of the WCIP also appears to provide support in moving many of these efforts forward, particularly Section 27, which addresses the issue of "access and repatriation of ceremonial objects and human remains", something that continues to be a point of contention in Japan.

While the government officially adopted a cabinet decision for the establishment of the "Symbolic Space" and guidelines for repatriation of Ainu ancestral remains in June, these have been subject to criticism from some Ainu activists. First, the guidelines established are specific to "repatriation of those remains whose person is identified", meaning that the guidelines apply to only 23 of the over 1,600 remains held by universities. Furthermore, the ancestral remains are often poorly accounted for by the universities, with many of them dismembered and different parts being stored separately. This exacerbates the hurdles in identifying and repatriating the remains. Indeed, there are cases where universities are refusing to repatriate remains to local communities, citing the government guidelines and claiming that the identity of the remains cannot be established based on their own poor accounting. Some Ainu activists are opposed to the very idea of consolidating ancestral remains in a "Symbolic Space", arguing that they should all be returned to local communities instead. Many are also wary that the remains will continue to be used for research in the "Symbolic Space" established by the government, and that its establishment will be used to quietly ignore the universities' crimes against the Ainu, without holding them fully to account. For Ainu activists and leaders working both inside and outside the Japanese government, what they want most of all is for the ancestral remains to simply be treated with the dignity that the remains of human beings deserve.

The Okinawans

Futenma-Henoko campaigns continue

Okinawans' most pressing problems continue to stem from US military presence and the Japanese government's deference to its relationship with the United States in the Okinawan context. 2014 was dominated by the politics surrounding the 19-year-long struggle to close the US military's Futenma Air Station, located in the center of densely-populated Ginowan City, and to prevent the construction of a new US military complex on Nago City's rural Cape Henoko (for background see *The Indigenous World 2011, 2012, 2013*). Tensions and protest increased this year as the Japanese government began construction in earnest.

A new sit-in emerged at the Camp Schwab entrance when Japanese government contractors began construction in July. Rallies throughout the year attracted tens of thousands and polls consistently showed an overwhelming majority of Okinawans opposed to the new base and desiring Futenma's closure. Popular sentiments were manifested in electoral politics as well. The Prefectural Assembly began the year by calling for the resignation of Governor Nakaima Hirokazu, who had reversed his opposition to base construction in 2013. By the end of the year, Okinawans as a whole had ousted Nakaima, instead electing anti-base construction candidates to the governorship and all four of the prefecture's lower house seats in Japan's National Diet. Nago City residents also re-elected anti-base mayor, Inamine Susumu.

With the Obama Administration increasing its pressure, Tokyo responded on different levels. Concentrating initial construction within Camp Schwab made protest more difficult, and the government announced it would transfer control over a prefectural road in Takae to the US military. Government officials refused to meet with governor-elect Onaga Takeshi and, soon after, cut 10 percent from the 2015 Okinawa budget. Many expect the cancellation of a long-awaited north-south railway on Okinawa Island.

Okinawans often point to everyday experiences of the bases to explain the unshakable dedication within the Futenma and Henoko campaigns and broad support for a reduction of US presence more generally. In February, military officials announced the results of soil tests from a 2013 military helicopter crash in Ginoza. It found lead and arsenic levels at 74 and 21 times safety standards respectively. This helps explain official and popular condemnation of the nine incidents involving military aircraft malfunction in 2014. The year also saw a continuation of crimes by US service members, such as sexual assault, breaking and entering, drink driving and hit-and-run incidents.

The year ended with the government suspending construction at Henoko after a series of typhoons and new uncertainties following the strong showing of anti-base candidates at the polls. Construction was expected to resume in January but the project will face an emboldened opposition.

Transnational intervention

Transnational strategies continue, reflecting a lack of faith in Japanese institutions to resolve problems associated with the bases. This year, Nago Mayor Inamine met directly with lawmakers and officials in Washington D.C. Litigation also continued in the *Dugong v. US Secretary of Defense* lawsuit. Filed in the U.S. Federal District Court in 2003 by a coalition of Okinawan, Japanese and American environmental organizations, the suit uses the US National Historical Preservation Act (NHPA), which requires US agencies operating internationally to take into account the effects of their actions on the official cultural assets of host nations. Expansion of Camp Schwab involves extensive landfill of the primary habitat of the critically-endangered Okinawa dugong (sea manatee), a protected "natural monument" under Japan's Law for the Protection of Cultural Properties. In April 2014, the Department of Defense (DoD) filed a court-ordered report determining that the base expansion would have "no adverse effect" on dugongs. Plaintiffs filed a new action in July, citing the DoD's improper fulfillment of NHPA requirements and its refusal to release the studies informing its determination. A new round of hearings began in December.

Sustained participation in United Nations fora by Okinawans has compelled the Japanese government to discuss Okinawan rights in the context of ratified conventions. In August, Keiko Itokazu became the first Diet member to make a direct appeal to the UN, in a Committee on the Elimination of Racial Discrimination (CERD) hearing and at the World Conference of Indigenous Peoples. So far, Tokyo has steadfastly rejected the indigenous identity of Okinawans and charges of discrimination against them. In its August 2014 report, CERD questioned the Japanese government's position, citing UNESCO's recognition of Ryūkyūan languages and Okinawans' unique ethnicity and culture. Government representatives responded that Okinawans "were not subject to 'racial discrimination' as provided for in the Convention", and that the Ryūkyūs were among "many islands in [Japan's] archipelago, on many of which traditions with unique traits had been developed".[3]   ○

Notes and references

1   Population figure for Hokkaido taken from the 2013 Survey of Ainu Livelihoods conducted by the Hokkaido prefectural government in cooperation with the Ainu Association (Hokkaido Government, Environment and Lifestyle Section. 2013. *Hokkaido Ainu Survey on Livelihood Report*, Accessed 6 January 2015, http://www.pref.hokkaido.lg.jp/ks/ass/ainu_living_conditions_survey. pdf). Population figure for rest of Japan taken from 2011 Survey of Non-Hokkaido Ainu Livelihoods conducted by the Council for Ainu Policy Promotion. 2011. *Non-Hokkaido Ainu Survey on Livelihood Report*, Accessed 6 January 2015, http://www.kantei.go.jp/jp/singi/ainusuishin/dai3/

siryou3_3.pdf). Many with Ainu ancestry do not publicly identify as Ainu due to discrimination and stigma in Japanese society. Ainu observers estimate the actual population of those with Ainu ancestry to be between 100-300,000, with 5,000 in the greater Kanto region alone.

2   See report in *The Indigenous World 2014* for details.

3   http://www.ohchr.org/EN/NewsEvents/Pages/DisplayNews.aspx?NewsID=14957&LangID=E#st hash.DQxguRsO.dpuf

W. Lonnie Ding-Everson, *the author of the section on the Ainu, is the founder of AINU PRIDE PRODUCTIONS (http://www.ainupride.com) and a former Ainu language instructor for the Foundation for Research and Promotion of Ainu Culture's language program in Tokyo.*

Kelly Dietz *is the author of the section on the Okinawans. She is assistant professor in the Department of Politics at Ithaca College in New York.*

CHINA

Officially, China proclaims itself a unified country with a multiple ethnic make-up, and all ethnic groups are considered equal before the law. Besides the Han Chinese majority, the government recognizes 55 ethnic minority peoples within its borders. According to China's sixth national census of 2010, the population of ethnic minorities is 113,792,211 persons, or 8.49 % of the country's total population.

The national "Ethnic Minority Identification Project", undertaken from 1953 to 1979, settled on official recognition for 55 ethnic minority groups. However, there are still "unrecognized ethnic groups" in China, numbering a total of 734,438 persons (2000 census figure). Most of them live in China's south-west regions of Guizhou, Sichuan, Yunnan and Tibet. The officially-recognized ethnic minority groups have rights protected by the Constitution. This includes establishing ethnic autonomous regions, setting up their own local administrative governance and the right to practise their own language and culture. "Ethnic autonomous regions" constitute around 60% of China's land area.

The Chinese (PRC) government does not recognize the term "indigenous peoples", and representatives of China's ethnic minorities have not readily identified themselves as indigenous peoples, and have rarely participated in international meetings related to indigenous peoples' issues. It has therefore not been clearly established which of China's ethnic minority groups are to be considered indigenous peoples. The Chinese government voted in favor of the UNDRIP but, prior to its adoption, had already officially stated that there were no indigenous peoples in China, which means that, in their eyes, the UNDRIP does not apply to China.

Conference on Nationality Affairs in Beijing

The Chinese state government convened the fourth national-level "Central Working Conference on Nationality Affairs" in Beijing, on 28 and 29 September 2014. The previous conference took place nine years ago. Top Chinese officials realized that the state had been experiencing new challenges and dissent with regard to ethnic nationality affairs and its ethnic policy programs and it was thus deemed a critical time to convene the high-level conference for a re-assessment of and new decision-making on ethnic nationality policies.

Three main resolutions were passed to guide future policy-making. The first resolution deals with the economic and living conditions of ethnic minorities. For the less advanced regions, the local governments must carry out poverty alleviation programs, bring about "leapfrog economic development", improve social service and security facilities in border areas, upgrade basic public infrastructure, and open up for border trading. Other points under this resolution include programs for safe drinking water and road construction, environmental conservation projects, compensation for environmental damage, and enhancing the ability of local communities to develop economically. There were also recommendations to promote tourism as an economic pillar for ethnic minority regions, upgrading hygiene and medical facilities in these regions, and providing support to train more local health workers.

The second resolution deals with education and culture. It calls for plans to construct new "ethnic minority villages" to showcase the local region's special cultural and geographical features. The resolution also recommends the standardization of compulsory education and boarding school programs, free vocational training at secondary level, and improvement of bilingual education programs.

The third resolution focuses on the "thoughts and minds" of ethnic nationalities. It calls for the application of the law to protect ethnic harmony and unity, for an enhanced understanding of legal concepts among all ethnic groups, and it emphasizes the government's opposition to Han Chinese chauvinism and narrow ethnic nationalism. It calls for the implementation of programs to promote ethnic nationality self-awareness in order to "preserve national unity and harmony among all groups" and for enhanced measures to prevent "infiltration by enemy ideological propaganda", along with a prohibition on thoughts and actions which discriminate against ethnic minority groups.

For long-term observers of Chinese ethnic minority policies, the resolutions and guidelines from the "Central Working Conference on Nationality Affairs" seem to be the usual grandiose political slogans, and raise doubts as to the political will to actually achieve concrete results.

Mongolian herdsmen protest over land

More conflicts over grazing land occurred in ethnic Mongolian regions last year. More than 30 pastoral herdsmen protested in front of the city government at Inner Mongolia's Bayannur City in April. They were local herdsmen from the area's Middle and Rear Urat Banner regions.

Due to the expropriation of vast tracts of pastureland for economic development by government and private companies, the Mongolian herdsmen have been unable to maintain their traditional pastoralist lifestyle and have been forced to find other means of subsistence. Their protest was sparked by the local government's action to withhold the payment of subsidies and compensation for ceasing to graze on the pastureland. During the protest, many of them were beaten up and injured by the police, and scores were arrested.

More strife was to follow in the Inner Mongolia's Tongliao City (original Mongolian name Tungliy'oo Xota) in Zalute Banner region. The local government forcibly expropriated 80,000 mu (800 ha) of pastureland at the officially-decreed price of 8 RMB (USD 1.25) per mu as compensation for local residents. Despite the opposition of most people, the land-grab program proceeded. During the eviction, riot police knocked down many *yurts* (traditional dwellings of the nomadic Mongolian herders) and beat up those residents who refused to leave.

Judicial persecution against Mongolians

Professor Borjigin Delger, a leading Mongolian academic, tried to sign his name in Mongolian for a money transaction at a bank in Hohhot City during the year but the bank refused to accept it. Delger is a renowned researcher on Mongolian language and traditional culture, and teaches at the Inner Mongolia University in Hohhot.

Hada, leader of the Southern Mongolian Democracy Alliance (SMDA), a dissident writer and a rights advocate for Mongolian people, was finally released from prison on 9 December 2014, after spending close to 19 years in jail. The Chinese authorities arrested him in 1995, and handed out a 15-year sentence on charges of "dividing the nation and engaging in espionage", later adding four more years to his prison term. However, SMDA officials reported that, after his release, Hada was under heavy restriction and constant monitoring by Chinese authorities, thus still living under virtual house arrest.

The case against Huugjilt, a Mongolian teenager, received Chinese media attention when the court overturned his conviction in December 2014. Huugjilt, 18 years old at the time, was wrongly convicted and executed in 1996 for the alleged rape and killing of a woman in Hohhot City. A Chinese man named Zhao, a serial rapist and killer, confessed to the murder after he was arrested in 2005. Huugjilt's family had been petitioning the court for a retrial of the case since 2006. Chinese media coverage of the exoneration highlighted other wrongful convictions in China, and activists viewed the teenager's death as a symbol of the miscarriage of justice in capital punishment cases, advocating steps toward judicial reform.

Religious persecution against Tibetans

In the Tibetan Autonomous Prefecture of Garze in Sichuan Province, 22-year-old Tibetan monk, Sonam Yarphel, was arrested in November for a street demonstration in which he demanded freedom for the Tibetan people. Shortly after his arrest, local police and military officers occupied the Mongyal Monastery he had come from. The local authorities then conducted "education programs" to instill patriotic sentiment in the monks, and stopped any Tibetans under the age of 18 from entering the monastery. Tibetan dissident and writer, Tsering Woeser, reported that 11 Tibetan monks died from self-immolation during 2014.

Uyghur incidents in Kunming and Xinjiang

The crackdown on Uyghur people was intensified in the aftermath of the railway station attack in Kunming (capital city of Yunnan Province) in March 2014. The incident, which left 29 civilians and four perpetrators dead, along with over 140 others injured, was carried out allegedly by a group of eight ethnic Uyghurs, according to Chinese state media. Three Uyghur individuals said to be members of the group received the death penalty in a court ruling in September, while a female member of the group was given a life sentence.

In Xinjiang Uyghur Autonomous Region, the government forced over 1,000 headmasters and principals of schools at all levels to swear allegiance to the Chinese national flag. The ceremony required them to take an oath to block all religious thoughts and ideas from "infiltrating" the schools. The education bureau in Kashgar had also mandated a blanket ban on Uyghur youth under 18 engaging in any religious activities in schools and kindergartens. The ban even covered activities outside the schools, where youngsters are prohibited from participating in any religious functions at home and during holiday periods.

For the Uyghur people, the Islamic belief is an integral part of their cultural and ethnic identity. The government's prohibition on religious practice at home is likely to exacerbate the discontent among the Uyghur people.

Besides the Kunming attack in March by the alleged Uyghur group, scores of violent incidents and protests were reported in Xinjiang throughout the year.

Ilham Tohti case

Prominent Uyghur academic, Ilham Tohti, was arrested and detained in January 2014. A court in Urumqi found him guilty of "separatism" in September and sentenced him to life imprisonment. All his assets were seized. Tohti had founded the "Uyghur Online" website in 2006 to discuss Uyghur issues but it was shut down by the authorities in 2008. He had previously been arrested in 2009 but was released later that year. His case has received extensive international media attention.

Tohti, an economist at Beijing's Central Nationalities University, is considered a moderate spokesperson for the Uyghur people but was still sentenced to life imprisonment. This reveals the Chinese government's harsh repression of any dissenting voice in the Uyghur community.

Power consolidation and more ethnic repression

In the two-year period since Xi Jinping assumed the highest post as General Secretary of the Chinese Communist Party (CCP), he has waged a widely-publicized campaign against corruption. The campaign has had an effect on corruption and graft practice at all levels of government, and reduced the squandering of public funds by officials. Many officials, from local bureaucrats to high-ranking heads of government departments and senior leaders, have been caught in the anti-corruption campaign. Its effect can be felt in the CCP hierarchy, military units, central and local government agencies, state corporations, universities, schools and research institutions.

Most Chinese citizens support the campaign because they have seen too many corrupt and graft practices by government and party officials. It has garnered applause for Xi but also enabled the expedient removal of his political enemies, and thus strengthened his power.

It is worth noting in this context that the Chinese government has placed more dissidents under arrest over the past two years than the previous ten. The government's vision of the "Chinese Dream" is still central to the state propaganda effort, along with trumpeting the results of the anti-corruption campaign. Most Chinese citizens were won over by the touted successes but some people fear the increasing authoritarianism, silencing of dissent and concentration of power in the hands of a few top political figures.

Observers said the Chinese government policies in the troubled ethnic nationalities regions, especially in Xinjiang, were still following the same cycle of harsh repression, leading to more conflicts and escalating violence. As the government has not dealt with the root cause of these issues, a recurrence of social convulsions and protests in ethnic minority regions is a likely future scenario. ○

Huang Chi-ping is an associate professor at the Ethnology Department of the National Cheng-chi University in Taiwan, where she is teaching and doing her research on the Yi group of China's ethnic minority peoples. Her field of speciality is Ethnography and Ethnic Literature. She also serves as editor of the "Aboriginal Education World" journal. Her article was translated from Chinese by **Jason Pan,** Director of the indigenous rights activist organization, TARA Ping Pu, and a former executive council member of the Asia Indigenous Peoples Pact (AIPP). Jason is an indigenous Pazeh (one of the lowland Ping Pu groups) of Liyutan village, Miaoli County.

TAIWAN

The officially-recognized indigenous population of Taiwan[1] numbers 534,561 people (2013), or 2.28% of the total population. Fourteen indigenous peoples are officially recognized. In addition, there are at least nine Ping Pu ("plains or lowland") indigenous peoples who are denied official recognition.[2] Most of Taiwan's indigenous peoples originally lived in the central mountains, on the east coast and in the south. However, nearly half of the indigenous population has migrated to live in urban areas.

The main challenges facing indigenous peoples in Taiwan continue to be rapidly disappearing cultures and languages, low social status and very little political or economic influence. The Council of Indigenous Peoples (CIP) is the state agency responsible for indigenous peoples. A number of national laws protect their rights, including the Constitutional Amendments (2000) on indigenous representation in the Legislative Assembly, protection of language and culture, and political participation; the Indigenous Peoples' Basic Act (2005), the Education Act for Indigenous Peoples (2004), the Status Act for Indigenous Peoples (2001), the Regulations regarding Recognition of Indigenous Peoples (2002) and the Name Act (2003), which allows indigenous peoples to register their original names in Chinese characters and to annotate them in Romanized script. Unfortunately, serious discrepancies and contradictions in the legislation, coupled with only partial implementation of laws guaranteeing the rights of indigenous peoples, have stymied progress towards self-governance.

Since Taiwan is not a member of the United Nations it has not been able to vote on the UN Declaration on the Rights of Indigenous Peoples, nor to consider ratifying ILO Convention 169.

Conflict over forest resources

In two separate cases, indigenous customary law and state laws on the ownership and utilization of forest resources came into conflict over the handling of
fallen trees last year. When trees have fallen due to natural causes, the traditional practice in most of Taiwan's indigenous communities living in mountainous
areas is to leave it on the ground for the natural decaying process to take over, or
alternatively to decide how to handle it at a communal council meeting.

The two cases got tangled up with other interest groups because they involved the valuable wood of the Taiwan red cypress, and conflicting claims over
territorial jurisdiction between indigenous communities, the government sector
and academia: in the Nantou County case, the fallen wood was removed by staff
from the National Taiwan University's Experimental Forest Research Center, who
said they had jurisdiction over the area. In Tongmen village of Hualien County, the

fallen wood was taken away by Forestry Bureau personnel. Tongmen villagers had already had quarrels with the Hualien County Government for not limiting the number of tourists entering Mugumugi Leisure Park, which had resulted in considerable damage to the local river and forest. Attempts were made to put up barriers to restrict tourists from entering, and this led to conflict with government officials.

Natural resource management issues were supposed to have been clarified with the promulgation of the Indigenous Peoples' Basic Law of 2005. However, all sides involved in the two cases, i.e. indigenous communities, local and central government agencies, academia and private sector actors, still have to come to grips with the interpretation and application of the law.

Puyuma hunters on firearms charge

The annual Mangayau Festival of the Puyuma people in Taitung County on the east coast was held in December. According to Puyuma tradition, male hunters camp out in the forest to hunt wild animals which are then taken back to be cooked for the festival. However, nine hunters from Papuru village were arrested by Taitung County police for illegally possessing firearms. Police officials said they had violated the firearms control law, and detained the men. Five of them did not have the proper firearm registration for their rifles, and were taken to the prosecutor's office in Taitung City for further questioning, although they were subsequently released. Papuru villagers protested at the police action, and the incident again generated public controversy over the preservation of wildlife versus traditional indigenous cultural practices. Officials from the Council of Indigenous Peoples (CIP) released press statements drawing attention to the fact that Taiwan's firearms control law had been modified in recent years, resulting in wider interpretations and applications. They noted particular sections according to which indigenous peoples shall not be subject to criminal prosecution but rather an "administrative punishment". The CIP statement called on the judiciary to be more careful in the application of the law and its officials said they would co-ordinate with relevant government agencies on this issue.

Aftermath of the November election

The November 2014 countrywide city and municipal elections saw large gains by the opposition Democratic Progressive Party (DPP), and are widely considered to have been a humbling defeat for the ruling Kuomintang (KMT) party and its leader, President Ma Ying-jeou. In the main elections, the KMT held on only to the New Taipei City mayoral seat, while the DPP won in the capital Taipei City, Kaohsiung City, Tainan City, Taoyuan City and Taichung City. In the aftermath of the November elections, the new city administrations will have a change of guard in all major departments. Since each of these six major cities has an Indigenous Affairs Commission under its government structure, new directors have also been appointed to the Indigenous Affairs Commissions.[3] One of these, Mayaw Kumud, is an indigenous activist, once jailed by the KMT government for organizing protests against the government's assimilation policy denying indigenous peoples their right to land, language and culture. Another is a female indigenous journalist, Kolas Yotaka, who used to head the news section of the Taiwan Indigenous Television network.

Ping Pu lowland groups continue to demand official recognition

Taiwan's top research institute, Academia Sinica, held a major academic conference at its campus at the end of the year, with its main theme being relationship and dialogue between the recognized indigenous peoples and the Ping Pu lowland indigenous groups.

Representatives from the Siraya community in Tainan area and Ping Pu aboriginal groups filed another appeal to the Ministry of Interior in November for the restoration of their indigenous status, which was invalidated by the Chinese KMT regime in the 1950s. This was the continuation of an earlier lawsuit requesting their inclusion as officially-recognized indigenous groups. Uma Talavan and her father, Cheng-hiong Talavan, presented their case on behalf of the Siraya and Ping Pu aboriginal groups at the hearing to the ministry's Petition and Appeals Committee. They were accompanied by attorneys for this latest in a series of litigation procedures against the government, initiated in 2010. Uma Talavan called the CIP's and the Taiwanese government's denial of their aboriginal status morally wrong, and a violation of human rights and the UN Declaration on the Rights of Indigenous Peoples.

Indigenous peoples in the military and police

KMT's indigenous legislator, Chien Tung-ming (Paiwan), organized a conference in 2014 to discuss indigenous peoples' military service, and their training programs and promotion in the three branches of the armed forces. The most senior indigenous military officers, ranked as colonels or above, along with five with major generals, attended the conference, which was presided over by Minister of National Defense Yen Ming. Legislators and attendees called for continued programs to cultivate indigenous military officers and to value their services.

Government officials also convened several meetings over the year with administrators from the two main academic institutions for the training of law enforcement officers, the Taiwan Police College and the Central Police University. The meetings were convened in recognition of the need to adjust the national examination system in light of the past years' declining numbers of indigenous police officers. Many senior-ranking indigenous officers who can speak the indigenous languages and are familiar with the local community culture are also near retirement. In many communities, the lack of indigenous police officers stationed in the local precincts has led to communication problems and cultural misunderstanding. To remedy the situation, government agencies and officials recommended adding "indigenous affairs administration" as an additional subject to the special national examination for indigenous quota police officers in the civil service. The aim is to broaden the entry base for qualified indigenous examinees, and encourage more police staff to work in indigenous areas. 〇

Notes and references

1   The currently ruling Kuomintang (KMT) party uses the "Republic of China".
    (*Note by the editor.* The People's Republic of China does not recognize the existence and political independence of Taiwan or the "Republic of China". Throughout this article, Taiwan is therefore solely used to refer to a geographical region, without taking any position regarding the political status of the island).
2   The officially-recognized groups are: the Amis (also known as Pangcah), Atayal (also called Tayal), Paiwan, Bunun, Puyuma (also called Pinuyumayan), Tsou, Rukai, Saisiyat, Sediq (also

called Seediq), Yamei (also called Tao), Thao, Kavalan, Truku and Sakizaya. The nine non-recognized Ping Pu groups are: the Ketagalan, Taokas, Pazeh, Kahabu, Papora, Babuza, Hoanya, Siraya and Makatao.
3   The new directors are Mayaw Kumud (Amis) for Taichung, Kolas Yotaka (Amis) for Taoyuan, Kuchung Kalavangan (Bunun) for Kaohsiung, Chen Hsiu-hui (Amis) for Taipei City, Wang Chih-min (Tsou) for Tainan, Yang Hsin-yi (Amis) for New Taipei City.

*Professor **Pasuya Poiconu** is from the indigenous Tsou people of central Taiwan. He teaches at the Taiwan National Chung Cheng University and his research focuses on indigenous literature and mythology. He has published a number of books on these subjects. He was previously the director of the Taiwan National Museum of Prehistory and is currently also serving as a committee member of the government agency responsible for civil service examinations.*

*This article was translated from Chinese by **Jason Pan**, an indigenous Ping Pu Pazeh writer and journalist from Liyutan village of central Taiwan. Jason is the Director of the indigenous rights activist organization, TARA Ping Pu, and a former executive council member of the Asia Indigenous Peoples Pact (AIPP).*

PHILIPPINES

The latest census conducted in the Philippines in 2010 included an ethnicity variable for the first time but no official figure for the indigenous peoples has yet come out. The country's indigenous population thus continues to be estimated at between 10% and 20% of the national population, which has been projected to currently lie at 102.9 million. The indigenous groups in the northern mountains of Luzon (Cordillera) are collectively known as *Igorot* while the groups on the southern island of Mindanao are collectively called *Lumad*. There are smaller groups collectively known as *Mangyan* in the central islands as well as even smaller, more scattered groups in the central islands and Luzon, including several groups of hunter-gatherers in transition.

Indigenous peoples in the Philippines have retained much of their traditional, pre-colonial culture, social institutions and livelihood practices. They generally live in geographically isolated areas with a lack of access to basic social services and few opportunities for mainstream economic activities, education or political participation. In contrast, commercially valuable natural resources such as minerals, forests and rivers can be found mainly in their areas, making them continuously vulnerable to development aggression and land grabbing.

Republic Act 8371, known as the Indigenous Peoples' Rights Act (IPRA), was promulgated in 1997. The law has been lauded for its support for respect for indigenous peoples' cultural integrity, right to their lands and right to self-directed development of these lands. More substantial implementation of the law is still being sought, however, apart from there being fundamental criticism of the law itself. The Philippines voted in favor of the United Nations Declaration on the Rights of Indigenous Peoples (UNDRIP) but the government has not yet ratified ILO Convention 169.

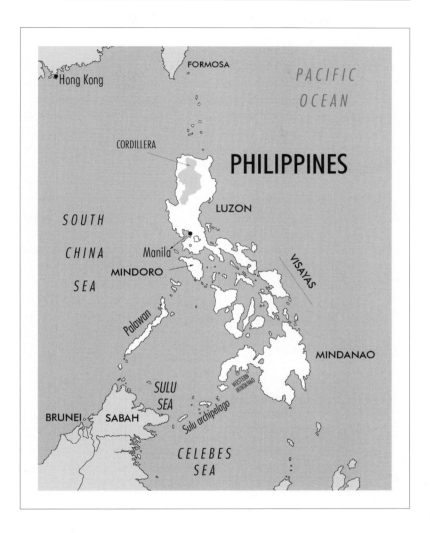

Mindanao peace process

Peace talks between the Government of the Philippines and the Moro Islamic Liberation Front (MILF) advanced with the signing of the Comprehensive Agreement on the Bangsamoro (CAB) on 27 March 2014 *(see Indigenous World*

2013 and *2014).* CAB will replace the Autonomous Region of Muslim Mindanao to "enhance existing systems and procedures, as well as establish a new set of institutional arrangements and modalities between the central government and the autonomous government with respect to power-sharing, wealth- and revenue-sharing, transitional aspects, and normalization." [1] The CAB was translated into legal provisions through the draft Bangsamoro Basic Law (BBL) or House Bill 4994, which was submitted to Congress in September 2014. BBL seeks to establish the new Bangsamoro political entity and provide for its basic structure of government, in recognition of the Bangsamoro people.[2]

While the draft BBL is perceived as a step forward in resolving the long-running armed conflict in Mindanao, indigenous peoples' organizations are urgently lobbying for a categorical inclusion of the rights of indigenous peoples in the draft BBL.[3] After a lobbying mission to Manila in May by indigenous representatives, the National Cultural Communities (NCC) Committee of Congress conducted a "Public consultation on the hopes and aspirations of the indigenous peoples regarding the BBL and the peace process" on 24 June whereby around 800 participants from academia, NGOs, churches and indigenous peoples' communities gathered in Upi, Maguindanao. Indigenous Teduray, Lambangian, Dulangan Manobo and Erumanen ne Menuvu shared their position and demands relating to their socio-cultural, economic and political future under the Bangsamoro.

Regional autonomy in the Cordillera

Article X of the 1987 Constitution of the Philippines mandates the creation of autonomous regions in Muslim Mindanao and the Cordillera in northern Philippines. In the Cordillera region, a renewed attempt at establishing a Cordillera Autonomous Region is being undertaken through House Bill 4649 (Act to Establish the Cordillera Autonomous Region), which was filed in Congress on 11 June 2014 and authored by all seven Congressmen in the Cordillera region.

House Bill (HB) 4649, the third attempt at establishing a Cordillera Autonomous Region, was met with opposition by Cordillera indigenous peoples. During the Cordillera Indigenous Peoples' Summit on Genuine Regional Autonomy and Self Determination, held on 18 August 2014 in Baguio City, more than 300 indigenous leaders from the six provinces of the region reflected on the Cordillera's past experiences and lessons on regional autonomy, and lessons shared from the failed experience of the Autonomous Region of Muslim Mindanao in the southern Philippines.[4] The first two attempts at establishing a Cordillera Autonomous Region were rejected in plebiscites in 1990 and 1998 as these were seen to lack substance in promulgating indigenous peoples' rights over their land and resources, indigenous culture and socio-political systems, political representation, basic social services and protection against institutionalized discrimination.

The Summit resulted in the Cordillera People's Declaration on Genuine Regional Autonomy, which criticized HB 4649 as lacking in features of genuine regional autonomy, and as being divisive as it threatens to revert the Cordillera provinces back to their former regions, with no categorical recognition of the Cordillera Ancestral Domain and no grounding in the urgent issues experienced by the Cordillera indigenous peoples. The Summit also agreed on recommendations and an action plan to pursue genuine regional autonomy.

Free, Prior and Informed Consent (FPIC)

Nationwide, indigenous territories continue to be a target for natural resource extraction and energy generation. In a 2014 report by KAMP, a national federation of indigenous peoples' organizations in the Philippines, there are 281 approved applications for large-scale mining operations covering at least 532,356 hectares of indigenous lands. This is on top of already ongoing large-scale mining operations. KAMP estimates that around 100,000 people belonging to 39 indigenous peoples will be displaced or will lose their livelihood as a result of the current administration's push for mining liberalization.

The year also witnessed the implementation of various energy projects in indigenous peoples' territories, including hydro-electric dams and geothermal and coal-fired power plants. In President Benigno Simeon Aquino III's State of the Nation Address[5] in July 2014, he boasted of the Jalaur River Multipurpose Dam in Panay, which is threatening the lives and livelihood of an estimated 17,000 people belonging to the Tumandok indigenous people. Other dam projects are having a similar impact, including the Laiban Dam, which is threatening to submerge eight indigenous communities and displace around 21,000 farmers and people belonging to the Agta, Dumagat and Remontado indigenous peoples in Rizal and Quezon provinces.

In these projects, the rights of indigenous peoples to FPIC, as enshrined in the Indigenous Peoples' Rights Act (IPRA), are constantly being violated. In most cases, the National Commission on Indigenous Peoples (NCIP)[6] has been instrumental in manipulating FPIC in favor of the corporations and government agencies interested in the mining and energy projects by withholding complete information on the projects, creating fake councils of elders, fast-tracking FPIC process without the full participation of affected communities, and deceiving the people into signing a resolution of consent. This is a continuing experience among Cordillera indigenous peoples, such as the Kalinga in relation to the Makilala Mining Project of Freeport-Macmoran or the Chevron geothermal project. In Abra province, the 50th Infantry Battalion of the Armed Forces of the Philippines interfered in the FPIC process for the mining application of Golden Lake and Philex mining companies by threatening, harassing and coercing the indigenous people into signing a Memorandum of Agreement between the mining company and the local government unit on 27 November 2014.[7] Similar experiences are reported by indigenous peoples throughout Philippines.

During the Thirteenth Session of the UN Permanent Forum on Indigenous Peoples, the Cordillera Peoples Alliance[8] called for the abolition of the NCIP for not fulfilling its mandate of upholding indigenous peoples' rights and for serving as an instrument for the violation of FPIC and other fundamental rights of indigenous peoples. It also called for the repeal of the IPRA.[9]

Human rights violations and militarization of schools

During 2014, KAMP documented a total of 15 indigenous victims of extrajudicial killings, the highest number in any year since President Benigno Aquino III assumed the presidency in 2010. The perpetrators of the killings belong to the state's military forces, which are conducting military operations in indigenous territories. KAMP noted that a common feature of the victims is that they were all vocal opponents of destructive mining projects, militarization, or had criticized government neglect and corruption. Some of the victims were killed during military operations of the Armed Forces of the Philippines. Extrajudicial killings are a consequence of the state counter-insurgency program known as Operation Plan Bayanihan, which targets legitimate organizations and activists, including indigenous peoples. Apart from this, there are numerous cases of harassment and intimidation committed by the military against indigenous peoples.

In 2014, militarization resulted in extrajudicial killings in Abra province,[10] the forced evacuation of some 2,000 Lumads in the province of Surigao del Sur in October 2014[11] and occupations of and attacks on schools or alternative learning systems that have been collectively set-up by the community and NGOs in Lumad communities in Mindanao. According to Salinlahi, a child rights organization, nine out of ten Lumad children have no access to education.[12] Recurring violations of children's rights, especially to education, through militarization and military operations, led to the formation of the Save Our Schools (SOS) network in 2012.[13] The Statement of the Second SOS Conference in September 2014 denounced the military encampments and attacks on alternative schools, and various human rights violations committed against children and other members of Lumad communities.[14] The SOS network, together with other indigenous peoples' organizations and advocates, are seeking the repeal of government policies, in particular the Department of Education Memorandum 221 of December 2013 (known as the Guidelines on the Protection of Children During Armed Conflict) and the Letter Directive 25 by the AFP in July 2013, which legitimize the conducting of armed forces' activities on the premises of schools and other public facilities, and which is stifling the growth of alternative schools.[15]

In November and December 2014, Lumads, including children, were among the 300 participants of the "Manilakbayan ng Mindanao 2014", a 14-day advocacy caravan, partly on foot and by boat from Mindanao to Manila, during which dialogues, campaigns and solidarity activities were organized to draw attention to the issues and concerns of indigenous peoples such as mining, extrajudicial killings, human rights violations and militarization of communities and schools. A dialogue was held with the Secretary of the Department of Education, Armin Luistro, who promised to take concrete steps to address the issue of militarization of schools.[16]

National consultation with the UN Special Rapporteur on the rights of indigenous peoples

In celebration of International Day of the World's Indigenous Peoples on 8 August 2014, the new UN Special Rapporteur on the rights of indigenous peoples (UN-

SRRIP), Ms Vicky Tauli-Corpuz, held a consultation with indigenous peoples' organizations, government agencies, UN agencies, multilateral banks, academia, religious groups and NGOs.[17] The consultation served as a venue for indigenous peoples to report on their situation and to hear from government agencies and other bodies on their policies and programs on indigenous peoples, and on the mandate, vision and tentative plans of the UNSRRIP.

Ms Corpuz, a Kankanaey from the Cordillera, assumed her mandate as UN-SRRIP in June 2014. As former chairperson of the Cordillera Peoples Alliance and a long-time activist and defender of women, human rights and indigenous peoples' rights, Ms Corpuz's appointment is highly regarded and supported by Philippine indigenous peoples.

World Conference on Indigenous Peoples (WCIP) Outcome Document

The WCIP Outcome Document is seen as another milestone in the promulgation of indigenous peoples' rights all over the world. However, the challenge is how the Philippine government will seriously implement it at the local and national level. During the WCIP, some indigenous leaders from the Philippines delivered statements bearing critiques of and recommendations on the implementation of the Outcome Document, saying that it failed to incorporate the particular concern of indigenous communities regarding militarization.[18] Philippine indigenous peoples fear that this will mean a continuation of impunity and the violation of the human rights, FPIC and collective rights of indigenous peoples. Nevertheless, the Outcome Document is seen as another important tool for indigenous peoples in pushing for genuine recognition of their rights by the Philippine government. ○

Notes and references

1   House Bill No. 4994 (http://www.gov.ph/2014/09/10/document-the-draft-bangsamoro-basic-law/)
2   Q and A: The draft Bangsamoro Basic Law (http://www.gov.ph/2014/09/10/q-and-a-the-draft-bangsamoro-basic-law/)
3   Position Paper on the House Bill 4994 (http://www.scribd.com/doc/244052247/Full-Inclusion-of-the-Indigenous-People-s-in-the-Bangsamoro#scribd)
4   Ti Similla. The Official Newsletter of the Academic Staff of University of the Philippines Baguio. (http://www.upb.edu.ph/attachments/article/65/October.pdf)

5   The State of the Nation Address of the President of the Republic of the Philippines is held annu-
    ally in the month of July
    (http://www.gov.ph/2014/07/28/english-benigno-s-aquino-iii-fifth-state-of-the-nation-address-ju-
    ly-28-2014/).
6   The NCIP is a government agency that is mandated to implement the Indigenous Peoples Rights
    Act of 1997.
7   2014 Human Rights Report by the Cordillera Human Rights Alliance, a federation of human
    rights organizations and advocates in the Cordillera.
8   The Cordillera Peoples Alliance is a federation of grassroots-based indigenous peoples organi-
    zations in the Cordillera region in northern Philippines.
9   A copy of the statement may be downloaded at
    http://papersmart.unmeetings.org/media2/3309514/cordillerapeoplesalliance.pdf
10 "Initial Result of the National Solidarity Mission in Lacub, Abra".
    (http://www.karapatan.org/node/1035).
11 "Militarization triggers evacuation of 2,000 Lumads in Surigao del Sur".
    (http://bulatlat.com/main/2014/10/30/bakwet-%c7%80-militarization-triggers-evacuation-of-
    2000-lumads-in-surigao-del-sur/#sthash.eV3MyqMC.dpuf).
12 "The Indigenous Peoples Under BS Aquino: Four Years of Deception, Dispossession, and De-
    struction" released by Kalipunan ng mga Katutubong Mamamayan ng Pilipinas (KAMP) or the
    National Federation of Indigenous Peoples' Organizations in the Philippines.
13 Website of the Save Our Schools network
    https://saveourschoolsnetwork.wordpress.com/about/
14 Statement of the 2nd Save Our Schools Conference.
    (http://www.rmp-nmr.org/articles/2014/10/04/stop-attacks-our-schools-and-communities-educa-
    tion-not-militarization).
15 "New DepEd, AFP memos allow military presence in schools".
    (http://kabataanpartylist.com/blog/new-deped-afp-memos-allow-military-presence-in-schools/).
16 "DepEd Sec. Luistro commits to ordering pull-out of military forces in schools".
    (http://www.rmp-nmr.org/articles/2014/12/03/deped-sec-luistro-commits-ordering-pull-out-mili-
    tary-forces-schools)
17 "Philippine Celebration of the World's Indigenous Peoples' Day highlights UNSRRIP.
    (http://www.tebtebba.org/index.php/content/318-ip-day-celebration-highlights-unsrrip).

*Sarah Bestang K. Dekdeken is a Kankanaey from the Cordillera region of north-
ern Philippines and a staff member of the Cordillera Peoples Alliance, a federation of progressive peoples' organizations, mostly grassroots-based organizations of indigenous communities in the Cordillera region.*

*Jill K. Cariño, an Ibaloi, is the current Vice Chairperson for External Affairs of the
Cordillera Peoples Alliance, and Convenor and Program Director of the Philippine
Task Force for Indigenous Peoples' Rights (TFIP), a network of non-governmen-
tal organizations in the Philippines advancing the cause of indigenous peoples.*

INDONESIA

Indonesia has a population of approximately 250 million. The government recognises 1,128 ethnic groups. The Ministry of Social Affairs identifies some indigenous communities as *komunitas adat terpencil* (geographically-isolated indigenous communities). However, many more peoples self-identify or are considered by others as indigenous. Recent government Acts and Decrees use the term *masyarakat adat* to refer to indigenous peoples. The national indigenous peoples' organisation, Aliansi Masyarakat Adat Nusantara (AMAN), estimates that the number of indigenous peoples in Indonesia falls between 50 and 70 million people.

The third amendment to the Indonesian Constitution recognises indigenous peoples' rights in Article 18b-2. In more recent legislation, there is implicit recognition of some rights of peoples referred to as *masyarakat adat* or *masyarakat hukum adat*, including Act No. 5/1960 on Basic Agrarian Regulation, Act No. 39/1999 on Human Rights, and MPR Decree No X/2001 on Agrarian Reform. Act No. 27/2007 on Management of Coastal and Small Islands and Act No. 32/2010 on Environment clearly use the term *masyarakat adat* and use the working definition of AMAN. The Constitutional Court in May 2013 affirmed the constitutional rights of indigenous peoples to their land and territories, including their collective rights over customary forest.

While Indonesia is a signatory to the UN Declaration on the Rights of Indigenous Peoples (UNDRIP), government officials argue that the concept of indigenous peoples is not applicable as almost all Indonesians (with the exception of the ethnic Chinese) are indigenous and thus entitled to the same rights. Consequently, the government has rejected calls for specific needs by groups identifying themselves as indigenous. On 22 December 2014, the Ministry of Environment and Forestry agreed to be the trustee of 4.8 million hectares of indigenous maps to be included in the One Map Initiative.

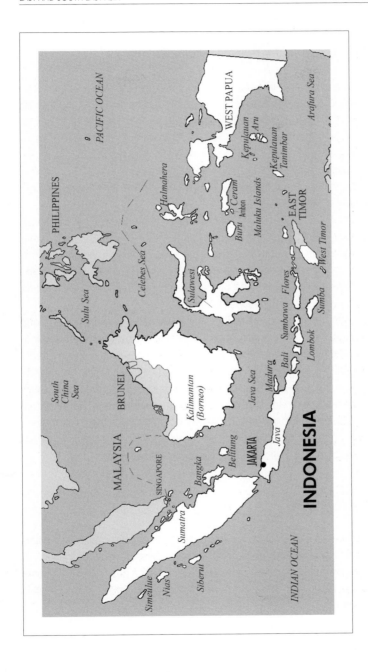

A new government under President Joko Widodo

2014 marked an important transition for Indonesian politics, with President Joko "Jokowi" Widodo assuming office alongside Vice-President Jusuf "JK" Kalla. In his official vision and mission, "Nawa Cita", Jokowi-JK outlined six main priorities for the protection of indigenous peoples.[1] Jokowi-JK undertook to push for the adoption of the Indigenous Peoples Act (see below), conduct policy reform and establish an independent commission on indigenous peoples. Jokowi-JK's commitments were unanimously endorsed by the members of the Indigenous Peoples' Alliance of the Archipelago (AMAN).

On 22 October 2014, President Jokowi announced a new cabinet composed of 34 ministries. AMAN welcomed his decision to merge the Ministry of Environment with the Ministry of Forestry to create the Ministry of Environment and Forestry with a commitment to sustainability. AMAN also welcomed the establishment of the Ministry of Agrarian and Spatial Planning as the main entry point for including and recognising indigenous territories.

Indeed, with President Jokowi at the helm, there is tremendous hope among indigenous peoples that he will initiate a reconciliation process between the Indonesian state and indigenous peoples. These actions must include, as a matter of urgency, official recognition of the systematic prejudice and injustice that indigenous peoples continue to suffer and immediate release and rehabilitation of indigenous victims of violence and criminalisation. In the medium term, the President must fulfil his commitment to establish a permanent and independent commission on indigenous peoples in order to ensure the full enjoyment of their collective rights as constitutionally afforded them as citizens of Indonesia.

Policy developments

At the national level, indigenous peoples continued to engage closely with different government entities and decision-making processes throughout the year in order to push for recognition and protection. Years of effort have resulted in some policy progress here. The status of relevant policy developments during 2014 is provided below:

Acceptance of indigenous maps

In 2014, the government launched the much-anticipated "one-map policy" as stipulated in Law No. 4/2011 on geospatial information, which is aimed at helping to resolve disagreements resulting from the use of different data and maps, which often result in land disputes and overlapping permits for plantation and mining operations.[2] On 22 December, the National REDD+ Agency and the Ministry of Environment and Forestry officially agreed to include 4.8 million hectares of indigenous maps in the One Map Initiative.[3] This is a very important step in helping the government identify and recognise where indigenous peoples live, and to ensure that indigenous peoples are included in decision-making, particularly regarding land allocation and issuance of permits. In cases of permits issued to private companies where the target areas overlap with indigenous territories, a special procedure will apply with regard to indigenous rights. This is particularly important given the current administration's focus on accelerating the business permit process, particularly that of land allocation.

The national initiative on the recognition and protection of indigenous peoples

On 1 September 2014, the Indonesian Vice-President launched a National Program for the Recognition and Protection of Indigenous Peoples. The Declaration was signed by nine ministries/institutions.[4] The Program has a number of targets ranging from the establishment of laws and regulations, legal reform, administrative tools, recovery and institutional strengthening of indigenous peoples and local government. The Program covers most of Jokowi's *Nawa Cita* (see above) and will be able to serve as a bridge between the previous government and the new one.

Draft Law on the Recognition and Protection of the Rights of Indigenous Peoples

Despite progressive national policy developments during the course of 2014, the government and Parliament have failed to adopt the Indigenous Peoples Act. Since 2012, indigenous peoples have harboured great hopes for fundamental change in Indonesian law, from the status quo to a system whereby indigenous peoples will finally gain recognition and protection. This hope was strengthened with the inclusion of the Bill on the Recognition and Protection of the Rights of Indigenous Peoples in the National Legislation Program and priorities for 2013 (see *The Indigenous World* 2013 and 2014). The Constitutional Court's Ruling on Customary Forest in May 2013 provided another push for the Indigenous Peoples Act. However, despite a series of public consultations, dialogues and hearings held by parliamentarians and indigenous organisations throughout 2013 and 2014, Parliament failed to adopt the Act when its term ended in September 2014. The Chair of the Special Committee publicly noted that the Ministry of Forestry had stalled the process, sending only low-ranking officials to the meetings with Parliament, without authority to take any decisions on behalf of the government.

Many argue that the failure to adopt the Indigenous Peoples Act indicates that the President did not have enough political commitment to fulfil the promises he had made to indigenous peoples when he first acknowledged the importance of a law to protect indigenous peoples during the commemoration of International Day of the World's Indigenous Peoples on 9 August 2006 in Jakarta. More worryingly, the then Ministry of Forestry has continued to pose a deep-rooted threat to the recognition and protection of the rights of indigenous peoples, in direct violation of Indonesia's 1945 Constitution.

A year of politics

In July 2014, 17,216 new legislators were elected at district, provincial and national levels, with at least 25 legislators officially backed by indigenous organisations and communities through different political parties. Earlier, these individual indigenous-backed legislators had signed agreements agreeing to work towards the recognition and protection of the rights of indigenous peoples and to report back to their constituents on progress at least twice a year. As of December 2014, these legislators have shown some promising progress, with the protection of indigenous peoples being included in the Local Regulation Program for 2015 in seven districts.

Continued violations of indigenous peoples' rights

As in previous years, conflicts involving indigenous peoples continued in 2014. The highly restrictive Forestry Law has led to the continued criminalisation of indigenous peoples who try to access their forests, with many members of indigenous communities coming into conflict with the law. In addition, the Law on Prevention and Eradication of Forest Destruction, which was adopted three months after the Constitutional Court ruling, continued to bar indigenous peoples from living in their forests. While legal reform at national level is increasingly recognising and protection indigenous peoples, this progress does not translate into enforcement on the ground. In fact, the majority of law enforcement officers are directly violating reform procedures, often making arrests without warrants and so on. In some cases it appears that these officials even directly position themselves as the protector of companies.

The Semende in Banding Agung, Bengkulu Province: On 24 April 2014, the District Court sentenced four members of the Semende community of Banding Agung, Sumatra to three years imprisonment and a fine of 1.5 billion rupiah. The appeal at the higher court was rejected and the sentence then confirmed by decision of the Supreme Court. The four villagers were charged under the Prevention and Eradication of Forest Destruction Act as the Ministry of Forestry has claimed their ancestral territory as National Park.

The Tungkal Ulu in South Sumatera Province: On 21 October 2014, the District Court of Palembang in South Sumatra sentenced five indigenous leaders to two years and six months in jail, a fine of 50 million rupiah. Mr. M. Nur and four others from Tungkal Ulu were charged with violating the Conservation Law as the government claims their ancestral territory is conservation area.

The arrest of Bachtiar M. Sabang in South Sulawesi: Mr. Sabang of Turunan Baji community has been held since October 2014 and his case is currently proceeding through the Sinjai District Court. He is facing at least three years in jail in accordance with the Conservation Law as the government claims his ancestral territory is protected forest.

Nusa Tenggara Timur cases: The Golo Lebo of East Manggarai district are constantly under pressure from the local government as they are resisting PT. Manggarai Manganese, a mining company operating on their ancestral territory. In fact, the company's permit expired on 7 December 2013. Also in Nusa Tenggara Timur, the Tana Ai in Sikka District are facing eviction by the local government and PT. Diocese Court, a coconut plantation whose permit expired in 2013.

The inquiry into violations of indigenous peoples' rights

Indigenous peoples continue to be the victims of systematic land grabbing through various policies, although the most significant threat remains that of the government's designation of ancestral territories as part of the State Forest Estate, covering approximately 70% of the country. During 2014, the National Commission on Human Rights (Komnas HAM) led a National Inquiry on Indigenous Peoples' Rights to their Territories in Forest Areas. The National Inquiry is based on the Commission's mandate to monitor human rights violations. The inquiry was also mandated by the Joint Memorandum of Agreement with 12 ministries/institutions to resolve conflicts within forest areas, in line with the effort to implement the Constitutional Court's Ruling No. 35 regarding Customary Forests. The National Commission on Women and Children joined the inquiry to ensure the inclusion of issues related to women and children. The inquiry included data and information gathering, study and examination of cases, public hearings and dialogues with government and company officials.

Initial findings from the series of regional public hearings show individual and collective human rights violations against indigenous peoples, with indigenous women and children in the most vulnerable position. The problems are wide-ranging and often unresolved, including but not limited to: unclear and overlooked boundaries of indigenous peoples' territories; overlapping licenses; manipulation of licenses by the government and companies; unresolved legal cases brought against defendants for various forms of violence against, criminalisation of and systematic crimes against indigenous peoples; the bias and consolidated use of military and private security guards by corporations; and a lack of just, thorough and multi-sectoral conflict resolution. The Commission's initial conclusions noted that all cases also contained significant internal conflicts fostered by companies and governments in order to take advantage of community divisions. The Com-

mission is preparing its final report, which will include a set of policy recommendations for the new administration and Parliament.

The situation in West Papua

The end of 2014 was shaken by the fatal shootings of at least five young civilians
by the security forces in Paniai District on 8 December 2014. The Indonesian
security forces are accused of having opened fire on a crowd of 800 peaceful
demonstrators, including women and children. Five protesters were killed and at
least 17 others — including elementary school students — were injured, according to a report by Human Rights Watch.[5] The National Police Chief initially denied
any involvement on the part of the security forces but the Provincial Papuan Police Chief later deployed an investigation team.[6] The shootings have raised national concerns and, in January 2015, the National Human Rights Commission
announced that it had formed a team to conduct an extensive investigation into
possible human rights abuses committed in the Paniai shootings.[7]

The region of West Papua has never been free from human rights violations.
Earlier in the year, on 28-29 November, in Abepura, Papua, a regional public
hearing of the National Inquiry into indigenous land rights violations, conducted
by the National Human Rights Commission, concluded that natural resource exploitation in Papua had had serious consequences in the form of physical conflicts involving torture; intimidation, environmental degradation and pollution; and
consequences for the people's health status, particularly women's reproductive
health. They are exposed to chemicals used in the operations of the gold mines
and oil palm plantations.[8] The National Commission recommended that the government review the licenses of private corporations in West Papua and also
called on the police to develop a rights-based Standard Operating Procedure for
dealing particularly with conflicts between indigenous peoples, the government
and private corporations.   ◯

Notes and references

1   http://kpu.go.id/koleksigambar/VISI_MISI_Jokowi-JK.pdf
2   http://www.thejakartapost.com/news/2014/12/26/one-map-policy-helps-resolve-land-disputes-
     overlapping-permits.html

3   Indonesia's One Map policy is stipulated in Law No. 4/2011 on geospatial information and was launched to help resolve disagreements resulting from the use of different data and maps that often cause land disputes and overlapping permits for plantation and mining operations

4   The Coordinating Ministry of Peoples' Welfare; Ministry of Environment; Ministry Home Affairs; Ministry of Law and Human Rights; Ministry of Forestry; National Defence Agency; Geospatial Information Agency; National Commission on Human Rights; and the REDD+ Agency

5   See: http://www.hrw.org/news/2014/12/10/indonesia-security-forces-kill-five-papua

6   See: http://www.thejakartapost.com/news/2014/12/09/police-investigate-paniai-shooting.html

7   See: http://thejakartaglobe.beritasatu.com/news/human-rights-committee-readies-papua-investigation-paniai-shooting/

8   See: http://www.komnasham.go.id/sites/default/files/dokumen/temuan%20awal%20inkuiri%20adat_papua.pdf

*Abdon Nababan is a Toba Batak from North Sumatera. He is the Secretary General of Aliansi Masyarakat Adat Nusantara/AMAN. **Erasmus Cahyadi** belongs to the Terre Clan from Flores, and has been working with AMAN since 2004. He is currently serving as Director of Legal and Human Rights. **Rukka Sombolinggi** is a Toraya from Sulawesi, and is Deputy to AMAN's Secretary General on Policy Advocacy, Legal Issues and Politics.*

MALAYSIA

In 2014, the indigenous peoples of Malaysia represented around 12% of the 28.6 million population.[1] They are collectively called *Orang Asal*. The *Orang Asli* are the indigenous peoples of Peninsular Malaysia. The 18 Orang Asli subgroups within the Negrito (Semang), Senoi and Aboriginal-Malay groups account for 180,000 or 0.6% of the national population. In Sarawak, the indigenous peoples are collectively called *Orang Ulu* and *Dayak*. They include the Iban, Bidayuh, Kenyah, Kayan, Kedayan, Murut, Punan, Bisayah, Kelabit, Berawan and Penan. They constitute around 1,198,200 or 45.5% of Sarawak's population of 2,633,100 million people. In Sabah, the 39 different indigenous ethnic groups are called natives or *Anak Negeri* and make up about 2,140,800 or 60.5% of Sabah's population of 3,540,300. The main groups are the Dusun, Murut, Paitan and Bajau groups. While the Malays are also indigenous to Malaysia, they are not categorised as *Orang Asal* because they constitute the majority and are politically, economically and socially dominant.

In Sarawak and Sabah, laws introduced by the British during their colonial rule recognising the customary land rights and customary law of the indigenous peoples are still in place. However, they are not properly implemented, and are even outright ignored by the government, which gives priority to large-scale resource extraction and the plantations of private companies over the rights and interests of the indigenous communities. In Peninsular Malaysia, while there is a clear lack of reference to Orang Asli customary land rights in the National Land Code, Orang Asli customary tenure is recognised under common law. The principal Act that governs Orang Asli administration, including occupation of the land, is the Aboriginal Peoples Act 1954. Malaysia has adopted the United Nations Declaration on the Rights of Indigenous Peoples (UNDRIP) and endorsed the Outcome Document of the World Conference on Indigenous Peoples.

Follow-up to SUHAKAM's National Inquiry into the Land Rights of Indigenous Peoples

A Task Force was established in 2013 with the mandate, among other things, of assessing the findings of the Human Rights Commission of Malaysia (SUHAKAM) during its National Inquiry into the Land Rights of Indigenous Peoples (See *The Indigenous World 2012, 2013, 2014*) with a view to implementing the recommendations made. The Task Force completed its work in September 2014. Its report was apparently delivered to the cabinet soon after but neither the cabinet nor parliament have thus far made any announcements as to how or when the SUHAKAM Land Inquiry recommendations are to be implemented.

Various calls have been made on the government to fully recognise indigenous peoples' customary laws on land, to remedy and redress land loss and to address development issues by respecting the right to Free, Prior and Informed Consent. NGOs have been demanding the implementation of the SUHAKAM recommendations[2] but it appears that the government is dragging its feet and the creation of the Task Force is seen by indigenous peoples as yet another delaying tactic.

Indigenous customary laws, while recognised as a legal definition by the Malaysian Federal Constitution, continue to be debated and limited only to the codified aspects of these laws. *Jaringan Orang Asal SeMalaysia* (JOAS), the national umbrella body of indigenous organisations in Malaysia, conducted its own research and presented the results at a seminar organised in conjunction with the World Indigenous Peoples' Day celebrations in August 2014. The participants endorsed the finding that customary laws continue to be relevant but felt that the qualifier in Federal Constitution Article160(2) that customs and usages have the force of law only when they are codified and the limited interpretations used in courts by lawyers and the government are discriminating against customary laws. Efforts to boost indigenous customary institutions are hampered by political interventions in the appointment of *Ketua Kampung* (village heads) and key positions in Native Courts, by the erosion of customary laws among young people due to external influences, and by the fact that customary institutions are male dominated. As a follow-up to its advocacy work for the recognition of indigenous customary laws and rights to land, JOAS will conduct further research on, and mapping of, traditional territories in 2015.

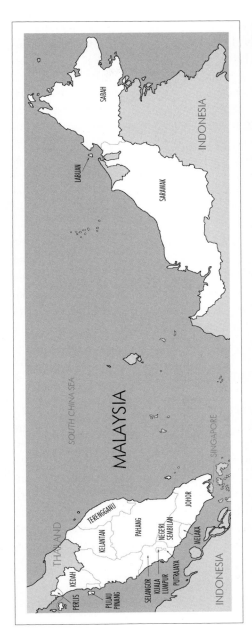

Development of laws, including Prior and Informed Consent

In 2014, the Natural Resources and Environment Ministry continued its consultation on a draft law on Access and Benefit Sharing (ABS), which has relevant provisions on access to indigenous knowledge and on Prior and Informed Consent (PIC). This proposed ABS law is the first to make specific reference to PIC and to include mutually-agreed terms for benefit sharing derived from the use of resources and traditional knowledge. The current draft does not include the term "free" but does provide that the PIC of indigenous and local communities be obtained in accordance with the customary laws and practices, community protocols and procedures of said communities. The draft law is expected to be tabled in Parliament in 2015 and the Ministry also has an open feedback mechanism.[3]

Another important development is the holding of the 5th ASEAN Social Forestry

Network (ASFN) Conference in Sabah, Malaysia, at which civil society organisations (CSOs) had an opportunity to provide input. The ASFN adopted key strategies and recommendations to further strengthen its commitment on social forestry. These included the setting up and monitoring of social forestry targets at national and regional levels; the adoption of a rights-based approach to social forestry policy formulation, planning and implementation; and the provision of secure tenure to indigenous and other local communities (especially customary forest users and rotational agriculturalists).[4] As a follow-up, the Sabah Social Forestry Working Group was formed, comprising the Sabah Forestry Department and indigenous organisations. Its aim is to pursue the possibility of drafting a Social Forestry Law for Sabah, to extend the indigenous resource management practice or *tagal* for forest resources, and to strengthen the community economy and livelihoods.

Additionally, making the most of Malaysia's role as chair of ASEAN in 2015, Malaysian CSOs, including indigenous organisations, organised several activities in preparation for the ASEAN Summits in April and November 2015. This included a study by JOAS on the impacts of ASEAN economic integration and of the socio-cultural and political security blueprints on indigenous peoples. These are to be used by CSOs for advocacy and awareness-raising efforts.

Challenging encroachment on indigenous lands

Indigenous peoples affected by encroachment and aggressive economic development interventions on their lands have stepped up their struggle, using various strategies including press releases, police reports, complaints to the government and, ultimately, filing their case in court. However, a general trend towards questioning witnesses and the credibility of experts in court cases on land claims continues to be used as a tactic to prolong them. Using the courts as an avenue for substantiating their rights is just one of the challenges faced by communities and their lawyers. Nevertheless, communities continued to file cases in court to prove their legitimate claims to their land in 2014, including in Pahang, Kelantan, Sarawak and Sabah.[5]

Anti-dam campaign

In September, over 150 *Orang Asal* from Pahang, Kelantan, Sarawak, Sabah and Kuala Lumpur gathered to issue a joint warning to the 2014 ASEAN Power Week sponsors and delegates that they should withdraw and stay away from planning or investing in mega-dams. They had to protest outside the building as no representatives of indigenous communities or CSOs were invited to the conference itself. Community representatives called on two of the sponsors of ASEAN Power Week, Sarawak Energy Berhad (SEB) and Tenaga Nasional Berhad, to respect the provisions of Malaysia's constitution and the UNDRIP by immediately withdrawing their proposals for the Baram Dam and Telom Dam, and halting their dam-project bidding processes, land acquisition and preparatory site work, including logging.[6]

In another protest, activists criticised the International New York Times for organising a sustainable-energy conference that included the SEB, which is spearheading a dam-building drive that the *Orang Asal* say is uprooting them from their ancestral lands.[7] SEB was one of two "gold sponsors" of the "Energy for Tomorrow" conference in November and the International New York Times was rapped for not considering the implications of featuring SEB as a sponsor and having its controversial CEO as a panellist.

The campaign was stepped up by Malaysian and international human rights organisations, which publicly denounced the actions taken by police to intimidate indigenous peoples in Sarawak at the proposed site of the Baram Dam.[8] In October, a group of residents from the villages of Long Na'ah and Long Kesseh were prevented from entering the blockade area by over 30 police from the General Operation Force (GOF) and at least 10 enforcement officers of the Sarawak Forestry Corporation (SAPU). Since then, GOF and SAPU personnel have remained encamped in the area.

United Nations Special Rapporteur on the right to health

In November, the UN Special Rapporteur on the right to health conducted a two-week official visit to Malaysia. He was able to visit two indigenous communities in Sabah and also met with NGOs and government representatives in Peninsular

Malaysia and Sabah but was unable to visit Sarawak. His report will be presented to the UN Human Rights Council in June 2015.

In his End Of Mission statement,[9] the Special Rapporteur noted that health indicators among indigenous populations were significantly worse than those of the general population and gave the example of life expectancy, which is around 53 years for indigenous peoples while the Malaysian average is over 70. He also highlighted the serious problem of birth registration, which is affecting communities living in remote areas and causing problems in accessing healthcare. He recommended that the right to health be promoted and protected through cross-sectoral programmes that address socio-economic and environmental factors, guided by a human rights-based approach that emphasises non-discrimination, participation and accountability. Equally emphasised were threats due to changes in land use as a result of development projects, which are leading to a substantial loss of access to traditional land and sources of livelihood and having a direct and negative impact on health.

On his visit to the communities, he said: "I received testimonies indicating that there is no meaningful dialogue between authorities and indigenous communities, and that these communities do not have access to basic information about development projects in their region and the potential environmental impact. Uncertainties about their livelihood security in the future is having a serious effect on the mental health and emotional well-being of indigenous communities, leading to chronic stress and anxiety, at the same time that it violates principles of prior and informed consent".

He felt that the current share of healthcare financing within the GDP, which stands at 4.3%, was low and should be increased to allow more resources to be injected for the further development of the sector. He also called for the financial barriers that restrict access to healthcare, especially for groups in vulnerable situations, to be removed.

Malaysia rejects UPR recommendations on indigenous peoples

In March 2014, the Malaysian government rejected all six key recommendations to strengthen indigenous rights made under the Universal Periodic Review. These included requests to allow visits on the part of the UN Special Rapporteur on the rights of indigenous peoples; the establishment of an independent body to investigate conflicts over land, territories and resources; implementation of the SU-HAKAM Inquiry recommendations; ensuring that laws on indigenous peoples comply with the UNDRIP; guaranteeing legal rights to forests; and the establishment of an independent National Commission on Indigenous Peoples. The government said that the Task Force had already been established to study these issues. The national indigenous network, which felt betrayed by the government, issued a scathing statement that was supported by many local and international NGOs stating that they could not respect a government that did not respect their rights. Four other recommendations concerning indigenous peoples, relating to poverty eradication and welfare, were, however, adopted.

World Conference on Indigenous Peoples (WCIP)

While in New York for the WCIP, representatives of indigenous peoples met with the 19-member government delegation from Malaysia headed by the Minister for Rural and Regional Development. Four indigenous representatives participated in the WCIP and, prior to the WCIP, JOAS also lobbied hard to ensure government support. The Minister expressed his support for the Outcome Document of the WCIP and committed the government to follow-up actions. Follow-up plans to press the government to implement the Outcome Document include translating and disseminating the text, holding a national training workshop and meeting with the Minister to hold him to his commitment.

Indigenous women

As a result of a series of workshops on women leaders in Sabah, Sarawak and Peninsular Malaysia, an indigenous women's network under JOAS, Wanita-JOAS, was launched in August 2014 and a statement marking International Women Human Rights Defenders' Day on 29 November was issued to bring to the attention of the authorities the fact that this is a critical time for indigenous women across Malaysia, confronted as they are with the need to defend their livelihoods and protect their heritage in the face of threats to the very survival of their communities from large-scale mining, rampant logging, the expansion of palm oil plantations, and the building of large-scale dams. They are not only standing alongside the men in their communities in this effort but also taking on important leadership roles. It is more important than ever that indigenous women have the space to share information, strategies and perspectives and develop a platform to help strengthen their collective resolve. As a follow-up, the leaders have planned a series of seminars all over Malaysia on women and political participation.   ○

Notes and references

1   Data sourced from the Statistics Department on 27.1.2015 at http://pqi.stats.gov.my/searchBI. php. Click "current population estimates" for ethnic groups for the whole of Malaysia (Other Bumiputra), Sabah and Sarawak. No current population data is available for Orang Asli. For Sabah and Sarawak, the Malays are included in the calculation, as some include the indigenous "Brunei Malays" (Sabah) and "Malays"(Sarawak), while some indigenous individuals identify as "Malay" for various reasons.
2   http://www.sarawakreport.org/campaign/joint-statement-on-human-rights-day-respect-the-affected-natives-and-peoples-of-sarawaks-rights/
3   http://www.nre.gov.my/ms-my/Lists/papar-pengumuman.aspx?ID=%20%20%20%20218
4   file:///C:/Users/user/Downloads/ASFN%20Adopted%20Strategies%20form%20Recommendations%20of%20the%20ASFN%204th%20&%205th%20Conferences.pdf
5   See examples at http://www.coac.org.my/main.php?section=news&article_id=126   - Kelantan ("Pos Belatim Temiar get another chance in court"); http://coac.org.my/main. php?section=news&article_id=129   - Pahang ("Landmark decision of the Court of Appeal of the Orang Asli case of Yebet binti Saman & Ors."); http://www.themalaysianinsider.com/malaysia/ article/natives-scuttle-sarawak-bid-to-take-their-ancestral-land   - Sarawak ("Natives scuttle Sarawak bid to take their ancestral land"); http://www.theborneopost.com/2014/10/10/ranau-villagers-lose-bid-for-stay-of-order-in-land-case/ - Sabah ("Ranau villagers lose bid for stay of order in land case").
6   file:///C:/Users/user/Downloads/Press%20Release%20-%20Mega%20dam%20protest%20 -%2010%20Sept%202014.pdf
7   http://www.themalaysianinsider.com/malaysia/article/new-york-times-rapped-over-malaysia-clean-energy-conference
8   http://www.suaram.net/?p=6679
9   http://www.ohchr.org/EN/NewsEvents/Pages/DisplayNews.aspx?NewsID=15370&LangID=E#st hash.362RDFpB.dpuf

*Jannie Lasimbang is a Kadazan from Sabah, Malaysia. She currently works as the Secretariat Director of the **Jaringan Orang Asal SeMalaysia (JOAS)** or Indigenous Peoples' Network of Malaysia. JOAS is an umbrella network of 87 community-based indigenous organisations and 6 NGOs that focuses its work on indigenous peoples' issues.*

ernment could lead to further intensification of conflict between communities and the government authorities. Bearing in mind the concerns of the potentially affected communities, the Karen Network for Culture and Environment (KNCE) and its allied organisations have recommended to the IUCN, as an advisor to the Bureau of the World Heritage Committee, that a number of measures taken prior to the establishment of the KKFC as a natural World Heritage site. These include the resolution of all conflicts between the government agencies and communities living in and around KKFC, in particular the evictions of Karen communities from the Kaeng Krachan National Park; that the concerned government agencies organise workshops for all affected communities to provide full information on both the advantages and disadvantages of establishing the proposed World Heritage site and that a public hearing should be conducted with the full and effective participation of all stakeholders. The KNCE further recommended that the proposed World Heritage site should clearly recognise the rights of indigenous peoples and other communities living in and around the KKFC, including the right to their livelihood practices, to access forests, and that the Karen be recognised as equal partners in the conservation and management of the World Heritage site; the need to clearly demarcate the village areas, lands and territories used by indigenous communities and to issue community land titles; and that a fair and clear conflict resolution and redress mechanism that is easily accessible and just for affected villagers be established.

Implementation of a new Forestry Master Plan

Deforestation due to encroachment on state land for the building of tourist resorts, for commercial plantations and illegal logging prompted the National Council for Peace and Order (NCPO) to issue NCPO Order Number 64/2014 and 66/2014 and to pass a Master Plan on Resolving Deforestation, State Land Encroachment and Sustainable Natural Resource Management. The master plan aims to increase forest cover by up to 40% and outlines three steps for achieving this. Step one is to stop deforestation and reclaim forestlands from the encroachers. This will be undertaken in the first year. Step two is to revamp the forest management system. This will be done within two years. The last step is to restore the condition of the forests. This will be carried out over a 10-year period.[6]

The implementation of this policy led to the arrest of 39 Karen villagers at Thung Pakha, Mae La Luang Sub-district, Mae La Noi district, Mae Hong Son province on 4 May 2014. They were later charged with illegal possession of timber, clearing of forest land, causing disturbance to wildlife habitat and "obstructing official business" (villagers stopped forest rangers from leaving their village after they arrested some community members). In reality, the arrested Karen were only cutting wood for building and maintaining their houses. However, on 19 October, the Mae Sariang Court of the northern province of Mae Hong Son sentenced 24 of them to between one and seven years in prison for illegal deforestation. The jail term, however, has been suspended for one year. The 15 others who faced similar charge were fined between 10,000 and 20,000 Baht (330 to 660 USD) depending on the quantity of timber found in their possession. Most of those arrested were released on bail. Their cases will be petitioned before the Appeal Court.

Adoption of the National Council of Indigenous Peoples

After several years of discussion and deliberation, the National Council of Indigenous Peoples (NCIP) in Thailand was finally adopted at the first Indigenous Peoples' Council Assembly held at Phothiwichalai Srinakarinwirote University at Mae Sot, Tak province on 28 November 2014. Thirty-nine indigenous peoples' networks from all over the country attended the event. This is a step forward in advancing and asserting the rights of indigenous peoples in Thailand. Four major decisions were reached by consensus. These include adopting the draft indigenous peoples' law, the Constitution of the National Council of Indigenous Peoples, a short-term work plan and a joint statement to be submitted to the National Reform Council and the Constitution Drafting Committee.

National reform

At the end of 2013, the political conflict between pro-government and anti-government groups led by the People's Democratic Reform Committee (PDRC) turned into violence. Nearly 30 innocent lives were lost, more than 700 people were injured, public and private properties were destroyed and some government buildings were taken over.[7] The strong division and prolonged conflict had led to political deadlock and administrative paralysis. On 22 May 2014, the military, under its newly-formed National Council for Peace and Order (NCPO), thus decided to take control of the national administration in order to prevent further deterioration of the situation. In order to restore peace and order in the country, the NCPO presented a three-step national roadmap of reconciliation, reform and election. The roadmap is expected to be completed by early 2016.

Indigenous peoples submitted proposals in the name of the National Council of Indigenous Peoples in Thailand to both the National Reform Council and the Constitution Drafting Committee on 11 key issues that the committee is currently dealing with. In addition, indigenous peoples' representatives have also worked closely with the People's Reform Committee, a parallel body established by civil society organisations to ensure that the concerns and proposals of civil society and ordinary people are included in the constitution and policies.   ○

Notes and references

1   Ten groups are sometimes mentioned, i.e. the Palaung are also included in some official documents. The directory of ethnic communities of 20 northern and western provinces of the Department of Social Development and Welfare of 2002 also includes the Mlabri and Padong.
2   The figure given is sometimes 1,203,149 people, which includes immigrant Chinese in the north.
3   For further information on the disappearance of Porlachi Rakchong Chareorn, see Human Rights Watch: http://www.hrw.org/news/2014/04/20/thailand-prominent-activist-feared-disappeared
4   Human Rights Violation Report, National Human Rights Commission dated 17 September 2014 case no. 317/2557.
5   See also, Bangkok Post, 'Ray of Hope in Forest Fight', 27 September, 2014 for English language media coverage of the NHRC of Thailand report: http://www.bangkokpost.com/opinion/opinion/434545/ray-of-hopein-forest-fight
6   http://www.prachatai.com/english/node/4450
7   http://www.thaiembassy.org/ankara/contents/files/news-20141203-165908-999042.pdf

Kittisak Rattanakrajangsri is a Mien from the north of Thailand. He has worked with indigenous communities and organisations since 1989. He is currently General Secretary of the Indigenous Peoples' Foundation for Education and Environment (IPF) based in Chiang Mai, Thailand.

CAMBODIA

Cambodia is home to 24 different Indigenous Peoples, who speak either Mon-Khmer or Austronesian languages.[1] As of late 2014, the name "Indigenous Peoples" had not yet been fully adopted in Cambodia, in either the legal system or the media. More commonly, these people are referred to as "ethnic minorities" or "indigenous ethnic minorities".[2] They live mainly in the six north-eastern upland provinces of Ratanakiri, Mondulkiri, Stung Treng, Kratie, Preah Vihear and Kampong Thom but Indigenous communities are also located in nine other provinces around the country. With an estimated population of 200,000 to 400,000 overall, Indigenous Peoples are generally estimated to account for 1 to 2% of the national population although they are not clearly disaggregated in national census data.

The 1993 National Constitution guarantees all citizens the same rights "regardless of race, colour, sex, language, and religious belief" or other differences. National legislation and policies specifically recognize Indigenous Peoples and their rights.[3] The 2009 National Policy on Indigenous Peoples' rights in Cambodia is arguably the most progressive of all the countries in mainland Southeast Asia.[4] However, the main problem remains the lack of implementation and Indigenous Peoples continue to see their lands and forests grabbed up through state-granted "concessions" of their lands to commercial companies.[5]

The Cambodian government has ratified many of the main international human rights conventions, including the International Convention on the Elimination of Racial Discrimination (CERD). In 2007, the Cambodian government supported the adoption of the UN Declaration on the Rights of Indigenous Peoples (UNDRIP) but has still not ratified ILO Convention 169.

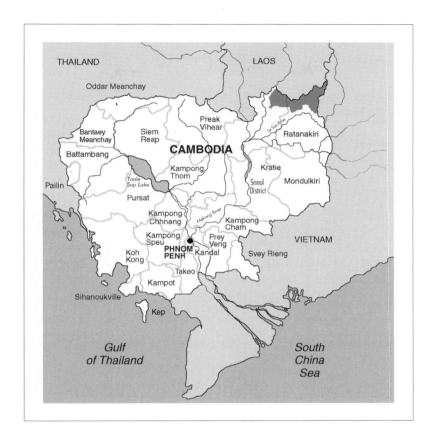

Human Rights Council's Universal Periodic Review of Cambodia

On 28 January 2014, Cambodia underwent the Second Cycle of the Human Rights Council's Universal Periodic Review (UPR) of its human rights record. In its presentation to the Working Group on the UPR, Cambodia's delegation affirmed the existence of national policies and laws recognizing Indigenous Peoples' land rights. It also affirmed that the state engages in "consultations" with Indigenous communities about their lands but made no mention of seeking their free, prior and informed consent to development projects that impact on their lands.[6] There is extensive literature documenting Cambodian state and corporate practices of dispossessing Indigenous Peoples of their lands.[7] "Consultation" – when it does happen – is usually an asymmetrical "take it or leave it" offer, accompanied by threats.

The World Conference on Indigenous Peoples

A single delegate from the Indigenous Peoples' movement in Cambodia was able to attend the World Conference on Indigenous Peoples (WCIP) that took place in New York in September 2014. He went home, as did many other Indigenous activists, feeling the event had been anti-climactic and disappointing. It did not produce any firm commitments from states to substantively act to better recognize, promote and protect Indigenous Peoples' rights. There was no participation by the Cambodian government in the WCIP. The Ambassador of Cambodia declined to meet with the delegate and, through his secretary, stated that the Embassy was too busy with other things to participate in the WCIP. The use of the WCIP outcome document in Cambodia is therefore not at all clear.

Indigenous Peoples in Cambodia take on the International Finance Corporation

One constructive development for the Indigenous rights movement in Cambodia in 2014 was the deployment of a new strategy for stopping, or at least slowing down, the rampant land grabbing that has marked so much of north-eastern Cambodia since the 1990s. Rather than simply appealing to the national government on largely moral grounds to implement its already adopted laws and policies on Indigenous Peoples' land rights, this new strategy involves effectively bypassing an unresponsive government. Instead, they are seeking a remedy from the financiers who are underwriting the companies that are grabbing their land, and who have a greater concern for maintaining an image of adhering to human rights principles; in this case, this is the International Finance Corporation (IFC), which is the private sector financing arm of the World Bank (WB). This strategy was developed through Indigenous Peoples' collaboration with several non-governmental organizations (NGOs) and Indigenous Peoples' organizations (IPOs).[8] In February 2014, the NGOs and IPOs filed a complaint on behalf of 17 largely Indigenous communities with the IFC's "internal watchdog", the Compliance Advisor Ombudsman (CAO) with regard to the IFC's financing of the Hoang Anh Gia Lai (HAGL) company which, in turn, has been responsible for the recent grabbing of tens of thousands of hectares of Indigenous lands and forests in Ratanakiri Province, much of which is being cleared or already has been cleared for rubber plantations.[9] These land grabs have been carried out without the free, prior and informed consent of the affected communities, and have not included any satisfactory compensation. The complaint sheds some light on the complicated transnational financing structures that Indigenous Peoples are up against when claiming their rights to their traditional lands, territories and resources. The finance structure described in the complaint appears to support recent arguments that land grabbing in Cambodia may have more to do with Asian money laundering than it does with simple resource capture.[10] It is likely that the structure of this case is variably reproduced elsewhere in the Southeast Asia region, if not globally.[11]

The complaint describes the problem as follows: during the first decade of the 21st century, the IFC invested approx. US$ 27 million in an equity fund run by the Dragon Capital Group Ltd (DCGL), a self-described "integrated investment group" with offices in Vietnam but whose CEO is British. This DCGL equity fund is known as the Vietnamese Enterprise Investments Ltd (VEIL) fund, which DCGL describes as its "bellweather [sic] fund...Cayman Islands incorporated, and listed on the Irish Stock Exchange".[12] DCGL/VEIL capital was then invested in the HAGL company which, in turn, was used to fund operations in Ratanakiri Province, carried out by approximately seven of its subsidiary companies. They then began bulldozing Indigenous lands, cutting down forests and developing rubber plantations. One might describe this financial arrangement as a four-tiered shell enclosure that varies by scale: IFC/DCGL/HAGL/HAGL subsidiaries or, as an alternative image, like a Babushka doll, with the IFC on the outside, and the subsidiaries with their bulldozers at the core. But what facilitates this structure in the first place is the role played by the Cambodian state, in granting the concessions of land to HAGL, cumulatively estimated at over 40,000 hectares.

The filed complaint describes the harm suffered by the 17 communities as a result of this flow of capital. The loss of collective lands is the primary cause of this harm. With the conversion of lands to rubber plantations has come deforestation, a loss of biodiversity and the pollution of water sources. The effects of territorial dispossession have severely impacted upon peoples' livelihoods, disrupted children's education, limited religious expression, triggered food insecurity and, in general, have foreclosed on peoples' hopes for their children's future. In short, these are all outcomes that are contrary to the World Bank's stated mission of "reducing poverty".[13]

As of the end of 2014, the IFC CAO was reported to have intervened on behalf of the Indigenous communities who are parties to the complaint, and IFC-mediated negotiations between the communities and the HAGL group are scheduled to take place during the first half of 2015. The NGOs and IPOs who assisted the communities in preparing the complaint are now supporting the communities' preparations to fully engage in these negotiations. The communities hope to regain their lands, including those that have been converted to rubber plantations. The HAGL group has reportedly agreed to a temporary halt in any further land clearing (until June 2015).

Should the negotiations result in the outcome hoped for by the communities, it may well represent a new phase in the Cambodian Indigenous rights movement, in which Indigenous Peoples begin to find remedies for land rights violations within the circuits of finance capital that drive the demand side of land grabbing, rather than waiting for the state to find the political will to recognize and protect Indigenous land rights. The other large Vietnamese company engaged in rubber plantation development in Cambodia, the Vietnamese Rubber Group (VRG), also appears to be responding to this kind of strategy.[14] Yet not all the companies engaged in Cambodian land grabs are so concerned with their public images. Indeed, it seems many prefer to have no image at all.   ◯

Notes and references

1   There is variation in the estimates of how many peoples there are because different writers per-
     ceive linguistic boundaries differently, cf., past editions of *Indigenous World*, as well "Indigenous
     Groups in Cambodia 2014: An Updated Situation" by Frédéric Bourdier (published by Asia Indig-
     enous Peoples Pact). The term, Indigenous, is capitalized here to reflect its growing acceptance
     as a name, a proper noun; rather than as an adjective.
2   The official Khmer proxy term for Indigenous Peoples – *chuncheat daoem pheak tech* – literally
     translates as "original ethnic minority people".
3   Cf. the 2001 Cambodian National Land Law: NS/RKM/0801/14; the 2002 National Forestry Law:
     NS/RKM/0802/016. 2009 legislation affecting Indigenous Peoples includes a "National Policy on
     the Development of Indigenous People," prepared by the Ministry of Rural Development, a "Sub-
     Decree on Procedures of Registration of Land of Indigenous Communities" (No.83 ANK/BK),
     both approved by the Council of Ministers on 24 April 2009; and a "Circular of the Ministry of

Rural Development on the Procedures and Methods of Implementing National Policy on the Development and Identification of an Indigenous Community," approved on 22 July 2009. Another circular was approved on 31 May 2011, from the Ministry of Interior and the Ministry of Land Management, Urban Planning and Construction, an "Inter-ministerial Circular on Interim Protective Measures Protecting Lands of Indigenous Peoples that Have Been Requested for Collective Ownership Titling, While Awaiting Titling Process According to Procedure to be Completed".

4   Although this is not saying all that much. All of the others (Vietnam, Thailand, Myanmar and Laos) maintain the common Asian stance that there are no Indigenous Peoples in their countries, or that everybody is Indigenous. Either way, the result is that there is no recognition of Indigenous rights at all. That Cambodia does recognize the existence of Indigenous Peoples is progressive but its recognition is quite limited, and does not meet the standards of international law, according to the UN Special Rapporteur on the rights of Indigenous Peoples. This is discussed at length in Keating, N. B. (2013), "Kuy Alterities: The Struggle to Conceptualize and Claim Indigenous Land Rights in Neoliberal Cambodia." *Asia Pacific Viewpoint* 54(3):309-322.

5   Global Witness (an NGO) has documented at length the state-corporate practices of Cambodian land concessions, which involve logging, plantations, mining and land speculation.
    All of their research is available at http://www.globalwitness.org/campaigns/corruption/oil-gas-and-mining/cambodia.

6   Cf. para. 13, UN document A/HRC/26/16. Report of the Working Group on the Universal Periodic Review - Cambodia

7   These include every entry for Cambodia in past editions of *The Indigenous World*. Bourdier (2014) – cf. note 1 above – provides a good current overview of this situation.

8   These include Indigenous communities of Tampuan, Jarai, Kachok and Kreung peoples; ethnic minority communities of Lao, Vietnamese and Khmer people; the NGOs Global Witness, Equitable Cambodia, and Inclusive Development International; and the Cambodia Indigenous Youth Association, Indigenous Rights Active Members, and Highlander Association IPOs. Cf. http://www.inclusivedevelopment.net/cambodia-and-laos-hagl-rubber-plantations/

9   Cf. http://www.globalwitness.org/rubberbarons/; accessed on 13 Feb 2015

10 The linkage between land-grabbing in Cambodia and Asian money-laundering is explored in Baird, I. G. (2014) "The Global Land Grab Meta-Narrative, Asian Money Laundering and Elite Capture: Reconsidering the Cambodian Context," *Geopolitics* 19(2):431-453.

11 Cf. http://www.globalwitness.org/campaigns/corruption/anonymous-companies; accessed on 13 Feb 2015

12 Cf. http://www.dragoncapital.com/dragon-capital-funds/vietnam-enterprise-investments-limited; accessed on 13 Feb 2015

13 Inclusive Development International and Equitable Cambodia conducted a human rights assessment study that documents all these outcomes. Forthcoming at http://www.inclusivedevelopment.net/

14 http://www.globalwitness.org/library/vietnam-rubber-group-says-its-doors-are-now-open-people-affected-plantations-cambodia-and; accessed on 13 Feb 2015

Neal B. Keating, *Associate Professor of Anthropology, State University of New York, Brockport, with contributions from Indigenous Peoples' networks in Cambodia.*

VIETNAM

As a multi-ethnic country, Vietnam has 54 recognized ethnic groups; 53 are ethnic minority groups with an estimated 13 to 14 million people, accounting for around 14% of the country's total population of 90 million. Each ethnic minority group has its own distinct culture and traditions.

The ethnic minorities live scattered throughout the country but are concentrated mostly in the Northern Mountains and in the Central Highlands (*Tay Nguyen*) in the south. The Vietnamese government does not use the term "indigenous peoples" for any groups but it is generally the ethnic minorities living in the mountainous areas that are referred to as Vietnam's indigenous peoples. The term ethnic minorities is thus often used interchangeably with indigenous peoples in Vietnam.

Poverty is still high among ethnic minorities. While the national poverty rate fell from 14.2% in 2010 to 9.6% in 2012, in the north-western mountains, mostly inhabited by ethnic minorities, it was still 28.55%.

All ethnic minorities have Vietnamese citizenship, and Vietnam's constitution recognizes that all people have equal rights. There is no specific law on ethnic minorities but a ministry-level agency, the Committee on Ethnic Minority Affairs, is in charge of ethnic minority affairs. The Government of Vietnam has not ratified ILO Convention 169 but voted in favour of the UNDRIP, although it does not recognize ethnic minorities as indigenous peoples.

New policies on disaster mitigation and poverty alleviation

In 2014, the Vietnam government issued three decisions that were important for ethnic minorities given that the target areas of these decisions were mainly inhabited by ethnic minorities: the first was on disaster prevention, helping poor households prone to natural diseases, storms and floods in Central Vietnam to build houses suitable for these conditions. The second was on identifying admin-

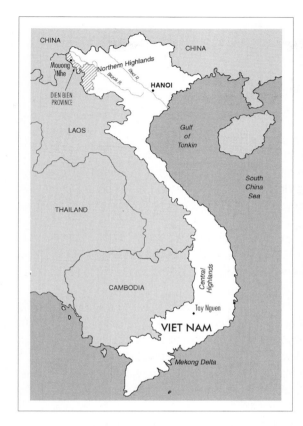

istrative units in areas having difficulty implementing policies on economic and social development and sustainable poverty reduction over the 2014 – 2015 period. The third concerned revised criteria for identifying communes in border areas and other security-sensitive areas for investment prioritization in the 2014 – 2015 period under Program 135, the government's poverty reduction programme targeting poor communes in mountainous areas. The Committee for Ethnic Minority Affairs also completed its report on the feasibility study for the continuation of Program 135 over the 2016 – 2020 period.

Ministry-level agencies issued five documents of importance to ethnic minorities. These were firstly the Guidelines on implementing Program 135 along with the Action Program of the Committee for Ethnic Minority Affairs on international integration, i.e. establishing contacts with similar agencies working on "ethnic minorities" in other countries over the 2014 – 2020 period. A Joint Circular was also issued guiding the implementation of policies on the recruitment of ethnic-minority public servants by agencies of the Vietnam Communist Party, including state agencies as well as the state mass organizations (e.g. Women's Union, Youth Union, Trade Unions, Farmers' Union etc.). A decision was made to approve implementation of the project "Propagandizing and disseminating laws for the ethnic minorities", which seeks to generate an awareness of and knowledge about national laws among ethnic minorities and, finally, a Joint Circular was produced with guiding principles for identifying and recognizing elders and customary leaders within ethnic minority groups.

REDD+ and ethnic minority rights and roles

Three-quarters of the territory of Vietnam is mountainous, covered with forest and inhabited by ethnic minorities. Since 2009, Vietnam has been one of the pilot countries implementing a national REDD+ (Reduced Emissions from Deforestation and Forest Degradation) programme. Vietnam was a pioneer with regard to implementing Free, Prior and Informed Consent (FPIC) in REDD+, with the K'Ho indigenous group in Lam Dong province. After the pilot FPIC process was conducted, draft guidelines were completed in late 2013 and tested in 2014 in Dien Bien, Lam Dong and Quang Binh provinces.

The national REDD+ network has been set up with six sub-technical working groups (Forest Governance, Finance and Benefit Sharing, Measurement, Reporting and Verification, Safeguard Measures, Private Sector Collaboration and Local Implementation). The National REDD+ Action Programme (NRAP) included most of the REDD+ network recommendations on ethnic minority peoples' roles in forest management and development programmes, and on safeguard measures in the implementation of REDD+, among other things. The REDD+ network facilitates the broad participation of all interested stakeholders. However, most of Vietnam's civil society organizations have little if any knowledge of REDD+ processes, and are unable to make a significant contribution. Many are still learning and are looking for collaboration opportunities.

According to the decisions of the United Nations Framework Convention on Climate Change (UNFCCC) at the 16th Conference of the Parties in 2010, social and environmental safeguards (SES) are one of the mandatory requirements for implementing REDD+. The safeguards include several provisions important for indigenous peoples, e.g. on participation and tenure security, among other things. One of the key tasks will be to come up with national information systems that provide information on how safeguards are being ensured. In Vietnam, construction of the safeguards information system is behind schedule due to a lack of human resources. Although the draft roadmap for implementing SES measures as part of the NRAP was introduced at the fifth meeting of the technical sub-group on SES in 2013, thus far the roadmap has not yet been officially approved.

During the preparation period (the so-called "readiness phase") for REDD+ in Vietnam, the following steps have been taken with the aim of complying with the UNFCCC decision on safeguards: Vietnam has made a number of achievements with regard to respecting the knowledge, rights and interests of indigenous people. According to the rural, agriculture and fisheries census of 2011, 1,338,000 households have rights over forestry land, accounting for 27% of all forest-dependent households in the mountainous areas, which are predominantly inhabited by indigenous peoples. The natural forest areas managed by households account for 18% of the total area of natural forest in Vietnam. It is expected that implementing REDD+ will encourage local governments to further strengthen the use and tenure rights of local people, including ethnic minorities, over forest land and forest resources. For example, the Dien Bien provincial government has authorized the communities' right to use natural forests. Quang Binh, Quang Tri and Dak Nong provinces are planning to acquire forest land owned by state enterprises and allocate it to local households and communities.

The FPIC framework currently being established in Vietnam is an important tool with which to meet SES requirements. Benefit-sharing mechanisms have also been designed for Vietnam since 2009 but these are not yet approved. Vietnam is one of the leading countries in implementing Payment for Forest Environmental Services (PFES). Over the last three years, the Forest Protection and Development Trust Fund of Vietnam, which is a trust fund mandated to collect money from people using forest ecosystem services (mainly hydropower and water supply companies) in order to pay forest owners in watershed areas, has received and paid out 3016 billion Vietnamese dong (approximately USD 140 million). PFES has been paid directly to ethnic minority and other forest owners, while in provinces where forests are not allocated to households, PFES is paid to state forest management boards who then pay the ethnic minority people, as forest protection contractors. According to the assessment conducted for the Ministry of Agriculture and Rural Development and presented at a workshop in September 2014, the implementation of PFES has contributed positively to forest protection.

According to the mid-term assessment of the Forest Carbon Partnership Facility (FCPF), despite attempts to promote the participation of ethnic minorities and other forest-dependent people in its REDD+ programme, they have only played a role of passive implementers at the local level and have not participated in decision making at all levels. There have been no representatives of ethnic minorities either on the National REDD+/FCPF Executive Committee or on the Provincial REDD+ Executive Committee in the NRAP. The programmes lack specific plans for building representative mechanisms for ethnic minorities at the decision-making level and strengthening the capacities of local people to ensure the full and effective participation of ethnic minorities in REDD+.

Universal Periodic Review of Vietnam

Vietnam underwent its second periodic review at the United Nations Human Rights Council (UNHRC) in Geneva on 5 February 2014. Vietnam's record came under fire from several countries during the review, and many of the diplomats who attended condemned Hanoi's continued restrictions on freedom of expression.

The UNHRC issued a list of 227 recommendations aimed at improving Vietnam's human rights record, including calls to abolish the death penalty, improve freedom of religion and end harassment of government critics. Vietnam rejected 45 of the recommendations and accepted the remaining 185 at the June 20 meeting of the UN Human Rights Council in Geneva, which concluded the Universal Periodic Review (UPR) process. Among other things, Vietnam rejected recommendations to sign the Optional Protocols to the International Covenant on Civil and Political Rights and other international human rights treaties it has ratified. The Optional Protocols are very important because they enshrine the right of individuals to make complaints against the government for violations of these treaties. Several of the recommendations are important for indigenous peoples in Vietnam, particularly those regarding freedom of expression, freedom of religion and an end to the prosecution of peaceful protesters. In the Central Highlands, in particular, indigenous peoples have in past decades suffered a lack of these rights due to their opposition to the dispossession of their land and resources and suppression of their religious beliefs.   ○

Notes and references

Asian Development Bank web-site. Workshop to Review Viet Nam's Payments for Forest Environmental Services Program.

http://www.gms-eoc.org/events/national-workshop-to-review-viet-nam-s-payments-for-forest-envi-ronment-services

Government of Vietnam, Circular No. 01/2014/TTLT-UBDT-BTC. Joint Circular on guiding the implementation of the policy on prestigious people of EM communities, 2014.

Government of Vietnam, Circular No. 02/2014/TTLT-BNV-UBDT. Joint Circular on guiding the implementation of the policy on EM officers, 11 September 2014.

Government of Vietnam, Circular No. 46/2014/ TT-BNNPTNT. Circular guiding the implementation of supporting production in extremely difficult communes, boundary communes, communes in security areas, and villages, 5 December 2014.

Government of Vietnam, Decision No. 1049/ QD-TTg. Decision on List of administrative units of difficult areas, 26 June 2014.

Government of Vietnam, Decision No. 21/QD-UBDT. Decision approving the implementation of the project "Propagandizing and disseminating laws to ethnic minorities", 2014.

Government of Vietnam, Decision No. 358/QD-UBDT. Decision on Action Program of the Committee on Ethnic Minorities on international integration, 2014 – 2020 period, 2014.

Government of Vietnam, Decision No. 48/ QD-TTg. Decision on the policies supporting poor households to build houses and to prevent storms and floods in the Central Region, 28 August 2014.

Government of Vietnam, Decision No. 495/ QD-TTG. Decision on the list of extremely difficult communes, boundary communes, communes in security areas for Program 135 2014 – 2015 period, 2014

UN-REDD Programme 2003. UN-REDD Viet Nam Phase II Programme: Operationalising REDD+ in Viet Nam. http://www.vietnam-redd.org/Upload/CMS/Content/REDD%20projects/UN-REDD%20 VN%20Phase%202/PD-signed.pdf

UNDP Vietnam website. http://www.vn.undp.org/content/vietnam/en/home/presscenter/articles/2014/02/24/ viet-nam-undergoes-second-universal-periodic-review/

Vietnam Rights Now website. https://www.vietnamrightnow.com/vietnam-rejects-45-human-rights-recommendations-from-upr/

Luong Thi Truong is director of the Vietnamese NGO, the Centre for Sustainable Development in Mountainous Areas (CSDM). She belongs to the Thai ethnic minority in Vietnam. She was selected as the ethnic minority representative to the Program Executive Board of UN-REDD Vietnam in 2014.

LAOS

Despite its support for the UN Declaration on the Rights of Indigenous Peoples (UNDRIP), Laos does not recognize its indigenous population, although there is some informal recognition of indigenous peoples on a regional level. Laos is officially a multi-ethnic state but it only recognizes one nationality – Lao. Officially, the government classifies indigenous peoples as "ethnic groups".[1] Self-identification as indigenous varies among the non-Lao population. There are 49 officially-recognized ethnic groups in Laos (with 160 sub-groups). The ethnic Lao comprise around one-third of the total population of nearly 7 million. Around another third consists of other Tai-Kadia language speakers. As for the remaining people, 30% speak one of the 30+ Mon Khmer languages, 5% speak the Sino-Tibetan language and 10% speak Hmong or Iu-Mien.

Laos' growing economy is a strong cause of social change among indigenous peoples, as is the evolving national legislation focusing on natural resource governance and the commodification of water (hydropower and irrigation), land and forests (agriculture, wood and non-wood forest products and carbon pools). Decision-making power over these resources is controlled mainly by a small, politically-dominant group (ethnic Lao) and an increasing number of indigenous people are being separated from their means of production.[2] Poverty is most common in the mountainous regions, where the majority of the country's indigenous peoples live,[3] with the greatest marginalization and poverty found among indigenous rural women.[4] The poorest groups in the lowlands are often those that have been resettled from the mountain regions. Social isolation and marginalization from mainstream Lao culture occurs due to different languages, customs and religion. Indigenous communities are now gaining better access to education and health services but information that would enable them to improve their living standards, especially as this relates to their rights as Lao citizens, is limited and sometimes blocked.

Laos has ratified the ICERD (1974) and the ICCPR (2009). The Lao government, however, severely restricts fundamental rights, including freedom of speech (media), association, assembly and religion, and civil society is closely controlled. Organizations openly focused on indigenous peoples or using related terms in the Lao language are not allowed and open discussions about indigenous peoples with the government can be sensitive, especially as the issue is seen as pertaining to special (human) rights. In 2014, the Universal Periodic Review of the Lao People's Democratic Republic (Lao PDR or Laos) made no direct reference to indigenous peoples.

National development

The Lao government is deeply influenced by the concept of development, and many of its policies (e.g. National Socio-Economic Development Plans 1 – 7) and goals are framed in the jargon of international bodies (UN Millennium Development Goals, World Bank and Asian Development Bank poverty indicators) and overseas development agencies, and in the context of ASEAN (Association of Southeast Asian Nations) membership. Gross Domestic Product (GDP) is the main indicator of development, and attracting direct foreign investment is crucial to maintaining growth in GDP. In 2014, the Lao economy came under severe stress, with revenue shortages resulting in delays to civil servant salaries, including teachers and health care workers,[5] especially in remote areas with high indigenous populations.

The main drivers of the economy continue to be the construction and operation of hydropower dams along the Mekong River and its tributaries, plus mineral and precious metal mining. These industries make up 60% of exports but have a negative impact on indigenous peoples across the country, involving the loss of land and forests and associated livelihoods,[6] village relocations, air and water pollution, migration, and changes to traditional ways of life. In June 2012, the government issued a three-year moratorium on mining, rubber and eucalyptus concessions, and this remained in effect for 2014.[7] Thousands of indigenous people no longer have access to their traditional agricultural and forest lands and have thus been forced to move into the wage labour economy.[8] However, the employment opportunities claimed by investors have not fully materialized, with many jobs going to foreign workers.[9] It is unclear how food security is being impacted but weak resource tenure rights are likely to be a core factor in decreasing security.[10]

With no tenure security and decreasing land, indigenous peoples are forced to turn to alternative livelihood systems or migration. Opium production is an important source of income for remote indigenous communities in the north of the country. Overall production/yield and the area cultivated increased for the eighth consecutive year in 2014. Donor support (United Nations Office on Drugs and Crime) to suppress the cultivation of opium involves aerial surveying and human resource expertise.[11] There are a wide range of traffickers involved, with many coming from indigenous groups straddling international borders. Arrests of traffickers, local suppression and violence occur.

International human trafficking in Southeast Asia is complex and government statistics are not disaggregated by ethnicity. However, international civil society organizations (CSOs) working on the topic report that indigenous peoples are among those trafficked and are at higher risk due to their lack of familiarity with the lowland areas and language. Those repatriated have been forced into exploitative labour conditions and the sex industry.[12]

Overseas Development Assistance

Government policy goals, some of which have negative impacts on indigenous peoples (the halting of shifting cultivation, village relocations, expansion of commercial agriculture, land concessions etc.), are mixed with donor development agendas and jargon, such as the UN Millennium Development Goals. The main donors in Laos do not promote a human rights-based approach or the specific rights and recognition of indigenous peoples but are instead often aligned with government efforts to stabilize pioneer shifting cultivation and informally bring the uplands under greater state control through market expansion and greater regional economic integration. Specific strategies such as the "Forest Strategy to the Year 2020" and the "Upland Development Strategy to the Year 2020", which are supported by donors, continue to be implemented with the aim of improving forest governance, food security and commercial agriculture. Policy and investment support for the expansion of commercial agriculture continues to increase, connecting remote indigenous communities to a growing network of agricultural buyers, both national and international (mainly China, Vietnam and Thailand).[13] Efforts to increase forest cover, an indicator of MDG 7 "Ensure Environmental Sustainability", has worked against swidden agriculture systems and includes industrial tree plantations.

Research published in 2014 revealed a strong bias towards hiring non-indigenous peoples in international aid agencies. The findings show that "a disproportionate number of aid agency staff (80%) come from the dominant Lao-Tai linguistic family even though they make up less than 65% of the Lao population" and that "none of the 23 aid agencies interviewed during the survey has hiring or employment policies for indigenous people".[14] Without affirmative action, such figures will not balance themselves out, so a much greater commitment is needed from aid agencies.

Natural resource legislation

In 2014, CSOs continued to lobby international donors and government on the content of the first National Land Policy. This policy was drafted with input from international civil society organizations, including key recommendations such as the right to refuse (via a vote) economic land concessions in village territories (i.e. withhold consent), formal recognition of customary land and forest tenure rights, and formal titling of communal land and forests. The recommendations are of particular importance given that the vast majority of land occupied by indigenous peoples is under communal ownership and is untitled. The December 2014 session of the National Assembly did not include the National Land Policy and it is not certain when it will be debated in 2015. Pressure is building, however, as revisions of both the Land and Forestry Laws require this policy to have been approved for guidance.

Laos formally began engagement in the European Union's Forest Law Enforcement Governance and Trade (FLEGT) process in 2014, with the support of the German government.[15] If completed, this trade agreement will give Laos' timber products preferential treatment on the EU market. A unique aspect of FLEGT is the EU-required multi-stakeholder process, which creates opportunities for local CSOs (including those with indigenous affiliations) to participate. The creation of the "Timber Legality Definition" has also begun and will offer a space in which to consider how indigenous peoples use forests and the possibility of expanding the formal rights of forest-dependent communities. The outcomes of the FLEGT-related work are expected to influence the content of the Forestry Law.

Payment for Environmental Services (PES), including REDD+, expanded in 2014 with the World Bank (Forest Investment Program) and Finnish government-funded "Scaling-Up Participatory Sustainable Forest Management Project". The third phase of the project has expanded to Xaiyaboury, Luang Namtha, Oudomxay and Bokeo provinces and is attempting to implement free, prior and informed consent (FPIC). Over 300, mainly indigenous, communities have been asked to take a decision on whether to participate in the project. All except one has given their consent.[16] With no legal basis in national legislation, the legitimacy of the

FPIC process remains in question, however.[17] Previous attempts at FPIC were facilitated by a local non-profit association from 2011 to 2012 under a GIZ (German development cooperation) bilateral REDD+ project but were never completed (see *The Indigenous World 2013*). In 2014, the GIZ FPIC process was taken over by the Lao Front for National Construction which, as an arm of the party, decreases the legitimacy of the process.

Indigenous resistance

Non-transparent and top-down land acquisitions facilitated by the government have increased the intensity of social conflicts, many of which go unaddressed as there are no judicial recourse options independent of party involvement and interference. Dam construction in southern Laos is, for example, having a devastating impact on indigenous communities and involves militarily-enforced village relocations to make way for the rubber plantations that hold shares in the dams.[18] Previous high-profile cases (Xekong Province) dating back several years (see *The Indigenous World 2013*) also continue to go unresolved, with national and provincial authorities unable to arrive at suitable conclusions. New channels for conflict resolution are, however, being piloted: the Vietnamese state-owned Rubber Group (VRG) has announced that it will establish a complaints mechanism and test a community consultations and compensation scheme for its plantations in Savanakhet and Champasak provinces,[19] in response to international media attention created by the human rights advocacy organization, Global Witness.[20] In Attapeu and Xekong provinces, conflicts between the Vietnamese Hoang Anh Gia Lai Group and indigenous communities over land lost to rubber plantations are being prepared for submission to the IFC complaints mechanism, as the company has received financial support from the World Bank's International Finance Corporation. However, outsider access to the affected indigenous communities is monitored by the government and it remains difficult to acquire information. Meanwhile, communities continue to show resistance (cutting down and destroying tree plantations, active local petitioning, unwillingness to cooperate with companies and the government).

Relevance of the Outcome Document of the World Conference on Indigenous Peoples

The September 2014 World Conference on Indigenous Peoples reiterated the content of the UNDRIP and produced an action-oriented Outcome Document to ensure its greater implementation. Although Laos supported the UNDRIP, using the Outcome Document would be very challenging and likely be ineffective in the country. No CSO, local or national, grounds its work in a human rights-based approach or openly advocates for the rights of indigenous peoples. Doing so would be counter to the party doctrine of unity among ethnic groups and would not be well received by the government. Attempting to engage the government in the Outcome Document would best be done by the UN Country Office or international government donors (Swiss Development Agency, German Development Cooperation, French Development Cooperation, etc.). ○

Notes and references

1   The term "ethnic minority" was officially used in the past but this was halted as the government believed it created a minority identity that did not align with the state's efforts to create a national identity. It could also be interpreted that, being minorities, these groups qualified for specific attention (i.e. rights), something which the state does not support.

2   **Molina R., 2011:** *CAMPS, CHILDREN, CHEMICALS, CONTRACTORS & CREDIT: Field Observations of Labour Practices in Plantations & other Social Developments in Savannakhet and Champasak.* Unpublished report.

3   **Epprecht M., Minot N., Dewina R., Messerli P., Heinimann A., 2008:** *The Geography of Poverty and Inequality in the Lao PDR.* Swiss National Center of Competence in Research (NCCR) North-South, University of Bern, and International Food Policy Research Institute (IFPRI), Bern: Geographica Bernensia. P. 38.

4   **Elizabeth M. King and Dominique van de Walle, 2010:** Catching up slowly: ethnic and gender inequalities in Lao PDR. *Indigenous People. Lao PDR Country Brief Number 2.*

5   Laos freezes salary increase for civil servants. www.TheEpochTimes.com/World, 14 August 2014.

6   Miners digging up controversy in northern provinces. *Vientiane Times,* 2 Jan 2015.

7   Govt to consider suspending large mining, land concessions. *Vientiane Times,* 8 May 2012.

8   Human Rights Council Working Group on the Universal Periodic Review Twenty first session 19–30 January 2015. *Summary prepared by the Office of the United Nations High Commissioner for Human Rights in accordance with paragraph 15 (c) of the annex to Human Rights Council resolution 5/1 and paragraph 5 of the annex to Council resolution 16/21.*

9   Rapid growth fails to generate jobs in Attapeu. *Vientiane Times*, 29 Jan 2014.

10   Miles Kenney-Lazar. 2014. *Dynamics of the Land Tenure and Food Security Nexus in Laos.* University of Clarke. National Research for Development Forum on Pathways for Sustainable Development in Laos 17-18 December 2014.

11   UNODC Regional Office for Southeast Asia and the Pacific. *Southeast Asia Opium Survey 2014. Lao and Myanmar.*

12   The International Fund for Agriculture Development and the Asian Indigenous Peoples Pact report that: "Teenagers and young Lao from ethnic minority groups, aged between 14 and 24, constitute the majority of illegal migrants; most of those migrants are women and girls. Of great concern are the estimated 30,000 children under 15 years of age who are currently working in Thailand." Country Technical Notes on Indigenous Peoples' Issues: Lao People's Democratic Republic. IFAD and AIPP, November 2012.

13   Switzerland supports upland smallholder farmers. *Vientiane Times*, 18 December 2014.

14   **Daviau, Steeve, 2014:** *Work Place Diversity in Aid Agencies in Laos – Indigenous Peoples Representation.* JVC, IWGIA, Oxfam Novib and McKnight Foundation.

15   EU and Laos prepare for timber agreement negotiations. *Vientiane Times,* 27 February 2014.

16   Anonymous personal communications, Vientiane, January 2015.

17   Portions of the process can be viewed on YouTube: https://www.youtube.com/watch?v=sXV-hr-NAGrI.

18   http://www.internationalrivers.org/blogs/294-1

19   Vietnam rubber giant to address issues raised by displaced communities. *Vientiane Times,* 28 August 2014.

20   http://www.globalwitness.org/library/vietnam-rubber-group-says-its-doors-are-now-open-people-affected-plantations-cambodia-and

Due to the sensitivity of some of the issues covered in this article, the author prefers to remain anonymous.

BURMA

Burma's diversity encompasses over 100 different ethnic groups. The Burmans make up an estimated 68 percent of Burma's 51 million people. The country is divided into seven mainly Burman-dominated divisions and seven ethnic states. The Burmese government refers to those groups generally considered indigenous peoples as "ethnic nationalities". This includes the Shan, Karen, Rakhine, Karenni, Chin, Kachin and Mon. However, there are many more ethnic groups that are considered or see themselves as indigenous peoples, such as the Akha, Lisu, Lahu, Mru and many others.

Burma has been ruled by a succession of Burman-dominated military regimes since the popularly-elected government was toppled in 1962. The current president Thein Sein (installed in 2011) and his nominally civilian administration have taken positive steps towards reform, releasing hundreds of political prisoners, easing certain media restrictions, taking steps to liberalize the economy and engaging in ceasefire talks with ethnic armed groups. However, many critical issues remain unaddressed, such as ongoing serious human rights violations in ethnic nationality areas, military offensives in Kachin and Northern Shan States, and a lack of significant legislative and institutional reforms.

Burma voted in favour of the UN Declaration on the Rights of Indigenous Peoples, adopted by the UN General Assembly in 2007, but has not ratified ILO Convention 169.

Conflict in Kachin and Northern Shan States hinders ceasefire prospects

Armed conflict between the *Tatmadaw* (Burma's Army) and the Kachin Independence Army (KIA), which began in June 2011, continued in Kachin and Northern Shan States throughout 2014. Clashes also continued with other ethnic

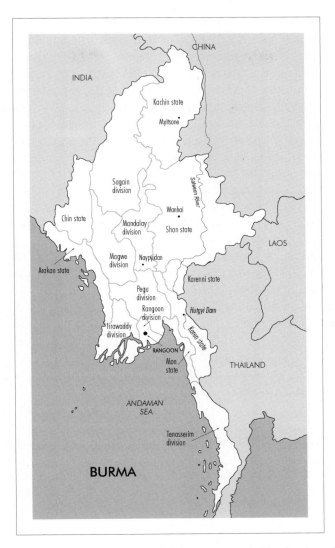

armed groups. Throughout the year, fighting was reported in nine townships in Kachin State and 18 townships in Shan State. *Tatmadaw* troops also attacked the Karen National Liberation Army (KNLA) twice in 2014, in violation of a 2012 ceasefire agreement.

In 2014, the government formally met five times with the Nationwide Cease-fire Coordination Team (NCCT), a coalition of 16 ethnic armed groups,[1] to negotiate the signing of a nationwide ceasefire agreement. However, ceasefire negotiations moved slowly due to renewed *Tatmadaw* offensives during the year and the government's continued refusal to address the key demands of ethnic armed groups – chiefly the demand to establish a genuine federal union for all of Burma and hold political dialogue before the signing of an agreement. The lack of coordination between the government and the *Tatmadaw* further undermined the government's commitment to ceasefire negotiations. In May, the government told ethnic armed groups that federalism would be considered and that the *Tatmadaw's* demands, namely to abide by the 2008 Constitution, would not be a prerequisite for the ceasefire agreement. However, in August, *Tatmadaw* Commander-in-Chief Sr Gen Min Aung Hlaing repeated the *Tatmadaw's* demands to ethnic leaders as a precondition for the ceasefire agreement.

In November, the *Tatmadaw* attacked a KIA military academy near the Kachin Independence Organization (KIO)'s headquarters in Laiza, Momauk Township, Kachin State. Twenty-three cadets from various ethnic armed groups undergoing training there were killed and 20 were injured in the attack. The United Nationalities Federal Council (UNFC), a coalition of ethnic armed groups,[2] (see *The Indigenous World 2014*) said the attack posed a "serious obstacle" to the peace process, while the KIO said it was "deliberate" and proved that the peace process was "dead". The government claimed the attack was "not intentional", describing the incident as an "accident".

IDPs and civilians face aid shortages and human rights abuses

As a result of the ongoing conflict, the total number of Internally Displaced Persons (IDPs), which was estimated at 91,000[3] for Kachin State at the beginning of the year, had reached 98,000 for Kachin and Northern Shan States by December.[4]

On 26 July, UN Special Rapporteur on human rights in Burma, Yanghee Lee, said access to KIA-controlled areas remained limited for aid agencies.[5] Between October and December, the government blocked the delivery of humanitarian assistance to some 27,500 IDPs living in KIA-controlled areas.[6]

In contravention of the UN General Assembly's resolution on the World Conference on Indigenous Peoples, *Tatmadaw* soldiers also continued to commit serious human rights violations against ethnic nationalities, including attacks on civilians, arbitrary detention, torture, sexual violence against women and girls, and forced labour. In January, the Women's League of Burma (WLB) released a report entitled *"Same Impunity, Same Patterns"*, which documents the *Tatmadaw's* use of rape and sexual violence as a weapon of war. The report detailed more than 100 cases of sexual violence perpetrated by *Tatmadaw* soldiers against women, almost solely in ethnic nationalities' areas.[7]

In June, the Bangkok-based organization Fortify Rights released the report: *"I Thought They Would Kill Me. Ending Wartime Torture in Northern Myanmar,"* exposing the *Tatmadaw's* systematic use of torture against ethnic minorities in Kachin and Northern Shan States since the resumption of the conflict in 2011.[8]

Sectarian violence against Muslim Rohingya

In Arakan State, the situation of Muslim Rohingya has remained dire since sectarian violence erupted in June 2012 (see *The Indigenous World 2013*). Sectarian violence between Buddhist Rakhine and the Muslim Rohingya minority flared up again when police and Buddhist Rakhine in Du Chee Yar Tan Village, Maungdaw Township, attacked and killed at least 48 Muslim Rohingya in the first half of January.[9]

Investigations into the incident by government-appointed commissions failed to hold anyone accountable for the violence, instead suggesting that Arakan State police be issued with better quality weapons. In February, then-UN Special Rapporteur on human rights in Burma, Tomás Ojea Quintana, said that the investigations had "failed to satisfactorily address" the allegations of violence.[10] Ojea Quintana later reiterated the fact that the widespread and systematic human rights violations in Arakan State could amount to crimes against humanity.[11]

In March and December respectively, the Human Rights Council and the General Assembly adopted resolutions expressing serious concerns over "the situation of the Rohingya" in Arakan State and calling on the government to give them "equal access" to citizenship.[12]

Unresolved tensions kept the number of IDPs in Arakan State at a constant level in 2014, while living conditions and access to healthcare steadily worsened due in part to the expulsion of several aid agencies.[13] In December, an estimated 139,000 Rohingya remained displaced in Arakan State. UN officials visiting Arakan State in June and July expressed grave concern at the conditions in Rohingya IDP camps, terming the situation "appalling" and "deplorable".[14] In 2014, around 53,000 people, including many Rohingya, attempted to seek safety abroad, leaving Burma and Bangladesh on boats bound for Malaysia and Thailand.[15]

Throughout the year, the government continued to enforce its anti-Rohingya agenda, including requiring Rohingya to seek permission to marry or travel (Regional Order 1/2009) and restricting Rohingya to two children (Regional Order 1/2005). In September, reports of the government's draft plan – the "Rakhine State Action Plan" – emerged. The plan intends to permanently segregate Buddhist Rakhine and Muslim Rohingya communities and to deport or intern Rohingya who cannot prove their right to citizenship.

Burma's census excludes members of ethnic nationalities

Burma conducted its first census in more than three decades from 30 March to 10 April last year. However, the census excluded 1.2 million people from Arakan, Kachin and Karen States, including an estimated 1.09 million Rohingya.

Despite the government's assurances to the contrary, on 29 March, President Thein Sein's spokesman Ye Htut announced that Rohingya would not be allowed to self-identify in the census. Rohingya who tried to self-identify were thus subjected to intimidation by security forces and were only allowed to participate if they agreed to identify as "Bengali", implying that they were illegal immigrants from Bangladesh. In April, then-UN Special Rapporteur on human rights in Burma, Tomás Ojea Quintana, said that the government's decision not to allow Rohingya to self-identify meant the census was not in line with international standards.[16]

In addition, the *Tatmadaw* heavily increased its militarization in March and April under the guise of preparing for the census. After the KIO rejected the government's request to collect census data in KIA-controlled areas, *Tatmadaw* troops threatened to take the census by force. *Tatmadaw* soldiers and police accompanied census enumerators to parts of Kachin and Shan States to collect data.

Legislative reforms fail to make progress for ethnic nationalities

Burma's Parliament convened in Naypyidaw for three sessions in 2014 but failed to enact legislation addressing important issues for ethnic nationalities. Despite the People's Assembly's 22 July vote to approve a draft Minority Rights Bill aimed at protecting minority rights and creating an Ethnic Affairs Ministry, no further progress was made on the bill. In a positive development, at least two state parliaments (Mon and Karenni) voted in favour of allowing ethnic languages to be taught in local schools. However, the initiative has yet to be implemented.

The Parliament failed to repeal or amend oppressive laws, such as the Unlawful Association Act, which had frequently been used by the authorities to detain citizens, activists and politicians in ethnic nationalities' areas. On 22 September, the National Parliament approved a law amending the Political Parties Registration Law, removing the right of temporary ID holders – which include many Rohingya – to form political parties.

In 2014, the debate on constitutional amendments continued to no avail. In January, the 109-member committee to review the 2008 Constitution (see *The Indigenous World 2014*) failed to propose any real changes to contested articles, including Article 338, which requires all armed forces to come under the command of the Defence Services.[17] In February, Burma's Parliament approved the formation of a 31-member committee to implement the findings of the review committee. However, the committee included only a handful of MPs from ethnic nationality parties.[18]

In December, the President's Office submitted a set of four draft bills, referred to as the "National Race and Religion Package", to Parliament. The bills restrict marriage, reproductive and religious conversion rights, imposing fines and prison sentences on violators, and will affect religious minorities, many of whom are from ethnic nationalities' states.   ○

Notes and references

1   The 16 groups are: Arakan Liberation Party (ALP); Arakan National Council (ANC); Arakan Army (AA); Chin National Front (CNF); Democratic Karen Benevolent Army (DKBA); Kachin Independence Organization (KIO); Karen National Union (KNU); KNU/KNLA Peace Council; Karenni National Progressive Party (KNPP); Lahu Democratic Union (LDU); Myanmar National Democratic

Alliance Army (NDAA); New Mon State Party (NMSP); Palaung State Liberation Front (PSLF); PaO National Liberation Organization (PNLO); Shan State Progress Party (SSPP); and Wa National Organization (WNO).

2   The 11 groups are: Chin National Front (CNF); Kachin Independence Organization (KIO); Karen National Union (KNU); Karenni National Progressive Party (KNPP); Lahu Democratic Union (LDU); National Unity Party of Arakan (NUPA); New Mon State Party (NMSP); Palaung State Liberation Front (PSLF); PaO National Liberation Organization (PNLO); Shan State Army - North (SSA-N); and Wa National Organization (WNO).

3   OCHA, *Myanmar: Humanitarian Bulletin, Issue 1*, 1-31 January 2014.

4   OCHA, *Myanmar: Humanitarian Bulletin, Issue 12*, 1-31 December 2014.

5   UNIC Yangon, *Statement of the Special Rapporteur on the Situation of Human Rights in Myanmar*, 26 July 2014.

6   OCHA, *Myanmar: Humanitarian Bulletin, Issue 11*, 1-30 November 2014.

7   Women's League of Burma (WLB), 2014, *Same Impunity, Same Patterns*, 14 January 2014.

8   Fortify Rights, 2014, *I Thought They Would Kill Me, Ending Wartime Torture in Northern Myanmar*, 9 June 2014.
     http://www.fortifyrights.org/downloads/Fortify%20Rights_Myanmar_9_June_2014.pdf

9   UN News Centre, *Top UN officials calls for probe into latest violence in Myanmar's Rakhine state*, 23 January 2014.

10   UNIC Yangon, *Statement of the Special Rapporteur on the Situation of Human Rights in Myanmar*, 19 February 2014.

11   UN Human Rights Council 2014; 25th session, 12 March 2014. Report of the Special Rapporteur on the situation of human rights in Myanmar, Tomás Ojea Quintana. UN Doc. A/HRC/25/64. OHCHR, *Myanmar: UN expert raises alarm on Rakhine State*, 7 April 2014.

12   UN Human Rights Council 2014: 25th session, 26 March 2014. Situation of human rights in Myanmar. UN Doc. A/HRC/25/L.21; UNGA 2014: 69th session, 29 December 2014. Situation of human rights in Myanmar. UN Doc. A/RES/69/248.

13   OCHA, *Myanmar: Humanitarian Bulletin, Issue 5*, 1-31 May 2014. CNN: *Caught between a hammer and an anvil: Myanmar's Rohingya "internment camps"*, 29 October 2014.

14   OCHA, *Assistant Secretary-General and Deputy Emergency Relief Coordinator, Kyung-Wha Kang Press Remarks on Myanmar*, 17 June 2014. UNIC Yangon, *Statement of the Special Rapporteur on the Situation of Human Rights in Myanmar*, 26 July 2014.

15   UNHCR, *Irregular Maritime Movements 2014*, 5 December 2014.

16   OHCHR, *Myanmar: UN expert raises alarm on Rakhine State*, 7 April 2014.

17   Irrawaddy, *Burma Parliament Committee: Keep Main Points of Constitution*, 31 January 2014.

18   Myanmar Times, *NLD leader backs new constitution review body*, 9 February 2014.

Diane Lewis *is currently a Research Officer at the Bangkok-based ALTSEAN-Burma.*

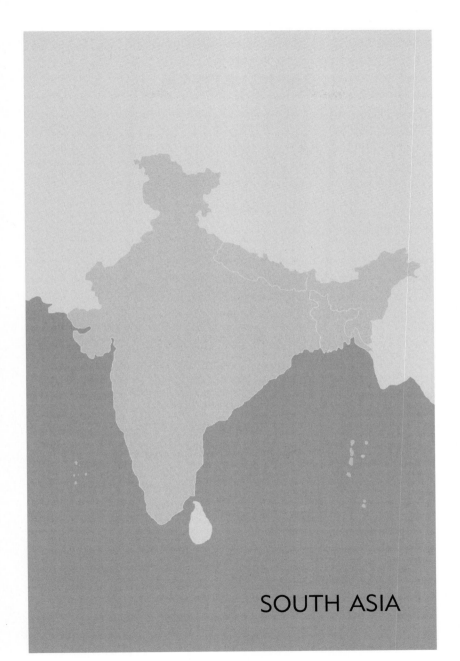

SOUTH ASIA

BANGLADESH

The majority of Bangladesh's 142.3 million[1] people are Bengalis but ap-proximately 3 million are indigenous peoples.[2] They belong to at least 54 different ethnic groups. These peoples are concentrated in the north-west (Rajshahi-Dinajpur), central north (Mymensingh-Tangail), north-east (Syl-het), south and south-east (Chittagong, Cox's Bazar and Greater Barisal), and in the Chittagong Hill Tracts (CHT) in the south-east of the country. In the CHT, the indigenous peoples are commonly known as Jummas for their practice of swidden cultivation (crop rotation agriculture), locally known as jum.

The Government of Bangladesh does not recognize indigenous peoples as "indigenous". A 2011 amendment to the constitution refers to them as "tribes", "minor races" and "ethnic sects and communities". Other legislation uses the term "*adibashi*", the Bengali equivalent of indigenous or aboriginal.[3] Bangladesh has ratified ILO Convention 107 on Indige-nous and Tribal Populations but not ILO Convention 169, and it abstained from voting when the UN Declaration on the Rights of Indigenous Peoples (UNDRIP) was adopted in the General Assembly in 2007.

Indigenous peoples remain among the most persecuted of all minori-ties, facing discrimination not only on the basis of their religion and ethnic-ity but also because of their indigenous identity and their socio-economic status. In the CHT, the indigenous peoples took up arms in defense of their rights in 1976. The civil war ended in 1997 with a CHT "Peace" Ac-cord,[4] recognizing the CHT as a "tribal inhabited" region. The traditional governance system and the role of its chiefs is specifically recognized, and the Accord provides building blocks for indigenous self-determina-tion. It remains, however, largely unimplemented, which has resulted in continued widespread human rights violations, violent conflicts and mili-tary control.

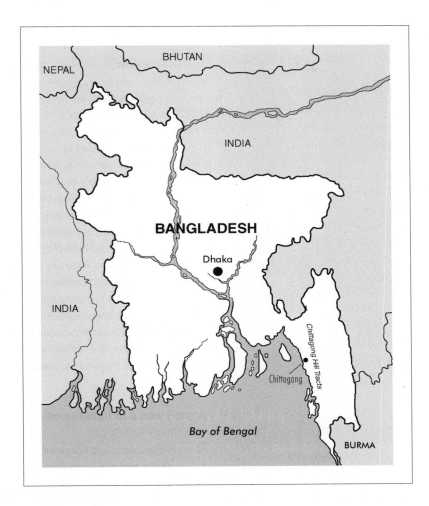

Law and policy development

On 1 July 2014, the CHT Development Board Act 2014 was passed by Parliament, turning the Board into a statutory body. The Act was passed despite opposition from the CHT Regional Council, which argued that turning the Board into a statutory body would create complexity in administration and development, as the main institutions that constitute the special administrative system in the

CHT, according to the CHT Accord, are the three Hill District Councils (HDC) at district level, and the CHT Regional Council at region level.[5]

On 23 November 2014, Parliament passed three Hill District Council amendment acts despite strong opposition from the indigenous community. The Ministry of Chittagong Hill Tracts Affairs tabled the Rangamati Hill District Council (Amendment) Bill 2014, the Khagrachari Hill District Council (Amendment) Bill 2014, and the Bandarban Hill District Council (Amendment) Bill 2014 on 1 July. As a result of this new legislation, the number of interim members of the Hill District Councils[6] will be increased to 11 from the existing five, including three non-indigenous members. By increasing the number of members without an election, the government has violated the CHT Accord, which stipulates the preparation of a voter list comprising only the permanent residents of the three hill districts, and obliges the government to consult the CHT Regional Council before enacting or amending any law which has an adverse effect on the development of the three hill districts, and the welfare of the tribal people.[7]

In September, during its 3rd regular parliamentary session, the government passed the 16th amendment to Bangladesh's Constitution, mandating Parliament to investigate and sack top judges on the grounds of incapability and misconduct.[8] Despite strong demands from indigenous peoples to be recognized as *Adivasi* / indigenous peoples in the Constitution during the last constitutional amendment in 2011 (see *The Indigenous World 2012*), this issue was not considered in the 16th amendment.

Status of Chittagong Hill Tracts Accord implementation

Only minor initiatives were taken in 2014 to implement the provisions of the CHT Accord that still remain either partly or fully unimplemented. The government transferred five subjects to the HDCs: shifting cultivation, secondary education, birth and death and other statistics, money lending businesses and tourism (local).[9] Some of the most important subjects are, however, yet to be transferred, including supervision, preservation and development of law and order in the district, land and land management and local police.

In the October 2013 parliamentary session, the government came close to passing the Amendment Bill of the CHT Land Dispute Resolution Commission Act 2001 but failed to do so in the end (see *The Indigenous World 2014*). Given the government's repeated expressions of commitment to amending the act, it was expected that the bill would be placed in any of Parliament's sessions in 2014. This did not happen, however, despite the governing party's absolute majority in Parliament.

Throughout 2014, the non-implementation of the CHT Accord continued to cause severe violations of indigenous peoples' human rights. For instance, the Border Guard Bangladesh (BGB) has taken an initiative to acquire around 32 acres of the recorded lands of the indigenous people of three villages in Dighinala upazila of Khagrachari Hill District to establish its battalion headquarters. The land acquisition has resulted in the eviction of at least 21 indigenous Jumma families. A primary school with 200 students and a Buddhist temple also face uncertainty. On 10 June, a clash between the indigenous people and BGB personnel over the establishment of the battalion headquarters resulted in at least 18 villagers, including several women, receiving injuries.[10]

Bangladesh becomes a member of the Human Rights Council

In October, Bangladesh was elected as one of the members of the Human Rights Council for the 2015 to 2017 period. In connection with the candidature, the Government of Bangladesh made a number of voluntary pledges, including to "intensify its efforts, while framing its national policies and strategies, to uphold the fundamental principles enshrined in the Constitution, the Universal Declaration of Human Rights, and international and regional human rights instruments to which it is a party" and to "continue to promote and protect the rights of the religious and ethnic minorities and work towards maintaining the traditional communal harmony by upholding the secular, pluralist and inclusive values of the State and the society in general".[11]

Land rights and displacement

Dispossession of indigenous peoples' land by influential land grabbers who receive support from the local administration intensified significantly in 2014. According to a report from the Kapaeeng Foundation, around 3,911 acres of land in the CHT were grabbed by state and non-state actors in 2014 alone, while 84,647 acres of land in the CHT were in the process of being occupied and acquired. The Forest Department intensified its steps to acquire more than 84,542 acres of land, declared as reserved and protected forest, while the BGB violated the customary land rights of indigenous peoples as well as provisions of the Hill District Councils Act of 1998 in its land acquisitions.[12]

Further, over the course of the year, around 102 indigenous families (2 from plain lands, 100 from the CHT) were evicted from their ancestral homesteads, 886 indigenous families (300 in plain lands and 586 in the CHT) were under threat of eviction, and 153 indigenous families (89 from plains and 64 from CHT) were attacked with the aim of grabbing their land. Furthermore, 10 indigenous persons were arrested by the police and 150 indigenous persons (106 in the CHT and 44 in plain lands) were accused in false and fabricated cases. As in previous years, indigenous women were subjected to violence in many land-related incidents across the country in 2014.[13]

This situation is exacerbated by the lack of government initiatives to prevent land dispossession by Bengali settlers and influential land grabbers under the direct patronage of local administrations. An increasing influx of other actors, such as private corporations, criminal syndicates and politically powerful individuals, has also worsened the problem.

Violence against indigenous women

As a result of the almost complete impunity that perpetrators of violence against indigenous women enjoy, the number of victims of violence increased from 67 in 2013 to 122 in 2014. For example, Bichitra Tirki, 36, an indigenous female leader of the *Jatiya Adivasi Parishad* (JAP), an elected member of the *Union Parishad* (local government body), and a prominent indigenous woman activist from Jinarpur village in Chapainawabgonj district, was tortured and sexually abused by a group of 30-35 people on 4 August 2014. The attack was linked to a land dispute. Bichitra filed a case with Gomstapur Police Station and, of the 18 accused, the police arrested ten. However, the person believed to be the mastermind behind the attack, and some of the main perpetrators, still have not been charged. Despite protests and demands from civil society, the District and Sessions Judge's Court granted bail to the perpetrators on 24 September.[14]

In September 2014, the Bangladesh Indigenous Women's Network (BIWN) organized the Second National Indigenous Women's Conference, at which the situation of violence against indigenous women and its causes were discussed and analyzed. The participants, among other things, highlighted how indigenous women are affected by land grabbing and the many obstacles to accessing justice, including falsification of medical reports in rape cases, inefficiency and discrimination in the legal system, and deficient legal aid. The conference concluded with the Dhaka Declaration, which included recommendations on exemplary punishment for the perpetrators of violence against indigenous women and children, and the need to ensure the participation of indigenous women in decision-making processes, among other things.[15]

Applying the Outcome Document from the World Conference on Indigenous Peoples (WCIP)

The Outcome Document from the World Conference on Indigenous Peoples 2014 is considered by indigenous organizations and activists as significant in terms of promoting indigenous peoples' rights at the national level, by providing a guide for the promotional activities of the UNDRIP. The provision relating to FPIC and legislative and administrative measures could, for example, be used to push for the direct participation of indigenous peoples in the drafting and implementation of legislation and administrative measures in Bangladesh. While laws and policies are drafted, indigenous peoples are very rarely consulted or approached. The right to be consulted is enshrined in the CHT Accord but rarely applied, as described above. Indigenous leaders and activists are currently planning a series of discussions on how to apply the Outcome Document and implement it at the national level, which is expected to result in a concrete action plan.   O

Notes and references

1   **Bangladesh Bureau of Statistics, 2011:** *Population & housing census 2011,* Government of the People's Republic of Bangladesh, Dhaka, p. 3.
2   **Kamal M (ed.), 2014:** *Parliamentary caucus on indigenous peoples: a genesis of parliamentary advocacy in Bangladesh,* Research and Development Collective, Dhaka.

3 The Small Ethnic Groups Cultural Institution Act 2010 uses the term "*khudro nrigoshthhi*" (small ethnic groups) to refer to the indigenous peoples but defines these as "adibashi", the Bengali equivalent of indigenous or aboriginal.

4 The Peace Accord was signed by the Government of Bangladesh, and the *Parbattya Chattagram Jana Samhati Samiti* (PCJSS, United People's Party of CHT), which led the resistance movement.

5 Press statement by Parbatya Chattagram Jana Samhati Samiti (PCJSS) entitled "Implementation of CHT Accord on the Occasion of the 17th Anniversary of CHT Accord" 29 November 2014

6 No election has been held to the HDCs for 21 years. The members are selected by the ruling parties and therefore not accountable to the people in the CHT. (See also http://unpo.org/article/16995).

7 Statement by the Chittagong Hill Tracts Commission, 2 December 2014 (http://chtcommission.org/).

8 http://bdnews24.com/bangladesh/2014/09/17/16th-amendment-passed-to-restore-parliaments-power-to-sack-judges

9 Press statement by Parbatya Chattagram Jana Samhati Samiti (PCJSS) entitled "Implementation of CHT Accord on the Occasion of the 17th Anniversary of CHT Accord" 29 November 2014

10 http://www.dhakatribune.com/bangladesh/2014/jul/01/indigenous-families-and-government-dispute-over-land-ownership-khagrachhari

11 A/69/393, para 7.

12 Kapaeeng Foundation 2015, Human rights report 2014 on indigenous peoples of Bangladesh, Kapaeeng Foundation, Dhaka.

13 Kapaeeng Foundation 2015, Human rights report 2014 on indigenous peoples of Bangladesh, Kapaeeng Foundation, Dhaka.

14 http://kapaeeng.org/an-indigenous-women-activist-raped-and-three-indigenous-persons-including-a-woman-killed-in-a-week-in-bangladesh/; http://kapaeeng.org/update-on-attack-upon-bichitra-tirki-in-chapainawabganj-18-alleged-attackers-granted-bail/

15 http://kapaeeng.org/2nd-national-indigenous-women-conference-held-in-dhaka-indigenous-women-declared-dhaka-declaration-for-united-movement/

Binota Moy Dhamai is a Jumma belonging to the Tripura people of the Chittagong Hill Tracts, and an activist in the movement for the rights and recognition of indigenous peoples in Bangladesh. He is an active member of the Bangladesh Indigenous Peoples Forum, Bangladesh and Executive Council Member of the Asia Indigenous Peoples Pact (AIPP) (bdtripura@gmail.com).

Pallab Chakma belongs to the Chakma people of the Chittagong Hill Tracts (CHT) of Bangladesh. He is an active indigenous peoples' rights activist and currently the Executive Director of Kapaeeng Foundation, a human rights organization of indigenous peoples of Bangladesh (pallab.rangei@gmail.com).

NEPAL

According to the 2011 census, the indigenous nationalities (*Adivasi Jana-jati*) of Nepal comprise 36% of the total population of 26.5 million, although indigenous peoples' organizations claim a larger figure of more than 50%. The 2011 census listed the population as belonging to 125 caste and ethnic groups, including 63 indigenous peoples, 59 castes (including 15 Dalit castes[1]) and 3 religious groups (Muslim, Sikh and Bangali). The Government of Nepal has, however, since 2002 recognized only 59 indigenous peoples.

Even though indigenous peoples constitute a significant proportion of the population, throughout the history of Nepal indigenous peoples have been marginalized by the dominant groups in terms of land, territories, resources, language, culture, customary laws, and political and economic opportunities.

The 2007 Interim Constitution of Nepal promotes cultural diversity and talks about enhancing the skills, knowledge and rights of indigenous peoples.[2] Nepal's indigenous peoples are waiting to see how these intentions will be made concrete in the new constitution, which is still in the process of being promulgated. Nepal has ratified ILO Convention 169 on Indigenous and Tribal Peoples and voted in favour of the UN Declaration on the Rights of Indigenous Peoples (UNDRIP). The implementation of ILO Convention 169 and UNDRIP is still wanting, however, and it is yet to be seen how the new constitution will bring national laws into line with the provisions of either of them.

Constituent Assembly polarized on "Process" versus "Agreement"

Throughout 2014, the 601 members of the second Constituent Assembly (CA) were polarized into ruling and opposition camps, arguing about whether to opt for a "process path", or an "agreement path". The former prioritizes the adoption of a new constitution by the given deadline of 22 January 2015, solving the remaining disputes via a vote (majority rule), while the latter seeks broader political agreements, arguing that this approach is a prerequisite for upholding the commitment to the ongoing peace process and the spirit of the interim constitution. The ruling camp was led by the ruling parties, led jointly by the Nepali Congress and the Communist Party of Nepal (CPN)-Unified Marxist-Leninist (UML), and supported by other political parties who together muster a 2/3 majority of the 601 CA members. The opposition camp comprises 19 political parties led by the Unified Communist Party of Nepal (UCPN) Maoist, supported by the Madhesi and indigenous political parties. They oppose the "process" of deciding disputed issues via a vote in the CA. The main reason is that, in the first CA, the Maoist and the Madhesi political parties had a two-thirds majority but did not pursue the "process path" (majority rule via a vote), instead opting for a consensus-seeking "agreement path". In the second CA, the Nepali Congress and CPN-UML want to go through the "process" (voting), as they believe that they have a comfortable majority to pass the constitution in the way they want.

The main task for the current CA was to try to resolve, through formal and informal processes, the remaining disputed issues, including federalism, a restructuring of the state, electoral system and judiciary. This work rested with the Political Dialogue and Agreement Committee of the CA. Despite claiming that 90 percent of the outcome of the first CA's work was owned by the second CA, the ruling parties very strongly opposed both the 14 identity-based provinces recommended by the first CA (see *The Indigenous World 2011*), and the 10 identity-based provinces recommended in 2012 by the State Restructuring Commission formed by the first CA. Instead, they proposed 5 to 7 provinces by carving out provinces based on geographical criteria, without separating the Terai lowland from the Hills while doing so. They fully opposed a proportional electoral system, which indigenous peoples argue is needed to ensure proper representation of the marginalized groups. They also wanted to undo certain provisions of the interim constitution and past agreements with movements of indigenous peoples, Madhesis, Muslims and Dalits, including Article 138 of the interim constitution,[3] replacing the term "secularism" with "religious freedom".

The year ended with heightened polarization, indicating two main possibilities: one is the continuation of the stalemate, as the current CA theoretically has three more years to run, and the other is that the ruling parties may use force,

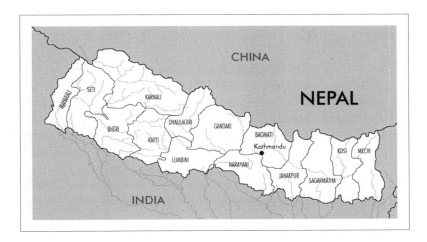

including the army, to come up with a new constitution that denies the rights of indigenous peoples, Madhesis,[4] Dalits, Muslims, and other minorities. If this should happen, it is likely to provoke some sort of violent reaction.

Supreme Court order concerning representation of indigenous peoples

On 28 April 2014, the Supreme Court of Nepal issued an order relating to the nomination of the 26 CA members that remained to be nominated directly by the government,[5] in line with a 2013 order on guaranteeing the direct representation of indigenous peoples in the constitution-making process.[6] The court ruled that the nominations should include indigenous peoples who had not been represented in the First-Past-the-Post- and Proportional Representation elections, and prominent personalities who were not members of political parties. The government and the main political parties largely ignored the ruling, nominating persons who were either members of their respective political parties or kith and kin of the leaders of those political parties. The CPN-UML, however, nominated the General Secretary of the Nepal Federation of Indigenous Nationalities (NEFIN), thus making it difficult for NEFIN and other indigenous peoples' organizations to file a case against the ruling political parties for contempt of court.

Coalitions promoting identity-based federalism

To counter the opposition to identity-based federalism from the ruling parties in the CA, the opposition parties, led by UCPN-Maoist in alliance with Madhesi and indigenous political parties represented in the CA and other allies not represented in the CA, formed a coalition of 22 political parties in September with a slogan to "ensure federalism with identity, constitution with federalism". They called on people to take to the streets in order to muster support for their efforts inside the CA.

Indigenous peoples formed several political parties as part of their movement towards forging coalitions based on identity.[7] A new indigenous peoples' national struggle committee was also formed at the initiative of Mr. Pdmaratna Tuladhar, former advisor to NEFIN, and the leaders of some of the numerically-large indigenous communities. It was, however, soon contested by NEFIN itself, in a parallel initiative. The desired unity and strength of the country's indigenous movement thus continues to be challenged by party affiliations and other political aspirations, and the movement appears fragmented.

Formation of indigenous caucus(es) in the CA

Although the CA regulation does not allow for the formal establishment of caucuses, there is an ongoing effort to form a caucus that would include most of the indigenous CA members belonging to various mainstream political parties, including the Nepali Congress, CPN-UML and UCPN-Maoist. CA members representing political parties that were established from within the indigenous peoples' movements have already formed the *Sajha Muddaka lagi Smyukta Manch Gathabandhan* (Joint Forum Coalition for Common Issues, i.e. Indigenous CA Members' Forum or Caucus). Ten political parties are represented in this caucus. Likewise, 41 Tharu CA members have formed the Tharu Caucus to ensure the Tharu people's rights in the new constitution, and to promote the formation of the Tharuwan/Tharuhat province. Following suit, the Magar and Rai CA members also formed their respective caucuses. When the Nepali Congress and CPN-UML filed a suggestion to have seven provinces based on geography in the Political Dialogue and Agreement Committee (feeling confident that they could muster the needed 2/3 majority if the proposition was put to a vote in the CA), the Tharu

Caucus publicly disagreed with the proposal. This drained the confidence of both the Nepali Congress and CPN-UML to push forward as, at the end of the day, during the vote in the CA, most of the indigenous CA members would likely have defied their whip in order to protect their indigenous peoples' rights.

Unification of five Limbuwan[8] political parties

After months of effort on the part of *tututumyang* (intellectuals and elderly leaders), five Limbuwan political parties merged in 2014.[9] The integration of the five parties into one (the Limbuawan Party, Nepal) has injected fresh hope into the leaders, cadres, supporters, well-wishers and activists of the indigenous peoples' movement with regard to the launch of a strong movement to secure Limbuwan autonomy in the new constitution, and has also inspired other indigenous peoples' movements and political parties to unify in order to gain strength at this critical historical juncture.

Rising demand for effective implementation of free, prior and informed consent (FPIC)

Violations of indigenous peoples' rights to their ancestral lands and natural resources continued to occur in 2014. One example was in Upper Marsyangdi, where a hydropower project will affect at least five Gurung and Tamang villages. According to local villagers, no meaningful consultation has been held with the communities, and the Environmental Impact Assessment data is incorrect. The project was slated to be completed by July 2015 but work on the project was held up due to joint protests by indigenous peoples and project workers demanding better working conditions.[10] As a result of the protests, the project management held talks with representatives of the project workers on 3 March 2014 in relation to their demands, thus creating divisions between project workers and indigenous peoples and isolating the latter. Local indigenous human rights defenders later initiated a dialogue with project staff on the FPIC process and a meeting has been agreed for early 2015.

NEFIN has finalized and passed FPIC guidelines to be implemented by itself and its affiliated District Coordination Committees. The guidelines were drafted because most of the local level IPOs and their leaders are not familiar with the procedures for a proper dialogue between indigenous peoples and project/program staff on the impact of such projects/programs on indigenous peoples' lands and resources.

Presentation of Nepal's issues at the World Conference on indigenous peoples 2014

The High Level Plenary of the United Nations General Assembly, known as the World Conference on Indigenous Peoples, was held at the United Nations Headquarters, New York, from 21-22 September 2014. Yasso Kanti Bhattachan, who represented the National Indigenous Women's Federation (NIWF), Nepal, and Pratima Gurung, who represented the International Disability Forum, read out statements in Table Discussion 1: United Nations system action to implement the rights of indigenous peoples on 22 September 2014.   ◯

Notes and references

1   Hindu cosmology divides the population into hereditary caste groups, who are ranked according to ritual purity. The Dalit castes form the lowest tier of the caste system and are highly marginalized to this day. (-Ed. note)
2   Indigenous peoples in Nepal gained official recognition from the government under the 1990 Constitution and the 2002 (2059) National Foundation for the Development of Indigenous Nationalities Act (known as the NFDIN Act), which lists 59 distinct indigenous communities in the country. Although a task force was formed to make recommendations for revising the list so far no such revision has been made.
3   Article 138 stipulates: 1) To bring an end to discrimination based on class, caste, language, gender, culture, religion and region by eliminating the centralized and unitary form of the state, the state shall be made inclusive and restructured into a progressive, *democratic federal system.
    #(1A) Accepting the aspirations of indigenous ethnic groups and the people of the backward and other regions, and the people of Madhes, for autonomous provinces, Nepal shall be a Federal Democratic Republic. The provinces shall be autonomous with full rights. The Constituent Assembly shall determine the number, boundary, names and structures of the autonomous provinces and the distribution of powers and resources, while maintaining the sovereignty, unity and integrity of Nepal.
    2) A High Level Commission shall be constituted to make recommendations for the restructuring of the State in accordance with clause (1) and (1A). The composition, function, duty, power and terms of service of such Commission shall be as determined by the Government of Nepal.

3) The final decision relating to the structure of the state and federal system shall be made by the Constituent Assembly.

4   Madhesis are inhabitants of the lowland Terai region of Nepal. Madhei leaders include indigenous peoples of Terai, including the Tharus, as Madhesi but indigenous peoples do not accept this.

5   The CA comprises 240 members elected through a first-past-the-post voting system (the candidate who gains the highest number of votes in each of the 240 constituencies wins the seat), 335 members elected through proportional representation (each of the country's diverse communities is ensured representation, in line with their overall proportion of the population), and 26 members nominated directly by the Cabinet (these 26 members are to represent "distinguished personalities" and indigenous peoples who fail to be represented through election). Source: United Nations Mission in Nepal Archive Site (http://www.un.org.np/unmin-archive/?d=peaceprocess&p=election_system).

6   See *The Indigenous World 2014*.

7   The new indigenous parties include *Khambuwa Rastriya Morcha, Tharuhat Terai Party, Rastriya Janamukti Party, Manch Sambadda Sanghiya Limbuwan Rajya parishad, Nepa: Rastriya Party, Adibasi Janjati Party,* and *Samajik Loktantrik Party*.

8   Limbuwan is a territory covering the existing nine districts that lie to the east of the Arun river. It is one of the provinces recommended by both the State Restructuring and State Power Division Committee of the CA and the Sate Restructuring Commission formed by the CA.

9   These were the *Munch Sambaddha Sanghiya Limbuwan Rajya Parishad, Limbuwan Mukti Morcha, Limbuwan Mukti Morcha Nepal, Sanghiya Ganatantrik Party,* and *Limbuwan Rajya Parishad*.

10   "*The glimpse of Indigenous Peoples' human rights violation in Nepal*" produced by Lawyers' Association for Human Rights of Nepalese Indigenous Peoples (LAHURNIP), 2011; http://www.ekantipur.com/2014/08/16/business/upper-marsyangdi-project-running-behind-schedule/393664.html (accessed on 20 January 2015)

Krishna B. Bhattachan belongs to the Thakali indigenous peoples. He is one of the founder faculty members and former Head of Department of Sociology and Anthropology at Tribhuvn University in Nepal and has published several books and articles on indigenous issues.

INDIA

In India, 461 ethnic groups are recognized as *Scheduled Tribes*, and these are considered to be India's indigenous peoples. In mainland India, the Scheduled Tribes are usually referred to as *Adivasis*, which literally means indigenous peoples. With an estimated population of 84.3 million, they comprise 8.2% of the total population. There are, however, many more ethnic groups that would qualify for Scheduled Tribe status but which are not officially recognized. Estimates of the total number of tribal groups are as high as 635. The largest concentrations of indigenous peoples are found in the seven states of north-east India, and the so-called "central tribal belt" stretching from Rajasthan to West Bengal.

India has several laws and constitutional provisions, such as the Fifth Schedule for mainland India and the Sixth Schedule for certain areas of north-east India, which recognize indigenous peoples' rights to land and self-governance. The laws aimed at protecting indigenous peoples have numerous shortcomings and their implementation is far from satisfactory. The Indian government voted in favour of the UNDRIP in the UN General Assembly. However, it does not consider the concept of "indigenous peoples", and thus the UNDRIP, applicable to India.

High-Level Committee report submitted

In August 2013, the then United Progressive Alliance government constituted a High-Level Committee headed by tribal expert and eminent sociologist, Virginius Xaxa, to examine the socio-economic, health and educational status of Scheduled Tribes (STs) and "suggest policy initiatives as well as effective outcome-oriented measures to improve development indicators and strengthen public service delivery to STs." [1] The Committee submitted its report to the new government led by Bharatiya Janata Party on 29 May 2014. The High-Level Committee made several major recommendations, some of which are briefly summarized here:

Legal and administrative framework

The High-Level Committee recommends that laws and policies enacted by the Parliament and State legislatures should not be automatically applied in the Fifth Schedule Areas (tribal areas in mainland India) but that their applicability should be decided by the Governor with the advice of the Tribes Advisory Council (TAC), the mandatory advisory bodies on "tribal welfare and advancement" in states with Fifth Schedule Areas. The Committee recommends broadening the mandate of the TAC and transforming it into the Tribes Advisory, Protective and Developmental Council. All constitutional provisions, laws, policies and administrative matters pertaining to the Scheduled Tribes should come under its ambit, and the Tribal

Welfare Department should be made accountable to it. A state's tribal development plan should be approved by the TAC (or its replacement, the Tribes Advisory, Protective and Developmental Council) before it is placed before the Legislative Assembly.

The model of the Autonomous Councils, local self-rule bodies at district level with limited autonomy in Sixth Schedule areas (tribal areas in Northeast India), should be extended to the Fifth Schedule Areas, as has been provided for in the Provisions of Panchayat (Extension to Scheduled Areas) Act, 1996.

Funding of Autonomous Councils in Sixth Schedule areas should not be left to the arbitrary discretion of the state governments any more. Instead, Autonomous Councils should be covered by the State Finance Commission, which is empowered to lay down appropriate principles of resource distribution between the state and the Autonomous Council.

Livelihoods and employment

According to the High-Level Committee report, credit and marketing facilities need to be extended to the STs. Delivery of social justice must be monitored by the National Commission for Scheduled Tribes, both at the national and state levels.

The government should follow a transparent policy with regard to employment opportunities for STs in the public sector. Special attention should be given to the Particularly Vulnerable Tribal Groups (PVTGs) among the tribes. The Ministry of Tribal Affairs should ensure that all states having PVTGs should utilize the grants received under Special Central Assistance to implement micro-projects specifically targeting individual PVTGs.

A National Institute of Tribal Development should be created as an autonomous research organization exclusively for undertaking research on STs.

Education

The High-Level Committee stresses that the Right of Children to Free and Compulsory Education Act, 2009 should be strictly implemented in tribal areas. Institutions of Integrated Tribal Development Projects/Agencies and micro-project support to tribal schools should be strengthened to prevent dropouts. Furthermore, the report recommends that the government establish well-run residential schools up to class 12 within a radius of ten kilometres from their homes in order to pro-

vide comprehensive facilities for marginalized children, including quality education, health care and academic support classes. Residential schools should be
set up specifically for Nomadic Tribes.

Health

The Committee recommends that the Ministry of Health and Family Welfare
should adopt a "Tribal Health Plan" with proposed goals such as attaining the
United Nations Millennium Development Goals on health and nutrition for the
Scheduled Tribe population in India by the year 2020, and bringing the health,
sanitation and nutrition status of the Scheduled Tribe population up to the same
level as that of the non-Scheduled Tribe population in the respective states by the
year 2025. Annual Tribal Health Plans should be generated at all levels by the year
2017 and 8.6 percent of the total Health Sector Plan and non-plan budget allocated
and spent, in proportion to the Scheduled Tribes population, plus 10 percent of the
Tribal Sub Plan budget for the implementation of the Tribal Health Plan.

Instead of deploying unwilling doctors and health staff from outside into the
Scheduled Areas, the Committee recommends the selection, training and deployment of local Scheduled Tribe candidates at village, block and district levels as an
effective long term solution.

Land alienation, displacement and enforced migration

According to the report of the High-Level Committee, the exercise of "eminent
domain" and definition of "public purpose", which are used by the state to legitimize land alienation for development and public infrastructure projects, should be
severely limited in tribal areas. The right of tribal communities to say "no" to acquisition of their land, and their right to access and manage forests and other
common property resources should be recognized. Furthermore, the Committee
recommends that the Right To Fair Compensation and Transparency in Land
Acquisition, Rehabilitation And Resettlement Act, 2013 should be amended by
incorporating a suitable provision to safeguard tribal land and community resources in Scheduled Areas, and disallow acquisition by a non-tribal, including private
companies.

In view of the widespread discontent among tribal people who have been displaced from their lands regarding poor resettlement and rehabilitation, a High-Level Fact-finding Committee/Enquiry Committee should be set up to investigate the quality of resettlement and rehabilitation in all medium and major development projects undertaken in the last 50 years in Scheduled Areas and tribal-dominated districts of states without Scheduled Areas.

The Committee also recommends that, in order to prevent illegal land alienation of tribal land, the Land Transfer Regulations/Tenancy laws of all Fifth Schedule Areas should be suitably amended to ensure Gram Sabha (village council) participation in the identification, investigation and restoration of lands to tribal people; plenary powers could be given to Gram Sabhas to fight cases of tribal land alienation collectively, as an individual tribal cannot afford to face prolonged legal battles; and the Gram Sabha should be empowered to restore the alienated land on detection, pending the long legal battle, in order to potentially discourage a prospective non-tribal buyer of land in Scheduled Areas.

Legal and constitutional issues

The High-Level Committee recommends strengthening the implementation of laws, notably the Provisions of Panchayats (Extension to Scheduled Areas) Act, 1996 and the Scheduled Tribes and Other Traditional Forest Dwellers (Recognition of Forest Rights) Act, 2006. The Committee also recognizes the need to set up a Judicial Commission to investigate cases filed against tribals and their supporters who have been jailed for so-called "naxal offences", i.e. for alleged collaboration with the Maoist (Naxalite) insurgents, or for their resistance and protest against projects.

However, the present government has not yet implemented any of the recommendations of the High-Level Committee. On the contrary, on 29 December 2014 the Union Cabinet came up with an Ordinance to amend the Right to Fair Compensation and Transparency in Land Acquisition, Rehabilitation and Resettlement Act, 2013 in order to make land acquisitions easier by doing away with the requirement for consent of the affected people, and for a social impact assessment for projects in the areas of defence and defence production, rural infrastructure (including rural electrification), affordable housing, industrial corridors and social infrastructure projects, including public-private partnerships.[2]

A more positive development is the introduction of The Scheduled Castes and Scheduled Tribes (Prevention of Atrocities) Amendment Bill, 2014 in the Lok Sabha (Lower House of Parliament) by the Minister for Social Justice and Empowerment on 16 July 2014. The Bill seeks to reinforce the Scheduled Castes and the Scheduled Tribes (Prevention of Atrocities) Act, 1989, which addresses atrocities committed against the Scheduled Castes (SCs) and Scheduled Tribes. While the Prevention of Atrocities Act, 1989 already states that a non-SC or non-ST public servant who neglects his duties relating to SCs or STs shall be punishable with imprisonment of six months to one year, the Bill specifies these duties, including, among other things, registering a complaint or First Information Report, reading out information given orally before taking the signature of the informant, and giving a copy of this information to the informant, etc. The Bill also provides for the establishment of an Exclusive Special Court at the district level (or a Special Court in districts with fewer cases) to try offences against SCs and STs and for the establishment of an adequate number of courts to ensure that cases are disposed of within two months.[3]

Human rights violations against indigenous peoples

India has witnessed an increase in atrocities against indigenous peoples/tribals in recent years. According to the "Crime in India 2013" report, published in 2014 by the National Crime Records Bureau (NCRB) of the Ministry of Home Affairs, a total of 6,793 crimes committed against tribals were reported in the country during 2013, as compared to 5,922 cases in 2012, an increase of 14.7%.[4] These are only the reported cases of atrocities committed by non-tribals, and do not include cases of human rights violations by the security forces.

Human rights violations by the security forces

During 2014, large areas of central and Northeast India remained affected by armed conflicts and the security forces continued to be responsible for human rights violations against indigenous peoples. In these areas, the tribals are sandwiched between the armed opposition groups (AOGs) and the security forces. On 3 September, two innocent tribal villagers were killed by the security forces in an alleged fake encounter in Gumla district of Jharkhand.[5] In Chhattisgarh, at least

26 local tribals were beaten up by Central Reserve Police Force (CRPF) personnel at Kokenar and Chote Tongpal region in Sukma district on 26 November, after
they protested against the detention of a woman for her alleged involvement with
Maoist insurgents. Six of the victims, including three elderly women, were taken
to Jagdalpur hospital with fractures and critical injuries. After 14 CRPF personnel
were killed in a major Maoist ambush in Sukma district on 1 December, five tribals
from Kasalpadh village, also in Chhattisgarh, were allegedly beaten and dragged
to the nearest CRPF camp by CRPF personnel for failing to alert them about the
Maoists' movements.[6]

Human rights violations by armed opposition groups

Armed opposition groups continued to be responsible for gross violations of international humanitarian law, including killings, during 2014. On the night of 23 December, militants of the National Democratic Front of Boroland, Songbijit faction (NDFB-
S) launched serial attacks on Adivasi villages. These Adivasis are the descendants
of labourers brought to Assam by the British to work in tea plantations, who are now
living in the Bodo areas. At least 80 persons including women and children were
killed in the attacks in Assam's Sonitpur, Kokrajhar, Chirang and Udalguri districts.
The NDFB-S cadres reportedly targeted the Adivasis, suspecting them of passing
information to the security forces, which had conducted a counterinsurgency operation against the group, killing three of its cadres on 21 December.[7] Furthermore, five
Bodo tribals were also killed in retaliatory attacks by miscreants from the Adivasi
communities.[8] The attacks led to a humanitarian crisis, displacing over 300,000
people, mainly Adivasis.[9] Earlier, on 21 August, NDFB-S militants killed a 16-year-
old schoolgirl at Dwimuguri village in Chirang district of Assam. The militants reportedly arrived at Dwimuguri village and forced the villagers to gather at a place, where
they shot Priya dead for allegedly passing on information that had led to the killing
of five NDFB-S cadres by the security forces a day earlier.[10]

The Maoists continued to kill innocent tribals on charges of being "police informers", or simply for not obeying their diktats. During 2014, the Maoists targeted tribals
mostly in Malkangiri and Koraput districts of Odisha state. Some of the alleged killings by the Maoists in 2014 took place at Ralegada village in Malkangiri district of
Odisha on 2 April,[11] at Talagoluru village in Koraput district on 11 May,[12] at Pilibadi
and Upar Renga villages in Koraput district on 19 July,[13] at Badliguda village in
Malkangiri district on 24 July,[14] at Dasini village in Koraput district on 26 July,[15] at

Erbanpalli village in Malkangiri district on 29 September,[16] at Materu village in Malkangiri district on 24 October,[17] in Kalimela area in Malkangiri district on 29 October,[18] and at Sriguda village in Koraput district on 6 November,[19] among others.

Alienation of tribal land

The 5th and 6th Schedule to the Constitution of India provide stringent provisions for the protection of land belonging to tribal peoples. In addition, at the state level, there is a plethora of laws prohibiting the sale or transfer of tribal lands to non-tribals, and providing for the restoration of alienated lands to the tribals. Yet these laws remain ineffective, as the lands of tribals continue to be alienated. While the latest data on alienation of tribal land is not available, in April 2012, the Government of India informed Parliament that 437,173 cases of tribal land alienation had been registered, covering 661,806 acres of land in the country, out of which 217,396 cases were disposed of in favour of the tribals, and 190,573 cases were decided against the tribal landowners in the courts.[20] As of 28 July 2014, in Assam alone, around 190,000 bighas (in Assam, equal to 25,460 ha) of land in the state's 30 tribal blocks and 17 tribal belts were reportedly under encroachment by non-tribals.[21]

The Government of India's lack of a serious response towards the land alienation of tribals can be gauged from its failure to make public the report of the High-Level Committee, which includes radical recommendations on land alienation, at the end of 2014.

Internally displaced tribal peoples

Conflict-induced displacement
As mentioned above, the murderous attacks by the NDFB-S on Adivasis in Assam on 23 December displaced over 300,000 persons, who have taken shelter in 85 relief camps in Sonitpur, Kokrajhar, Udalguri and Chirang districts of Assam. Out of these IDPs, there are 287,182 Adivasis sheltered in 65 relief camps, and 13,091 Bodos in 20 relief camps. In addition, many Adivasis have also fled to the neighbouring states of Arunachal Pradesh and West Bengal. The IDPs are living in dismal conditions in overcrowded relief camps that lack basic facilities.[22]

Development–induced displacement

The government admits that the displacement of Scheduled Tribe people is taking place as a result of various development projects. However, there is no official figure available of the displacement caused by development projects. During 2014, the tribals continued to resist attempts by the government to acquire their lands for mining and other industrial projects.[23] Thousands of tribals from nearly 27 villages in Manavar Tehsil of Dhar district in Madhya Pradesh are facing displacement due to the acquisition of their agricultural land for a proposed cement plant. The tribals have protested against this land acquisition.[24]

Repression under forest laws

The Scheduled Tribes and Other Traditional Forest Dwellers (Recognition of Forest Rights) Act, 2006 (hereinafter the Forest Rights Act) has been touted as a progressive piece of legislation aimed at undoing the "historic injustice" committed against the forest-dwelling Scheduled Tribes and other traditional forest dwellers who have lived in the forests for centuries. However, the rights of a large number of forest-dwelling tribals continue to be denied under the Act. According to the Ministry of Tribal Affairs, as of 30 September 2014, a total of 3,853,977 land claims had been received across the country under the Forest Rights Act. Of these, a total of 3,189,324 claims (82.75% of the total received) have been disposed of, for which 1,494,933 titles were distributed and 33,765 titles were ready for distribution. However, 1,694,391 claims (52.87% of the total disposed of) were rejected.[25] There have been credible reports of arbitrary rejections of claims made under the Forest Rights Act. Yet the Ministry of Tribal Affairs claimed that: "No such cases where violation of this Act has been established have come to the notice of the Government." It merely places the onus of implementing the Forest Rights Act on the state governments.[26]

Across India, tribal peoples are being illegally evicted from their ancestral homelands in the name of conservation, particularly for tiger reserves. Those who resist such evictions face threats and harassment from the forest authorities. The tribals are promised land, housing and money as compensation but often receive very little or nothing.[27] Three tribal villages are currently facing imminent eviction from Similipal Tiger Reserve in Odisha. In September 2014, members of the

Munda tribe in Similipal Tiger Reserve met India's Forest Department where they were "threatened" and "cheated" into signing an eviction document drawn up by the foresters.[28] Three out of six villages have already been removed from the Similipal Tiger Reserve. However the 32 families of the Khadia tribe who were evicted from Similipal in December 2013 are now living in dire conditions in makeshift tents, having to rely on government hand-outs for their survival and have not received the compensation they were promised.[29]

Nagalim

Approximately 4 million in population and comprising more than 45 different tribes, the Nagas are a transnational indigenous people inhabiting parts of northeast India and north-west Burma. The Nagas were divided between the two countries with the colonial transfer of power from Great Britain to India in 1947. Nagalim is the name coined to refer to the Naga homeland transcending the present state boundaries, and is an expression of their assertion of their political identity and aspirations as a nation. The Naga people's struggle for the right to self-determination dates back to the colonial transfer of power from Great Britain to India. Armed conflict between the Indian state and the Nagas' armed opposition forces began in the early 1950s and it is one of the longest armed struggles in Asia. In 1997, the Indian government and the largest of the armed groups, the National Socialist Council of Nagaland Isaac-Muivah faction (NSCN-IM), agreed on a ceasefire and, since then, have held regular peace talks. Largely as a result of India's divide-and-rule tactics, the armed movement was split into several factions fighting each other. In 2010, a reconciliation process started among the main armed factions, the NSCN-IM, the Government of the People's Republic of Nagaland/National Socialist Council of Nagaland (GPRN/NSCN) and the Naga National Council (NNC).

2014 did not see much progress in the efforts to find a permanent settlement to the Indo-Naga political problem. The talks between the Government of India (GoI)and the NSCN-IM were low profiled and did not take center stage in the public discussions. The reconciliation process facilitated by Forum for Naga Reconciliation (FNR) moved a step forward by signing the "Lenten Agreement" among the armed groups but it still faces the challenge of translating agreements into reality. Further, the hope for an alternative political arrangement for the Nagas in Manipur too took a backstage with the toppling of the Congress-led central government.

The peace talks and the reconciliation process

The Bharatiya Janata Party led National Democratic Alliance g(NDA) overnment was sworn into office in May 2014. Following this, the government appointed a new interlocutor, RN Ravi, Chairman of the Joint Intelligence Committee for the Indo-Naga peace talk. The NDA government remained silent over the issue of peace talks until Kiren Rijiju, Mister of State for Home on 29th June spoke to reporters on the sidelines of the 6th Asian Ministerial Conference on Disaster Risk Reduction in Bangkok, Thailand. He announced to the reporters that the peace processes in the Northeast will develop gradually under the new government and noted that peace talks will be action-oriented[30]. However, without explanation, he made a categorical remark that it will take more time to bring the National Socialist Council of Nagaland and the United Liberation Front of Assam on board and to find a solution. This remark sent out waves of skepticism among news readers of the region. Newspapers reported a few rounds of official negotiations between the government and NSCN-IM but nothing on concrete results. In was in this context that the Nagaland unit of the Congress on 2nd December expressed disappointment over Prime Minister Narendra Modi's silence on the Naga peace process during his two-day visit to the state.

The demand for an alternative arrangement for the Nagas in Manipur

The Nagas in southern Nagalim, led by the United Naga Council (UNC), has been demanding for an interim alternative political arrangement for the Nagas of Manipur state since 2010. According to the UNC, during the 7th tripartite talk held on 6th February 2014, it was agreed that the government would institute a high-profile committee to translate the demand for an alternative arrangement into a political reality[31]. This committee was not constituted before the national general election that took place in April-May, and the new BJP-led NDA government has not shown any interest in instituting the committee or in taking the issue forward.

The human rights situation in southern Nagalim also did not improve in 2014. Mr. Ngalangzar Malue, an Autonomous District Council member of Ukhrul District was killed by an unidentified gunman on the 12th of July about 22 kms away from

Ukhrul District Headquarter. The Manipur government sent hundreds of Manipur Police Commando (MPC) and Indian Reserved Battalion (IRB) to Ukhrul District Headquarters and arrested eight cadres of the NSCN-IM. Further, the government imposed *Section 144* of the Criminal Procedure Code (*S.144 CrPC*) which prohibits free movement and the assembly of more than five people. The law is intended to provide for an emergency when there is a major violence or where there is an apprehension of a serious disturbance of the public tranquility. The imposition of S.144 CrPC suspended the freedom of movement and association of the public for nearly two month causing harm to the social, economic and mental health of the people in and around Ukhrul District Headquarters. This unexplained action of the state was condemned by several national and international human rights organisations and the outraged public protested for weeks. On 30th August, two young men, Mr. Mayopam Ramror and Ramkashing Vashi were killed when the MPC and IRB commandos indiscriminately open fired on the peaceful protestors.   ○

Notes and references

1   Now, a high-level committee to map status of tribals. *The Hindu*, 18 August 2013. http://www.thehindu.com/news/national/now-a-highlevel-committee-to-map-status-of-tribals/article5033054.ece
2   Nod for ordinance to amend Land Act. *The Hindu*, 29 December 2014. http://www.thehindu.com/news/national/cabinet-approvesordinanceto-amend-land-acquisition-act/article6735783.ece
3   PRS Legislative Research, http://www.prsindia.org/billtrack/the-scheduled-castes-and-the-scheduled-tribes-prevention-of-atrocities-amendment-bill-2014-3327/
4   NCRB: "Crime in India 2013".
5   Complaint filed by the Jharkhand Human Rights Movement dated 17/11/2014 with the National Human Rights Commission.
6   Torture prevented tribals from tipping off CRPF of Maoist movement. *The Times of India*, 6 December 2014.
7   Asian Centre for Human Rights: *Assam: The largest conflict induced IDPs of the world in 2014 reel under a massive humanitarian crisis.* ACHR, 2 January 2015.
8   Assam violence toll mounts to 75. *The Hindu*, 25 December 2014.
9   Asian Centre for Human Rights: *Assam: The largest conflict induced IDPs of the world in 2014 reel under a massive humanitarian crisis.* ACHR, 2 January 2015.
10   NDFB(S) guns down schoolgirl. *The Assam Tribune*, 22 August 2014.
11   Maoists kill tribal in Malkangiri. *The Indian Express*, 3 April 2014.
12   Maoists kill two abducted tribal leaders. *The Hindu*, 13 May 2014.
13   Maoists kill another tribal. *The Hindu*, 25 July 2014.

14   Maoists kill 2 villagers in Malkangiri district calling them informers. *The Indian Express*, 25 July 2014.
15   Maoists kill tribal in border village. *The Times of India*, 28 July 2014.
16   'Maoists' kill tribal in Malkangiri. *The Times of India*, 1 October 2014.
17   Odisha: Tribal sarpanch killed by Maoists. *The Indian Express*, 25 October 2014.
18   Maoists abduct and kill tribal youth in Odisha. *Business Standard*, 30 October 2014.
19   Tribal villager killed in Narayanpatna block, Maoist hand suspected. *The Samaya*, 7 November 2014. http://odishasamaya.com/news/tribal-villager-killed-in-narayanpatna-block-maoist-hand-suspected/
20   Lok Sabha Unstarred Question No.3495, available at: http://164.100.47.132/LssNew/psearch/QResult15.aspx?qref=122082
21   1.9 lakh bighas of tribal land under encroachment in State. *The Sentinel*, 28 July 2014.
22   Asian Centre for Human Rights: *Assam: The largest conflict induced IDPs of the world in 2014 reel under a massive humanitarian crisis*. ACHR, 2 January 2015.
23   Tribal villagers resist attempts to deny them their forest rights. *The Hindu*, 7 January 2014.
24   Tribal protest against acquisition of land for cement factory. *The Times of India*, 10 February 2014.
25   *Status report on implementation of the Scheduled Tribes and Other Traditional Forest Dwellers (Recognition of Forest Rights) Act, 2006 [for the period ending 30 September 2013]*. Ministry of Tribal Affairs; available at: http://www.tribal.nic.in/WriteReadData/CMS/Documents/2013110112 05276091728MPRforthemonthofSeptember2013.pdf
26   Reply of Minister of State in the Ministry of Tribal Affairs Shri Mansukhbhai Dhanjibai Vasava, in the Lok Sabha, Unstarred Question No.3392, answered on 01.08.2014
27   Survival International: *India: Tiger Reserve tribe faces eviction*, 14 October 2014. http://www.survivalinternational.org/news/10488
28   Survival International: *India: Tiger Reserve tribe faces eviction*, 14 October 2014. http://www.survivalinternational.org/news/10488
29   Survival International: *India: tribes face harassment and eviction for "tiger conservation"* 13 May 2014, http://www.survivalinternational.org/news/10239
30   http://www.dnaindia.com/india/report-northeast-peace-process-will-develop-gradually-under-new-government-minister-of-state-kiren-rijiju-1998487
31   United Naga Council: Statement on Alternative Arrangement dated Tahamzam, 01.08.2014.

Paritosh Chakma *is Programme Coordinator at the Asia Indigenous and Tribal Peoples Network (AITPN) based in Delhi, India.*

The section on Nagalim was written by **Gam A. Shimray**. *He is a member of the Naga Peoples Movement for Human Rights and currently holds the position of Director of the Indigenous Knowledge and Peoples Network (IKAP) based in Chiang Mai, Thailand.*

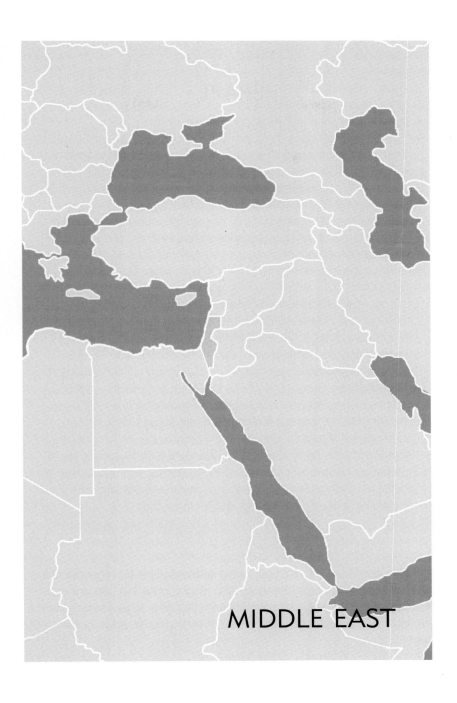

MIDDLE EAST

ISRAEL

Israel's Arab Bedouin are indigenous to the Negev-Naqab desert. Centuries ago, they were semi-nomadic. Bedouin combined herding with agriculture in villages linked by kinship systems, which largely determined land ownership. Prior to 1948, about 90,000 Bedouin lived in the Negev. After 1948 most were expelled to Jordan and Sinai. Only about 11,000 survived in Israel. In the early 1950s, the Israeli government concentrated this population within a restricted geographical area that was about ten percent of the Bedouin's former territory, with a promise of return to their original lands within six months. This promise has yet to be fulfilled. According to the Central Bureau of Statistics (2009), around 75,000 Bedouin currently live in 35 "unrecognized villages", which lack basic services and infrastructure. Another 150,000 Bedouin live in seven townships and 11 villages that have been "recognized" over the last decade. However, these townships and villages hinder the traditional Bedouin way of life and provide few employment opportunities. The Bedouin are today politically, socially, economically and culturally marginalised and experience many forms of discrimination. Their representatives regularly attend and address UN bodies on indigenous peoples' issues but their indigenous status is not officially recognized by the state of Israel. Israel has not ratified ILO Convention No. 169 and has violated many of its provisions. Additionally, Israel did not participate in the vote on the UN Declaration on the Rights of Indigenous Peoples and has failed to meet this Declaration's provisions.

House demolitions and crop destructions remained on the 2014 agenda in the Negev and a slim hope of reaching a fair solution to the Al-Araqib land claim was crushed by bulldozers. On the whole, the situation in the Negev was characterized by Israel's continuous defiance of most international human rights standards.

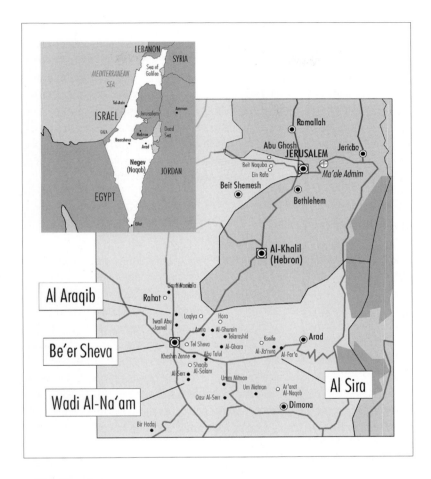

House demolitions

The freezing of the Prawer bill on the arrangement of Bedouin settlement in the Negev by the Knesset[1] in 2013 did not shelve the Be'er Sheva Metropolitan Plan, and the government continued to implement some of its provisions in 2014 by issuing demolition orders against Bedouin villages. According to the Negev Coexistence Forum (NCF), 86 such cases were reported in 2014, including the demolition of several hundred structures, the uprooting of olive trees and the destruction of crops.[2] Although the purpose of house demolitions is to concentrate the Bedouin in townships and recognized villages, 54% of the reported destructions occurred in these very same places. Indeed, due to the lack of public development plans, their residents are unable to obtain construction permits and their houses are therefore just as vulnerable to demolition as the "unrecognized villages". One new trend is that many Bedouin owners choose to destroy their homes themselves. This is not only due to the fact that the state authorities threaten to make the owners pay the demolition expenses but also because it allows the owners to salvage some equipment and construction materials while also minimizing the resulting trauma experienced by family members.

The Al-Araqib land claim

The Al-Araqib unrecognized village north-west of Be'er Sheva was among those that experienced demolitions in 2014. This village has to date been "destroyed" more than 70 times and has become a symbolic case of Bedouin resilience when it comes to defending their land rights. The plight of Al-Araqib dates back to 1951 when members of the Al-Ukbi tribe were expelled from their homes and lands and forced to resettle in Hura, some 20 km away. Their land was subsequently expropriated and classified as "state land" but some families returned and settled there again. In 2009, Al-Araqib was chosen as the site of a new forest sponsored by the Jewish National Fund[3] and the entire village, with a population of 300 people, was destroyed. Its inhabitants, however, were soon back raising makeshift homes and refusing to leave their land —just as they would continue to do each time their village was destroyed.

Adopting a counter-claim policy, the state of Israel decided in 2011 to put a final stop to what it calls "trespassing on state land" and filed a NIS 1.8 million (approx. USD 450,000) lawsuit against the heirs of Sheikh Suleiman Al-Ukbi, thereby placing the burden on these latter to prove ownership of their ancestral lands at Al-Araqib and Zazhilika.[4] The case was heard in March 2012 but, in keeping with the Dead Negev Doctrine which, since the 1970s, has classified all land in the Negev region as "*mewat*"—i.e. unoccupied and uncultivated land – and hence as state lands, Judge Sarah Dovrat rejected the claims of the Al-Ukbi tribe. The judgment was immediately appealed but, while waiting for the appeal case to be heard, Al-Araqib suffered several more demolitions and, in May, eight eviction orders were delivered for enforcement between 12 June and 12 July.

The appeal case opened in the Supreme Court in Jerusalem on 2 June 2014. Starting by comparing the Dead Negev Doctrine with the Terra Nullius doctrine,[5] the applicability of which is today totally rejected internationally, Attorney Michael Sfard, representing the appellants, went on to present various research findings obtained from archives, aerial photos and Bedouin testimonies that provided strong evidence of the Bedouins' land rights in the northern Negev. These rights were further confirmed by documents showing that vast Bedouin-owned tracts of land in the Negev had been formally purchased during Ottoman and British times by Zionist organizations and Jewish individuals—land on which 11 thriving kibbutzim[6] were built and exist to the present day. The state attorneys, on the other hand, spent considerable time arguing that the Bedouins were not indigenous to the Negev since they were "descended from 18th century invaders". They also stated that the Bedouins' assertion of private land titles rather than a collective one proved their non-indigenous status. The state furthermore claimed that the UN Declaration on the Rights of Indigenous Peoples did not constitute "customary international law" and hence was not binding upon Israel. After deliberating, the judges expressed their displeasure with the extremely long delay in dealing with claims filed by the Bedouin more than 50 years ago and suggested holding a conciliation process in order to reach a fair solution on the question of Bedouin land ownership at Al-Araqib. The Al-Ukbi members agreed, and the court awarded the state a fortnight to consider.

Before the fortnight was over, however, the slim hope of a fair solution had been crushed as structures in the cemetery were razed to the ground in a three-day action starting on 12 June. An order to freeze the demolitions while the case was ongoing was not respected by the police and, by the time the court had decided to order a new freeze, it was too late as there was nothing left to be destroyed.[7] The Al-Ukbi members nevertheless soon returned and, by the end of 2014, they had been dislodged a further six times.

No shelters and sirens for Bedouin villages

Bomb shelters and air-raid sirens are a common sight all over Israel, but not in Bedouin communities.[8] During the Protective Edge military operation in July

2014,[9] several rockets fired from Gaza hit Bedouin villages across the Negev. Two of those hits were fatal, killing at least one person[10] and severely injuring six others. On 16 July, the Association for Civil Rights in Israel (ACRI) issued an urgent petition to the Supreme Court demanding immediate protection for the recognized and unrecognized Bedouin villages in the Negev. On 20 July, the court determined that there was no reason for an immediate intervention in the policy of protection for the communities. Nonetheless, the Justices held that the long-term preparedness needed to be clarified, and gave the respondents —the Ministry of Defence and the Regional Councils— 30 days to give their response.[11]

The denial of basic human rights

Besides being denied their rights to land and to a secure environment, the Bedouin are also being denied other basic human rights. One of these is the internationally-recognized human right to water as enshrined by the UN General Assembly in the International Covenant on Economic, Social and Cultural Rights (CESCR). A recent report shows that many unrecognized villages have no access to the water network. Those that do are provided with insufficient quantities and the residents have to install and maintain the necessary infrastructure at their own cost. The quality of water is not supervised and is often a health risk. Finally, they have to pay the highest water rates in the entire country.[12]

The Bedouin community's freedoms of expression, speech and assembly are also at risk after suffering a critical blow following a demonstration last year in Hura against the Prawer Plan. As described in a Negev Coexistence Forum Report, hundreds of Bedouin and their supporters experienced the use of shock grenades, tear gas and mounted police during this "day of rage". They also suffered lengthy detentions and had to pay high legal costs. All this indicates to the Bedouin community, as well as to their supporters, that when they go out to protest it is not considered a legitimate civil demonstration but rather a security event, and hence the ability of the Bedouin community to exercise their rights to freedom of speech and assembly is seriously jeopardized.[13]   ○

Notes and references

1   The Knesset is the legislative branch of Israel's government. Regarding the Prawer Plan, see *The Indigenous World 2014*, pp. 354-356.
2   See website of the Negev Coexistence Forum (NCF) and their report, "The House Demolition Policy in the Negev-Naqab" (2014) at http://www.dukium.org
3   JNF was created in 1901 with the purpose of buying land for exclusive Jewish settlement. See *The Indigenous World 2010*, p. 433-435.
4   The only way for Bedouins to prove land ownership is either to prove the existence of a village or cultivation in 1858, or to show that ownership was registered at the British Land Registry Office no later than 1921, the beginning of the British Mandate. This makes it virtually impossible for Bedouins to prove their ownership.
5   This concept, which considers land as "belonging to no-one" has been used, for instance, in Australia to negate the land rights of the Australian Aborigines.
6   Communal settlements, typically farms.
7   This entire section draws on NCF (http://www.dukium.org); Gush Shalom (http:// http://zope. gush-shalom.org/index_en.html) and Mondoweis (http://mondoweiss.net/2014/06/bedouin-de-molished-proceedings).
8   According to Israel's 1951 Civil Defense law, all homes, residential buildings and industrial buildings are required to have bomb shelters or access to protected spaces.
9   Israeli military operation launched against Gaza on 8 July 2014.
10 This Arab Bedouin was among the five Israeli civilians killed during the conflict.
11 See ACRI at http://www.acri.org.il/en/2014/07/20/bedouin-protection-denied/
12 See NCF Report "Thirsty for (the right to) Water: the Policy of not Supplying Water to the Unrecognized Arab-Bedouin Villages in the Negev" (2014). At http://www.dukium.org/reports-and-position-papers/
13 See "'Days of Rage': Deprivation of Freedom of Speech of the Bedouin Community in the Negev-Naqab". NCF, 2014 at http://www.dukium.org.

Diana Vinding is an anthropologist and former and former member of IWGIA's Board. She has followed the situation of the Bedouin for many years.

PALESTINE

Following Israel's declaration of independence in 1948, clans from the Jahalin Bedouin together with clans from four other tribes from the Negev Desert (al-Kaabneh, al-Azazmeh, al-Ramadin, and al-Rshaida) took refuge in the West Bank, then under Jordanian rule. These refugee tribes, who number approximately 17,000 people, are semi-nomadic agro-pastoralists living in the rural areas around Hebron, Bethlehem, Jerusalem, Jericho and the Jordan Valley, today part of the so-called "Area C" of the Occupied Palestinian Territory (OPT). "Area C", the administration of which was provisionally - and temporarily - granted to Israel in 1995 by the Oslo Accords, represents 60% of the West Bank. It is home to all West Bank Israeli settlements, industrial estates, military bases, firing ranges, closed military zones, nature reserves or settler-only by-pass roads, all under Israeli military control, and all of which surround and control Palestinian areas.

Israeli policies dash "High Hopes" of peace

A decade ago, Israel developed the E-1 Plan, calling for a mass forcible population transfer of Palestinian Bedouin refugees from Jerusalem's periphery, for the development of Ma'ale Adumim settlement.

The 3,000-acre E-1 settlement plan was red-lined in 2005 by the international community, responding to peace activists' advocacy, as representing "the end of the Two State Solution." Diplomatic pressure on Israel froze it - until now. Today, E-1 development is back on the agenda.

Now, with Gaza's urgent rehabilitation, the discriminatory Jewish state bill, and exploding tensions in Jerusalem as the focus, new Israeli settlement plans are forging ahead. Nearly 1,000 acres have been expropriated for a new settlement, G'vaot (illegal under international law). Silwan, Har Homa and Givat Hama-

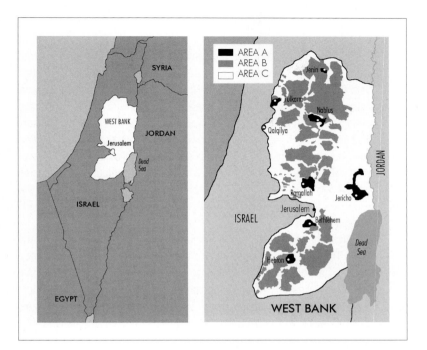

tos settlements have seen major development. The Nuweimeh Plan also went public, calling for forced ethnic displacement (a grave breach of the Geneva Convention, to which Israel is a signatory e.g. article 49 and 147) of some 12,500 Bedouin herders to a purposefully built urban township on arid wasteland north of Jericho. They will be forced to live there against their will, and at the expense of their traditional desert culture and pastoral economy. Prof. Dawn Chatty of Oxford stated that if this Israeli military plan for forced displacement goes ahead, it will be cultural genocide and a form of ethnic cleansing. During a closed experts' workshop in January 2015, Prof. Marco Sassoli of Geneva articulated that the plan, if implemented, will be a war crime.

Similarly, next to Jerusalem's main waste dump in Azaria - near E-1 and East Jerusalem, close to the site where in the 1990s 1,000 Bedouin were forcibly transferred - land is now being massively levelled in order to facilitate the forcible transfer of hundreds more Bedouin refugees. Israel seems to be deliberately attempting to deculturalize the Bedouin by depriving them of their herding culture, especially access to grazing.

E-1 development on land where Bedouin live will utilize all open land required for natural expansion of Palestinian East Jerusalem. By removing the only Palestinians from that region, "judaizing" East Jerusalem to Jericho and making Greater Jerusalem demographically Jewish, Israel is foreclosing a viable Palestinian state. Closing off the only open access to Jerusalem for Palestinian West Bankers (south and north access is already closed off by settlements, the Wall, settler-only roads and checkpoints), the E-1 plan denies Palestine access to its economic heart, religious sites, centre of social life, university campuses and specialist hospitals. A newly leaked EU document refers to E-1 development as a red line that may lead to EU sanctions against Israel. Carrot diplomacy exhausted, the EU now considers sticks.

The implications of forcible transfer into urban sites for Bedouin are similarly catastrophic. They are likely to lapse into increasing poverty and unsustainability, dependent on handouts from international taxpayers which the international NGOs or UN agencies deliver as humanitarian aid. Most indigenous Bedouin have already suffered under Israel's forced transfers: inside Israel in the Negev, where Israel refuses to recognize Bedouin land title deeds, and as Palestine refugees under Israeli occupation in the West Bank.

Even without this planned displacement, the situation is untenable in their current rural locations where planning permission is denied. West Bank Bedouin are not allowed to build, denied free access to education, forbidden access to electricity, have no vehicle access to the settler-only road systems or access to their Jerusalem market and holy sites. They suffer problematic access to health services, water, grazing lands or employment, endure regular, high rates of home demolition and live in constant threat of settler violence.

Women's rights are also a matter of concern in this conservative community. Because they can no longer freely range with their animals, work outside the home or go to market, their lives have been hugely limited.

The Bedouin refugees in the West Bank call for their Right of Return to their lands inside Israel, from which they were forcibly displaced in 1948. If they cannot return to Tel Arad in the Negev, they wish to remain where they are but with planning permission. Their minimal demands are for respect for their cultural needs and full consultation as to plans for their future: preferably by the Palestinian Authority, not Israel's military. Military rule of Area C (60% of the West Bank, where settlements are found, now being annexed *de facto* by Israel) under the Oslo Accords was supposed to be temporary, until 1999. As the support system for Areas A and B (Palestine's towns and villages), Area C contains almost all water aquifers, farmland, road systems, access to markets and border. ◯

*Angela **Godfrey-Goldstein*** co-directs The Jahalin Association [Nabi Samwel], at whose website www.jahalin.org is further information on this subject. Producer of HIGH HOPES, which screened recently in New York, she is an Israeli peace activist and human rights defender

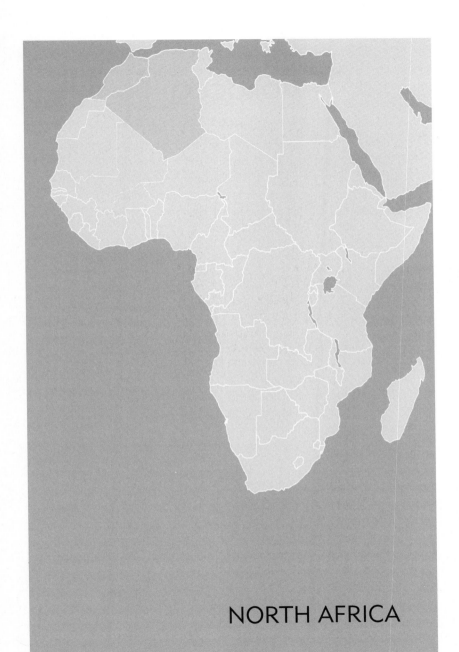

NORTH AFRICA

MOROCCO

The Amazigh (Berber) peoples are the indigenous peoples of North Africa. The most recent census in Morocco (2006) estimated the number of Amazigh speakers to be 28% of the population. However, the Amazigh associations strongly challenge this and instead claim a rate of 65 to 70%. This means that the Amazigh-speaking population may well number around 20 million in Morocco, and around 30 million throughout North Africa and the Sahel as a whole.

The Amazigh people have founded an organisation called the "Amazigh Cultural Movement" (ACM) to advocate for their rights. There are now more than 800 Amazigh associations established throughout the whole of Morocco. It is a civil society movement based on universal values of human rights.

The administrative and legal system of Morocco has been highly Arabised, and the Amazigh culture and way of life is under constant pressure to assimilate. Morocco has for many years been a unitary state with a centralised authority, a single religion, a single language and systematic marginalisation of all aspects of the Amazigh identity. The new Constitution of 2011 now officially recognises the Amazigh identity and language. This could be a very positive and encouraging step forward for the Amazigh people of Morocco but unfortunately its official implementation is still pending enactment of the organic law that would establish rules as to how Tamazight is to be officially implemented, along with methods for incorporating it into teaching and into life generally as an official language. Work to harmonise the legal arsenal with the new Constitution has not, in fact, yet commenced and no steps have been taken to implement the Constitution.

Morocco has not ratified ILO Convention 169 and did not vote in favour of the UN Declaration on the Rights of Indigenous Peoples.

Implementing the official status of the Amazigh language

In comparison with the constitutions of other North African countries, the Moroccan Constitution of 2011 represents a significant and progressive legal instrument for both Amazigh language (Tamazight) and identity. It lays down specific provisions regarding the Amazigh people. Its recitals note the Amazigh identity as a specific component of state identity.

Article 5 of the Constitution confirms the official status of Tamazight, noting that:

An organic law shall set out the process for implementing the official status of this language, along with ways of incorporating it into education and into the priority areas of public life, with the aim of it eventually being able to play its role as official language[1]

However, three years have passed since the Constitution was adopted and the government has as yet made no moves to implement this official recognition, despite calls from the Amazigh Cultural Movement (ACM) to do so. Until such an organic law is implemented, the situation of Amazigh rights will remain in a state of limbo.

Implementation of this official status cannot take place without legal regulation and, until this is done, the Moroccan state will continue to rely on laws that are incompatible with the new constitution, for example, Law No 3.64 on the unification of Moroccan courts of 26 January 1965, which requires the Amazigh people to use only Arabic in the national courts. It is clear that the work to bring Moroccan legislation into line with the 2011 Constitution is not on this government's agenda as we are now more than halfway through its term in office. This means that, in practice, the situation of Amazigh rights continues unchanged.

Civil and political rights of the Amazigh people

The situation of Amazigh political parties remains at an impasse. The Amazigh Democratic Party (PAD), banned by the government, has still not been given the right to exist. The same goes for the people's right to organise and implement human rights activities. The Amazigh organisation, Azetta, was prohibited from organising a training on human rights at Oujda on 12 April 2014 even though its leaders complied with all the legal conditions.

Azetta was also banned from putting up information posters for its 4th Congress in Rabat. This is in flagrant violation of the right of expression and a prevention of civil society's role.[2] Violations of the rights of Amazigh activists continue despite the government's rhetoric on freedoms and human rights. Saïd Awragh, an Amazigh activist, was arrested in early October 2014 at Casablanca airport on his return from the United States. He was taken before the Imtghren (Errachidia) Court on Thursday 13 November 2014 charged with having been involved in the bloody altercations that occurred on 5 May 2011 between Amazigh students and pro-Arabist students at Errachidia University in the south-east of Morocco. Aw-ragh, a former student at this university, was in the United States at the time of the events and could therefore not have been involved. According to the Amazigh association Tiddukla in Washington, of which this activist is a member, it was because of his activism on behalf of the Amazigh in the United States that he was arrested on his return to the country.[3]

This situation has led the Amazigh Cultural Movement (ACM) to protest on a number of occasions. Several Amazigh organisations seized the opportunity of the World Human Rights Forum taking place in Marrakech to show their anger at the marginalisation of the Amazigh. The World Amazigh Assembly (AMA), for example, in coordination with Amazigh activists from Marrakech and from other place in Morocco, demonstrated outside the Palais des Congrès on 29 November 2014, where the World Human Rights Forum was sitting.

Grabbing of Amazigh land

As an indigenous people, the Amazigh have a close bond with their traditional lands. The Amazigh tribes are still calling for the return of their lands taken during colonial times.

The Amazigh organisations have exhausted all domestic recourse aimed at resolving the problem of land grabbing, and this year they decided to bring the problem to international attention. The Confederation of Amazigh Associations (Tamunt n Iffus) and Tamaynut, the biggest Amazigh organisation in the whole of North Africa, organised an international meeting on 19 and 20 April 2014 on the theme of "rights to land, forest and resources". Several Amazigh associations from Morocco participated. The meeting ended with the signing of a memoran-dum on land by more than 100 Amazigh associations, which was sent to the King and Head of Government of Morocco.

This same document was presented to the UN Permanent Forum on Indige-nous Issues by Mr Mohamed Handaine[4], who among other things reported that "several tribes are going to be driven off of their ancestral lands. The 4,000 or so inhabitants of the village of Tadwart, 20 km from Agadir, have received an eviction notice although they have lived on their territory for two centuries".[5]

Despite all these efforts, the problem still remains unresolved. Quite the con-trary, the Waters and Forests Board is continuing to demarcate lands and forests in which the Amazigh have lived for centuries. The government is announcing a speeding up of the demarcation of lands, without considering the demands of people who hold documents proving their ownership. Such is the case in both the Chtouka Ait Baha region near Agadir and the Tafrawt region of Tiznit.

Amazigh language teaching

Teaching of Tamazight is essential for the Amazigh people and for continuity of their identity. More than 10 years have now passed since the introduction of the language into the Moroccan education system but, faced with a lack of political will and the absence of an organic law regulating official recognition of the language, its teaching has reached no more than 10% of primary school pupils. In 2014, the Ministry abandoned even this, claiming a lack of educational and staff resources, an unfounded argument given that "80 posts were given this year to successful teachers specialising in the Amazigh language but they were surprised to be allocated to posts teaching Arabic and French" according to the Amazigh Observatory for Rights and Freedoms in a press release published on 20 September 2014.[6] The situation of Tamazight teaching continues to deteriorate or even be ignored completely within the school system, as for example in the official document of the Ministry of Education entitled "A new school for tomorrow's citizens", which sets out a strategic vision for 2030 in which the Amazigh language is neglected and marginalised despite its official recognition in the Constitution. This document is in flagrant violation of Amazigh rights and an attack on the Constitution.

Information

The situation with regard to information on the Amazigh language and culture remains unchanged since last year. The only Amazigh TV channel in existence has few resources, and its budget does not live up to Amazigh desires for a professional broadcaster that can take up the enormous challenges of promoting an Amazigh identity and culture in the competitive world of information technology. The ACM is continually demanding the adoption and application of fair and balanced Terms of Service that would take into account all the components of Moroccan identity and culture, as noted in the Constitution, on an equal basis. ○

Notes and references

1   See the Moroccan Constitution.
2   www.reseauamazigh.org
3   http://www.tamazgha.fr/La-monarchie-marocaine-s-acharne.html
4   Declaration of the Amazigh delegation to the Permanent Forum 13th session May 2014. In :
    http://www.gitpa.org/web/AFN%20AMAZIGH%20HANDAINE%20.pdf
5   Ibid.
6   http://www.amazighnews.net/20140922993/situation-de-l-enseignement-de-la-langue-
    amazighe-maroc.html

Dr. Mohamed Handaine is the President of the Confederation of Amazigh Associations of South Morocco (Tamunt n Iffus), Agadir, Morocco. He is a university graduate, historian and writer, and board member of the Coordination Autochtone Francophone (CAF). He is a founder member of the Amazigh World Congress and has published a number of works on Amazigh history and culture. He is also the IPACC North African Regional Representative as well as a member of the steering committee of the ICCA Consortium in Geneva.

ALGERIA

The Amazigh, the Mozabite and the Tuareg are the indigenous peoples of Algeria, as well as of other countries of North Africa and the Sahara, and have been present in these territories since ancient times. They can primarily be distinguished from other inhabitants by their language (Tamazight), but also by their way of life and their culture (clothes, food, beliefs). The Algerian government, however, does not recognise their indigenous status, wherefore no official statistics on their demographics exist. Associations defending and promoting the Amazigh culture estimate the Tamazight-speaking population at around 11 million people, or 1/3 of Algeria's total population.

The Amazigh of Algeria are concentrated in five large regions in the north-east, the east, the west, the South-west and the south of the country.[1] Large cities such as Algiers, Blida, Oran, Constantine, etc., are home to several hundred thousand people who are historically and culturally Amazigh, but who have been partly arabised over the course of the years, succumbing to a gradual process of acculturation.

After decades of demands and popular struggles, the Amazigh language was finally recognised as a "national language" in the Constitution in 2002. Despite this achievement, the Amazigh identity continues to be marginalised and folklorised by state institutions, and Arabic remains the country's only official language. There has to date been no law ensuring the protection and promotion of Amazigh political, economic, social, cultural and linguistic rights in Algeria. Consequently, state resources remain entirely directed at promoting the Arabo-Islamic identity of Algeria, while the Amazigh identity remains concealed or relegated to an inferior position.[2] At the same time, anti-Amazigh laws remain in place, and new ones have been enacted.[3]

Internationally, Algeria has ratified the main international standards, and it voted in favour of the UN Declaration on the Rights of Indigenous Peoples in 2007. However, these remain un-implemented, which has led to the UN treaty monitoring bodies making numerous observations and recommendations to Algeria in this regard.

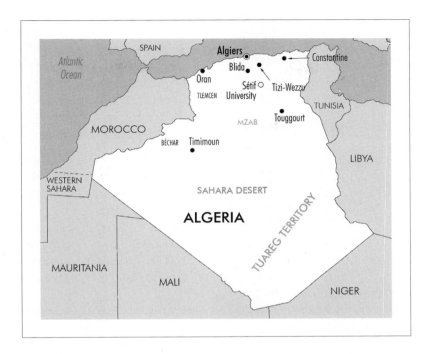

Deteriorating socio-economic conditions

The Amazigh in Algeria are unable to benefit from the natural resources found on their lands and territories (water, forests, oil and gas). In the Sahara, the Mozabite and Tuareg peoples receive none of the benefits of the energy resources that lie in their subsoil, and the water found in the Kabylie mountains and in Chenoua benefits cities such as Algiers first and foremost, with no compensation provided to the local population. Consequently, Amazigh living in rural and mountainous areas survive on remittances sent home by family members abroad. The unemployment rate in these areas is three times the national average. Young people, in particular, seek an escape in the form of alcohol and drugs, exile and suicide.[4]

On the pretext of the war on Islamist terrorists, the Algerian government has sent military reinforcements in particular to the Kabylie region. This region now has the greatest concentration of armed forces in Algeria but also suffers from the highest levels of insecurity (murders, armed robberies, kidnappings). Ransom demands are now very common but there are no official statistics in this regard because the Algerian authorities keep all matters of security highly confidential.

Police violence and judicial harassment

2014 was marked by police violence in the Kabylie and M'zab regions. In Kabylia, the April 2014 presidential elections were widely boycotted and peaceful demonstrations were organised in many areas of the region to denounce the undemocratic nature of these elections. During one of these demonstrations, in Haizer, Tuvirett Wilaya (Province) in Bouira, the police violently intervened to arrest 32 demonstrators who were subsequently sentenced to between two months and two years in prison. On 20 April, the anniversary of the "Arab Spring", a peaceful march of in Tizi-Wezzu was violently set upon by police who later brutally beat up the demonstrators they arrested.

Members of the Movement for the Self-Determination of Kabylie (*Mouvement pour l'Autodétermination de la Kabylie* / MAK), an unrecognised political movement, are systematically placed under surveillance, persecuted by the police force and harassed by Algeria's judicial system. Members of MAK were thus subjected to police violence and summoned to court in May in Vgayet, Tuvirett and Sidi-Aich; July in Tazmalt; and August in Tizi-Wezzu.

As in 2013, the region of M'zab was shaken throughout 2014 by serious clashes between the indigenous Mozabite population and Arab Chaambas settled unlawfully by the Algerian authorities on the Mozabites' traditional territories. According to the Algerian press, the riots resulted in the deaths of some 15 youths and the ransacking of thousands of houses, shops and farm sheds belonging primarily to the Mozabite population.[5] According to civil society organisations, the Algerian Human Rights League in particular, the Algerian authorities have stirred up the conflict by deliberately discriminating against the indigenous inhabitants. An activist was sentenced to two years in prison and a fine of 100,000 dinars in September 2014 for filming police officers looting a shop in Guerrara, Ghardaia Wilaya.

Although the state of emergency was lifted in February 2014, restrictions on freedom remain. All associational activity requires the authorisation of the administration and the police. Consequently, associations independent of the Algerian government no longer dare organise their activities.

The law on associations, adopted in December 2011,[6] is beginning to have an effect in terms of restricting Amazigh freedoms, particularly the requirement to communicate solely in Arabic and to respect Sharia law, and the ban on any relationship with Amazigh associations abroad or foreign NGOs.   ◯

Notes and references

1   Namely in Kabylia in the north-east, Aurès in the east, Chenoua, a mountainous region on the Mediterranean coast to the west of Algiers, M'zab in the south, and Tuareg territory in the Sahara. A large number of Amazigh populations also exist in the south-west of the country (Tlemcen and Béchar) and in the south (Touggourt, Adrar, Timimou), accounting for several thousands of individuals.
2   The few initiatives taken in the area of communication and teaching suffer from a severe lack of resources and a large number of obstacles are placed in the path of their implementation.
3   Law on the generalisation of the Arabic language, Law on associations and political parties, which stipulates exclusive use of the Arabic language, Family Code based on Sharia law, etc...).
4   See for example: http://www.tamurt.info/l-alcool-et-la-drogue-detruisent-la-structure-sociolo-gique-de-la-kabylie,4612.html
5   Mohamed Chaouchi. Algérie. Violences intercommunautaires à Ghardaïa: quels enjeux? http://www.diploweb.com/Algerie-Violences.html
6   Law No 12-06 of 12 January 2012 on associations, Official Journal of 15/01/2012.

Belkacem Lounes *is a Doctor of Economics, university teacher (Grenoble University), President of the Amazigh World Congress (NGO defending Amazigh rights), and the author of numerous reports and articles on Amazigh rights.*

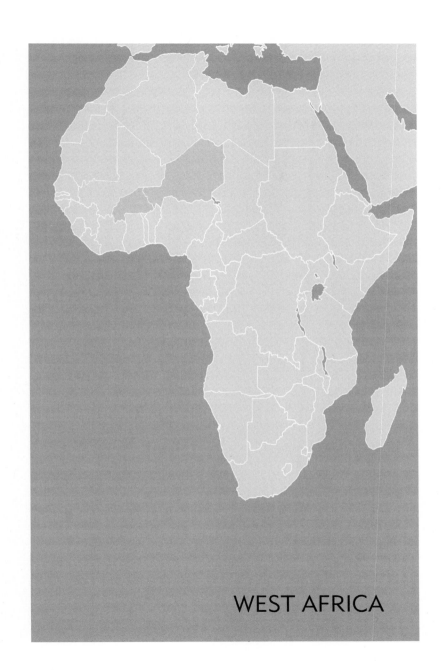

WEST AFRICA

NIGER

Niger's indigenous populations are the Peul, Tuareg and Toubou. These peoples are all transhumant pastoralists. Niger's total 2009 population was estimated at 14,693,110. 8.5% of the population are Peul, i.e. 1,248,914 individuals. They are mostly cattle and sheep herders but some of them have converted to agriculture because they lost their livestock during the droughts. They live in all regions of the country. The Peul can be further sub-divided into a number of groups, namely the Tolèbé, Gorgabé, Djelgobé and Bororo. 8.3% of the population are Tuareg, i.e. 1,219,528 individuals. They are camel and goat herders. They live in the north (Agadez and Tahoua) and west (Tillabery) of the country. 1.5% of the population are Toubou, i.e. 220,397 individuals. They are camel herders and live in the east of the country: Tesker (Zinder), N'guigmi (Diffa) and along the border with Libya (Bilma).

The Constitution of June 2010 does not explicitly mention the existence of indigenous peoples in Niger. The rights of pastoralists are set out in the Pastoral Code, adopted in 2010. The most important rights in the code include an explicit recognition of mobility as a fundamental right of pastoralists and a ban on the privatisation of pastoral spaces, which poses a threat to pastoral mobility. An additional important element in the Pastoral Code is the recognition of priority use rights in pastoral homelands (*terroirs d'attache*). Niger has not signed ILO Convention 169 but did vote in favour of the United Nations Declaration on the Rights of Indigenous Peoples.

Political context

In 2014, Niger continued to be affected by insecurity due to the situation in neighbouring countries: the conflict in Mali had a negative impact on the mobility of pastoralists in north-western Niger, despite the end of the French military operation *Operation Serval*.[1] Likewise, the eastern region was heavily influenced

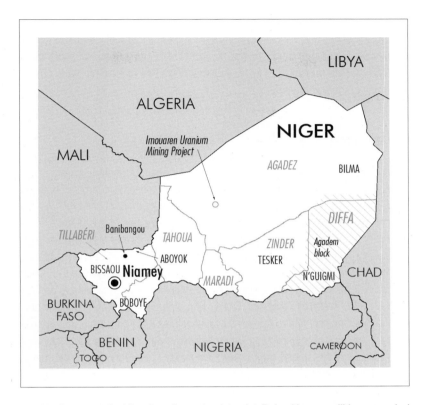

by developments in Nigeria, where the Islamist Boko Haram militia expanded their activities. The number of refugees in Niger's Diffa region has grown to approx. 100,000,[2] increasing the pressure on scarce resources in the area of Lake Chad, and making it difficult for Nigerien pastoralists to move southwards during the dry season.

However, as a response to the political crisis in the Sahel, several international and sub-regional commitments in favour of pastoralists were implemented. For example, the World Bank has initiated a regional formulation process for a new project supporting pastoralism in the Sahel with funding of USD 250 million over six years, and the Lomé Regional Agriculture and Food Agency has been established, whose duties include managing the animal feed component of a sub-regional food security reserve.

Unfortunately, at the national level, the government's commitments are slow in translating into action. No new decrees for implementation of the 2010 Pastoral Code were adopted this year, and 12 out of 14 existing decrees still await adoption. Without the decrees, it is not possible to make use of the new law to protect the rights of the pastoralists.

The human rights situation

Conflicts on the Niger borders with Mali and Nigeria put pastoralists practising cross-border transhumance in a situation of chronic insecurity in terms of both security forces and armed groups that constantly suspect them of collusion with the enemy. This undeclared war situation has resulted in several cases of brutal interrogations of young pastoralists by the military outside of any legal proceedings, particularly in the Baniboungou area, at the border of the Menaka region of Mali.

Similarly, there is persistent and regular discrimination vis-à-vis the Peul community, as evidenced by various cases of community reprisals by farmers on Peul herders in the areas of Konni and Torodi, where herders have been unjustly suspected of having committed offences they had nothing to do with. It is a vicious circle whereby the lack of a functioning justice system impels people to start defending themselves and this, in turn, aggravates the conflicts. The Peul remain most vulnerable to these attacks because they move around either alone or in small groups.

Land grabbing

AREN - the largest pastoralist association in Niger - has largely mobilized its members this year to map all pastoral areas in the Sahelian zone. This was part of a project funded by Danida[3] on the prevention of pastoral land grabbing by agricultural interests, illegal sales of land in the public domain and pollution of pastures by extractive industries. Seventy cases of land grabbing have thus been identified, and will be the subject of further study in terms of their administrative, legal and geographical implications. A lawsuit was even brought against a private operator wishing to subdivide pastoral lands near Niamey. The case is currently being investigated by the court. Finally, AREN intends not only to participate in the drafting of the national report on human rights for the next Universal Periodic Review scheduled for January 2016 in Geneva but also to produce its own alternative report. AREN will also initiate a campaign with members of the Human Rights Council to recommend the adoption of the decrees related to the Pastoral Code.

The situation of Indigenous women in Niger

The Billital Maroobé Network, composed of 400,000 pastoralist members across the Sahel region, set up a sub-regional Collective of Women Pastoralists in Africa and established seven national offices in 2014. They are currently in the process of formulating their action plans (capacity building and advocacy) with the support of CARE and OXFAM, with the expectation that their work will lead to the emergence of genuine political representation for women pastoralists in the sub-region.   ◯

Notes and references

1   Operation Serval was a French military operation in Mali authorized by UN Security Council Resolution 2085, adopted unanimously on 20 December 2012, and ending on 15 July 2014. According to the French President, François Hollande, Operation Serval had the following three objectives: 1) to stop the offensive from the terrorist groups; 2) to preserve the existence of the Malian state and to allow it to restore its territorial integrity; and 3) to prepare for the deployment of the African-led International Support Mission (AFISMA).
2   The Congregation of the People of Tradition for Proselytism and Jihad, better known by its Hausa name *Boko Haram*, is a radical Islamist militia based in the north-east of Nigeria. The jihadist Boko Haram follows the takfiri doctrine, which regards even non-militant Muslims as infidels.
3   Danish International Development Agency, Denmark's development cooperation under the Ministry of Foreign Affairs.

Dodo Boureima is Secretary General of AREN, which is the largest pastoral association of Niger. He is also Permanent Technical Secretary of the regional pastoral network, Billital Maroobé, covering seven countries of West Africa and representing 400,000 pastoralists. Dodo Boureima is himself a pastoralist.

Serge Aubague is Technical Advisor with CARE Denmark's sustainable development programme in Niger (www.care.dk), focusing on the rights of pastoralists and working in close collaboration with civil society in West Africa. He is an agronomic engineer from the University of Dijon and holds Master's degrees in Business Administration, Sociology and Livestock Sciences from the University of Montpellier.

BURKINA FASO

Burkina Faso has a population of 14,017,262 (4th General Census of Population and Housing, December 2006) comprising some 60 different ethnic groups. The indigenous peoples include the pastoralist Peul (also called the *fulbe duroobe egga hoddaabe*, or, more commonly, *duroobe* or *egga hoddaabe*) and the Tuareg. There are no reliable statistics on the exact number of pastoralists in Burkina Faso. They can be found throughout the whole country but are particularly concentrated in the northern regions of Séno, Soum, Baraboulé, Djibo, Liptaako, Yagha and Oudalan. The Peul and the Tuareg most often live in areas which are geographically isolated, dry and economically marginalised and they are often the victims of human rights abuses. Burkinabe nomadic pastoralists, even if innocent of any crime, have thus been subjected to numerous acts of violence: their houses burnt, their possessions stolen, their animals killed or disappeared, children and the elderly killed, bodies left to decay and their families forbidden from retrieving them.

Peul pastoralists are gradually becoming sedentarised in some parts of Burkina Faso. There are, however, still many who remain nomadic, following seasonal migrations and travelling hundreds of kilometres into neighbouring countries, particularly Togo, Benin and Ghana. Unlike other populations in Burkina Faso, the nomadic Peul are pastoralists whose whole lives are governed by the activities necessary for the survival of their animals and many of them still reject any activity not related to extensive livestock rearing.

The existence of indigenous peoples is not recognised in the Constitution of Burkina Faso. The Constitution guarantees education and health for all; however, due to lack of resources and proper infrastructure, the nomadic populations can, in practice, only enjoy these rights to a very limited extent. Burkina Faso voted in favour of the United Nations Declaration on the Rights of Indigenous Peoples.

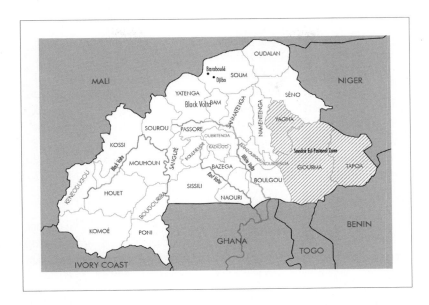

The *egga hoɗaaɓe* and the political context of Burkina Faso in 2014

2014 was marked by massive unrest in Burkina Faso that ended in the resignation of President Blaise Compaoré on 30 October. This discontent was manifested in acts of serious anti-social conduct in which the security forces were often powerless to defend men and women threatened with death by groups of individuals with unclear agendas. Saydou Diallo, chief of a clan of *egga hoɗɗaaɓe*, illustrates the problem clearly:

> On that day (July 2014), the first rains of the season fell. Around 10 in the morning, it was still raining when my son, Harouna, told me that our cattle had damaged a field. I told him we'd sort it out with the landowner when it stopped raining. So my son went over to the farmer's village, as is customary. A few hours later, there were people everywhere... Yacouba my son, a Koranic master, was stoned to death with stones from his own mosque. The crowd also wanted to kill me. When the police finally turned up, they told me to undress to show the others that I was unarmed, old and incapable of doing any harm. I told them that a Muslim should not undress in public. Blows from

sticks and stones all over made me change my mind. In any case, I had no choice: the corpses of my three children were lying a few metres from me, the fourth groaning in pain and near death. Just a few metres further away, 12 other members of my family were trapped in a round, straw-roofed hut. The thatch was set on fire and it began to burn fiercely. It was then that a woman, an elected representative of a local village and a friend of my wife, forced open the door and released the 12 occupants, some with serious burns... And so I lost my four sons before my very eyes, 25, 24, 22 and 18 years of age... I and the other members of my family were taken to the clinic where we were treated for nine days before being taken to a camp where we now live. We have not been visited by a state authority or official since.[1]

This testimonial shows that the Burkinabe state still works on the same old logic as before. When someone dies, there is no reparation. When a farmer is allegedly killed by a nomadic pastoralist, his dependents receive no compensation. Worse still, those who kill nomadic pastoralists become heroes in their community. As for the politicians, (locally-elected representatives, mayors, deputies, prefects, High Commissioners, ministers), they are conspicuous in their absence at a time when they should be considering how best to heal the wounds. They do not care about anyone, not the sedentary farmers or the nomadic pastoralists. And the above simply demonstrates that, even in 2014, the Burkinabe political context is very far from favourable to either harmonious co-existence between farmers and pastoralists or to the promotion of the human rights of these people.

The indigenous movement in Burkina Faso

Numerous awareness-raising meetings have been organised by different associations including the Association for the Protection of the Rights and the Promotion of Cultural Diversities of Minority Groups, in an attempt to link the indigenous peoples of Burkina Faso into the wider global indigenous movement with the aim of improving their security. Although the *egga hoɗɗaaɓe* still do not seem interested in making this connection, their discontent at the injustices they are suffering on a daily basis has led to a cultural isolationism that forced the leaders of Burkina's Peul communities, both rural and urban, to meet during 2014 in order to attempt to speak with a single voice about the injustices of the ongoing violence against nomadic pastoralists in the country.

On 2 and 4 April 2014 all the major traditional and religious Peul chiefs came together in Bobo Dioulasso, in the west of Burkina, to discuss the issue. Likewise, the leaders of the country's nomadic pastoralists met from 9 to 13 October in Fada, in the east of the country, to better understand what was going on. The Peul chiefs and pastoralist leaders have just received official recognition of their association, "Association Finaatawaa", established following the Bobo Dioulasso meeting.

These two major meetings of 2014 seem to have marked the birth of a movement of indigenous peoples that is fairly aware of the challenges facing it. This movement, which is still in its early stages, may well end up linking into a global movement based around the concept of *indigenous peoples*, as a way for the nomadic Peul pastoralists to "to try to address their situation, analyse the specific forms of inequalities and oppression they suffer from and overcome the violations by also invoking international law".[2]

Nomadic Peul pastoralists in Burkina Faso and ECOWAS

The nomadic pastoralists of Burkina Faso, shaken physically and emotionally by repeated attacks from sedentary farmers, are becoming poorer by the day. While climatic conditions are clearly no longer favourable to them, there is also a network of organised cattle rustlers in operation that even seems to be feared by the regular security forces.

2014 was thus marked by renewed troubles (silencing of nomadic pastoralists, cattle rustling, murders, etc.) in which the poor *egga ho aa e* were left to their fate. Not knowing which way to turn for help, their leaders trekked back and forth from the Malian/Nigérien Sahel (where they originally come from) to Ghana, through Burkina Faso, or from northern Nigeria to Ghana, through Benin and then Togo, seeking the blessings of one religious chief or another with the aim of improving their security. The fear is that one day they may decide they have to take up arms like some other nomadic pastoralists have already done in Nigeria. When that day comes, the Ecoomic Community of West African States (ECOWAS) will end up fighting not only the Tuareg and the Islamic militants but also the Peul.

Conclusion

As in previous years, the *egga hoddaaɓe* of Burkina Faso suffered murderous attacks from sedentary farmers in 2014 without putting up any resistance. The difference this year was that there is now a nascent movement of indigenous peoples taking shape, with the recognition of the association of Peul chiefs. Such a movement should clearly be encouraged given the extreme poverty to which some previously great pastoralists have now been reduced through cattle rustling, thefts and murders orchestrated by local farmers, or simply due to climate change. This situation means the *egga hoddaaɓe* are desperate to find a protector and, when one realises that such a scenario works in favour of their recruitment by all kinds of Islamists active in the ECOWAS area, it can but be concluded that, like the Tuareg of Mali and Boko Haram in Nigeria/Cameroon, the nomadic pastoralists may be next. It is to be hoped that it does not come to this and that these forgotten, marginalised, stigmatised and truly vulnerable people will instead find solace in the global indigenous movement.   ◯

Notes

1   Interview made by the author with Saydou Diallo.
2   Indigenous Peoples in Africa: The Forgotten Peoples? The African Commission's work on indigenous peoples in Africa. ACHPR & IWGIA, 2006, p.11.

Issa Diallo is senior research fellow at the National Center for Scientific and Technological Research in Ouagadougou. He is also president of the Association for the Protection of the Rights and the Promotion of Cultural Diversities of Minority Groups (ADCPM), officially recognized by the Government of Burkina Faso since 2005. ADCPM's objective is to promote human and cultural rights, especially for people from minority groups.

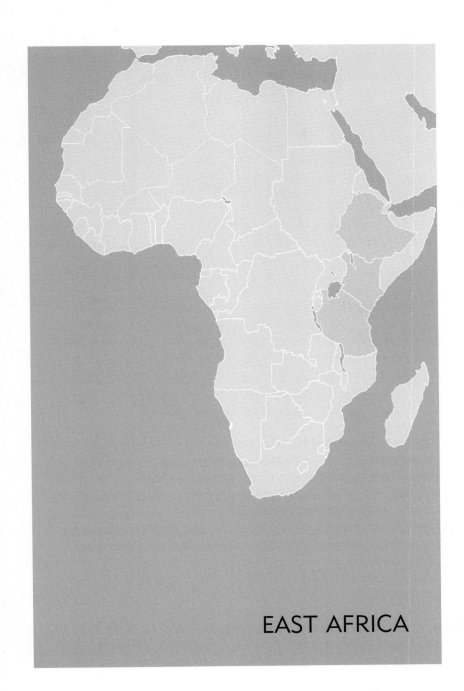

EAST AFRICA

ETHIOPIA

The indigenous peoples of Ethiopia make up a significant proportion of the country's estimated 95 million population. Around 15 per cent are pastoralists who live across Ethiopia, particularly in the Ethiopian lowlands, which constitute around 61 per cent of the country's total landmass. There are also a number of hunter-gathering communities, including the forest dwelling Majang (Majengir) who live in the Gambela region. Ethiopia has the largest livestock population in Africa, a significant amount of which is concentrated in pastoralist communities living on land that, in recent years, has become the subject of high demand from foreign investors. The Ethiopian government's policy of villagization has seen many pastoralist communities moved off of their traditional grazing lands, and indigenous peoples' access to healthcare provision, and to primary and secondary education, remains wholly inadequate. There is no national legislation protecting them, in addition to which Ethiopia has neither ratified ILO Convention 169 and nor was present during the voting on the UN Declaration on the Rights of Indigenous Peoples (UNDRIP).

2014 saw no improvement in national legislation that could offer protection to the indigenous peoples of Ethiopia. Instead, existing consultation mechanisms suffered further decline, prompting concerns from a number of international human rights organizations.[1] This lack of consultation must be seen within the context of wider concerns regarding the Ethiopian government's alleged use of anti-terror laws to curtail freedom of speech. These concerns intensified with the arrest of six members of the critical blogging group, Zone 9, and three other journalists in April 2014.[2]

Land grabbing

A key element in the deteriorating situation for indigenous peoples in Ethiopia is the ongoing policy of "land grabbing" where companies lease large tracts of land

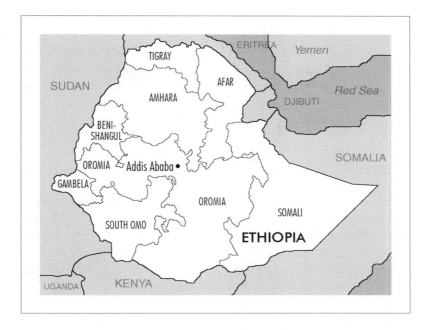

from the Ethiopian government in return for significant levels of foreign invest-ment. Since 2008, when widespread concern about the possibility of a potentially global food crisis increased demand for agricultural land, the Ethiopian govern-ment has leased millions of hectares of land throughout the country to agricul-tural investors, both foreign and domestic. The Ethiopian government says that investment such as this is important for guaranteeing food security. The policy is also seen as an important element of Ethiopia's development strategy because it means that land that is categorized as "under-utilized" can be used productively. However, much of this land is not, in reality, under-utilized but in fact is used by pastoralists, whose customary rights to the land are being consistently violated. Moreover, the way in which the land is used under the new leasing arrangements arguably does little for food security as there is, in fact, little food produced. In-stead, it is chiefly used for an array of non-food products such as flowers or for growing food products destined for the export market. Thus, for example, at the end of 2014, Saudi Star Agricultural Development announced plans to inject USD 100 million into the Gambela region of Ethiopia for a rice production project. Rice is not a staple food in Ethiopia so the overwhelming majority of the rice produced will be sold outside the country.

The Ethiopian government highlights the employment opportunities of such investment for those living in lowland areas, but much of the employment in these areas has gone to "highlanders" who have moved there to find work.[3] The latter has also increased the risk of ethnic tensions, something that has already materialized in the Gambela region and in the lower Omo valley.

Villagization

Part of the Ethiopian government's policy on land management includes the pursuit of a policy of villagization, which aims to resettle those who live in rural areas - often indigenous peoples - into communities with improved access to basic amenities, such as clean water, medical services and schools. In reality, however, such amenities have not been provided, and many of the communities have too little food for the population that now exists there. Many people find that, when they try and return to the land they have left in order to resume their previous way of life, it has been leased and they no longer have access to it. Indigenous communities thus find themselves displaced and deprived of their traditional livelihoods and of access to their natural environment, including access to water, grazing and fishing grounds, arable lands and forest resources.

Urgent need for legal protection and adherence to international law

Efforts by activists and NGOs calling on the government to introduce affirmative legal and administrative measures, including the government's ratification of ILO Convention 169 and other related international legal documents that would protect the most disadvantaged and the poorest members of Ethiopian society, have not been received favorably.

In addition, assessments of the social impact on pastoral and agro-pastoral communities, conducted in 2014, have confirmed the existence of gender disparities, especially amongst indigenous peoples in the South, Somali, Afar and Oromia regions. This is based on an evaluation of the livelihoods and socio-economic development needs of the agro-pastoral communities in the four regions of the country. The situation for indigenous women and children is thus particularly acute, with women having no access to land. Furthermore, these communities suffer from high levels of internal economic inequality – something that increases the likelihood of tribal conflict within and across ethnic borders.

The Ethiopian government's lack of a specific policy or program to address indigenous peoples' special needs and status has further aggravated their situation. Ethiopia is a key political actor in Africa, and the second most populous country on the continent. It is a glaring omission that such a significant political actor has not attempted - in consultation with the country's indigenous peoples and their representative institutions - to develop policies and programs that are in accordance with international law on indigenous peoples in terms of bridging the social and economic gaps.

During the session of the African Commission on Human and Peoples' Right - due to be held in The Gambia in December 2014 but postponed - the Ethiopian government's report had little to say about the status and protection of indigenous peoples. The report therefore ignored widely reported concerns regarding the human rights of indigenous people in the lower Omo valley, and in Gambela, Benishangul Gumuz, Afar, Somali and Oromia regions – all areas that have been part of the government's land lease policy and villagization program. It is important that any such report reflect the reality of the situation of indigenous communities rather than avoiding, or ignoring, their acute development and human rights needs.

Need for a strong movement

Considering the future for indigenous peoples' rights in Ethiopia, it is therefore important to establish a country-wide, inclusive and participatory movement that would be able to ensure that pastoralist and agro-pastoral peoples' concerns are considered as part of key government policies and programs. The country's lack of formal mechanisms within which to consider such issues, as well as legal restrictions on freedom of association and speech, appear to preclude this. This is despite the fact that the Ethiopian constitution - though lacking in clear provisions directly related to indigenous peoples – does include a provision for dealing with the development needs of pastoralist communities. However, despite this, the overall outlook for a nationwide indigenous peoples' movement is promising.

Consensus is underway amongst various groups, with indigenous peoples from different regions in Ethiopia meeting last year to discuss the further impact upon their livelihoods of ever-increasing human rights abuses and land grabbing policies. It is intended that a follow up discussion will be held to update the group on developments in the country as well as to consider how to work together in tackling these. With the support of international organizations, and if the government were to hold a more positive view, the country's marginalized communities would be able to face a more positive future.   ○

Notes and references

1   e.g. Human Rights Watch (HRW) http://www.hrw.org/news/2015/02/23/world-bank-address-ethiopia-findings.
2   Those arrested were Befekadu Hailu, Natanael Feleke, Mahlet Fantahun, Atnaf Berahane, Zelalem Kiberet, Abel Wabela, Edom Khassay, Tesfalem Waldyes and Asmamaw Hailegeorgis.

Nyikaw Ochalla is the Director of the Anywaa Survival Organisation, working on indigenous peoples' land rights and protection of their fundamental human rights and dignity.

Alison Watson is Professor of International Relations at the University of St Andrews in Scotland, and works on issues of indigenous rights in East Africa and in North America.

KENYA

In Kenya, the peoples who identify with the indigenous movement are mainly pastoralists and hunter-gatherers, as well as some fisher peoples and small farming communities. Pastoralists are estimated to comprise 25% of the national population, while the largest individual community of hunter-gatherers numbers approximately 79,000.[1] Pastoralists mostly occupy the arid and semi-arid lands of northern Kenya and towards the border between Kenya and Tanzania in the south. Hunter-gatherers and fisher peoples and small farming communities are strewn across the Rift Valley and Coastal regions. They all face land and resource tenure insecurity, poor service delivery, lack of political voice, back-handed treatment and exclusion. Their situation seems to get worse each year, with increasing competition for resources in their areas.

Indigenous peoples in Kenya are recognized under Article 260 of the 2010 Constitution; however, there is no specific legislation on indigenous peoples and Kenya has yet to support the adoption of the United Nations Declaration on the Rights of Indigenous Peoples (UNDRIP) or ratify the International Labour Organization (ILO) Convention No. 169. Kenya has, however, ratified the International Convention on the Elimination of All Forms of Racial Discrimination (ICERD), the Convention on the Elimination of Discrimination against Women (CEDAW), the International Covenant on Civil and Political Rights (ICCPR), the International Convention on the Elimination of All Forms of Racial Discrimination (CERD) and the Convention on the Rights of the Child (CRC). Chapter Four of the Kenyan Constitution contains a progressive Bill of Rights that makes international law a key component of the laws of Kenya and guarantees protection of minorities and marginalized groups. Under Articles 33, 34, 35 and 36, freedom of expression, the media, and access to information and association are guaranteed. However, the principle of Free, Prior and Informed Consent (FPIC) remains a pipedream for indigenous peoples in Kenya.[2]

Insecurity

The Bill of Rights under Article 29 of the Kenyan Constitution guarantees every Kenyan citizen the right to freedom and security of the person,[3] and specifically sub-article (c) categorically guarantees the rights of every person not to be *"subjected to any form of violence from either public or private sources"*. Yet in spite of this safeguard, Kenyans, especially indigenous peoples along the border with Somalia, Ethiopia and Turkana, have continued to suffer continued attacks from the Al-Qaeda affiliated Al-Shabaab terrorist group in Somalia, the Oromo Liberation Front (OLF) rebels in Ethiopia and Merile militia from Sudan.

Internally, competition among the leadership of indigenous peoples, cattle rustling[4] and territorial and natural resource-related conflicts have raged in Baringo, Isiolo, Samburu, Pokot, Turkana and Marsabit counties where the majority of the residents are indigenous peoples. These conflicts have led to widespread injuries and sometimes deaths and displacement of large sections of these communities. This has undermined indigenous peoples' economic, social and cultural rights as guaranteed under the Kenyan Constitution, the Convention on the Elimination of Discrimination against Women (CEDAW), the International Covenant on Civil and Political Rights (ICCPR) and the Convention on the Rights of the Child, which Kenya has ratified. Development and human rights actors, political commentators[5] and researchers on conflicts have blamed these conflicts and insecurity on internal issues[6] arising from corruption by government officials at border points, laxity by security agencies and the glaring lack of coordination between ordinary Kenyans and the state and its security agencies which has made terrorists, criminals and radicals continue to wreak havoc in the country.

Insecurity undermines the right to education

Pastoralist-dominated northern Kenya features prominently in the country's long-term development plan "Vision 2030" [7] because of the newly-found oil, gas and water reserves and the envisaged LAPSSET transport and logistics corridor (Lamu Port Southern Sudan-Ethiopia Transport Corridor), which will connect a new Kenyan port at Lamu to the South Sudanese and Ethiopian markets. However, insecurity has accelerated in the region and, in late 2014, alleged Al-Shabaab

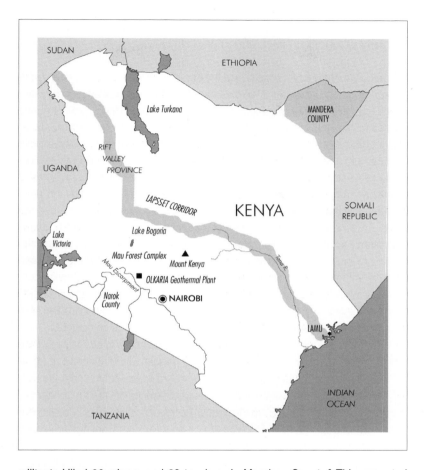

militants killed 36 miners and 28 teachers in Mandera County.[8] This prompted civil servants such as teachers and doctors to flee the region fearing for their lives. With the opening of schools in January 2015, at least 300 teachers staged a sit-in strike in Nairobi and refused to resume work because of the insecurity in Mandera, Wajir and Garissa counties. They are now seeking transfers to other parts of the country where their security can be guaranteed.[9] This insecurity has negatively affected the education of pastoralist children in the region.

Security amendment laws and impact on NGOs

Following the Al-Shabaab attacks in Mandera, the Kenyan Parliament held a special sitting on 18 December 2014 to deliberate the Security Laws (Amendment) Bill.[10] Opposition Members of Parliament (MPs) strongly opposed the Bill, warning that Kenya was becoming a "police state" since the Act contained provisions that violate Kenya's human rights obligations under the 2010 Constitution and various regional and international human rights instruments that Kenya has ratified. Some of the sections of the Bill include: restriction of freedoms of expression and assembly – giving powers to the Cabinet Secretary to designate where and when certain public gatherings may be held; limitations on access to justice and the rights of arrested and accused persons; broadening the powers of security agents to arbitrarily arrest and detain suspects with no possibility for bail; expanding the powers of the National Intelligence Service (NIS) to search and seize private property and monitor communications without court warrants. However, the government appeared very eager to ensure the passage of the controversial Bill, which was eventually passed on 19 December - amid refusal by opposition MPs to vote, fistfights, name-calling and utter chaos on the floor of parliament.

The Security Laws (Amendment) Bill of 2014 also seeks to arbitrarily categorize and monitor Public Benefit Organizations (PBOs). On 16 December, 2014, the Non-Governmental Organizations (NGO) Coordination Board under the Ministry of Devolution and Planning held a press conference in which it announced the de-registration of 522 PBOs. Subsequently, the opposition party (Coalition for Reforms and Democracy / CORD) and the Kenya National Commission on Human Rights (KNCHR) filed a suit at the High Court citing the unconstitutionality of the Bill.[11] [12] On 2 January 2015, the court suspended some sections of the Bill deemed injurious to the Bill of Rights of the Constitution but the government launched an appeal challenging this ruling. The case is ongoing and civil society organizations, the public and the media are following with keen interest. At the same time, following the court ruling, the NGO Coordination Board has been collecting views from the public and NGOs on the best way to manage the NGOs without infringing the rights of individuals and groups – something which should have been done prior to the drafting and passing of the Bill. Since 2013, the Kenyan authorities have repeatedly attempted to clamp down on dissenting voices, either through the adoption of restrictive legislation targeting NGOs and media, through violent police crackdowns on demonstrators, or through judicial harassment of protesters and human rights defenders.

Attacks on indigenous peoples by wild animals

Kenya is famous for its rich and diverse wildlife population. Indigenous peoples have interacted with and protected wildlife in Kenya for centuries, and indeed most of the wildlife conservation sanctuaries and famous national parks such as the Maasai Mara are within indigenous peoples' territories. However, due to a growing population and scarcity of open rangelands for the wildlife, interactions with wild animals have had negative impacts on indigenous people and their resources in recent years, and there has been a sharp increase in cases of injury and death of people, and destruction of their crops, water points, livestock and property. The new Wildlife Conservation and Management Act of 2013, the review of which involved the participation of indigenous peoples, has progressive provisions with regard to indigenous peoples that include: recognition of wildlife conservation as a form of land use; recognition of community wildlife conservancies and sanctuaries, and community representation in the Kenya Wildlife Service Board through nomination by community associations; establishment of a community compensation scheme; improved compensation for death, injury and permanent disability; development of incentives and benefit-sharing regulations; establishment of County Wildlife Conservation and compensation committees and recognition of community wildlife associations. However, while the Act has been in force since 2013, no compensation has been paid out to indigenous peoples for deaths, destruction of crops and property, or injuries suffered as a result of attacks by wild animals. Meanwhile, indigenous peoples have been arrested for retaliatory attacks on wild animals following attacks on people and livestock.

Ever-present land-grabbing menace

The 2010 Kenyan Constitution has a special provision for recognizing and protecting community lands.[13] This provided a ray hope for indigenous peoples who for a century had consistently lost their lands and territories through coercion, displacement and outright land grabbing. Indeed, previous commissions set up to investigate historical land injustices such as the *Charles Njonjo Commission* of 1999 and the *Paul Ndungu Commission* of 2003[14] (which both had a mandate to inquire into illegal and irregular allocation of public and other lands in Kenya) provided a wide range of recommendations, especially with regard to repossession and restitution of indigenous peoples' lands that had been illegally grabbed.

The National Land Commission, which was established in February 2013, has a mandate to manage public lands on behalf of the national and county governments and recommend a national land policy to the national government; advise the national government on a comprehensive programme for the registration of titles in land throughout Kenya; conduct research related to land and the use of natural resources, and make recommendations to appropriate authorities. It is also the prerogative of the National Land Commission to initiate investigations, on its own initiative or following a complaint, into present or historical land injustices, and recommend appropriate redress; and encourage the application of traditional dispute resolution mechanisms in land conflicts; assess tax on land and premiums on immovable property in any area designated by law; and monitor and have oversight responsibilities over land-use planning throughout the country.[15] However, despite the creation of the National Land Commission, redress for historical injustices and land grabbing appear to be getting lost in the intricacies of political machinations and patronage. The opposition party, Coalition for Reforms and Democracy (CORD), has accused the government of being unable to offer strategies and interventions too resolve the political, legal and moral questions around land grabbing in Kenya. Further, CORD has claimed that land grabbing has been "*officialized*" and that the National Land Commission suffers from structural failures in dealing with the land question.[16] This follows cases of land grabbing of school grounds and other public lands by well-connected and wealthy individuals and cartels.

The case of geothermal drilling in Olkaria

In 2014, about 8,000 Maasai of Olkiramatian and Shompole Group Ranches in the Nguruman Escarpment on the border between Narok and Olkejuado counties were faced with eviction following a legal battle with a private company called Nguruman Limited, owned by a South African investor that claimed ownership of the community land. According to media reports, the land grab started in 1986 when the South African investor, along with 14 officials from Narok and Olkejuado county councils, obtained the title deed to a small portion of the ranch that had been illegally registered. Over the course of the next few years, the investor quietly bought out his co-directors and, as sole proprietor, was able to dictate terms, preventing the surrounding Maasai communities from accessing the escarpment.[17] The community is protesting on the basis of constitutional Article 10 on the right to participation of people and protection of marginalized lands and Article 63, which vests community lands in communities –putting them at the centre of any discussions concerning their land.

Around 100 kilometres north of the Nguruman Escarpment, in the foothills of Mt. Longonot, another Maasai community resident is under siege in Olkaria. The Kenya Electricity Generating Company (KenGen) - the largest power-producing company in Kenya producing about 80 percent of the electricity consumed in the country - has been drilling and generating geothermal energy from land claimed by local Maasai as part of their ancestral land. KenGen has four geothermal power plants generating 158 megawatts, most of which are concentrated at Olkaria. KenGen has embarked on expansion plans to send an additional 560 megawatts of power to Kenya's national grid. The target for the expansion is Maasai land at Enarasha locality in Narok County. In 2013, hirelings under alleged police supervision raided Enarasha village and razed it to the ground. According to media reports, at least 2,300 people were rendered homeless, 20 calves were burnt to death and 247 houses were destroyed. It is reported that 300 bullets were fired by the police to disperse and scare away the Maasai villagers in order to pave way for exploration and harnessing of geothermal power.[18] These actions are in contravention of key provisions in the Constitution such the rights to participation and community involvement, to land, sustainable development and benefit sharing. The protests of the Maasai people against these violations continued in 2014 and a complaint was filed with the World Bank, which is involved in the financing of the project.

The case of wind power in Turkana

In Kenya's north-west, home to the Turkana indigenous peoples, a huge wind power project called the Lake Turkana Wind Power Project (LTWP) is underway. The USD 694 million project is being funded by the African Development Bank,

Aldwych International and Standard Bank with the aim of producing 300MW of electricity by 2016. While this project is expected to spur infrastructural development in these remote and marginalized areas and create employment among the local communities, the process by which community land was transformed to private land is suspect –and the extent to which the community was involved in determining the amount of land to be annexed from their communal land is unclear. The communities, who are mainly pastoralists and who traditionally utilize their land and resources communally, are seeking explanations as to how 40,000 acres of their land was hived off and offered to private corporations. This forms yet another violation of the right of indigenous peoples to their land and natural resources as prescribed under Article 63 of the Constitution of Kenya, which vests community land in communities identified on the basis of ethnicity, culture or similar community of interest. This action further contravenes the right of communities to be consulted and involved in any activities affecting them, and to be the voice in the management and development of their lands.

The case of the LAPSSET infrastructure project

The Lamu Port, South Sudan and Ethiopia Transport Corridor Project (LAPSSET) - which includes a major thoroughfare, oil pipeline, railway network and port connecting Kenya and its northern and western neighbours - forms part of the major infrastructural projects being spearheaded by the Government of Kenya in its quest to realize the country's 2030 development vision. Plans are already underway for the construction of the first three berths for the port in Lamu, consisting of general cargo, bulk cargo and container cargo, to serve what is being called the Great Equatorial Land Bridge. On 6 March 2013, the Kenyan President signed a UDS 480 million agreement with China Communications Construction Company Ltd for the construction of the three berths.[19] These developments are taking place despite the fact that Lamu is a UNESCO World Heritage site. With plans being at an advanced stage, indigenous peoples in Lamu - who constitute the historically marginalized Bajuni, Sanye, Aweer (Boni) and Orma people - are concerned that there is a lack of adequate information, consultation and participatory decision-making relating to the project, as well as a lack of social and environmental impact assessments. These communities face imminent threats to their livelihoods, land rights and access to natural resources.

A 2014 Kenya Human Rights Commission (KHRC) position paper on Lamu and the LAPSSET project indicates that the rights of indigenous peoples are at risk and a number of issues have to be addressed before initiating any further activities.[20] These issues include the fact that the oil and industrial infrastructure development should not displace existing and potential livelihoods but rather complement and even boost local capacities for production; and that communities should be enabled to compete effectively in emerging economic activities. Further, the paper calls upon the actors in the LAPSSET project to immediately address the historical economic marginalization of communities and persons, and put in place mitigating measures to prevent the project from exacerbating this. The KHRC paper calls for the protection and promotion of the rights of indigenous communities in light of the pressure they face to "modernize", and in light of their continued vulnerabilities. The KHRC calls for the application of an equality and non-discrimination policy to the benefit of marginalized communities, groups and persons, by establishing equalization models and benefit-sharing standards that seek to rebalance age-old disparities. Further, the KHRC calls for "Public Participation" with regard to the constitutional thresholds of public involvement in government decision-making as part of the broader aim of good governance and accountability.

Implementation of the Truth Justice and Reconciliation Commission report

Indigenous peoples and their organizations continued to call for the implementation of the recommendations of the report of the Truth Justice and Reconciliation Commission (TJRC) during 2014. The TJRC, which was created by an Act of Parliament in 2008 and whose mandate is to investigate the gross human rights violations and other historical injustices that took place in Kenya between 12 December 1963 and 28 February 2008, launched its report on 3 May 2013. Under the specific theme of Minority and Indigenous Peoples, the TJRC recommended that:

- Within two years of issuing the report, the government should ratify the following international and regional instruments: ILO Convention No. 169; Convention on the Prevention and Punishment of the Crime of Genocide;

Convention on the Protection of the Rights of All Migrant Workers and Members of Their Families; Convention against Discrimination in Education; and Statelessness Conventions.

- The President, within six months of issuing the report, should issue an official, public and unconditional apology to minority and indigenous communities in Kenya for the state's systematic discrimination against these groups and communities.

- The Kenya Law Reform Commission should examine all Kenyan legislation to ensure that it does not result in *de jure* or *de facto* discrimination against minority groups. In consultation with minority and indigenous groups, national legislation governing state-sponsored or private development programs should be developed that requires the *free, prior and informed* consent (FPIC) of affected communities and which includes specific guidelines as to how to engage in a process of consultation with communities.

- The government should develop a plan on data collection and disaggregation on minority and indigenous communities, with special attention to ensuring disaggregation of data related to minority and indigenous women. The process should incorporate the principles of the United Nations Expert Workshop on Data Collection and Disaggregation for Indigenous Peoples.

Most of these recommendations, which are central to the realization of the fundamental human rights of indigenous peoples, are yet to be implemented.[21] This is despite the fact that, since 2013, there have been numerous calls from civil society and the official opposition party (CORD) for the implementation of the TJRC report.[22]

Implementation of the ACHPR ruling on the Endorois people

Following the 2010 African Commission on Human and People's Rights' (ACHPR) ruling on the Endorois indigenous peoples, which found that the Government of Kenya had violated, among other things, the Endorois people's rights to freedom of religion, to property, to culture, to the free disposition of natural resources and to development, under the African Charter (Articles 8, 14, 17, 21 and 22, respectively), the process of implementing the ruling has proved lethargic. However, in September 2014, the Kenyan government formed a task force for implementing the ACHPR ruling.[23] This development raised concerns among the Economic, Social and Cultural Rights Network and other civil society organizations in Kenya which are involved in advocating for the implementation of the ruling. The concerns related to the mandate and composition of the Task Force and the process for its establishment, and included among other things: (i) lack of provisions for information on the formation of the task force and lack of consultation with the Endorois peoples or their representatives; (ii) the task force is comprised of government officials only, and (iii) the taskforce's objective is merely to "study the decision", and advise the state on the political, security, economic and environmental implications of the ruling and not to make recommendations for its actual implementation. Within a year, the task force is expected to present the final report to the Kenyan President. While this is a positive step towards implementing the ACHPR ruling, government's tendency to fail to include, involve and consult indigenous peoples on matters that have a direct bearing on their well-being and survival is a cause for worry, and there is a need for more concerted efforts on the part of Kenya's indigenous peoples and the global indigenous peoples' movement to press for the fast-tracking of the implementation of the Endorois ruling by the Kenya government.

Progress of the Ogiek case

The hearing of the Ogiek case against the state of Kenya - referred to the African Court on Human and Peoples' Rights by the ACHPR - took place on Thursday 27 November 2014 in Addis Ababa, Ethiopia. According to media reports, the ACHPR submitted that the Kenya government had violated the Ogiek community's rights to life, property, natural resources, development, religion and culture due to persistent harassment and evictions from their ancestral lands, in contravention of the international human rights standards of free, prior and informed consent. During this first hearing, the Kenyan government denied the Ogiek community's claims and insisted that the Court lacked jurisdiction in the case because the Ogiek had not exhausted local legal mechanisms. The African Court is expected to deliver its ruling in 2015.

Indigenous peoples and the Universal Periodic Review

Indigenous peoples in Kenya have, through their organizations and other human rights institutions, continued to advocate for the implementation of the 2010 UPR recommendations on the rights of indigenous peoples. On 22 January 2015, the state of Kenya will undergo a UPR review for the second time. Prior to the review, the Pastoralist Development Network of Kenya (PDNK) - on behalf of the "Indigenous and Minority Peoples Thematic Group" under the coalition of "Civil Society Coalition on Kenya's Universal Periodic Review (CSCK-UPR)", which is chaired and coordinated by the Kenya National Commission on Human Rights - presented a stakeholder report to the Human Rights Council, which among other things recommended that Kenya adhere to the United Nations Declaration on the Rights of Indigenous Peoples and ratify ILO Convention 169.   ◯

Notes and References

1   Kenyan National Bureau of Statistics: *Census 2009 Results: Ethnic Affiliation*, http://www.knbs. or.ke/censusethnic.php. Read more about the Kenyan Population census in: *Soft Kenya: Kenya population: http://softkenya.com/kenya/kenya-population/* and in: *Daily Nation:* "Census: Kenya has 38.6m people": http://www.nation.co.ke/News/-/1056/1000340/-/11l14rlz/-/index.html
2   Read more about the Kenyan Constitution in: Korir Sing'Oei, 2012: *Kenya at 50: unrealized rights of minorities and indigenous peoples.* Minority Rights Group: London. Available at: http://www2. ohchr.org/english/bodies/hrc/docs/ngos/MRG_Annex1_Kenya_HRC105.pdf And in: Dr. Adams Oloo: *Elections, Representations and the New Constitution:* Constitution Working Paper No. 7. Society for International Development (SID): Nairobi. Available at: http://www.sidint.net/docs/WP7.pdf
3   See Article 29 of Chapter Four (Bill of Rights of the 2010 Kenyan Constitution).
4   Cattle rustling is the terminology often used in the Horn of Africa to describe raiding or stealing cattle.
5   See insecurity in Kenya by Kethi Kilonzo on the Standard newspaper of 29 June 2014 at: http://www.standardmedia.co.ke/?articleID=2000126397&story_title=rising-insecurity-is-a-threat-to-kenya-s-stability; accessed on 9 March 2015
6   See more at: http://www.the-star.co.ke/news/why-insecurity-africa-will-remain-big-challenge-2015-#sthash.BXaHTqWW.dpuf
7   Kenya *Vision 2030* is the national long-term development blue-print that aims to transform Kenya into a newly industrializing, middle-income country by the year 2030. Read more on Vision 2030 at: www.vision2030.go.ke/cms/vds/Popular_Version.pdf
8   See more at: http://www.the-star.co.ke/news/lesuuda-calls-protection-teachers-northern-kenya-#sthash.xGPOmEA1.dpuf

9   See; http://www.businessdailyafrica.com/Corporate-News/Teachers-posted-to-northern-Kenya-remain-defiant/-/539550/2607174/-/kam5di/-/index.html

10 See; https://www.fidh.org/International-Federation-for-Human-Rights/Africa/kenya/16696-kenya-the-security-laws-amendment-act-must-be-repealed

11 See: http://www.standardmedia.co.ke/article/2000148056/high-court-sets-dates-to-hear-security-laws-suit

12 Read more on: http://www.businessdailyafrica.com/Opinion-and-Analysis/Allow-NGOs-to-speak-up-and-look-for-funds/-/539548/2210420/-/format/xhtml/-/ad6ws5/-/index.html, by Suba Church-ill.

13 Article 63 of the Constitution of Kenya: *Community Land.*

14 Government of Kenya 1999, 2003.

15 Article 67 of the Constitution of Kenya establishing the National Land Commission with specific mandates

16 See: http://www.news24.co.ke/MyNews24/Jubilee-coalition-behind-land-grabbing-says-CORD-20150121

17 Read the original article on Theafricareport.com : How African politicians gave away $100bn of land | News & Analysis: *www.afronline.org/?p=25881/* http://countypress.co.ke/govt-probe-how-nguruman-land-was-stolen/

18 Read more on Enarasha evictions at: www.shomonews.com/the-faces-behind-the-brutal-enara-sha-*olkaria*-attack/ and
www.culturalsurvival.org/.../forceful-evictions-maasai-narasha-recipe-tri...

19 Read more on the Lamu births deal at: http://www.coastweek.com/3731-latest-news-China-Com-munications-Construction-to-build-three-berths-in-Lamu-Port.htm

20 Kenya Human Rights Commission: *A call to avert development induced poverty as is a common consequence of mammoth development projects that displace people and alter their way lives*: http://www.khrc.or.ke/media-centre/news/230-forgotten-in-the-scramble-for-lamu.html

21 See: civil-society-ignites-debate-on-tjrc-report: http://www.capitalfm.co.ke/news/2014/05/

22 See: cord-digs-in-wants-tjrc-report-implemented: http://standardgroup.co.ke/lifestyle/article/2000126390/

23 See: http://www.escr-net.org/sites/default/files/Government%20Task%20Force%20%28Gazette%-20Notice%29.pdf

Michael Tiampati *has worked as a journalist in Kenya and East Africa for Reuters Television and Africa Journal. He has been working with indigenous peoples' organizations in Kenya for more than 13 years, including the Centre for Minority Rights Development (CEMIRIDE), Maa Civil Society Forum (MCSF) and Mainyoito Pastoralist Integrated Development Organization (MPIDO). He is currently the National Coordinator for the Pastoralist Development Network of Kenya (PDNK).*

TANZANIA

Tanzania is estimated to have a total of 125 – 130 ethnic groups, falling mainly into the four categories of Bantu, Cushite, Nilo-Hamite and San. While there may be more ethnic groups that identify as indigenous peoples, four groups have been organizing themselves and their struggles around the concept and movement of indigenous peoples. These four groups are the hunter-gatherer Akie and Hadzabe, and the pastoralist Barabaig and Maasai. Although accurate figures are hard to arrive at since ethnic groups are not included in the population census, population estimates[1] put the Maasai in Tanzania at 430,000, the Datoga group to which the Barabaig belongs at 87,978,[2] the Hadzabe at 1,000[3] and the Akie at 5,268. While the livelihoods of these groups are diverse, they all share a strong attachment to the land, distinct identities, vulnerability and marginalization. They also experience similar problems in relation to land insecurity, poverty and inadequate political representation.

Tanzania voted in favour of the UN Declaration on the Rights of Indigenous Peoples in 2007 but does not recognize the existence of any indigenous peoples in the country and there is no specific national policy or legislation on indigenous peoples *per se*. On the contrary, a number of policies, strategies and programmes that do not reflect the interests of the indigenous peoples in terms of access to land and natural resources, basic social services and justice are continually being developed, resulting in a deteriorating and increasingly hostile political environment for both pastoralists and hunter-gatherers.

Constitutional review process in Tanzania

During 2014, Tanzania continued its historic process of constitutional review.[4] Indigenous peoples in Tanzania realized from the very beginning that this represented a very important opportunity for them and so their civil society or-

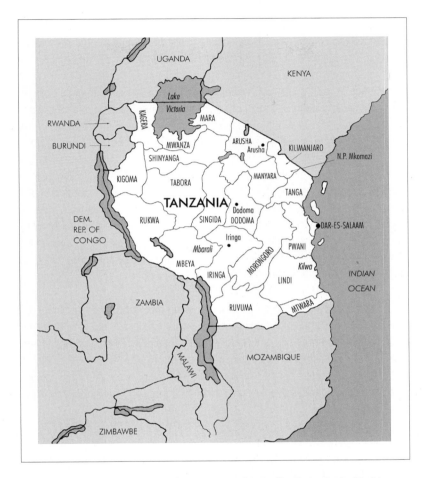

ganizations (CSOs) decided to form a network specifically to deal with this process. This network is called the Pastoralists and Hunter-Gatherers Katiba Initiative (Katiba Initiative/KAi) and is coordinated by PINGOs Forum, an umbrella organization of indigenous pastoralists and hunter-gatherers in Tanzania. The engagement of Tanzania's indigenous peoples in the constitutional review process began in 2012[5] when they proposed candidates for appointment as members of the Constitutional Review Commission (CRC) but, unfortunately, these candidates were not successful. Indigenous peoples have since then been engaged in all stages of the process, in accordance with the Constitutional Review Act. They have mobilized communities to participate in the process, collected community opinions, conducted civic education and submitted written submissions to the CRC. Indigenous peoples also lobbied for pastoralists and hunter-gatherers to be represented in the Constituent Assembly,[6] and they succeeded in getting seven representatives appointed. These representatives have been fundamental in advocating pastoralist and hunter-gatherer recommendations for inclusion in the revised constitution, which will be put to a referendum by the end of April 2015.

The revised constitution that has been proposed by the Constituent Assembly is being finalized at a time when tensions and fears, and violations of indigenous peoples' human rights, are the talk of the day. It is also being released at a time when many members of the opposition parties – UKAWA (Umoja wa Katiba ya Wananchi), which loosely translates as "The Union of Defenders of the People's Constitution" - have boycotted sessions of Parliament in response to allegations of foul play by members of the Constituent Assembly allied to the ruling party, the CCM. Since then, the public have become highly divided over the legitimacy of the process and the final proposed constitution.

Pastoralists and hunter-gatherers have given their input and recommendations at different stages of the constitutional review process to both the Constitutional Review Commission and the Constituent Assembly. The major recommendations were submitted to the Constituent Assembly in May 2014 and focused on recognizing indigenous peoples' livelihoods, making land a constitutional category, protecting indigenous peoples' land and making rights to livelihood a constitutional matter.[7]

What has been incorporated into the proposed new constitution?

Some of the recommendations made by pastoralists and hunter-gatherers have (at least to some extent) been included in the current draft constitution, which is to be tabled for referendum in April 2015. These include:

1. Equal recognition of pastoralism as a livelihood system on a par with farming
The first demand that pastoralists and hunter-gatherers made was a modest one – simply equal recognition with other livelihood systems in the country,

such as farming and fishing. Pastoralism is not recognized in the current constitution and this lack of recognition has implications for national policy directions and the allocation of resources for development. This demand received a positive response as the proposed constitution does indeed now recognize pastoralism on the same footing as other livelihoods. This progress is captured mostly in Chapter Two, which deals with guiding principles, and Chapter Three, which deals with land and other natural resources. The chapter on guiding principles gives the government a mandate to promote associations of different producers (pastoralists included), to build processing factories for the produce of pastoralists and other groups, and to set aside land for their use (Article 13 of the proposed constitution).

2. Protection of minorities

The constitutional recognition of minorities and the promulgation of special provisions for their protection is perhaps where the greatest progress has been made by KAi and its constituency. Article 56 of the proposed constitution defines minorities as peoples whose livelihood is dependent on biodiversity and provides, in great detail, the special measures that must be taken to ensure minorities' participation in political affairs and the country's administration, and to ensure that they have special access to development opportunities, employment and education. The same article mandates the government to provide measures that will make sure that minorities are granted rights to the land where they have traditionally lived and which they have used for accessing food. This is important because it is an explicit recognition of a livelihood as well as an opportunity for minorities to access and gain rights to traditional lands from which they have been dispossessed by other users/uses.

3. Inclusion of pastoralist group rights in the Bill of Rights

Another important area of progress is the creation of a special category of rights in the Bill of Rights section. This relates to the creation of pastoralists' and other small producers' rights. Article 46 of the proposed constitution provides for the human rights of pastoralists, fishermen, farmers and artisanal miners. These rights include the right to own, use and manage land for their own specific activities, the right to participate in the formulation of laws, policies and strategies and to obtain the information and knowledge necessary for these groups to improve their livelihoods and economy. The draft constitution requires the government to undertake land-use planning with a view to setting aside land for the use of each group. Security of tenure for these groups is further buttressed by Article 47, which provides for mandatory compensation for lands that may be taken for development and any other community uses.

4. Making land and other natural resources a constitutional category

Pastoralists and hunter-gatherers fought hard to get a chapter on land included, and this has resulted in Chapter Three of the proposed constitution, which deals with land, natural resources and the environment. This is the shortest chapter in the whole constitution but it contains some important demands made by pastoralists and hunter-gatherers. The proposed constitution restricts the right of ownership to Tanzanian citizens and groups (pastoralists, farmers, hunter-gatherers) with foreigners only able to access land for investment purposes. The chapter is also very strong on women's rights to land, as they are given the same status as their male counterparts. In terms of providing protection of group rights, the proposed constitution requires the government to undertake land-use planning and demarcate land for different groups. It also requires prompt and just compensation to be paid to groups whose lands are alienated for national interests (Article 47).

The general provision that emphasizes that all natural resources are public goods to be managed for the benefit of present and future generations is, however, maintained. The use of the phrase "public" is very unfortunate because it has the effect of placing control and management of natural resources in the hands of the government. Allegedly for the benefit of all, admittedly, but experience shows that this often means denying local communities the opportunity to have a say in the management and control of those resources.

One important achievement relates to traditional hunter-gatherer communities' use of wildlife resources in protected areas. Existing laws and policies outlaw hunting and gathering for all, including communities who traditionally rely on these practices for their subsistence. According to the proposed constitution, the government will be required to set aside lands for hunter-gatherers who have traditionally been using these lands to live on and to access food (Article 56). This could be interpreted to mean that even an area that has been designated as a protected area will be made accessible to hunter-gatherers, provided they have been using it traditionally.

5. Protection, promotion and development of culture and intellectual property rights

Another area in which pastoralists and hunter-gatherers made a great deal of effort during the review process relates to culture and intellectual property. This is because these groups are still strongly attached to their cultures and are differentiated from the mainstream population by these strong cultural elements. Despite this, their cultures are also on the verge of extinction due to the intrusion of popular culture. Their intellectual property rights have fallen prey to piracy and pastoralists and hunter-gatherers often do not share in the economic benefits that accrue from their cultures and intellectual property transactions. Their demands therefore involved constitutional protection of their cultures and intellectual property as well as mechanisms to ensure that they are the first to obtain benefits from them.

The proposed constitution has, to some extent, included these demands. For example, Article 15 makes it clear that one of the objectives of the constitution is to promote and protect national heritage and the cultures of Tanzanians. To implement these objectives, the proposed constitution demands that measures be put in place to protect, preserve and develop the cultures of the different communities in the country.

6. Special equalization fund and equitable development

Pastoralists and hunter-gatherers made very strong recommendations for the establishment of a special equalization fund to address inequalities in development between different parts of the country and communities. The first and second drafts of the constitution did take on board these recommendations, and Article 250 (a) (ii) of the current proposed constitution has maintained the issue albeit not couched in exactly the same language as the original proposal. According to Article 250(a) (ii), one of the guiding principles of national resource allocation is the need to prioritize certain areas and groups that are lagging behind in development. This provision is highly significant for pastoralist and hunter-gatherer areas, which are historically delayed in this regard.

Recommendations that have not been included

While important recommendations made by pastoralists and hunter-gatherers have been taken on board, there are also important recommendations that have been left out. The following are the major gaps in the proposed constitution:

1. The first major gap relates to land and other natural resources. While there is a chapter on this issue, it is of a general nature and has fallen short of including the recommendations made by pastoralists and hunter-gatherers. The management and control of natural resources continues to be in the hands of central government and nothing has been done to democratize this by establishing a National Land Commission to manage national lands or giving village assemblies more power to make decisions over village land. By the same token, the proposal for establishing a new category of "community land" has not been included.

2. Another major gap in the recommendations on land is the issue of historical injustices. Pastoralists and hunter-gatherers recommended remedies in the form of restitution and compensation for those persons and communities who have suffered historical land-related injustices but this was not included.

3. It was also recommended that the new constitution should provide opportunities for pastoralists to access protected areas. This recommendation has not been taken on board. Furthermore, the inclusion of natural resources in the constitution unfortunately does not include the need to devolve management and provide mechanisms for the equitable distribution of benefits to communities living in and around conservation areas.

4. In terms of the management of national lands, pastoralists and hunter-gatherers advocated that the new constitution should place the management and control of land and other natural resources in the hands of democratically-elected representative institutions, thereby departing from the present situation where these resources are under the control of the President and other executive organs of government. This recommendation did not see the light of the day.

5. Finally, none of the cardinal recommendations of pastoralists and hunter-gatherers dealing with recognition of customary law and traditional institutions within the official systems of law and governance have been included in the proposed constitution. These recommendations were made in recognition of the role that customary law and traditional institutions play in the preservation of culture, conflict management and management of land and other natural resources. These recommendations did not see the light of the day despite the fact that culture as a general principle has been incorporated.

6. Despite the gaps, the proposed constitution has undoubtedly taken on board many important recommendations made by indigenous peoples. The next process of engagement will be the referendum in 2015, when pastoralists and hunter-gatherers will vote for or against the proposed constitution.

Major violations of indigenous peoples' rights in 2014

Conflicts between indigenous peoples and other land users continued throughout 2014. These conflicts often arose in connection with attempts to grab pastoralists' lands. These conflicts have led to human rights violations, and claimed the lives of both pastoralists and farmers.

In Morogoro region, the year was characterized by bloodshed between pastoralists and farmers in Kambala and Mabwegere villages. A fight broke out between the two groups, leading to the death of one farmer in December 2014 in Mgongola Valley. This triggered a series of attacks against any Maasai persons in Morogoro township irrespective of who they were and whether or not they had any connection with Kambala village or the Mgongola Valley. The cause of the conflict was the invasion of farmers into the pastoralist Mabwegere village, whose lands are designated as grazing land. Although Mabwegere village has been registered as a pastoralist village, the Morogoro regional authorities continue to deny recognition of the village and the political leaders continue to provide support to farmers from outside the village to invade the village land.

The year witnessed a near fatal fight between five villages bordering Ndarakwai Ranch and the company owning the ranch (which also contains a tented camp) in West Kilimanjaro. The controversy stems from the fact that the alleged owners obtained the land dubiously in 1995. Colonialists during the days of German East Africa forcibly evicted Maasai pastoralists to establish ranches and farms in the area. According to the Maasai pastoralists, when the investor moved in in 1995, he razed many Maasai *bomas* (settlements) to the ground. Ever since, they have been resisting the occupation of their ancestral land. Serious conflict began on 21 October 2014 when the company attempted to survey the property and erect markers without involving the Maasai pastoralists and their respective village councils. On 14 November, the police shot a young man attempting to water his cattle at the only generous spring bordering the property. In reaction to this, furious Maasai pastoralists razed the tented camp to the ground and destroyed 10 cars. Tourists and staff were evacuated and taken to safety. This was followed by mass arrests of villagers, including women. In total 18 people were arrested and denied bail. By the end of the year, 16 people were still in custody awaiting trial.

In another case, the government has been trying to extend Kilimanjaro Airport from 5.6 square kilometers to 110 square kilometers, threatening more than 20,000 people, mainly Maasai pastoralists, with eviction from seven villages in Hai and Meru districts. The pastoralists have been struggling against this threat for years. On 13 February, however, the conflict took a new turn when pastoralists invaded the investor's camp and demanded that he vacate their land. The regional authority has allowed the residents to remain on the land they have been occupying for years while attempts are made to sort out the matter.[8] On 13 March, the government attempted to erect temporary markers demarcating the contested area. The pastoralists, however, were having none of this.[9] The conflict has not yet been resolved, and tensions are still running high as the pastoralists are worried about being evicted from the land.   ◯

Notes and references

1   www.answers.com/Maasai ; www.answers.com/Datoga; www.answers.com/Hadza.
2   The Datoga is an ethnic Nilotic group of pastoralists in Manyara region, especially in Hanang district, where the Barabaig forms a minority.
3   Other sources estimate the Hadzabe at between 1,000 – 1,500 people. See, for instance, **Madsen, Andrew, 2000:** *The Hadzabe of Tanzania. Land and Human Rights for a Hunter-Gatherer Community.* Copenhagen: IWGIA.
4   The Constitutional Review Process was established by enacting Constitutional Review Act No. 83 of 2011.

5   A first meeting of pastoralist indigenous peoples to discuss the Constitutional Review process
    was conducted in November 2011.
6   The constituent assembly made up of the ordinary members of parliament plus 201 other mem-
    bers. The 201 new members included 10 representatives from pastoralists and 10 representa-
    tives from groups with similar interests.
7   www.pingosforum.or.tz
8   *Daily News*, Dar es Salaam, 21 April 2014.
9   *Daily News*, Dar es Salaam, 21 April 2014.

Edward T. Porokwa *is the Executive Director of Pastoralists Indigenous NGOs Forum (PINGOs Forum), an umbrella organization for pastoralists and hunter-gatherers in Tanzania. He is an indigenous lawyer and an Advocate of the High Court of Tanzania. He has been working on indigenous human rights issues for the last 15 years.*

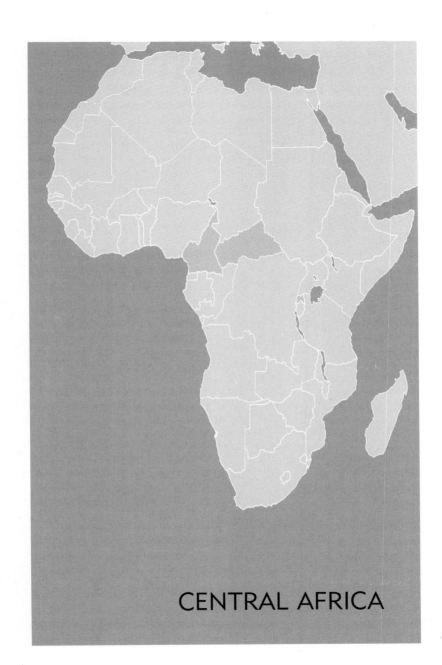

CENTRAL AFRICA

RWANDA

The Batwa[1] population of Rwanda is known by various names: hunter-gatherers, forest peoples, Batwa (or Twa), Pygmies, *Potiers*/Potters, *abasangwabutaka,*[2] or a "historically marginalized people", or "HMP". The Batwa live throughout the country and number between 33,000 and 35,000 people out of a total population of around 11,000,000, i.e. 0.3% of the population.[3] They have a distinct culture, often associated with their folkloric and traditional dance and the intonation of their specific language.

Prior to 1973, when national parks were created in Rwanda, the Batwa lived mainly from hunting and gathering in the territory's natural forests. They were expelled from their ancestral lands with no warning, compensation or other means of subsistence and they now constitute the poorest and most marginalized ethnic group in Rwanda.

Their complete lack of representation in governance structures has been a great problem for the Batwa. However, Article 82, para 2 of the Rwandan Constitution, amended by Revision No. 2 of 8 December 2005, stipulates that eight members of the Senate must be appointed by the President of the Republic, who shall also ensure representation of the historically marginalized communities. However, at the moment the Batwa have only one representative in the Senate.

The Rwandese government still does not recognize the indigenous or minority identity of the Batwa and, in fact, all ethnic identification has been banned since the 1994 war and genocide, even though the government voted in favour of the UN Declaration on the Rights of Indigenous Peoples. Because of this unwillingness to identify people by ethnic group, there is no specific law in Rwanda to promote or protect Batwa rights. Rwanda is not a signatory to ILO Convention 169.

The 1994 Genocide 20th Commemoration

In April 2014, Rwanda commemorated the 20th anniversary of the 1994 Genocide. During the national commemoration ceremony at Amahoro Stadium in Kigali, it was mentioned only once that the Batwa were also victims of the genocide. UN Secretary-General Ban Ki-Moon stated: "More than 800,000 people were systematically killed, overwhelming the Tutsi, as well as moderate Hutu, Twa and others." Earlier in January 2014, the Security Council adopted a resolution that officially recognized the 1994 Genocide as the "genocide against the Tutsi in Rwanda, during which Hutu and others who opposed the genocide were also killed". This official narrative does not shed light on the Batwa, who were also targeted during the 1994 Genocide because of their historical relationship with the Tutsi. An account of the Batwa during the genocide has yet to come to light on a national level in Rwanda.[4]

Genocide survivors

The 20th anniversary of the 1994 Genocide highlights the continued discrimination of Batwa genocide survivors in terms of receiving the same government assistance as Tutsi genocide survivors. Article 14 of the Rwandan Constitution states:

> *"The State shall, within the limits of its capacity, take special measures for the welfare of the survivors of genocide who were rendered destitute by the genocide committed in Rwanda from October 1st, 1990 to December 31st, 1994, the disabled, the indigent and the elderly as well as other vulnerable groups."*

Not only are many Batwa survivors of the 1994 Genocide but the severe vulnerability of the Batwa as a cultural minority has been documented by numerous international organizations, including the African Peer Review Mechanism, the UN Independent Expert on Minority Issues, Minority Rights Group International, and the Unrepresented Nations and Peoples Organization. Studies consistently show the Batwa to be falling behind nationally in literacy, access to medical treatment, land ownership, mortality rates and life expectancy. The Rwandan government must take serious steps to ensure Batwa communities enjoy the same rights as other Rwandans.

Land rights

Girinka Program
The Girinka Program,[5] also known as "one cow per poor family", has revealed itself to be inherently flawed in its implementation vis-à-vis Batwa communities, despite its benevolent intentions to help poor families develop self-sufficiency by providing a dairy cow. In order for families to be eligible for the Girinka Program, they must already own at least 0.25-0.75 hectares of land and construct a shed.

As land is an incredibly contentious issue in Rwanda, given the extremely high population density, programs that require land ownership for eligibility, by nature, exclude that portion of the Rwandan population that has no access to land. The vast majority of Batwa do not own land, nor do they have the resources to build a shed for the cow. Consultations with Batwa communities in 2014 furthermore revealed that officials at the local level were giving out the cattle in a nepotistic manner.

Ancestral lands

During the 20th century, Twa communities were removed from the Gishwati forest, Nyungwe forest and Volcanoes National Park as a result of national and international conservation efforts. The Batwa, who were removed from their land under the principle of *terra nullius*, or "nobody's land", have yet to receive adequate compensation from the Rwandan government for the loss of their land and destruction of their culture and livelihoods, as provided for by the UN Declaration on the Rights of Indigenous Peoples.

Marshlands

Furthermore, the Twa communities have been restricted in their access to marshlands, from where they obtain the clay needed to produce their traditional pottery. As pottery is a traditional occupation that is of historic, cultural and socio-economic significance in Batwa communities, the government is urged to provide an affordable alternative source of clay if marshlands are to be restricted to public use.

Political rights

The "Historically Marginalized" label

Since the 1994 Genocide, the label of "Historically Marginalized People" has been used as a pseudonym for the Batwa by the Rwandan government without consultation with the Batwa, which goes against the principles outlined by UNDRIP and the Outcome Document from the 2014 World Conference on Indigenous Peoples. The Rwandan government is requested to consult and cooperate with Batwa civil society before any policies that directly affect their livelihoods are enacted.

Adequate representation

Furthermore, despite the fact that there is one Batwa sitting in the Senate, it should be noted that, over the last three years of government assignments, no Batwa have been placed in any other office. This lack of representation is extremely disconcerting as this continues a historic legacy of discrimination and exclusion from decision-making processes.

Continued discrimination

There have been reported cases whereby the Batwa have been denied the right to express their concerns over their socio-economic and political rights and have been consequently accused of ethnic divisionism. One example of such abuse was reported in 2014, when a young Mutwa delegate from the Batwa-led organization, COPORWA, who was traveling to a community gathering, was arrested in Eastern Province, incarcerated and tried in court.[6]

It was also reported in 2014 that Batwa homes were attacked in Nyaraguru District in 2013 due to suspected thefts, although there was no evidence in this regard.

Housing and health issues

Bye Bye Nyakatsi

The Bye Bye Nyakatsi Housing Program[7] has significant problems, which the Rwandan government needs to address immediately. Although the program was developed to eliminate thatched roof housing, or *"Nyakatsi"*, in an effort to increase Rwandan living standards, the means by which this program has been implemented have been destructive to many Batwa communities. The Batwa have traditionally built and resided in *Nyakatsi* for practical reasons, such as the separation of living quarters between family members and supplies storage. The tin roofs that are provided following the destruction of *Nyakatsi* are insufficient compensation to remedy the shaken livelihoods of the Batwa. The lack of education on how to construct tin-roofed houses has resulted in collapsed housing and subsequent deaths. Furthermore, many Batwa have sold their tin roofs for money and are now living in makeshift housing or with other Batwa families. There is also overcrowding of Batwa homes, reportedly leading to incest, rape, child pregnancies and increased exposure to disease. This lack of understanding afforded to Batwa communities by the Rwandan government in the implementation of the program has resulted in Bye Bye Nyakatsi's benevolent intentions being overshadowed by its dark realities.

COPORWA (Community of Rwandan Potters, an NGO working for the promotion and protection of the rights of Twa people) lobbied the Rwandan government on the *Bye Bye Nyakatsi* programme in 2011/12, and the government recognized that it had implemented the programme poorly among Twa people, promising to revise its policy. However, the problem was still ongoing in 2014. ○

Notes and references

1   Batwa and Mutwa are the plural and singular forms used in Kinyarwanda to refer to the Twa people, and will be used accordingly in this article.
2   Abasangwabutaka is loosely translated from Kinyarwanda as "those who were on the land first".
3   According to a socio-economic survey carried out in 2004 by CAURWA (*Community of Indigenous Rwandans*), now known as COPORWA (*Community of Rwandan Potters*), in collaboration with the Statistics Department of the Ministry of Finance and Economic Planning. The exact number of Twa today is unknown.
4   Likewise, the Batwa perspective is missing from the "*Ndi Umunyarwanda*" program started in 2013 by the Government of Rwanda with the aim of telling the truth on the history of the 1994 Genocide.
5   The program is funded by the Government of Rwanda (2006-2015) with a view to reducing child malnutrition rates and increasing household incomes of poor farmers. These goals are directly achieved through increased access to and consumption of milk, by providing poor households with a heifer.
6   The reported event took place in 2012.
7   The Bye Bye Nyakatsi Housing Program was launched in 2011with a view to eliminating insecure housing in Rwanda by 2020.

Richard Ntakirutimana is Twa and is the director of the African Initiative for Mankind Progress Organization.

Bennett Collins is a research fellow in the School of International Relations at the University of St Andrews in Scotland.

CENTRAL AFRICAN REPUBLIC

There are two groups of indigenous people in the Central African Republic (CAR), the Mbororo and the Aka. The indigenous Mbororo are essentially nomadic pastoralists in constant search of pastureland. They can be found in the prefectures of Ouaka, in the centre-west region; M'bomou, in the south; Nana-Mambéré in the north-west; and Ombella-Mpoko and Lobaye in the south-west. The 2003 census gave an estimated Mbororo population of 39,299 individuals, or 1% of the total population. A higher proportion of Mbororo live in rural areas than in urban, accounting for 1.4% and only 0.2% of the population respectively. The indigenous Aka population is also known by the pejorative name of Pygmies. The exact size of the Aka population is not known but it is estimated at several tens of thousands of people. The Aka live primarily (90%) in the forests, which they consider their home and where they are able to carry out their traditional activities of hunting, gathering and fishing. The Aka are found in the following prefectures: Lobaye and Ombella M'poko in the south-west; Sangha Mbaéré in the south-west; and Mambéré Kadéi in the west.

The Central African Republic voted in favour of the UN Declaration on the Rights of Indigenous Peoples in September 2007 and ratified ILO Convention No. 169 on indigenous and tribal and peoples in August 2010. It is the first and only African state to have ratified this Convention which, under the terms of the ILO Constitution, entered into force on 11 August 2011. Since then, the country has been in the process of implementing it although this has been very challenging given the war situation and political instability the country has suffered since 2012.

The situation of indigenous peoples during and since the conflict

Along with other communities in the country, the situation of indigenous peoples in the Central African Republic (CAR) deteriorated during the conflict

and has not improved since. Because of their livestock, the Mbororo very quickly
became subjected to pillaging, theft, kidnapping and ransom demands on the part
of armed groups. Many of them ended up as members of these groups. The
armed groups have arms, commit some of the worst violations and are the cause
of insecurity in some towns. They are directly acknowledged as being the perpetrators of several crimes and find themselves accused and rejected by other communities. In contrast, the Pygmies have suffered atrocities at the hands of the
armed groups and many have left their usual camps to find protection elsewhere,
resulting in loss of life and property but, above all, loss of their natural environment. It is their situation that has deteriorated the most. They find themselves
once again, as in the past, under the domination of other communities.

Implementation of ILO Convention No. 169

Under the terms of the ILO's Constitution, Convention No. 169 has now come into force in the CAR. The first report on the Convention's implementation was considered by the Committee of Experts of the International Labour Office at its 2014 session, where it expressed serious concerns at the exacerbation of inter-community tensions and violence, aimed particularly at the Aka and Mbororo peoples. The group recognised the difficulties in implementing the Convention, given the conflicts in the country, but encouraged the government to put in place measures to protect indigenous groups. This report was not made public.

Legal reforms in favour of indigenous peoples

The "Support for the Promotion of Indigenous Rights in the CAR" (APPACA) pro-ject, funded by the Secretariat of the United Nations Indigenous Peoples' Partner-ship (UNIPP) and implemented by the UN Population Fund (UNFPA), in partner-ship with the ILO and the CAR's High Commission for Human Rights and Good Governance, came to an end without any evaluation, raising issues as to whether the outcomes were achieved. The overall project objective was to improve indig-enous peoples' enjoyment of their rights in relation to national and international legal instruments by supporting legal and institutional reforms and building the capacity of different actors on indigenous issues. The continuing and extremely vulnerable situation that indigenous peoples have found themselves in since the conflict, however, is sufficient demonstration that the project's objective has not been achieved.

In 2012, the government officially launched a process to harmonise the CAR's land legislation. One of the major concerns in this regard was to ensure recogni-tion of indigenous peoples' customary and community land rights and get them incorporated into legislation. The process was suspended due to the violence that broke out in 2012 and the ensuing political instability.

In 2007, the High Commission for Human Rights and Good Governance initi-ated a draft bill of law on the promotion and protection of indigenous peoples' rights in the CAR. Civil society and some National Councillors are in the process of submitting a draft bill of law to the Parliament.

In the context of the current drafting of the new Constitution, civil society in the CAR has mobilised strongly to lobby for the inclusion of ILO Convention No. 169, along with other conventions ratified, and recognition of indigenous rights, into the new Constitution. The national transition councillors seem highly favourable to this work and, at the current time, it seems to have been well accepted by them.

Representation and participation of indigenous peoples

Although a number of indigenous individuals, particularly Mbororo, currently occupy positions of responsibility, there are some state institutions and decision-making bodies, such as the National Transitional Council, in which no major action, either political or legal, has been taken by the CAR's government to promote the representation and participation of indigenous peoples. Civil society in the Central African Republic is working on a number of projects aimed at obtaining their involvement in the different political processes underway, such as the Voluntary Partnership Agreement with the European Union on timber trade,[1] forest conservation known as Reducing Emissions from Deforestation and Forest Degradation (REDD), Extractive Industries Transparency Initiative (EITI), etc.

Before the 2012 conflict, some indigenous peoples, with NGO help, had set up associations and were participating in the national and international meetings underway, independently expressing their points of view and jointly signing declarations of national and international import. This momentum came to a halt with the conflict and increased climate of fear, causing the indigenous people to abandon their involvement and the promotion of their rights. Large-scale information-sharing and awareness raising is therefore still needed in these communities. ○

Notes and references

1   Voluntary Partnership Agreement between the European Union and the Central African Republic on forest law enforcement, governance and trade in timber and derived products to the European Union (FLEGT).

Jean Jacques Urbain Mathamale, *is a jurist by training and a human and community rights activist. An expert in forest governance, he has worked since 2008 on the issue of promoting and protecting indigenous rights in the CAR, and been involved in key legal processes on these issues. He is coordinator of the Centre for Environmental Information and Sustainable Development (CIEDD), one of the objectives of which is to lobby for projects, programmes and policies for indigenous communities in their own environment. Since 2014, he has worked to include indigenous rights, as set out in ILO Convention No. 169 and the UN Declaration, in the CAR's new Constitution.*

CAMEROON

Among Cameroon's more than 20 million inhabitants, some communities self-identify as indigenous. These include the hunter/gatherers (Pygmies), the Mbororo pastoralists and the Montagnards or mountain communities.

The Constitution of the Republic of Cameroon uses the terms indigenous and minorities in its preamble; however, it is not clear to whom this refers. Nevertheless, with the developments in international law, civil society and the government are increasingly using the term indigenous to refer to the above-mentioned groups.

Together, the Pygmies represent around 0.4% of the total population of Cameroon. They can be further divided into three sub-groups, namely the Bagyeli or Bakola, who are estimated to number around 24,000 people, the Baka - estimated at around 40,000 - and the Bedzan, estimated at around 1,500 people. The Baka live above all in the Eastern and Southern regions of Cameroon. The Bakola and Bagyeli live in an area of around 12,000 square kms in the south of Cameroon, particularly in the districts of Akom II, Bipindi, Kribi and Lolodorf. Finally, the Bedzang live in the central region, to the north-west of Mbam in the Ngambè Tikar region.

The Mbororo people living in Cameroon are estimated to number over 1 million people and they make up approx. 12% of the population. The Mbororo live primarily along the borders with Nigeria, Chad and the Central African Republic. Three groups of Mbororo are found in Cameroon: the Wodaabe in the Northern Region; the Jafun, who live primarily in the North-West, West, Adamawa and Eastern Regions; and the Galegi, popularly known as the Aku, who live in the East, Adamawa, West and North-West Regions.

The Montagnards live high up in the Mandara Mountain range, in the north of Cameroon. Estimated to number 400,000 in 1976, their precise number today is not known.

Cameroon voted in favour of the UN Declaration on the Rights of Indigenous Peoples in 2007 but has not ratified ILO Convention 169.

Legislative changes

There were no major legislative changes in Cameroon during 2014, either in general terms or in relation to indigenous peoples in particular. Nevertheless, discussions on the issue of land tenure reform intensified in 2014 (see Law 74-1 and 74-2 of 6 July 1974), underway since 2012 within the Ministry for Land and State Property (MINDCAF). Civil society, including indigenous peoples' organizations, formulated and submitted recommendations to the committee in charge of the revision process. This action led MINDCAF to request a study on land tenure governance in Cameroon, which was finalized on 26 May 2014.

This study is not widely known and has not been published. It should be noted that the aim of the reform is to modernize land and cadastral management in order to facilitate the development of agribusiness, infrastructure and social housing. Cameroon's indigenous peoples and civil society mobilized to carry out extensive lobbying aimed at incorporating their concerns into the ongoing reforms. They have not, however, been officially invited to participate in the work of amending the documents produced as part of this reform.

The lead organizations in this process are MBOSCUDA, the Centre for Environment and Development (CED) and the Rights and Resources Initiative.

The Forest and Wildlife Law (See Law No 94/01of 20 January 1994), the reform of which commenced many years ago, has at last been finalized and is awaiting presentation to Parliament by the Department for Forests and Wildlife. This review, which among other things was to take local and indigenous communities' concerns into consideration, was championed by the Parliamentary Network for Ecosystems in Central Africa (REPAR).

Indigenous peoples are mentioned in the revised bill and were involved in its amendment and in the validation of REPAR's drafts. The customary or traditional rights of indigenous peoples, such as hunting and gathering and the sale of forest products, are to a limited extent recognized in the bill.

Nothing was said throughout 2014 with regard to the Pastoralist Code, which has been awaiting adoption since 2013.

Very often these reforms are carried out with a lack of institutional coordination between the departments concerned, and this can sometimes result in a failure to pass laws effectively.

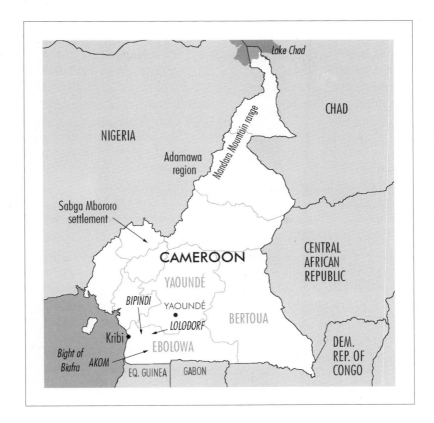

Policies and programs

The Ministry of Social Affairs has committed, as part of its 2014 Program Budget, to update, consolidate and validate the National Solidarity Policy for vulnerable groups, including indigenous peoples. A consultant conducted a background study for this document in 2008. The ministry validated the policy document at a workshop held from 15-16 December 2014. A draft law on national solidarity and a draft decree on the creation, organization and operation of a National Solidarity Fund have been developed for this purpose and sent to the Prime Minister.

This document forms part of a framework aimed at establishing policy coherence between solidarity actions and the social security reforms underway in Cameroon. It is intended to strengthen the economic independence of vulnerable groups and to fight social exclusion. The document is divided into three main parts, namely: a definition of national solidarity, the fields and priority actions of intervention and the management mechanisms for National Solidarity.

Indigenous peoples are mentioned in the document and are considered vulnerable populations alongside groups such as the blind, the physically disabled, those with learning difficulties, etc. They were not involved in the process but were invited for the validation ceremony.

Study on the identification of indigenous peoples in Cameroon

The second phase of the study on the identification of indigenous peoples in Cameroon was launched by the Ministry of External Relations without informing or involving the stakeholders. This procedure appears opaque and has many flaws. Before the second phase commenced, guidance was given to the consultants and some organizations working with indigenous peoples' to the effect that the Mbororo should not be counted as indigenous peoples. This situation is of great concern to the Mbororo but their association, MBOSCUDA, is hoping to denounce this situation publicly.

Celebrating International Day of the World's Indigenous Peoples

International Day of the World's Indigenous Peoples was celebrated on 9 August 2014 under the auspices of the department responsible within the Ministry of Social Affairs (MINAS) and in collaboration with other development partners.

The Mbororo pastoralists and Baka communities took part in the celebrations. The day was punctuated by dances, speeches and exhibitions of artefacts, food and traditional medicines.

Speeches were read out by two indigenous community leaders in which they criticized the lack of inclusive programs established by the Ministry of Social Affairs over the last decade as well as the lack of any effective indigenous involvement in initiating programs that concern them.

Climate change process

The REDD+ process in Cameroon is in its strategy planning phase after the adoption and validation of its Readiness Preparation Plan in 2012 by the World Bank.

The program is being implemented through a National Coordination Unit (CN) under the supervision of the Ministry of the Environment and for the Protection of Nature and Sustainable Development (MINEPDED). Indigenous people are represented and are participating in all relevant activities. The REDD+ process in Cameroon is highly participatory and transparent.

Funds from the World Bank have been made available through the department responsible for indigenous capacity building so that they can effectively participate in the process.

The funds are being managed by an indigenous organization, the African Indigenous Women's Organization Central African Network (AIWO-CAN), in partnership with other major indigenous organizations. The first two workshops on REDD+ mechanisms and on directives (CLIP) with regard to free, prior and informed consent in REDD+ were held during November and December and will continue throughout the course of 2015 and 2016. The workshops saw the strong participation of all indigenous organizations in the country.

Voluntary Partnership Agreement - FLEGT

Cameroon signed the Voluntary Partnership Agreement - "Forest Law Enforcement, Governance and Trade (VPA-FLEGT)" in October 2010 and then ratified the agreement in August 2011. This agreement came into force in 2013. Through this agreement, the country has undertaken to improve forest governance and ensure that wood imported into the European Union from Cameroon meets the established regulations. The position of indigenous peoples was emphasized during this procedure, in order to ensure their increased involvement in all the respective activities.

The 3rd Forum on Forest Governance was held in Yaoundé from 22-24 October 2014 with the effective participation of indigenous people. The Forum was organized by the NGO FODER (Forêt et Development Rural) in partnership with the University of Wolverhampton, the IDL Group (International Development Consultant Group), the European Union and DFID. Its objective was to share experiences and assess the implementation of the VPA-FLEGT in the countries of Central and West Africa. In other words, the forum focused on how to ensure legality and traceability of the wood used in these countries. The main conclusions of this forum were: the need for greater involvement of indigenous peoples through capacity-building sessions, the need to develop an appropriate information system for tracking timber from the felling site to the European market and the use of seized timber in local development projects.

Mobilization of indigenous people

With regard to indigenous peoples' mobilization in 2014, under the auspices of their umbrella organization (MBOSCUDA), Mbororo pastoralists met at the organization's regional headquarters in Mandjou, on the outskirts of Bertoua, in the East region of Cameroon to commemorate the 4th General Assembly of MBOSCUDA. Around 5,000 people gathered to celebrate, take stock and draw up their strategy plan for the coming three years. Women and youths were represented in the new national executive bureau.

Under the auspices of RACOPY, a network of indigenous peoples, forest peoples also met in Bertoua in 2014 to take stock of their activities.

Indigenous leaders from some 12 indigenous peoples' organizations met in Yaoundé during November and December 2014 to learn about the REDD+ process and mechanisms, in order to be able to better contribute to strategy building for the process and also take part in benefit-sharing when the time comes.

Civil society organizations also mobilized in the north-west capital of Bamenda to support the Mbororo community of Bandja, a place on the outskirts of Bamenda, whose homes were destroyed by the Catholic Mission. Strong mobilization and media coverage managed to get this forcible expropriation reversed.

Insecurity and the rise of terrorism in Cameroon

The escalation in terrorism in the far north of the country and the conflict in the Central African Republic have greatly affected indigenous communities in Cameroon.

Of the 200,000 refugees in the Eastern, Adamawa and Far North regions of Cameroon, approx. 90% are Mbororo pastoralists. Whole families and properties have been broken up by the various armed rebels involved in the conflict in the CAR. The pastoralists are vulnerable not only because they live in remote areas with their cattle but also, and even more so, because as a community they have been associated with the Seleka rebels, whose seizure of political power has led to chaos due to their religious identity.

The humanitarian situation has been overwhelming and beyond description. In a press conference, UNHCR acknowledged that the situation was out of control and called for stronger support from the international community and affected states. It condemned the growing insecurity along the Cameroon - CAR and Cameroon – Nigeria borders, which has given rise to an influx of thousands of refugees fleeing into the country. Many of these refugees are now safe in refugee camps.

Mbororo pastoralists are also vulnerable and are falling victim to the Nigerian terrorist group, Boko Haram. Their incursions into the far north of Cameroon to find food for their group have led to abductions of pastoralist herdsmen and their cattle.   ○

Hawe Hamman Bouba, *Vice-President of MBOSCUDA, member of the ACH-PR's WGIP and of the Cameroon National Commission for Human Rights and Freedoms.*

With contributions from **Hassoumi Abdoulaye***, Deputy Secretary General of MBOSCUDA.*

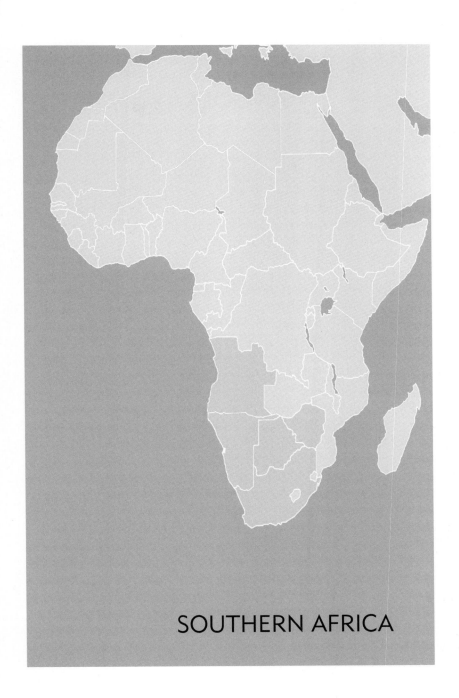

SOUTHERN AFRICA

ANGOLA

The indigenous peoples of Angola include the San and Himba, as well as other possibly Khoe-San descendent groups (including Kwisi and Kwepe) and groups with similarities to the Himba (including Kuvale and Zemba). Situated in Angola's southern provinces, together they represent approximately 0.1% of Angola's current population of 24.3 million.[1] The San number between 5,000 and 14,000. Often referred to as "*vassequele*" or "*kamussequele*", the San are found mainly in the southern provinces of Huila, Cunene, Cuando Cubango and Moxico. San groups in Angola include the Khwe and !Kung, who are also found in Namibia and Botswana, with the majority being !Kung. In general, the San have a subordinate social and economic relationship with neighbouring non-San groups, characterized by discrimination.

While in the past the San, and possibly Kwepe and Kwisi, were hunter-gatherers, most now live from a combination of subsistence agriculture, informal manual work and food aid, although a number of significant traditional livelihood practices remain. These include gathering of bush foods and, in some cases, hunting and crafts. Herero-speaking minority groups, including the Himba, Kuvale and Zemba, are traditionally semi-nomadic pastoralists.

There are no specific references to indigenous peoples or minorities in the Constitution, nor in other domestic law. The Government of Angola does not recognise the concept of indigenous peoples as affirmed in international law. Despite this, Angola has been a signatory to ILO Convention 107 on Indigenous and Tribal Populations since 1976, albeit with very limited reporting. Angola has not indicated any interest in considering the ratification of ILO Convention169 on Indigenous and Tribal Peoples, which to all intents and purposes superseded C107 in 1989. Angola became a signatory to ICERD in 2013, and has ratified CEDAW-OP, CRC, ICCPR and CESCR. Despite these ratifications, a number of core human rights remain unrealised in Angola.

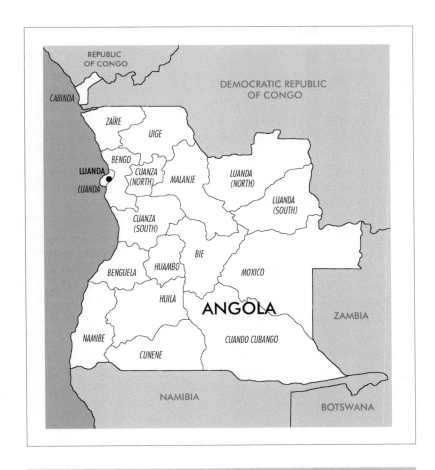

Angola has diverse national media, although direct criticism of the government is rare, and the San have only limited national public visibility through occasional coverage in the national press and television. A few civil society organisations work with San communities, some in cooperation with local and national governments; however, San and other minorities do not have their own formal representative structures.

Limited knowledge of indigenous peoples and minorities in Angola

A ngola's San have a turbulent history, sharing similar social and economic challenges and deprivation with San living in neighbouring countries. The San of Angola have experienced more than 25 years of civil and cross-border war, and many of them fled to Namibia (then South-West Africa), Zambia and South Africa as refugees. Those San who left the country are now resident in Namibia or South Africa, and there are reports of a small number remaining in Zambia.

Some Khoe-San or Khoe-San descendent groups are found in small numbers in south-west Angola, including the Kwepe and Kwisi. It should be noted that although the term "Kwisi" is frequently used, it is considered derogatory by the people themselves who prefer to identify according to the areas in which they live, including "Vátua". Knowledge of the indigenous and minority groups in these areas is restricted by a lack of local resources and capacity, and concrete data is limited or outdated. Other factors limiting the availability of information are the poor level of state and civil society engagement with indigenous peoples on a local and international level; a lack of data collection and media reporting; a lack of dissemination of available information to international audiences; the vast geographical distances involved;[2] and difficulties working in remote areas with poor infrastructure, including the risks associated with mines left over from the wars. This article therefore focuses on the situation of the !Kung and Khwe San groups, who are predominantly found in the south and south-east of Angola.

Current challenges

Reports from the early 2000s[3] produced by the Working Group of Indigenous Minorities in Southern Africa (WIMSA), Trōcaire, OCADEC (*Organização Cristã de Apoio ao Desenvolvimento Comunitário*), ACADIR (*Associação de Conservação do Ambiente e Desenvolvimento Integrado Rural*) and others assessed the challenges facing certain San communities in southern Angola in detail. These reports, and past meetings or conferences on Angola's San, some of which included government participation, have repeatedly identified problems relating to food security, health care, education, access to clean water, livelihoods and the availability of identity documents. These issues remain substantial challenges for Angola's San, and food security, in particular, was a problem for many of them in 2014, compounded by the severe droughts of previous years.

Local organisations furthermore highlight the lack of the San's social and economic inclusion in Angola, the expropriation of their land, and their discriminatory labour and social relations with neighbouring Bantu groups. Additionally, the potential effects of the development of the Kavango Zambezi Trans Frontier Conservation Area (KAZA TFCA), which includes a substantial area in south-east Angola, require close monitoring.

Information on the challenges faced by Angolan Himba, Kuvale and Zemba is scarce, although relevant issues will undoubtedly include land tenure and access to services and natural resources, as is the case in Namibia where these cross-border groups also live. The planned development of the Orokawe/Baynes Dam on the Cunene River, which forms the border between Angola and Namibia, prompted protests by the Himba and Zemba of Namibia in March 2014 due to loss of their territory.

Civil society support

A handful of civil society organisations provide some support to Angola's San, including three Angolan NGOs (MBAKITA, ACADIR and OCADEC) that work both with the state and in cooperation with international organisations, including the Open Society Initiative for Southern Africa (OSISA), Terre des Hommes (TdH) and, previously, Tr caire. None of them work exclusively with indigenous peoples but do include community projects with the San within wider programmes, mainly in the fields of agriculture, livelihood, health, education and community-based natural resource management.

In 2014 MBAKITA, working in the provinces of Cuando Cubango, Bie, Huambo, Huila and Cunene, was implementing community programmes on human rights, food security, preventive health care and education, information and communication. ACADIR, an NGO working on natural resource management, environmental and community issues, has supported registration and identity issues, access to clean water, food security, health and education. OCADEC has a number of programmes focused on San education and representation. In March 2014, a number of Angolan San, through the facilitation of OCADEC, took part in the Regional San Rights Conference in Namibia funded by Terre des Hommes, which focused on self-determination and human rights as promoted by the African Commission on Human and Peoples' Rights, the UN Declaration on the Rights of Indigenous Peoples and ILO 169.[4]

Government engagement and national inclusion

Several government ministries and local government bodies have programmes that involve San and other indigenous communities, while other arms of government refuse point blank to recognise these indigenous peoples. The overall support provided to and recognition of indigenous peoples by the Government of Angola is thus inconsistent and limited, and civil society organisations note that the concept of self-determination is largely absent from the programmes that are implemented.

In January 2014, the Ministry of Culture commented on the "process of reintegration" of the San in Angola, stating that an increase in development programmes, and inclusion in the 2014 national census, was assured. The ministry also noted that assessments and consultations with communities were needed, and that San language radio programmes would be developed.[5] However, in the same speech, a communication by an NGO to the UN regarding San human rights was seemingly criticised.[6]

Also in early 2014, the Ministry of Social Welfare (MINARS), supported by OCADEC with funding from the Embassy of France, supplied oxen, ploughing equipment, seed and food relief to 150 San families in Huila Province, as part of a two-year project that commenced in 2013.[7]

In July 2014, Governor António Didalelwa of Cunene Province acknowledged the food insecurity, housing challenges, lack of education and health care provision that San communities faced, as well as the disparity between San and Bantu groups. He pledged that San communities in the province would, in future, be better integrated into provincial development plans, including agriculture and fishery cooperatives.[8] Also in Cunene, the provincial office of the Ministry of Agriculture and Rural Development (MINAGRI) had a wide-ranging programme with the Vátua in 2014,[9] aimed primarily at increasing food security through agriculture and livestock projects in areas where communities are traditionally reliant on hunting and gathering.

The Ministry of Public Administration, Employment and Social Security (MAPESS) did not report to the ILO Committee of Experts (CEACR) on Convention No.107 in Geneva as requested in 2014. A repeated Direct Request to the Government of Angola has been adopted by the CEACR,[10] requesting further information on government, private and civil society projects, demographics, equality and non-discrimination issues related to minority tribal communities, and that ratification of ILO Convention 169 be considered.   ○

Notes and references

1   However, estimates vary, no disaggregated data is currently available and information on Angola's minority and indigenous populations remains very limited.
2   Moxico and Cuando Cubango provinces in south and south-west Angola cover areas of around 200,000 km².
3   For example, see Trōcaire, WIMSA and OCADEC (2004) Where the First are Last: San Communities Fighting for Survival in Southern Angola or Robins, Madzudzo and Brenzinger (2001) An Assessment of the Status of the San in South Africa, Angola, Zambia and Zimbabwe, Windhoek: LAC
4   http://tdh-southern-africa.org/cms/?q=node/42
5   http://allafrica.com/stories/201402080122.html
6   http://www.portalangop.co.ao/angola/pt_pt/noticias/lazer-e-cultura/2014/1/6/Ministra-Cultura-quer-mais-divulgacao-sobre-reintegracao-das-comunidades-Kohisan,be3040a7-8f31-4a9a-a95b-45a1a675cb9c.html
7   http://jornaldeangola.sapo.ao/regioes/huila/grupo_khoisan_com_apoio_na_integracao_social
8   http://jornaldeangola.sapo.ao/regioes/cunene/integracao_social_do_grupo_khoisan
9   http://www.portalangop.co.ao/angola/pt_pt/noticias/economia/2014/11/49/Cunene-Exito-programa-integracao-dos-vatuas-agricultura-depende-sua-fixacao,26f1e781-76e2-4940-ad3b-c46438fde073.html
10 http://www.ilo.org/dyn/normlex/en/f?p=NORMLEXPUB:13100:0::NO:13100:P13100_COMMENT_ID:3183873:NO

Ben Begbie-Clench is a consultant working on San issues and former director of the Working Group of Indigenous Minorities in Southern Africa (WIMSA), benbegbie@gmail.com

Pascoal Baptistiny is the Director of MBAKITA, an Angolan NGO that works with San communities, baptistinysabatiny@gmail.com

Antonio Chipita is the Executive Director of ACADIR, an Angolan NGO working on natural resource management, environmental and community issues, antoniochipita2012@gmail.com

NAMIBIA

The indigenous peoples of Namibia include the San, the Nama, the Himba, Zemba and Twa. Taken together, the indigenous peoples of Namibia represent some 8% of the total population of the country.

The San (Bushmen) number between 27,000 and 34,000, and represent between 1.3% and 1.6% of the national population.[1] They include the Khwe, the Hai||om, the Ju|'hoansi, the !Xun, the Naro and the !Xoo. Each of the San groups speaks its own language and has distinct customs, traditions and histories. The San were mainly hunter-gatherers in the past but, today, many have diversified livelihoods. Over 80% of the San have been dispossessed of their ancestral lands and resources, and are now some of the poorest and most marginalised peoples in the country.

The Himba number some 25,000. They are pastoral peoples, and reside mainly in the semi-arid north-west (Kunene Region). The Zemba and Twa communities live in close proximity to the Himba in north-western Namibia.[2] The Nama, a Khoe-speaking group, number some 70,000.

The Constitution of Namibia prohibits discrimination on the grounds of ethnic or tribal affiliation but does not specifically recognise the rights of indigenous peoples or minorities. The Namibian government prefers to use the term "marginalised communities", and no national legislation deals directly with indigenous peoples.[3] Namibia voted in favour of the UN Declaration on the Rights of Indigenous Peoples when it was adopted but has not ratified ILO Convention No. 169. Namibia is a signatory to several other binding international agreements that affirm the norms represented in the UNDRIP, such as the African Charter on Human and Peoples' Rights, the Convention on the Rights of the Child (CRC), the International Convention on the Elimination of All Forms of Racial Discrimination (ICERD, and the International Covenant on Civil and Political Rights (ICCPR).

The Division of San Development under the Office of the Prime Minister (established in 2009) is mandated to target the San, Himba, Zemba and Twa, and represents an important milestone in promoting the rights of indigenous peoples/marginalised communities in Namibia.[4]

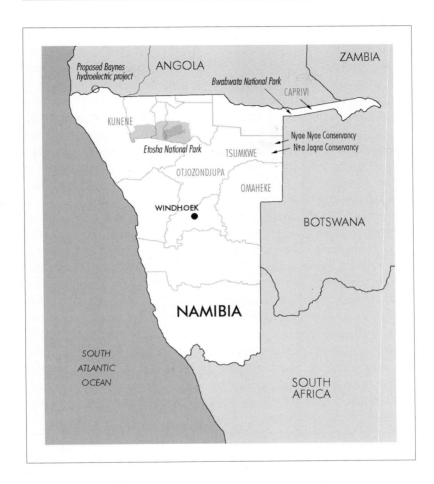

Participation and political representation

The Government of Namibia has increased its efforts to guarantee the consultation, participation and representation of Namibian indigenous peoples in recent years, primarily by recognising some of their traditional authorities (TAs). However, many indigenous peoples, especially the San, are poorly represented in mainstream politics. For example, no San individual is currently a Member of

Parliament and only one San, a Juǀ'hoan woman from Tsumkwe district, is a regional councillor.[5]

Five San traditional authorities (TAs) have been recognised by the government. Other San have no separate TA but fall under the traditional authorities of neighbouring groups. As a result, the interests of these San communities lack any form of political representation. Two chiefs of recognised TAs have died in the last two years and successors have not yet been appointed. Moreover, some of the recognised TAs have faced serious complaints from their communities in recent years on issues including corruption, a lack of transparency, favouritism and nepotism. Nevertheless, San communities still perceive the institution of traditional authority to be an important tool for making their voices heard.

A number of TAs from various Himba communities have tried to obtain official recognition from the government for years without any progress. Furthermore, a group of community members held a demonstration to demand the removal of Chief Hikumine Kapika in March 2014, a strong and internationally-known key player in negotiations with the government in connection with the a hydropower scheme at the Kunene River since the 1990s.[6] The demonstrators claimed Chief Kapika to be a "sell-out" and raised other concerns. However, despite these complaints, the Kapika Royal Family and the respective traditional community leaders decided that Kapika should remain as a chief. Some traditional councillors, however, stressed that they would not recognise Kapika as their chief. It is not clear whether or not these internal conflicts will have an effect on the future negotiations between Himba and the government regarding the construction of the controversial hydropower scheme.[7]

Another representative body of San, the Namibian San Council, was established in around 2006 with strong NGO support. This council currently consists of 14 members of various of Namibia's San communities. It has the potential to play an important role for the San in Namibia in terms of representing their interests in decision-making processes – especially given the perception of many San that their TAs are not fulfilling this responsibility. During 2014, the San Council participated in three capacity-building workshops focussing on consultation, representation and advocacy. It remains to be seen whether the Namibian San Council can eventually become an important representative organization both nationally and internationally. The lack of funding is a major obstacle.

In 2014, with the support of the Indigenous Peoples of Africa Co-ordinating Committee (IPACC), efforts were made to establish a Namibian Indigenous Platform comprising Himba, Nama and San representatives. However, this platform only met once in 2014. It is therefore not yet certain whether or not it will become a strong and united political voice for indigenous peoples in Namibia.

Land

In general, the vast majority of San still have no *de jure* land rights and many have difficulties in securing such rights. The Division of San Development is trying to address the land dispossession of San communities with the purchase of resettlement farms, employing a group resettlement model. At least eight resettlement farms have been bought for San communities in three regions since 2008.[8] Two more San communities in the Omaheke region are supposed to be resettled in the coming years. The farms have already been identified but a lack of infrastructure is hampering the resettlement. Nonetheless, the lack of substantial post-settlement support, the remoteness of the resettlement farms and difficult access to public services, the lack of secure title and the uncontrolled influx of newcomers all remain major challenges.

In terms of San living in conservancies on communal land, despite strong legal support from NGOs over the years, the San living in the N≠a Jaqna Conservancy and the Nyae Nyae Conservancy (Otjozondjupa region) have not yet been able to prevent outsiders from other ethnic groups from grazing their cattle on the land (Nyae Nyae) or erecting illegal fences (N≠a Jaqna).

Education

Research has consistently highlighted the fact that San communities are by far the most disadvantaged ethnic groups in the education system and few San complete their secondary education.[9] The reasons for this include poverty, discrimination, the remote location of villages, cultural mismatch (language, and differences related to cultural and social practices), inappropriate curricula, lack of role models and teenage pregnancies.

The government started to offer free primary education in 2013, in accordance with Article 20 of the Namibian Constitution. Free secondary education is expected to start in around 2016. Additionally, the San Development Programme (now targeting other marginalised communities as well) supported 453 learners in 2014 to enrol at various levels to improve their educational qualifications.[10]

Policy development

The Office of the Ombudsman began the process of developing a White Paper on the Rights of Indigenous Peoples in Namibia in 2013, with the support of the ILO programme "Promoting and Implementing the Rights of the San Peoples of the Republic of Namibia".[11] Two consultants and a Namibian legal NGO assisted the Ombudsman in drafting the White Paper. The current draft covers topics such as access to rights, education, sustainable livelihood options, policy and legislation, gender, non-discrimination, consultation, participation and representation. The draft is currently under review with the Office of the Prime Minister. It still remains to be seen whether or not there is currently enough political will to take the initiative further.

Furthermore, in December 2014, the President of Namibia launched the first National Human Rights Action Plan (NHRAP) 2015-2019, which was prepared by the Office of the Ombudsman (as the National Human Rights Institution in Namibia), with broad stakeholder consultation.[12] The 2012 Baseline Study on Human Rights in Namibia established that ordinary Namibians recommended prioritising so-called second-generation rights under the auspices of the International Covenant on Economic, Social and Cultural Rights (ICESCR). The most pressing issues were identified in the areas of health, education, housing, land, water & sanitation, justice and discrimination. These areas are now all included in the NHRAP. Many of them are of particular concern to so-called vulnerable or marginalised groups in Namibia – including women, children, indigenous peoples and sexual minorities, among others. Although the President of Namibia, Hifikepunye Pohamba, did not explicitly mention indigenous peoples as one of the vulnerable groups in Namibia in his keynote address at the launch of the Action Plan, the NHRAP explicitly speaks of indigenous peoples, in the internationally accepted use of the term. Some proposed key interventions in the sectors of health, education, land and discrimination specifically target indigenous people, among others. The NHRAP also includes a chapter on monitoring and evaluating its implementation.

Advancement of indigenous peoples' rights in Namibia in 2014

Namibia participated in the WCIP and reaffirmed its commitment to implementing the United Nations Declaration on the Rights of Indigenous Peoples, in accordance with Namibia's Constitution.[13] Some progress was made during 2014 in terms of advancing indigenous peoples' rights in Namibia. More specifically, the initiatives aimed at establishing functional indigenous representative structures with the support of the ILO and INGOs (the Namibian San Council and the Namibian Indigenous Platform), the development of a White Paper, and the launch of the NHRAP can all be seen as promising steps. It remains to be seen, however, whether there is enough political will to take the latter initiatives further. The establishment of representative indigenous structures still remains highly dependent on extensive outside support and funding. ○

Notes and references

1   The latest available quantitative data come from the Namibian population and housing census 2011, which suggests that the San constitute 0.8% of the Namibian population (Republic of Namibia, n.d. "Namibia 2011 Population and Housing Census Basic Report". Windhoek: Republic of Namibia: 171). However, since the census only provides data on rough language groups, the number of San in Namibia is certainly much higher (for more information on the challenges of quantitative data in relation to San see Di**eckmann, Ute et al., 2014: "Scraping the Pot": San in Namibia Two Decades** after Independence. Windhoek: Legal Assistance Centre: P. 13ff.

2   The Twa have traditionally been hunters and gatherers in the mountains, while the Himba and Zemba (also written Tjimba) are cattle breeders and small-scale agriculturalists (see http://www.norad.no/en/tools-and-publications/publications/reviews-from-organisations/publication?key=403144).

3   The government defines "indigenous" by reference to European colonialism.

4   It was preceded by the San Development Programme (SDP, established in 2004). In 2007, the SDP's mandate was expanded to cover other marginalised communities as well as the San (the Twa, Zemba and Himba).

5   As of 21 March 2015, a Juǀ'hoansi from Tsumkwe East, ǀUiǀoǀo Royal will be a Member of Parliament again, see "Die 96 Mitglieder des sechsten Parlamentes seit der Unabhaengigkeit", Allgemeine Zeitung, Namibia, 3.12.2014, p. 7.

6   For more information on the planned hydropower scheme, see The Indigenous World 2014, p. 466 (IWGIA 2014).

7   "Chief Kapika retains his throne after backing from paternal line", The Namibian, 14.5.2014.

8   **Republic of Namibia, 2014**: Statement at the World Conference on Indigenous Peoples (WCIP), United Nations, NY, 22-23 September 2014.

9   See, for example, the **Ministry of Education, Namibia (Ed.), 2010**: EMIS (Education Management Information system). Windhoek.

10 **Republic of Namibia, 2014**: *Statement at the World Conference on Indigenous Peoples (WCIP)*, United Nations, NY, 22-23 September 2014.
11 The Namibia component of the Indigenous Peoples Programme under the 2008/12 partnership programme of the Spanish Agency for International Development Cooperation and the International Labour Organization, which was extended until 2014.
12 **Republic of Namibia, 2014**: *National Human Rights Action Plan 2015-2019*. Windhoek: Republic of Namibia.
13 **Republic of Namibia, 2014**: *Statement at the World Conference on Indigenous Peoples (WCIP)*, United Nations, NY, 22-23 September 2014.

Ute Dieckmann *is research coordinator at the Land Environment and Development Project of the Legal Assistance Centre in Namibia. Her research over the last decade has focused on San and land reform in Namibia. She coordinated the reassessment of the status of San in Namibia and is currently assisting with the capacity building of the Namibian San Council.*

ZIMBABWE

While the Government of Zimbabwe does not recognise any specific groups as indigenous to the country, two peoples self-identify as indigenous: the Tshwa (Tyua, Cuaa) San found in western Zimbabwe, and the Doma (Vadema) of north-central Zimbabwe. Population estimates indicate there are 2,600 Tshwa and 1,050 Doma in Zimbabwe, approximately 0.03% of the country's population.

The Tshwa and Doma have histories of foraging and continue to rely to a limited extent on wild plants, animals and insect resources. Most households tend to have diversified economies, often working for members of other groups. Many Tshwa and Doma live below the official poverty line and together make up some of the poorest people in the country. While available socio-economic data on Tshwa communities has increased (baseline data collected in 2013), up-to-date information on the Doma is very limited. Often referred to by the derogatory term of "Ostrich People" due to the relatively high incidence of ectrodactyl foot malformation within their population, reports suggest the Doma face similar discrimination, food insecurity and lack of access to social services as the San.[1]

Zimbabwe has no specific laws on indigenous peoples' rights. However the "Koisan" language is included in the Constitution as one of 16 official languages, and there is some recognition within government of the need for more information and improved approaches to minorities. Realisation of core human rights in Zimbabwe continues to be challenging. Zimbabwe is a signatory to the CERD, CRC, CEDAW, ICCPR and ICESCR; reporting on these conventions is largely overdue but there have been recent efforts to meet requirements. In recent years, Zimbabwe has also participated in the United Nation's Universal Periodic Review (UPR) process. Zimbabwe voted in favour of the adoption of the United Nations Declaration on the Rights of Indigenous Peoples (UNDRIP) but, as with other African states, with the exception of the Central African Republic, Zimbabwe has not adopted ILO Convention No. 169.

Recognition, policy and programmes

The terms "indigenous", "indigeneity" and "indigenisation" are widely utilised by the Government of Zimbabwe when referring to Zimbabweans who were considered disadvantaged before independence in April 1980. The San and Doma are not identified as indigenous peoples as such but are referred to as part of the category of "marginalised persons, groups and communities" in government documents. Awareness of minority groups in Zimbabwe has grown in previous years, although political and economic barriers persist as key factors in limiting effective engagement. None of the 2014 UPR mid-term reports therefore mentioned the issues facing San or Doma, or other minorities specifically, other than to say that access to justice has been improved through the provision of a new court house in Tsholotsho.[2]

In late 2013, a study was carried out on by Ben Begbie-Clench, Robert Hitchcock and Ashton Murwira on the San in Tsholotsho District, Matabeleland North Province, and this report was circulated to the Zimbabwe government in 2014. Support for this work was provided by the Ministry of Local Government, Public Works and National Housing and the Ministry of Primary and Secondary Education.[3] Responses were obtained from several ministries, which are in the process of following up on recommendations made. The finalised report, funded by IWGIA and OSISA (Open Society Initiative of Southern Africa), will be available in early 2015.

While the concept of indigenous peoples is not included in the Zimbabwe Constitution of 2013, some sections relate to indigenous and minority groups. The government carried out limited work in 2014 on the protection and promotion of "indigenous knowledge systems, including knowledge of the medicinal and other properties of animal and plant life", as described in the revised Zimbabwean Constitution.

The government also continues to maintain that it will promote the teaching of the "Koisan" language as one of the 16 official languages, as stipulated in the Constitution.[4] Planning for increased provision of educational materials in mother tongues was carried out with support from UNICEF and other donors, although an orthography has yet to be developed for Tshwao. Efforts to implement the teaching and recording of the critically endangered Tshwao language have been made

almost solely by local NGOs and community associations, supported by University of Zimbabwe linguists.[5]

Livelihoods and food security

The extreme poverty of the San persisted throughout 2014,[6] and was exacerbated by severe flooding in January and February in Tsholotsho District, where the majority of the Tshwa San reside. The flooding, which occurred after heavy rain caused the Gariya Dam to overflow and the Gwayi and Zumbani rivers to burst their banks, destroyed houses and crops, displacing over 400 families in the area. The allegedly delayed and limited response by the Zimbabwe government was criticized heavily, and media reports indicated that some families were still living in tents in October. Also in October, the international NGO, Médecins Sans Frontières (MSF), announced the handover of its 14-year HIV/AIDS programme in Tsholotsho District to the Ministry of Health. MSF had provided a range of critical support and specific programmes for the Tshwa over the preceding years.

Unconfirmed media reports in July highlighted apparently severe food insecu-rity among San in Tsholotsho District. The Tshwa have a marked reliance on food relief, provided in the majority by NGOs, with substantial additional sources from small scale-agriculture, wild plants and insects. However, the provision of tools and advice for local agriculture has remained limited for the San in Tsholotsho and this, coupled with unreliable deliveries of food relief and limited access to natural resources, has contributed to low levels of food security.

Government and NGO projects in Tsholotsho District, including CAMPFIRE (Communal Areas Management Programme for Indigenous Resources), have had some albeit relatively minor effects on income levels in a few remote com-munities.[7]

Resettlement and judicial issues

An unknown number of San, Ndebele and Kalanga households were moved away from the southern boundary of Hwange National Park in September 2013, in response to issues of cyanide-related deaths of elephants and other animals in southern Hwange and areas to the south of the park (see *The Indigenous World 2014*).

In November 2014, some 22 people were arrested, tried and jailed for in-volvement in the 2013 cyanide poisoning, at least two of whom were San.[8] One Tshwa San received a US$200,000 fine and a 16-year prison sentence with la-bour, as compared to lighter jail sentences, fines and acquittals for members of other groups. There are indications of a high level of involvement on the part of government officials in the alleged poaching rings, which were involved in the killing of elephants, rhinoceros and other high value animals in Zimbabwe in 2014.[9] The Minister of Environment, Water and Climate made a statement in the National Assembly on 27 August 2014 stating that anti-poaching operations had been stepped up in and around Hwange National Park.[10]

Limited impact of government programmes and policies

The Zimbabwe government espouses what it terms "indigenisation", which means, in effect, localization, empowerment and expansion of economic opportunities for all Zimbabwean groups considered disadvantaged before independence, in line with the *Indigenisation and Economic Empowerment Act* (IEEA). The government's indigenisation policy is aimed in part at expanding employment and income-generating opportunities for youth and marginalised groups. However, this policy has had relatively little impact in Tsholotsho District or in the Zambezi Valley where the Doma reside,[11] both groups with high unemployment and low income levels. The Fast Track Land Reform process in Zimbabwe, which was touted by the government as enhancing access to land by marginalised groups, had few direct impacts on the Tshwa and Doma in 2014.

Indigenous language, culture and identity issues

Tshwao is part of the Eastern Kalahari Khoe group of languages, and is relatively little spoken. In August, Tshwao language activist, Banini Moyo, passed away, further reducing the small number of Zimbabwean San who speak the Tshwao language fluently. Some work has been done to promote the Tshwao language by the Creative Arts and Educational Development Association (CAEDA), including through International Mother Language Day in Dlamini, Tsholotsho on 21 February[12] in which the Tshwa San participated.

Meetings on indigenous issues

A regional San planning meeting was held in Bulawayo from 25-27 June 2014, including representatives from the Tshwa community, and organised by the Southern African Development Community and several NGOs. A Working Group of Indigenous Minorities in Southern Africa (WIMSA)/Southern African Development Community Council of Non-Governmental Organisations (SADC-CNGO) discussion of indigenous issues also took place in Bulawayo in June 2014.

There were issues raised about San and other indigenous groups' human rights at a Southern African Development Community (SADC) side event in Harare on 28 July 2014, attended by the Open Society Initiative for Southern Africa (OSISA) and other non-government organisations, including the Tsoro-o-tso San Development Trust.

Visits were paid to western Zimbabwe by OSISA in September-October 2014 in which discussions were held regarding assistance for the Tsoro-o-tso San Development Trust and San community development and empowerment activities.

In July 2014, a representative of the Tshwa community, Christopher Dube, attended the launch of "United Nations Declaration on the Rights of Indigenous Peoples: A Manual for National Human Rights Institutions" in Cape Town, South Africa. This meeting and its follow-ups had an impact on the Tsholotsho San in that connections with international-level activities on human rights were strengthened. No San or Zimbabwe government representatives took part in May's 13th United Nations Permanent Forum on Indigenous Issues (UNPFII) meeting in New York.

Relevance of the 2014 World Conference on Indigenous Peoples

There were a number of issues discussed at the WCIP in New York in September which were relevant to Zimbabwe, including civil and political rights, the right to Free, Prior and Informed Consent (FPIC), land rights, the right to development, the right to health, cultural rights including the right to learn and speak mother tongue languages, and the right to education. Neither Zimbabwe nor any Zimbabwean indigenous representatives took part in the World Conference on Indigenous Peoples, although there were discussions sponsored by NGOs at the local level in western Zimbabwe on some of the issues raised at the conference, including issues associated with development, land and resource access, and intellectual property rights.   ○

Notes and references

1   https://www.newsday.co.zw/2014/06/21/relief-doma-people/
2   http://www.hrforumzim.org/news/zim-civil-society-organisations-mid-term-report-of-the-universal-periodic-review-process/
3   **Hitchcock, Robert K., Ben Begbie-Clench, and Ashton Murwira, 2014a:** *The San of Zimbabwe: An Assessment Report.* Report to the Government of Zimbabwe (GOZ), the Open Society Initiative of Southern Africa (OSISA), and the International Work Group for Indigenous Affairs (IWGIA).
4   This effort has been called "half-hearted"; see **Maseko, Busani and Noziziwe Dlhamini, 2014:** Mother Tongue Language Instruction for Lower Primary School Level in Zimbabwe: A Half-hearted Commitment to the Development of her Indigenous Languages, *Journal of Education and Practice* 5(6):59-65.

5   Tshwao language cultural and language days were held several times in 2014 by the Tsoto-o-tso San Development Trust and the Creative Arts and Educational Development Association in Tsholotsho and Bulalima-Mangwe districts.

6   See **Zhou, Mangarai, 2014:** The Persistence of Extreme Poverty among Ethnic Minorities in Zimbabwe: A Case of the San Community in Tsholotsho District, Matabeleland North. BA Dissertation, Development Studies, Midlands State University, Zimbabwe and **Hitchcock, Robert K., Ben Begbie-Clench, and Ashton Murwira, 2014:** Indigenous Space, "Indigenisation", and Social Boundaries among the Tshwa San of Western Zimbabwe. Paper presented at the Association of Social Anthropologists of the United Kingdom and Commonwealth (ASA) Conference No. 14, University of Edinburgh, Edinburgh, United Kingdom, 19 - 22 June 2014.

7   There were reports by community leaders that CAMPFIRE programmes did not distribute benefits widely to communities in western Tsholotsho in 2014.

8   **Mabuko, N., V. Muphoshi, T. Tarakini, E. Gandiwa, S. Vengesayi, and E. Makuwe, 2014:** Cyanide Poisoning and African Elephant Mortality in Hwange National Park, Zimbabwe, A Preliminary Assessment. *Pachyderm* 55:92-94; **Gogo, Jeffrey, 2014:** Anti-Poaching Efforts under Pressure from Corruption. *The Herald*, 10 November 2014.

9   **Gogo, Jeffrey, 2014:** Anti-Poaching Efforts under Pressure from Corruption. *The Herald*, 10 November 2014.

10   Statement by Minister Kasukuwere, Minister of Environment, Water, and Climate in the Parliament of Zimbabwe, 27 August 2014.

11   See **Machinya, Johannes, 2014:** The Role of the Indigenisation policy in Community Development : A Case of the Zvishavane Community Share Ownership Trust, Zvishavane District, Zimbabwe. MA thesis, University of Witwatersrand, Johannesburg, South Africa.

12   **Ndlovu, Davy, 2014:** *In Their Own Words: A Contemporary History of the Lost and Forgotten San People in Zimbabwe.* Revised edition. Dlamini, Zimbabwe: Creative Arts and Educational Development Association.

Ben Begbie-Clench *is a consultant working on San issues and former director of the Working Group of Indigenous Minorities in Southern Africa (WIMSA), benbegbie@gmail.com*

BOTSWANA

The Botswana government does not recognize any specific ethnic groups as indigenous to the country, maintaining instead that all citizens of the country are indigenous. However, 3.3% of the population identifies as belonging to indigenous groups, including the San (known in Botswana as the Basarwa) who, in July 2014, numbered some 61,000. In the south of the country are the Balala, who number some 1,700 and the Nama, a Khoekhoe-speaking people who number 2,100. The majority of the San, Nama and Balala reside in the Kalahari Desert region of Botswana. The San in Botswana were traditionally hunter-gatherers but nowadays the vast majority consists of small-scale agro-pastoralists, cattle post workers, or people with mixed economies who reside both in rural and urban areas. They are sub-divided into a large number of named groups, most of whom speak their own mother tongue in addition to other languages. These groups include the Ju/'hoansi, Bugakhwe, Khwe-ǁAni, Ts'ixa, ǂX'ao-ǁ'aen, !Xóõ, ǂHoan, ǂKhomani, Naro, G/ui, G//ana, Tsasi, Deti, Shua, Tshwa, Danisi and /Xaise. The San, Balala, and Nama are among the most underprivileged people in Botswana, with a high percentage living below the poverty line.

Botswana is a signatory to the Convention on the Elimination of All Forms of Discrimination against Women (CEDAW), the Convention on the Rights of the Child (CRC) and the Convention on the Elimination of All Forms of Racial Discrimination (CERD). It also voted in favor of the United Nations Declaration on the Rights of Indigenous Peoples when it was adopted but has not signed the only international human rights convention that deals with indigenous peoples, ILO Convention No. 169. There are no specific laws on indigenous peoples' rights in the country nor is the concept of indigenous peoples included in the Botswana Constitution.

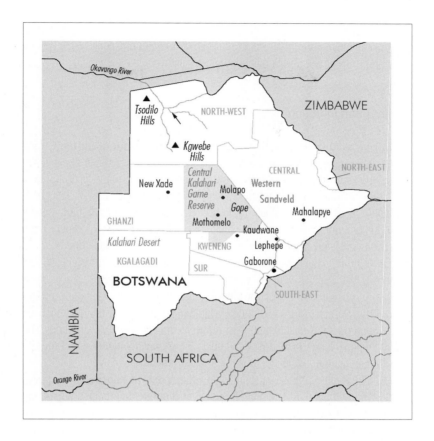

National and local elections held in October

On 24 October 2014, national elections were held in Botswana. President Lieutenant General Seretse Khama Ian Khama and the Botswana Democratic Party were victorious. The San in the CKGR and Ghanzi organized to vote for the opposition party, the Umbrella for Democratic Change (UDC).[1] One San, Jumanda Gakelebone, was elected to a district council, representing New Xade in Ghanzi District.[2]

President Khama's State of the Nation Address, given to the Botswana Parliament on 14 November 2014, made no specific mention of issues facing indigenous and minority peoples in the country.

Hunting ban imposed

On 1 January 2014, President Khama imposed a nationwide hunting ban.[3] However, public uncertainty continued regarding the ban and to whom it applied. Apparently, private land was exempt, allowing land owners to sell hunting rights to safari hunters from outside the country, who are willing to pay between US$5,000-US$20,000 to hunt. While government spokespersons initially said that subsistence hunters would be allowed to continue to operate, dozens of people have since been arrested and jailed for alleged contravention of wildlife laws.

On 4 January 2014, two San were taken from their homes in New Xade and beaten by the Special Support Group (SSG) of the Botswana Police on false charges of possessing "illegal" bushmeat. Their injuries required hospital treatment. The SSG members said they were making an example of the men "in order to dissuade others from attempting to return to the Central Kalahari Game Reserve".[4] Ghanzi District officials stated that six police officers were being investigated in connection with the assault.[5]

On 13 February, President Khama attended the 2014 Conference on Illegal Wildlife Trade in London. There were demonstrations outside the meeting on the Botswana hunting ban and the treatment of people in the Central Kalahari Game Reserve, an issue that resonated throughout 2014.[6]

In August 2014, the Botswana High Court threw out the case of four San men accused of "poaching" in the CKGR. Also in August 2014, four CKGR residents sued the Botswana government over the hunting ban, claiming that the order conferred arbitrary powers on the Minister of Environment, Wildlife and Tourism. They also claimed that the ban violated the Constitution of Botswana by excluding those who hunt on private game farms from the ban.[7] In general, community trusts, including ones with San majorities, are having difficulties as a result of changes in the way community-controlled hunting areas are being handled.[8]

Indigenous people living near World Heritage sites are endangered

On 22 June, the Okavango Delta became the world's 1,000[th] World Heritage site and the second World Heritage site in the country (the Tsodilo Hills were the first). The World Heritage property encompasses an area of 2,023,590 ha (20,236 km²) with a buffer zone of 2,286,630 ha (22,866 km²), making a total of 43,102 km². A Khwe San man participated in the ceremony, which was held in Qatar. At that meeting, it was underlined in the discussions that Botswana was required to re- spect the rights of indigenous people in the territory. However, there are indica- tions from reports in the Okavango that the North West District Council and the Tawana Land Board have been telling San-majority communities in the Okavango Delta and in the buffer zone that they will have to move to new places.[9] These communities include, but are not limited to, Gudigwa, Mababe, Khwaai, Xaxana- ga and Diseta Island.[10] Questions also continued to be raised about what would happen to San and other livestock owners in the Okavango with the expansion of commercial tourism operations. [11]

On 19 December, the President of Botswana officially opened the Gcwihaba National Monument tourism facilities in western Ngamiland. This site is a pro- posed World Heritage site, and it is a cooperative effort between the Department of Environment, Wildlife and Tourism and the /Xai /Xai (Cgae Cgae) Tlhabololo Trust, whose members celebrated the dedication with a dance and other cultural activities.[12]

Gcwihaba and Botswana's first World Heritage site, the Tsodilo Hills, saw expanded mineral exploration on the part of Tsodilo Resources, a Botswana- based mining company, throughout the year. The Ju/'hoansi residents of Tsodilo, whose identity as indigenous peoples has not been recognized by the Botswana government, have felt increasingly marginalized from decision-making relative to their neighbors, as external interests become increasingly important in the Tsodi- lo region.[13]

San citizens of Ranyane take the government to court – again

In July 2013, the San residents of Ranyane in southern Ghanzi District took the government to court and won the right to remain in their community. However, the government terminated all services, including the maintenance of and fuel supply for the engine that pumps water from their borehole. Some desperate residents sold their livestock to buy a new engine and supply it with fuel. On 15 November 2014, Ranyane residents sued the government in an attempt to restore services, which, in addition to the maintenance and supply of the borehole engine, included health, and employment services.[14]

Conditions in the CKGR continue to deteriorate

As far as the Central Kalahari Game Reserve (CKGR) issue is concerned, as of the end of 2014 there were still problems with former residents of the reserve not being allowed to enter, having goods and water confiscated, not being provided with medicines such as those for HIV (antiretrovirals) and tuberculosis, and being harassed at the gates of the reserve. At present, the government only allows those people into the CKGR who are on the list of the original 243 applicants in the first CKGR legal case. A case that was brought against the government regarding entrance rights was thrown out on a technicality by a High Court Judge in 2014.

The President of Botswana inaugurated a new diamond mine in the CKGR in September. The Ghagoo (Gope) Diamond Mine is located in the south-eastern portion of the CKGR and is estimated to hold US$4.9 billion worth of rough diamonds. The Botswana government said its share of the proceeds would be used to provide services for San outside the CKGR.[15]

Visit by the UN Special Rapporteur on cultural rights

The United Nations Special Rapporteur in the field of cultural rights, Farida Shaheed, visited Botswana from 14-26 November. She went to several San settlements, Ghanzi, D'Kar, Old Xade, New Xade, CKGR, and met with Roy Sesana, a prominent San activist, in addition to meeting numerous government officials and residents. The Special Rapporteur noted the lack of mother-tongue education for cultural minorities; the unfairness of the House of Chiefs system, which fails to include minorities; and the restrictions that prevent residents born in the CKGR from remaining there. She also mentioned the new World Heritage site at

Okavango and underlined the government's agreement to consult with and respect Okavango's residents.

The UN Special Rapporteur did not mention the hunting ban, either explicitly or implicitly.[16]

Indigenous attention to international meetings

In May 2014, Leburu Andrias, a San from Shakawe, attended the 13th United Nations Permanent Forum on Indigenous Issues, which met in New York City from 12-23 May. A spokesperson for the Botswana government, the Director of the Department of Community Development in the Ministry of Local Government and Rural Development, made a statement at the UNPFII meeting on the Botswana government's position on human rights.[17] The statement did not mention anything about indigenous peoples, only saying that the government was providing assistance to people through the Remote Area Development Program and that Botswana supported human rights for all people in the country.

No San from Botswana were able to attend the September 2014 World Conference on Indigenous Peoples in New York.

General trends affecting indigenous peoples of Botswana

Uncertainty over government policies regarding social, economic and cultural rights for indigenous peoples was a major issue for the country's citizens in 2014. Other important developments and trends in 2014 included large amounts of tribal land (71% of the country) being turned into commercial leasehold fenced ranches. There was both an expansion and contraction of mining operations, with some workers on the Boseto Copper Project in the Toteng area of Ngamiland being laid off, some of whom were San. Work continued on the Khoemacau Copper Mining project, which will have a direct impact on the environment and people of the north-western corner of the Central Kalahari Game Reserve, northern Ghanzi District and southern Ngamiland. Questions continued to be raised about what would happen to San and other livestock owners in Okavango with the expansion of commercial tourism operations.[18]

Access to water continued to be a problem in many remote area communities. The private companies designated by the Botswana government to oversee water resources and manage facilities – and to set fees – provide poor management and maintenance at high costs to the consumers.[19]

As of the end of 2014, the Directorate on Corruption and Economic Crime (DCEC) had not yet completed its promised investigations of the land issues in various parts of the country. No indictments of the Botswana Department of Wildlife and National Parks or Botswana Police had been filed for mistreatment of Botswana citizens as of the end of 2014. Had these cases been pursued, they would have had a significant and positive impact on Botswana's indigenous peoples.   ○

Notes and references

1   **Baaitse, Francinah, 2014:** Basarwa Rebel against BDP. *Weekend Post*, 1 December 2014.
2   **Letsididi, Bashi, 2014:** Honourable Councilor Jumanda Gakelebone of New Xade. *Sunday Standard*, 17 November, 2014.
3   **Republic of Botswana, 2014a:** *Supplement C. Wildlife Conservation and National Parks (Prohibition of Hunting, Capturing, or Removal of Animals Order, 2014). Statutory Instrument No. 2 of 2014. Botswana Government Gazette, Volume LII, No. 2, 10 January 2014.* Gaborone: Botswana Government Gazette.
4   As said by the officers to reporter Mongaedi Gaothobogwe.
5   **Gaothobogwe, Monkagedi, 2014:** Six Police Officers under Investigation for Torturing Basarwa Suspects. *The Monitor*, 22 January 2014.
6   **Letsididi, Bashi, 2014:** Truth a Casualty in the War for the CKGR. *Sunday Standard*, Monday, 20 October 2014; We Neither Hunt Naked nor with Bows and Arrows, *Sunday Standard*, December 8 2014; **Sylvain, Renee, 2014:** Essentialism and the Indigenous Politics of Recognition in Southern Africa. *American Anthropologist* 116 (2):1-34; **Letsididi, Bashi, 2014:** Are Basarwa Better Conservationists? *Sunday Standard*, 24 November 2014.
7   **Morula, Morula, 2014:** CKGR Residents Sue Govt. over Hunting Ban. *Sunday Standard*, 18 August 2014.
8   **Morula, Morula, 2014:** Community Trusts Face Collapse as Hunting Ban Bites. *Sunday Standard*, 22 July 2014.
9   Observations and reports by personnel from the Botswana Khwedom Council, the Kuru Family of Organisations, and the San Studies Centre and researchers working in and around the Okavango.
10 See, for example, **Konopo, Joel, 2014:** Fisherman Says Khama Stole His Land. *Botswana Guardian*, 19 December 2014; **Ontebetse, Khonani and Basadi Morokotso, 2015:** Fight for Okavango Delta – Khama Caught in the Cross Fire. *Sunday Standard*, 12 January 2015.
11 **Ontebetse, Khonani and Basadi Morokotso, 2015:** Fight for Okavango Delta – Khama Caught in the Cross Fire. *Sunday Standard*, 12 January 2015, p. 1.

12 **Mmolai, Esther, 2014:** Xaixai Community Showcases Culture. *Botswana Daily News*, 21 December 2014. Some of the San at /Xai/Xai were opposed to G/wihaba becoming a World Heritage Site

13 **Taylor, Michael, 2014:** 'We Are Not Taken as People': Ignoring the Indigenous Identities and History of Tsodilo Hills World Heritage Site, Botswana. In *World Heritage Sites and Indigenous Peoples' Rights*, Stefan Disko and Helen Tugendhat, eds. pp. 119-129. Copenhagen: International Work Group for Indigenous Affairs. p. 124.

14 **Baaitse, Francinah, 2014:** Basarwa Back in Court. *Mmegi Online*, 15 December, 2014.

15 **Dibela, Lebogang, 2014:** The Gope Gem Diamonds Mine: A Jewel or Blight in the History of Basarwa Resistance? *Sunday Standard*, 7 September 2014.

16 Preliminary Conclusions and Observations by the Special Rapporteur in the field of Cultural Rights at the end of her visit to Botswana – 14 / 26 November, 2014, on the Office of the High Commissioner for Human Rights website, accessed, 26 February, 2014. http://www.ohchr.org/EN/NewsEvents/Pages/DisplayNews.aspx?NewsID=15345&LangID=E#sthash.C0ZzP4i1.dpuf

17 **Republic of Botswana, 2014b:** *Statement by Mr. Steven Ludick, Director Department of Community Development, Ministry of Local Government and Rural Development of the Republic of Botswana, Item.4, Human Rights.* Paper presented at the 13th Session UN Permanent Forum on Indigenous Issues, 12-23 May 2014, New York. Gaborone, Botswana: Government of Botswana.

18 **Ontebetse, Khonani and Basadi Morokotso, 2015:** Fight for Okavango Delta – Khama Caught in the Cross Fire. *Sunday Standard*, 12 January 2015, p. 1.

19 See, for example, **Tsiane, Leinyana, 2014:** Water Wars Boil Over in D'Kar. *Mmegi on-Line* August 22, 2014.

Robert Hitchcock *is a member of the board of the Kalahari Peoples Fund (KPF), a non-profit organization devoted to assisting people in southern Africa. rkhitchcock@gmail.com*

Judith Frost *is an editor and researcher based in New York who has been involved with indigenous people's issues for many years. frostjjaa@verizon.net*

Wayne A. Babchuk *holds a joint Assistant Professor of Practice position in the Department of Educational Psychology and in the Department of Anthropology at the University of Nebraska-Lincoln (UNL), Lincoln, Nebraska. wbabchuk1@unl.edu*

SOUTH AFRICA

South Africa's total population is around 50 million, of which indigenous groups are estimated to comprise approximately 1%. Collectively, the various First Indigenous Peoples groups in South Africa are known as Khoe-San, comprising the San and the Khoekhoe. The San groups include the ‡Khomani San who reside mainly in the Kalahari region, and the Khwe and !Xun who reside mainly in Platfontein, Kimberley. The Khoekhoe include the Nama who reside mainly in the Northern Cape Province, the Koranna mainly in the Kimberley and Free State provinces, the Griqua in the Western Cape, Eastern Cape, Northern Cape, Free State and KwaZulu-Natal provinces and the Cape Khoekhoe in the Western Cape and Eastern Cape, with growing pockets in the Gauteng and Free State provinces. In contemporary South Africa, Khoe-San communities exhibit a range of socio-economic and cultural lifestyles and practices.

The socio-political changes brought about by the current South African regime have created the space for a deconstruction of the racially determined apartheid social categories such as "Coloureds". Many previously "Coloured" people are now exercising their right to self-identification and identify as San and Khoekhoe or Khoe-San. First Nations indigenous San and Khoekhoe peoples are not formally recognized in terms of national legislation; however, this is shifting with the pending National Traditional Affairs Bill 2013, which is intended to be tabled before parliament in 2015. South Africa has voted in favour of adopting the UN Declaration on the Rights of Indigenous Peoples but has yet to ratify ILO Convention 169.

In 2014, the Khoi and San communities continued to advocate for formal recognition of their collective rights to their lands, resources, indigenous institutions and indigenous languages in post-apartheid South Africa. Through their respective institutions, they have been able to make incremental progress towards these collective rights due to the enabling legislative environment that exists in South Africa, particularly the national regulatory framework for implementation of the Nagoya Protocol on access and benefit-sharing under the Convention on Biological Diversity (see example below).

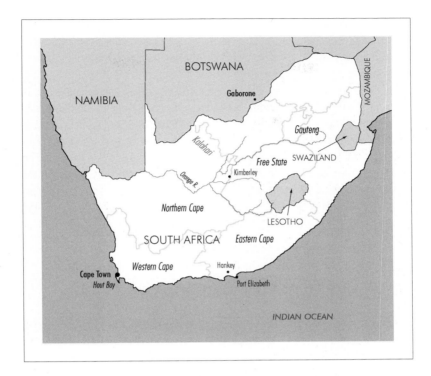

Benefit-sharing agreements – the Nagoya Protocol (CBD)

The National Khoi & San Council (NKC) and the San Council continued their work to secure rights to their associated traditional knowledge of South African indigenous biological resources under the strong South African law on Access and Benefit-Sharing,[1] in line with the Nagoya Protocol under the Convention of Biological Diversity (CBD). During 2013, the NKC and the San Council signed the first agreement collectively with a commercial company recognizing the Khoi and San peoples' traditional knowledge associated with an endemic shrub called Buchu. During 2014, the NKC and San Council met with an additional two commercial companies. These meetings negotiated benefit-sharing arrangements for the Khoi and San people relating to two plant species endemic to South Africa. The San and Khoi are regarded as the modern-day holders of traditional knowledge and they are the "indigenous community" as defined by the South African regulatory framework on access and benefit-sharing, and whose traditional uses have initiated or contributed to bioprospecting by these commercial companies.

Further, the NKC also included specific Khoisan farming communities as beneficiaries. Apartheid and colonialism caused disruption to the Khoi and San historical community structures. The NKC is therefore putting special measures in place for greater inclusion of the Khoi and San historical farming communities in the benefit-sharing processes where they are affected. The South African government is playing a mediating role in helping to ensure that the private sector complies with its legal obligation to share benefits with the Khoi and San peoples. The challenge currently being faced is that of ensuring that more actors within the private sector comply with the regulatory framework on access and benefit-sharing. Greater compliance with this South African (SA) regulatory framework by the private sector will ensure that more benefits are shared with indigenous communities.[2]

The Amendment to the Restitution of Land Rights Act 2014

The programme of land restitution in South Africa is based around the provisions of the Restitution of Land Rights Act, 1994 (Act No. 22 of 1994), which enables individuals and groups that have been dispossessed of their land on the grounds of race since 16 June 1913 to claim compensation and reparations.[3] The Act provided a cut-off date for claims of 31 December 1998 and did not provide for dispossessions that occurred prior to the date of 1913.

The Restitution of Land Rights Amendment Act, 2014 was passed by the South African national parliament and the provincial parliaments in June 2014, and soon thereafter signed by President Jacob Zuma. This Amendment extends the opportunity to make land claims for another five years. The right to restitution was officially reopened on 1 July 2014. Claimants who were dispossessed of land after 1913 will have the opportunity to claim it back until June 2019. An explanatory note to the Amendment Act indicates that the government will conduct research into the historical land claims of the Khoi and San communities since their land dispossession occurred well *before* 1913. As noted above, the Restitution of Land Rights Act, 1994 makes provision for land restitution only where land dispossession occurred *after* 1913.[4]

During 2014, the SA government met with 900 Khoi and San representatives to discuss this process of land restitution. A working group of different Khoi and San representatives was established to work with the SA government to develop policy proposals and make recommendations to address their historical land claims. The working group process anticipates provincial participation from Khoi and San groupings in this dialogue process.

As the national representative body of the Khoi and San, the NKC has welcomed this dialogue process in principle. It has, however, expressed concern at the lack of meaningful participation in this policy development process. The structure of the working group does not ensure full representation and participation of the NKC. This is relevant as existing historic communities represented on the NKC have been vetted through a government-led process, as noted in official SA government reports during 1999. This is also the official body with which the SA government is negotiating the recognition of their traditional institutions and communities in the process of the National Traditional Affairs Bill, 2013. And yet it is unclear who the current representatives on the working group are actually representing.[5]

Khomani San

The Khomani San successfully claimed back 65,000 hectares of land through the post-apartheid South African restitution process in 1999. This land was part of their ancestral lands lost during the apartheid era in 1931 with the formation of the Kalahari Gemsbok Park. In addition, they were also granted extensive land-use rights within the recently named Kgalagadi Transfrontier Park.[6] Under the terms of this agreement, six title deeds for six Kalahari farms were transferred to the community property association of the San community. The San community members moved back onto this land but little development occurred and there was no significant improvement in the welfare of this community. Things have started to turn around since then, with all the different stakeholders recommitting to their various roles.[7] An office administrator was finally appointed in 2014 and a farm manager will soon also be in post. These appointments are key in helping to implement post-settlement responsibilities.

Khoekhoegoewab language

The Khoi and San indigenous languages are mentioned in the South African Constitution. The indigenous languages of the Khoi and San, however, still do not
enjoy official language status on a par with the other 11 official South African
languages.

Some Khoisan revivalist groupings in the Western Cape have started to offer
informal classes in the Khoekhoegoewab/ Nama language. This is important
given the extent of the loss of this indigenous language among the Khoisan communities.

Cultural expressions – "Riel dancing"

A competition in "rieldance", one of the oldest dance styles that was previously
performed by the Khoisan ancient peoples, was held in December 2014. Key
Khoisan groupings participated, and Khoisan youth are generally showing an increasing interest in the dance. Traditionally, it is performed in circles, and requires
footwork and imitations of animals. The dance later became expressed through
farmworkers and sheep shearers working as labourers on commercial farms in
the Western Cape. The revival of this cultural expression will contribute to creating a stronger sense of community among the Khoisan people.[8]   O

Notes and references

1   Called the National Environmental Management: Biodiversity Act 10 of 2004 and its BABS Regu-
     lations.
2   Interview with Mr. Cecil le Fleur, Chair of National Khoi & San Council.
3   http://www.justice.gov.za/lcc/docs/1994-022.pdf
4   The Amendment to the Restitution of Land Rights Act, 2013.
5   Interview with Mr. Cecil le Fleur, Chair of National Khoi & San Council.
6   The claimant community instituted formal legal proceedings against the relevant state structures
     involved. After a series of failed attempts at obtaining satisfactory responses from the govern-
     ment, their appointed legal representatives finally lodged formal litigation documents in the High
     Court in October 2012. The state parties opted not to oppose the court action, and negotiated a
     settlement proposal. In 2013, the Khomani San people agreed to and accepted the settlement
     agreement developed by the state in order to honour and implement the land claim.

7   http://www.khomanisan.com/about-us/#HistoryOfTheSan
8   http://www.iol.co.za/capeargus/khoisan-dance-experiencing-riel-revival-1.1791530#.VPQnw9j-9nlU

Lesle Jansen *is a First Nations Indigenous lawyer from South Africa. She holds a Master's degree in Indigenous Peoples in International Law from the University of Arizona (USA). She also completed a second Master's degree in the Rule of Law for Development from Loyola University, Chicago, at its centre in Rome, Italy. She serves as an expert member on the ACHPR's Working Group on Indigenous Populations/Communities in Africa. She is currently working with a team of environmental lawyers known as Natural Justice (naturaljustice.org). They work with indigenous and local communities on their relationship with natural resources. She is based in Cape Town.*

PART II

INTERNATIONAL PROCESSES

WORLD CONFERENCE ON INDIGENOUS PEOPLES

The year of the High-Level Plenary Meeting of the UN General Assembly to be known as the World Conference on Indigenous Peoples 2014

On 21 December 2010, the UN General Assembly adopted a resolution (A/RES/65/198) to organize a high-level plenary meeting of the General Assembly to be known as the World Conference on Indigenous Peoples (HLPM/WCIP). This meeting was held in New York, 22-23 September 2014, the objective being to share perspectives and best practices on the realization of the rights of Indigenous Peoples, including pursuing the objectives of the UN Declaration on the Rights of Indigenous Peoples (the Declaration). The name of this meeting was misleading as it was in reality a special session of the General Assembly and not a fully-fledged World Conference. Regardless of its name, Indigenous Peoples saw fit to engage in the HLPM/WCIP process to ensure it upheld and realized Indigenous Peoples' rights. In 2014, the HLPM/WCIP process faced a number of political challenges and it was not clear whether UN General Assembly resolution A/RES/66/296 (the modalities resolution), which set out the logistics for the meeting as well as a process for the drafting of the outcome document, would be upheld in a way that would provide for the full and effective participation of Indigenous Peoples. After concerted lobbying on a number of fronts by both Indigenous Peoples and states, the modalities resolution was implemented; however, the planning process was now six months behind schedule. Indigenous lobbying began in June 2014, focusing on the content of the HLPM/WCIP outcome document. Indigenous representatives also participated in the informal consultations and the interactive hearing in New York. All of this work culminated in the adoption of an outcome document at the HLPM/WCIP session that upheld many of the priorities that Indigenous Peoples had set out in the Alta outcome document (AOD).

Difficulties in appointing the indigenous co-facilitators

Following the adoption of the AOD during the global indigenous conference held in Alta in June 2014, Indigenous Peoples took an optimistic but cautious view that the remaining work on the modalities resolution on organizational matters would begin to be implemented in late 2013 with the reappointment of two co-facilitators. The two facilitators would be composed of one state representative and one indigenous representative, following a precedent established during the 66th session of the General Assembly when the modalities resolution had been adopted. It was understood that the President of the 68th session of the General Assembly, Ambassador John Ashe of Antigua and Barbuda, did not oppose the appointment of two co-facilitators and that it was only a matter of time before this would take place. However, by the end of 2013 no appointments had been made. Both states and Indigenous Peoples were aware that there was much work to do before the HLPM/WCIP including agreement on the themes of the conference as well as a definition of the consultation process by which the outcome document would be drafted.

With no clear direction from the President of the General Assembly (PGA), the global indigenous coordinating group (GCG) wrote to him on 13 January 2014, lending their support to the reappointment of two co-facilitators and naming Mr. John Henriksen as their preferred choice for the position of indigenous co-facilitator.[1] There was no response to that letter. On 29 January 2014, the PGA issued his first aide-memoire outlining three options to address the appointment of co-facilitators. After consultation, the GCG responded by supporting only those options that provided for indigenous participation equal to that of states and rejecting those that did not. No consensus was reached among states as regards to any of the three options so the PGA issued a second aide-memoire on 26 February 2014[2] whereby he stated that there would be no co-facilitators, there would be two parallel consultation processes instead, one for states and one for indigenous "groups" and that indigenous groups could make their views known to states via informal briefings. The aide-memoire also noted that consultations would begin the following week, on 3 March 2014, and that a focal point for the remaining organizational work had been appointed within the PGA's office, Mr. Crispin Gregoire of Dominica. The proposal for two separate consultation processes was strongly rejected by the GCG and Indigenous Peoples regionally and prompted the North American Indigenous Peoples' caucus to call for the cancellation of the HLPM/WCIP and to formally withdraw from the GCG. Other regions made it clear to the PGA[3] that his proposed framework was inconsistent with the right of Indigenous Peoples to participate in matters affecting them and that they would find it very difficult, if not impossible, to continue to engage in the process if the framework was not adjusted. During this time, states who supported the HLPM/WCIP held bilateral discussions with the PGA urging him to reconsider his latest proposal. The PGA seemed adamant in his course of action and issued a letter on 5 March 2014 confirming that Mr. Andrej Logar, Permanent Representative of Slovenia and Mr. Eduardo Ulibarri, Permanent Representative of Costa Rica would assist him with consultations.

On 20 March 2014, the newly-appointed focal point of the HLPM/WCIP within the PGA's office, Mr. Crispin Gregoire, issued a letter proposing an adjustment to the PGA's aide-memoire of 26 February 2014. The PGA would appoint four advisers - two state and two indigenous - to assist him with the consultations; these consultations would be informal and inclusive. On the basis of the consultations, the PGA would then prepare a zero draft outcome document for the consideration of states and Indigenous Peoples. This zero draft would form the basis on which the final outcome document would be negotiated. This development was viewed as a positive move that upheld both the status of Indigenous Peoples as equal to states and the right of Indigenous Peoples to participate in decisions affecting them. Indigenous Peoples quickly responded in writing welcoming the adjusted framework and nominating Mr. Les Malezer and Dr. Myrna Cunningham for the roles of indigenous advisers. Mr. John Henriksen had by that time confirmed that he no longer wished to be considered for the role of indigenous co-facilitator.

With the 13th session of the Permanent Forum on Indigenous Issues (PFII) fast approaching and the modalities resolution requiring the interactive hearing to be held no later than June, it was hoped that the new framework would be formally adopted, thus allowing the remaining preparatory work to begin. However, the PGA continued to show a lack of leadership and, by the end of the first week of the PFII, there had been no confirmation as to a way forward. On 19 May 2014, the PGA sent a letter to the five UN regions confirming his proposal of 21 March 2014. He also set a deadline of 20 May 2014, noting that if no objections were received, the proposal would be implemented. The deadline passed with no clear direction being issued by the PGA. On the last day of the PFII, Mr. Crispin Gregoire delivered a statement to the PFII meeting which provided no further direction on a way forward. In response, the GCG expressed their extreme disappointment that the PGA had failed to exercise decisive leadership.

A week later, the PGA issued another letter[4] - the first to be addressed specifically to Indigenous Peoples - advising that the first informal consultation would take place on 3 June 2014 and confirming his appointment of four advisers, including those selected by Indigenous Peoples, Mr. Les Malezer and Dr. Myrna Cunningham. Indigenous Peoples breathed a collective sigh of relief as it seemed that the HLPM/WCIP process could finally recommence in a way that was acceptable to them. The first logistical challenge was that of getting indigenous delegates to New York for 3 June 2014 given that there were only four days available in which to make travel arrangements. As a result, all regions except Africa were able to send one or two delegates to the first meeting. Although the North American Indigenous Peoples' caucus had officially withdrawn from the process, a number of North American tribes and not-for-profit organizations participated under their own mandates in the first and successive rounds of informal consultations.

The informal consultations

The first round of informal consultations was followed by the interactive hearing on 17 and 18 June 2014 as well as two further rounds of informal consultations on 16 July 2014 and 18 and 19 August 2014. At each consultation, Indigenous Peoples prepared themselves ahead of time with regional and sometimes cross-regional positions and agreed to limit their oral statements to areas of priority and specific wording in order to ensure that states had ample opportunity to present their positions.

Not only were Indigenous Peoples actively and strategically engaging in these rounds of consultations but a lobbying team made up of representatives from the regions of the Arctic, Asia, Latin America and the Caribbean, the Pacific, Russia and the women's caucus was also permanently based in New York from June to September 2014. This group met daily to review the current drafting of the outcome document, prioritize issues from the AOD and engage in lobbying with those states considered friendly to the process and to Indigenous Peoples' priorities. They also met regularly with the indigenous advisers who were, by that time, also based in New York. A strong relationship was established with a group of states known as the friends of the HLPM/WCIP. There were frequent exchanges of views and positions, with the lobbying team setting out their priorities and the states then providing technical and political feedback based on their experience of drafting UN documents.

The indigenous advisers were actively engaged in the drafting of the outcome document as well as assisting the PGA's office with the logistical arrangements that needed to be made. Due to the stalemate in the first half of the year, all remaining preparatory work had to be carried out with some urgency. The lobbying team also provided feedback to the PGA's office on Indigenous Peoples' expectations of the process and, at times, lobbied to ensure that such expectations were met.

The lobbying team was able to positively influence the content of the outcome document by prioritizing those issues and rights deemed of utmost importance according to the AOD. While the best outcome would have been to incorporate all aspects of the AOD, given the limited time available to draft a final document, along with the restrictive positions of some states, prioritizing certain areas and advocating for their inclusion was both necessary and strategic. The prioritized areas were:

Cluster 1 - international oversight mechanism, permanent status for Indigenous Peoples within the UN and other international measures;
Cluster 2 - lands, territories and resources and demilitarization;
Cluster 3 - national policy direction;
Cluster 4 - indigenous women, youth and children;
Cluster 5 - traditional knowledge and livelihoods.

Different regions focused on specific clusters, working on drafting language and producing non-papers that were used to explain the relevance and importance of the specific rights that each cluster addressed, and which elaborated specific mechanisms that were important in order to realize such rights. These non-papers also proved to be very advantageous, with many states commenting on how they allowed them to more fully understand the importance of certain issues and the mechanisms proposed to address such issues.

The draft outcome document and the intergovernmental process

Following the August consultation, a final draft outcome document was prepared by the PGA's office. This document was then the subject of an intergovernmental process in which the states and the four advisers participated. As such, there was limited input from Indigenous Peoples and the two indigenous advisers played a critical role in reminding states of the reasons why Indigenous Peoples had prioritized certain issues and advocating for the draft outcome document to remain as close as possible to the original draft given that it had a high level of legitimacy, being the product of numerous consultations between states and Indigenous Peoples. The indigenous lobbying team spent a number of days based outside the meeting rooms where the intergovernmental process was taking place, receiving regular updates from the indigenous advisers as well as from the friends of the HLPM/WCIP. During these debriefs, the lobbying team was able to present its position on suggested word changes which, in turn, provided the friends of the HLPM/WCIP and the indigenous advisers with clear direction as to the priorities and specific wording that was required. According to those who participated, it was a difficult period in which many states who had not spoken during the consultation process or who had only made general statements tried to redraft the outcome document. Such tactics were strongly resisted by a number of the friends of the HLPM/WCIP, who were now largely responsible for maintaining the integrity of the outcome document.

The adoption of the WCIP's Outcome Document

When the HLPM/WCIP session finally took place on 22 and 23 September, Indigenous Peoples from all seven geopolitical regions gathered in New York. This was not without several logistical and political challenges, including interference by the Russian authorities in the travel arrangements of a number of Russian indigenous delegates as well as some US entry visas not being issued in time for delegates from the African and Asian regions.

The adoption of the outcome document[5] was scheduled for the first day of the meeting in order not to conflict with a summit organized by the UN Secretary-General on climate change the following day. While the drafting of the outcome document had encountered a number of challenges, it was an historic moment when it was finally adopted. Indigenous Peoples had proactively influenced the themes and content of the final outcome document so that it mirrored many of the priorities set out in the AOD. The highest body of the UN had committed to concrete actions with which to implement the Declaration, with the overwhelming majority of those actions directed at the national level. This was a significant achievement that heralded greater recognition of Indigenous Peoples' rights. As such it was a cause for celebration.   ○

Notes and references

1   GCG Letter to the President of the General Assembly regarding the Indigenous Co-Facilitator, (15 Jan. 2014): http://wcip2014.org/wp-content/uploads/2014/01/Letter-to-PGA-with-letterhead-to-send.pdf
2   President of the General Assembly Aide-Memoire regarding Co-Facilitators, (26 Feb. 2014): http://wcip2014.org/wp-content/uploads/2014/03/Aide-memoire-of-PGA-26-Feb-2014.pdf
3   GCG letter to the President of the UN General Assembly: Analysis of the Aide-Memoire on organisational issues:
      http://wcip2014.org/wp-content/uploads/2014/03/GCG-letter-to-PGA-4-March-20141.pdf
4   President of the General Assembly new proposal for implementation of the Modalities Resolution A/66/296, 19 May 2014:
      http://wcip2014.org/wp-content/uploads/2014/05/World-Conference-on-Indigenous-Peoples-19-May-2014.pdf
5   Outcome Document of the World Conference on Indigenous Peoples: http://wcip2014.org/wp-content/uploads/2013/03/N1446828.pdf

Tracey Whare was the Secretariat for the Indigenous Peoples' Global Coordinating Group. Email: wharetracey@gmail.com

A/RES/69/2

United Nations

General Assembly

Distr.: General

25 September 2014

Sixty-ninth session
Agenda item 65

Resolution adopted by the General Assembly on 22 September 2014

[without reference to a Main Committee (A/69/L.1)]

69/2. Outcome document of the high-level plenary meeting of the General Assembly known as the World Conference on Indigenous Peoples

The General Assembly,

Adopts the following outcome document:

Outcome document of the high-level plenary meeting of the General Assembly known as the World Conference on Indigenous Peoples

1. We, the Heads of State and Government, ministers and representatives of Member States, reaffirming our solemn commitment to the purposes and principles of the Charter of the United Nations, in a spirit of cooperation with the indigenous peoples of the world, are assembled at United Nations Headquarters in New York on 22 and 23 September 2014, on the occasion of the high -level plenary meeting of the General Assembly kno wn as the World Conference on Indigenous Peoples, to reiter-

---

* Reissued for technical reasons on 22 September 2014.
* A/69/150.

ate the important and continuing role of the United Nations in promoting and protecting the rights of indigenous peoples.

2. We welcome the indigenous peoples' preparatory processes for the World Conference, including the Global Indigenous Preparatory Conference held in Alta, Norway, in June 2013. We take note of the outcome document of the Alta Conference[1] and other contributions made by indigenous peoples. We also welcome the inclusive preparatory process for the high-level plenary meeting, including the comprehensive engagement of the representatives of indigenous peoples.

3. We reaffirm our support for the United Nations Declaration on the Rights of Indigenous Peoples, adopted by the General Assembly on 13 September 2007,[2] and our commitments made in this respect to consult and co-operate in good faith with the indigenous peoples concerned through their own representative institutions in order to obtain their free, prior and informed consent before adopting and implementing legislative or administrative measures that may affect them, in accordance with the applicable principles of the Declaration.

4. We reaffirm our solemn commitment to respect, promote and advance and in no way diminish the rights of indigenous peoples and to uphold the principles of the Declaration.

5. In addition to the Declaration, we recall the other major achievements of the past two decades in building an international framework for the advancement of the rights and aspirations of the world's indigenous peoples, including the establishment of the Permanent Forum on Indigenous Issues, the creation of the Expert Mechanism on the Rights of Indigenous Peoples and the establishment of the mandate of the Special Rapporteur on the rights of indigenous peoples. We commit ourselves to giving due consideration to recommendations and advice issued by those bodies in cooperation with indigenous peoples.

1 A/67/994, annex.
2 Resolution 61/295, annex.

6. We encourage those States that have not yet ratified or acceded to the International Labour Organization Indigenous and Tribal Peoples Convention, 1989 (No. 169),[3] to consider doing so. We recall the obligation of ratifying States under the Convention to develop coordinated and systematic action to protect the rights of indigenous peoples.

7. We commit ourselves to taking, in consultation and cooperation with indigenous peoples, appropriate measures at the national level, including legislative, policy and administrative measures, to achieve the ends of the United Nations Declaration on the Rights of Indigenous Peoples and to promote awareness of it among all sectors of society, including mem bers of legislatures, the judiciary and the civil service.

8. We commit ourselves to cooperating with indigenous peoples, through their own representative institutions, to develop and implement national action plans, strategies or other measures, where re levant, to achieve the ends of the Declaration.

9. We commit ourselves to promoting and protecting the rights of indigenous persons with disabilities and to continuing to improve their social and economic conditions, including by developing targeted measur es for the aforementioned action plans, strategies or measures, in collaboration with indigenous persons with disabilities. We also commit ourselves to ensuring that national legislative, policy and institutional structures relating to indigenous peoples are inclusive of indigenous persons with disabilities and contribute to the advancement of their rights.

10. We commit ourselves to working with indigenous peoples to disaggregate data, as appropriate, or conduct surveys and to utilizing holistic indicator s of indigenous peoples' well-being to address the situation and needs of indigenous peoples and individuals, in particular older persons, women, youth, children and persons with disabilities.

---

3 United Nations, *Treaty Series*, vol. 1650, No. 28383.

11. We commit ourselves to ensuring equal access to high-quality education that recognizes the diversity of the culture of indigenous peoples and to health, housing, water, sanitation and other economic and social programmes to improve well-being, including through initiatives, policies and the provision of resources. We intend to empower indigenous peoples to deliver such programmes as far as possible.

12. We recognize the importance of indigenous peoples' health practices and their traditional medicine and knowledge.

13. We commit ourselves to ensuring that indigenous individuals have equal access to the highest attainable standard of physical and mental health. We also commit ourselves to intensifying efforts to reduce rates of HIV and AIDS, malaria, tuberculosis and non-communicable diseases by focusing on prevention, including through appropriate programmes, policies and resources for indigenous individuals, and to ensure their access to sexual and reproductive health and reproductive rights in accordance with the Programme of Action of the International Conference on Population and Development,[4] the Beijing Platform for Action[5] and the outcome documents of their review conferences.

14. We commit ourselves to promoting the right of every indigenous child, in community with members of his or her group, to enjoy his or her own culture, to profess and practise his or her own religion or to use his or her own language.

15. We support the empowerment and capacity-building of indigenous youth, including their full and effective participation in decision-making processes in matters that affect them. We commit ourselves to developing, in consultation with indigenous peoples, policies, programmes and resources, where relevant, that target the well-being of indigenous youth, in particular

4 *Report of the International Conference on Population and Development, Cairo, 5-13 September 1994* (United Nations publication, Sales No. E.95.XIII.18), chap. I, resolution 1, annex.

5 *Report of the Fourth World Conference on Women, Beijing, 4-15 September 1995* (United Nations publication, Sales No. E.96.IV.13), chap. I, resolution 1, annex II.

in the areas of health, education, employment and the transmission of traditional knowledge, languages and practices, and to taking measures to promote awareness and understanding of their rights.

16. We acknowledge that indigenous peoples' justice institutions can play a positive role in providing access to justice and dispute resolution and contribute to harmonious relationships within indigenous peoples' communities and within society. We commit ourselves to coordinating and conducting dialogue with those institutions, where they exist.

17. We commit ourselves to supporting the empowerment of indigenous women and to formulating and implementing, in collaboration with indigenous peoples, in particular indigenous women and their organizations, policies and programmes designed to promote capacity-building and strengthen their leadership. We support measures that will ensure the full and effective participation of indigenous women in decision-making processes at all levels and in all areas and eliminate barriers to their participation in poli tical, economic, social and cultural life.

18. We commit ourselves to intensifying our efforts, in cooperation with indigenous peoples, to prevent and eliminate all forms of violence and discrimination against indigenous peoples and individuals, in particular, women, children, youth, older persons and persons with disabilities, by strengthening legal, policy and institutional frameworks.

19. We invite the Human Rights Council to consider examining the causes and consequences of violence against indigenous women and girls, in consultation with the Special Rapporteur on violence against women, its causes and consequences, the Special Rapporteur on the rights of indigenous peoples and other special procedures mandate holders within their respective mandates. We also invite the Commission on the Status of Women to consider the issue of the empowerment of indigenous wo men at a future session.

20. We recognize commitments made by States, with regard to the United Nations Declaration on the Rights of Indigenous Peoples, to consult and

cooperate in good faith with the indigenous peoples concerned through their own representative institutions in order to obtain their free and informed consent prior to the approval of any project affecting their lands or te rritories and other resources.

21. We also recognize commitments made by States, with regard to the Declaration, to establish at the national level, in conjunction with the indigenous peoples concerned, fair, independent, impartial, open and transparent processes to acknowledge, advance and adjudicate the rights of indigenous peoples pertaining to lands, territories and resources.

22. We recognize that the traditional knowledge, innovations and practices of indigenous peoples and local communities make an important contribution to the conservation and sustainable use of biodiversity. We acknowledge the importance of the participation of indigenous peoples, wherever possible, in the benefits of their knowledge, innovations and practices.

23. We intend to work with indigenous peoples to address the impact or potential impact on them of major development projects, including those involving the activities of extractive industries, including with the aim of managing risks appropriately.

24. We recall the responsibility of transnational corporations and other business enterprises to respect all applicable laws and international principles, including the United Nations Guiding Principles on Business and Human Rights[6] and to operate transparently and in a socially and environmentally responsible manner. In this regard, we commit ourselves to taking further steps, as appropriate, to prevent abuses of the rights of indigenous peoples.

25. We commit ourselves to developing, in conjunction with the indigenous peoples concerned, and where appropriate, policies, programmes and resources to support indigenous peoples' occupations, traditional subsistence activities, economies, livelihoods, food security and nutrition.

6 A/HRC/17/31, annex.

26. We recognize the importance of the role that indigenous peo ples can play in economic, social and environmental development through traditional sustainable agricultural practices, including traditional seed supply systems, and access to credit and other financial services, markets, secure land tenure, health care, social services, education, training, knowledge and appropriate and affordable technologies, including for irrigation, and water harvesting and storage.

27. We affirm and recognize the importance of indigenous peoples' religious and cultural sites and of providing access to and repatriation of their ceremonial objects and human remains in accordance with the ends of the Declaration on the Rights of Indigenous Peoples. We commit ourselves to developing, in conjunction with the indigenous peop les concerned, fair, transparent and effective mechanisms for access to and repatriation of ceremonial objects and human remains at the national and international levels.

28. We invite the Human Rights Council, taking into account the views of indigenous peoples, to review the mandates of its existing mechanisms, in particular the Expert Mechanism on the Rights of Indigenous Peoples, during the sixty-ninth session of the General Assembly, with a view to modifying and improving the Expert Mechanism so that it can more effectively promote respect for the Declaration, including by better assisting Member States to monitor, evaluate and improve the achievement of the ends of the Declaration.

29. We invite the human rights treaty bodies to consider the Declarat ion in accordance with their respective mandates. We encourage Member States to include, as appropriate, information on the situation of the rights of indigenous peoples, including measures taken to pursue the objectives of the Declaration, in reports to those bodies and during the universal periodic review process.

30. We welcome the increasingly important role of national and regional human rights institutions in contributing to the achievement of the ends of the Declaration. We encourage the private sector, civil society and academic

institutions to take an active role in promoting and protecting the rights of indigenous peoples.

31. We request the Secretary-General, in consultation and cooperation with indigenous peoples, the Inter-Agency Support Group on Indigenous Peoples' Issues and Member States, to begin the development, within existing resources, of a system-wide action plan to ensure a coherent approach to achieving the ends of the Declaration and to report to the General Assembly at its seventie th session, through the Economic and Social Council, on progress made. We invite the Secretary - General to accord, by the end of the seventieth session of the Assembly, an existing senior official of the United Nations system, with access to the highest lev els of decision-making within the system, responsibility for coordinating the action plan, raising awareness of the rights of indigenous peoples at the highest possible level and increasing the coherence of the activities of the system in this regard.

32. We invite United Nations agencies, funds and programmes, in addition to resident coordinators, where appropriate, to support the implementation, upon request, of national action plans, strategies or other measures to achieve the ends of the Declaration, in accordance with national priorities and United Nations Development Assistance Frameworks, where they exist, through better coordination and cooperation.

33. We commit ourselves to considering, at the seventieth session of the General Assembly, ways to enable the participation of indigenous peoples' representatives and institutions in meetings of relevant United Nations bodies on issues affecting them, including any specific proposals made by the Secretary General in response to the request made in paragraph 40 below.

34. We encourage Governments to recognize the significant contribution of indigenous peoples to the promotion of sustainable development, in order to achieve a just balance among the economic, social and environmental needs of present and future generations, and the need to promote har-

mony with nature to protect our planet and its ecosystems, known as Mother Earth in a number of countries and regions.

35. We commit ourselves to respecting the contributions of indigenous peoples to ecosystem management and sustainable development, including knowledge acquired through experience in hunting, gathering, fishing, pastoralism and agriculture, as well as their sciences, technologies and cultures.

36. We confirm that indigenous peoples' knowledge and strategies to sustain their environment should be respected and taken into account when we develop national and international approaches to climate change mitigation and adaptation.

37. We note that indigenous peoples have the right to determine and dev elop priorities and strategies for exercising their right to development. In this regard, we commit ourselves to giving due consideration to all the rights of indigenous peoples in the elaboration of the post-2015 development agenda.

38. We invite Member States and actively encourage the private sector and other institutions to contribute to the United Nations Voluntary Fund for Indigenous Peoples, the Trust Fund on Indigenous Issues, the Indigenous Peoples Assistance Facility and the United Nations Indigenous Peoples' Partnership as a means of respecting and promoting the rights of indigenous peoples worldwide.

39. We request the Secretary-General to include relevant information on indigenous peoples in his final report on the achievement of the Millennium Development Goals.

40. We request the Secretary-General, in consultation with the Inter-Agency Support Group on Indigenous Peoples' Issues and Member States, taking into account the views expressed by indigenous peoples, to report to the General Assembly at its seventieth session on the implementation of the present outcome document, and to submit at the same session, through

the Economic and Social Council, recommendations regarding how to use, modify and improve existing United Nations mechanisms to achieve the ends of the United Nations Declaration on the Rights of Indigenous Peoples, ways to enhance a coherent, system-wide approach to achieving the ends of the Declaration and specific proposals to enable the participation of indigenous peoples' represen tatives and institutions, building on his report on ways and means of promoting participation at the United Nations of indigenous peoples' representatives on the issues affecting them. [7]

4th plenary meeting
22 September 2014

7 A/HRC/21/24.

INDIGENOUS WOMEN

Over half of the world's indigenous peoples are women, living in over 90 countries. In the last 20 years, indigenous women have increasingly participated in international processes to assert the rights of indigenous peoples, of women and related rights. As it may be known, 20 years ago in Beijing, during the United Nations 4th Conference on Women, indigenous women approved and signed the **Beijing Declaration of Indigenous Women,** setting the basis of indigenous women's claims as indigenous people and as women. The conference was the first time that indigenous women had the chance to highlight collectively their diverse cultures at the international level. Since the Beijing landmark, indigenous women have been advocating and gained more space within the women's movement and the indigenous peoples' movement.

Indigenous Women Advancements and pending challenges 2014

2014 was a year of challenges as well as many accomplishments for the indigenous women's movement at the international level. Indeed, 2014 was the first time ever that the United Nations General Assembly held a High Level Plenary Meeting on Indigenous Peoples - known as the World Conference on Indigenous Peoples (WCIP). The World Conference was an opportunity for indigenous women from different regions to advocate, connect, raise awareness on their achievements and needs, and to and continue fighting for their rights. As an outcome of indigenous women's hard work and advocacy efforts, many of their demands were included in the WCIP's Outcome Document, especially in paragraphs 17 to 19, that focus on empowerment of indigenous women through political participation, capacity building and leadership, on data disaggregation by gender and ethnicity, holistic indicators, on sexual and reproductive rights, and on violence against indigenous women and girls.[1]

Such process was possible thanks to an intense preparatory process in which indigenous women actively advocated and reached consensus for their voices to be heard and fully considered. Indeed, indigenous women from the seven socio-cultural regions gathered in Lima, Peru in 2013 at the World Conference of Indigenous Women, where they adopted the Lima Position Document and Plan of Action, as a political advocacy roadmap in face of the international processes of the next year, including the World Conference on Indigenous Peoples, CSW 59-Beijing+20, Cairo+20 and the Post 2015 Development Agenda.

Another sphere of active engagement of indigenous women and their organizations has been the preparatory process for the International Fund for Agricultural Development (IFAD) 2015 Forum on Indigenous Peoples. Indigenous women played a key role in the organization and participated in the four regional preparatory workshops that were held in Africa, Asia, Latin America and the Caribbean, and the Pacific.

Within the women's movement, indigenous women have increasingly participated at the United Nations Commission on the Status of Women (CSW). As a result, in past years they advocated and achieved the adoption of two resolutions on indigenous women by the CSW: "Indigenous women: beyond the ten-year review of the Beijing Declaration and Platform for Action", which urges the adoption of measures that ensure the full and effective participation of indigenous women in all aspects of society;[2] and "Indigenous women: key actors in poverty and hunger eradication",[3] which urges States and agencies of the United Nations system to adopt measures aimed at promoting the empowerment of indigenous women and the realization of their rights. Both resolutions help set an agenda and more focus on indigenous women's particular situation and, along with the WCIP Outcome Document recommendations, support their current advocacy efforts within the frame of CSW, where they demand to consider the issue of the empowerment of indigenous women at a future period of sessions.[4]

Indigenous women still face discrimination, structural and physical violence, invisiblization, poverty and marginalization. Their efforts show that their struggle and their articulation prove effective as they struggle and progress in making their voices heard, so that their rights will be ensured and fully exercised at the local, national, regional and global levels. Our accomplishments step by step, year by year, help us continue our road with more strength and confidence.   ○

Notes and references

1   A/69/L.1
2   Resolution E/2005/27
3   Resolution E/CN.6/2012/L.6
4   A/RES/69/2, 19

This article has been written by the **International indigenous Women's Forum-FIMI**. The International Indigenous Women's Forum/ Foro Internacional de Mujeres Indígenas (FIMI by its Spanish acronym) was born in 1995. FIMI is a coordinating global body with the mission to bring together indigenous women leaders and human rights activists from different parts of the world in order to coordinate agendas, build capacities and to develop leadership skills for participation in international decision-making processes by ensuring the consistent and serious inclusion of indigenous women's perspectives in all discussions regarding human rights.

FIMI, as a global network that articulates indigenous women leaders of Africa, Asia the Americas, the Arctic and the Pacific has actively participated in each of the annual sessions of the United Nations Permanent Forum on Indigenous Issues (UNPFII), and in the UN Commission on the Status of Women (CSW). FIMI is currently developing four strategic programs: the Political Participation and Advocacy Program, the Indigenous Women Global Leadership School, Indigenous Women's Watch against Violence and the Indigenous Women's Fund-AYNI.

For more information please contact us at:
www.fimi-iiwf.org
info@iiwf.org
https://www.facebook.com/pages/Foro-Internacional-de-Mujeres-Indigenas/130945820519@iiwf

THE PERMANENT FORUM ON INDIGENOUS ISSUES

Established in 2000, the UN Permanent Forum on Indigenous Issues (PFII) is an advisory body to the UN Economic and Social Council (ECOSOC). It is composed of 16 independent experts functioning in their personal capacity, who serve for a term of three years as Members and may be re-elected or re-appointed for one additional term. Eight are nominated by governments and eight by Indigenous peoples. The PFII addresses Indigenous issues in the areas of economic and social development, environment, health, human rights, culture and education. In 2008, the PFII expanded its mandate to include the responsibility to "promote respect for and full application of the Declaration and to follow up the effectiveness of the Declaration". According to its mandate, the PFII provides expert advice to ECOSOC and to UN programmes, funds and agencies; raises awareness about Indigenous issues; and promotes the integration and coordination of activities relating to Indigenous issues within the UN system.

The annual session of the PFII is held in April or May, at the UN Headquarters (or any other venue decided by the PFII) for two weeks. The PFII has a biannual working method that comprises one year devoted to a theme and one year devoted to reviewing the recommendations made by the PFII.

At its public session, the PFII provides the opportunity for Indigenous peoples from around the world to have direct dialogue and communication with the PFII expert members, the UN specialized agencies, the Special Rapporteur on the rights of indigenous peoples as well as other Human Rights Special Rapporteurs, other expert bodies, and UN Member States.

International Expert Group meeting on Sexual Health and Reproductive Rights

In January 2014, the Permanent Forum organized an expert group meeting on sexual health and reproductive rights at the UN Headquarters in New York. Attended by six regional experts and representatives of Indigenous peoples' organizations, governments and UN agencies, the participants discussed how international human rights standards and policies could be more responsive to advancing sexual health and reproductive rights for Indigenous peoples. The meeting was also an opportunity to exchange information, analysis and good practices. The conclusions and recommendations of the meeting called for an increased emphasis on the provision of intercultural healthcare that responds to and engages with indigenous peoples' notions of health and illness, traditional medicinal knowledge and practices, as well as a conceptual framework that links their biological, spiritual and emotional lives. The final report and recommendations of the expert group meeting were submitted to the 13th Session of the UN Permanent Forum on Indigenous Issues in May 2014.[1]

The Pre-Sessional Meeting (Mexico)

From 26 to 28 March 2014, PFII members met for a pre-sessional meeting in Mexico City at the invitation of the Government of Mexico. This meeting constituted a crucial element in the preparatory process for the 13th session because nine of the 16 members were new, so it was their first PFII meeting. In addition to the session preparations, the meeting provided an opportunity for the members to discuss issues related to the mandate of the Permanent Forum and its relation to ECOSOC, as well as for the secretariat to provide an overview of its work throughout the year.

Forum members also met with Indigenous peoples' representatives, government officials, parliamentarians and the UN country team in Mexico. Discussions at these meetings covered issues such as the concerns of Indigenous peoples in the region over current consultation procedures with governments, violence against Indigenous peoples and the slow progress of implementing the UN Declaration on the Rights of Indigenous Peoples and corresponding member state commitments. In addition, upon departure from Mexico, the PFII issued a communication concerning the alarming treatment of Indigenous peoples in various states within Mexico.

World Conference on Indigenous Peoples

Secretariat staff spent considerable time over the course of 2014 in preparations for the high-level plenary meeting of the General Assembly, known as the World Conference on Indigenous Peoples. A few PFII members had limited participation in the consultations convened by the President of the General Assembly to discuss the draft outcome document of the World Conference, which were held on 3 June, 17 and 18 June, 16 July and 18 August 2014.

Among the numerous dignitaries that spoke at the opening ceremony of the World Conference on 22 September was the PFII Chairperson, Dr. Dalee Sambo Dorough. In addition, 12 members of the PFII, from all seven regions, were able to attend the high-level plenary meeting, solely as observers.

The Outcome Document from the World Conference (A/Res/69/2) contains a number of solemn commitments made by states with respect to the implementation of the human rights of Indigenous peoples and reaffirmation of indigenous peoples' substantive rights. The significant reaffirmation of the purposes and principles of the UN Charter, as well as the reaffirmation of support for the UN Declaration on the Rights of Indigenous Peoples, as formal commitments, is crucial to the future of Indigenous peoples, nations and communities.

The 13th session of the Permanent Forum on Indigenous Issues

The 13th session of the Permanent Forum on Indigenous Issues took place at UN Headquarters from 12 to 23 May 2014. The two-week session was attended by over 1,200 participants with a large number of representatives of Member States, including high-level officials, UN agencies, funds and programmes, Indigenous peoples' delegates and NGOs. There were also significant numbers of Indigenous women and youth, and Indigenous persons with disabilities.

This year's **special theme** focused on "principles of good governance consistent with the UN Declaration on the Rights of Indigenous Peoples". The theme attempted to give voice to Indigenous legal traditions that emulate and represent good governance. During discussions, Member States and Indigenous peoples provided examples of cooperation around developing governance structures that could improve conditions within Indigenous communities, and which include Indigenous peoples' direct involvement in every stage of project design. Such instances helped to emphasize the importance of Indigenous participation in decision-making and the design of meaningful and effective governance approaches. The PFII theme was selected from the overall list of sustainable development goals because it transcends and impacts on all of the fundamental human rights of Indigenous peoples. Furthermore, it was identified as a way of highlighting the principles of transparency, responsiveness, consensus, equity and inclusiveness, effectiveness and efficiency, accountability, participation, consultation and consent, human rights and the rule of law in order to potentially influence both the World Conference on Indigenous Peoples and the ongoing dialogue on Sustainable Development Goals.

One day of the Permanent Forum's session was dedicated to **human rights**. Under this agenda item, the Permanent Forum congratulated Professor James Anaya on the successful conclusion of his service as Special Rapporteur on the rights of indigenous peoples. The Forum also welcomed the appointment of Ms Victoria Tauli-Corpuz as the new Special Rapporteur and stated that it looked forward to working closely with her. Also speaking during the agenda item on human rights was Mr. Wilton Littlechild on behalf of the Expert Mechanism on the Rights of Indigenous Peoples; Mr. Francisco Cali, President of the Committee on the Elimination of Racial Discrimination; Ms Soyata Maiga, on behalf of the African Commission on Human and Peoples' Rights; Mr. Emilio Alvarez, Executive Secretary of the Inter-American Commission on Human Rights; and Mr. Kenneth Deer on behalf of the Voluntary Fund for Indigenous Peoples.

The regional focus this year was on **Asia**, which yielded a range of recommendations to Asian states as well as to the UN system and Asian Indigenous peoples' organizations. Despite concern over the fact that most of the recommendations had not yet been implemented, the PFII noted some positive developments. In particular, the legal recognition of the Ainu as the Indigenous peoples of Japan; the decision of the Constitutional Court of Indonesia to recognize the customary rights of Indigenous peoples with regard to forests; and the increased engagement and partnerships of national human rights institutions and agencies of the United Nations system with Indigenous organizations and institutions were all notable outcomes of this half-day focus. However, the PFII expressed concern at the increasing adverse impacts of climate change, the large hydroelectric dams, nuclear power plants, biofuel plantations, windmills and geothermal plants, which are all adversely impacting Asian Indigenous peoples' territories and being pursued without the free, prior and informed consent or the full and effective participation of Indigenous peoples.

In addition, the Forum focused on: (i) preparations for the World Conference on Indigenous Peoples; (ii) the work of UN agencies, funds and programmes related to Indigenous peoples' issues; (iii) Indigenous children and youth; (iv) the Second Decade of the World's Indigenous Peoples (2005-2014); (v) Indigenous peoples' inclusion in the post-2015 development agenda; and (vi) the future work of the PFII, including emerging issues.

The reports by PFII members addressing sexual health and reproductive rights (EGM report of January 2014, E/C.19/2014/8); a study on an optional protocol to the UNDRIP (E/C.19/2014/7); best practices and examples in respect of resolving land disputes and land claims (E/C.19/2014/4); the situation of Indigenous children in Latin America and the Caribbean (E/C.19/2014/5); impacts of the doctrine of discovery on Indigenous peoples (E/C.19/2014/3); and on challenges in the African region to protecting traditional knowledge, genetic resources and folklore (E/C.19/2014/2) were all presented.

During its annual substantive session in July 2014, the UN Economic and Social Council unanimously adopted the PFII report of its 13th session, immediately following its presentation by PFII Chairperson, Dr. Dalee Sambo Dorough.

Annual Meeting of the Inter-Agency Support Group

The annual meeting of the Inter-Agency Support Group on Indigenous Issues was held on 2 and 3 December 2014 at OHCHR, Geneva and was attended by 40 UN agency focal points for Indigenous peoples' issues; PFII Chairperson Dalee Sambo Dorough; and Joan Carling, PFII focal point for the IASG.

The meeting was opened by the host, OHCHR, followed by statements from the PFII Chairperson, outgoing IASG Chair (UNICEF), and the Special Rapporteur on the rights of indigenous peoples. Mr. Wu Hongbo, Under Secretary General of the Department of Economic and Social Affairs and recently appointed Senior Official of the United Nations system responsible for coordinating follow up action for the World Conference on Indigenous Peoples, delivered a video message. Consistent with the Outcome Document, Mr. Wu requested the assistance of the IASG in the development of a system-wide action plan (SWAP) to ensure a coherent approach to achieving the ends of the UN Declaration. In response, the IASG established a small, informal working group to develop its own terms of reference and to prepare a realistic timeline for the development of the SWAP.

The meeting also discussed the development and operationalization of indicators based upon the UN Declaration by a IASG working group, to be led by the Secretariat of the Convention on Biological Diversity. The meeting also addressed the need to enhance the participation of national human rights institutions as well as opportunities for inter-agency collaboration in 2015. ○

Notes and references

1   The report of the meeting is available at: http://www.un.org/esa/socdev/unpfii/documents/2014/8.
     pdf.

*Dr. **Dalee Sambo Dorough** (Inuit-Alaska) is an Associate Professor of Political Science at University of Alaska Anchorage and Expert Member of the UN Permanent Forum on Indigenous Issues for which she was the Chairperson in 2014.*

UNITED NATIONS
SPECIAL RAPPORTEUR ON THE RIGHTS
OF INDIGENOUS PEOPLES

The Special Rapporteur on the rights of indigenous peoples is one of numerous "special procedures" of the UN Human Rights Council. The special procedures are independent human rights experts with mandates to report and advise on human rights from a thematic or country-specific perspective. The Special Rapporteur on the rights of indigenous peoples has a mandate to gather information and communications from all relevant sources on violations of the human rights of indigenous peoples; to formulate recommendations and proposals on measures and activities to prevent and remedy violations of the rights of indigenous peoples; and to work in coordination with other special procedures and subsidiary organs of the Human Rights Council, relevant UN bodies and regional human rights organizations.

In accordance with this mandate, the Special Rapporteur can receive and investigate complaints from indigenous individuals, groups or communities, undertake country visits and make recommendations to governments on the steps needed to remedy possible violations or to prevent future violations. The work of the Special Rapporteur has tended to concentrate on four principal areas: promotion of good practices; responding to specific cases of alleged human rights violations; country assessments; and thematic studies. The Special Rapporteur also works in collaboration with other UN mechanisms dealing with indigenous peoples.

The first Special Rapporteur, Mr. Rodolfo Stavenhagen, was appointed by the then Commission on Human Rights in 2001, serving two three-year periods which ended in 2008. The second Special Rapporteur, Professor James Anaya, was appointed by the Human Rights Council in 2008, and 2014 marked the final year of his mandate as Special Rapporteur. Ms Victoria Tauli-Corpuz from the Philippines was appointed the new Special Rapporteur by the Human Rights Council and she assumed her position in June 2014. She is the first woman and the first person from the Asia region to assume the position.

Final months of Professor James Anaya as Special Rapporteur

From January to May 2014, the Special Rapporteur (SR) James Anaya, continued to carry out work within his four principal work areas. These are the promotion of good practices; responding to specific cases of alleged human rights violations; country assessments; and thematic studies. In 2013, the SR presented his final two thematic studies to the Human Rights Council[1] and the General Assembly.[2] His final report to the Human Rights Council focused on extractive industries affecting indigenous peoples and his final report to the General Assembly provided reflections on his mandate and on implementation of the Declaration on the Rights of Indigenous Peoples.

With respect to country visits, the SR made public his final three country reports developed over the past year in connection with visits to Panama, Canada and Peru. Each of these reports[3] was based on research and information gathered by the SR, including during visits to these countries in July, October and December 2013 respectively. The report on Peru focuses especially on the situation of indigenous peoples in the context of extractive industries and contains an annex on the proposed expansion of the Camisea natural gas extraction project within Lote 88 in Cusco, Peru. The SR briefly discussed these reports during this statement and interactive dialogue before the Permanent Forum on Indigenous Issues in May 2014.

With respect to his examination of specific cases, the SR presented his final report on the cases of alleged violations of human rights of indigenous peoples he had examined in September 2014.[4] The report refers to 37 cases examined from September 2013 through communications sent up to 1 June 2013 and replies received up to 31 May 2014. Cases related to the following countries are included in the report: Argentina, Bangladesh, Bolivia, Brazil, Cameroon, Canada, Chile, Colombia, Costa Rica, Ethiopia, France, Guatemala, Honduras, India, Israel, Kenya, Papua New Guinea, Philippines, Russia, Tanzania and the United States of America. The report also contains letters addressed to corporations and to UNESCO's World Heritage Committee regarding the nomination of World Heritage sites. In his report, the SR provided a series of brief conclusions and recommendations related to each case. The SR's observations may highlight aspects or comment on the adequacy of any response to the allegations transmitted, reiterate recommendations previously made to the government or other actor concerned, or make reference to relevant international standards.

During 2014, the SR James Anaya also issued two press releases, and followed up on a case previously addressed in the context of one of his country visits. In January, he urged the Government of Kenya to ensure respect for the human rights of the Sengwer indigenous peoples in the context of what was an upcoming forcible eviction from their homes in the Embobut. In April 2014, the SR called on the owners of the Washington Redskins football team in the United States to consider "the hurtful reminder that the term 'redskins' represents of the long history of mistreatment of Native American people in the United States". Further, in January 2014, the SR met with indigenous activist and leader, Leonard Peltier, at the federal penitentiary located in Florida, United States, where Mr. Peltier is incarcerated. In his 2012 report on the situation of indigenous peoples in the United States of America, the SR had requested that the government renew its consideration of clemency for Mr. Peltier, as part of measures for reconciliation with the country's indigenous peoples.

Finally, during the final five months of his mandate, the SR James Anaya carried out several activities relevant to his work of promoting good practices. In January 2014, he discussed the importance of giving focused attention to sexual health and reproductive rights, during an international expert group meeting of the UN Permanent Forum on Indigenous Issues (UNPFII) on that same theme. In February, he gave the keynote speech at the indigenous panel entitled "Intellectual Property and Genetic Resources: What is at Stake for Indigenous Peoples?" which opened the 26th session of the World Intellectual Property Organization Intergovernmental Committee on Intellectual Property and Genetic Resources, Traditional Knowledge and Folklore.

As part of his efforts to promote good practices, the SR also carried out working visits to two countries, Bolivia and Chile. In March 2014, he delivered a lecture on international human rights and indigenous peoples at a conference hosted by the Andean University Simón Bolivar and the Office of the High Commissioner for Human Rights, in La Paz, Bolivia. During his stay, the SR conducted informal meetings with representatives of indigenous peoples and the Government of Bolivia regarding key issues affecting indigenous peoples in the country, including issues related to the development of a law on consultation. In April 2014, the Special Rapporteur visited Chile to give a lecture on the duty of the state to consult with indigenous peoples during a conference organized by the Universidad Diego Portales. He also made a keynote speech during a meeting of various business enterprises organized by Global Compact Chile. While he was in Chile, the SR also met with several representatives of the state, as well as delegations of representatives of indigenous peoples, NGOs and academics. During the meeting, views on the key challenges for the protection of the rights of indigenous peoples in Chile were exchanged.

In April 2014, the SR James Anaya hosted a meeting in Tucson, Arizona, United States to provide reflections on his mandate as Special Rapporteur. The meeting brought together the newly-appointed Special Rapporteur, Victoria Tauli-Corpuz, academics, United Nations representatives, non-governmental organizations, and representatives of the UNPFII and the Expert Mechanism on the Rights of Indigenous Peoples (EMRIP). Participants welcomed the new mandate holder and discussed the working methods of and lessons learned from the Special Rapporteur on the rights of indigenous peoples.

Work of the new Special Rapporteur, Victoria Tauli-Corpuz, in 2014

Ms Victoria Tauli-Corpuz assumed her mandate as new Special Rapporteur on the rights of indigenous peoples on 2 June 2014. Ms Tauli-Corpuz is a well-known Kankanay Igorot activist from the Cordillera (the Philippines). She was a member of the UN Permanent Forum on Indigenous Issues, where she served as Chair for the period 2005-2010 and has also been chairperson-rapporteur of the UN-OHCHR Voluntary Fund for Indigenous Populations. She is an expert on issues such as sustainable development, indigenous women's rights, the impact of investments on the rights of indigenous peoples and climate change. She has been a negotiator in the process of the UNFCCC for some years, both as indigenous and governmental representative. She was the founder and Executive Director of Tebtebba Foundation, an indigenous peoples' international centre for policy research and education based in Baguio. She has been advisor to several NGO and UN programs and agencies.

Thematic reports

Ms Tauli-Corpuz submitted her first report to the Human Rights Council on 17 September 2014, during its 27th session. In her report,[5] the Special Rapporteur noted that there was already a strong legal and policy foundation for, and some advances in, the implementation of indigenous peoples' rights. However, serious obstacles remain such as the failure of some governments to recognize indigenous peoples; a lack of practical implementation measures; the need to complete reconciliation and redress for past wrongs; discrimination and negative attitudes on the part of the broader society; and social and economic conditions that prevent the full exercise of indigenous peoples' rights. The Special Rapporteur expressed her intention to offer solutions to address these ongoing challenges through her country visits, thematic studies and communications work according to her mandate. Over the next three years, she intends to focus particularly on issues surrounding the economic, social, cultural and environmental rights of indigenous peoples. She also stated the need for a thematic report on indigenous women and children. The SR also introduced to the Human Rights Council (HRC) the mission reports of her predecessor, Professor James Anaya, to Peru, Panama and Canada, as well as the report containing his communications.[6]

On 20 October, the Special Rapporteur submitted her report to the Third Committee of the UN General Assembly.[7] The SR focused on indigenous peoples' economic, social and cultural rights within the context of development and, particularly, within the framework of ongoing UN discussions on the post-2015 Agenda for sustainable development. The SR analyses the historic context of the concept of development and its implications for indigenous peoples, the link between economic, social and cultural rights and self-determination and non-discrimination, and the need for special and truly effective measures in order to fully implement those rights. She also assesses the failure of the Millennium Development Goals in terms of promoting human rights, including the rights of indigenous peoples, and points out the main challenges that should be taken into account in the new sustainable development goals in order to overcome such failure.

Country visits

From 21 to 28 November, the SR undertook her first official country mission to Paraguay. During her visit, the SR had the chance to meet with government representatives, civil society organizations and indigenous peoples' organizations and communities in several parts of the country. In her statement upon conclusion of the visit,[8] the SR made some preliminary observations and recommendations. While recognizing the positive legal framework in the country with regard to indigenous peoples' rights, the SR expressed her concern at the lack of land rights security for indigenous peoples in the country, as nearly half of the indigenous communities do not have legally-recognized lands and, even when lands have been titled to the communities, land security is not ensured and members of the communities are subject to encroachment and harassment by agro-business, logging companies, cattle ranchers and others. She recommended establishing effective land adjudication mechanisms to solve indigenous peoples' claims to lands, territories and resources. She also underlined the striking poverty situation faced by many indigenous peoples in Paraguay, even in a national context of overall economic growth, as shown by relevant socio-economic indicators. She referred to the lack of adequate basic social services, particularly health and education, and the need to upgrade and provide adequate funding to the national institution in charge of indigenous affairs (INDI) so that it can respond to these challenges. The SR also called for the Paraguayan government to develop an adequate legal framework for the implementation of indigenous peoples' rights to consultation, consent and participation, and underlined the key concern of a lack of access to justice. She called for the full implementation of the Inter-American Court on Human Rights' decisions on the Sawhoyamaxa, Yakye Axa and Xamok Kasek cases. She concluded by stating that racism and discrimination were at the root of many of the problems faced by indigenous peoples in the country. The SR will submit the report of her mission to the HRC in September 2015.

Communications and public statements

The SR has continued working on the area of communications to respond to allegations of violations of the rights of indigenous peoples. Apart from communicating with several governments, the SR, together with Baskut Tuncak, SR on the implications for human rights of the environmentally sound management and disposal of hazardous substances and wastes, issued a press released on the situation in block 192 (formerly block 1 AB) in the Peruvian Amazon on 15 December 2014. The SRs referred to information on the proposed new licensing of the block, and reminded the Peruvian government of the need to respect indigenous peoples' rights, including their rights of consultation and consent, and to comply with commitments to solve the serious health problems and clean up the lands and waters heavily polluted after 44 years of oil exploration and exploitation in the area, prior to any new concession.[9]

The SR released a public statement on the occasion of the UN International Day of the World's Indigenous Peoples, calling on states to address human rights violations and to ensure the participation of indigenous peoples in formulating and implementing their national and local development strategies and plans. The SR underlined the importance of access to justice, which remains "elusive for many indigenous peoples in many parts of the world".[10]

In December 2014, the SR signed a joint public letter by 28 special procedures addressed to the President of the World Bank drawing the attention of this international financial institution to its human rights obligations and expressing the concerning weaknesses of the new environmental and social policies under consideration, including with respect to the rights of indigenous peoples.[11]

Collaboration with other specialized UN bodies

In line with her mandate and established practice, the SR has collaborated with the UN Permanent Forum on Indigenous Peoples (UNPFII) and the Expert Mechanism on the Rights of Indigenous Peoples (EMRIP) over this period. Before formally assuming her mandate, she participated - together with SR Anaya - in the 13th session of the UNPFII, which took place in May in New York. In July, she participated in the 7th session of the EMRIP, where she delivered a statement on the forthcoming UN World Conference on Indigenous Peoples (WCIP) and took part in a discussion roundtable on the post-2015 agenda on sustainable development.[12] The three specialized mechanisms issued a public statement[13] on this issue calling on the Open-ended Working Group on the Sustainable Development Goals to use the term "indigenous peoples" and to give due attention to their rights and concerns in the outcome of their deliberations.

During her participation in those meetings, the SR pursued the established practice of holding meetings with indigenous representatives attending the sessions to hear about allegations of violations of their human rights.

Other activities

On 21 and 22 September 2014, the World Conference on Indigenous Peoples, a thematic high-level meeting, was held in New York during the 69th session of the UN General Assembly. The SR actively participated in the WCIP, both as speaker in several side events and in the official roundtable on "UN system-wide actions for the implementation of the rights of indigenous peoples".[14]

The SR was also invited to speak on a panel on "integrating the Guiding Principles in UN human rights mechanisms" organized by the UN Working Group on Business and Human Rights during the third session of the UN Forum on Business and Human rights, which took place in Geneva from 1 to 3 December 2014. She also participated in an event on indigenous peoples and access to remedy, coordinated by indigenous organizations and support groups.[15]

The SR participated in the COP20 of the UNFCCC, held in Lima, Peru, and delivered several interventions in relevant side events. The SR has been invited by indigenous organizations to meetings and activities in several countries. The SR has established a website where her reports, statements and other activities can be accessed: www.unsrvtaulicorpuz.org ○

Notes and references

1   A/HRC/24/41
2   A/68/317
3   A/HRC/27/52/Add.1 The situation of Indigenous peoples in Panama; A/HRC/27/52/Add.2 The situation of Indigenous peoples in Canada; A/HRC/27/52/Add.3 The situation of indigenous peoples' rights in Peru with regard to the extractive industries.
4   A/HRC/27/52/Add.4 Observations on communications.
5   A/HRC/27/52
6   A/HRC/27/52/Add.1; A/HRC/27/52/Add.2; A/HRC/27/52/Add.3; A/HRC/27/52/Add.4
7   A/69/267 Rights of indigenous peoples, including their economic, social and cultural rights in the post-2015 development framework. 6 August 2014.
8   See http://unsr.vtaulicorpuz.org/site/index.php/en/news/notes/45-conclusion-visit-paraguay
9   http://unsr.vtaulicorpuz.org/site/index.php/es/declaraciones-comunicados/55-peru-oil-project
10   http://unsr.vtaulicorpuz.org/site/index.php/en/statements/24-indigenousday-2014
11   Reference OL OTH/13/2014. At http://unsr.vtaulicorpuz.org/site/index.php/en/statements/53-joint-letter-to-worldbank
12   http://unsr.vtaulicorpuz.org/site/index.php/en/news/notes/21-unsr-participates-emrip

13 Signed by Ms Dalee Sambo Dorough, Chair of the UNPFII, Mr. Albert Deterville, Chair of the EMRIP and the SR. See http://unsr.vtaulicorpuz.org/site/index.php/en/statements/22-statement-indigenous-post2015

14 http://unsr.vtaulicorpuz.org/site/index.php/en/statements/31-statement-un-wcip2014

15 All the information on the 3rd session of the UN Forum can be found at http://www.ohchr.org/EN/Issues/Business/Forum/Pages/2014ForumonBusinessandHumanRights.aspx

Maia Campbell worked for the Special Procedures Branch of the OHCHR in Geneva supporting the work of the SR Prof. James Anaya. She now works in the Secretariat of the PFII at the UN headquarters in New York.

Patricia Borraz works as an assistant to the SR Victoria Tauli Corpuz as part of the project to support the UN SRRIP.

UN EXPERT MECHANISM ON THE RIGHTS OF INDIGENOUS PEOPLES

The United Nations Expert Mechanism on the Rights of Indigenous Peoples was established in 2007 by the Human Rights Council under resolution 6/36 as a subsidiary body. The mandate of the Expert Mechanism is to provide the Human Rights Council with thematic expertise, mainly in the form of studies and research, on the rights of indigenous peoples as directed by the Council. The Expert Mechanism may also make proposals to the Council for its consideration and approval. It comprises five experts on the rights of indigenous peoples, one from each of the world's five geopolitical regions, with indigenous origin a relevant factor in their appointment. They are appointed by the Human Rights Council for terms of three years, and may be re-elected for one additional period.

The Expert Mechanism meets in a plenary session once a year for up to five days and these sessions are open to representatives of indigenous peoples, states, NGOs, UN entities, national human rights institutions and academics. The sessions of the Expert Mechanism provide a unique space for focused multilateral discussions on the scope and content of the rights affirmed to indigenous peoples under international law, and how the implementation of these rights can be advanced. The Office of the United Nations High Commissioner for Human Rights (OHCHR) services the Expert Mechanism and also provides technical and financial support.

New membership

In March 2014, the Human Rights Council reappointed International Chief Wilton Littlechild (Canada) to a second three-year term. The Council also appointed Mr. Edtami Mansayagan (Philippines), who replaced Ms Jannie Lasimbang (Malaysia).

International Expert Seminar

On 18 and 19 February 2014, the University of Auckland hosted an Expert Seminar on Restorative Justice, Indigenous Juridical Systems and Access to Justice for Indigenous Women, Children and Youth and Persons with Disabilities. The objective of the seminar was to support the Expert Mechanism in its drafting of the 2014 study on this theme.

The event was organized by the Faculty of Law of the University of Auckland and the Office of the High Commissioner for Human Rights, in cooperation with the Expert Mechanism. Panellists and participants addressed issues including the relationship between indigenous juridical systems and international human rights law; discrimination against indigenous women, children and youth and persons with disabilities in criminal justice systems; and the concept and practice of restorative justice, including its links with peace and reconciliation.

7th Session of the Expert Mechanism

The annual session of the Expert Mechanism took place in Geneva from 7 to 11 July 2014. In addition to the five members of the Expert Mechanism, participants included representatives of states, indigenous peoples, United Nations entities, non-governmental organizations, national human rights institutions and academics.

The Expert Mechanism held a panel discussion on the Post-2015 Development Agenda. The 7th session also provided an opportunity to discuss the World Conference on Indigenous Peoples, which took place on 22 and 23 September 2014, including the zero draft of its outcome document.

The Expert Mechanism presented two studies for discussion. The first was a follow-up study on access to justice, with a focus on indigenous juridical systems, restorative justice, and access to justice for indigenous women, children and youth and persons with disabilities. The second addressed the theme of promotion and protection of the rights of indigenous peoples in disaster risk reduction initiatives.

The 7th session also included a discussion of the United Nations Declaration on the Rights of Indigenous Peoples, comprising a panel discussion on the role of parliaments in the implementation of the Declaration.[1]

Proposals

At its 7th session, the Expert Mechanism made the following proposals to the Human Rights Council:

Theme of the Expert Mechanism's new study
The Expert Mechanism proposed that the Human Rights Council authorize the Expert Mechanism to undertake a study on the promotion and protection of the right of indigenous peoples to their cultural heritage, including sports and traditional games.[2]

World Conference on Indigenous Peoples
The Expert Mechanism proposed that the Human Rights Council organize a panel on the outcome of the World Conference on Indigenous Peoples and its implications for the implementation of the United Nations Declaration on the Rights of Indigenous Peoples.

Business and human Rights
The Expert Mechanism proposed that the Human Rights Council request the Expert Mechanism to convene a technical expert seminar, in collaboration with the Working Group on the issue of human rights and transnational corporations and other business enterprises, and with the participation of the Special Rapporteur on the rights of indigenous peoples and the Permanent Forum on Indigenous Issues, to elaborate guidance on the issue of indigenous peoples' access to justice and remedy in the context of business operations affecting their human rights.

United Nations Declaration on the Rights of Indigenous Peoples
The Expert Mechanism proposed that the Human Rights Council:

- Urge states and indigenous peoples to report on the measures taken to implement the rights enshrined in the Declaration through the continuation of the Expert Mechanism's questionnaire survey.

- Call upon states to establish, with the full and effective participation of indigenous peoples, independent mechanisms to oversee and promote the implementation of the rights contained in the Declaration.
- Encourage the General Assembly to adopt appropriate permanent measures to ensure that indigenous peoples' governance bodies and institutions, including traditional indigenous governments, indigenous parliaments, assemblies and councils, are able to participate at the United Nations as observers with, as a minimum, the same participatory rights as non-governmental organizations in consultative status with the Economic and Social Council.

Post-2015 development agenda

The Expert Mechanism proposed that the Human Rights Council urge states to address the concerns of indigenous peoples in the post-2015 development agenda and to take measures to ensure the participation of indigenous peoples, and in particular indigenous youth, in national processes for the implementation of the new development goals.

Indigenous human rights defenders

The Expert Mechanism proposed that the Human Rights Council pay particular attention to indigenous human rights defenders in its work on this theme, drawing in particular on the work of the Special Rapporteur on the situation of human rights defenders and on Council resolution 25/18.

Adoption of studies and reports

During its 7th session, the Expert Mechanism also adopted its follow-up study and advice on indigenous peoples' access to justice[3] and its study and advice on the promotion and protection of the rights of indigenous peoples in disaster risk reduction initiatives.[4] The report on the summary of responses to the questionnaire seeking the views of states and indigenous peoples on best practices regarding possible appropriate measures and implementation strategies to attain the goals of the Declaration was also adopted.[5]

27th session of the Human Rights Council

The Expert Mechanism conducted its interactive dialogue with the Human Rights Council during its September session jointly with the Special Rapporteur on the rights of indigenous peoples. Mr. Albert Deterville, Chair-Rapporteur of the Expert Mechanism, presented the work of the Expert Mechanism. He introduced the follow-up study and advice on access to justice and the study and advice on the promotion and protection of the rights of indigenous peoples in disaster risk reduction initiatives, and briefed the Council on some of the Expert Mechanism's inter-sessional activities, particularly with respect to the World Conference on Indigenous Peoples. Mr. Deterville also urged the Council to provide the financial resources necessary to facilitate the Expert Mechanism's inter-sessional activities, including the annual expert seminar.

The interactive dialogue was followed by the annual half-day discussion on indigenous peoples, which was devoted to the theme of the promotion and protection of the rights of indigenous peoples in disaster risk reduction initiatives. The half-day discussion included statements by Ms Margareta Wahlström (SRSG for Disaster Risk Reduction), Mr. Albert Deterville, Ms Aissatou Oumarou (representative of the Association of Peul Indigenous Women of Chad), Mr. Giovanni Reyes (Secretary-General of the National Coalition of Indigenous Peoples in the Philippines) and Mr. Alejandro Maldonado (Executive Secretary of the National Coordination Office for Disaster Reduction of Guatemala). Ms Victoria Tauli-Corpuz, Special Rapporteur on the rights of indigenous peoples, moderated the discussion. During the ensuing discussion, statements from the floor were made by a number of states, as well as civil society organizations. Speakers welcomed the Expert Mechanism's study and agreed on the need to engage indigenous peoples in disaster risk reduction and ensure their participation and their right to be consulted in disaster risk reduction initiatives, including indigenous women and children.

World Conference on Indigenous Peoples

The Chair-Rapporteur represented the Expert Mechanism at the World Conference on Indigenous Peoples (WCIP), which took place in New York on 22 and 23

September 2014, and served as a panellist at the discussion on Indigenous Priorities for the Post-2015 Sustainable Development Agenda. He underlined the importance of indigenous peoples' participation in the Post-2015 process, both at national and international level.

Paragraph 28 of the WCIP Outcome Document makes specific reference to the Expert Mechanism, inviting the Human Rights Council to review its mandate, "with a view to modifying and improving the Expert Mechanism so that it can more effectively promote respect for the Declaration, including by better assisting Member States to monitor, evaluate and improve the achievement of the ends of the Declaration." [6]   ◯

Notes and references

1   UN document A/HRC/27/64
2   The final title of the study, as requested by the Human Rights Council in resolution 27/13 is *Promotion and protection of the rights of indigenous peoples with respect to their cultural heritage, including through their participation in political and public life.*
3   UN document A/HRC/27/65
4   UN document A/HRC/27/66
5   UN document A/HRC/27/67
6   General Assembly Resolution 69/2.

Juan Fernando Núñez is Human Rights Officer in the Indigenous Peoples and Minorities Section of the Research and Right to Development Division of the Office of the United Nations High Commissioner for Human Rights.

ILO CONVENTION Nº 169

The International Labour Organisation (ILO) Indigenous and Tribal Peoples Convention No. 169 (C169) is an international treaty, adopted by the International Labour Conference of the ILO in 1989. C169 is, along with the United Nations Declaration on the Rights of Indigenous Peoples adopted by the UN General Assembly in 2007, a cornerstone of the international framework on the rights of indigenous peoples. To date, 22 countries have ratified the Convention, with some two-thirds of ratifying States found in Latin America. In Europe, the most recent ratification, that of Spain, dates back to 2007. The Asian continent is yet to record a second ratification of the Convention after that of Nepal in 2007. In Africa, the Central African Republic remains the only country that has ratified this instrument (in 2010).

Seminar on learning from 25 years' experience of ILO Convention No. 169

In 2014, the C169 turned 25. In order to mark this anniversary, a seminar entitled "Enabling rights-based development for indigenous and tribal peoples: Learning from 25 years' experience of ILO Convention No. 169" was held in Geneva on 27 and 28 November 2014. This seminar was organised by the ILO, the Ministry of Foreign Affairs of Denmark, the Permanent Mission of Mexico to the International Organisations, IWGIA and the University of Lucerne, with more than 100 people attending from the ILO, UN agencies, ratifying and non-ratifying states, indigenous peoples and NGOs, plus employers' and workers' organisations.

The objectives of the meeting were: to take stock of ILO Convention No. 169 (C 169) as an enabling tool for indigenous peoples' rights-based and self-determined development; to provide a platform for sharing lessons learned and identifying key challenges and future actions for the effective implementation of indigenous peoples' rights as enshrined in the Convention; and to develop concrete recommendations for its enhanced implementation. Although there were a diverse array of visions expressed at the event, there was broad agreement among the participants regarding the positive effects the Convention has had since its approval but also regarding the many weaknesses that remain in terms of its implementation.

On the positive side, many constitutional reforms and decisions taken by international and domestic courts have drawn on the Convention and it has contributed to resolving conflicts between indigenous peoples and states, as well as influencing policies and programmes, particularly but not exclusively within the ratifying states. One noted weakness was the fact that it has been ratified by only 22 states, 15 of which are in Latin America, meaning that C 169 covers less than 15% of the world's indigenous population (some 50 million out of an estimated 370 million).

The participants also agreed that the Convention's implementation remains a challenge as there are significant implementation gaps in many states and these have negative consequences for indigenous peoples, in the form of poverty and human rights violations, particularly of their collective rights to land, territories and natural resources in the context of development activities.

Some of the recommendations to emerge from this event involved a commitment from the participants to promote the Convention's ratification and to contribute to tackling and closing the implementation gaps through the adoption of regulatory frameworks and measures that ensure its effective application. It was considered particularly important to complete the demarcation of indigenous lands, and to ensure the effective consultation – and participation – of indigenous peoples and communities in decision-making processes and benefit-sharing agreements. Participants also agreed that the ILO needed to play a more active role in disseminating information on the Convention, both at national, regional and local level, and in building the capacity of all actors, including government officials, indigenous peoples and the private sector, as well as employers' and workers' organisations, to implement the Convention. There was also agreement on the need to ensure better access for indigenous peoples to the ILO's supervisory mechanisms. The UN plan of action proposed at the World Conference on Indigenous Peoples was highlighted as an opportunity to strengthen links between UN agencies, states and indigenous peoples in order to support ratification and implementation.[1]

Given that the greatest number of ratifications of C 169, and thus the greatest application, has been in Latin America, the seminar considered the implications of this instrument for indigenous rights in that region in some depth. Central to this was a presentation of the report on "Challenges facing the implementation of ILO Convention No. 169 in Latin America on its 25th anniversary", produced at IW-GIA's request by a group of researchers and indigenous rights defenders, both indigenous and non-indigenous, from across the region.[2] The analyses given in this report, which focus among other things on indigenous peoples' rights to their lands, territories and natural resources, the right to prior consultation, the right to set their own development priorities, customary law and indigenous justice systems, plus the rights of indigenous women (some of which were presented at the event by the authors), are conclusive in demonstrating that this international treaty has had a significant impact on the recognition (at least formal - constitutional, legal, jurisprudential, and partial implementation of indigenous rights in Latin America. The importance of the Inter-American Human Rights System's case law on indigenous rights is clearly demonstrated, both in this report and in the seminar's contributions, as it has drawn on C 169 to resolve demands related to the rights to land, consultation and free, prior and informed consent, as well as indigenous peoples' political participation in the region. The observations and recommendations of the ILO supervisory bodies when applying C 169 in the region have also been important but sadly not followed up in terms of fulfilment by the relevant states.

One of the areas of greatest concern noted at the seminar with regard to the implementation of C 169 in Latin America was the exercise of indigenous peoples' right to consultation in the face of administrative actions relating to investment projects on indigenous lands and territories. Several of the speakers noted that getting states to fulfil their duty in this regard remains a challenge.

One issue that caught people's attention during the seminar was the studies commissioned by the ILO on the effects of the application of C 169 on investment projects, the results of which were presented by representatives of the employers' organisations. According to these studies, conducted in a number of Latin American countries, the application of C 169 has been a disincentive to investment. It was rather worrying that the ILO should give a platform to this business rhetoric, which questions the validity of a rights-based framework in order to guarantee investments which are very often in direct conflict with indigenous peoples' right to set their own development priorities.

All in all, it was an important seminar that successfully identified the challenges facing the different actors - ILO, states, indigenous peoples, employers and human rights organisations - in terms of enforcing the rights recognised in C 169. In relation to the ILO, there was agreement that indigenous peoples and their territories are now suffering from unprecedented pressure caused by the imposition of a development vision that does not respect their lands, resources or life plans, and that the ILO needs to strengthen its action on C 169 so that this instrument can, over the next 25 years, become a powerful tool for intercultural dialogue that will enable justice to be done for indigenous peoples, and which will encourage societies to be more respectful of ethnic and cultural diversity both in the Latin America region and throughout the world.   ◯

Notes and references

1   Summary of Discussion Seminar on "Enabling rights-based development for indigenous and tribal peoples:
    Learning from 25 years' experience of ILO Convention No. 169", Geneva 27-28 November 2014.
2   Available at http://www.iwgia.org/iwgia_files_publications_files/0701_convenio169OIT2014.pdf

José Aylwin, Co-Director Observatorio Ciudadano, Chile.

THE UNITED NATIONS FRAMEWORK CONVENTION ON CLIMATE CHANGE

The United Nations Framework Convention on Climate Change (UNFC-CC) is an international treaty created at the Earth Summit in Rio in 1992 to tackle the growing problem of global warming and the related harmful effects of a changing climate, such as more frequent droughts, storms and hurricanes, melting of ice, rising sea levels, flooding, forest fires, etc. The UNFCCC entered into force on 21 March 1994, and has near universal membership, with 195 countries as ratifying parties. In 1997, the Convention established its Kyoto Protocol, ratified by 184 parties, by which a number of industrialized countries have committed to reducing their greenhouse gas emissions in line with legally binding targets.

In 2007, the Convention's governing body, the Conference of the Parties (COP), adopted the Bali Action Plan. The elements of the Bali Action Plan (a shared vision, mitigation, adaptation, technology development and transfer, provision of financial resources and investments) were negotiated in the Ad Hoc Working Group on Long-Term Cooperative Action (AWG-LCA). Apart from the Kyoto Protocol's working group (AWG-KP) and the AWG-LCA, the Convention has two permanent subsidiary bodies, namely the Subsidiary Body for Scientific and Technological Advice (SBSTA) and the Subsidiary Body for Implementation (SBI). In December 2012, during the COP18 in Doha, the AWG-LCA concluded its work and most discussions were terminated or moved to the SBSTA and SBI. COP18 adopted the Durban Platform for Enhanced Action (ADP) that will lead the COP discussions towards an overall binding agreement on emissions reductions in 2015.

Indigenous peoples are organized in the International Indigenous Peoples Forum on Climate Change (IIPFCC), which serves as a mechanism to develop the united positions/statements of indigenous peoples and continue effective lobbying and advocacy work in the UNFCCC meetings/sessions. Indigenous rights and issues cut across almost all areas of

> negotiation but have been highlighted most significantly within the REDD+ (Reducing Emissions from Deforestation and Forest Degradation, Conservation, Enhancement of Carbon Stocks and Sustainable Management of Forests), one of the mitigation measures negotiated under the AWG-LCA.

The 2014 negotiations under the UNFCCC were marked by the fast approaching deadline for a new climate agreement, which should fall into place in Paris at COP21 in 2015. COP20, which took place in Lima, Peru in December 2014, was therefore seen as a crucial step towards the new climate agreement.

Indigenous Peoples' rights in the 2015 Climate Change Agreement

For indigenous peoples, getting their rights recognized and secured in the 2015 Climate Change agreement is vital. Indigenous peoples have a very close relationship with their lands, territories and resources. It is because of this close relationship with nature that indigenous peoples, including indigenous women, are disproportionately affected by the adverse impacts of climate change. These adverse effects also undermine the equitable development of present and future generations and have a range of direct and indirect implications on the full and effective enjoyment of their human rights. The 2015 climate change agreement must therefore address indigenous peoples' climate change concerns, acknowledge their potential contribution to climate change solutions and respect, protect and fulfill their collective rights to their lands, territories and resources, unlike the Kyoto Protocol, which does not mention indigenous peoples at all.

On 17 October 2014, a group of human rights experts submitted an open letter calling on the States Parties to include language in the 2015 climate agreement that provides that the parties shall, in all climate change-related actions, respect, protect, promote and fulfill human rights for all. The letter also specifically mentioned respecting the principle of free, prior and informed consent of indigenous peoples.

Indigenous peoples' dialogue with states in Lima, Peru

In 2013, during COP19 in Warsaw, indigenous representatives had initial meetings with the delegation of Peru to arrange a global dialogue between indigenous peoples and states before COP20 in Lima, Peru. Such pre-COP meetings have been organized twice before by Mexico and were valuable venues for indigenous peoples to develop advocacy-focused strategies. The International Indigenous Peoples Forum on Climate Change (IIPFCC) set up a global steering committee that met several times during 2014 and prepared the pre-COP meeting while a technical team developed an indigenous peoples' position paper for COP20 and COP21. The meeting took place before the official COP20, with around 80 indigenous participants and 10 state representatives.[1] The meeting was a key venue for indigenous peoples to dialogue with friendly states in order to exchange views and position on different elements of the negotiations.

Indigenous peoples at COP20 in Lima, Peru

The indigenous peoples' position paper for COP20 and COP21 comprises six key messages. These are as follows:

1. Recognition of a human rights-based approach which respects indigenous peoples' rights in climate change agreements and related actions
2. Respect for indigenous peoples' rights to lands, territories and resources
3. Recognition of, and respect for, indigenous traditional knowledge and the role of indigenous peoples in adaptation and mitigation
4. Recognition and support of indigenous peoples' community-based monitoring and information system (CBMIS)
5. Respect indigenous peoples' rights to full and effective participation in all climate change actions and UNFCCC institutions
6. Ensure indigenous peoples' direct access to finance and capacity building.

Indigenous representatives lobbied on these messages throughout COP20 in all interventions provided to indigenous constituents. The IIPFCC has also arranged meetings with both outgoing and incoming COP Chairs (Lima and Paris) in order to create a regular venue in which to deliver indigenous positions and exchange views.

With the support of the Peruvian Ministry of the Environment, Norway and UNDP, the Inter-ethnic Association for the Development of the Peruvian Forest (AIDESEP) organized the Indigenous Pavilion during the first week of COP20, during which thematic panels on different issues took place, and where an exhibition was established. Indigenous peoples hope that future hosts of COP meetings will continue to support the organization of Indigenous Pavilions.

As a parallel event to COP20, civil society, including six indigenous organisations from Peru, organized the Peoples' Summit on Climate Change from 8-11 December. The Peoples' Summit also included a Global March of Peoples in Defence of Mother Earth on 10 December, which was joined by many indigenous representatives from all over the world.

Reducing Emissions from Deforestation and Forest Degradation (REDD+) in 2014

The negotiations around REDD+ remain one of the most crucial for indigenous peoples in forest areas and are hence closely followed by the IIPFCC. Many indigenous organizations are today involved in the national development of REDD+, which is described in several articles in this volume.

In 2014, the SBSTA discussed the issues of non-carbon benefits (NCBs) in REDD+ and Safeguards Information Systems (SIS). Parties and observers submitted their views on NCBs in March, and these were taken into consideration by the 40th session of SBSTA. However, no agreement on this methodological issue could be reached. The draft text of SBSTA dated 10 June 2014 noted that non-carbon benefits were specific to national circumstances. This has serious implications for indigenous peoples, as land rights are one of the crucial non-carbon benefits for indigenous peoples. Indigenous peoples raised their grave concerns on the emerging situation, which could potentially give rise to excuses among the parties in relation to accelerating the disbursement of results-based payment without addressing land tenure issues and the IIPFCC called for the formulation of international guidance on methodological issues regarding non-carbon benefits.[2] As the parties could not agree on the issue, the SBSTA will continue its consideration in June 2015.

The 41st session of the SBSTA, which met during COP20, could not reach a consensus on further guidance for Safeguards Information Systems (SIS) due to deep divisions between the parties. Some parties expressed support for additional guidance and for the need to have clarity on the types of information SIS should entail. The Philippines, for example, stated that further detail on the type of information would be useful for both developed and developing countries.[3] Indigenous peoples' representatives in COP20 also advocated for additional guidance on SIS and called on the parties to take the opportunity to strengthen the rights of indigenous peoples and local communities.[4] However, Guyana, India, Tanzania, Indonesia, Brazil, Colombia, Ecuador, Costa Rica and Thailand were opposed to additional guidance on SIS, stating that national circumstances should guide the type of information to be provided. The discussion will continue in June 2015.

Adaptation in 2014

Indigenous peoples and communities have demonstrated their ability and wisdom to adapt to climate variability, generating knowledge, developing technologies and forms of social organization that determine the collective management of their territory. This was also recognized in the 5th Assessment Report of the Intergovernmental Panel on Climate Change (IPCC) in 2013 (see *The Indigenous World 2014*).

In Lima, UNEP launched its *Adaptation Gap Report,* which provides a framework for defining adaptation gaps and a preliminary assessment of the gap between adaptation needs and reality. It will support discussions under the UNFCCC, including on adaptation aspects of the 2015 agreement, the discussion on defining a global goal for adaptation, aspects of loss and damage, and the National Adaptation Plan (NAP) process.

Indigenous peoples have gained ground in the discussions on adaptation to climate change. A joint meeting on available tools for the use of indigenous and traditional knowledge and practices for adaptation, the needs of local and indigenous communities and the application of gender-sensitive approaches and tools for adaptation was organized by the Adaptation Committee under the Nairobi

Work Program on 1-4 April 2014 in Bonn, Germany. Some of the indigenous representatives from different regions were invited to the meeting, where they contributed by sharing their good practices, opportunities, challenges and recommendations regarding the use of indigenous knowledge and practices for adaptation. This sharing helped to raise the awareness of UNFCCC parties, relevant international and intergovernmental organizations and non-governmental organizations (NGOs) as to the good practices of indigenous knowledge pertinent to climate change adaptation.

The COP20 Report and indigenous peoples

The decisions adopted by COP20, after much wrangling and division between the opinions of developed and developing countries, mention "indigenous peoples" four times. Furthermore, indigenous peoples' rights are recognized in the preamble to the "*Elements for a draft negotiating text*", which is the basis coming out of Lima on which to negotiate a 2015 agreement:

> *Stressing that all actions to address climate change and all the processes established under this agreement should ensure a gender-responsive approach, take into account environmental integrity / the protection of the integrity of Mother Earth, and respect human rights, the right to development and the rights of indigenous peoples*

It is positive that indigenous peoples' rights and the need for a gender-responsive approach are included in the preamble to the draft negotiating text. However, the sections of the draft negotiating text on mitigation; adaptation and loss and damage; finance; technology development and transfer and capacity building, among others, have not operationalized indigenous peoples' rights as undertaken by the UNFCCC parties. It is therefore very important that indigenous peoples sustain their strategic advocacy and lobbying throughout 2015 in order to maintain what is in the negotiating text and further try to include human rights language, including the key messages of the indigenous peoples' advocacy document drafted in Peru, in all elements of the 2015 climate change agreement. This needs a great deal of collective preparation on the part of indigenous peoples from all regions of the world.   ○

Notes and references

1   The states present were Brazil, Peru, Panama, Mexico, Norway, USA, Tuvalu, Bolivia, France and Canada.
2   Statement of the International Indigenous Peoples Forum on Climate Change (IIPFCC) in the closing session of SBSTA 40, June 2014.
3   TWN Lima News Update No.33: Divisions on safeguards remain on REDD-plus; no outcome in Lima.
4   Statement of IIPFCC in the opening session of SBSTA 41, December 2014.

Shree Kumar Maharjan is an indigenous Newar from Nepal. He is a conservation ecologist and the Deputy Secretary-General of the Asia Indigenous Peoples' Pact (AIPP).

Gideon Sanago is a Maasai from Tanzania. He works for the Association for Law and Advocacy for Pastoralists (ALAPA).

Lakpa Nuri Sherpa belongs to the Sherpa indigenous group of Nepal and is currently working for AIPP as Regional Coordinator for the Climate Change Partnership with Indigenous Peoples.

Rodion Sulyandziga is an indigenous Udege from the Russian Far East. He chaired the IIPFCC throughout 2014.

Kathrin Wessendorf is a Swiss anthropologist working for IWGIA as Environment and Climate Programme Coordinator.

CONVENTION ON BIOLOGICAL DIVERSITY

The Convention on Biological Diversity (CBD) is an international treaty under the United Nations. The CBD has three objectives: to conserve biodiversity, to promote its sustainable use and to ensure the equitable sharing of the benefits arising from its utilization.

The Convention has developed programs of work on thematic issues (such as marine, agricultural or forest biodiversity) and cross-cutting issues (such as traditional knowledge, access to genetic resources or protected areas). All these programs of work have a direct impact on indigenous peoples' rights and territories. The CBD recognizes the importance of indigenous knowledge and customary sustainable use for the achievement of its objectives (articles 8(j) and 10(c)) and emphasizes their vital role in biodiversity. In 2010, COP10 adopted the Nagoya Protocol on Genetic Resources and the Fair and Equitable Sharing of Benefits Arising from their Utilization (ABS)[1], the Aichi Targets and a new multi-year program of work.

The International Indigenous Forum on Biodiversity (IIFB) was established in 1996, during COP3, as the indigenous caucus in the CBD negotiations. Since then, it has worked as a coordination mechanism to facilitate indigenous participation in, and advocacy on, the work of the Convention through preparatory meetings, capacity-building activities and other initiatives. The IIFB has managed to get many of the CBD programs of work to consider traditional knowledge, customary use or the effective participation of indigenous peoples, and has been active in the negotiations regarding access to genetic resources in order to defend the fundamental rights of indigenous peoples that should be included therein.

The 12th Conference of the Parties (COP 12)

With the theme of "Biodiversity for Sustainable Development", the 12th meeting of the Conference of the Parties to the Convention on Biological Diversity (CBD COP 12) was held from 6th to 17th October 2014 in Pyeongchang, South Korea. The meeting was aimed at raising international awareness of the essential role of biodiversity and its contribution to sustainable development, as well as highlighting biodiversity in the context of the post-2015 Development Agenda and the Sustainable Development Goals (SDGs). This meeting also covered the 1st COP to the CBD, serving as the *Meeting of the Parties* (MOP) to the Nagoya Protocol.

Indigenous representatives from the seven indigenous geopolitical regions gathered in the International Indigenous Forum on Biodiversity (IIFB) to present the indigenous views on biodiversity conservation and to advocate their positions with State Parties on issues related to sustainable development, climate change and synthetic biology; a Global Strategy for Plant Conservation, Marine and Coastal Biodiversity; the 4th Global Biodiversity Outlook (GBO-4); the place of traditional knowledge in the CBD process; ABS mechanism; Multi-year Programme of Work of the Conference of the Parties up to 2020 etc.[2]

At COP12, a Global Plan of Action on Customary Sustainable Use was adopted with the aim of positively contributing to poverty eradication and sustainable development. Indigenous peoples remain hopeful that this plan of action will be incorporated by states into their National Biodiversity Strategies and Action Plans and be further developed at the national and local levels.   In its closing statement, the IIFB expressed its "satisfaction and support for the decisions adopted at COP12 and the commitments made by the Parties for stronger, deeper, more inclusive and joined up implementation of the CBD" but noted that there was still much work ahead for everyone in terms of taking responsibility for the well-being of the Earth, and that many meetings would be needed to discuss how to achieve the biodiversity targets.

National reports, strategies and action plans

172 Parties attended the Conference, 152 provided national reports on biodiversity, and 31 provided National Biodiversity Strategies and Action Plans (NBSAPs).

Some countries made reference to indigenous peoples and acknowledged indigenous peoples' traditional knowledge and practice. Many of the NBSAPs included consultations with indigenous peoples' organizations for their development. The IIFB representatives actively engaged to enhance an understanding of indigenous knowledge and customary practices as a centrally important and cross-cutting theme that can potentially have a major positive effect in terms of implementing biodiversity targets and that full and effective participation of indigenous peoples and local communities should therefore be ensured at all levels.

CBD agrees on using "Indigenous Peoples" terminology

COP12 noted with appreciation the outcome document of the World Conference on Indigenous Peoples. However, among the most difficult and time-consuming negotiations for IIFB during the COP was the use of the term *"Indigenous Peoples and Local Communities"*.

For many years, representatives of the IIFB have raised the need to revise the outdated terminology of the CBD and, in particular, to change the term "indigenous and local communities" to a legally correct "indigenous peoples and local communities". With the adoption of the UN Declaration on the Rights of Indigenous Peoples (UNDRIP) in 2007 and the subsequent recommendations of the UN Permanent Forum on Indigenous Issues, IIFB insisted that the CBD should use the term "indigenous peoples and local communities" (IPLCs) in the context of the future work of the CBD.

Finally after long and exhausting negotiations during the last day of the COP12, the term *"indigenous peoples and local communities"* was adopted,[3] albeit with some reservations.

After the new terminology had been adopted, Canada made a lengthy statement during which it asserted its commitment to respect and protect the human rights of indigenous peoples but then stated that it saw this decision as highly flawed and undermining the integrity of the Convention on Biological Diversity.

The Nagoya Protocol enters into force

The Nagoya Protocol entered into force on 12 October 2014 after receiving the required 57 ratifications, and its 1st COP-MOP was held from 13 to 17 October.

During the meeting, the Parties and IIFB thoroughly discussed the procedures and institutional mechanisms for promoting compliance with the provisions of the Nagoya Protocol and how to address cases of non-compliance. As a result, it was decided to establish a Compliance Committee. Two indigenous observers and one alternate are nominated by IIFB during each COP-CBD. For the coming two years, the observers are: Preston Hardison, a representative of the Tullalip tribe (North America) and Onel Masardule, a representative of the Guna people (Panama, Latin America). As an alternate, IIFB proposed Jennifer Corpuz, an indigenous representative from the Philippines (Asia).   ○

Notes and references

1   The Nagoya Protocol on Access to Genetic Resources and the Fair and Equitable Sharing of Benefits Arising from their Utilization to the Convention on Biological Diversity was adopted by the 10th COP to the CBD on 29 October 2010 in Nagoya, Japan and entered into force 13 October 2014. The Nagoya Protocol is "an international agreement which aims at sharing the benefits arising from the utilization of genetic resources in a fair and equitable way, including by appropriate access to genetic resources and by appropriate transfer of relevant technologies, taking into account all rights over those resources and to technologies, and by appropriate funding, thereby contributing to the conservation of biological diversity and the sustainable use of its components" (http://www.cbd.int/abs/).
2   The documents under the discussion of the COP12 can be found at http://www.cbd.int/cop12/doc/
3   In Session document UNEP/CBD/COP/12/L.26 ARTICLE 8(j) AND RELATED PROVISIONS - Terminology "indigenous peoples and local communities" http://www.cbd.int/doc/meetings/cop/cop-12/insession/cop-12-L-26-en.pdf

Tatiana Degai is a PhD candidate at the University of Arizona majoring in American Indians Studies with a minor in linguistics. Tatiana is an Itelmen person from Kamchatka, Russian Far East, working on language revitalization and ethnoecological educational programs for indigenous youth. Tatiana has been participating in the CBD meetings since 2006 on behalf of the indigenous peoples of Kamchatka.

Polina Shulbaeva is head of the Information Law Center of Indigenous Peoples of the North of Tosmkaya Oblast, Russia. Polina has been following the CBD process since 2006 and is currently a regional coordinator on the CBD work for the indigenous peoples of Russia and Eastern Europe. Polina is Selkup herself, working mostly on ethno-ecological and law programs in her home Tomsk area.

WORLD HERITAGE CONVENTION

The Convention concerning the Protection of the World Cultural and Natural Heritage ("World Heritage Convention") was adopted by UNESCO's General Conference in 1972. With 191 States Parties, it is today one of the most widely ratified multilateral treaties. Its main purpose is the identification and collective protection of cultural and natural heritage sites of "outstanding universal value" (OUV). The Convention embodies the idea that some places are so special and important that their protection is not only the responsibility of the states in which they are located but also a duty of the international community as a whole.

The implementation of the Convention is governed by the World Heritage Committee (WHC), an intergovernmental committee consisting of 21 States Parties. The WHC keeps a list of sites which it considers to be of outstanding universal value ("World Heritage List") and ensures that these sites are adequately protected and safeguarded for future generations. Sites can only be listed following a formal nomination by the State Party in whose territory they are situated. Although a large number of World Heritage sites are fully or partially located in indigenous peoples' territories, no guidelines exist under the Convention to ensure the participation of indigenous peoples in processes and decisions affecting them.

The WHC is supported by three advisory bodies. The International Union for Conservation of Nature (IUCN) and the International Council on Monuments and Sites (ICOMOS) provide technical evaluations of World Heritage nominations and help in monitoring the state of conservation of World Heritage sites; the International Centre for the Study of the Preservation and Restoration of Cultural Property (ICCROM) provides advice and training related to cultural sites. An indigenous proposal to establish a "World Heritage Indigenous Peoples Council of Experts" (WHIPCOE) as an additional advisory body was rejected by the WHC in 2001.

Since the adoption of the 2007 UN Declaration on the Rights of Indigenous Peoples (UNDRIP), international human rights bodies and mechanisms have repeatedly urged the WHC and its advisory bodies to align the implementation of the World Heritage Convention with the standards affirmed in the Declaration. In November 2013, the UN Special Rapporteur on the Rights of Indigenous Peoples, James Anaya, sent a letter to UNESCO's World Heritage Centre, the Secretariat of the WHC, noting the many concerns raised by indigenous peoples regarding the nomination and management of World Heritage sites and calling on the WHC to take action towards:

- Ensuring meaningful participation of indigenous peoples in the nomination of World Heritage sites;
- Safeguarding indigenous peoples' land and resource rights during the nomination process;
- Consulting indigenous peoples with a view to obtaining their free, prior and informed consent regarding the establishment of World Heritage sites that may affect them;
- Ensuring transparency throughout nomination and implementation processes;
- Safeguarding against misuse and distortion of indigenous peoples' culture, practices and knowledge;
- Ensuring that indigenous peoples derive benefits from World Heritage sites that affect them; and
- Providing redress for past injustices and violations of indigenous peoples' rights.[1]

UNESCO/IUCN report on the state of conservation of the Kenya Lake System

One case that has drawn a great deal of international criticism is the WHC's 2011 inscription of **Lake Bogoria National Reserve in Kenya** on the World Heritage List (as part of the "Kenya Lake System"), without involving the indigenous Endorois community in the decision-making process (see *The Indigenous World 2012* and *2013*). In early 2014, the World Heritage Centre sent letters to the State Party of Kenya requesting its comments on information received from the African

Commission on Human and Peoples' Rights (ACHPR) (see *The Indigenous World 2014*) regarding the "lack of free, prior and informed consent from the Endorois community for the inscription of Lake Bogoria…, and concerns on the lack of participation of the Endorois in management and decision making". Having received no comments from the State Party, the Centre and IUCN submitted a State of Conservation (SOC) report to the WHC in May 2014 in which they noted the concerns raised by the ACHPR among the "current conservation issues" and recommended that the WHC urge Kenya to take measures to address these concerns.[2]

This engagement of UNESCO and IUCN seems to have encouraged the relevant Kenyan government agencies to enter into a Memorandum of Understanding (MoU) with representatives of the Endorois community, which recognizes Lake Bogoria National Reserve as Endorois ancestral land and requires Endorois inclusion in its management.[3] The extent to which this MoU will give the Endorois a real voice and decision-making power in the Reserve's management, and lead to an equitable sharing of benefits, remains to be seen.

38th session of the World Heritage Committee, Doha, June 2014

Highly significant for indigenous peoples in terms of the overall implementation of the Convention is a WHC decision requesting the World Heritage Centre and the Advisory Bodies prepare a "draft policy for integrating a sustainable development perspective into the processes of the World Heritage Convention" for examination by the WHC in 2015. The policy will consist of policy statements on eight "key dimensions" of sustainable development, including "Local Communities/Indigenous Peoples" and "Human Rights".[4] The draft document will also include suggestions for specific operational procedures and working modalities that could help translate the new policies into practice. Unfortunately, the possibilities for indigenous peoples to participate in these efforts are very limited.[5]

Another important decision adopted by the WHC relates to the processes for the listing of "mixed" cultural/natural World Heritage sites. The WHC requested that the World Heritage Centre, IUCN and ICOMOS prepare a report including options for changes to the listing criteria and evaluation process for mixed nominations, for consideration by the WHC in 2015.[6] These efforts are a response to difficulties encountered in the case of the indigenous-led nomination of Pimachiowin Aki (Canada) in terms of appropriately acknowledging indigenous peoples' relationship to the land, and the interconnectedness of natural and cultural values, under the existing criteria. They are highly relevant for future World Heritage nominations involving indigenous peoples' territories and Special Rapporteur James Anaya has "emphasize[d] the importance of consulting with indigenous peoples throughout the entirety of such a review process".[7]

Noteworthy decisions on specific sites

As recommended by the World Heritage Centre, the WHC adopted a decision on the state of conservation of the Kenya Lake System which "[n]otes the resolutions of the ACHPR with regard to the recognition of rights of the Endorois in relation to Lake Bogoria, and urges the State Party to respond to ACHPR regarding these resolutions and to ensure full and effective participation of the Endorois in the management and decision-making..., through their own representative institutions". **Kenya** must submit a report on the implementation of this decision to the WHC's 39th session in 2015.[8]

Also noteworthy is a WHC decision on the state of conservation of **Virunga National Park in the DRC,** which contains a strong message to extractive industries not to operate in World Heritage sites. The decision requests the State Party "cancel all the oil exploitation permits granted within the property and reiterate its position that oil, gas and mineral exploration and exploitation are incompatible with World Heritage status".[9]

The WHC again added several new sites to the World Heritage List that incorporate indigenous peoples' territories. The **Okavango Delta in Botswana**, home to various groups of San, became the 1,000[th] site inscribed on the List. Although San leaders were supportive of the Delta becoming a World Heritage site, the original nomination contained little information on the San and their cultural heritage, and no recognition of their rights to land and resources.[10] In evaluating the nomination, IUCN therefore requested that the State Party provide additional recognition of the cultural heritage of the San, as well as assurances that their rights to access natural resources and cultural sites would be respected and no evictions would be undertaken.[11] Supplementary information provided by Botswana in February 2014 contains additional documentation on the San relationship to their land, as well as confirmation that the cultural heritage and user access rights of communities living within the property are legally guaranteed.[12] The WHC's decision calls for continued efforts to "reinforce the recognition of the cultural heritage of indigenous inhabitants" and to "sensitively accommodat[e] traditional subsistence uses and access rights". It underlines the need to ensure that indigenous peoples' views are respected and integrated into management planning, and that they have access to tourism benefits.[13]

Another newly-listed site is the **Mount Hamiguitan Range Wildlife Sanctuary in the Philippines**. The WHC had already considered the nomination in 2013 but referred it back to the State Party requesting it continue to work with indigenous peoples "to resolve any outstanding land claims to ensure there is broad based support for the nomination of the site".[14] In the updated nomination, the Philippine government provided evidence of the affected indigenous communities' support for the nomination and commitment to protecting the site, as well as proof that they had freely relinquished their ancestral domain claims over areas within the site, including its buffer zone. The Provincial Government of Davao Oriental in return pledged to provide technical assistance and support to the relevant tribal groups in the preservation of their culture and in the pursuit of a sustainable livelihood in the periphery of the World Heritage area.[15] The WHC's decision encourages the State Party "to continue efforts to work collaboratively with local communities and indigenous peoples on the management of the property and to ensure the equitable access and sharing of benefits".[16]

Another site, the **Great Himalayan National Park in India**, was listed after intense lobbying by local NGOs and community-based organisations to get it postponed. They were concerned over the lack of inclusion of local communities in the drafting of the nomination, a lack of consideration of cultural and spiritual values, a lack of implementation of the 2006 Forest Rights Act in the nominated area, and potential adverse implications of World Heritage listing for traditional forest dwellers' livelihoods.[17] In particular, local people strongly opposed plans to convert the Tirthan and Sainj Wildlife Sanctuaries, included in the nominated area, to national park status, as this would imply the relocation of three villages and the extinguishment of traditional resource use rights in the sanctuaries.[18] IUCN had supported these plans in its Advisory Body Evaluation, recommending that the WHC request India to "expedite the formal designation of Tirthan and Sainj Wildlife Sanctuaries as national parks to improve their legal protection".[19] However, following persistent campaigning by community-based organisations, it was announced on the day of the inscription that India had "indicated that it may not now pursue this transfer of protection status".[20] The WHC refrained from encouraging India to designate the wildlife sanctuaries as national parks but requested that it "expedite… the resolution of community rights-based issues with respect to local communities and indigenous peoples in the Tirthan and Sainj Wildlife Sanctuaries, including in relation to the phasing out of grazing in the Tirthan Wildlife Sanctuary".[21]

A proposal by **Panama** for 31,628 ha to be added to the **Darien National Park World Heritage site** (minor boundary modification) was referred back to the State Party, among other things to "confirm, and provide supporting information, on the necessary consultation with indigenous and local peoples in support of the proposed addition".[22] The increasing number of such decisions in recent years reflects the IUCN's increased attention to the need to ensure indigenous peoples' participation in decisions affecting them.

18th ICOMOS General Assembly, Florence, November 2014

The ICOMOS General Assembly adopted a resolution entitled "Our Common Dignity: advancing rights-based approaches to heritage conservation", which requests "Continued consideration of rights-based approaches in the work of ICOMOS in relation to its role as an Advisory Body to the World Heritage Convention".[23] In April 2014, ICOMOS, IUCN and ICCROM organised a workshop on "World Heritage and Rights-Based Approaches", the findings of which were presented at a side event during the WHC's 38th session.[24] ICOMOS has been very slow to integrate human rights considerations into its work and, unlike IUCN, has never officially endorsed the UNDRIP.

IUCN World Parks Congress, Sydney, November 2014

The 2014 IUCN World Parks Congress was held under the theme "Parks, People, Planet: Inspiring Solutions" and was meant to help bridge the gap between the conservation and sustainable development agendas. Several workshops and events discussed the role of indigenous peoples and their rights in relation to World Heritage.

The outcome document of the Congress, "The Promise of Sydney", underlines the need for all states and relevant organisations to ensure that indigenous peoples are fully involved in the creation, designation and management of protected areas that overlap with their territories, that their collective land and resource rights are respected, their livelihoods supported, and past and continuing injustices redressed and remedied. With regard to World Heritage sites specifically, the Promise of Sydney highlights the need for the World Heritage Convention to be aligned with the UNDRIP and for the Convention's Operational Guidelines to be amended accordingly, with the full and effective participation of indigenous peoples. It calls for the effective involvement of indigenous peoples in the management, evaluation and monitoring of World Heritage sites that overlap with their territories and recommends that the "conceptual and management gap between natural and cultural World Heritage Site designations" be eliminated.[25]

The WPC saw the launch of a new book on "World Heritage Sites and Indigenous Peoples' Rights" published jointly by IWGIA, Forest Peoples Programme and the Gundjeihmi Aboriginal Corporation. The book includes 20 case studies on World Heritage sites from around the world that explore indigenous peoples' experiences with World Heritage sites and Convention processes. Also launched at the Congress was a joint UNESCO and UNDP/GEF Small Grants Programme publication on "Engaging Local Communities in Stewardship of World Heritage" (World Heritage Papers 40). ○

Notes and references

1   See UN Doc. A/HRC/25/74, p. 127.
2   UNESCO Doc. WHC-14/38.COM/7B.Add, p. 111ff.
3   "Kabarnet Declaration on Lake Bogoria National Reserve as a World Heritage Site", 26 May 2014.
4   Decision 38 COM 5D.
5   For details on the process for developing the draft policy, see Doc. WHC-14/38.COM/5D and the working document available at http://whc.unesco.org/document/128769
6   Decision 38 COM 9B. For background information, see Doc. WHC-14/38.COM/9B.
7   Letter to UNESCO, see UN Doc. A/HRC/25/74, p. 127.
8   Decision 38 COM 7B.91.
9   Decision 38 COM 7A.37.
10 See http://www.ipacc.org.za/eng/news_details.asp?NID=330, "San leaders endorse World Heritage Site nomination in the Okavango Delta", 3 September 2013.
11 See IUCN's Advisory Body Evaluation and pp. 392-393 of the nomination file, both available at http://whc.unesco.org/en/list/1432/documents/
12 Ibid., at p. 420ff.
13 Decision 38 COM 8B.5.

14   Decision 37 COM 8B.12.
15   See p. 443ff. of the nomination file, available at http://whc.unesco.org/en/list/1403/documents/
16   Decision 38 COM 8B.8.
17   See, e.g., Himalaya Niti Abhiyan, Open Letter to UNESCO, 14 June 2014, https://himnitiabhiyan.
     files.wordpress.com/2014/06/open_letter_to_unesco_whc.pdf
18   See pp. 627-629 of the nomination, available at http://whc.unesco.org/en/list/1406/documents/
19   See Doc. WHC-14/38.COM/INF.8B2.ADD, p. 9.
20   See http://whc.unesco.org/en/sessions/38COM/records/ (23 Jun 2014 - 12:03 PM, at 3:02:10).
21   Decision 38 COM 8B.7.
22   Decision 38 COM 8B.46.
23   ICOMOS Resolution 18GA 2014/36.
24   For the workshop report and recommendations, see http://www.icomos.no/whrbareport
25   See http://worldparkscongress.org/about/promise_of_sydney.html. See in particular the "Vision"
     and the "Innovative Approaches to Change" relating to Stream 6, Stream 7 and World Heritage.

Stefan Disko *works as a consultant for IWGIA on issues related to World Herit-age. He holds an M.A. in ethnology and international law from LMU Munich and an M.A. in World Heritage Studies from BTU Cottbus.*

BUSINESS AND HUMAN RIGHTS

In June 2011, the Human Rights Council unanimously endorsed the Guiding Principles on Business and Human Rights: Implementing the United Nations "Protect, Respect and Remedy" Framework (hereafter: "the Guiding Principles"). This was the first time a UN intergovernmental body had endorsed a normative document on the traditionally very divisive issue of how the human rights responsibility of transnational and other enterprises can be framed in international law. The Council's endorsement effectively established the Guiding Principles as the authoritative global standard for preventing and addressing adverse impacts on human rights arising from business-related activity.

The Council also decided to establish a Working Group on the issue of human rights and transnational corporations and other business enterprises (the Working Group) with a mandate, *inter alia*, to promote the effective and comprehensive dissemination and implementation of the Guiding Principles worldwide. At its 18th session in September 2011, the Council appointed five independent experts, of balanced geographical representation, for a period of three years, as members of the Working Group. The member representing Europe is Russian veteran indigenous rights activist Pavel Sulyandziga. The Working Group started its work in January 2012. The Working Group meets three times a year in closed sessions within which it can organise stakeholder consultations. Furthermore, it is responsible for organising a yearly Forum on Business and Human Rights. The Working Group's mandate and strategy of work can be found on its website.[1]

Binding treaty discussion and extension of working group mandate

Major initiatives were underway in the area of business and human rights in 2014 which, to varying degrees, relate to the rights of indigenous peoples.

The topic that gained most publicity internationally was the initiative to create a binding international treaty on business and human rights, which would eventually supersede the 2011 UN Guiding Principles on Business and Human Rights developed under the leadership of Prof. John Ruggie. In 2013, Ecuador proposed the development of a binding international instrument to address corporate human rights abuses. Initiatives to create such a binding treaty have been in existence since the early 1970s; however, a previous attempt to introduce binding human rights norms for transnational corporations was unsuccessful.[2] Since Ecuador's renewed attempt, heated discussions between proponents and opponents of a binding instrument have dominated the debate on business and human rights. On the side of the states, the most vocal proponents include Ecuador and South Africa, while most EU states, along with Canada, USA and Australia, are among the opponents, clearly favouring the voluntarist approach of the Guiding Principles. Besides states, a large coalition of civil society organisations has also taken up the issue and started its own campaign in favour of a binding instrument.[3]

During the negotiations, attempts were made to obtain a single Human Rights Council resolution on the issue of business and human rights, including both the work on the Guiding Principles and the future binding treaty. The two camps were, however, ultimately unable to come to an agreement and two separate resolutions were therefore drafted.

In June, during the 26th session of the UN Human Rights Council, the representatives of Ecuador and South Africa introduced a draft resolution[4] proposing the establishment of an open-ended intergovernmental working group on the elaboration of an international legally-binding instrument on transnational corporations and other business enterprises with respect to human rights. The resolution was co-sponsored by Bolivia, Cuba Venezuela, Algeria, El Salvador, Nicaragua and Senegal. It was eventually adopted by 20 votes to 14 with 13 abstentions, as resolution 26/9.[5]

In a second resolution, the mandate of the UN Working Group on Business and Human Rights was extended by a further three years (2015-17) in its present composition.[6]

No major steps were taken to implement the first resolution in 2014, and the open-ended working group had not been established by the end of the year. The indigenous peoples' response to the binding treaty initiative has been mixed, with concerns raised over the leading role of Ecuador, as a country allegedly working to weaken the inter-American human rights system, and over the long, protracted process that is to be expected. One key consideration for indigenous peoples is to ensure that any future treaty on business and human rights properly reflects indigenous peoples' rights as set out in the UN Declaration on the Rights of Indigenous Peoples (UNDRIP) and ILO Convention 169.[7]

The Outcome Document of the UN World Conference on Indigenous Peoples makes reference to Guiding Principles but does not address the issue of a possible binding instrument.[8]

National action plans on business and human rights

Throughout 2014, a major focus of the UN Working Group on Business and Human Rights was the issue of providing guidance for the development of national action plans (NAP) on business and human rights.

The first countries to come up with such action plans were the United Kingdom in September and the Netherlands in December 2013. In 2014, several other European countries followed suit: Denmark, Finland, Italy and Spain (draft, July 2014).[9] Of these, most do not stipulate specific action regarding indigenous peoples' rights, with no mention at all in the Dutch NAP, and two casual mentions but no actions stipulated in the Danish NAP. Finland pledges to "continue the dialogue related to the human rights impacts of business activities with the UN bodies for indigenous peoples and ensure that the effects of business activities on the realisation of the rights of indigenous peoples will be brought forward in the World Conference on Indigenous Peoples in autumn 2014"[10] The UK NAP mentions indigenous peoples twice in a laundry list of vulnerable groups entitled to consultation and with regard to whom business awareness should be raised.[11] The Italian baseline document makes one rather accidental mention of indigenous peoples in passing.[12] The Spanish Draft NAP was the only one available in 2014, and this makes explicit reference to ILO Convention 169 and the UNDRIP.

In 2014, both the Working Group on Business and Human Rights and a joint effort by the Danish Institute for Human Rights (DIHR) and the International Corporate Accountability (ICAR) sought to address the lack of guidance in the current NAP processes. Firstly, the Working Group on Business and Human Rights developed a guidance document for the development of national action plans. This document includes three references to indigenous peoples, all within laundry lists

of vulnerable groups, without reference to specific rights,[13] and one footnote referring to the Working Group's 2013 thematic report on indigenous peoples.[14]

Secondly, in June, the DIHR and ICAR released a detailed toolkit aimed at
providing guidance and quality control for the elaboration of NAPs.[15] It introduces
the concept of National Baseline Assessments to be carried out before the actual
NAP development. The baseline assessment measures the current state of human rights and human rights impacts of businesses, aiding the later step of identifying specific needs and appropriate actions. The toolkit is largely process-ori-
ented and does not premeditate specific outcomes or reference specific rights
and frameworks such as the UNDRIP. However, it puts strong emphasis on the
need to adequately consult groups that are at increased risk of human rights violations. In December, the DIHR and ICAR undertook a joint assessment of existing NAPs in relation to the toolkit, and for which IWGIA contributed an assessment of the Danish NAP with a view to indigenous peoples' rights.[16]

In 2014, several states launched their NAP processes, including Germany,
which envisages a two-year process starting with a National Baseline Assessment, as proposed by the toolkit. In September, the USA launched its NAP process, starting with a civil society consultation phase until 15 January 2015.[17]
While the trend is still dominated by wealthy industrial nations, several African,
Latin American and Asian states have also committed to developing NAPs or are
in the process of doing so, including Colombia, Mozambique, Myanmar and Mexico.[18]

Business initiatives regarding Free, Prior and Informed Consent

In 2014, two business associations, the International Council on Mining and Metals and IPIECA, the global oil and gas industry association for environmental and
social issues, undertook activities related to indigenous peoples' right to Free,
Prior and Informed Consent (FPIC). Both processes were informed by the project
"Making Free, Prior and Informed Consent a Reality" carried out by the UK-based
group Philippine Indigenous Peoples Links (Piplinks) and its partners.[19] In 2013,
the ICMM adopted a position statement on indigenous peoples and mining[20] and,
in 2014, worked on developing guidance for its practical application to come into
effect in May 2015.[21] IPIECA has been running a project on FPIC, announced in
late 2013, although this has not yet produced any public outputs.[22]

European Network on Indigenous Peoples

During the 2014 session of the UN Expert Mechanism on the Rights of Indigenous Peoples, the European Network on Indigenous Peoples (ENIP), which comprises IWGIA (Denmark), Piplinks (UK), Forest Peoples Programme (UK), Almaciga (Spain) and INFOE (Germany), launched a study on the UN Guiding Principles and their interpretation with regard to indigenous peoples' rights. The launch included presentations by the UN Special Rapporteur on the rights of indigenous peoples, along with representatives of the UN EMRIP and the Permanent Forum on Indigenous Issues.[23] Indigenous peoples also actively participated in the 3rd UN Forum on Business and Human Rights, held in Geneva from 1-3 December, after a one-day indigenous preparatory caucus meeting. Indigenous peoples' issues were not, however, a particular focus of the meeting. Unlike in 2013, no dedicated panel discussion on indigenous issues was scheduled and the model of holding per-group pre-sessions was abandoned because it was limiting the level of interaction between the groups. By implication, there was no dedicated indigenous pre-session either. However, several side events addressed various aspects of indigenous peoples' rights. A high-profile event featuring the UN Special Rapporteur on the rights of indigenous peoples, Ms Vicky Tauli-Corpuz, the President of the UN Permanent Forum on Indigenous Issues, Dalee Sambo Dorough, and Working Group member Mr. Pavel Sulyandziga, addressed the issue of indigenous peoples' access to justice and reparation within the context of the UN Guiding Principles. The Asia Indigenous Peoples Network on Extractive Industries and Energy (AIPNEE) hosted a side event on challenges concerning extractive industries and FPIC as an approach to solutions.

Policy reviews of development banks

On 30 July 2014, the World Bank opened its new draft Environmental and Social Framework (ESF) for consultation.[24] Environmental and Social Standard (ESS) 7 spells out the Bank's future policy regarding indigenous peoples. On the positive side, the draft framework strengthens indigenous peoples' right to give or withhold their Free, Prior and Informed Consent and increases protection against forced relocation.[25] On the downside, it dilutes established safeguards in several key areas. ESS 7, para 9 contains a clause which allows governments to completely opt out of its application and take an "alternative approach", if "applying this ESS would create a serious risk of exacerbating ethnic tension or civil strife, or where the identification of culturally-distinct groups as envisioned in this ESS is inconsistent with the provisions of the national constitution". This clause is a loophole of amazing magnitude and has drawn widespread criticism, as it would effectively allow the Bank and its borrowers to completely sidestep its own policy and the provisions of the UNDRIP. Apart from ESS 7, the standard dealing with "Land Acquisition, Restrictions on Land Use and Involuntary Resettlement" has been blasted by rights groups, as it is seen to contain major dilutions in regard to proper resettlement planning and exempts land rights and land-use regulation activities from its application, meaning that that "people whose land rights are made insecure through a Bank-financed land administration project, because, for example, they are not determined to have ownership rights, are left completely vulnerable to forced eviction by their government, without any safeguards protections from the Bank." [26] This opt-out clause was also among the changes criticised in a joint letter by 29 UN mandate holders and experts submitted to the Bank on 12 December 2014. The signatories included the UN Special Rapporteur on the rights of indigenous peoples and the UN Working Group on Business and Human Rights.[27]

O

Notes and references

1   http://www.ohchr.org/EN/Issues/Business/Pages/WGHRandtransnationalcorporationsandother-business.aspx
2   The "Draft Norms on the Responsibilities of Transnational Corporations and Other Business Enterprises with Regard to Human Rights", E/CN.4/Sub.2/2003/12 (2003) were rejected by the Human Rights Commission in 2004, see http://business-humanrights.org/en/united-nations-sub-commission-norms-on-business-human-rights-explanatory-materials
3   See http://www.treatymovement.com/
4   A/HRC/26/L.22/Rev.1.
5   See Report of the Human Rights Council on its twenty-sixth session, A/HRC/26/2, 11 December 2014, resolution regarding the binding instrument: A/HRC/26/L.22/Rev.1.
6   Human Rights Council Resolution 26/22 " Human rights and transnational corporations and other business enterprises", A/HRC/RES/26/22, dated 15 July 2014.
7   For an analysis from an indigenous perspective, see Luis Vittor: Los pueblos indígenas y el tratado sobre empresas transnacionales y derechos humanos, 2 February 2015, http://alainet.org/active/80526

8   Para 24: "We recall the responsibility of transnational corporations and other business enterprises to respect all applicable laws and international principles, including the United Nations Guiding Principles on Business and Human Rights: Implementing the United Nations 'Protect, Respect and Remedy' Framework, and to operate transparently and in a socially and environmentally responsible manner. In this regard, we commit ourselves to taking further steps, as appropriate, to prevent abuses of the rights of indigenous peoples." A/69/2, 15 September 2014.

9   See overview at http://business-humanrights.org/en/un-guiding-principles/implementation-tools-examples/implementation-by-governments/by-type-of-initiative/national-action-plans

10 Ministry of Employment and the Economy: "National Action Plan for the implementation of the UN Guiding Principles on Business and Human Rights" http://www.tem.fi/files/41214/TEM-jul_46_2014_web_EN_21102014.pdf

11 Good Business: Implementing the UN Guiding Principles on Business and Human Rights https://www.gov.uk/government/publications/bhr-action-plan

12 Indigenous peoples are mentioned once, where the document discusses differences between the original and a revised version of the OECD "Common Approaches on Environment and Officially Supported Export Credits". The Foundations of the Italian Action Plan on the United Nations "Guiding Principles On Business And Human Rights", http://business-humanrights.org/sites/default/files/media/documents/foundations-ungps-nap-italy.pdf

13 Guidance on National Action Plans on Business and Human Rights http://www.ohchr.org/Documents/Issues/Business/UNWG_%20NAPGuidance.pdf

14 Report of the Working Group on the issue of human rights and transnational corporations and other business enterprises A/68/279, 7 August 2013.

15 National Action Plans on Business and Human Rights: A Toolkit for the Development, Implementation, and Review of State Commitments to Business and Human Rights Framework http://accountabilityroundtable.org/analysis/napsreport/

16 ICAR & ECCJ Release Assessments of Current National Action Plans on Business & Human Rights http://accountabilityroundtable.org/analysis/napsassessments/

17 See dedicated ICAR website http://nationalactionplan.us/

18 Full list at http://business-humanrights.org/en/un-guiding-principles/implementation-tools-examples/implementation-by-governments/by-type-of-initiative/national-action-plans

19 Report: Making Free Prior & Informed Consent a Reality - Indigenous Peoples and the Extractive Sector, http://www.piplinks.org/report%3A-making-free-prior-%2526amp%3B-informed-consent-reality-indigenous-peoples-and-extractive-sector

20 Indigenous Peoples and Mining Position Statement http://www.icmm.com/publications/icmm-position-statement-on-indigenous-peoples-and-mining

21 ICMM to launch public consultation on updated Indigenous Peoples & Mining Good Practice Guide on 30 January, 14 January 2015 http://goxi.org/profiles/blogs/icmm-to-launch-public-consultation-on-updated-indigenous-peoples

22 New project on Free, Prior and Informed Consent, 06 Sep 2013, http://www.ipieca.org/news/20130906/new-project-free-prior-and-informed-consent

23 ENIP launches study on UN Guiding Principles 11 July 2014, http://www.enip.eu/web/enip-launches-study-on-un-guiding-principles-at-emrip-7th-session/

24 Available from http://documents.worldbank.org/curated/en/2014/07/19898916/environmental-social-framework-setting-standards-sustainable-development

25 cf. Land, Housing and Indigenous Peoples' Rights in the Draft World Bank Environmental & Social Framework ROUNDTABLE OUTCOME DOCUMENT, October 6, 2014. Washington DC,

    http://consultations.worldbank.org/Data/hub/files/land_rights_in_the_draft_esf_roundtable_out-
    come_document_final.pdf
26 Forest Peoples Programme: "World Bank's Draft Safeguards Fail to Protect Land Rights and
    Prevent Impoverishment: Major Revisions Required http://www.forestpeoples.org/sites/fpp/files/
    news/2014/07/Statement%20on%20Land%20Rights%20in%20Draft%20World%20Bank%20
    ESF%20%28FINAL%29.pdf
27 http://www.forestpeoples.org/sites/fpp/files/news/2014/12/OL%20Other%20%28World%20
    Bank%29%2011.12.14%20%2813.2014%29%20FINAL.pdf

Johannes Rohr *is a historian and independent consultant working on indigenous
peoples' rights. From 2012 on, he has supported UN working group member
Pavel Sulyandziga in his efforts to promote indigenous rights in the business
context.*

POST-2015 DEVELOPMENT AGENDA AND THE SUSTAINABLE DEVELOPMENT GOALS

In 2012, the Rio +20 UN Conference on Sustainable Development decided to establish an inclusive and transparent intergovernmental process that would be open to all stakeholders with a view to developing global Sustainable Development Goals (SDGs) that address the challenges and short-comings of the Millennium Development Goals (MDGs).[1] It is widely agreed that indigenous peoples were not granted enough attention in the MDGs. They were excluded from the process and are mentioned in neither the goals nor their indicators. Dealing with issues directly related to indigenous peoples, such as ending poverty, ensuring human rights and inclusion for all, ensuring good governance, preventing conflict, ensuring environmental sustainability and protection of biodiversity and climate change, the Post-2015 development framework and the SDGs will, for the next decade, set the standards for global sustainable development and will directly influence the lives of millions of indigenous peoples. The SDGs present a unique opportunity to remedy the historical injustices resulting from racism, discrimination and inequalities long suffered by indigenous peoples across the world. In the post-2015 development process, indigenous peoples are striving to ensure that the SDG targets and indicators reflect indigenous peoples' rights and their relationship to their lands, territories and natural resources and take their special vulnerabilities and strengths into consideration.

The Rio+ 20 Outcome Document mandated the creation of an intergovernmental Open Working Group (OWG)[2] to discuss and propose goals, targets and indicators for the SDGs. The OWG's working methods include the full involvement of relevant stakeholders and expertise from civil society, the scientific community and the UN system, in order to provide a diversity of perspectives and experience. All nine UN Major Groups, among them the Indigenous Peoples' Major Group and other stakeholders, were thus engaged in the OWG sessions in 2013 and 2014, and will be expected to continue their participation, interventions and lobbying in 2015.

In January 2014, together with the International Indigenous Peoples' Centre for Policy Research and Education (Tebtebba) and the UN Secretariat Permanent Forum for Indigenous Issues (UNSPFII), IWGIA facilitated a **Technical Workshop on indigenous peoples' priorities and targets for the SDGs.**

The outcome of the workshop was the development of an indigenous peoples' position paper and draft ideas for targets and indicators relevant to indigenous peoples in the SDGs. The position paper was endorsed by the international indigenous constituency and used by indigenous peoples, primarily the IP Major Group as guiding principles and was disseminated during the OWG meetings and used to lobby governments and other relevant stakeholders.

Report of the Open Working Group on Sustainable Development Goals

On 1 August, 2014, the OWG submitted a report to the 68th session of the UN General Assembly (GA) containing a proposal for SDGs for consideration and appropriate action.[3] In December 2014, the GA adopted a draft resolution deciding that these proposals[4] "shall be the basis for the integration of the SDGs into the post-2015 development agenda, while recognizing fully that other inputs may also be considered in this intergovernmental negotiation process at the 69th session of the GA".[5]

Indigenous peoples noted with concern that many references to "indigenous peoples" were deleted from this final Outcome Document. Despite indigenous peoples' lobbying efforts, the OWG outcome document, in its current form, contains only two references to indigenous peoples among its proposed 17 goals and 169 targets. Under Goal 2 on "agricultural productivity and the incomes of small-scale food producers", indigenous peoples are mentioned between commas along with women, family farmers, pastoralists and fishers; Goal 4 on education reads "ensure equal access to all levels of education and vocational training for the vulnerable, including persons with disabilities, indigenous peoples, and children in vulnerable situations". The goals, on the other hand, do not reflect, for example, land rights or culturally-sensitive education – both key priorities for indigenous peoples. The invisibility of indigenous peoples in this document raises a serious risk of repeating the mistakes from the Millennium Development Goals

(MDGs) and once again leaving behind 15% of the world's poorest in the global development agenda.

Interactive meeting with civil society on contributions to the synthesis report

On 10 September 2014, an interactive meeting took place with civil society in relation to the high-level stocktaking event on the post-2015 development agenda being arranged by the President of the 68th Session of the General Assembly, John Ashe. During the meeting, civil society representatives articulated their views on the post-2015 and sustainable development discussions to date. IWGIA funded an indigenous representative to attend the meeting in New York and supported her work, which served as an important contribution to the Secretary General's Synthesis Report.

The Secretary General's Synthesis Report

In December 2014, a Synthesis Report by United Nations Secretary General Ban Ki-moon "The Road to Dignity by 2030: Ending Poverty, Transforming All Lives and Protecting the Planet"[6] was published affirming that the United Nations Sustainable Development Goals and the Post-2015 development agenda should "leave no one behind" and recognizing that "people are at the center of sustainable development".

The Indigenous Peoples' Major Group commends the report's call for genuine commitment to work together to promote sustained and inclusive economic growth, social development and environmental protection and thereby to benefit all, as well as its overall commitment towards using a human rights-based approach to development.

While the Secretary General's Synthesis Report makes no specific mention of Major Groups, the report affirms that the "meaningful participation" of essential actors, new partnerships and key constituencies are critical for a true, transformative agenda. A specific reference to Major Groups would have been desirable since the "Major Groups and other stakeholders'" participatory framework has proved successful during the UN Commission on Sustainable Development and the Open Working Group on Sustainable Development Goals. Furthermore, data disaggregation is one of the major issues for indigenous peoples. The synthesis report places special emphasis on the issue of data disaggregation as well as data gaps.

World Conference on Indigenous Peoples

In September 2014, the high-level plenary meeting of the General Assembly known as the World Conference on Indigenous Peoples (WCIP) reaffirmed the UN General Assembly's commitments in support of indigenous peoples and sustainable development arising from the Rio+20 Conference on Sustainable Development. The Rio+20 Outcome Document[7] recognizes "the importance of the participation of indigenous peoples in the achievement of sustainable development" and "the importance of the United Nations Declaration on the Rights of Indigenous Peoples in the context of global, regional, national and subnational implementation of sustainable development strategies". The WCIP adopted an action-oriented outcome document aimed at implementing the principles set out in the UN Declaration on the Rights of Indigenous Peoples, affirming that "indigenous peoples have the right to determine and develop priorities and strategies for exercising their right to development" and committing to "giving due consideration to all the rights of indigenous peoples in the elaboration of the post-2015 development agenda". These achievements must be reflected in the post-2015 development agenda, consistent with the rights of indigenous peoples and their valuable contributions to achieving sustainable development for all.

Indigenous peoples' Indicator meeting

In November 2014, a meeting took place in Baguio City entitled the "Global Workshop on Indigenous Peoples' Sustainable Development Goals and Post-2015 Development Agenda".[8] The meeting discussed and agreed on indicators relevant to indigenous peoples in the SDGs and built on the experiences of the Indigenous Peoples' Major Group in its earlier engagement and advocacy work in relation to the Open Working Group on the SDGs and the Post-2015 Development Agenda. A revised version of the indigenous peoples' position paper and the indicators developed at this meeting will form the basis of an international lobbying tool during the course of 2015 focusing on the Post-2015 summit and beyond. Part of the meeting also therefore considered strategies and planned future entry points for lobbying.

Next steps towards post-2015

Looking beyond 2014, there is still much work for indigenous peoples to do if they are to ensure that their concerns and contributions are taken into consideration in the work streams ahead and in the post-2015 development framework and that their rights are reflected in the SDGs, both in their indicators and their implementation.

Finance for Development (FfD) is an important piece of a larger puzzle, and several pieces will need to dovetail carefully into other processes in 2015 and beyond, most notably the UN Summit on the Post-2015 Development Agenda in September 2015, and the UNFCCC Conference of the Parties in December 2015. The relationship between the processes is still unclear and there is a need to find synergies rather than overlaps. As the Secretary General's Synthesis Report does not mention FfD, there is speculation that finance will most probably form a parallel negotiation alongside the post-2015 negotiations. The issue of Finance for Development is of prime importance to indigenous peoples in terms of eradicating poverty, accessing basic services and protecting their lands and territories and the world's biodiversity from aggressive industrial development, especially in light of the increased emphasis on private sector financing of development. There will be several FfD drafting sessions during 2015, culminating in the **"Third International Conference on Financing for Development"**, which will be held in Addis Ababa in July 2015 at the highest possible political level, including Heads of State or Government, relevant ministers ministers of finance, foreign affairs and development cooperation and other special representatives.

Another process that is worth taking note of is a universal intergovernmental **High-Level Political Forum (HLPF)**. The HLPF is another critical outcome of Rio+20. The HLPF will be the main United Nations platform dealing with sustainable development from 2015 and beyond. It will provide political leadership and guidance; follow up and review progress in implementing sustainable development commitments and address new and emerging sustainable development challenges. There are still many uncertainties regarding the HLPF; for example, how civil society will participate, how the HLPF will conduct reviews of the future work of sustainable development in all countries and at the UN, and how the review sessions will be carried out, to name but a few of the questions that remain to be answered.   ○

Notes and references

1   http://www.uncsd2012.org/content/documents/727The%20Future%20We%20Want%2019%20June%201230pm.pdf
2   http://sustainabledevelopment.un.org/owg.html
3   The reports and relevant documents resulting from the OWG session can be downloaded at: http://sustainabledevelopment.un.org/index.php?menu=1549
4   http://www.un.org/ga/search/view_doc.asp?symbol=A/68/L.61&referer=/english/&Lang=E
5   UN Resolution A/68/L.61
6   http://www.un.org/disabilities/documents/reports/SG_Synthesis_Report_Road_to_Dignity_by_2030.pdf
7   http://www.uncsd2012.org/content/documents/727The%20Future%20We%20Want%2019%20June%201230pm.pdf?ref=driverlayer.com
    The meeting was organized by Tebtebba, AIPP, Forest Peoples Programme, IWGIA and ILO with support from the European Commission and Brot Für die Welt.

Ida Peters Ginsborg is a Danish Sociologist working for IWGIA. As IWGIA's focal point for the post-2015 development process, Ida follows, supports and reports on indigenous peoples' full and effective participation.

ARCTIC COUNCIL

The Arctic Council is a high-level intergovernmental forum of the Arctic States (Canada, Kingdom of Denmark, Finland, Iceland, Norway, Russia, Sweden, USA), established in 1996 at a meeting in Ottawa, Canada by expanding the mandate of the then Arctic Environmental Protection Strategy (AEPS) from a purely environmental cooperation to accommodate sustainable development and a focus on the lives and well-being of the peoples of the Arctic. The eight member States in turn hold the chairmanship for two years. From 2013-2015 it was held by Canada and from 2015 by the USA. When Canada embarked on a second cycle of chairmanships in 2013, it appointed federal Minister for the Environment and Northern Economic Development, Leona Aglukkaq, an Inuk from Nunavut, as Minister for the Arctic Council.

A unique feature of the Council is that the indigenous peoples are represented as Permanent Participants at the negotiating table along with the Arctic governments. Permanent Participants currently represent six organizations of Arctic indigenous peoples (Arctic Athabaskan Council, Aleut International Association, Gwich'in Council International, Inuit Circumpolar Council, Russian Association of Indigenous Peoples of the North, Saami Council). The Arctic Council has an extensive list of observers, including non-Arctic states, intergovernmental organizations and NGOs.

The Arctic Council's core activities concern interaction among Arctic States, and coordination, promotion and publication of scientific research on climate, environmental and biodiversity issues, linked with Arctic shipping and marine safety issues, health and mental well-being. Activities are based around six working groups, programmes, task forces and expert groups. The work of the Arctic Council is monitored and promoted by the Standing Committee of Parliamentarians of the Arctic Region, which was established in 1994 in support of the creation of the Arctic Council.

Climate change

Arctic cooperation has become increasingly important due, mainly, to climate change, which has shown to affect the Arctic rapidly and in extraordinary ways. The Arctic Council is known for its substantial contribution to climate change research and policy recommendations. Climate change has, among other things, opened up access to Arctic waterways such as the North West and North East Passages. Increased access to and awareness of the Arctic has also resulted in increased pressure on the Arctic Council to accommodate observers in its activities. Following the Arctic Climate Impact Assessment flagship project (2004), the new cross-cutting cooperation is the Adaptation Action for a Changing Arctic, which aims to integrate knowledge from different fields of expertise and thus also has an increasing focus on local and indigenous knowledge (TK).

Traditional knowledge

Arctic indigenous peoples play an important role in the Arctic Council and are very active in the Sustainable Development Working Group (SDWG) where culture and language retention and development, mental wellness and traditional knowledge, along with economic development issues, are high on the agenda. Under the theme "development for the people of the North", Canada has reinforced the focus on the integration of traditional knowledge and ways of life into the work of the Arctic Council. This plays out in the various areas of cooperation from climate change adaptation and mitigation through biodiversity monitoring to sustainable economic, social and cultural development.

The Arctic Council has primarily met in Canada's Northern Territories for the past two years, where participants have been able to meet indigenous peoples and learn about their language, culture and traditional livelihood by visiting small communities on the outskirts of northern cities. In October 2014, the SDWG hosted a community outreach event focusing on the incorporation of traditional knowledge into the work of the Council, in N'dilo, Northwest Territories.

The inclusion and application of traditional and local knowledge is by no means new to the Arctic Council or to the SDWG. Despite many efforts over the years to incorporate traditional knowledge into the work of the Arctic Council, however, it remains a challenge as to how best to integrate traditional and Western science and research and progress is thus slow.

Health and well-being

Mental wellness was the focus of a follow-up to the "Hope and Reconciliation in Suicide Prevention Conference" held in Nuuk in 2009. Under the heavy title of "The Evidence Base for Promoting Mental Wellness and Resilience to Address Suicide in Circumpolar Communities", the SDWG held a workshop in Tromsø in May 2014 on the important issue of intervention.

The workshop was a capacity-building exercise with four primary objectives, namely to share good practices, to provide networking opportunities and to provide a venue for the guidance of research teams and government representatives by community representatives and experts. Finally, the workshop aimed to plan and optimize research activities across the Arctic and was successful in developing a concrete work plan for the initiative up to its concluding symposium, planned for 2015.

Arctic Economic Council

Sustainable economic development in the Arctic remains a huge challenge. In order to provide opportunities for business to engage with the Arctic Council and to promote circumpolar economic development, an Arctic Economic Council (AEC), an independent body of business representatives, was established in Iqaluit, Canada in September 2014. The AEC operates under the auspices of the AC. The AEC has been long in the coming. Preparations for a forum for business development commenced during the Swedish chairmanship of the AC from 2011 - 2013 but only took off late in Canada's chairmanship.

The overall aim of the AEC is: "Fostering sustainable development, including economic growth, environmental protection and social development in the Arctic Region." In a press statement from the inaugural meeting of the AEC, the emphasis was put on traditional indigenous knowledge, stewardship and a focus on small businesses as playing a central role.

The AEC, which consists of 42 business representatives appointed by the Arctic states and indigenous organizations, has decided to establish a number of working groups under the following headings: stewardship in the Arctic; maritime transport; extractive industries; the promotion of business opportunities across the Arctic; business scenarios 2040; and renewable energy. Each working group will produce a report with recommendations on how to promote business opportunities in these areas and report back to the Arctic Council at its next meeting in April 2015.

Indigenous Peoples' Secretariat

The Indigenous Peoples' Secretariat (IPS) was established at the initiative of the governments of Denmark and Greenland in 1993 to support the participation of indigenous peoples in the Arctic Environmental Protection Strategy, AEPS, later to become the Arctic Council.

The IPS celebrated its 20-year anniversary at its offices in Copenhagen on 27 November 2014. The event gathered peoples from across the Arctic, including representatives of Permanent Participants, indigenous artists, former staff and government representatives for the workshop: "Building on Indigenous Achievements in the Arctic Council" and a celebration.

The IPS is scheduled to relocate to Tromsø, which is the administrative headquarters of the Arctic Council, in 2015 when Canada hands over the chairmanship to the United States at the next Ministerial Meeting of the Arctic Council, to be held in Iqaluit, capital of the self-governing territory of Nunavut.   ◯

Marianne Lykke Thomsen has a background in Inuit studies and anthropology and has been living and working in Greenland in various capacities for close to 30 years. In her earlier capacity as senior policy advisor to the Government of Greenland, she played an active part in UN work on human and indigenous peoples' rights and in the Arctic Council process. Prior to this, she worked with the Inuit Circumpolar Council on environmental issues and Traditional Knowledge. Marianne Lykke Thomsen was elected a member of IWGIA's Board in January 2015.

AFRICAN COMMISSION ON HUMAN AND PEOPLES' RIGHTS

The African Commission on Human and Peoples' Rights (African Commission) was officially inaugurated on 2 November 1987 and is the main human rights body of the African Union (AU). In 2001, the African Commission established its Working Group on Indigenous Populations / Communities in Africa (WGIP), which was a remarkable step forward in promoting and protecting the human rights of indigenous peoples in Africa. The Working Group has produced a thorough report on the rights of indigenous peoples in Africa, and this document has been adopted by the African Commission as its official conceptualization of the rights of indigenous peoples.

The human rights situation of indigenous peoples has, since 2001, been on the agenda of the African Commission and has since then been a topic of debate between the African Commission, states, national human rights institutions, NGOs and other interested parties. Indigenous representatives' participation in the sessions and in the Working Group's continued activities – sensitization seminars, country visits, information activities and research – plays a crucial role in ensuring this vital dialogue.

Linking up civil society organizations in North Africa to the African Commission's WGIP

On 5-6 February 2014, the WGIP, in collaboration with the World Amazigh Congress (*Congrès Mondial Amazigh*), organized a regional sensitization seminar on indigenous peoples' rights in Tunis, Tunisia. The seminar was the first to be held by the WGIP in the northern region of Africa, and representatives from Egypt, Tunisia, Algeria, Libya, Morocco and the Canary Islands were present.

The purpose of the seminar was mainly to create an opportunity for representatives from indigenous organizations, human rights organizations and national human rights institutions to meet, network and learn about the African Commission's work. At the seminar, participants worked to identify the main challenges faced by indigenous communities in the northern region of Africa, and to start a strategic collaboration among the stakeholders present, taking into account the actual political situation in the region and the relatively new open space available for indigenous peoples to articulate their rights. Many issues were discussed, including a review of the state of indigenous peoples and the key challenges they are facing in North Africa. This was considered in parallel with the increasing recognition and legal protection of indigenous populations' rights at the regional and international level, and some best practices in Africa were shared with the participants.

The seminar was attended by the WGIP, the Office of the High Commissioner for Human Rights (OHCHR), an expert from the Human Rights Centre of the University of Pretoria, representatives of national human rights institutions in Algeria and Egypt, civil society organizations, journalists and indigenous peoples' representatives from the North African sub-region.

Working towards influencing the policies of the World Bank

During 2014, the WGIP provided its input to the revision process of the World Bank's Environmental and Social Policy (ESP) and associated Environmental and Social Standard (ESS). The WGIP highlighted the fact that the proposed so-called "Alternative Approach" to the application of safeguards for indigenous peoples would undermine the results achieved by the African Commission across the continent with regard to the increasing recognition and protection of indigenous peoples.

The WGIP sent two letters to the World Bank dated 8 July 2014 and 1 September 2014 to raise its concerns and the WGIP members participated in various consultations organized by the Safeguard Review Team of the World Bank. In response to this, the Safeguard Review Team of the World Bank invited the WGIP to meet with them in Washington, on 6 February 2015 to discuss the revision process and the concerns raised by the WGIP and many other stakeholders in Africa. The WGIP is continuing the dialogue with the World Bank and hopes that the proposed "Alternative Approach" will be dropped.

Continuing lobbying for the implementation of the UN Declaration on the Rights of Indigenous Peoples: the World Conference on Indigenous Peoples

The WGIP participated actively in the preparatory process leading up to the World Conference on Indigenous peoples (WCIP) and played a key role in lobbying African embassies at the United Nations. The African Commission adopted a resolution on the WCIP in which it called on AU Member States to:

- participate fully and actively in the preparation and deliberations of the World Conference;
- support the full and active participation of indigenous peoples and civil society organizations in the preparation and deliberations of the World Conference;
- ensure that the drafting of the WCIP Outcome Document is done with the participation of indigenous peoples;
- engage in constructive dialogue with the WGIP and civil society organizations working on indigenous issues;
- ensure that the WCIP Outcome Document recognizes the work of regional human rights mechanisms, including the work of the Commission in promoting and protecting the rights of indigenous peoples in Africa.

The resolution was widely distributed and thoroughly discussed with the African embassies at the United Nations during the preparatory process and this led to a more favorable approach and a better understanding of the WCIP Outcome Document on the part of the African governments. This was reflected in the fact that the Outcome Document was endorsed by acclamation by all states, including all African states.

The Ogiek case heard by the African Court on Human and Peoples' Rights

The African Court of Human and Peoples' Rights heard the case brought by the indigenous Ogiek community against the Government of Kenya on 27-28 November 2014. The case was originally lodged with the African Commission on Human and Peoples' Rights but was referred to the Court by the Commission on the basis that it implied serious human rights violations. It is the first Commission-referred case to be heard by the Court.

The Ogiek peoples are the first inhabitants of the Mau Forest in Kenya. Their land case deals with their forced displacement from the Mau forest and the reha-bilitation of their land and natural resource rights. The Ogiek communities' sur-vival and livelihood depend on the resources found in the forest and, for many years now, they have increasingly been dispossessed of their ancestral forest land by neighboring communities, settlers, logging activities and government eviction exercises. Before taking their case to the African Commission, they had tried to obtain justice from the Kenyan courts for many years with no success. The African Court has not yet issued its decision.

Ongoing sensitization of African states and other stakeholders on indigenous rights

In September 2014, with the support of the WGIP, the Centre for Human Rights of the University of Pretoria in South Africa conducted its fourth one-week inten-sive course on indigenous peoples' rights.[1] This course was targeted at senior government officials, civil society and academics in Africa. The lecturers were all well-known experts on the topic, including members of the WGIP and an expert from the Inter-American Commission on Human Rights.

Mindful of the impact of extractive industries on the lives of indigenous peo-ples in Africa, the WGIP carried out a "Study on Extractive Industries, Land Rights and the Rights of Indigenous Communities/Populations in East, Central and Southern Africa". This study is based on case studies from Kenya, Cameroon, Uganda and Namibia. It will be validated at a workshop in Windhoek, Namibia, on 3-4 March 2015.

The WGIP conducted a Research and Information Visit to Tanzania in 2013. The delegation met and discussed the general situation of indigenous popula-tions with the representatives of various ministerial offices, embassies, UN spe-cialized agencies, international and local NGOs, including indigenous peoples' organizations, and several indigenous communities living in different parts of the country. The report of the visit was adopted by the African Commission in 2014 and will be published in 2015. ○

Notes and references

1   For more information about the course, please refer to: http://www1.chr.up.ac.za/index.php/ahrc-2014/ipr-course.html

Geneviève Rose is project coordinator for IWGIA's African Commission on Human and Peoples' Rights Programme. She holds an M.A. in Conflict Resolution and International Studies from the University of Bradford, UK.

THE INTER-AMERICAN HUMAN RIGHTS SYSTEM

Respect for indigenous peoples' rights is of particular importance for the Inter-American Human Rights System (IHRS) and it has therefore developed relevant jurisprudence that has - through decisions to Member States of the Organisation of American States (OAS) - enabled individual and collective rights to be recognised, victims to be compensated and guidelines to be produced with the aim of preventing or resolving matters of domestic jurisdiction.[1] The Inter-American Commission on Human Rights (IACHR) has, in particular, used its different mechanisms to protect indigenous peoples' rights, and this area of its work is being developed primarily through its Rapporteurship on the Rights of Indigenous Peoples, created in 1990.

Thematic and country reports

On 30 December 2013, the Commission approved the report entitled **"Indigenous Peoples in Voluntary Isolation and Initial Contact in the Americas: Recommendations for the full respect of their human rights"**.[2] The Commission publicly presented this report on 29 July 2014, in which it noted that the American continent is home to the greatest number of indigenous peoples in voluntary isolation and initial contact in the world. More specifically, the Commission indicated that their presence was known in Bolivia, Brazil, Colombia, Ecuador, Paraguay, Peru and Venezuela. It added that there were signs of their presence in Guyana and Suriname.[3]

In the report, the Commission expanded on the scope of the principle of no contact in relation to self-determination and summarised the sources of international law that establish the rights of indigenous peoples in voluntary isolation and initial contact. In terms of their situation, the Commission noted that there were different levels of recognition of the rights of indigenous peoples in voluntary isolation and initial contact in the Americas, notwithstanding the fact that, in practice, these peoples are "highly vulnerable and many of them are in danger of disappearing completely".[4] The Commission identified the main threats facing them as being those resulting from contact, pressure on their lands and territories, natural resource extraction, contagious diseases and illnesses, direct aggression, tourist projects and drugs trafficking.[5]

The report concluded with a series of specific recommendations aimed at encouraging states to fulfil their obligations to respect and guarantee the rights of indigenous peoples in voluntary isolation and initial contact. These were divided into the following sections: i) recognition and self-determination; ii) protection of territory; iii) natural resources; iv) free, prior and informed consultation; v) health; vi) inter-ethnic conflicts; vii) no contact; and viii) collaboration and coordination with other actors.[6]

On 21 December 2014, the Commission approved the report entitled: **"Missing and Murdered Indigenous Women in British Columbia, Canada"**,[7] following a visit made to Canada between 6 and 9 August 2013 with regard to this problem.

The Commission found the figures of missing and murdered indigenous women particularly concerning given that indigenous peoples represent a very small proportion of Canada's overall population.[8] In the report, the Commission described the nature of these events and found that these disappearances and murders formed part of a broader pattern of violence and discrimination in which indigenous women and girls are one of the most disadvantaged groups in Canada.[9] According to the Commission, this situation is exacerbated by "poverty, inadequate housing and economic and social relegation", along with discriminatory and stereotypical attitudes related to their gender and race.[10]

The Commission also analysed the Canadian government's response, indicating that it had not adequately prevented these deaths and disappearances nor thoroughly investigated them. The Commission highlighted the experience of families in the investigation procedures.[11]

While recognising the Canadian state's openness and willingness to resolve the issues, the Commission made a series of recommendations.[12]

On 31 December 2013, the Commission approved the report **"Truth, Justice and Reparation: Fourth Report on the Human Rights Situation in Colombia"**.[13] This report, which was publicly presented on 28 August 2014, addressed the human rights situation from the fundamental aspect of how these rights have been affected by the armed conflict and the current context of the possible signing of a peace accord.

Section C. of Chapter 6, entitled: "Differential Impact of the Armed Conflict and Process of Disappearance of the Indigenous Peoples in Colombia" considered the following issues: i) land and territory as affected by the armed conflict; ii) continuing murders, disappearances, threats and accusations against indigenous peoples and the special impact on their traditional authorities and leaders; iii) the militarisation of and armed clashes on indigenous peoples' ancestral territories; iv) how indigenous peoples and their ancestral territories are affected by anti-personnel mines and unexploded munitions; v) fumigations that affect indigenous territories; vi) forced displacement; vii) multiple discrimination and violence against women exacerbated by the armed conflict; viii) armed conflict, megaprojects and prior consultation; ix) impact on indigenous peoples' health and food; x) impunity and lack of access to justice on the part of indigenous peoples and their members; and xi) reparation and restitution of rights of victims from indigenous peoples and communities.[14]

On the basis of this assessment of the situation of indigenous peoples in the armed conflict, the Commission made specific recommendations to the Colombian state.[15]

IACHR country visit to Chile

From 24 to 26 November 2014, the Rapporteur for Indigenous Peoples, Commissioner Rose-Marie Belle Antoine, visited Chile with, among other things, the aim of "closely examining the human rights situation of indigenous peoples in Chile, in particular in the context of development and investment projects, and concessions for the extraction of natural resources".[16]

In her press release at the end of the visit, the Rapporteur stressed her concern at the information received on the lack of constitutional recognition of Chile's indigenous peoples, on barriers in the process for granting titles over their ancestral territories, on the lack of free, prior and informed consultation with regard to the implementation of a number of development projects and extractive industries, on the inadequate control indigenous peoples have over the education of their children in order to ensure the preservation of their cultural heritage, and on violence and intimidation against indigenous communities, among other things.[17]

The Commission called on the state to establish an institutionalised mechanism for consultations with indigenous peoples, to include a multicultural perspective in the design of legislation and public policies, to accelerate the process of restitution of their ancestral lands, to prevent any excessive use of force by law enforcement authorities aimed at countering the expression of their social demands, and to ensure access to a culturally-pertinent education.[18]

Thematic hearings before the IACHR [19]

The following thematic hearings took place during the IACHR's 150th Ordinary Period of Sessions, held from 20 March to 4 April 2014:

- Human rights situation of the indigenous community of Apetina in Suriname.
- Right to prior consultation on the part of Chile's indigenous peoples.
- Human rights situation of Nicaragua's indigenous peoples.
- Human rights situation of the indigenous peoples of the Kugapakori, Nahua, Nanti and others Territorial Reserve (RTNKN) in Peru.

The following thematic hearings took place during the IACHR's 153rd Ordinary Period of Sessions, held from 23 October to 7 November:

- Reports of human rights violations against indigenous peoples in Costa Rica.
- Right of indigenous peoples to legal status and property in Peru.
- Reports of destruction of the biocultural heritage of Mexico due to the construction of megadevelopment projects.
- Impact of the activities of Canadian mining companies on human rights in Latin America.
- Human rights situation of indigenous peoples in Ecuador.

Reports on petitions and individual cases

In 2014, the Commission approved admissibility reports on the rights of indigenous peoples:

- Report on Admissibility No. 96/14. Petition 422-06, Tagaeri and Tarome-
  nane Indigenous Peoples in Isolation (Ecuador).[20]
- Report on Admissibility No. 20/14. Petition 1566-07, Communities of the
  Sipakepense and Mam Mayan People of the Municipalities of Sipacapa
  and San Miguel Ixtahuacán (Guatemala).[21]
- Report on Admissibility No. 62/14. Petition 1216-03, People of Quishque-
  Tapayrihua (Peru).[22]

Submission of cases to the Court

During 2014, the Commission took two cases to the Inter-American Court in relation to indigenous peoples' rights.

On 26 January 2014, the Commission took the case of *Kaliña and Lokono
Peoples v. Suriname* to the Inter-American Court.[23] As described in the press release issued by the Commission at the time, this involves:

> a series of violations of the rights of the members of eight communities of
> the Kaliña and Lokono indigenous peoples of Suriname's Lower Marowi-
> jne River. Specifically, the violations have to do with an existing legal fra-
> mework that prevents recognition of the indigenous peoples' juridical
> personality, a situation that to this day continues to keep the Kaliña and
> Lokono peoples from being able to protect their right to collective proper-
> ty. In addition, the State has failed to establish the regulatory foundations
> that would allow for recognition of the right to collective ownership of the
> lands, territories, and natural resources of the Kaliña and Lokono indige-
> nous peoples. This lack of recognition has been accompanied by the is-
> suance of individual land titles to non-indigenous persons; the granting of
> concessions and licenses to carry out mining operations in part of their
> ancestral territories; and the establishment and operation of three nature
> reserves in part of their ancestral territories.[24]

This case is pending judgment by the Inter-American Court.

On 5 August 2014, the Commission took the case of *Members of the Village
of Chichupac and Neighbouring Communities, Municipality of Rabinal vs. Guatemala*, to the Inter-American Court. This involves massacres, extrajudicial execu-

tions, torture, forced disappearances and rape of members of the village of Chichupac and neighbouring communities, municipality of Rabinal, perpetrated as part of the operations carried out by the National Army and its collaborators during the internal armed conflict in Guatemala.[25] The Commission determined that the events in this case were part of the genocide perpetrated against the Mayan indigenous people in Guatemala.[26]The Commission also emphasised that "more than three decades have passed since the events of this case; more than two decades have passed since the first complaint was filed, and yet no one has been made to answer for these crimes".[27]

This case is with the Inter-American Court, pending public hearing.

Hearings held by the Inter-American Court

During the 103rd Ordinary Period of Sessions of the Inter-American Court, held from 12 to 30 May 2014, a public hearing took place for the case of the *Garífuna Community of Triunfo de la Cruz and its members v. Honduras*. The Commission took this case to the Court arguing a violation of various components of this community's right to collective property. The Commission thus explained to the Court that: i) the community has no suitable and culturally appropriate property title to its ancestral territory; ii) recognition of part of the ancestral territory has been slow and they continue to be denied a single title to the whole territory based on the community's historic occupation and customary use; iii) the community has not been able to peacefully occupy and hold their ancestral lands because of a lack of appropriate determination and demarcation of the titled lands, the lack of legal certainty over the titles granted, restrictions on access to areas of the ancestral territory due to the creation of protected areas and a failure to effectively protect their territory from occupation and dispossession by third parties or to guarantee that it is exclusively indigenous; iv) the expansion of the urban conurbation by the state authorities and the sale of community lands have also affected the right to collective property; v) the state has failed to conduct free, prior and informed consultation of the community with regard to decisions relating, for example, to tourism projects, the creation of a protected area on part of the ancestral territory and the sale of community lands; and vi) the community has had no recourse that would take account of their specific features, their economic and social characteristics, their customary law, values, habits and customs in the context of the processes related to collective ownership.[28]

This case is pending judgment by the Inter-American Court.

During the 51st Extraordinary Period of Sessions of the Inter-American Court, held in Asunción, Paraguay from 1 to 4 September 2014, the public hearing took place for the case of the *Garífuna Community of Punta Piedra and its members v. Honduras*. The Commission submitted this case explaining that it involved a violation of the right to collective property as a result of a failure to fulfil the duty of guarantee in the face of encroachment by non-indigenous persons onto lands and territories belonging to the community and which were subsequently recognised by the state through the granting of full ownership titles. According to the Commission, this titling was conducted without an adequate process of regularisation, despite knowing that a group of settlers had occupied various parts of the community's lands and territories, especially Río Miel and the forest area. The Commission emphasised that this situation has meant that the Garífuna Community of Punta Piedra has been able to exercise effective possession of only half of the territory to which the state granted legal title, with a resulting negative impact on their way of life, means of subsistence, and traditional culture, uses and customs.[29]

This case is pending judgment by the Inter-American Court.

Judgments issued by the Inter-American Court

On 29 May 2014, the Inter-American Court issued a judgment in the case of *Norín Catrimán et al (Leaders, Members and Activist of the Mapuche Indigenous People) v. Chile*. The case was submitted on behalf of eight victims convicted of "terrorist" crimes in application of Law No. 18,314, known as the "Antiterrorist Law" for actions that took place in 2001 and 2002 in Regions VIII (Biobío) and IX (Araucanía) of Chile. Of the victims, three were traditional authorities of the Mapuche indigenous people, four were members of that people and one was an activist demanding the rights of that people. In addition, accessory penalties of disqualification were imposed which restricted their exercise of the right to freedom of expression and political rights.

The Court concluded that the state had violated the rule of law and the presumption of innocence to the detriment of the eight victims in this case by maintaining and implementing "Article 1 of Law No. 18,314, which contained a legal presumption of the subjective element of terrorist activity, a basic element of Chilean law with which to distinguish terrorist behaviour from non-terrorist behaviour". The Court also concluded "that the substantiation on which the convictions were based used a rationale of a stereotypical and prejudiced nature, in violation of the principle of equality and non-discrimination and of the right to equal protection under the law". The Court found that the accessory penalties resulted in further violations of the rights to personal freedom, to judicial guarantees, to freedom of expression and political rights, which had an aggravated impact on those who were traditional authorities, and to the right to protection of the family.[30]

As a consequence, the Court ordered the state to implement the following measures of reparation:

(i) adopt all necessary judicial, administrative or other measures to revoke, in every aspect, the convictions of Messrs. Segundo Aniceto Norín Catrimán, Pascual Huentequeo Pichún Paillalao, Víctor Manuel Ancalaf Llaupe, Florencio Jaime Marileo Saravia, Juan Patricio Marileo Saravia, José Huenchunao Mariñán, Juan Ciriaco Millacheo Licán and Ms Patricia Troncoso Robles; (ii) provide free and immediate medical and psychological or psychiatric treatment to all victims of the case that request it; (iii) disseminate the publications and radio broadcasts as noted in the Judgment; provide study grants in Chilean public institutions for the children of the eight victims of this case if requested; (iv) clearly and safely regulate the procedural measures for protecting witnesses in terms of confidentiality of their identity, ensuring that this is an exceptional measure, subject to judicial control and based on need and proportionality, and that this means of evidence is not used decisively as the basis for a conviction, and regulate the corresponding counterbalance measures; (v) pay each of the eight victims the sum stated in the Judgment by way of reparation for pecuniary and non-pecuniary damage; (vi) pay the sums stated in the Judgment by way of reimbursement of costs and expenses.[31]

This case is currently at the stage of monitoring fulfilment of the judgment.

On 14 October 2014, the Inter-American Court issued its judgment in the case of the *Kuna Indigenous Peoples of Madungandí and Emberá Indigenous People of Bayano and their members v. Panama*. The background to the case involves the construction of a hydroelectric dam in the Alto Bayano zone, Panama province, in 1972. This construction involved flooding part of the indigenous reserve in the area and the displacement of the indigenous communities living there to other alternative lands.

The Court ruled a violation of the right to collective property due to: i) a failure to delimit and title the territories of the Kuna people of Madungandí for approximately six years; ii) a failure to demarcate the territories of the Kuna people of Madungandí for approximately 10 years; iii) a failure to delimit the territories of the Emberá of Ipetí and Piriatí communities for 23 years; iv) a failure to title the territories of the Piriatí Emberá community for approximately 24 years; v) a failure to demarcate the territories of the Piriatí Emberá community for approximately 24 years; vi) a failure to demarcate and title the territories of the Ipetí Emberá community for approximately 24 years; and vii) a failure to guarantee the effective enjoyment of the collective property title of the Piriatí Emberá community, given that the private property title conferred on an individual has still not been revoked. The Court also found that the state had failed in its duty to adapt its domestic law as it had not provided rules enabling the delimitation, demarcation and titling of collective lands prior to 2008. The Court also established violations of the rights to judicial guarantees and judicial protection.[32]

As a consequence of these violations, the Court ordered the state to implement the following measures of reparation:

> a) publish the Judgment of the Inter-American Court and its summary and conduct radio broadcasts in this regard; b) hold a public act recognising international responsibility with regard to the events in this case; c) demarcate the lands corresponding to the Ipetí and Piriatí Emberá communities and title the Ipetí lands as the collective property of this community; d) adopt the necessary measures to revoke the private property title granted to Sr Melgar within the territory of the Emberá of Piriatí community; e) pay the amounts set in the Judgment by way of reparation for pecuniary and non-pecuniary damage and as reimbursement of costs and expenses.[33]

This case is currently at the stage of monitoring fulfilment of the judgment.   ○

Notes and references

1   See *inter alia* the report: **IACHR.** *Indigenous and Tribal Peoples' Rights over their Ancestral Lands and Natural Resources.* OEA/Ser.L/V/II. Doc. 56/09. 30 December 2009.. This report compiles and analyses the norms and jurisprudence of the Inter-American Human Rights System regarding the rights of indigenous and tribal peoples on their territories, lands and natural resources. Available at: https://www.oas.org/en/iachr/indigenous/docs/pdf/AncestralLands.pdf

2   **IACHR.2013.** *Indigenous Peoples in Voluntary Isolation and Initial Contact in the Americas: Recommendations for the full respect of their human rights.* Available at: http://www.oas.org/en/iachr/indigenous/docs/pdf/Report-Indigenous-Peoples-Voluntary-Isolation.pdf

3   Id. para. 15.

4   Id. para. 17.

5   Id. Pgs. 43 - 76.

6   Id. Pgs. 77 - 81.

7   IACHR. Missing and Murdered Indigenous Women in British Columbia, Canada. 2014. Available at: https://www.oas.org/en/iachr/reports/pdfs/Indigenous-Women-BC-Canada-en.pdf

8   IACHR. Press release dated 12 January 2015. *IACHR Presents Report on Murdered and Missing Indigenous Women in British Columbia, Canada.* Available at: http://www.oas.org/en/iachr/media_center/PReleases/2015/003.asp

9   Id.

10   Id.

11   Id.

12   **IACHR. 2014.** Missing and Murdered Indigenous Women in British Columbia, Canada. Available at: https://www.oas.org/en/iachr/reports/pdfs/Indigenous-Women-BC-Canada-en.pdf paras 304 and ss.

13   **IACHR. 2013.** *Truth, Justice and Reparation: Fourth Report on the Human Rights Situation in Colombia.* Available at: http://www.oas.org/es/cidh/docs/pdfs/Justicia-Verdad-Reparacion-es.pdf.

14   Id. Pgs. 297 – 344.

15   Id. Pg. 346.

16   IACHR. Press release dated 11 December 2014. *IACHR concludes visit to Chile.* Available at: http://www.oas.org/en/iachr/media_center/PReleases/2014/150.asp

17   Id.

18   Id.

19   Recordings of these nine thematic hearings held during 2014 can be found at the following link: http://www.oas.org/es/cidh/audiencias/topicslist.aspx?lang=en&topic=17

20   Available at: http://www.oas.org/en/iachr/decisions/2014/ECAD422-06EN.pdf

21   Available at: http://www.oas.org/en/iachr/decisions/2014/GTAD1566-07EN.pdf

22   Available at: http://www.oas.org/en/iachr/decisions/2014/PEAD1216-03EN.pdf

23   IACHR. Press release dated 4 February 2014. *IACHR Takes Case involving Kaliña and Lokono Peoples v. Suriname to the Inter-American Court.* Available at: http://www.oas.org/en/iachr/media_center/PReleases/2014/009.asp.

24   Id.

25 IACHR. Press release dated 17 September 2014. *IACHR Takes Case Involving Guatemala to the Inter-American Court of Human Rights.* Available at: http://www.oas.org/en/iachr/media_center/PReleases/2014/100.asp.
26 Id.
27 Id.
28 See http://www.corteidh.or.cr/docs/comunicados/cp_07_14.pdf. For information regarding the Commission's submission of the case see:
http://www.oas.org/es/cidh/decisiones/corte/12.548NdeResp.pdf.
29 See http://www.corteidh.or.cr/docs/comunicados/cp_18_14.pdf. For information on the Commission's submission of the case see:
http://www.oas.org/en/iachr/media_center/PReleases/2013/076.asp.
30 I/A Court HR. *Case of Norín Catrimán et al (Leaders, members and activist of the Mapuche Indigenous People) v. Chile. Merits, Reparations and Costs.* Judgment of 29 May 2014. Series C No. 279. Available at: http://www.corteidh.or.cr/docs/casos/articulos/seriec_279_esp.pdf.
31 Extract taken from the Official Abstract of the Judgment, available at: http://www.corteidh.or.cr/docs/casos/articulos/resumen_279_esp.pdf.
32 I/A Court HR. *Case of the Kuna Indigenous Peoples of Madungandí and the Emberá Indigenous People of Bayano and their Members v. Panama.* Preliminary Objections, Merits, Reparations and Costs. Judgment of 14 October 2014. Serie C No. 284. Available at: http://www.corteidh.or.cr/docs/casos/articulos/seriec_284_esp.pdf.
33 Extract taken from the Official Abstract of the Judgment, available at: http://www.corteidh.or.cr/docs/casos/articulos/resumen_284_esp.pdf.

Silvia Serrano Guzmán *is a Human Rights Specialist of the Inter-American Commission on Human Rights. The information and opinions expressed in this article are those of the author alone. They in no way represent the OAS, the IAHRC or its secretariat.*

PART III

GENERAL INFORMATION

ABOUT IWGIA

IWGIA is an independent international membership organization that supports indigenous peoples' right to self-determination. Since its foundation in 1968, IWGIA's secretariat has been based in Copenhagen, Denmark.

IWGIA holds consultative status with the United Nations Economic and Social Council (ECOSOC) and has observer status with the Arctic Council, the African Commission on Human and Peoples Rights (ACHPR) and United Nations Educational, Scientific and Cultural Organization (UNESCO).

Aims and activities

IWGIA supports indigenous peoples' struggles for human rights, self-determination, the right to territory, control of land and resources, cultural integrity, and the right to development on their own terms. In order to fulfil this mission, IWGIA works in a wide range of areas: documentation and publication, human rights advocacy and lobbying, plus direct support to indigenous organisations' programmes of work.

IWGIA works worldwide at local, regional and international level, in close cooperation with indigenous partner organizations.

More information about IWGIA can be found on our website, www.iwgia.org

Become a member of IWGIA

Membership is an important sign of support to our work, politically as well as economically. Members receive IWGIA's Annual Report and *The Indigenous World*. In addition, members get a 33% reduction on the price of other IWGIA publications when buying from our Web shop.

Read more about IWGIA membership and join us at: http://www.iwgia.org/iwgia/membership

IWGIA PUBLICATIONS 2014

Publications can be ordered online at:
www.iwgia.org

In English

The Indigenous World 2014
Ed. by Cæcilie Mikkelsen
IWGIA, Copenhagen
ISBN: 978-87-927864-18

Annual Report 2013
IWGIA, Copenhagen

World Heritage Sites and Indigenous Peoples' Rights
Ed. by Stefan Disko and Helen Tugendhat
IWGIA, Forest Peoples Programme & Gundjeihmi Aboriginal Corporation, Copenhagen
ISBN: 978-87-92786-54-8

Land Rights of Indigenous Peoples in Africa - Revised and updated 2014
By Albert Kwokwo Barume
IWGIA, Copenhagen
ISBN: 978-87-92786-40-1

Business and Human Rights: Interpreting the UN Guiding Principles for Indigenous Peoples. IWGIA Report 16
By Johannes Rohr & José Aylwin
Ed. by IWGIA
IWGIA & ENIP, Copenhagen
ISBN: 978-87-92786-44-9

Indigenous Peoples in the Russian Federation. IWGIA Report 18
By Johannes Rohr
Eds. Diana Vinding and Kathrin Wessendorf
IWGIA, Electronic copy only
ISBN: 978-87-92786-49-4

Work Place Diversity in Aid Agencies in Laos
By Steeve Daviau
The Japanese International Volunteer Center, Oxfam Novib,
The McKnight Foundation and IWGIA, Electronic copy only

Shifting Cultivation, Livelihood and Food Security New and Old Challenges for Indigenous Peoples in Asia
By Christian Erni and Joan Carling
AIPP & IWGIA, Chiang Mai

Marginalisation and Impunity
Violence against Women and Girls in the Chittagong Hill Tracts
By Dr. Bina D'Costa
Chittagong Hill Tracts Commission (CHTC), IWGIA, and Bangladesh
Indigenous Women's Network, Dhaka

Tribes States and Colonialism: The Evolution of the Concept of Indigenous Peoples and its Application in Asia
By Christian Erni
IWGIA, Electronic copy only

Constitutional Politics and Indigenous Peoples in Nepal
By Christina Nilsson & Sille Stidsen
IWGIA, Electronic copy only

A study on the socio-economic status of indigenous peoples in Nepal
By Dr. Chaitanya Subba, Pro. Dr. Bishwamber Pyakuryal, Mr. Tunga
Shiromani Bastola, Mr. Mohan Khajum Subba, Mr. Nirmal Kumar Raut,
and Mr. Baburam Karki
LAHURNIP & IWGIA, Kathmandu
ISBN: 993728861-4

The Glimpses of Indigenous Peoples' human rights violation in Nepal
LAHURNIP & IWGIA, Kathmandu

Indigenous Peoples in Voluntary Isolation and Initial Contact in the Americas: Recommendations for the Full Respect of Their Human Rights
IACHR. OAS Official Document. Elaborated with the financial support of IWGIA
ISBN: 978-0-8270-6113-2

Report on the State of Pastoralists' Human Rights in Tanzania: Survey of Ten Districts of Tanzania Mainland 2010/2011
PAICODEO, Arusha. Elaborated with the financial support of IWGIA
ISBN: 978-9987-9726-1-6

Non-Carbon Benefits in REDD+
Indigenous Peoples Perspectives and Recommendations to the Subsidiary Body for Scientific and Technological Advice (SBSTA)
By Joan Carling and Lakpa Nuri Sherpa
AIPP & IWGIA, Chiang Mai

Safeguards Information System (SIS) in REDD+:
What should it deliver for indigenous peoples?
By Joan Carling and Lakpa Nuri Sherpa
AIPP & IWGIA, Chiang Mai

Indigenous Women in REDD+
Making their Voice Heard
By Christian Erni, Kathrin Wessendorf, Joan Carling, Tunga Bhadra Rai & Pheap Sochea
AIPP & IWGIA, Chiang Mai

The crucial role of indigenous peoples in nurturing forest and maintaining forest cover - An important Non-Carbon Benefit of REDD+
IWGIA, AIPP, IBIS, AMAN, Forest of the World, CARE & NEFIN, Electronic copy only

Case study: Titling of indigenous territories protects and increases tropical forest cover in the Peruvian Amazon
IWGIA, AIPP, IBIS, AMAN, Forest of the World, CARE & NEFIN, Electronic copy only

Case study: The capacity of local communities to monitor biodiversity and resources in Madagascar, Nicaragua, Philippines and Tanzania
IWGIA, AIPP, IBIS, AMAN, Forest of the World, CARE & NEFIN, Electronic copy only

Fact Sheet: Indigenous Peoples' Right to Land
The Threat of Land Grabbing
IWGIA, Electronic copy only

Fact Sheet: Indigenous peoples in the post-2015 development framework
IWGIA, Tebtebba & International Indian Treaty Council, Electronic copy only

Post 2015 Development Process: Governance
IWGIA & Tebtebba, Electronic copy only

Post 2015 Development Process: Inequality
IWGIA & Tebtebba, Electronic copy only

Post 2015 Development Process: Health
IWGIA & Tebtebba, Electronic copy only

Post 2015 Development Process: Women
IWGIA & Tebtebba, Electronic copy only

Post 2015 Development Process: Education
IWGIA & Tebtebba, Electronic copy only

Post 2015 Development Process: Energy
IWGIA & Tebtebba, Electronic copy only

Post 2015 Development Process: Water
IWGIA & Tebtebba, Electronic copy only

Post 2015 Development Process: Environmental Sustainability
IWGIA & Tebtebba, Electronic copy only

In Spanish

El Mundo Indígena 2014
Ed. by Cæcilie Mikkelsen
IWGIA, Copenhagen
ISBN: 978-87-92786-42-5

La rebelión ciudadana y la justicia comunitaria en Guerrero
By Marcos Matías Alonso, Rafael Aréstegui Ruiz & Aurelio Vázquez
Villanueva
Instituto de Estudios Parlamentarios "Eduardo Neri" del H. Congreso
del Estado de Guerrero, Centro de Estudios Sociales y de Opinión
Pública de la Cámara de Diputados del Congreso de la Unión & IWGIA,
Mexico City
ISBN: 978-607-7919-94-0

Convenio 169 de la OIT:
Los desafíos de su implementación en América Latina a 25 años de su aprobación
Ed. by José Aylwin & Leonardo Tamburini
IWGIA, Lima
ISBN: 978-87-92786-55-5

Pueblos de la yuca brava: Historia y culinaria
By Alberto Chirif
IWGIA, ORE Media, Nouvelle Planète & Instituto del Bien Común, Lima
ISBN: 978-87-92786-39-5

La batalla por "Los Nanti"
Informe IWGIA 17
By Frederica Barclay & Pedro García Hierro
Perú Equidad – Centro de Políticas Públicas y Derechos Humanos &
IWGIA, Copenhagen/Lima
ISBN: 978-87-92786-45-6

El derecho a la consulta de los pueblos indígenas:
Análisis del derecho nacional, internacional y comparado
Informe IWGIA 19
Ed. by Paulina Acevedo
Norwegian Embassy, Observatorio Ciudadano & IWGIA, Santiago de Chile
ISBN: 978-87-92786-46-3

Desplazados ambientales, globalización y cambio climático
Informe IWGIA 20
By Paulina Acevedo Menanteau
Observatorio Ciudadano & IWGIA, Santiago de Chile
ISBN: 978-87-92786-50-0

Pueblos indígenas en aislamiento voluntario y contacto inicial en
las Américas: recomendaciones para el pleno respeto a sus
derechos humanos
IACHR. OAS, Official Document. Elaborated with financial support
from IWGIA
ISBN: 978-0-8270-6113-2

Mujeres indígenas y REDD+ hacerse escuchar
By Christian Erni, Kathrin Wessendorf, Joan Carling, Tunga Bhadra
Rai & Pheap Sochea
AIPP & IWGIA, Chiang Mai

Sistema de información de salvaguardas en REDD+
¿Que debería aportar a los pueblos indígenas?
By Joan Carling & Lakpa Nuri Sherpa
AIPP & IWGIA, Chiang Mai

Beneficios más alla del carbono: perspectivas de los pueblos indígenas y recomendaciones al OSACT
By Joan Carling & Lakpa Nuri Sherpa
AIPP & IWGIA, Chiang Mai

El Pueblo Caquinte: recuento de un amargo consentimiento
By Yaiza Campanario Baqué
IWGIA, Electronic copy only

In Portuguese

Suicídio adolescente em povos indígenas – 3 estudos
UNICEF & IWGIA, Panama City
ISBN: 978-85-64377-19-6

VIDEOS

The Sylvan Call - DVD
A production by JJBA & BIRSA, India